Handbook of Research on Interdisciplinary Studies on Healthcare, Culture, and the Environment

Mika Markus Merviö
Kibi International University, Japan

A volume in the Advances in Public Policy and Administration (APPA) Book Series

Published in the United States of America by
IGI Global
Information Science Reference (an imprint of IGI Global)
701 E. Chocolate Avenue
Hershey PA, USA 17033
Tel: 717-533-8845
Fax: 717-533-8661
E-mail: cust@igi-global.com
Web site: http://www.igi-global.com

Copyright © 2022 by IGI Global. All rights reserved. No part of this publication may be reproduced, stored or distributed in any form or by any means, electronic or mechanical, including photocopying, without written permission from the publisher. Product or company names used in this set are for identification purposes only. Inclusion of the names of the products or companies does not indicate a claim of ownership by IGI Global of the trademark or registered trademark.
Library of Congress Cataloging-in-Publication Data

Names: Mervio, Mika Markus, 1961- editor.
Title: Handbook of research on interdisciplinary studies on healthcare, culture,
  and the environment / Mika Merviö, editor.
Description: Hershey, PA : Information Science Reference, [2022] | Includes
  bibliographical references and index. | Summary: "This book discusses
  problems that the world and all societies are facing and contain
  insights and ideas that help to understand the rapidly changing terrain
  of the complex interactions within the fields of healthcare, culture,
  environment, society and economy"-- Provided by publisher.
Identifiers: LCCN 2021042336 (print) | LCCN 2021042337 (ebook) | ISBN
  9781799889960 (hardcover) | ISBN 9781799889984 (ebook)
Subjects: LCSH: Health services administration. | Public health. |
  Environmental quality.
Classification: LCC RA971 .I485 2022 (print) | LCC RA971 (ebook) | DDC
  362.1--dc23/eng/20211029
LC record available at https://lccn.loc.gov/2021042336
LC ebook record available at https://lccn.loc.gov/2021042337

This book is published in the IGI Global book series Advances in Public Policy and Administration (APPA) (ISSN: 2475-6644; eISSN: 2475-6652)

British Cataloguing in Publication Data
A Cataloguing in Publication record for this book is available from the British Library.

All work contributed to this book is new, previously-unpublished material. The views expressed in this book are those of the authors, but not necessarily of the publisher.

For electronic access to this publication, please contact: eresources@igi-global.com.

Advances in Public Policy and Administration (APPA) Book Series

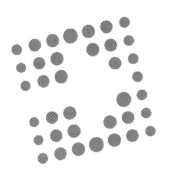

ISSN:2475-6644
EISSN:2475-6652

Mission

Proper management of the public sphere is necessary in order to maintain order in modern society. Research developments in the field of public policy and administration can assist in uncovering the latest tools, practices, and methodologies for governing societies around the world.

The **Advances in Public Policy and Administration (APPA) Book Series** aims to publish scholarly publications focused on topics pertaining to the governance of the public domain. APPA's focus on timely topics relating to government, public funding, politics, public safety, policy, and law enforcement is particularly relevant to academicians, government officials, and upper-level students seeking the most up-to-date research in their field.

Coverage

- Government
- Law Enforcement
- Political Economy
- Politics
- Public Administration
- Public Funding
- Public Policy
- Resource Allocation
- Urban Planning

> IGI Global is currently accepting manuscripts for publication within this series. To submit a proposal for a volume in this series, please contact our Acquisition Editors at Acquisitions@igi-global.com or visit: http://www.igi-global.com/publish/.

The Advances in Public Policy and Administration (APPA) Book Series (ISSN 2475-6644) is published by IGI Global, 701 E. Chocolate Avenue, Hershey, PA 17033-1240, USA, www.igi-global.com. This series is composed of titles available for purchase individually; each title is edited to be contextually exclusive from any other title within the series. For pricing and ordering information please visit http://www.igi-global.com/book-series/advances-public-policy-administration/97862. Postmaster: Send all address changes to above address. Copyright © 2022 IGI Global. All rights, including translation in other languages reserved by the publisher. No part of this series may be reproduced or used in any form or by any means – graphics, electronic, or mechanical, including photocopying, recording, taping, or information and retrieval systems – without written permission from the publisher, except for non commercial, educational use, including classroom teaching purposes. The views expressed in this series are those of the authors, but not necessarily of IGI Global.

Titles in this Series

For a list of additional titles in this series, please visit: www.igi-global.com/book-series/advances-public-policy-administration/97862

Challenges and Barriers to the European Union Expansion to the Balkan Region
Bruno Ferreira Costa (University of Beira Interior, Portugal)
Information Science Reference • © 2022 • 372pp • H/C (ISBN: 9781799890553) • US $195.00

Smart Cities, Citizen Welfare, and the Implementation of Sustainable Development Goals
Ana Cristina Pego (Nova University, Portugal)
Information Science Reference • © 2022 • 402pp • H/C (ISBN: 9781799877851) • US $195.00

Faith-Based Influences on Legislative Decision Making Emerging Research and Opportunities
Karla L. Drenner (Purdue University Global, USA)
Information Science Reference • © 2022 • 353pp • H/C (ISBN: 9781799868071) • US $195.00

Contemporary Politics, Communication, and the Impact on Democracy
Dolors Palau-Sampio (University of Valencia, Spain) Guillermo López García (University of Valencia, Spain) and Laura Iannelli (University of Sassari, Italy)
Information Science Reference • © 2022 • 420pp • H/C (ISBN: 9781799880578) • US $195.00

Analyzing Current and Future Global Trends in Populism
Adrian David Cheok (Professional University of Information and Management for Innovation, iUniversity, Tokyo, Japan)
Information Science Reference • © 2022 • 271pp • H/C (ISBN: 9781799846796) • US $195.00

Contemporary Politics and Social Movements in an Isolated World Emerging Research and Opportunities
Emily Stacey (Rose State College, USA)
Information Science Reference • © 2022 • 167pp • H/C (ISBN: 9781799876144) • US $175.00

Handbook of Research on Special Economic Zones as Regional Development Enablers
Paulo Guilherme Figueiredo (City University of Macao, Macao) Francisco José Leandro (City University of Macao, Macao) and Yichao Li (City University of Macao, Macao)
Information Science Reference • © 2022 • 470pp • H/C (ISBN: 9781799876199) • US $275.00

Public Affairs Education and Training in the 21st Century
Onur Kulaç (Pamukkale University, Turkey & University of Southern California, USA) Cenay Babaoğlu (Selçuk University, Turkey) and Elvettin Akman (Süleyman Demirel University, Turkey)
Information Science Reference • © 2022 • 468pp • H/C (ISBN: 9781799882435) • US $195.00

701 East Chocolate Avenue, Hershey, PA 17033, USA
Tel: 717-533-8845 x100 • Fax: 717-533-8661
E-Mail: cust@igi-global.com • www.igi-global.com

List of Contributors

Aboagye, Dacosta / *Kwame Nkrumah University of Science and Technology, Ghana* 233
Aridi, Amalisha / *Capitol Technology University, USA* 1
Asante, Felix / *Kwame Nkrumah University of Science and Technology, Ghana* 233
Bongarzoni, Paolo / *Swiss School of Management, Italy* 204
Bowers, Seleste / *University of Phoenix, USA* 41
Burrell, Darrell Norman / *The Florida Institute of Technology, USA* 1, 41, 75
Dai, Yan / *Auburn University, USA* 21
Dávalos-Aceves, Jessica / *Escuela de Ciencias Económicas y Empresariales, Universidad
    Panamericana, Mexico* 178
Ferri, Adriano / *Swiss School of Management, Italy* 204
Garcia, Maria Jesus Garcia / *University of Valencia, Spain* 164
Jang, Hyun Sung / *Auburn University, USA* 21
Kaur, Mandeep / *Punjabi University, Patiala, India* 87
Kyeremeh, Emmanuel / *Berekum College of Education, Ghana* 233
Lewis, Eugene J. / *Capitol Technology University, USA* 1
Mercedes, D'Alizza / *The Chicago School of Professional Psychology, USA* 1
Merviö, Mika Markus / *Kibi International University, Japan* 263, 279
Paxton, Simon Regin / *Komazawa University, Japan* 250
Rajeshwari, T. / *Gayatri Chetna Kendra, Kolkata, India* 54
Rastogi, Rohit / *Dayalbagh Educational Institute, India & ABES Engineering College, India* 54
Sagar, Sheelu / *Amity University, Noida, India* 54
Salisbury-Glennon, Jill D. / *Auburn University, USA* 21
Saxena, Mamta / *Government of India, Delhi, India* 54
Schneider, Rainer / *RECON, Germany* 219
Shufutinsky, Anton / *Cabrini University, USA* 1, 41
Singh, Baljit / *Sri Guru Teg Bahadur Khalsa College, Sri Anandpur Sahib, India* 87
Singh, Bhavna / *G. S. Ayurved Medical College and Hospital, Pilkhuwa, India* 54
Strunk, Kamden K. / *Auburn University, USA* 21
Tandon, Neeti / *Vikram University, Ujjain, India* 54
Vargas-Hernández, José G. / *Instituto Tecnológico José Mario Molina Pasquel y Henríquez,
    Mexico* 104, 124, 143, 178
Wang, Chih-hsuan / *Auburn University, USA* 21
Wright, Jorja B. / *University of Charleston, USA* 1, 41

Table of Contents

Preface xvi

Chapter 1
Managing High Performing Safety Cultures in US Healthcare Organizations During COVID-19 1
    Darrell Norman Burrell, The Florida Institute of Technology, USA
    Anton Shufutinsky, Cabrini University, USA
    Jorja B. Wright, University of Charleston, USA
    D'Alizza Mercedes, The Chicago School of Professional Psychology, USA
    Amalisha Aridi, Capitol Technology University, USA
    Eugene J. Lewis, Capitol Technology University, USA

Chapter 2
A Cross-Cultural Comparison of College Student Self-Efficacy, Self-Regulation, and Resilience
Between the US and China During the COVID-19 Pandemic 21
    Yan Dai, Auburn University, USA
    Hyun Sung Jang, Auburn University, USA
    Jill D. Salisbury-Glennon, Auburn University, USA
    Chih-hsuan Wang, Auburn University, USA
    Kamden K. Strunk, Auburn University, USA

Chapter 3
Due to COVID-19, Food Insecurity and Access to Healthy Food Have Become Significant Public
Health Problems 41
    Darrell Norman Burrell, The Florida Institute of Technology, USA & Capitol Technology
        University, USA
    Anton Shufutinsky, Cabrini University, USA
    Jorja B. Wright, University Charleston, USA
    Seleste Bowers, University of Phoenix, USA

Chapter 4
Ionization, Gadget Radiation Analysis, and Disease Control by Yajna: An Ancient Vedic Wisdom for Human Health Relevant Amidst Pandemic Threats 54
    Rohit Rastogi, Dayalbagh Educational Institute, India & ABES Engineering College, India
    Mamta Saxena, Government of India, Delhi, India
    T. Rajeshwari, Gayatri Chetna Kendra, Kolkata, India
    Sheelu Sagar, Amity University, Noida, India
    Bhavna Singh, G. S. Ayurved Medical College and Hospital, Pilkhuwa, India
    Neeti Tandon, Vikram University, Ujjain, India

Chapter 5
The Need for Adaptive Organizational Systems Concerning Proactive Health Literacy Approaches in the Misinformation State of COVID-19 75
    Darrell Norman Burrell, The Florida Institute of Technology, USA & Capitol Technology University, USA

Chapter 6
A Review of the Healthcare System in the State of Punjab, India.. 87
    Mandeep Kaur, Punjabi University, Patiala, India
    Baljit Singh, Sri Guru Teg Bahadur Khalsa College, Sri Anandpur Sahib, India

Chapter 7
Theoretical and Empirical Approaches and Typologies Into Failures and Enhancement of Organizational Resilience Analysis 104
    José G. Vargas-Hernández, Instituto Tecnológico José Mario Molina Pasquel y Henríquez, Mexico

Chapter 8
Organizational Resilience Capability and Capacity Building.. 124
    José G. Vargas-Hernández, Instituto Tecnológico José Mario Molina Pasquel y Henríquez, Mexico

Chapter 9
Implications of Implementing Operational Multi-Levels: Individual, Organizational, Community, and Societal Resilience 143
    José G. Vargas-Hernández, Instituto Tecnológico José Mario Molina Pasquel y Henríquez, Mexico

Chapter 10
Renewable Energies and the Urban Environment in Spain 164
    Maria Jesus Garcia Garcia, University of Valencia, Spain

Chapter 11
Welfare State, Income, and Public Debt: Their Implications for Latin American Life Satisfaction .. 178
    Jessica Dávalos-Aceves, Escuela de Ciencias Económicas y Empresariales, Universidad
        Panamericana, Mexico
    José G. Vargas-Hernández, Instituto Tecnológico José Mario Molina Pasquel y Henríquez,
        Mexico

Chapter 12
US Dependance on Chinese Pharma in the Pandemic Era and the Nationalization of the US System 204
    Paolo Bongarzoni, Swiss School of Management, Italy
    Adriano Ferri, Swiss School of Management, Italy

Chapter 13
Does It Hold Water? An Empirical Investigation on the Usefulness of Filtering Tap Water to Treat Health Complaints 219
    Rainer Schneider, RECON, Germany

Chapter 14
Assessing Differential Vulnerability to Health Risks Associated With Microbial Contamination of Vegetables 233
    Emmanuel Kyeremeh, Berekum College of Education, Ghana
    Dacosta Aboagye, Kwame Nkrumah University of Science and Technology, Ghana
    Felix Asante, Kwame Nkrumah University of Science and Technology, Ghana

Chapter 15
Japanese Stone Gardens: Diversity, Sustainability, and Consumerism 250
    Simon Regin Paxton, Komazawa University, Japan

Chapter 16
Art and Environment Seen Through the Lens of Politics in Japan 263
    Mika Markus Merviö, Kibi International University, Japan

Chapter 17
Japanese Visual Arts: Representation and Perfectioning of Reality – Mimesis and Understanding of Japanese Visual Arts 279
    Mika Markus Merviö, Kibi International University, Japan

Compilation of References 303

About the Contributors 357

Index 363

Detailed Table of Contents

Preface xvi

Chapter 1
Managing High Performing Safety Cultures in US Healthcare Organizations During COVID-19 1
    Darrell Norman Burrell, The Florida Institute of Technology, USA
    Anton Shufutinsky, Cabrini University, USA
    Jorja B. Wright, University of Charleston, USA
    D'Alizza Mercedes, The Chicago School of Professional Psychology, USA
    Amalisha Aridi, Capitol Technology University, USA
    Eugene J. Lewis, Capitol Technology University, USA

The increasing complexity of the United States healthcare system has compounded the likelihood of mistakes. One of the 10 leading causes of death and disability is safety issues with patient care. Medical errors put undue hardship on the economy resulting in the loss of billions of dollars. The current COVID-19 pandemic revealed gaps in public health strategies, medical treatments, comprehensive patient safety, and human resources strategy. Implementing human resources and performance management processes that promote safety, safe decision making, and reduce medical errors is critical. Adopting methods used by high-reliability organizations (HRO) may reduce medical errors and improve patient safety. Qualitative focus groups were used to collect data around creating organizational cultures focused on safety. This research aims to improve performance by providing healthcare leaders with tools to enhance organizational culture, reduce medical errors, and improve patient safety in the age of COVID-19.

Chapter 2
A Cross-Cultural Comparison of College Student Self-Efficacy, Self-Regulation, and Resilience
Between the US and China During the COVID-19 Pandemic 21
    Yan Dai, Auburn University, USA
    Hyun Sung Jang, Auburn University, USA
    Jill D. Salisbury-Glennon, Auburn University, USA
    Chih-hsuan Wang, Auburn University, USA
    Kamden K. Strunk, Auburn University, USA

The unprecedented COVID-19 global pandemic has created many challenges across the educational domains experienced by many cultures around the world. The present study elucidates a cross-cultural comparison of college students' self-efficacy, self-regulation, and resilience between college students in the United States and China during these challenging times. A total of 479 college students from the United States and China were recruited to participate in the present study. Multivariate analyses of variance (MANOVA) were conducted, and results indicated that U.S. college students demonstrated significantly higher self-efficacy and resilience and significantly lower self-regulation than Chinese college students. Further, the implications of the present study provide suggestions for effective teaching and learning strategies that can be used to establish supportive learning environments for students from different cultural backgrounds.

Chapter 3
Due to COVID-19, Food Insecurity and Access to Healthy Food Have Become Significant Public Health Problems 41

    Darrell Norman Burrell, The Florida Institute of Technology, USA & Capitol Technology
        University, USA
    Anton Shufutinsky, Cabrini University, USA
    Jorja B. Wright, University Charleston, USA
    Seleste Bowers, University of Phoenix, USA

Since the onset of COVID-19, food insecurity and access to healthy food have become significant public health problems. Inequalities in dietary behaviors have been unambiguously correlated to the food environment, including access to healthy and fresh foods. The Coronavirus Disease, also known as the COVID-19 pandemic, has led to significant fluctuations in the distribution, sale, purchase, preparation, and food consumption in the United States (U.S.). In addition, in the United States (U.S.), substantial socioeconomic and racial disparities exist in dietary behaviors. Limited access to fresh food, coupled with a greater prevalence of fast-food outlets in lower-income and minority neighborhoods, is partially responsible for sub-optimal eating patterns among residents. The purpose of this research is to highlight the factors and influences concerning childhood obesity, food education, community gardening, and healthy eating.

Chapter 4
Ionization, Gadget Radiation Analysis, and Disease Control by Yajna: An Ancient Vedic Wisdom for Human Health Relevant Amidst Pandemic Threats 54

    Rohit Rastogi, Dayalbagh Educational Institute, India & ABES Engineering College, India
    Mamta Saxena, Government of India, Delhi, India
    T. Rajeshwari, Gayatri Chetna Kendra, Kolkata, India
    Sheelu Sagar, Amity University, Noida, India
    Bhavna Singh, G. S. Ayurved Medical College and Hospital, Pilkhuwa, India
    Neeti Tandon, Vikram University, Ujjain, India

The use of electronic items like computers, laptops, tablets, television, LED lights, mobile phones, microwaves, etc. are mandatory necessity of lifestyle today. Electro-magnetic radiation is emitted from the electronic devices and are very harmful to human beings its excessive use leads to growth of cancer cells. Therefore, we need to find a way out to prevent ourselves from the harmful effect EMR level at workplace and homes. It is time to adopt modern way from traditional techniques and forward a model that involves the community, with a stakeholder-focused approach. Ancient Indian scriptures have described Yagya to absorb the harmful effect of cosmic waves. Hence, in the present study, the authors have done test to find the impact of Yagya on effect of radiation on human beings emitted from electronic devices. Results of the experiment showed significant decrease in EMR with Yagya, indicating Yagya can be one of the useful solutions as non-conventional method for reducing indoor EMR level.

Chapter 5
The Need for Adaptive Organizational Systems Concerning Proactive Health Literacy
Approaches in the Misinformation State of COVID-19 75
    Darrell Norman Burrell, The Florida Institute of Technology, USA & Capitol Technology
        University, USA

When it comes to COVID-19 in America, the country represents four percent of the global population but accounts for 22% of global COVID-19 deaths. The convergence of misrepresentation and rapid growth contagious are considered interrelated. Social media has played a significant role in the spread of myths and misconceptions concerning COVID-19, and as a result, health literacy has become critical to fighting the virus. Misinformation has come to define COVID-19 due to unrelenting public fables misinformation on everything from the virus being a hoax, untested cures, and the uselessness of wearing facemasks. Health literacy is the extent to which the public and patients can acquire and understand essential health knowledge required to make proper health choices and decisions. The inquiry employs a content analysis of current literature and qualitative interviews to explore practical organizational adaptive approaches that promote COVID-19 health literacy.

Chapter 6
A Review of the Healthcare System in the State of Punjab, India... 87
    Mandeep Kaur, Punjabi University, Patiala, India
    Baljit Singh, Sri Guru Teg Bahadur Khalsa College, Sri Anandpur Sahib, India

This study attempted to analyse the healthcare system in the state of Punjab at a community level, village level, and district level. In the chapter, an attempt is made to review the literature concerned with different aspects such as organizational structure, institutions and infrastructure, service delivery, and healthcare expenditure. It will enable the reader to have a look at the past trends and present functioning of healthcare system of the state and give the reader a direction for further research in the potential areas. This review accounts for various studies conducted in the healthcare in the state of Punjab, India. A thematic comprehensive presentation of literature review is done in this chapter.

Chapter 7
Theoretical and Empirical Approaches and Typologies Into Failures and Enhancement of
Organizational Resilience Analysis 104
    José G. Vargas-Hernández, Instituto Tecnológico José Mario Molina Pasquel y Henríquez,
        Mexico

The aim of this chapter is to analyze the implications of theoretical, empirical, and typologies into failures and enhancement of organizational resilience. It is assumed that the application of conceptual, theoretical, and empirical knowledge base to specific knowledge and practice integrated into organizational resilience will help, but it is unclear to what extent it can be designed and supported because of lack of empirical evidence. The method employed is the analytical reflection sustained in the review of theoretical and empirical literature and observation. It is concluded that each organizational system transformation needs different and specific conceptual, theoretical, and empirical knowledge bases to take advantage of failures and enhance organizational resilience.

Chapter 8
Organizational Resilience Capability and Capacity Building.. 124
    José G. Vargas-Hernández, Instituto Tecnológico José Mario Molina Pasquel y Henríquez,
      Mexico

The objective of this chapter is to analyze the implications of organizational resilience capability and capacity building and development processes and the posed challenges to its design and implementation. It is based on the conceptual and theoretical assumptions underpinning the capabilities of resilience that can be learned and designed by organizations to be implemented and applied to adverse conditions. These underlying assumptions affect the organizational resilience capabilities building. It is concluded that building and development organizational resilience capabilities processes has increased the research agenda on the theoretical and conceptual literature and the notions, factors, elements, and challenges.

Chapter 9
Implications of Implementing Operational Multi-Levels: Individual, Organizational, Community, and Societal Resilience 143
    José G. Vargas-Hernández, Instituto Tecnológico José Mario Molina Pasquel y Henríquez,
      Mexico

The purpose of this study is to analyze the operational implications of implementing resilience at the multi-levels of individual, organizational, community, and societal resilience. It is assumed that the implementation of resilience requires identifying the concepts, antecedents, fundaments, principles regarding the nature, processes, orientations, and outcomes. The method employed is the analytical-reflective based on conceptual, theoretical, and empirical literature review and observation of specific situations. This chapter considers a wide range of research related to resilience to be comprehensive. It is concluded that resilience is critically relevant at multi-level for individuals, organizations, communities, and society that must remain capable and strong even when all the events are adverse and seem incapable and consider ad hoc responses based on the nature of experienced major incidents. Neither academic research nor the practitioners are fully considering the implementation of resilience to solve problems.

Chapter 10
Renewable Energies and the Urban Environment in Spain 164
    Maria Jesus Garcia Garcia, University of Valencia, Spain

Sustainable development is a type of development that advocates first of all the harmonization between economic development and environmental protection. Adding social progress, it would therefore be development in which high and stable growth in the production of goods and services is compatible with widespread social progress, environmental protection, and prudent and efficient use of natural resources. It is therefore a delicate building supported by three main pillars—social, economic, and environmental—in which none of them prevails over the other. Accordingly, sustainability has an integrated character, preceded as it is by the objectives of economic recovery, environmental sustainability, and social cohesion. It is a general principle with transversal or horizontal projection capable of crossing different and varied sectoral areas, as many as are relevant to achieve its integrating objectives.

Chapter 11
Welfare State, Income, and Public Debt: Their Implications for Latin American Life Satisfaction .. 178

    Jessica Dávalos-Aceves, Escuela de Ciencias Económicas y Empresariales, Universidad Panamericana, Mexico
    José G. Vargas-Hernández, Instituto Tecnológico José Mario Molina Pasquel y Henríquez, Mexico

The effect of economics on the subjective well-being of people has been studied by treating country information in the same way as data from individuals. The objective of this chapter is to analyze 17 Latin American countries with data from 2016 by including both effects handled into two different levels. This work contributes to extend the current debate regarding the impact of economics on subjective well-being of people by applying the multilevel method. Some of the findings revealed that both the individual economic situation as well as the welfare state and the rule of law of a country generate effects on subjective well-being. Similarly, the effect of interaction between some variables was analyzed, and it was concluded that people with great economic difficulties have a stronger relationship with subjective well-being in areas of higher government spending and higher tax burden.

Chapter 12
US Dependance on Chinese Pharma in the Pandemic Era and the Nationalization of the US System 204

    Paolo Bongarzoni, Swiss School of Management, Italy
    Adriano Ferri, Swiss School of Management, Italy

The severe impact of the coronavirus pandemic has indeed prompted several questions about economic and social security. Among them is placed the current concern about the possible nationalization of the U.S. pharmaceutical industry due to the fear of a possible generic drug shortages. More importantly, since the United States imports most of its drugs from other countries (e.g., China), is the impact of Covid-19 on the pharmaceutical industry the catalyst for a future nationalization for the U.S. pharmaceutical industry? Are there real reasons to support this prospect, or is it an old argument renewed by fear?

Chapter 13
Does It Hold Water? An Empirical Investigation on the Usefulness of Filtering Tap Water to Treat Health Complaints 219

    Rainer Schneider, RECON, Germany

Recently, it was shown that regular consumption of a standardized amount of filtered tap water over a period of three weeks improved self-reported physical complaints. However, since individuals were fully aware of the type of water they consumed, it was unclear to what extent this effect was ascribable to placebo effects. This chapter tests the effectiveness of an in-home water filter system (AcalaQuell®) by comparing it with a sham water filter containing no significant filter ingredients. Both filters were concealed, and participants knew that the probability to receive the clinically proven filter was 50%. There were large differences with regard to symptom reduction between the two groups. For individual-specific complaints, the reduction was 38% for the filtered water group while the reduction in the placebo group was about 8%. Subjective health complaints are considerably reduced after daily intake of AcalaQuell®-filtered tap water during a three-week administration period. This effect is specific and independent from placebo effects.

Chapter 14
Assessing Differential Vulnerability to Health Risks Associated With Microbial Contamination of Vegetables 233
> Emmanuel Kyeremeh, Berekum College of Education, Ghana
> Dacosta Aboagye, Kwame Nkrumah University of Science and Technology, Ghana
> Felix Asante, Kwame Nkrumah University of Science and Technology, Ghana

In the Sunyani Municipality, rapid population growth and uncertainties in rainfall have encouraged the use of untreated surface water for irrigating vegetables. However, microbial levels of ready-to-eat vegetables remain untested, and the differences in exposure unexplored. Further, there is a paucity of studies that compare the quality of local and exotic vegetables. A mixed method approach was used to collect and analyse primary data for the study. Forty-one farmers were sampled whilst 24 vegetable samples were used. The results showed on-farm vegetables in the municipality had microbial counts beyond the acceptable World Health Organization (WHO) threshold. Comparatively, the microbial counts of on-farm vegetables in rural and peri-urban locations differed, and the quality of local and exotic vegetables also differed. Also, vulnerability to on-farm microbial contamination differed across space and among producers. It is recommended that vegetable farmers should be educated on the safety of vegetables by the Agricultural Extension Officers in the municipality.

Chapter 15
Japanese Stone Gardens: Diversity, Sustainability, and Consumerism 250
> Simon Regin Paxton, Komazawa University, Japan

It has been suggested that the modern Japanese garden contains a wide variety of garden types. While some scholars have acknowledged the diversity of modern Japanese gardens, recent developments in Japanese stone gardens, known as karesansui, have gone largely unnoticed. Preconceived notions of karesansui do not encapsulate the true diversity which exists today. Moreover, the general public has tended to exoticize karesansui. Scholarly work on karesansui has, however, dispelled many of the myths and misrepresentations related to these gardens. In this chapter, the author will extend previous research and shed light on recent developments in karesansui and the myths that surround them. This chapter will examine karesansui from several perspectives: diversity, sustainability, and finally, from the perspective of consumerism.

Chapter 16
Art and Environment Seen Through the Lens of Politics in Japan 263
> Mika Markus Merviö, Kibi International University, Japan

This chapter analyses the changing diversity of politically and socially relevant interpretations, ideas, and opinions concerning the environment in Japan with a special reference given to visual arts and how environment and environmental issues have been dealt with in Japanese art. Politics involves constant reinterpretation and rearranging of everything around us. Art and especially visual images allow endless opportunities for reconstruction and to be used, recomposed, and combined rhizomatically. The art world in Japan has been directly influenced by the changing political and social context, but within the art community in Japan, power relations have deeply influenced what ideas reach the public. Politicization of environment and art has a long history in Japan as environment and art both are an indispensable part of Japanese society and history. Shaping the interpretations for them has always had profound political and social significance. Moreover, the digitizing and internet together have made the spreading of images much easier and have made visual images more important than ever.

Chapter 17
Japanese Visual Arts: Representation and Perfectioning of Reality – Mimesis and Understanding of Japanese Visual Arts 279

Mika Markus Merviö, Kibi International University, Japan

In this chapter, the author has analysed the Japanese visual traditions in the context of changing social, cultural, and political environment. He has provided detailed discussions about different phases of Japanese art history, and towards the end of the chapter, he has focused especially on the present situation of Japanese visual art scene. In addition, he has tried to add something new to the analysis by applying the concept of mimēsis in the sense that the human beings are mimetic beings and feeling an urge to create texts and art that reflect and represent reality. The Japanese visual art does much more than just copies the reality: it represents the reality and perfections it, and by accomplishing these acts, Japanese art remains dynamic and provides a means for artists in Japan to express themselves and the society around them.

Compilation of References 303

About the Contributors 357

Index 363

Preface

This book uses as its inspiration *The International Journal of Public and Private Perspectives on Healthcare, Culture, and the Environment (IJPPPHCE)*, one of IGI Global's Core Journals. It is a genuinely international journal with an innovative and interdisciplinary approach to issues of Healthcare, Culture, and the Environment. It is particularly these issues that have proved to be at the core of social transformation of modern societies and areas where there are very strong linkages between different issue areas. The ongoing COVID 19 pandemic has strongly demonstrated how these three thematic areas are linked with public and private perspectives. Furthermore, effective interactions reaching beyond all types of boundaries are indispensable in order to cope with the types crises and emergencies that we are dealing with.

In times of crisis it has become very clear that there is a particular need for both interdisciplinary and transdisciplinary approaches in finding solutions to issues that tend to defy disciplinary and other borders, both physical and mental. The Journal bears the dichotomy of 'Public and Private Perspectives' to indicate an openness to analyze social and cultural phenomena from the point of view of different actors and stakeholders. Public policy remains important but it is important to be able to bring all the relevant perspectives to the analysis. The global approach in the journal means that we have been serious about inviting scholars from all parts to the world to contribute fresh and original research that in many different ways may well turn out to challenge the borders of our disciplines and many other borders and limitations that still exist in the world. This book continues the best traditions of our journal and maintains its interdisciplinary and transdisciplinary approach as well as the global perspective.

This book consists of chapters that have been invited from selected authors among the scholars who have contributed their articles to the journal and asked them to enhance and update their articles to turn them into book chapters. Furthermore, this book also includes several articles that have not yet been published elsewhere and which are fresh chapters dealing with the theme of the book. What is common to all these research works is that they fit into the general theme and provide innovative approaches that could well be termed as being transdisciplinary, moving beyond fixed disciplines and combining in an innovative ways tools to analyze topics that are central for contemporary societies.

Our experience among the authors has been that healthcare, welfare, culture and the environment are probably the most important and contested issue areas in international discourses concerning the contemporary societies. It is exactly these areas where the modern state as well as the civil society and all individuals are facing the biggest challenges to adjust to new realities, in terms of politics, culture, economy or ethics. These areas are often overlapping and in many countries there are already scholars working in some of these interdisciplinary fields and there surely is a need to encourage better communication across cultural and disciplinary borders as well as moving to all new directions.

Preface

To summarize about the issue areas of this book I will introduce briefly the main areas of study and how we have approached them.

1) Healthcare: 'Health' as a concept has a long history of having been seen intricately entangled with a plethora of human activities. Healthcare as a system is directly connected with politics, administration, education, ethics, religion, culture and economy. Healthcare has significantly improved our quality of life and it is no wonder that its role in societies keeps growing. In short, health care is not only an industry directly covering more than ten percent of GDP in most industrialized countries. The close relationship between health and welfare extends its impacts to all human activities and in the age of Anthroposcene that includes also the environment. This book will give some of the answers what healthcare and welfare are all about and where they are moving within the societies that themselves are rapidly changing.

2) Culture: While 'health' easily leads us to analyze from within the framework of social sciences and natural/ medical sciences 'culture' is more elusive and requires an understanding of philosophy and humanities. However, in our global society cultural differences and socially and culturally based forms of understanding/ construction are central to social analysis. Including "Culture" and encouraging research on the topic opens the discussion to cultural differences concerning the public and private as well as the "culture" and cultural understanding itself and their relevance to policy and society. In short, "Culture" is included to encourage new kinds of innovative pieces of research both in terms of developing the theory and paying attention to cultural diversity and the importance of culture in every society, as well as to the historical roots of social issues and forms of understanding in different societies. Culture is particularly suitable when it is combined with other issue areas that the journal covers. The result both in terms of issue areas as well as the theoretical approach often becomes transdisciplinary and helps to make new fresh contributions to international research and theory in various fields. Of course, the most important contribution will be the relevance of research for finding solutions to acute social problems.

3) Environment is the physical and cultural setting of human endeavors and the stage where everything else happens. In this era of our reflexive relationship with the threatened and beleaguered natural environment it is clear that the sheer survival of all living things is at stake and that their health, culture and everything they hold important is closely connected to the environment. Environmental issues are of primary importance for all the living things, including all the humans on this planet. Therefore, it makes very much sense to discuss environmental issues in the context of social issues of our time. We hope that our efforts will help to find solutions to environmental and social problems and we do recognize that all these efforts are closely linked.

Scope and Approach of the Book

This book introduces discourses and analytical discussions of many different related topics, all adding to understanding on changing realities within the realms of healthcare, culture and the environment. In this book the idea has been to link discussions of in social, environmental and cultural sphreres in new ways to be able to understand the issues better both in the global and their own social and cultural context. This book aims to transcend all kind of boundaries, including the national boundaries and boundaries of academic disciplines to search explanations to developments in contemporary world. Area-specific or culture-specific discussions, of course, are closely linked to developments elsewhere, but there is also a need to analyze the impact of local cultures and traditions – without being blind to changes in these traditions.

Transdisciplinary approach is used here to promote depth of understanding as well as adaptability to skills needed to succeed in our changing world. In short, the problems that we are facing in contemporary world require both deeper understanding and a broader set of skills. The idea is to include multiple disciplines with a human centered goals. In the end the analysis not only integrates the perspectives of multiple disciplines but helps to find all new perspectives.

INTRODUCTION OF CONTENTS BY HIGHLIGHTING HOW THEY RELATE THE CURRENT SITUATION AND FUTURE TRENDS IN THE FIELDS OF HEALTHCARE, CULTURE, AND THE ENVIRONMENT

Chapter 1: Managing High Preforming Safety Cultures in US Healthcare Organizations During COVID-19

The increasing complexity of the United States healthcare system has compounded the likelihood of mistakes. One of the ten leading causes of death and disability is safety issues with patient care. Medical errors put undue hardship on the economy resulting in the loss of billions of dollars. The current COVID-19 pandemic revealed gaps in public health strategies, medical treatments, comprehensive patient safety, and human resources strategy. Implementing human resources and performance management processes that promote safety, safe decision making, and reduce medical errors is critical. Adopting methods used by high-reliability organizations (HRO) may reduce medical errors and improve patient safety. Qualitative focus groups were used to collect data around creating organizational cultures focused on safety. This research aims to improve performance by providing healthcare leaders with tools to enhance organizational culture, reduce medical errors, and improve patient safety in the age of COVID 19.

The authors use in their analysis the Nuclear Organization Framework (NOF) model of organizational design, where changes in the organization's elements can affect the entire system. This includes the organizational design components and subcomponents that fall within them, such as policies, leadership capacity, data, skilled professional staff, patient involvement, and others, such as safety culture—all necessary for executing and maintaining effective safety programs in health care settings.

Patient harm occurs when these five components are inconsistent. Among the leading ten causes of death and disability globally is safety failure during patient care. Specifically, in the United States, up to 440,000 deaths occur every year due to medical errors. Additionally, 10% of patients are injured while receiving health care, and almost half of these injuries are preventable. Moreover, 40% of patients worldwide are harmed during primary and outpatient health care services. These preventable medical errors account for approximately 15% of total hospital activity and expenditures. Researchers suggest medical errors can occur purposely or accidentally.

The increased complexity of our society and the current healthcare system warrants that human resources drives interventions focused on creating new organizational cultures to reduce the chances and occurrences of medical errors. The COVID-19 crisis is a catalyst for current public health methodologies, medical therapies, and overall patient safety. This recent turbulent healthcare environment causes necessity, uncertainty, and drastic upheaval, which is influencing innovative leadership practices that

Preface

are connected to the strategic fit of an organization. A recent descriptive study of a Turkish university hospital revealed that operating rooms (OR) are among the most complex healthcare areas prone to medical errors. Reasons for these errors include multi-disciplinary staff, varied educational objectives, and complicated team dynamics. Up to 50% of medical errors occur in the OR. These factors all contribute to higher rates of medical errors. Researchers posit that these errors are preventable through corrective feedback, reviewing the errors, and better teamwork. Therefore, implementing organizational processes that improve these factors is tantamount to effective prevention.

The authors identify that errors arise from poor technique and inadequate knowledge, and human factors, including workplace fatigue, perception failures, and misjudgments. Quantifying the magnitude of harmful incidents and engaging in behaviors is critical to reducing errors and being ethical and honest when engaging patients and making errors. The healthcare culture understandably focuses on caring for patients, even at the expense of security and safety. There is a complex tension around ethics and safety concerning patients' interests, the interests of the healthcare organization, and the interests of finding quicker paths to treating patients. The ethical challenge is the need, to be honest when patients are impacted by avoidable actions, errors, and unsafe behaviors. The threat of legal action and expensive payments can create a culture that dissuades divulging knowledge about mistakes and ethical violations. Changes in organizational culture are critical to reducing errors and medical errors with the propensity to harm. As a means of managing reputational risk, organizations do not openly disclose the nature and extent of medical errors and unsafe operational practices. Often the public finds out when a whistleblower reveals the offense. Patient-centered decision-making necessitates the requirement to appreciate the importance of organizational cultures that drive employees to make ethical and safe decisions or disclose those instances when the organization or employees engage in hazardous activities.

Among the impacts of the COVID-19 was that it created a serious shortage in health care staff. Thereby, healthcare staff faced increased workloads, high fatigue and exhaustion, and workplace stress. It is noteworthy to discuss how compassion fatigue (CF) among healthcare personnel affects an organization's totality and compromises patient safety. Compassion fatigue was conceived to describe the phenomenon of stress resulting from exposure to a traumatized individual rather than from exposure to the trauma itself.

The COVID-19 pandemic revealed many loopholes in the existing public health supply chain methodologies, patient safety procedures, and human resources processes. All healthcare personnel is challenged to establish cultures driven by both ethical and safe behavior. In the past, healthcare organizations did not openly disclose the severity of medical errors and patient safety issues. The present culture in medicine does not encourage a safe and open space to report errors and patient safety violations. Human resources as to play leadership role in changing that. This study shows how organizational cultures in healthcare organizations must be addressed from the lens of organizational design. The interconnectedness of organization design components must be understood and carefully and appropriately managed to foster and develop effective organizational safety cultures, including patient safety cultures, and drive transformative organizational change.

Chapter 2: A Cross-Cultural Comparison of College Student Self-Efficacy, Self-Regulation, and Resilience Between the US and China During the COVID-19 Pandemic

Culture shapes students' learning beliefs and we need a psychological theory that focuses on both cross-cultural similarities as well as cross-cultural differences, as the majority of the research studies in this area focus on cross-cultural similarities and neglect cross-cultural differences. Contrasts often tell far more than similarities. Dramatic differences in individuals' learning have been found between Eastern and Western cultures and this article adds greatly to our understanding of the American and Chinese cultures, especially in the educational setting. Moreover, this chapter provides valuable information and insights how the organizations and individuals in China and the United States cope during the COVID-19 global pandemic.

The unprecedented Coronavirus (COVID-19) global pandemic forced many colleges and universities around the world to abruptly abandon their long-established practices and rapidly develop new ones that would be safe while also make best of the available online educational options. This event marked the first time that college students uniformly attended online college courses throughout the world. On the one hand, online learning provided virtual learning accessibility and flexibility in times of a potential natural disaster, civil emergency, and crisis. On the other hand, however; regardless of the course format, online learning environments also caused many college students around the world to develop a sense of isolation and loneliness due to a lack of interpersonal relationships with their instructors and peers.

Further, most, if not all, college students evacuated from their on-campus or off-campus residential settings to move back home with their parents or guardians. Thus, college students now had to face these unique online learning contexts alone without the support of their college peers. The various challenges faced by college students during the pandemic may also have been a function of their social and cultural backgrounds.

The more personal variables such as self-efficacy, metacognitive self-regulation, and resilience have all been demonstrated to serve as important factors contributing to college students' learning and academic achievement, especially while they are engaged in online learning environments. In addition, some preliminary research into the effects of the COVID-19 global pandemic on college students' learning has demonstrated that during the spring of 2020, parental support was a statistically significant predictor of college students' motivation, which was a significant predictor of their cognitive and metacognitive strategies.

Thus, it is suggested here that during the COVID-19 global pandemic, while college students were learning away from their college or university setting while engaged in online learning, self-efficacy, metacognitive self-regulation, and resilience may have been especially critical to their academic success. Further, significant differences in individual self-efficacy, self-regulation, and resilience have been found between college students from Eastern and Western cultures, which may further lead to differences in learning academic performance. These are the reasons why the study sought to investigate a cross-cultural comparison between American and Chinese students' self-efficacy, metacognitive self-regulation, and resilience during the COVID-19 global pandemic.

As for the method, volunteer participants (N = 479) were recruited from a large Southeastern university in the U.S. and two large universities in China during the Spring semester of 2020. Participants received extra course credit as an incentive for their participation. The anonymous survey consisted of demographic questions, the Self-efficacy for Learning and Performance and Metacognitive Self-regulation

Preface

subscales of the Motivated Strategies for Learning Questionnaire and the Resilience Evaluation Scale. For the Chinese participants, all original items, which were in English, were translated into Chinese. To guarantee the content validity of the Chinese version of the measure, a standard translation and back-translation procedure was used. A certified translator who is bilingual and fluently in both English and Chinese translated the English questionnaires into Chinese. The Chinese version was evaluated by the researcher, who is fluent in English and Chinese. Then, back translation was conducted by the researcher and checked by the certified translator. All participants completed the anonymous surveys in Qualtrics.

As for the results, the study demonstrated that self-efficacy, self-regulation, and resilience differed between American and Chinese college students. First, the results showing that American students' self-efficacy was reported as being higher than that of Chinese students is aligned with previous research demonstrating that Asian students' self-reported self-efficacy was weaker than that of participants from the Western region. In previous research there was also be found a lower level of self-efficacy among Asian students as compared to non-Asian students. The American college students' self-regulation was found to be slightly lower than their Chinese counterparts in the present study. This finding echoes the previous research, which showed that Chinese children showed more adaptive self-regulation skills as compared to children from the United States. In terms of the gender effect, in this study there was no significant gender difference in self-efficacy, self-regulation, or resilience. In general, the result of present study provided evidence of the difference in self-efficacy, self-regulation, and resilience between American and Chinese college students. Future studies may fully explore the factors that impact self-efficacy, self-regulation, and resilience for different cultural groups in diverse learning contexts with more comprehensive perspectives and insights to develop proper pedagogical and learning strategies and establish an educationally supportive learning environment for students from different cultural backgrounds.

Chapter 3: Due to COVID-19, Food Insecurity and Access to Healthy Food Have Become Significant Public Health Problems

Since the onset of COVID-19, food insecurity and access to healthy food have become a significant public health problem. Inequalities in dietary behaviors have been unambiguously correlated to the food environment, including access to healthy and fresh foods. The COVID-19 pandemic has led to significant fluctuations in the distribution, sale, purchase, preparation, and food consumption in the United States and elsewhere. In addition, in the United States, substantial socioeconomic and racial disparities exist in dietary behaviors. Limited access to fresh food, coupled with a greater prevalence of fast food outlets in lower-income and minority neighborhoods, is partially responsible for sub-optimal eating patterns among residents. The purpose of this chapter is to highlight the factors and influences concerning childhood obesity, food education, community gardening, and healthy eating.

Child obesity has attained an epidemic level not only in the U.S. but all over the world. The Centers for Disease Control identify overweight as a BMI at or above the 85th percentile and below the 95th percentile for children and teens of the same age and sex. Children and teens who have a BMI above the 95th percentile of their peers of the same age and sex are considered obese.

Childhood obesity is influenced by genetics, high sugar consumption, unhealthy snack food, portion size, activity level, environment, socio-culture, family, and psychological factors. Each area plays a significant role in shaping the lives of young children. Genetics is one of the leading factors for developing obesity; however, it does not contribute to its increase entirely. Physical activity plays a significant role in personal and preventative health in which exercising could reduce chronic diseases and premature mortality by 6 to 10 percent. Some epidemiologists classify obesity as a non-communicable disease; however, it is just as deadly as a biological virus. Numerous factors contribute to non-communicable health conditions. The cause of being overweight and obese is a lot more complicated and is influenced by (a) diet and insufficient physical activity, (b) heredity and genetics, (c) family and social factors, (d) behavioral and cultural factors, (e) environmental and socioeconomic status, and (f) media marketing. Children who are overweight and obese are likely to remain unhealthy into adulthood and develop other non-communicable diseases.

Researchers are continuously seeking methods to reduce childhood obesity, which includes leveraging technology and develop innovation. For example, telemedicine uses "interactive synchronous video" to deliver medical care to patients (or communities) that lack the accessibility to healthcare services. Healthcare professionals and scientists have concluded that telemedicine is a viable delivery platform for behavioral healthcare services to rural areas. These technologies have become invaluable during the COVID-19 pandemic, where social distancing has become very important.

To combat obesity, nutrition alone is not enough. Physical activity is a crucial part of any dietary and health program. Guidelines established by the U.S. and the WHO recommend at least 60 minutes of moderate-to-vigorous physical activity daily, including "muscle and bone strengthening three days a week". However, only about 25% of children and youth participate in the required physical activity.

The concept of community gardens and how it benefits the health of children and families is rooted in the theory of experiential learning. Experiential learning is learning by experience and doing, followed by reflection. It is through the process of thoughtfully caring for a garden, through the seasons of planting and harvesting, that an individual learns the value of the food they are purposefully cultivating for consumption. The research regarding the benefits of community gardens has led may agencies and local governments to promote community gardens as a way to access nutritious food and increase physical activity. In a study that looked at pre and post BMI measures of primarily low socio-economic status Hispanic families after participating in various activities including a tending to a community garden, children diagnosed as obese and overweight saw a 13% and 23% decrease in weight, respectively. Additionally, there was an increase of the reported fruits and vegetables available at home and consumed at post-measures.

Increasing access to and consumption of fresh vegetables is an important public health goal. Gardening can contribute to food security at all income levels by providing access to fresh, culturally acceptable produce and encouraging a more nutritious diet. Food security is defined as access by all people at all times to enough food for an active and healthy life. It is a concept that encompasses food's quantity, quality, and cultural acceptability.

Many families in the United States have increasing rates of food insecurity since the emergence of COVID-19. Feeding America, the largest hunger-relief organization in the U.S., estimates that more than 54 million people in the country, including 18 million children, are currently experiencing food insecurity. Household food insecurity has excessively impacted African-American and Latinx households at nearly twice the rate of Caucasian families. As many urban residents struggle with access to fresh fruits and vegetables and continue to face food insecurity, community gardens have helped alleviate these nutritional gaps. Inhabitants in the U.S. face a range of threats to health and well-being, which could theoretically be adopted by proposals such as community gardening. These hazards incorporate non-communicable diseases and their causative risk considerations, such as minimal physical activity

Preface

levels and poor diet. Thus, neighborhood gardening is a multifaceted multi-factorial endeavor, likely to have numerous influences (direct and indirect) on the health and well-being of those taking part

Chapter 4: Ionization, Gadget Radiation Analysis and Disease Control by Yajna – An Ancient Vedic Wisdom for Human Health and Relevant Amidst Pandemic Threats

This chapter provides very original blend of culture, environment and technology. In particular, it provides insights of Indian culture and helps to understand how environment and technology are in different parts of the world always seen through cultural lenses and that the use of technology is never free from culture and values. Furthermore, the use of technology is also closely linked with different kind of risks to living things and the environment in general. This chapter can not ascertain the actual risks levels of each and every technology but it surely provides a good collection of insights and wisdoms embedded in Indian culture and helps to test the open mindedness of academic communities. Of course, the risks and worries listed in the chapter have also been addressed in many other communities around the world, with different degrees of seriousness. After all we are dealing with issues that are very much related to the life-styles of most people in the world and challenging dominant attitudes and economic powers may not be easy.

The use of electronic items like computers, laptops, tablets, television, Led lights, mobiles phones, microwaves etc. are mandatory necessity of lifestyle today. The Electro-Magnetic Radiations are emitted from the electronic devices and are very harmful to human beings its excessive use leads to growth of cancer cells and have other detrimental impacts to health. Therefore, the authors argue that we need to find a way out to prevent ourselves from the harmful effect EMR level at workplace and homes. It is time to adopt modern way from traditional techniques and forward a model that involves the community, with a stakeholder-focused approach. Ancient Indian scriptures have described Yagya to absorb the harmful effect of cosmic waves. Hence, in the present study, author's team have done test to find the impact of Yagya on effect of radiation on human beings emitted from electronic devices. Results of the experiment showed significant decrease in EMR with Yagya, indicating Yagya can one of the useful solutions as non-conventional method for reducing indoor EMR level.

As for the cellular phone use and whether it is connected with an increased risk for intracranial tumours glioma the results are still not decisive. A study analysis on two case-control done on malignant brain tumours, that comprised 1498 cases and 3530 controls, revealed that mobile phone use increased the risk of glioma. The result analysis showed that there was increased risk of meningioma or glioma with using mobile phones for more than 10 years. IARC then classified electromagnetic radiofrequency fields as possibly carcinogenic to humans, as per the report of World Health Organization.

After presenting these serious concerns the authors proceed to introduce Surya Namaskar as an ancient Indian method in which we infuse the infinite energy of the Sun within us through some simple yoga postures. By practicing yogic postures, breathing process and chanting Omkar mantra, while the energy centers located in the body are activated, it also purifies the person's aura. By doing Surya Namaskar, our lungs, heart and heartbeat are free from disorder. While practicing this, our attention should be on the seven chakras located on the sushumna nadi. Since ages, Sun has been worshiped as the basis of life. The sun not only gives us the energy and spiritual power of life, but many beneficial nectar-like elements present in its rays make our body disease free. When the balance of chemicals present in the body deteriorates, many diseases and ailments start growing in our body.

As a specific technique, the authors introduce Mudrās. Hands and fingers are capable to do some extra ordinary things besides assisting in holding, eating and doing physical work. Hands are the instrument to everything. They are like the control panel to everything. In science of yog and meditation there are hundreds of Mudrās, some are used for health, some for wellbeing, some Mudrās are done for creating processes. In fact, different features of life can be denoted with the Mudrās. For example, in yoga a particular asana has a unique Mudrā, and a specific kind of breathing another Mudrā is useful, to derive the best result from within the human body.

In yoga, different gestures of fingers and hand (mudrās) are used in conjunction with pranayama (the yogic breathing exercises) and are generally done while seated in the pose of Padmasana or Vajrasana. Each mudrās formations stimulate and activates different organs and body parts. Mudrās when done with breathing exercise it affect the flow of energy and also help to change the mood of an individual. Each hand gestures and its positions during Mudrā act as locks it guide energy flows and reflexes to the brain. During Mudrā making crossing, curling, pressing, stretching or touching thumb with different fingers of the hand we can help to manipulate the mind body. Mudrās allows a physical connection with an intangible wish that this is possible because each area of the hand corresponds to a certain part of the mind or body. There are different mudrās formation however by meditating on a specific Mudrā helps manifest certain hopes, energies, or devotions into your life. At a higher spiritual level, practicing on specific mudrās shows the outward representation of one's inward intentions. Mudrās show what a practitioners' desires and what he intends to be!. Please refer annex for more details and related contents.

After further specific instructions the authors proceed to recommendations and try to convince that Yagya is effective when done properly. As well as on our body a result oriented research based work just asking for medicine is not going to cure, buying a medicine is not going to cure, even worshipping and praising is not going to cure. The practice of Yoga, Pranayama Meditation and Mudrā practices are claimed to develop positive psychology with mental and physical well-being, personality development with fulfilment of joyous living can be attained with its basic practice as propounded by Ved Murti Pt. Sri Ram Sharma Acharya. The authors recommend that Yoga Practice may be prescribed by the doctors as an additional therapy to common people who have suffered health loss due to Covid 19 pandemic or due any physiological disorder of the body system. It is also recommended to consider the clear instruction on breath work, postures, relaxation techniques, and meditation on different methods of Hatha Yoga, Ashtanga yoga, Iyengar yoga and Bikram yoga and meditation techniques. This chapter takes as granted that the Indian traditions can help to provide cures that are effective in modern times and apparently this view has plenty of support in India. The success of these cures apparently depends very much on the ability of people to change their life-styles and mindset. In order to effectively adopt the practices described here one obviously needs to believe in the values that accompany these practices. It is not only in Indian traditions where the benefits of meditation techniques are recognized. Mind and body certainly work together. Everyone should be far more open to recognize the existence different cultural understandings and practices and only then critically examine how these practices contribute or fail to contribute to mental or physical health in different parts of the world.

Chapter 5: The Need for Adaptive Organizational Systems Concerning Proactive Health Literacy Approaches in the Misinformation State of COVID-19

When it comes to COVID-19 in America, the country represents 4 percent of the global population but account for 22 percent of global COVID-19 deaths (Bagherpour & Nouri, 2020). The convergence of

Preface

misrepresentation and rapid growth contagious are considered interrelated. Social media has played a significant role in the spread of myths and misconceptions concerning COVID-19, and as a result, health literacy has become critical to fighting the virus. Misinformation has come to define COVID-19 due to unrelenting public fables misinformation on everything from the virus being a hoax, untested cures, and the uselessness of wearing facemasks. Health literacy is the extent to which the public and patients can acquire and understand essential health knowledge required to make proper health choices and decisions. The inquiry employs a content analysis of current literature and qualitative interviews to explore practical organizational adaptive approaches that promote COVID-19 health literacy. This chapter provides a wealth of valuable recommendations for medical providers to promote adaptive organizational systems by incorporating health literacy programs to identify patients with low health literacy, improve health literacy, and impact health outcomes concerning disease and health condition management.

Low health literacy is a public health travesty. Health information and health literacy around COVID 19 is a miscalculated public health conundrum. The COVID 19 can be understood not only as a pandemic but an info-demic because of the need for patients to be more health literate when they are being bombarded by inaccurate or misleading information from social media, public officials, and family. During a global pandemic, the need to understand and explore health literacy's nuances has never been more pressing. This qualitative exploratory study uses the expertise of subject matter experts on health literacy to classify the barriers to health information literacy, the best practices for improving health information literacy, and the additional measures are taken by medical providers during the COVID 19 outbreak ensure that patients have the most accurate and useful health information. Health literacy is an area in need of significant attention in health information management and health services delivery because it is often a critical factor in disease risk management. Health literacy is essential with the outbreak of COVID 19, especially in an age when so much inaccurate health information is readily available.

Patients will often mask their lack of comprehension of instructions, directions, or information to evade the embarrassment not being health literate. Patients with low literacy skills have a 50% increased risk of hospitalization than patients with adequate literacy skills Low health literacy leads to poor illness management skills including improper management of medications and inappropriate prevention activities. Research indicates that patients with low health literacy are less likely to follow treatment protocols, are less effective at following medical directions, have higher risks of hospitalizations, and have more prescription miscalculations.

Nurses and doctors are often unmindful that a patient has poor health literacy and often do not have the tools or the training to diagnose a patient's degree of health literacy or improve a patient's health literacy level. Strategies for addressing the issue are often low-priority or absent in medical organizations. Research has outlined that frequently nursing and other clinicians have limited understanding of health literacy, a limited understanding of how increasing health literacy can improve health outcomes and that health literacy is a low priority in patients' treatment protocols. The nurse plays a vital role in direct patient care and delivering health services. Educating nurses, doctors, physician assistants, and medical center office staff on the issue and reaching them better communications approach is critical to increasing health literacy among patients.

As for the method of this study, interviews were conducted with 12 researchers with expertise and research on health literacy. Interviews were conducted using ZOOM video conferencing software due to COVID 19 social distancing restrictions. All participants had a doctorate degree with more than five post-doctorate years of academic research. All participants also had to have a minimum of 5 years of professional healthcare experience. Six participants were male, and six were female. They were selected based on peer-reviewed research studies indexed in Google Scholar, ResearchGate, and Academia.edu. All participants had over 300 citations on Google Scholar. They were asked questions about their perceptions of health literacy barriers and the best practices to improve health literacy by patients with COVID 19. The iterviews were asked such questions as: "Because there was so much misinformation on social media about COVID 19, what do you recommend as additional practices that should be explicitly implemented to promote more accurate health literacy around COVID 19?" The replies show a wide variety of practical advice and a real concern about the lack of health literacy among the present crisis situation.

Healthcare leaders can change the conversation to diminish miscommunication through engagement in activities that support improving patient care through health literacy, which is critical as people continue to lose their lives and become hospitalized due to COVID 19. All too often, stagnation in adaptive organizational systems provides barriers to health literacy. This chapter clearly demonstrates that changing, increasing, and improving health literacy conversations would provide higher quality patient care, give hope to patients in recovery, and bring faith to a system designed to save lives.

Chapter 6: A Review of Health Care System in the State of Punjab, India

In Indian healthcare system, services are delivered through a decentralised approach and organized by a complex network of public and private healthcare providers of states. India's healthcare sector has federal structure and federal-state divisions and state governments are responsible for providing and organizing health services in their respective states. The central government is responsible for health related treaties, national disease control, framing national health policies and regulating the healthcare system. Private sector in the country is not well regulated and most of the facilities are not registered with the concerned medical council and about 40% of the private care is provided by unqualified providers. The government sponsored schemes in the country are also relying on private sector hospitals as part of public-private partnerships. There is lack of clarity about the fact that which councils or entities are responsible for the regulation of private sector. Approximately 70% of population in country is availing services from private health sector. The private sector is comprised of single clinic, multi-speciality clinic, single hospital, multi-speciality hospital, super-speciality hospital, trust hospital, corporate hospital and medical colleges.

This chapter focuses on the situation of health care system in the state of Punjab. Punjab is a prosperous state and has growing economy and therefore may provide ideas how the Indian health care system will develop in the future also in other parts of India. The Punjab Health System Corporation (PHSC), Department of Health & Family Welfare, Government of Punjab is responsible for providing preventive, promotive and curative health services to the people of state through a 3-tier structure. PHSC functions under the DOH&FW and it monitors and coordinates public hospitals in implementation of various schemes. At village level, department is playing very crucial role in facilitating program delivery and spreading awareness in rural areas. It consists of Subsidiary-Health Centres (SHCs) at below providing basic healthcare services, above it there are Primary Health centres (PHCs). To support PHCs there is secondary level healthcare system, which spread over the district through civil hospitals, sub-divisional and district hospitals. Above all there is tertiary level health care system, which provides services of specialised hospitals & medical colleges.

There are total 1060 private hospitals in the state of Punjab. Private sector has created 63% of total hospital beds in the country from the year 2002 to 2010 and currently providing 80% of outpatient care and 60% of inpatient care. There is high rate of vacancies and absenteeism at public health facilities

Preface

and it is the major reason for difficulty in improvement of healthcare. Either the public clinics are not open or are understaffed. Despite having high income relative to others, Punjab has a vacancy rate of around 20%. There is high rate of absenteeism by health workers and there is almost 15% of absences without any reason. The predominant factor behind the absenteeism is whether a health worker lives close to the facility or not. There is slow increase in number of medical institutions as well as beds in Punjab during last 3 decades, which is insufficient to meet the demand of growing population. There is also a gap in allocation of health institutions among the districts within Punjab. Approximately 64% population have confidence in medical institutions of Punjab and 80%-95% of times people in Punjab visit private facilities without considering the fact that whether they live in urban or rural areas and also whether they are suffering from short term or long term illness. Infrastructure of the government hospitals is always insufficient for its patients and private hospitals have advance amenities more than that of govt. hospitals as they get many corporate & private investments. Although private hospitals have best equipment, advanced technology, high bed-patients ratio, but these hospitals provide services only to those patients who can afford the treatment costs.

One of the major causes of ill-state of healthcare in Punjab is decreasing state-govt. expenditure on health which leads to other problems like lack of medicines, limited doctor salaries and poor infrastructure. The private healthcare is dominating the delivery of primary and secondary healthcare system; state expenditure on public health decreased because of centrally sponsored NRHM, which is to fill gaps in the delivery of rural healthcare services; the expenditure on health & family welfare for Punjab has increased at a lower speed than its GSDP for past years. The reasons which affected the delivery of healthcare services in public sector are absenteeism and unfilled vacancies in Punjab Public Health System.

In their conclusion the authors point out that the previous studies related to healthcare systems have concentrated on other states than Punjab and even in Punjab also very limited area (maximum 3 districts) has been chosen for the studies. The low-income rural & urban population differences have been ignored while evaluating the accessibility and affordability of health services. The reasons for accessing healthcare institutions by the rural population in urban areas, reduced per-capita expenditure in the state and beds-shortage in public healthcare institutions have not been properly identified.

By considering these gaps of research in the area of healthcare system, it would be necessary to review the policy-making strategies and the implementation programmes of these policies. There is a requirement to study the healthcare system in Punjab from the view-point of low income population of the state and also the perceptions of the service providers must be better considered for a proper assessment of the public & private healthcare performance.

Furthermore, more districts or areas in a state can be evaluated to know the ground realities of a state. It is required to compare the public and private health care units to know the reasons for their good or worst working situations as well as for their performances. Job satisfaction of doctors, nurses and other staff plays a major role in the performance and service quality of the hospitals, so job satisfaction of employees can also be studied with the performance of the hospitals. This study has carefully analysed the past, present and likely future of health care in Punjab as well as placed the analysis within the context of wider Indian social, political and economic context. Furthermore, this chapter can be used to analyse the mechanisms of interaction between the public and private sectors, especially in issues of health care and social welfare.

Chapter 7: Theoretical and Empirical Approaches and Typologies Into Failures and Enhancement of Organizational Resilience Analysis

The concept of resilience become first relevant after 9/11 when the world was facing abruptly changing realities and resilience was a concept that helped to address the events and find ways to cope with uncertainties. The ongoing pandemics provide the opportunity to apply this concept and develop it further and show its full potential. Organizational resilience is active and purposeful to cope with unknown unexpected events. Organizational resilience is the capacity to maintain positive adjustment, bounce back and maintain desirable functions and outcomes under challenging conditions, from untoward events during strain. Organizational resilience is the system property that confers the ability to remain functional despite the threats. Organizational resilience is the ability to bounce back from unanticipated events with adverse effects.

People have positive contributions towards resilience. Organizational resilience should get the right people in the right positions and roles to achieve the organization's success. The dynamic nature of resilience provides the foundation for the development of organizational resilience. To address each of these types of resilience requirement areas, this chapter highlights key terms and concepts in the literature, along with several empirical studies, that demonstrate general wisdom and lessons learned for each case. Descriptive and outcome focused analysis of organizational resilience after a threatening situation is required

The aim of this chapter is to analyze the implications of theoretical, empirical, and typologies into failures and enhancement of organizational of organizational resilience. It is assumed that the application of conceptual, theoretical, and empirical knowledge base to specific knowledge and practice integrated into organizational resilience, it is unclear to what extent can be designed and supported because of lack of empirical evidence. The method employed is the analytical reflective sustained in the review of theoretical an empirical literature and observation. It is concluded that each organizational systems transformation needs different and specific conceptual, theoretical, and empirical knowledge base to take advantage of failures and enhance organizational resilience.

Conceptualizations of organizational resilience focuses on the detection on variables. The conceptualization of resilience is related to several events, among which the nature of change described as a specific phenomenon, is the most cruc. Organizational resilience is the ability to absorb and recover from shocks. Organizational resilience is the ability to develop effective plans for both short-term resuming and long-term restoration following disruptive events.

Organizational resilience is the ability to withstand stress and bounce back or recover from traumatic events. Organizational resilience is the ability to bounce back from adverse effects of unanticipated events. Organizational resilience is the ability of affected parties to communicate and reorganize across periods of rapid change or chaos

Organizational resilience is the capacity to absorb the impact and recover from the occurrence of extreme weather events. Organizational resilience is the characteristic to deal with unexpected abrupt and or extreme change. Organizational resilience is the capacity to maintain positive adjustment, bounce back and maintain desirable functions and outcomes under challenging conditions, outward events and during strain.

An organizational collaborative approach towards anticipation of risks to respond more effectively to any threats coming from unknow events and disruptions. Theoretical and empirical factors of organizational resilience and their effects on climate change and extreme weather are limited and sparse.

Preface

There are two schools of thought regarding the organizational resilience. From a sociological perspective, the findings of Richardson support correlations among self-efficacy, personal resilience, psychological empowerment, and leadership style with organizational resilience. The sociological organizational resilience theory. The sociological resilience theory assumes that may be multiple possible equilibriums in each organizational system. In organizational theory, organizational resilience incorporates insights from contingency and coping theories. Organizational resilience is contextually specific to a certain situation. Contextual organizational resilience is situational or oriented toward specific situations.

The empirical research is difficult to conduct. Resilience is a source of sustainable advantage for organizations. Preliminary results of empirical research indicates that resilience indicators including awareness issues and stakeholders' responsibilities in organizational recovery priorities contribute to enhance the overall organizational resilience.

This chapter analyzes the conceptual, theoretical, and empirical knowledge base of organizational resilience to find some implications of its typologies into failures and enhancement of organizational of organizational resilience. Despite the limited empirical evidence of knowledge base of organizational resilience, it can be integrated into practice in specific organizational systems. Therefore, each organizational systems transformation needs different and specific conceptual, theoretical, and empirical knowledge base to take advantage of failures and enhance organizational resilience. Organizational resilience incorporates both coping and contingency theories. Resilience is a source of knowledge for sustainable competitive advantage based on the organizational ability directed toward organizational development and advancement. It seems like there will be no shortage of problems and shocks and, therefore, there is plenty of need for organizational resilience. The more practical aspects of the theory are elaborated in the following chapter.

Chapter 8: Organizational Resilience Capability and Capacity Building

In his chapter organizational resilience is analyzed especially from the perspective of capability and capacity building. This approach is particularly valuable to avoid and limit the impacts of adverse events and generally to prepare for things to come. The objective of this paper is to analyze the implications of organizational resilience capability and capacity building and development processes and the posed challenges to its design and implementation. It is based on the conceptual and theoretical assumptions underpinning the capabilities of resilience that can be learned and designed by organizations to be implemented and applied to adverse conditions. These underlying assumptions affect the organizational resilience capabilities building. It is concluded that building and development organizational resilience capabilities processes has increased the research agenda on the theoretical and conceptual literature and the notions, factors, elements, and challenges.

Organizational resilience may be considered the ability, capability, and property which can be improved over time despite the difficulties to find the right elements that may contribute to handle disruptive events. Organizational resilience is a desirable property, an ability, capacity, and capability to deal with changes, jolts, and risks. Some characteristics of organizational resilience are the potential capability and capacity under emergent, disruptive, and discontinuous internal and external environment not always perceived in operational activities. Some characteristics of organizational resilience are the development of potential capabilities that take advantage under emergent and discontinuous, emergent, and disruptive environment. The essence of organizational resilience capabilities is the dealing with change, risks, and environmental jolts.

The integral and capability-based resilience model provides a frame of reference structure to ongoing debate. The capability-based perspective contributes to organizational resilience capabilities for the organization for survival and prosperity despite the adversity and turbulence. Resilience based on the perspective of capabilities that become effective in situations of complexity of risks contributes with applying stability while addressing the disruptions through incorporating non-linearity quantum thinking replacing the Newtonian thinking. Organizational resilience capability building is context-dependent on the specific exposure to desirable characteristic dealing with unexpected, abrupt, and extreme change.

Organizational resilience is an ability of a system to meet operating, maintaining, and recovering critical capabilities under pressures, tensions and stressors of disasters and unexpected events. Specific resilience is the capability to maintain functions during and after specific threat or unexpected event. Organizational resilience is the emergent capability to investigate, learn, act, and improve and those overall capabilities without knowing in advance what one will be called to act upon.

The theory of organizational resilience may help to build resilience capabilities to overcome the challenges of adversity, no continuous and disruptive environment, manage disasters and crisis. Organizational resilience has a diversity of responses to adversity using functional resources and capabilities to respond in a specific context and operate under several conditions. Organizational resources and capabilities facilitate resilience.

An interdisciplinary approach to organizational resilience theory is useful to expand the conceptualization to include transformative changing levels of ecological adversity to develop resources and capabilities aimed to mitigate the negative impacts. Conceptual advancements of organizational resilience combine the ecological, psychological, and economic perspective linked to the capability building as a formative construct. The functional dimensions of biodiversity aids ecological resilience leading organizations to prepare resources and building capability redundancies to anticipate adversities.

The interplay of cognitive and behavioral elements of organizational resilience, the contextual factors such as power, resources, social capital, etc. are necessary to develop the resilience capabilities and success full resilience processes. The behavioral resilience enables to learn the situation, to use the resources and capabilities and to move the organization forward through collaborative actions. Moreover, resilience capabilities in organizations are complex, socially embedded and path-dependent to be analyzed by the use of observational and conversational methods of analysis on environments, developments and competitive advantages management.

This chapter illustrates well the need to study the interdependencies and interactions to capture resilience capabilities in different organizational contexts to build a strong theoretical framework for more effective organizational resilience management. It is urgently needed to find more robust conceptual foundations of organizational resilience and its underlying assumptions about capabilities building to cope with disruptions and threats.

Organizational resilience adopts the best practice to deliver continual organizational improvement, competence, and capabilities. Organizational resilience requires to adopt best habits and practices to deliver improvement by embedding capabilities and competences, from vision, values, behaviors, and culture. The improvement of organizational resilience is challenged by their inability to rely on trial and error.

Individuals like organizations can build capabilities and abilities in resilience to become more competent and confident, create a growing positive organizational culture able to face organizational change as a less stressful opportunity while achieving more control over the trends of the environment in the future.

Organizations must manage resilience to climate changes and extreme weather by using efficiently organizational resources, capabilities, and ideologies through the transferable and underlying mecha-

Preface

nisms and processes to different contexts and sectors. The entrepreneurial and resilience mindset as an organizational capability can emerge from the identification and recognition that organizations are vulnerable and organizational crisis events are part of the normal life.

Chapter 9: Implications of Implementing Operational Multi-Levels – Individual, Organizational, Community, and Societal Resilience

This chapter analyzes the operational implications of implementing resilience at the multi-levels of individual, organizational, community and societal resilience. It is assumed that the implementation of resilience requires to identify the concepts, antecedents, fundaments, principles regarding the nature, processes, orientations, and outcomes. The method employed is the analytical-reflective based on conceptual, theoretical, and empirical literature review and observation of specific situations. This paper considers a wide range of research related to resilience to be comprehensive. It is concluded that resilience is critically relevant at multi-level for individuals, organizations, communities, and society that must remain capable and strong even when all the events are adverse and seem incapable and consider ad hoc responses based on the nature of experienced major incidents. Neither academic research nor the practitioners are fully considering the implementation of resilience to solve these serious problems.

Information, operational and supply resilience are domains of organizational resilience. Organizational resilience may occur through managing inter-organizational relationships such as in the case of supply chain resilience. Resilience is an alternative to face supply chain risks and disruptions. Interpretations of the concept of organizational resilience aimed to prioritize risks and challenges to improve its objectives conceived as the maturity levels.

Every organization must develop and harness its own right resilience as a value driver underpinned by its values, brand, interactions, and practices in the face of growing threats. The components of organizational resilience are the behavioral, cognitive, and contextual. Organizational resilience blends behavioral, cognitive, and contextual properties to increase the ability to develop responses to deal with the current situation. The organizational context entails the need of resilience. Organizational resilience focuses on organizational context. The cognitive component enables the capacities of noticing, interpreting, analyzing, and formulating responses, supported by the elements to building cognitive resilience are the constructive sensemaking and the ideological identity. The sensemaking processes laid the foundations for organizational resilience.

Organizational resilience must be supported by information technology in connection, coordination, and creation of a context before, during and aftermaths of the recovery crisis. The recovery level and time are relevant parameters to certify the quality of organizational resilience. The process of embedding and disembodying communication and information systems facilitate or reduce the organizational resilience. Information systems can be risk or enabling factors to organizational resilience. Resilience is likely to be improved using Internet and enforcing internal security

Organizational resilience assessed used to identify actions to alter climate and weather extremes is under methodological inquiry and interpretation. The assessment of organizational resilience to climate variability and weather extremes needs to identify the factors of organizational resilience and the physical variabilities of climate and weather extremes. The physical aspect of resilience is a biological survival and implies the ability to grow and prosper.

Regional climate projections may be able to provide quantitative information for organizational resilience assessments while for some classes of extremes may only provide qualitative data. To estimate resulting organizational resilience losses needs specific data of the event. Exceeding the coping range does not mean that the critical organizational resilience threshold has passed, although it is difficult to define.

Resilience is survivability, resumption, restoration and optimize support to the community resilience. Resilience focuses on local community and social perspectives and sectorial and industry perspective. Resilience collective capacities building is an inclusive process that involves the individuals, organizations, and communities' actors to interact, use and build its capability endowments. These endowment capabilities are cognitive, behavioral, emotion and relational.

Societal resilience can be proactive and reactive. A proactive resilience response is questioned due to the bounded rationality of individuals. A proactive resilience response is questioned due to the bounded rationality of individuals. Organizational resilience is a critical component of community resilience which are very interrelated and interdependent to provide a systematic approach in an ability to plan, respond and recover from crisis and emergencies as well as actions to strengthen resilience.

Organizational resilience thrives in the context of a community. Resilience contextual transformation and changing conditions are guided in the manipulation of variables time and space or location. The greater the time needed for recovery indicates the lower resilience at the same level of vulnerability. Resilience degrades is unaltered if the variables change slow with impact only on routines.

The objective of the organizational resilience is to accept that incidents may occur with negative consequences. The analysis of organizational resilience must have a relative tendency towards more objective and rational implementation taking into consideration the reactive and proactive approaches.

Neither academic research nor the practitioners are considering the organizational resilience to solve problems. Conventional thinking and problem-solving do not facilitate organizational resilience. Organizations may consider resilience as ad hoc responses based on the nature of experienced major incidents.

Resilience is the ability to respond according to the societal needs and rebound from crisis. Resilience is the ability to be able return to original shape after being stretched, bent, and pressed. Organizational resilience is the harmonious integration of the functions of risk, compliance, and governance to enable proactive organizational decision-making. Ensuring an appropriate level of organizational resilience, compliance on development effectiveness and sustainability and transparency outcomes define the required balance by involving personnel in the operational process of the organization. Organizations must develop the ability to deal with stress derived from disruptions based on risks applied to the different levels of organizational resilience.

Organizational resilience drives benefits by the anticipation of existing and creating new market needs and in response to the corporate environments. Organizational resilience applies principles that should resonate with all sectors and stakeholders. Accepting to assume lower level of organizational resilience gives an opportunity to speak up and share feelings and thoughts about the situation and how to get away and advance. This chapter clearly illustrates with many examples how to implement the theory of organizational resilience and how the concept is of great importance in interdisciplinary research that responds to the problems and risks that societies are facing.

Chapter 10: Renewable Energies and the Urban Environment in Spain

This chapter analyzes the all the essential aspects of sustainable development and then proceeds to analyze the situation with renewable energies and urban environment in Spain by paying special attention to the evolving Spanish and European Union legislation and jurisdiction. Sustainable development is a type of development that advocates first of all the harmonization between economic development and environmental protection, adding social progress; it would therefore be development in which high and stable growth in the production of goods and services is compatible with widespread social progress, environmental protection and prudent and efficient use of natural resources.; it is therefore a delicate building supported by three main pillars: social, economic and environmental in which none of them prevails over the other. Accordingly, sustainability has an integrated character, preceded as it is by the objectives of economic recovery, environmental sustainability and social cohesion. It is a general principle with transversal or horizontal projection, capable of crossing different and varied sectoral areas, as many as are relevant to achieve its integrating objectives.

Since sustainable development is an integrative concept, its influence on the urban and housing sector could not fail to have these same connotations, insofar as sustainable urbanism is nothing but a projection of sustained development in a specific area. Urban planning must respond to the requirements of sustainable development, minimizing its commitment to growth and betting on the regeneration of the existing city in order to achieve a sustainable and inclusive urban model, environmentally, socially and economically that improves the quality of life of citizens in urban spaces. In short, we are talking about the integrated objectives of sustainability applied to urban planning, in which the duty of conservation plays a fundamental role.

Spanish Constitution is devoid of explicit references to sustainable development, since it is a relatively new concept in our domestic law. However, the relationship between this principle and certain constitutional rights is evident, since the idea of sustainable urbanism advocates the preservation of urban spaces and buildings in which the constitutional right to decent housing and an adequate environment can be realized. From the perspective of the principle of sustainability, urban planning must be oriented towards renovation in order to comply with article 45 of the Constitution, since renovation does not consume land and makes it possible to exploit and use, rather to reuse, the existing heritage. In this sense, the implications between sustainable development and protection and the right to an adequate environment that guarantees the quality of life are fully established.

The Law 8/2013 introduced within the duty of urban conservation the realization of additional works that had as a common denominator the fact that its imposition is based on reasons of general interest, and that the Consolidated Text of the Land Law of 2008 considered as works of improvement. Royal Legislative Decree 7/2015, of 30 October, refers to them in article 15.1 c). These additional works include those carried out for tourism and cultural reasons, to which are added those focused on improving the quality and sustainability of the urban environment, introduced by Law 2/2011 of 4 March on Sustainable Economy and where those actions related to energy efficiency are framed. The content of these additional works for the improvement of quality and sustainability is determined as we have indicated, by reference to the Technical Building Code.

These works additional to the duty of conservation which now also include those related to the improvement of the quality and sustainability of the urban environment, has a particular legal regime, since the law establishes the possibility for the administration to force the landlord to the realization of the same, even once exceeded the limit of the duty of conservation. In this case, the administration that orders or imposes the realization of such works must pay the economic excess that entails the realization of the same. And this economic excess is fixed by reference to the limit of the duty of conservation referred to above. In this way, the limit of the duty of conservation (half of the current value of construction of a building of a new plant, equivalent to the original in connection with the construction features and the useful surface, taken with the conditions necessary for their occupation is approvable or, in your case is in a position to be legally intended for use by own) it is also the limit of the works to be executed at the expense of the owners when the Administration of the order to the improvement of the quality or sustainability of the urban environment. The Law assumes the criterion of the joint participation of the owner and the Administration in the maintenance of the property, as deduced from article 9.1 of the Land Law after the wording given to it by the Law on urban renovation, regeneration and renovation.

Royal Legislative Decree 7/2015, of 30 October, considers the importance of these renovation actions in the urban environment and the need to adapt them to the limits of the legal duty of conservation through the economic viability report, regulated in article 22. This memory, it is expected not only in cases in which they carry out activities of regeneration and renewal, but also in the case of actions of renovation of building, isolated or included in a scope of work (by areas or spaces), establishing as one of its aims to ensure the least possible impact on the personal wealth of the individuals, adjusted in any case the limits of the duty to bequeath conservation.

Chapter 11: Welfare State, Income, and Public Debt and Their Implications for Latin American Life Satisfaction

The effect of Economics on the subjective well-being of people has been usually studied by treating country information in the same way as data from individuals. The objective of this paper is to analyze 17 Latin American countries with data from 2016, by including both effects handled into two different levels accordingly. The models that will be used in the present work will be multilevel, since they make it possible to involve different independent variables at more than one level. This is important because it offers a way to evaluate the effect on well-being in a more adequate way that takes into consideration the structure of data, and in consequence it turns out to be a more robust measurement. Therefore it will have results that reflect more closely what happens in reality, what could be useful in terms of creating public policy more accurate for bringing well-being to citizens in general.

This work contributes to extend the current debate regarding the impact of Economics on subjective well-being of people by applying the multilevel method. Some of the findings revealed that both the individual economic situation as well as the welfare state and the rule of law of a country generate effects on subjective well-being. Similarly, the effect of interaction between some variables was analyzed, and it was concluded that people with great economic difficulties have a stronger relationship with subjective well-being in areas of higher government spending and higher tax burden.

With respect to subjective well-being in Latin America, it was found that socio-demographic variables maintain a relationship with subjective well-being not very different from that of industrialized economies. However, as economies, the Latin American ones are more heterogeneous among them than they could be, for example, the European ones. So the context could have an even more important role for the Latin case. As an example, there are greater and more consistent effects of wage inequality on subjective well-being in Latin America in relation to the United States and Europe. A more recent study, identified a slightly positive association between income inequality and subjective well-being in Latin America, contrary to the negative association in other regions.

Among the findings of this study it was observed that both, the characteristics of individuals and the economic conditions of the context in which they operate are relevant to model the subjective well-being of people in Latin America. Due to the difference in the nature of data, using a multilevel model turned out to be an adequate strategy to carry it out.

Studies of Latin America regarding subjective well-being are scarce but these countries are particularly interesting for research purposes since they have many cultural similarities, and at the same time, they can show marked differences in terms of political and economic indicators. In the study the chosen dependent variable was 'life satisfaction', which was used as a measure of subjective well-being. Among the findings were such pieces of data as married people being more satisfied with their lives than singles, and less so if they are widowed or separated. In relation to race, where the mestizos were the reference group there were no significant differences of these with the whites, Asian and mulattos. However, African-Americans, indigenous people and people belonging to *other races* category were significantly less happy. Regarding education, illiterate people, people with complete secondary education, and individuals with incomplete, and complete higher education were happier than people with complete primary education. Also, non-religious people turned out to be statistically less happy than those who are. On the other hand, there is a negative correlation with age, that is, at younger age people are happier. People with employment have a greater satisfaction with life than those who do not.

In relation to public debt, it was found that it generates a negative effect on subjective well-being. However, the three highest economic strata resulted with a positive interaction effect in areas of higher public debt. Integrity of government and fiscal burden were not particularly significant. However, they showed to have a moderating effect for the individual economic situation. People with difficulties to cover needs onward showed a stronger relationship with subjective well-being in areas of greater government integrity. While the same three highest social strata maintained a more superficial relationship with happiness in countries with higher tax burdens. Probably this could be explained by the fact that people who belongs to the lowest strata is more likely to work in the informal economy, and therefore are not affected by tax increases.

Overall, economic conditions as well as the rule of law of a country predictably played a major influence on subjective well-being. However, the rich Latinobarometer survey data allowed to include more demographic variables such as race and educational level and, therefore, the study represents a multilevel analysis. Many of these demographic factors turned out to be very significant for subjective well-being and more sensitive in terms of cultural differences. This multilevel study would be highly useful for further comparative studies in Latin America. Moreover, it would also provide insights for researchers focusing on other regions such as the ASEAN countries, the European Union or the African countries.

The Latinobarometer survey allowed to include more demographic variables such as race and educational level. These factors were significant for subjective well-being. Regarding the impact caused by personal economic situation, there is a curvilinear effect of growth at decreasing rates. After people are able to meet their needs the positive effect begins to decrease. Regarding the second-level variables, it was found that GDP per capita PPP and government spending have a significant positive impact on the variable of interest. When the interaction term is included with the individual economic situation, two phenomena were observed. People with the ability to save tend to have a stronger relationship with subjective well-being when their country's GDP per capita PPP was higher than the reference group, and slightly lower when the country's government spending was sumptuous. Since government expense frequently is directed to social programs, this could explain such result.

In relation to public debt, it was found that it generates a negative effect on subjective well-being. However, the three highest economic strata resulted with a positive interaction effect in areas of higher public debt. As is known, as part of public debt government emits certificates and other instruments in order to obtain financing support from citizens in return of an interest rate chargeable at the end of the established period. This could explain the fact that people who is able to invest in this promissory notes which offer profit and safety, maintain a positive relation with public debt.

Integrity of government and fiscal burden were not significant. However, they showed to have a moderating effect for the individual economic situation. People with difficulties to cover needs onward showed a stronger relationship with subjective well-being in areas of greater government integrity. While the same three highest social strata maintained a more superficial relationship with happiness in countries with higher tax burdens. Probably this could be explained by the fact that people who belongs to the lowest strata is more likely to work in the informal economy, and therefore are not affected by tax increases. According to the report of the International Labour Organization (ILO) in 2013, 46.8% of jobs were informal in Latin America. The poorest quintile had an informal employment rate of 72.5%, while the richest quintile had 29.8% of participation.

Through this analysis it was clear that Economics indeed have an effect on subjective well-being of population, and multilevel technique helped to organize and consider these factors apart from the ones proper of the individual in an adequate way.

From 2018, diverse Latin American countries have been facing government and regime changes, mainly left-oriented, with the exception of Brazil, which has an extreme right-wing government. The common denominator between them are the presence of populist presidents. Future research works could study this in an attempt to identify if these type of transformations has led to significant differences in well-being terms among populations. Within countries, as is the case in Mexico, there is not always a union of ideologies between the president and state governors, which could imply changes in fiscal policy within the republic.

Another factor that could be of interest could be the way the different countries, through their governments, have decided to manage the present pandemic, a new variable that is having collateral effects not only in health terms, but in job positions, business survival and tax application.

Chapter 12: US Dependance on Chinese Pharma and the Nationalization of the US System

The United States has become increasingly dependent on foreign nations for their pharmaceutical supply. This chapter draws on many recent research works and provides a sharp analysis of the situation after which the authors explore different policy alternatives and recommendations. The starting point of this chapter is that China is by now responsible for the production of a vast majority of generic pharmaceuticals destined for consumption in the United States. Such phenomenon has the potential for catastrophic consequences for the American public, as the Chinese pharmaceutical supply chain has already faced disruptions during the Covid-19 pandemic. Furthermore, the United States could even be deprived of their generic drugs supply during a possible future conflict with China. In their conclusion the authors suggests that since Americans have a history of putting the interest of their community before the interests of the few, the current vulnerabilities of their pharmaceutical supply chain (as exposed by the impact of the Covid-19 pandemic) should lay down the foundation for a nationalized American pharmaceutical supply chain. Of course, we are discussing here a highly political issue that ties health, politics and economy in many different ways. Furthermore, the nationalized American pharmaceutical supply chain would certainly have a huge global impact and in the middle of ongoing COVID-19 pandemic in 2022 there is plenty of diversity in opinions concerning the optimal global regime of pharmaceutical production and supply chain as well as patent system.

Preface

Chapter 13: Does It Hold Water? An Empirical Investigation on the Usefulness of Filtering Tap Water to Treat Health Complaints

There is a fair amount of evidence that regular consumption of a standardized amount of filtered tap water improved the self-reported physical complaints. However, since individuals were fully aware of the type of water they consumed it was unclear to what extent this effect was ascribable to placebo effects. This paper tests the effectiveness of an in-home water filter system (AcalaQuell®), which was compared with a sham water filter containing no significant filter ingredients. Both filters were concealed, and participants knew that the probability to receive the clinically proven filter was 50 percent. There were large differences between the two groups (d = 0.7 < d < 2). For individual-specific complaints, the reduction was 38 percent for the filtered water group while the reduction in the placebo group was about 8 percent. Subjective health complaints are considerably reduced after daily intake of AcalaQuell®-filtered tap water during a three-week administration period. This effect is specific and independent from placebo effects.

There are several questions this work could not address. For instance, subjective health complaints and medical symptoms may or may not covary. Phenomenological (i.e. experienced) complaints may not have an actual clinical causation and therefore cannot be quantified organically or functionally (i.e. objectively). Rather, they may manifest as physical symptoms that are caused by psychological factors (e.g. life stress). Conversely, patients with a diagnosed illness may be symptom-free and thus do not experience complaints (e.g., hypertension). On average, subjective complaints and objective health issues only correlate moderately, and therefore the results of this study await confirmation beyond merely subjective health issues. Nonetheless, subjective complaints should not be dismissed as insignificant, as they exist even if they have no medical foundation. The fact that this study demonstrated a highly specific effect on subjective health complaints attests to that.

One aim of this study was to investigate a POU filter system in actual use and in a natural environment. As such, the results are externally valid. There are many factors, however, that could not be accounted for, for instance, adherence to the study protocol, water installations on site, or the supplier's water quality. Furthermore, only a relatively limited period of time was investigated and participants were not followed-up upon. Future studies should account for these factors and employ research designs that allow drawing conclusions for different types of ailments, outcome parameters (e.g. biomarkers, medical diagnoses), and samples (clinical vs. non-clinical).

With regard to the therapeutic use of the device future studies should shed more light on the filter's capacity to expedite or complement other treatments, e.g. during convalescence, recuperation and therapeutic treatment. Although the filter is not designed as a medical tool, its effectiveness could be utilized and extended to the clinical realm. Such studies should also employ techniques in more controlled environments that allow investigation of biomedical factors which act as mediating factors to restore health. In doing so, the questions if and how the filter actually structures water should be elucidated since this might substantially contribute to our understanding of the healing properties of water.

This research has carefully analyzed a POU filter system in actual use and in a natural environment. This kind of research has obvious benefits for both health and for better understanding of water that plays such a crucial role in environment. Filtered tap water may sound as a rather basic issue but there still seems be room for improvements and better understanding.

Chapter 14: Assessing Differential Vulnerability to Health Risk Associated With Microbial Contamination of Vegetables

In Ghana, Sunyani is increasingly becoming an important vegetable producing area. Vegetables cultivated there include cabbage, carrot, garden eggs (types of eggplant), tomatoes and okra for the increasing population in the Municipality taking advantage of the numerous surface water (streams) available to irrigate the vegetables. However, the Ministry of Food and Agriculture has already cautioned that, use of untreated water may contaminate vegetables produced.

In the Sunyani Municipality of Ghana, both the rapid population growth and uncertainties in rainfall have encouraged the use of untreated surface water for irrigating vegetables regardless of risks. Meanwhile, microbial levels of ready-to-eat vegetables remain untested and the differences in exposure unexplored. Further, there is paucity of studies that compare the quality of local and exotic vegetables. In this study, a mixed method approach was used to collect and analyse primary data for assessing the situation and finding solutions.

This study sought to assess bacterial quality of on-farm vegetables in rural and peri-urban location and farmers' differential vulnerability to the risks of bacterial infections in rural and peri-urban locations within the Sunyani Municipality. Samples of cabbage and tomatoes were collected and analysed at the laboratory. A survey was also conducted to gather primary data from vegetable farmers in the Municipality. The outcome of the study showed that on-farm vegetables in the study area were contaminated above the WHO and ICMSF standards with slight variation from one location to the other. This poses great danger to both producers and consumers of vegetables without proper decontamination of the vegetables. Again, it was observed that farmers' vulnerability to bacterial contamination risks varied between rural and peri-urban locations within the Municipality. The results showed that, majority of producers at the peri-urban community frequently consume vegetables produced and may be more vulnerable to the risk of microbial infections than those at the rural community. In the same vein, exotic producers were may be vulnerable to the risks of bacterial contamination than traditional producers. It was also found that farmers perception on the bacterial quality of vegetables produces were negative. Age and the educational level of farmers had no association with their perceptions. The study recommends that the quality of both on-farm vegetables and the water used to irrigate them in the study area should be regularly monitored by the Crops Research Institute of the CSIR and the Environmental Protection Agency in order to assess their microbial contamination levels and initiate appropriate mitigation measures to deal with possible health risks and build the resilience of farmers. Also, the authors strongly advice the vegetable farmers in the study area to be educated on the health and safety of vegetables by the Agricultural Extension Officers in the Municipality.

Chapter 15: Japanese Stone Gardens – Diversity, Sustainability, and Consumerism

Gardens certainly are widely recognized as a characteristic part of Japanese aesthetic tradition. Moreover, modern Japanese garden contains a wide variety of garden types, from a tiny tabletop Zen gardening kit to a large national park. While some scholars have acknowledged the diversity of modern Japanese gardens, recent developments in Japanese stone gardens, known as *karesansui*, have gone largely unnoticed. The author notes that preconceived notions of *karesansui* do not encapsulate the true diversity which exists today. Moreover, the general public has tended to exoticize *karesansui*. Scholarly work on

Preface

karesansui has, however, dispelled many of the myths and misrepresentations related to these gardens. In this chapter the author analyzes and extends previous research and sheds light on recent developments in *karesansui* and the myths that surround them. This chapter examines *karesansui* from several perspectives: diversity, sustainability, and, finally, from the perspective of consumerism.

Historical accounts of *karesansui* frequently cite the Muromachi era (1336-1573) as the starting point. However, reference to stone placement in gardens in Japan's seminal text on gardening *Sakuteiki* (作庭記), published in the latter part of the Heian era (794—1185), suggests that *karesansui* gardens were in existence much earlier. Nevertheless, the Muromachi era is significant and remains the period most closely associated with *karesansui* gardens and was been referred to as the "era of gardens" by the novelist Shiba Ryôtarô (司馬遼太郎). It is true that one of the main reasons that gardening skills developed so much during the Muromachi period was because of the rise of gardening specialists known as *niwamono* (庭者) and *sansui kawaramono* (山水河原者).

In the Edo period (1604—1868), *karesansui* gardens spread beyond Zen Buddhist temples to a variety of different locations and residences of people from various classes, including the imperial Palace, samurai family residences, and townsfolk. The artist, tea ceremony master and garden designer, Kobori Enshū (小堀遠州) (1579—1647) is said to have contributed greatly to this spread of *karesansui* gardens during this period. Perhaps Kobori Enshū's greatest influence was on the Tea Ceremony in which his school was referred to as *Enshū ryū* (遠州流). It was during this period that *karesansui* gardens became more full scale in size, and, arguably, became more accepted by the general public.

The Meiji era (1868—1912) saw a decline in *karesansui* gardens. During this period, *Ueji ryū* (植治流) style gardens, which are a modern style of garden which emphasize the natural state of nature, became particularly popular during this time and continued through to the Shôwa period (1926—1989). While this period saw a decline in *karesansui* gardens, there was a revival of these gardens by the gardener Shigemori Mirei (1896-1975), who designed gardens such as the *karesansui* garden at *Tōfukuji* (東福寺). Shigemori strived to not only revive Japanese stone gardens but emphasized both the design of the garden as well as its conceptual elements.

Karesansui gardens are traditionally divided into two main categories: *zenkishiki* (前期式), which refers to *karesansui* gardens from the *Azuchimomoyama* period (安土桃山時代) (1573—1603); and, *kōkishiki* (後期式), which refers to *karesansui* gardens after that period. According to Miyamoto (1998), *zenshiki karesansui* gardens are constructed on the slope of a mountain, while *kōkishiki karesansui* gardens are constructed on flat ground of temple grounds. The author, however, notes that these categories do not take into account more recent developments in design. For instance, public parks, many of which were daimyo gardens, are often neglected in discussions on Japanese gardens. Furthermore, there are many other types of gardens which tend to be overlooked, such as Isamu Noguchi's gardens, which incorporate sculptures and sculptural elements, and Japanese colonial gardens in Asia.

Given the ongoing fears of global warming and environmental degradation, as well as increased interest in creating sustainable living spaces, it is perhaps unsurprising that some recent developments in *karesansui* gardens have been motivated or influenced in some way by sustainable landscape design.

Sustainable landscape design strategies are becoming an important part of urban landscapes and many of the characteristics of *karesansui* gardens are compatible with the principles of sustainability. A sustainable garden is designed to be both attractive and in harmony with the environment.

Many of the features of *karesansui* gardens which are compatible with sustainability are self-evident. Perhaps the most obvious characteristic is that *karesansui* gardens conserve water. Moreover, they require very little maintenance. Gardens by their very nature change over time. Therefore, old gardens do not maintain their form over time. In the case of *karesansui* gardens, however, they do maintain their form to a much greater extent. Mental health has been included in the UN Sustainable Development Goals (SDGs), and as *karesansui* gardens promote reflection and introspection, it could be argued that they are beneficial on mental health. Moreover, the practical nature of *karesansui* gardens as well as their compatibility with sustainable design makes them particularly suitable for our everyday environment, and it could be argued that this can create an aesthetic experience.

The distinct and iconic patterns used in *karesansui* gardens are immediately recognizable and identifiable as symbolic of traditional Japanese culture. Therefore, the popular swirls and patterns of *karesansui* gardens have been incorporated into a number of consumer products, including jigsaw puzzles, games, confectionary, and even desserts. Indeed, there are a number of consumer items which have been produced for that purpose. For example, miniature *karesansui* kits, which allow people to make small *karesansui* gardens and can be used as ornamentation, are available for purchase. These miniature kits can also be purchased in "capsules" from popular *gacha gacha* games for children (and collectors). The close association between *karesansui* gardens and traditional Japan means that the *karesansui* patterns can be easily used to create a sense of "Japaneseness", which may be useful in marketing products to both domestic and foreign markets.

In the end, *karesansui* gardens will have different meanings to different people. While the narrative which these gardens are built on has an unmistakable element of cultural nationalism, and one that scholarly criticism has aptly revealed, the multitude of forms in which these gardens appear suggests that that they will continue to survive. Indeed, for the observer of *karesansui* gardens, in their many forms, these gardens may conjure up a feeling of nostalgic sentimentalism, reaffirm one's sense of cultural heritage, or simply provide respite from the drudge of daily life. What is apparent is that, regardless of the various forms these gardens take and individual observer's experiences, these gardens are here to stay.

This chapter contributes to our knowledge of these gardens and extends existing scholarship which questions previous attempts to categorize Japanese gardens. While traditional style *karesansui* gardens will no doubt continue to function as tourist destinations and glimpses into traditional Japanese culture, and while new approaches to these gardens may not reach similar heights of popularity as gardens such as at *Ryōanji*, these gardens will inevitably continue to evolve and appear in various forms in the future. That is to say, they will continue to function as a creative force in our society, and recent developments will continue to push the boundaries of garden design and create exciting possibilities for future living spaces.

Chapter 16: Art and Environment Seen Through the Lens of Politics in Japan

This chapter analyses the changing diversity of politically and socially relevant interpretations, ideas and opinions concerning the environment in Japan with a special reference given to visual arts and how environment and environmental issues have been dealt with in Japanese art. Politics involves constant reinterpretation and rearranging of everything around us. Art and especially visual images allow endless opportunities for reconstruction and to be used, recomposed and combined rhizomatically. Art world in Japan has been directly influenced by the changing political and social context, but within the art community in Japan power relations have deeply influenced what ideas reach the public. Politicization of environment and art has a long history in Japan as environment and art both are an indispensable part of Japanese society and history. Shaping the interpretations for them has always had profound political and

Preface

social significance. Moreover, the digitizing and Internet together have made the spreading of images much easier and have made visual images more important than ever.

Chapter 17: Japanese Visual Arts – Representation and Perfectioning of Reality: Mimesis and Understanding of Japanese Visual Arts

In this chapter the Japanese visual traditions are analysed in the context of changing social, cultural and political environment. There are detailed discussions about different phases of Japanese art history and about Japanese visual arts and towards the end of the chapter the focus moves to the present situation of Japanese visual art scene. The concept of mimēsis is used in the chapter in the sense that the human beings are mimetic beings and feeling an urge to create texts and art that reflect and represent reality. The Japanese visual art does much more than just copies the reality: it represents the reality and perfections it and by accomplishing these acts Japanese art remains dynamic and provides a means for artists in Japan to express themselves and the society around them. These two chapters, Chapter 16 and 17, both seek ways to link culture with society and other areas of life. In order to go beyond the borders of disciplines and find new fresh and relevant ways to deepen understanding new theoretical approaches and copceptial tools are needed. Hopefully these ideas will be found useful also in other cultural and social contexts.

Mika Markus Merviö
Kibi International University, Japan

Chapter 1
Managing High Performing Safety Cultures in US Healthcare Organizations During COVID-19

Darrell Norman Burrell
https://orcid.org/0000-0002-4675-9544
The Florida Institute of Technology, USA

Anton Shufutinsky
https://orcid.org/0000-0003-3819-0623
Cabrini University, USA

Jorja B. Wright
https://orcid.org/0000-0002-7028-995X
University of Charleston, USA

D'Alizza Mercedes
The Chicago School of Professional Psychology, USA

Amalisha Aridi
Capitol Technology University, USA

Eugene J. Lewis
https://orcid.org/0000-0002-2956-0760
Capitol Technology University, USA

ABSTRACT

The increasing complexity of the United States healthcare system has compounded the likelihood of mistakes. One of the 10 leading causes of death and disability is safety issues with patient care. Medical errors put undue hardship on the economy resulting in the loss of billions of dollars. The current COVID-19 pandemic revealed gaps in public health strategies, medical treatments, comprehensive patient safety, and human resources strategy. Implementing human resources and performance management processes that promote safety, safe decision making, and reduce medical errors is critical. Adopting methods used by high-reliability organizations (HRO) may reduce medical errors and improve patient safety. Qualitative focus groups were used to collect data around creating organizational cultures focused on safety. This research aims to improve performance by providing healthcare leaders with tools to enhance organizational culture, reduce medical errors, and improve patient safety in the age of COVID-19.

DOI: 10.4018/978-1-7998-8996-0.ch001

INTRODUCTION

The increasing complexity of the United States healthcare system has compounded the likelihood of mistakes. Expecting error-free performance from healthcare personnel working in exceedingly high stressed environments is idealistic (World Health Organization, 2019). This topic is essential because medical errors are related to patient safety. Medical errors are "preventable adverse" events occurring during medical care administration that can be harmful to the patient (Carver et al., 2020). Patient safety focuses on preventing and reducing safety hazards, errors, and risks that may happen while providers administer health care (World Health Organization, 2019). The following are five components necessary to execute patient safety:

- Clear-cut guidelines.
- Leadership capability.
- Data to lead safety enhancements.
- Competent health care specialists.
- Patient engagement (World Health Organization, 2019).

Additionally, these five components are not exclusive of one another. Each of these belongs within the organizational system and systematically interacts with the other parts through an inter-related organization design continuum. All these are influenced by human resources and organizational leadership.

HUMAN RESOURCES ORGANIZATION DESIGN AND SYSTEMS THEORY

Today's financial markets exist in a hypercompetitive industrial complex. Organizations strive to ensure that they create or maintain a competitive advantage over their market competitors to succeed and survive in this environment (Shufutinsky, 2018). This is achieved through innovation in products, processes, or services (Magretta, 2012), often designed and developed through strategy (Magretta, 2013), as well as through management of both internal and external factors, and align those factors, including organizational structure and processes, to achieve effective strategic change. To ensure this, human resources managers must plan and strategize adequately and engage in business process improvement focused on improving strategy, culture, and operations (Worley, Hitchins, & Ross, 1996). This is accomplished through human resources organizational assessment and design models (Shufutinsky, 2018).

Organizations are complex adaptive systems (Senge, 2014). Human resources and organizational development are grounded in systems thinking, one of the significant aspects that sets the field apart from those like it (Jamieson, 2017; Shufutinsky, 2017; Senge, 2014). Systems thinking addresses that every major part of an organization and its stakeholders (Jamieson, 2017). To expound, each element is part of a more extensive network of components, each with the potential to modify all others, directly or indirectly (Senge, 2014; Shufutinsky & Long, 2017; Shufutinsky et al., 2020). Organization design models, such as Jamieson's Strategic Organizational Design (SOD) model or Shufutinsky's Nuclear Organization Framework (NOF), as seen in Figure 1, contend that organizations cannot be effectively changed without changing the culture, which is at the core of the organization, but simultaneously cannot be altered without effectual changes made to the other components of the organizational system by human resources. Thus, there is a complex and ever-changing relationship between the elements in an

Figure 1. The Nuclear Organization Framework: model of systemic organizational design [Adapted from Shufutinsky, (2019)]

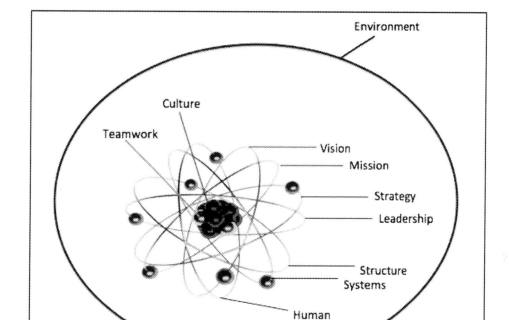

organization's design. Human resources practices and policies significantly influence this relationship. This relationship exhibits the systemic nature of organizations and the dynamic, holistic effects that variations make on the entire system, potentially causing significant shifts that result from adaptations to just a few components on their own (Jamieson, 2017; Shufutunsky, 2019).

The main inter-related components that comprise an organization have a dynamic relationship with one another, as exhibited in the NOF model (Fig. 1), revealing the nature of the components' interconnectedness critical to organizational design and function. The model displays the continuous movement of each of the elements regarding one another as part of the entire system (Shufutinsky, 2019). The atomic visual representation of the model expresses the inherent nature by which different components are continually shifting, interacting, and reacting with others, and symbolically addresses the energies and energy changes in the elements that affect an organization's core culture and vice versa, causing continuous dynamic change and necessity for agility concerning organizational structure, systems/processes, leadership, human factors and behavior, mission, leadership, strategy, teamwork & collaboration, and even vision and the competitive environment (Shufutinsky, 2019).

In the NOF model of organizational design, changes in the organization's elements can affect the entire system. This includes the organizational design components and subcomponents that fall within them, such as policies, leadership capacity, data, skilled professional staff, patient involvement, and others, such as safety culture—all necessary for executing and maintaining effective safety programs in health care settings.

Table 1. Medical errors and rates of the affected population (World Health Organization, 2019)

Types of Medical Errors	Rates/Statistics
Unsafe surgical care procedures	25% of patients
Unsafe injections practices	9.2 million Disability-Adjusted Life Years
Diagnostic errors	5% of adults in outpatient settings
Unsafe transfusion practices	8.7 severe reactions per 100,000 distributed blood components
Radiation errors	15 errors per 10,000 treatment courses
Sepsis	Affects 0.39% of the population worldwide
Venous thromboembolism (blood clots)	9.9 million cases globally

Patient harm occurs when these five components are inconsistent. Among the leading ten causes of death and disability globally is safety failure during patient care (World Health Organization, 2019). Specifically, in the United States, up to 440,000 deaths occur every year due to medical errors (Ugur et al., 2016). Additionally, 10% of patients are injured while receiving health care, and almost half of these injuries are preventable (World Health Organization, 2019). Moreover, 40% of patients worldwide are harmed during primary and outpatient health care services (World Health Organization, 2019). These preventable medical errors account for approximately 15% of total hospital activity and expenditures (World Health Organization, 2019). Researchers suggest medical errors can occur purposely or accidentally (Ugur et al., 2016).

Medical errors place additional hardship on the healthcare system and affect the economy, and account for approximately $42B of annual losses throughout the world (Ugur et al., 2016). During the COVID-19 pandemic, healthcare statistics exhibit a significant increase in healthcare-acquired infections; approximately 70% of hospitalized patients are due to this type of infection.

RESEARCH APPROACH

This qualitative research study employs a small focus group participatory action research design. This design has been effectively used in numerous social science disciplines, either as a standalone or a combined research approach.

LITERATURE REVIEW

Table 1 describes the distinct types of medical errors that can occur.

Medical errors, especially those around ethical and poor decision making, are detrimental to patient safety, too costly to fix, and lowers the overall quality of health care.

The increased complexity of our society and the current healthcare system warrants that human resources drives interventions focused on creating new organizational cultures to reduce the chances and occurrences of medical errors. As mentioned earlier, the COVID-19 crisis is a catalyst for current public health methodologies, medical therapies, and overall patient safety. This recent "turbulent healthcare environment" (Shafer et al., 2000, p. 8) causes necessity, uncertainty, and "drastic upheaval," which is influencing innovative leadership practices that are connected to the strategic fit of an organization (Carmeli et al., 2010, p. 340). Strategic fit is "change and adaptation;" this organizational competency is "crucial to a firm's ability to change and adapt to unforeseen contingencies" (Carmeli et al., 2010). In the end, this ever-changing environment warrants healthcare facilities to thrive "in the healthcare industry's rock and roll realities... without experiencing constant internal change and turmoil" (Shafer et al. 2000, p. 3). Moreover, Shafer et al. explain that organizational agility, the ability to respond to change swiftly, is an essential aspect of a healthcare organization's strategic fit and ultimately should be considered when analyzing how organizational processes affect health care workers and patients' safety.

A recent descriptive study of a Turkish university hospital revealed that operating rooms (OR) are among the most complex healthcare areas prone to medical errors (Ugur et al., 2016). Reasons for these errors include multi-disciplinary staff, varied educational objectives, and complicated team dynamics (Ugur et al., 2016). Up to 50% of medical errors occur in the OR, "despite the effective improvements in [patient safety] practices" (Ugur et al., 2016, p. 595). These factors all contribute to higher rates of medical errors. Researchers posit that these errors are preventable through "corrective feedback, reviewing the errors, and better teamwork" (Ugur et al., 2016, p. 595). Therefore, implementing organizational processes that improve these factors is tantamount to effective prevention. Table 2 illustrates other administrative functions researchers, healthcare employees, and policymakers should consider when reducing the rate of medical errors.

COLLABORATION

Human resources and organizational leadership should drive collaboration which is essential to reducing medical errors because of the complexity of the healthcare system. This compounds the consequences of mistakes and defects, whether they are due to unethical decision making, poor decision making, or accidental negligence. Conlon et al. (2008) discuss high-reliability organizations (HRO) principles, which are complex organizations in which major catastrophes can occur (including many casualties). Yet, their safety records are "exceptional" (p. 2). Healthcare organizations can be considered HROs due to the complex nature of these systems. Five factors contribute to an HRO:

- **Expect failures**. Training staff to expect errors improves recognition and increases response time.
- **Focus on root causes**. Reject the initial cause of an error and continue to find the root cause.
- **Frontline leadership**. Train staff at each level of the organizational structure to rectify errors at the lowest level.
- **Resiliency.** Having a resilient staff who works through errors "detect, contain, and mitigates" errors (Conlon et al., 2008, p. 2).
- **Respect at each level encourages employees to communicate during surgical time-out procedures as a form of error mitigation.**

All five of these components form "mindfulness," in which a "mindful" organization anticipates faults and is quick when correcting errors (Conlon et al., 2008, p. 2). Mindful organizations utilize sensemaking tools like strategic foresight and learning to gather information from "unexpected events" (Conlon et al., 2008, p. 2). Use that information to make decisions about possible future scenarios that could

Table 2. Organizational processes that can improve patient safety

Organizational Elements	Definition
Leadership	Singh et al. (2008) and Masson et al., 2020) describe the importance of effective leadership for improved patient safety. Healthcare organizations that score high with patient satisfaction have three things in common: patient safety is a top priority, management perceptions of safety, and scales of working conditions (Singh et al., 2008). Collaborative leadership efforts that include system-level efforts with all relevant stakeholders at the forefront ensure health organizations are not only prepared (i.e., COVID-19 pandemic), but employees can give. Patients receive the best care (Masson et al., 2020).
Standardization/Triage	Standardization/ triage procedures should be from patients' admission to discharge (Ugur et al., 2016). Each medical discipline has varied processes and methodologies and constitutes an enormous patient safety segment (Ugur et al., 2016). For standardization processes to be effective, healthcare personnel must work in harmony to reduce medical errors. For example, the current COVID-19 pandemic requires healthcare professionals to draft, edit, and execute surge plans (Masson et al., 2020).
Team building	Team building includes improving inter and intra-team dynamics and the flow of information among team members. Ugur et al. claim in-depth team meetings are essential in reducing medical errors because "detailed discussion" of patient care strategies "may improve patient outcomes and decrease complications" (Ugur et al., 2016, p. 595). For teams to work effectively, communication must be detailed and
Staffing	Supervisors and human resources managers are essential in patient safety initiatives because employee rotation and "unqualified staff" are some "…of the most common causes of [medical] errors" (Ugur et al., 2016, p. 595). Disrupting staff continuity and various team conflicts interrupt planning initiatives. Ultimately, having stable, consistent teams in which members have positive interactions significantly reduces medical error occurrences and results in higher patient safety (Ugur et al., 2016).
Time-out	Time-out procedures are part of the Joint Commission issued Universal Protocol (The Joint Commission, 2020). This guidance is for all healthcare professionals; however, operating room employees can benefit the most from time-out procedures because of their responsibilities regarding patient safety. During these four-minute meetings, patient information is dispersed among surgeons, anesthesiologists, nurses, and the rest of the OR staff before the surgery (Ugur et al., 2016). Time-out procedures prevent medical errors by 97% and increase patient safety by 93% (Ugur et al., 2016).
Accurate Error Reporting	Errors can occur before or during various medical processes. Nonetheless, feedback is still vital when tracking the occurrences of errors and determining causes (Ugur et al., 2016). A study showed that nurses only report two-thirds of identified errors, and a little under half of the identified reports were filled out correctly (Ugur et al., 2016). Lastly, eight of ten medical employees did not report medical errors within a year (Ugur et al., 2016).
Culture	Organizations' cultures strongly correlate with effective leadership because top management sets the tone. Cultivating a negative organizational environment consisting of "judgmental and punitive attitudes" hinders employees from reporting errors (Ugur et al., 2016).
Training	Constant and consistent training initiatives are essential to keep medical staff compliant with laws, policies, regulations and administer updated care to ensure patient safety is of the highest quality (Masson et al., 2020). Education and training strategies allow medical staff to understand risks; a more significant understanding of risks can reduce medical errors (Malm et al., 2008).
Logistics	The COVID-19 pandemic shows the gaps in the supply chain for medical personal protective equipment. There have been shortages of N-95 style face masks and ventilators, which has caused significant care management issues for many hospitals around the country. Evaluating inventory levels is vital when administering superior patient care. Health care executives and clinical leaders must also develop contingency plans in another pandemic event (Masson et al., 2020).
Technology	Technological advances in medicine have improved care and patient satisfaction because "there is a direct intervention in human life" (Ugur et al., 2016). Telehealth programs allow providers to give care from a distance. Therefore, telehealth has been incredibly beneficial during the current pandemic because it protects patients and providers by adhering to social distancing rules.

cause medical errors. Healthcare leaders should consider the habits of HROs because those factors can be easily adapted to medical centers to improve patient safety (Conlon et al., 2008).

ORGANIZATIONAL SAFETY CULTURE

Today is more than ever; it is critical for healthcare organizations at every level to develop organizational cultures that are obsessively focused on ethics and safety (Burrell et al., 2019). Even organizations with safety as a critical aspect of their corporate values still struggle with creating the ideal and most effective cultures (Burrell et al., 2019). One reason for this is that safety culture is often misunderstood regarding what it is and how it can be fostered and molded by human resources and organizational leadership. As a term, safety culture did not become a general term in the safety literature until after 1986 after the Soviet Union the Chernobyl nuclear power plant accident. Safety experts identified a low functioning safety culture as a significant cause of the atomic disaster (Shufutinsky & Long, 2017). Following the accident, safety culture has continued to be a general and essential term in safety practice and research, being identified as a critical element to establishing safe workplace conditions (Shufutinsky & Long, 2017).

Nevertheless, the term has still not been consistently defined (Burrell et al., 2019; Shufutinsky & Long, 2017). The actionable understanding of precisely what having an influential, ethical safety culture means an area in need of additional research and investigation Shufutinsky & Long, 2017). Generally, safety culture is characterized as a sub-component or subculture of an overarching organizational culture (Antonsen, 2009; Cooper, 2000; Geller, 1994; Parker, Lawries, & Hudson, 2006; Shufutinsky et al., 2015).

Edgar Schein (2007) describes a desired organizational culture as "…the pattern of basic assumptions which an organization's members have invented, discovered, developed, and consider valid and, therefore, transfer and teach to new members as a means of coping with occupational hazards and risks." Shufutinsky and Long (2017) and O'toole (2002) classify culture as one of the most critical aspects of shaping employees' actions and behaviors and strategy intended to perpetuate safety. With that definition holding, organizational safety culture is a subculture in an organization's total culture. This ultimately means that corporate culture is central to organizational effectiveness and managerial design (Jamieson, 2017; Kates & Galbraith, 2007). As a result, an organization's safety culture is critical to its safety strategy, programs, processes, and general organizational performance (Shufutinsky & Long, 2017). With that in mind, a patient safety culture contains collective principles, opinions, rules, and behavioral traits of healthcare workers and their actions when they interact with patients safely (Hemphill, 2015).

Errors arise from poor technique and inadequate knowledge, and human factors, including workplace fatigue, perception failures, and misjudgments (Burrell et al., 2019). Quantifying the magnitude of harmful incidents and engaging in behaviors is critical to reducing errors and being ethical and honest when engaging patients and making errors (Burrell et al., 2019). The healthcare culture understandably focuses on caring for patients, even at the expense of security and safety (Martin et al., 2017). There is a complex tension around ethics and safety concerning patients' interests, the interests of the healthcare organization, and the interests of finding quicker paths to treating patients (Hemphill, 2015). The ethical challenge is the need, to be honest when patients are impacted by avoidable actions, errors, and unsafe behaviors (Hemphill, 2015). The threat of legal action and expensive payments can create a culture that dissuades divulging knowledge about mistakes and ethical violations (Hemphill, 2015; Burrell et al., 2019). Changes in organizational culture are critical to reducing errors and medical errors with the propensity to harm (Hemphill, 2015).

As a means of managing reputational risk, organizations do not openly disclose the nature and extent of medical errors and unsafe operational practices. Often the public finds out when a whistleblower reveals the offense (Burrell et al., 2019). Patient-centered decision-making necessitates the requirement to appreciate the importance of organizational cultures that drive employees to make ethical and safe decisions or disclose those instances when the organization or employees engage in hazardous activities (Burrell et al., 2019).

A safe culture does not punish those that discover safety problems (Hemphill, 2015). It includes many mechanisms to report unethical and unsafe organizational practices that can harm patients (Hemphill, 2015). Perpetuating cultures with these kinds of measures improve safety and the quality of care (Hemphill, 2015). Unauthorized releases of medical information, poorly given discharge instructions, the absence of coordinated care between various clinicians, medication dispensing errors, and surgical mistakes are issues that can occur in health care settings (Hemphill, 2015). The utilization of innovative healthcare technologies and systems has been developed to improve healthcare delivery and the treatment of patients. One unintended consequence has been new risks around safety due to technical flaws, operating errors, and new complexities (Hemphill, 2015). Cultures that are ethical, transparent, tolerant, and constructively responsive to human mistakes are critical to developing healthcare cultures that will be safer (Hemphill, 2015). The result is building systems where blame, severe punishment, cover-ups are chosen to improve patient safety (Hemphill, 2015).

Hemphill (2015) outlines how healthcare mishaps can be observable as poor operational processes, poorly constructed business practices, outdated procedures, poor decision making, flawed organizational structures, equipment malfunction, and human error that could be or even unintentional. All of these issues are even magnified or addressed by human resources and executive leadership's interventions (Burrell et al., 2019). As a result, it becomes crucial for leadership to drive and perpetuate cultures guided by ethical decision-making and open honest communication when there are medical errors and unsafe practices (Burrell et al., 2019).

ETHICS AND EMOTIONAL ACUMEN IN DECISION MAKING

Catastrophic healthcare safety failures can result from weak organizational cultures that encompass a gradual introduction of lapses in ethical and safety-oriented behaviors and decisions (Hemphill, 2015). Organizations often have cultures that contain mixed and competing messages about productively, profit, and patent safety (Hemphill, 2015). These mixed messages often manifest themselves with employees developing shortcuts and workarounds that appear to improve speed around work completion and create vulnerabilities (Greenfield & Jensen, 2010; Swisher & Davis, 2005).

DATA COLLECTION

The data collection method included focus groups. These groups were comprised of 24 participants. Focus group participants included six healthcare compliance professionals, six healthcare risk managers, six nursing managers, and six patient safety administrators. All participants had over ten years of healthcare management experience, and all participants had advanced degrees. The participants were optimal because they were subject matter experts, representing the value of using focus groups (Morgan,

2018). Morgan (2018) states that focus groups are a trustworthy approach to gathering data for studies that investigate:

- Expert perspectives, concepts, and sentiments regarding a subject.
- Real-world problems that allow participants with an understanding of the nuances of the problem to analyze those problems.
- Distinct reflections and perceptions in an amassed or grouped way (Morgan, 2018).

Focus groups themes- An ethical safety culture includes all the following:

1. A code of ethics that all employees must follow that is tied to employee performance.
2. Reward and recognize employees that engage in safe and ethical practices.
3. Having regular and interactive training programs.
4. Have a "no fear" whistleblowing policy in which whistleblowers have protection from retaliation action for voluntarily disclosing information about unsafe, dishonest, or illegal activities occurring within the organization.
5. Develop a variety of mechanisms for employees to report unsafe and unethical behavior, either openly or anonymously.
6. Create a ZERO tolerance policy against retaliation towards employees that disclose violations to ethics and safety. a reporting employee will result in immediate disciplinary action.
7. Having a "no-fault" model may allow for increased reporting of medical errors, unsafe practices, and unethical behaviors, thus creating opportunities to analyze mistakes and personal and institutional learning.
8. Have staff or employees with job duties with ownership around safety and ethics compliance and conformity.

An ethical patient safety culture encompasses an emphasis on organizational strategy devoted to patient-centered care and selects safety ahead of profit (Hemphill, 2015). This requires that employees on all levels understand the importance and patent safety and their roles and ensuring the culture is ethical and safe (Hemphill, 2015).

The figure below represents a flowchart model proposed by D. Burrell and N. Bhargava (2018), representing the levels of safe, ethical, moral, and legal decision making around creating safe and ethical cultures in complex organizations.

Self-intelligence (SI) and emotional intelligence (EI) are critical to sensemaking, decision-making, and interactions in organizations (Shufutinsky & Long, 2017; Shufutinsky, 2019b; Shufutinsky, 2020), and these apply to making decisions and actions regarding safety practices, procedures, and policies in organizations. Individuals' shared values, behavioral norms, and emotional mindsets play pivotal roles in organizational change and organizational culture, and SI, including self-awareness of EI, allows individual members in the organization to be conscious of their contribution to and effect on culture. Self-intelligence embodies numerous aspects of self, including use-of-self (UoS), self-behavior, self-and situational-awareness, mindfulness and presencing, self-knowledge, self-monitoring (Shufutinsky, 2020), self-leadership, self-valuing, and agency. All of these elements of the self are considered fundamental building blocks of our ability to be effective agents in organizations (Seashore et al., 2004). Thus, SI can be a vital constituent to organizational design, development, and change, including safety culture

Figure 2. D. Burrell and N. Bhargava's Emotional Acumen Model for Safe, Ethical, Moral, and Legal Decision Making (2018)

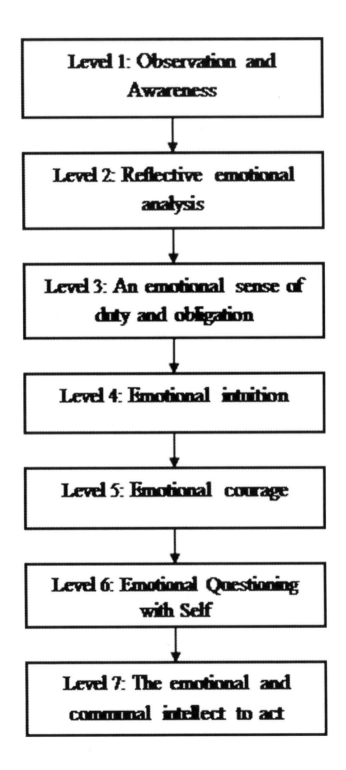

Table 3.

Model	D. Burrell and N. Bhargava's Emotional Acumen Model for Safe, Ethical, Moral, and Legal Decision Making (2018)
Level 1	Observation and Awareness – At this stage, there is a discovery, observation, and a witness of a safe, ethical, moral, or legal issue of concern.
Level 2	Reflective emotional analysis – At this stage, there is a level of significant disquiet that leads to a deeply reflective and critical emotional examination about the issue of concern and how serious it is or has the potential to be. At this stage, an individual must try his/her best to gather the facts and be as neutral as possible while describing or analyzing those facts. One should not be inclined towards distorting the facts or information for their personal benefits.
Level 3	An emotional sense of duty and obligation – At this stage, there is either an emotional inability to remain a bystander about the issue and not do anything about it. There is personal emotional onus and responsibility to act.
Level 4	Emotional intuition – This stage is about intuitions or conscience. When our emotions are cultivated by compassion, they sometimes highlight what our cognizant and coherent mind has overlooked. Our emotions are one mode to check or to see whether one is rationalizing.
Level 5	Emotional courage – At this stage, there is an in-depth exploration of the range of emotions that could include fear of retaliation and apprehension of the potential backlash. However, there are still compelling overriding reasons to take action and do something. Here, a prediction about the future is made, which is relevant to the situation(s) at hand. Though an individual can never predict the future, yet certain things are more likely than others.
Level 6	Emotional Questioning with Self – At this stage, an individual should always ask oneself before acting the following questions: a) Will I be able to live with myself if I made a particular choice? b) Will I feel better or worse about myself? c) Am I willing to let other people know about the situation or my decision to act? d) Will I feel guilty or ashamed of not taking any action sooner, or will I feel proud of my decision to act? e) Do I want everyone around me to act the way I did?
Level 7	The emotional and communal intellect to act – At this stage, there is an understanding of how to manage the emotional perceptions and emotional consequences required to act and navigate the social interactions, politics, and fallout.

in healthcare settings that may affect patient safety (Shufutinsky & Long, 2017; Shufutinsky, 2018; Shufutinsky, 2020).

Mindfulness and UoS have positive effects on human cognition, emotion, behavior, and physiological response. Individuals experienced with these SI practices tend to have trained attention that results in better real-time assessment, sensemaking, decision-making. This increased level of attentional breadth, including effective control and stability of attention on relevant tasks and less attention on distractions, essentially results in improved relationships, well-being, and ultimately increased performance (Dane, 2011; Good et al., 2016; Reb et al., 2014; Shufutinsky et al., 2020). This increased level of attention on the task at hand, reduction of focus on distractions, improved cognitive and emotional response, and improved relationality can have a considerable effect not only on a reduction of lapses, misses, and mistakes (Good et al., 2016; Shufutinsky et al., 2020), but also on ethically prioritizing patient safety over competing interests (Hemphill, 2015), effectively contributing to the reduction of medical errors and thus improved patient care.

COVID-19 created a shortage in health care staff (Xu, Intrator, Bowblis, 2020). Thereby, healthcare staff faced increased workloads, high fatigue and exhaustion, and workplace stress (Liu et al., 2020). It is noteworthy to discuss how compassion fatigue (CF) among healthcare personnel affects an organization's totality and compromises patient safety. Compassion fatigue was conceived to describe "the phenomenon of stress resulting from exposure to a traumatized individual rather than from exposure to the trauma itself" (Cocker & Joss, 2016, p. 618). Pfifferling & Gilley (2000) add psychological depth and dimension to the experience of CF by revealing that compassion fatigue is "a deep physical, emotional, and spiritual exhaustion accompanied by acute emotional pain" (p. 2).

From a systemic perspective, compassion fatigue affects the entire organization because, as exhibited in the NOF model, human factors serve as a critical component to organizational design and functions. Schein (1996) expounds on this outlook by offering that an organization's collective psychology merits attention. Schein (1996) proffers that "it is these norms or 'shared, tacit ways of perceiving, thinking, and reacting' embedded in an organization's culture and psychology that are perhaps the most powerful force operating in organizational systems" (p. 3).

There is harmony across organizational behavior literature to support the supposition that compassion fatigue diminishes patient safety, increases accidents, lessens the quality of care, and exacerbates organizational culture (Day & Anderson, 2011; Maiden et al., 2011; McHolm, 2006; Najjar et al., 2009; Nolte et al., 2017; Schultz et al., 2007; Slatten et al., 2011). Research indicates that compassion fatigue is typified by enervation, irritability, anger, apathy, maladaptive coping mechanisms such as alcohol and drug abuse, and "an impaired ability to make decisions and care for patients" (Cocker & Joss, 2016, p. 618). Simply stated, healthcare professionals may suffer adverse effects from the care they offer patients. Hormann and Vivian (2005) posit that staff's stressful emotions may worsen the organizational milieu because the distressing sentiments embed themselves in the system. Hormann and Vivian (2005) rationalize that in a trauma-organized workplace, "the internal atmosphere remains stressful, and stress becomes an organizing framework, a lens through which the work is experienced. The interplay of atmosphere and organizing framework results in a culture partially defined by its stress" (p. 164).

Consistent with the existing literature that highlights the psychological benefits derived from mindfulness (Yip et al., 2017), qualitative research underscores that "mindfulness was associated with less compassion fatigue and positive levels of patient care" (Yip et al., 2017, p. 460). From a quantitative perspective, research supports (Constantine Brown et al., 2017) the qualitative findings that there is a negative correlation between compassion fatigue and mindfulness. Stated differently, individuals experiencing elevated levels of compassion fatigue lack a sense of mindfulness. To assuage compassion fatigue among healthcare practitioners and improve patient safety and care, research asserts that mindfulness-based interventions (MBIs) improve and positively affect an organization's systemic elements (Lomas et al., 2019; Scheepers et al., 2020). Further, when "embedded in an organizational approach," MBIs help foster a "culture of wellness" (Scheepers et al., 2020, p. 139).

Analogous to the complexity of the United States health care system, implementing MBIs may be deemed a "complex intervention" (Demarzo et al., 2015, p. 167). Notably, Demarzo et al. (2015) emphasize that "there is a need for an appropriate theoretical model that allows for an understanding of how the intervention can cause changes in people's health or in the use of services and that identifies the weak points in the causal chain to strengthen them" (p. 167). Responding to Demarzo et al. (2015), utilizing Burrell & Bhargava's (2018) Emotional Acumen Model for Safe, Ethical, Moral, and Legal Decision Making may help mitigate the negative consequences associated with compassion fatigue in the healthcare system because the model illuminates how to address the human factor of emotions that may influence patient safety.

CONCLUSION

Now more than ever human resources play a significant role in influencing and creating safe cultures in healthcare. The increased complexity of the medical processes has increased the likelihood of medical errors, negatively affecting patient safety. Studies show that there are five components needed to execute patient care procedures safely and that medical errors cost the US healthcare system billions of dollars in lost revenue. The COVID-19 pandemic revealed many loopholes in the existing public health supply chain methodologies, patient safety procedures, and human resources processes. All healthcare personnel is challenged to establish cultures driven by both ethical and safe behavior. In the past, healthcare organizations did not openly disclose the severity of medical errors and patient safety issues. The present culture in medicine does not encourage a safe and open space to report errors and patient safety violations. Human resources as to play leadership role in changing that. Organizational cultures in healthcare organizations must be addressed from the lens of organizational design. The interconnectedness of organization design components must be understood and carefully and appropriately managed to foster and develop effective organizational safety cultures, including patient safety cultures, and drive transformative organizational change. Furthermore, The Emotional Acumen Model for Safe, Ethical, Moral, and Legal Decision Making is an instrument that healthcare leaders can use to improve the organizational culture, medical error reporting, and patient safety through organizational change.

Human resources, through the effective implementation, facilitation, and management of organizational design, the use of self-intelligence practices and mindfulness training, and the implementation of the Emotional Acumen Model, healthcare organizations can foster, create, and maintain effective safety cultures that include safe, ethical, moral, and legal decision-making to ensure improved patient safety, and thus improved patient outcomes and overall patient care.

REFERENCES

Abdullah, H. C., Hamed, S., Kechil, R., & Hamid, A. H. (2013). Emotional management skill at the workplace: A study at the government department in Seberang Perai Tengah. *International Journal of Social Science and Humanity*, *3*(4), 365–368. doi:10.7763/IJSSH.2013.V3.263

Acholiya, R. (2013). Corruption in Education System in India: A Study. *Pioneer Journal*, 100-105.

Annas, G. J. (2003). HIPAA Regulations— A New Era of Medical-Record Privacy? *The New England Journal of Medicine*, *348*(15), 1486–1490. doi:10.1056/NEJMlim035027 PMID:12686707

Antonsen, S. (2009). Safety Culture and the Issue of Power. *Safety Science*, *47*(2), 183–191. doi:10.1016/j.ssci.2008.02.004

Bagozzi, R. P., & Yi, Y. (1988). On the Evaluation of Structural Equation Models. *Journal of the Academy of Marketing Science*, *16*(1), 74–94. doi:10.1007/BF02723327

Beemsterboer, P. (2010). *Ethics and Law in Dental Hygiene* (2nd ed.). Saunders Elsevier.

Bentler, P. M., & Bonnet, D. C. (1980). Significance Tests and Goodness of Fit in the Analysis of Covariance Structures. *Psychological Bulletin*, *88*(3), 588–606. doi:10.1037/0033-2909.88.3.588

Bernstein, S. (2019). Being present. *Nursing*, *49*(6), 14–17. doi:10.1097/01.NURSE.0000558105.96903.af PMID:31124847

Boesz, C., & Lloyd, N. (2008). Investigating international misconduct. *Nature*, *452*(7188), 686–687. doi:10.1038/452686a PMID:18401384

Brewer, L. (2005). The whistleblower. *Accountants Today*, 10-12.

Brown, A. J. (2001). Internal witness management: An art or a science? *Ethics and Justice*, *3*(2), 45–61.

Burke, R., & Cooper, C. (2013). *Voice and Whistle-blowing in Organizations: Overcoming Fear, Fostering Courage, and Unleashing Candour*. Edward Elgar Publishing.

Burrell, D., Rahim, E., Juris, K., & Sette, Z. (2010). Developing knowledge transfer-oriented ethical cultures in US government agencies regulating the commercial use of nuclear power. *International Journal of Nuclear Knowledge Management*, *4*(2), 165. doi:10.1504/IJNKM.2010.032314

Burrell, D. N., Bhargava, N., Duncan, T., Lindsay, P. V., Cole, C. M., & Sangle, P. (2019). Exploring the Complex Nature of Ethical Cultures in Health Care Organizations. *International Journal of Applied Research on Public Health Management*, *4*(2), 29–46. doi:10.4018/IJARPHM.2019070103

Byrne, B. M., Oakland, T., Leong, F. T., van de Vijver, F. J., Hambleton, R. K., Cheung, F. M., & Bartram, D. (2009). A critical analysis of cross-cultural research and testing practices: Implications for improved education and training in psychology. *Training and Education in Professional Psychology*, *3*(2), 94–105. doi:10.1037/a0014516

Carmeli, A., Gelbard, R., & Gefen, D. (2010). The importance of innovation leadership in cultivating strategic fit and enhancing firm performance. *The Leadership Quarterly*, *21*(3), 339–349. doi:10.1016/j.leaqua.2010.03.001

Carroll, A. B., & Buchholtz, A. K. (2000). *Organization and society* (4th ed.). South-Western College.

Carver, N., Gupta, V., & Hipskind, J. (2020). *Medical Error*. StatPearls Publishing. https://www.ncbi.nlm.nih.gov/books/NBK430763/

Cocker, F., & Joss, N. (2016). Compassion Fatigue among Healthcare, Emergency, and Community Service Workers: A Systematic Review. *International Journal of Environmental Research and Public Health*, *13*(6), 618. doi:10.3390/ijerph13060618 PMID:27338436

Conlon, P., Havlisch, R., Kini, N., & Porter, C. (2008). Using an Anonymous Web-Based Incident Reporting Tool to Embed the Principles of a High-Reliability Organization. In *Advances in Patient Safety: New Directions and Alternative Approaches* (Vol. 1: Assessment). Agency for Healthcare Research and Quality. https://www.ncbi.nlm.nih.gov/books/NBK43630/

Constantine Brown, J. L., Ong, J., Mathers, J. M., & Decker, J. T. (2017). Compassion fatigue and mindfulness: Comparing mental health professionals and MSW Student Interns. *Journal of Evidence-Informed Social Work*, *14*(3), 119–130. doi:10.1080/23761407.2017.1302859 PMID:28388339

Cooper, M. D. (2000). Towards a model of safety culture. *Safety Science*, *36*(2), 111–136. doi:10.1016/S0925-7535(00)00035-7

Courtemanche, G. (1988, February). The Ethics of Whistle-Blowing. *Internal Auditor*, 36–41.

Currence, J. (2017). *Developing Business Acumen (Making an Impact in Small Business HR)*. Society for Human Resources Management.

Dane, E. (2011). Paying attention to mindfulness and its effects on task performance in the workplace. *Journal of Management, 37*(4), 997–1018. doi:10.1177/0149206310367948

Day, J. R., & Anderson, R. A. (2011). Compassion fatigue: An application of the concept to informal caregivers of family members with dementia. *Nursing Research and Practice, 2011*, 408024. doi:10.1155/2011/408024 PMID:22229086

Dellaportas, S., Gibson, K., Alagiah, R., Hutchinson, M., Leung, P., & Van Homrigh, D. (2005). *Ethics, governance, and accountability: A professional perspective*. John Wiley & Sons, Ltd.

Demarzo, M. M. P., Cebolla, A., & Garcia-Campayo, J. (2015). The implementation of mindfulness in healthcare systems: A theoretical analysis. *General Hospital Psychiatry, 37*(2), 166–171. doi:10.1016/j.genhosppsych.2014.11.013 PMID:25660344

Deshpande, S. P. (1996). Ethical climate and the link between success and ethical behaviour: An empirical investigation of a non-profit organization. *Journal of Business Ethics, 15*(3), 315–320. doi:10.1007/BF00382957

Elias, R. (2008). Auditing students' professional commitment and anticipatory socialization and their relationship to whistleblowing. *Managerial Auditing Journal, 23*(3), 283–294. doi:10.1108/02686900810857721

Fan, X., & Sivo, S. A. (2009). Using goodness-of-fit indexes in assessing mean structure invariance. *Structural Equation Modeling, 16*(1), 54–69. doi:10.1080/10705510802561311

Figley, C. (1995). *Compassion Fatigue: Coping with Secondary Stress Disorder in Those Who Treat the Traumatized*. Brunner/Mazel.

Fornell, C., & Larcker, D. F. (1981). Evaluating structural model with unobserved variables and measurement errors. *JMR, Journal of Marketing Research, 18*(1), 39–50. doi:10.1177/002224378101800104

Fu, W. (2014). The impact of emotional intelligence, organizational commitment, and job satisfaction on ethical behavior of Chinese employees. *Journal of Business Ethics, 122*(1), 137–144. doi:10.100710551-013-1763-6

Geller, E. S. (1994). Ten principles for achieving a total safety culture. *Professional Safety, 39*(9), 18–24.

Gillin, L. (2015). *Business acumen: In the workplace*. CreateSpace Independent Publishing.

Goleman, D. (2005). *Emotional Intelligence*. Bantam Publishing.

Goleman, D. (2007). *Social Intelligence. Social Intelligence: The New Science of Human Relationships*. Bantam Publishing.

Good, D. J., Lyddy, C. J., Glomb, T. M., Bono, J. E., Brown, K. W., Duffy, M. K., & Lazar, S. W. (2016). Contemplating mindfulness at work: An integrative review. *Journal of Management, 42*(1), 114-142.

Greenfield, B., & Jensen, G. M. (2010). Beyond a code of ethics: Phenomenological ethics for everyday practice. *Physiotherapy Research International, 15*, 88–95. doi:10.1002/pri.481 PMID:20564757

Hair, J. F., Black, W. C., Babin, B. J., & Anderson, R. E. (2010). *Multivariate data analysis* (7th ed.). Prentice-Hall.

Hastie, R., & Dawes, R. (2009). *Rational choice in an uncertain world: the psychology of judgment and decision making*. SAGE Publications.

Hemphill, R. (2015). Medications and the Culture of Safety. *Journal of Medical Toxicology, 11*(2), 253-6.

Hoffman, W., & McNulty, R. E. (2010). A business ethics theory of whistleblowing: Responding to the $1 trillion question. In M. Arszulowicz & W. Gasparski (Eds.), *Defense of proper action: The whistleblowing* (pp. 45–60). Transaction Publishers.

Hormann, S., & Vivian, P. (2005). Toward an understanding of traumatized organizations and how to intervene in them. *Traumatology, 11*(3), 159–169. doi:10.1177/153476560501100302

Hu, L. T., & Bentler, P. M. (1999). Cutoff criteria for fit indexes in covariance structure analysis: Conventional criteria versus new alternatives. *Structural Equation Modeling, 6*(1), 1–55. doi:10.1080/10705519909540118

Jaggar, A. M. (1989). Love and knowledge: Emotion in feminist epistemology. *An Interdisciplinary Journal of Philosophy, 32*(2), 151–176. doi:10.1080/00201748908602185

Jamieson, D. W. (2017). *Strategic organization design – Overview*. Lecture Presentation, Cabrini University Organizational Development Program.

Kates, A., & Galbraith, J. R. (2007). *Designing your organization: Using the Star Model to solve five critical design challenges*. Jossey-Bass.

Khan, M. A. (2009). Auditors and the whistleblowing law. *Accountants Today*, 12-14.

KPMG. (2015). *Health care and cybersecurity: increasing threats require increased capabilities*. KPMG. https://assets.kpmg.com/content/dam/kpmg/pdf/2015/09/cyber-health-care-surveykpmg-2015.pdf

Lee, E. (2005). Whistleblowers: Heroes or villains? *Accountants Today*, 14-18.

Levin, I. P., Schneider, S. L., & Gaeth, G. J. (1998). All frames are not created equal: A typology and critical analysis of framing effects. *Organizational Behavior and Human Decision Processes, 76*(2), 149–188. doi:10.1006/obhd.1998.2804 PMID:9831520

Liu, Q., Luo, D., Haase, J. E., Guo, Q., Wang, X. Q., Liu, S., Xia, L., Liu, Z., Yang, J., & Yang, B. X. (2020). The experiences of healthcare providers during the COVID-19 crisis in China: A qualitative study. *The Lancet. Global Health, 8*(6), 790–798. doi:10.1016/S2214-109X(20)30204-7 PMID:32573443

Lomas, T., Medina, J. C., Ivtzan, I., Rupprecht, S., & Eiroa-Orosa, F. J. (2019). A Systematic Review and Meta-analysis of the Impact of Mindfulness-Based Interventions on the Well-Being of Healthcare Professionals. *Mindfulness, 10*(7), 1193–1216. doi:10.100712671-018-1062-5

Magretta, J. (2012). Understanding Michael Porter: The Essential Guide to Competition and Strategy. *Harvard Business Review*.

Maiden, J., Georges, J. M., & Connelly, C. D. (2011). Moral distress, compassion fatigue, and perceptions about medication errors in certified critical care nurses. *Dimensions of Critical Care Nursing, 30*(6), 339–345. doi:10.1097/DCC.0b013e31822fab2a PMID:21983510

Malm, H., May, T., Francis, L., Omer, S., Salmon, D., & Hood, R. (2008). Ethics, Pandemics, and the Duty to Treat. *The American Journal of Bioethics, 8*(8), 4–19. doi:10.1080/15265160802317974 PMID:18802849

Martin, G., Martin, P., Hankin, C., Darzi, A., & Kinross, J. (2017). Cybersecurity and healthcare: how safe are we? *British Medical Journal, 358*.

Maruyama, G. (1998). *Basics of Structural Equation Modeling.* Sage Publishing. doi:10.4135/9781483345109

Masson, G., Vaidya, A., & Bean, M. (2020). *The coronavirus playbook: How 12 health systems are responding to the pandemic.* https://www.beckershospitalreview.com/infection-control/the-coronavirus-playbook-how-12-health-systems-are-responding-to-the-pandemic.html

Mathieu, F. (2007). Running on Empty: Compassion Fatigue in Health Professionals. *Rehab Community Care Med, 4*, 1–7.

McHolm, F. (2006). Rx for compassion fatigue. *Journal of Christian Nursing, 23*(4), 12–19. doi:10.1097/00005217-200611000-00003 PMID:17078229

Miceli, M., & Near, J. P. (1992). *Blowing the whistle.* Lexington Books.

Miceli, M. P., Near, J. P., & Dworkin, T. M. (2008). *Whistleblowing in organizations.* Routledge.

Morgan, D. (2018). Basic and Advanced Focus Groups. *Sage (Atlanta, Ga.).*

Morris, H. M. (2014). *Annals of entrepreneurship education and pedagogy.* Edward Elgar Publishing.

Najjar, N., Davis, L. W., Beck-Coon, K., & Carney Doebbeling, C. (2009). Compassion fatigue: A Review of the Research to Date and Relevance to Cancer-care Providers. *Journal of Health Psychology, 14*(2), 267–277. doi:10.1177/1359105308100211 PMID:19237494

Near, J. P., & Miceli, M. P. (1995). Effective whistleblowing. *Academy of Management Review, 20*(3), 679–708.

Nolte, A. G., Downing, C., Temane, A., & Hastings-Tolsma, M. (2017). Compassion fatigue in nurses: A meta-synthesis. *Journal of Clinical Nursing, 26*(23-24), 4364–4378. doi:10.1111/jocn.13766 PMID:28231623

O'Connor, F. J., & Baratz, J. M. (2004). Some assembly required: The application of state open meeting laws to email correspondence. *George Mason Law Review, 12*, 719.

O'Toole, M. (2002). The relationship between employees' perceptions of safety and organizational culture. *Journal of Safety Research, 33*(2), 231–243. doi:10.1016/S0022-4375(02)00014-2 PMID:12216448

Parker, D., Lawries, M., & Hudson, P. A. (2006). framework for understanding the development of organizational safety culture. *Safety Science, 44*(6), 551–562. doi:10.1016/j.ssci.2005.10.004

Pasupathi, M. (1999). *Socio-emotional influences on decision making: The challenge of choice-When I'm 64.* National Academies Press.

Pfifferling, J., & Gilley, K. (2000). Overcoming compassion fatigue. *Family Practice Management, 7*(4), 1–6.

Randall, M. D., & Gibson, M. A. (1990). Methodology in business ethics research: A review and critical assessment. *Journal of Business Ethics, 9*(6), 457–471. doi:10.1007/BF00382838

Rathbone, E. (2012). Can we be smarter about our feelings? *University of Virginia Magazine,* 21-22.

Reb, J., Narayanan, J., & Chaturvedi, S. (2014). Leading mindfully: Two studies on the influence of supervisor trait mindfulness on employee well-being and performance. *Mindfulness, 5*(1), 36–45. doi:10.100712671-012-0144-z

Rest, J. (1979). *Development in judging moral issues.* University of Minnesota Press.

Ross, E. (2013). *Emotion and decision making explained.* Oxford University Press.

Rummel, R. J. (1970). *Applied factor analysis.* Northwestern University Press.

Saxena, S., & Awasthi, P. (2010). *Leadership.* PHI Learning Private Limited.

Scheepers, R. A., Emke, H., Epstein, R. M., & Lombarts, K. M. (2020). The impact of mindfulness-based interventions on doctors' well-being and performance: A systematic review. *Medical Education, 54*(2), 138–149. doi:10.1111/medu.14020 PMID:31868262

Schein, E. H. (1996). Organizational culture: The missing concept in organization studies. *Administrative Science Quarterly, 41*(2), 229–240. doi:10.2307/2393715

Schein, E. H. (2007). The role of the founder in the creation of organizational culture. *Organization Science,* 439.

Schultz, R., Hebert, R. S., Dew, M. A., Brown, S. L., Scheier, M. F., Beach, S. R., ... Nichols, L. (2007). Patient suffering and caregiver compassion: New opportunities for research, practice, and policy. *The Gerontologist, 47*(1), 4–13. doi:10.1093/geront/47.1.4 PMID:17327535

Seashore, C. N., Shawver, M. N., Thompson, G., & Mattare, M. (2004). Doing good by knowing who you are: The instrumental self as an agent of change. *OD Practitioner, 36*(3), 42–46.

Senge, P. M. (2014). *The fifth discipline fieldbook: Strategies and tools for building a learning organization.* Crown Business.

Shafer, R., Dyer, L., Kilty, J., & Amos, J. (2000). *Crafting a human resource strategy to foster organizational agility: a case study* (CAHRS Working Paper #00-08). Cornell University, School of Industrial and Labor Relations, Center for Advanced Human Resource Studies.

Shufutinsky, A. (2018). Organizational Assessment of a Biotechnology Firm's Safety, Health, and Environmental Department through an Organizational Development Lens. *International Journal of Interdisciplinary & Multidisciplinary Studies, 4*(3).

Shufutinsky, A. (2019). Tribalism and Clone Theory in New Leaders and the Resulting Degradation of Organizational Culture. *Psychology and Behavioral Science International Journal, 10*(2).

Shufutinsky, A. (2019b). *From Salutes to Staff Meetings: A Triangulated Qualitative Inquiry Study of the Experiences of Wounded Warriors in Post-Military Corporate Positions.* ProQuest Dissertations.

Shufutinsky, A. (2020). Blackbird on a Bough: An Autoethnographic Conversation Regarding Personal Struggle, the Use-of-Self Journey, and Lessons that Inform Professional Practice. Accepted for publication in Practising Social Change (UK).

Shufutinsky, A., DePorres, D., Long, B., & Sibel, J. (2020). Shock Leadership Development for the Modern Era of Pandemic Management and Preparedness. *International Journal of Organizational Innovation*, *13*(1), 1–23.

Shufutinsky, A., & Long, B. (2017). The Distributed Use of Self-as-Instrument for Improvement of Organizational Safety Culture. *OD Practitioner*, *49*(4), 36–44.

Shufutinsky, A., Shanahan, P., Schaal, N., Madad, S., & Johnson, W. D. (2015). Applying conflict analysis and resolution strategies to assess organizational safety culture in accident investigations. *International Journal of Interdisciplinary and Multidisciplinary Studies*, *2*(3), 71–90.

Singh, G., Singh, R., & Thomas, E. J. (2008) Measuring Safety Climate in Primary Care Offices. In *Advances in Patient Safety: New Directions and Alternative Approaches* (Vol. 2: Culture and Redesign). Agency for Healthcare Research and Quality (US). https://www.ncbi.nlm.nih.gov/books/NBK43706/

Slatten, L. A., David Carson, K., & Carson, P. P. (2011). Compassion fatigue and burnout: What managers should know. *The Health Care Manager*, *30*(4), 326–333. doi:10.1097/HCM.0b013e31823511f7 PMID:22042140

Stewart, D. (1996). *Organization ethics*. McGraw-Hill Companies, Inc.

Swisher, L. L., & Davis, C. M. (2005). The realm-individual-process-situation (RIPS) model of ethical decision-making. *HPA Resource*, *5*(3), 1–8.

Thakkar, M., & Davis, D. C. (2006). Risks, barriers, and benefits of EHR systems: A comparative study based on the size of the hospital. *Perspectives in Health Information Management*, *3*, 5. PMID:18066363

The Joint Commission. (2020). *The Universal Protocol*. Retrieved from https://www.jointcommission.org/-/media/deprecated-unorganized/imported-assets/tjc/system-folders/topics-library/up_posterpdf.pdf?db=web&hash=57DC6A91EF83C142943961031B3626F9" https://www.jointcommission.org/-/media/deprecated-unorganized/imported-assets/tjc/system-folders/topics-library/up_posterpdf.pdf?db=web&hash=57DC6A91EF83C142943961031B3626F9

Thompson, K. (2015). *A systematic guide to business acumen and leadership using dilemmas: Includes organizational health, agility, resilience, and crisis management*. CreateSpace Independent Publishing.

Ugur, E., Kara, S., Yildirim, S., & Akbal, E. (2016). Medical errors and patient safety in the operating room. *JPMA. The Journal of the Pakistan Medical Association*, *66*(5), 593–597. https://jpma.org.pk/article-details/7750?article_id=7750 PMID:27183943

US Securities and Exchange Commission. (2018). *SEC Adopts Statement and Interpretive Guidance on Public Company Cybersecurity Disclosures*. https://www.sec.gov/news/press-release/2018-22

Weiss, J. W. (2006). Organization ethics (4th ed.). Thompson/South West.

Wilde, J. H. (2013). *Citizen watch in the accounting department? Tax and financial reporting responses to employee whistleblowing allegations* (Order No. 3608021). Available from ProQuest Dissertations & Theses Global. (1497226692). Retrieved from https://search-proquestcom.contentproxy.phoenix.edu/docview/1497226692?accountid=35812

World Health Organization. (2019). *Patient Safety.* https://www.who.int/news-room/fact-sheets/detail/patient-safety

Xu, H., Intrator, O., & Bowblis, J. R. (2020). Shortages of Staff in Nursing Homes During the COVID-19 Pandemic: What are the Driving Factors? *Journal of the American Medical Directors Association, 21*(10), 1371–1377. doi:10.1016/j.jamda.2020.08.002 PMID:32981663

Yip, S. Y., Mak, W. W., Chio, F. H., & Law, R. W. (2017). The mediating role of self-compassion between mindfulness and compassion fatigue among therapists in Hong Kong. *Mindfulness, 8*(2), 460–470. doi:10.100712671-016-0618-5

Chapter 2
A Cross-Cultural Comparison of College Student Self-Efficacy, Self-Regulation, and Resilience Between the US and China During the COVID-19 Pandemic

Yan Dai
https://orcid.org/0000-0003-1170-7776
Auburn University, USA

Chih-hsuan Wang
https://orcid.org/0000-0002-8361-8062
Auburn University, USA

Hyun Sung Jang
Auburn University, USA

Kamden K. Strunk
Auburn University, USA

Jill D. Salisbury-Glennon
Auburn University, USA

ABSTRACT

The unprecedented COVID-19 global pandemic has created many challenges across the educational domains experienced by many cultures around the world. The present study elucidates a cross-cultural comparison of college students' self-efficacy, self-regulation, and resilience between college students in the United States and China during these challenging times. A total of 479 college students from the United States and China were recruited to participate in the present study. Multivariate analyses of variance (MANOVA) were conducted, and results indicated that U.S. college students demonstrated significantly higher self-efficacy and resilience and significantly lower self-regulation than Chinese college students. Further, the implications of the present study provide suggestions for effective teaching and learning strategies that can be used to establish supportive learning environments for students from different cultural backgrounds.

DOI: 10.4018/978-1-7998-8996-0.ch002

INTRODUCTION

Cultural Differences in Education

In line with the increasing diversity in educational settings around the world, the study of culture has been espoused as increasingly essential (McInerney & King, 2018). The United Nations Educational Scientific and Cultural Organization (UNESCO) emphasizes cultural diversity and the need for reflecting it in the educational policy below:

Education should celebrate cultural diversity. Enhanced diversity in education can improve the quality of education by introducing both educators and learners to the diversity of perspectives and the variety of lived worlds. The cultural dimension of education must be stressed... (UNESCO, 2015, p. 67).

Culture shapes students' learning beliefs (McInerney & King, 2018). McInerney and King (2018) have further emphasized that we need a psychological theory that focuses on both cross-cultural similarities as well as cross-cultural differences, as the majority of the research studies in this area focus on cross-cultural similarities and neglect cross-cultural differences. Dramatic differences in individuals' learning have been found between Eastern and Western cultures (Herrman et al., 2011; Oettingen,1995; Steel et al., 2014; Trommsdorff, 2009).

Thus, most would agree that culture and education are inseparable and that an understanding of culture is essential. However, the definition of culture remains complicated and varied. Trumbull and Rothstein-Fisch (2011) mention, "Nearly everyone believes it [culture] exists, but few can agree on exactly what it is." (p. 26). Similarly, King and McInerney (2016) stated, "Numerous scholars have defined culture in different ways" (p. 276). Taras et al. (2016) specify how the definition of culture can be ambiguous in the literature. Taras and his colleagues further mention that 164 different definitions of culture were found by Kroeber and Kluckhohn (1952). Thus, researchers have noted the vague and non-universal definition of culture due to its complexity. As a result, different cultural models have been introduced in the literature. For the purposes of the present study, culture will be conceptualized from a subjective perspective that includes values, traditions, and beliefs that mediate the behavior of a particular group (McInerney, 2011; as cited in McInerney & King, 2018).

Hofstede's cultural model has been considered the most empirically impactful model for more than 40 years, and this cultural model was developed based on our traditional assumption that cultures reside within countries (Taras et al., 2016). That is why it is believed that many cross-cultural researchers equate country and culture because they believe that people's nationality may act as proxies for their cultural values. The present study was grounded in Hofstede's (1984) culture model, and it was presumed that Chinese students and American students are two different cultural groups. Hofstede's dimensions have been used extensively in a variety of research studies (Zainuddin et al., 2018). Hofstede's model consists of four dimensions that are used to identify what national culture is. Table 1 below summarizes Hofstede's model from Zainuddin et al. (2018).

Since Hofstede's model has been more utilized in the business setting, there remains a paucity of research espousing whether the model has leverage in the educational environment. Previous research examined how this dichotomous dimension would play a role in self-efficacy (Mahat et al., 2014), self-regulation strategies (Leung et al., 2006; Wu et al., 2020), and resilience (Stutman et al., 2002). Further, prior research offers the dimensions of individualism and collectivism to explain individual learning differences. Specifically, self-efficacy (Mahat et al., 2014) and self-regulation strategies (Leung et al., 2006; Wu et al., 2020) were reported differently in collectivist and individualist cultures. Similarly, students from collectivistic cultures were also different in resilience than their counterparts from individualistic cultures (Stutman et al., 2002). Researchers presumed that this was due to the fact that students in collectivistic cultures care more about others' opinions, expectations, and evaluations (Oettingen, 1995). Further they tend to focus more on obedience, correspondence of own profits with others, and collectivist goals (Camgoz et al., 2008). In contrast, students from more individualistic cultures emphasize the individual's moral worth, independence, and self-reliance, and they focus on individual achievement precedence over social groups (Merriam & Mohamad, 2000; Wood, 1972). Thus, the present study used the individualism versus collectivism dimension of Hofstede's model in the educational settings. Specifically, this chapter focused on students' cross-cultural differences in self-efficacy, self-regulation, and resilience.

Typically, Western Europe, the United States, Australia, and New Zealand are considered to operate from a more individualistic perspective (Takano & Osaka, 2018). Whereas, South and South-East Asia,and Central Asia are considered to be more collectivistic (Beugelsdijk et al., 2017; Minkov et al., 2017; Welzel, 2013). The authors followed this distinction as a guild. Consequently, the present study compared American college learners who tend to be reflective of a more Western individualistic culture and Chinese college learners as representatives of Eastern collectivist culture.

The COVID-19 Global Pandemic and Learning

The unprecedented Coronavirus (COVID-19) global pandemic forced many colleges and universities around the world to abruptly close and shift from face-to-face classes to online instruction during the spring of 2020 (Alexander et al., 2020; Rashid & Yadav, 2020). This event marked the first time that college students uniformly attended online college courses throughout the world. On the one hand, online learning provided virtual learning accessibility and flexibility in times of a potential natural disaster, civil emergency, and crisis (Mackey et al., 2012). On the other hand, however; regardless of the course format, online learning environments also caused many college students around the world to develop a sense of isolation and loneliness due to a lack of interpersonal relationships with their instructors and peers (Bowers & Kumar, 2015; Kaufmann & Vallade, 2020).

Further, most, if not all, college students evacuated from their on-campus or off-campus residential settings to move back home with their parents or guardians. Thus, college students now had to face these unique online learning contexts alone without the support of their college peers. The various challenges faced by college students during the pandemic may also have been a function of their social and cultural backgrounds.

Finally, the more personal variables such as self-efficacy, metacognitive self-regulation, and resilience have all been demonstrated to serve as important factors contributing to college students' learning and academic achievement, especially while they are engaged in online learning environments (Ayyash-Abdo, 2016; Cicha et al., 2021; Torun, 2020). In addition, some preliminary research into the effects of the COVID-19 global pandemic on college students' learning has demonstrated that during the Spring of 2020, parental support was a statistically significant predictor of college students' motivation, which was a significant predictor of their cognitive and metacognitive strategies (Salisbury-Glennon et al., 2021).

Thus, it is suggested here that during the COVID-19 global pandemic, while college students were learning away from their college or university setting while engaged in online learning, self-efficacy, metacognitive self-regulation, and resilience may have been especially critical to their academic success. Further, significant differences in individual self-efficacy, self-regulation, and resilience have been found between college students from Eastern and Western cultures (Herrman et al., 2011; Oettingen,1995; Steel et al., 2014; Trommsdorff, 2009), which may further lead to differences in learning academic performance (Herrman et al., 2011; Trommsdorff, 2009). Therefore, the present study sought to investigate a cross-cultural comparison between American and Chinese students' self-efficacy, metacognitive self-regulation, and resilience during the COVID-19 global pandemic.

LITERATURE REVIEW

Self-Efficacy

Bandura (1977) first coined the term self-efficacy, and defined it as "beliefs in one's capabilities to organize and execute the courses of action required to produce given attainments" (Bandura, 1997, p. 3). In the Motivated Strategies for Learning Questionnaire that the authors utilized for our research, Pintrich et al. (1991) define self-efficacy as self-appraisal of one's ability to master a task. As illustrated in both definitions, both Bandura and Pintrich believed that self-efficacy concerned an individual personal belief or appraisal, and ultimately, this self-efficacy would lead to generating higher outcomes in one's performance. In fact, self-efficacy has been considered a predictor of students' academic performance in education (Andrew, 1998; Komarraju et al., 2009; Travis & Bunde, 2020). It is believed that higher self-efficacy is related to higher academic performance. Specifically, self-efficacy theorists argue that if students have higher self-efficacy, they are likely to generate better academic performance due to their higher beliefs.

Bandura (1997) postulated that self-efficacy beliefs are formed through four sources: (1) mastery experience, (2) vicarious experience, (3) social persuasion, and (4) physiological or emotional state. Mastery experiences are formed through the collection of one's successful achievements, and they are considered the strongest source of self-efficacy. Second, vicarious experiences are formed when people observe others who are similar to themselves who succeed in their performance, and this observation will raise the observers' self-efficacy. Third, social persuasion occurs when people receive positive verbal feedback while performing their task (e.g., "you can do it"). Lastly, people's emotional, mental, and physical well-being is important for self-efficacy as these factors affect how they feel about their self-efficacy. All these resources involve social and cultural differences based on the environment in which individuals in and the social norm their culture held.

Klassen (2004a) raised the question, "Do efficacy beliefs operate in the same way across cultures?" (p. 731). Klassen generated this inquiry based on Eaton and Dembo's (1997) articulation; "researchers must focus on clarifying the underlying factors of motivation within each specific cultural group" (p. 438). More specifically, cross-cultural researchers have given attention to the role of self-efficacy in different cultural groups, and they have found that culture has an impact on students' self-efficacy (Wang et al., 2018).

For example, Klassen (2004a) conducted cross-cultural research to investigate the effects of self-efficacy in individualistic and collectivistic cultural groups. By researching Anglo (representative of individualistic culture) and Indo (representative of collectivistic culture) Canadian middle school students; Klassen (2004a) found that self-efficacy was a strong predictor of academic performance for both groups. Despite self-efficacy emerging in both groups as a strong predictor Klassen (2004a) reported that the source of predicting self-efficacy was different between the two cultural groups. Through these results, Klassen (2004a) argued that the operation of self-efficacy was the same between individualistic and collectivistic cultures, but how it operated appeared to be different between them. Self-efficacy and its effect actually had a different role between the two cultural groups. It has further been found that whether the type of feedback was focused on the individual or the group affected motivation (Early, 1990. Moreover, feedback involving collective goal settings increased students' self-efficacy in a collectivistic culture (Bonneville-Roussy et al., 2019)

Eaton and Dembo (1997) sought to investigate the differences in the motivational beliefs between Asian American and non-Asian 9th graders. Their results indicated that for the Asian American students, their fear of the consequence of academic failure explained their failure. In contrast, fear of failure least explained the results for the non-Asian students. Interestingly, while Asian American students reported lower levels of self-efficacy beliefs, they still significantly outperformed the non-Asian students. The researchers concluded that motivational beliefs fostered different responses in different cultural groups.

Metacognitive self-regulation

Although a variety of definitions of metacognition have been posited, Schunk (2008) argues that Flavell's definition is broad enough to encompass the widely diverse meaning of metacognition. According to Flavell (1985), the core meaning of metacognition is "cognition about cognition" (Flavell, 1985, p. 104), which is also known as "thinking of thinking." Our recommended definition of metacognition is excerpted from De Backer et al. (2015) and it is defined as "both the awareness and the active control students have over their cognitive activities when engaged in learning or academic problem-solving" (p. 470). In other words, metacognition refers to students' ability to monitor and regulate their thoughts, feelings, and behaviors.

Self-regulation is broadly defined in two ways. Schunk (2008) arguably notes that Bandura's self-regulation was aligned with his social cognitive theory; therefore, his view on self-regulation was related to the functions of self-observation, self-judgement, and self-reaction. In fact, Bandura calls self-regulation a triadic reciprocal interaction of personal, behavioral, and environmental processes (Bandura, 1977). Based on Bandura's version of self-regulation, Zimmerman viewed self-regulation as one's cognitive and behavior control to attain their learning goals (Schunk, 2008). The following definition presents Zimmerman's view on self-regulation; "the self-directive process by which learners transform their mental abilities into academic skills" (Zimmerman, 2002, p. 65). Thus, the definitions of metacognition and self-regulation vary depending on which educational philosophical lens is adopted.

Pintrich et al. (1991) perceived metacognitive self-regulation as controlling one's cognition through planning, monitoring, and regulating. These metacognitive self-regulatory activities are essential for successful academic performance. Pintrich et al. initially asserted that there was a synergistic relationship between motivation and cognition as they both interact in a "dynamic interplay" in the self-regulated learner (Pintrich et al., 1989).

Even though the three phases of metacognitive self-regulation seem to be readily generalizable, researchers have recognized the growing need for culturally-based assessment for self-regulation (McClelland et al., 2015; Pintrich, 1991). McInerney and King (2018) asserted that since self-regulatory skills are acquired through social modeling, and social collaboration, for example, cultural factors will most likely play a very central role in acquiring self-regulation. For instance, McClelland et al. (2015)

articulate that American students might be more likely to be perceived as lacking self-regulation as compared to Chinese students due to their more unstructured time in the classroom. In other words, McClelland et al. (2015) noted that Chinese parenting and teaching practices could be more supportive of the development of self-regulation. That is one reason why the cultural context should be taken into account to explain students' self-regulation. Furthermore, McClelland et al. (2015) illustrate that the form of self-regulation appears differently depending on culture. For example, McClelland and his colleagues explained that Chinese children with better working memory and attentional control (self-regulatory strategies) demonstrated in higher achievement in reading; however, the same effect was not found among American children.

Despite the potential variability of self-regulation being manifested, McClelland et al. (2015) mention that self-regulation is considerably related to academic achievement across different cultures, including those in the United States, China, Taiwan, South Korea, Japan, Australia, Germany, Iceland, and France. Previously, self-regulation has been found to be related to academic performance (Ariani, 2016), the depth of thinking and understanding (Jenson, 2011), and focus on the learning process (Reyna et al., 2019). Moreover, self-regulated learning strategies could be used to positively impact academic achievement (Ariani, 2016; Brady et al., 2021; Galla et al., 2019; Hromalik et al., 2018). Further, like self-efficacy, self-regulation could be constructed differently depending on different cultures (Shen et al., 2018). Therefore, it is suggested here that it is necessary to understand self-efficacy and self-regulation within the cultural context. Further, in their review, McInerney and King (2018) suggested that based on their review of the literature into culture and self-regulation in educational contexts, there were very few two-culture studies conducted during the time span of their review. Thus, there remains a need for further investigation into cultural differences in self-regulation using two-culture studies.

Resilience

Psychological resilience has drawn increasing attention in the education domain due to its crucial influences on an individual's coping strategies not only after trauma but also in response to academic failure (Ayyash-Abdo, 2016; Hernández et al., 2019; Moke, 2018; Tope-Banjoko, 2020). There are varying operational definitions of psychological resilience throughout the literature, which have evolved with increasing research. Connor and Davidson (2003) defined resilience as "a measure of stress coping ability and, as such, could be an important target of treatment in anxiety, depression, and stress reactions (p.76)." Cicchetti (2010) viewed resilience as "a dynamic developmental process encompassing the attainment of positive adaptation within the context of significant threat, severe adversity, or trauma (p.145)." Other researchers defined resilience more broadly as the protective factors and processes or mechanisms that contribute to a healthy outcome, despite experiences with stressors shown to carry significant risk for developing psychopathology (Hjemdal et al., 2006) and a dynamic process of positive adaptation in the context of significant adversity (Luthar & Cicchetti, 2000). There is a consensus among researchers that the definition of resilience consists of adverse experience, coping, and positive adaptation (Cicchetti, 2010; Connor & Davidson, 2003; Grotberg, 2003; Herrman et al., 2011; Luthar & Cicchetti, 2000; Luthar & Ziegler, 1991; Masten et al., 1990; Trigueros et al., 2019). That is, psychological resilience refers to the ability to mentally cope with adversity and bounce back (Herrman et al., 2011; Robertson et al., 2015). In a review of the resilience literature, there are two categories of factors that determine the resilience outcome: external factors such as the environment (i.e., culture, family, etc.) (Bonanno et al., 2010) and internal factors such as self-efficacy, self-control, and cultural and social sensitivity (Gunnestad, 2006; Ungar, 2008; Wagnild & Young, 1993).

Resilience differences exist among individuals across cultures (Herrman et al., 2011; Ungar, 2005, 2008). The home culture is one of the most critical factors that promote resilience (Connor & Davidson, 2003; Pieloch et al., 2016). Ungar's (2008) tri-cultural comparison with 1,500 youth from 14 sites globally revealed that there are global and cultural differences in youths' resilience. The results demonstrated that even when faced with similar adversities, there was great variation across cultures in how youth cope with adversity (Ungar, 2006). Arrington and Wilson (2000) found that cultural variation exerted a significant influence on children's resilience. Ungar (2005) posited that the resources available for survival might be very different among different cultures. Other researchers have suggested that variability in resilience may be caused by both personal factors, including self-efficacy, self-regulation, cognitive flexibility, adaptability (Joseph & Linley, 2008), and environmental factors, such as cultural factors, spirituality and religion, and social policy (Luthar & Cicchetti, 2000). It was believed by the researchers of the present study that a global pandemic could pose a potentially important time during which to assess resilience from a cross-cultural perspective (Ali et al., 2021; Cénat et al., 2020; Loree, 2020; Zheng et al., 2020). Therefore, we conducted this research during the COVID-19 global pandemic in an effort to compare college students' resilience during a significantly stressful event.

Hence, the present study was conducted in an effort to provide a cross-cultural comparison of college students' self-efficacy, self-regulation, and resilience between college students residing in the U.S. and China during the COVID-19 global pandemic. In addition, we also take gender into consideration because women remain underrepresented in Eastern cultures, especially in China, due to the deep-rooted male supremacy culture norms. Thus, the research questions posed in the present study are as follows: 1) Is there a difference based on the interaction of culture and gender on students' self-efficacy, self-regulation, and resilience? 2) What are the differences in the self-efficacy, self-regulation, and resilience between the American and Chinese college students? 3) What are the differences in the self-efficacy, self-regulation, and resilience between men and women? It is hoped that the results of the present study may be able to enlighten higher education professionals and policymakers to have a more comprehensive understanding of college students' differences in online learning contexts during the COVID-19 global pandemic as a function of culture. Specifically, using a cultural perspective, we hope to be able to suggest effective pedagogical and learning strategies to establish supportive learning environments for students from different cultural backgrounds.

METHODS

Participants

Volunteer participants ($N = 479$) were recruited from a large Southeastern university in the U.S. and two large universities in China during the Spring semester of 2020. Participants received extra course credit as an incentive for their participation. The entire sample consisted of 147 (30.69%) U.S. students and 332 (69.31%) Chinese students. With regards to gender, of U.S. participants, 24 (16.2%) self-identified as men, 120 (81.1%) as women, 1 (.7%) as agender, and 2 (1.4%) as Nonbinary/genderqueer/gender fluid; of Chinese participants, 106 (31.9%) identified as women, and 222 (66.9%) were men. In terms of ethnicity, of the U.S. participants, 123 (83.7%) reported that they were White, 17 (11.6%) reported that they were Asian or Pacific Islander, 6 (4.1%) reported that they were African American, and 1 (.7%) reported as "Other". All Chinese participants reported as Asian Chinese. The total survey completion rate was 86.15%.

Materials

The anonymous survey consisted of demographic questions, the Self-efficacy for Learning and Performance and Metacognitive Self-regulation subscales of the Motivated Strategies for Learning Questionnaire (MSLQ; Pintrich et al., 1991), and the Resilience Evaluation Scale (RES; van der Meer et al., 2018). The Self-efficacy for Learning and Performance and Metacognitive Self-regulation subscales have been previously used separately from the entire MSLQ (Aivaloglou & Hermans, 2019; Bong & Hocevar, 2002; Hilpert et al., 2013; Klassen & Kuzucu, 2009). They were used separately in present study for research purposes as well.

For the Chinese participants, all original items, which were in English, were translated into Chinese. To guarantee the content validity of the Chinese version of the measure, a standard translation and back-translation procedure was used (Hambleton & Patsula, 1998). A certified translator who is bilingual and fluently in both English and Chinese translated the English questionnaires into Chinese. The Chinese version was evaluated by the researcher, who is fluent in English and Chinese. Then, back translation was conducted by the researcher and checked by the certified translator.

The Self-efficacy for Learning and Performance subscale is an 8-item 7-point Likert-type scale, ranging from 1 (*not at all true me*) to 7 (*very true of me*). This subscale evaluates students' expectancy for success and self-efficacy (Pintrich et al., 1991) (Example question "I believe I will receive an excellent grade in this class"). The original internal consistency reliability of Cronbach's α is .93. The current sample demonstrated adequate reliability (Cronbach's $\alpha = .91$ for U.S. sample and Cronbach's $\alpha = .94$ for Chinese sample). The Metacognitive Self-regulation subscale is a 12-item 7-point Likert-type scale, ranging from 1 (*not at all true me*) to 7 (*very true of me*). This subscale evaluates students' control and self-regulation aspects of metacognition (Pintrich et al., 1991) (Example question "I ask myself questions to make sure I understand the material I have been studying in this class"). The original internal consistency reliability of Cronbach's α is .79. The current sample demonstrated adequate reliability (Cronbach's $\alpha = .81$ for both U.S and Chinese samples). The original RES (van der Meer et al., 2018) is a 9-item 5-point Likert-type scale ranging from 0 to 4. This study modified the RES 5-point Likert scale to a 7-point Likert scale ranging from 1 (*not at all true me*) to 7 (*very true of me*) to align the scales with other questionnaires. The RES scale evaluates students' psychological resilience (van der Meer et al., 2018) (Example question "After setbacks, I can easily pick up where I left off"). The original internal consistency reliability of Cronbach's α is .91. The current sample demonstrated adequate reliability (Cronbach's $\alpha = .88$ and .93 for the U.S and Chinese samples, respectively).

Procedures

Participants were invited to complete the survey through a third party (the faculty members as gatekeepers) who work at a four-year research university in a U.S. Southeastern University and two universities in Northeast and Southeast China. The anonymous survey was distributed through emails. Students clicked on the survey link provided in the invitation emails, then they read the Informed Consent and made a decision whether they were willing to participate in the study. All participants completed the anonymous surveys in Qualtrics. Participation was voluntary and participants were consented to participate in the study. Students were able to withdraw from completing the survey anytime by closing the website. The survey process was in compliance with American Psychological Association (APA) ethical guidelines, and this study was approved by the University Institutional Review Board (IRB).

Data Analytic Approach

14 out of the 161 U.S. participants did not answer any questions on the RES scale, listwise deletion was conducted. For the Chinese sample, among 332 participants, 4 did not report their gender. Other than that, there are only minor (< 5%) missing values. Data were analyzed via SPSS 27. A 2×2 Factorial MANOVA was conducted on two independent variables: culture and gender. The independent variables were students' cultural background (the United States vs. China) and their genders. As for gender, we excluded 3 U.S. participants because there is no comparison group in China. Thus, gender comparison was narrowed to men and women for research purposes in the present study. Preliminary assumption testing was tested to examine normality, linearity, univariate and multivariate outliers, homogeneity of variance-covariance matrices, and multicollinearity, with no serious violations noted.

RESULTS

To examine the difference in self-efficacy, self-regulation, and resilience between the U.S. and Chinese participants, we conducted a 2×2 Factorial MANOVA. Based on previous literature, our assumptions were that there were significant differences in students' self-efficacy, self-regulation, and resilience between American and Chinese students. There were significant differences in students' self-efficacy, self-regulation, and resilience between men and women students; culture and gender together would influence students' self-efficacy, self-regulation, and resilience.

A statistically significant Box's M test (Box's $M = 82.05, p < .001$) indicated inequality of variance-covariance matrices of the dependent variables across levels of the independent variables. Then, we conducted Pillai's Trace test. Bartlett's test of Sphericity indicated sufficient correlation between the dependent measures to proceed with the analysis, $\chi^2 = 349.30, df = 5, p < .001$. We conducted preliminary assumption testing to check for normality, linearity, univariate and multicollinearity, without finding any serious violations.

RQ1: Is there a difference based on the interaction of culture and gender on students' self-efficacy, self-regulation, and resilience?

The univariate interaction effect of culture × gender was not significant, Pillai's Trace = .02, $F(3, 465) = 2.57, p = .053$, with a small effect size $\eta^2 = .02$.

RQ2: What are the differences in the self-efficacy, metacognitive self-regulation, and resilience between the U.S. and Chinese students?

We examined the multivariate main effect of the culture. Results indicate that there was a significant main effect of culture on dependent variate, Pillai's Trace = .20, $F(3, 465) = 38.79, p < .001$, with a large effect size $\eta^2 = .20$. As we found the main effect statistically significant, we proceeded the assessment with an inspection of the Levene's Test of Equality of Error Variance. In this study, Metacognitive self-regulation had statistically significant Levene's tests ($p < .05$), indicating that the metacognitive self-regulation might violate the assumption of homogeneity of variance with $p_{\text{self-regulation}} = .01$, and data should be viewed with caution. However, there were no violations of normality was noted for variables, and the largest variance divided by the smallest variance was less than three, and the sample size was large in each group, and the presence of homoscedasticity for the three dependent variables. So the corrective remedies were not needed (Hair et al., 2009; Strunk & Mwavita, 2020). Both self-efficacy and resilience have statistically non-significant Levene's tests ($p > .05$), indicating that the self-efficacy and resilience meet the assumption of homogeneity of variance with $p_{\text{self-efficacy}} = .41$ and $p_{\text{resilience}} = .79$, respectively. Univariance ANOVA was conducted on these three variables separately. Results showed that culture had a statistically significance on all three dependent variables, $F(1, 467) = 41.70, p < .001, \eta^2 = .08$; $F(1, 467) = 4.25, p = .04, \eta^2 = .01$ and $F(1, 467) = 40.02, p < .001, \eta^2 = .08$, respectively. To be more specific, U.S. students reported higher levels of self-efficacy ($M = 5.63, SD = .99$) than their Chinese counterparts ($M = 4.74, SD = .95$); slightly lower levels of metacognitive ($M = 4.69, SD = .91$) than Chinese students ($M = 4.72, SD = .72$); and higher levels of resilience ($M = 5.54, SD = .1.01$) than Chinese students ($M = 4.70, SD = .99$), all with $p < .05$ (see Table 2).

RQ3: What are the differences in the self-efficacy, metacognitive self-regulation, and resilience between men and women?

Next, we examined the multivariate main effect towards gender. The results demonstrated there was no significant main effect of gender on the dependent variates, Pillai's Trace$_{\text{(gender)}} = .01, F(3, 465) = 1.74, p = .16, \eta^2 = .01$.

DISCUSSIONS AND CONCLUSIONS

Results of the present study demonstrated that self-efficacy, self-regulation, and resilience differed between American and Chinese college students. First, the results showing that American students' self-efficacy was reported as being higher than that of Chinese students is aligned with previous research demonstrating that Asian students' self-reported self-efficacy was weaker than that of participants from the Western region (Oettingen & Zosuls, 2006; Scholz et al., 2002). Wang et al. (2018) also noted that the previous research had found a lower level of self-efficacy among Asian students as compared to non-Asian students. Second, our American college students' self-regulation was found to be slightly lower than their Chinese counterparts in the present study. This finding echoes the previous research, which showed that Chinese children showed more adaptive self-regulation skills as compared to children from the United States (Jose & Bellamy, 2012). But it is also noteworthy that Jose and Bellamy (2012) also found that Japanese children did not have the advantage in self-regulation as compared with their Chinese counterparts, although the Asian culture generally prioritizes self-regulation in broad terms. These findings may call for future studies of Chinese parenting and teaching practices that uniquely support the development of self-regulation among Asian learners and probe into whether some specific cultural processes would support self-regulation and be adapted and incorporated into self-regulation interventions (McClelland et al., 2015).

Additionally, our study yielded a difference in resilience between U.S. and Chinese college students, which corroborated with previous research suggesting that there were resilience differences among individuals across cultures (Herrman et al., 2011; Luthar & Cicchetti, 2000; Panter-Brick, 2014; Ungar, 2008). The finding that U.S. students reported higher resilience levels than their Chinese counterparts mirrors previous research findings that American. and Chinese participants may exhibit significant differences in psychological well-being and coping strategies in dealing with adversity (Luong & Charles, 2014;

Zhang et al., 2007). It especially echoes Zheng et al.'s (2020) research finding that American. Participants were more resilient than the participants in Mainland China. This is probably because, as Zheng et al. (2020) supposed, resilience is a concept defined by Western researchers to measure dispositional traits at the individual level, which focuses on individualistic characteristics. In contrast, the Chinese culture may feature more collectivism and fatalism, which might render resilience capacity less relevant.

In terms of the gender effect, we did not find significant gender difference in self-efficacy, self-regulation, or resilience. Even though previous studies found that self-efficacy was higher in men than in women (Catherine, 2017; Hadley et al., 2017; Rachmajanti & Musthofiyah, 2017) and Kizkapan et al. (2018) found that girls reported higher self-regulation than boys. Another finding regarding resilience and gender indicated no significant difference in students' resilience between men and women, which is not consistent with previous research, which found that resilience differences did, in fact, exist among individuals across genders (Herrman et al., 2011; Ungar, 2005, 2008).

In general, the result of present study provided evidence of the difference in self-efficacy, self-regulation, and resilience between American and Chinese college students. Future studies may fully explore the factors that impact self-efficacy, self-regulation, and resilience for different cultural groups in diverse learning contexts with more comprehensive perspectives and insights to develop proper pedagogical and learning strategies and establish an educationally supportive learning environment for students from different cultural backgrounds.

LIMITATIONS AND IMPLICATIONS

Several limitations exist in the present study. First, of the U.S. sample, 24 (16.2%) self-identified as men, 120 (81.1%) as women, 1 (.7%) as agender, and 2 (1.4%) as nonbinary/genderqueer/gender fluid. With regards to the Chinese sample, 106 (31.9%) were women, and 222 (66.9%) were men. There might be potential validity issues for comparing the two samples and generalization to the whole U.S. and China college student population. Future, the present study was conducted during the COVID-19 pandemic period. Virtually all universities worldwide had to move to online learning platform. Therefore, on one hand, it provided an opportunity to investigate students' resilience during the adversity of a global pandemic. However, on the other hand, students may lack sufficient readiness and willingness to participate in online learning, which would impact their self-efficacy and metacognitive self-regulation. They may have needed more time to develop their adaptiveness, self-efficacy, and self-regulated skills in such an online learning context. In addition, the self-efficacy, self-regulation, and resilience concepts and instruments that we used in the present study were all created and developed by Western psychologists, and as Ungar (2013) stated that the language and methods we use to explore these constructs are entrenched in Western hegemony. These constructs measure dispositional traits at the individual level (Zheng et al., 2020), which may not be an ideal fit for multinational populations and are not culturally free.

Therefore, more empirically-based and cross-cultural studies are needed. The present study provides evidence of the differences in self-efficacy, self-regulation, and resilience between American and Chinese college students. Future studies may take age, ethnicity, and social status into consideration to more fully explore the factors that impact self-efficacy, self-regulated learning, and resilience across different cultural groups in diverse learning contexts with more comprehensive perspectives and insights. Additionally, culturally valid measures need to be developed to fit different cultural populations. Finally, there remains a need for more research into the effects of culture on learner's self-efficacy, metacognitive self-regulation and resilience using more mixed-methodological approaches.

Table 1. Hofstede's model

Types	Definitions
1. Power distance	how much individuals can tolerate or accept unequal distribution of power in organizations
2. Uncertainty avoidance	how much individuals can tolerate or accept uncertainty and ambiguity. Strong uncertainty avoidance indicates the possibility of having strict results and laws. Whereas more tolerable societies about uncertainty tend to avoid regulations but accept more different opinions.
3. Masculinity vs. femininity	how much societies possess male or female characteristics. Societies with higher masculinity are assertive and competitive. Whereas societies with high femininity are more modest and caring
4. Individualism vs. collectivism	how much individuals are related to each other in a society. Societies with high individualism emphasize self-interest and "I" consciousness, while societies with high collectivism emphasize group harmony, social bonding activities, and "We" consciousness.

Table 2. Mean score, standard deviations, and univariance analyses of variance in self-efficacy, self-regulation, and resilience

Measure	U.S. ($n = 144$)		China ($n = 327$)		F (3, 467)	η^2
	M	*SD*	*M*	*SD*		
Self-efficacy	5.63	.99	4.74	.95	41.70***	.08
Self-regulation	4.69	.91	4.72	.72	4.25*	.01
Resilience	5.54	1.01	4.70	.99	40.02***	.08

* $p < .05$. ** $p < .01$. *** $p < .001$

REFERENCES

Aivaloglou, E., & Hermans, F. (2019, February 27-March 2). Early programming education and career orientation: The effects of gender, self-efficacy, motivation and stereotypes. In *Proceedings of the 50th ACM Technical Symposium on Computer Science Education* (pp. 679-685). 10.1145/3287324.3287358

Alexander, B., Darby, F., Fischer, K., Jack, A. A., Le Sane, C. B., Staisloff, R., & Stout, K. A. (2002). The post pandemic college and the future of: The academic enterprise, teaching and learning, the student experience, enrollment, business models and community colleges. *The Chronicle of Higher Education*.

Ali, D. A., Figley, C. R., Tedeschi, R. G., Galarneau, D., & Amara, S. (2021, June 17). Shared trauma, resilience, and growth: A roadmap toward transcultural conceptualization. *Psychological Trauma: Theory, Research, Practice, and Policy*. Advance online publication. doi:10.1037/tra0001044 PMID:34138612

Andrew, S. (1998). Self-efficacy as a predictor of academic performance in science. *Journal of Advanced Nursing, 27*(3), 596–603. doi:10.1046/j.1365-2648.1998.00550.x PMID:9543047

Ariani, D. W. (2016). Why do I study? The mediating effect of motivation and self-regulation on student performance. *Business Management in Education, 14*(2), 153–178. doi:10.3846/bme.2016.329

Arrington, E. G., & Wilson, M. N. (2000). A re-examination of risk and resilience during adolescence: Incorporating culture and diversity. *Journal of Child and Family Studies, 9*(2), 221–230. doi:10.1023/A:1009423106045

Ayyash-Abdo, H., Sanchez-Ruiz, M. J., & Barbari, M. L. (2016). Resiliency predicts academic performance of Lebanese adolescents over demographic variables and hope. *Learning and Individual Differences, 48*, 9–16. doi:10.1016/j.lindif.2016.04.005

Bandura, A. (1997). Self-efficacy: The exercise of control. *The Freeman*.

Bandura, A., & McClelland, D. C. (1977). *Social learning theory* (Vol. 1). Prentice Hall. doi:10.1177/105960117700200317

Beugelsdijk, S., Kostova, T., Kunst, V. E., Spadafora, E., & van Essen, M. (2017). Cultural distance and firm internationalization: A meta-analytical review and theoretical implications. *Journal of Management, 44*(1), 89–130. doi:10.1177/0149206317729027 PMID:30443095

Bonanno, G. A., Brewin, C. R., Kaniasty, K., & Greca, A. M. L. (2010). Weighing the costs of disaster: Consequences, risks, and resilience in individuals, families, and communities. *Psychological Science in the Public Interest, 11*(1), 1–49. doi:10.1177/1529100610387086 PMID:26168411

Bong, M., & Hocevar, D. (2002). Measuring self-efficacy: Multitrait-multimethod comparison of scaling procedures. *Applied Measurement in Education, 15*(2), 143–171. doi:10.1207/S15324818AME1502_02

Bonneville-Roussy, A., Bouffard, T., Palikara, O., & Vezeau, C. (2019). The role of cultural values in teacher and student self-efficacy: Evidence from 16 nations. *Contemporary Educational Psychology, 59*, 101798. Advance online publication. doi:10.1016/j.cedpsych.2019.101798

Bowers, J., & Kumar, P. (2015). Students' perceptions of teaching and social presence: A comparative analysis of face-to-face and online learning environments. *International Journal of Web-Based Learning and Teaching Technologies, 10*(1), 27–44. doi:10.4018/ijwltt.2015010103

Brady, A. C., Kim, Y. E., & Cutshall, J. (2021). The what, why, and how of distractions from a self-regulated learning perspective. *Journal of College Reading and Learning, 51*(2), 153–172. doi:10.1080/10790195.2020.1867671

Camgoz, S. M., Tektas, O. O., & Metin, I. (2008). Academic attributional style, self-efficacy and gender: A cross-cultural comparison. *Social Behavior and Personality, 36*(1), 97–114. doi:10.2224bp.2008.36.1.97

Catherine, A. (2017). Investigating the relationship between science self-efficacy beliefs, gender, and academic achievement, among high school students in Kenya. *Journal of Education and Practice, 8*(8), 146–153.

Cénat, J. M., Noorishad, P. G., Blais-Rochette, C., McIntee, S. E., Mukunzi, J. N., Darius, W. P., Broussard, C., Morse, C., Ukwu, G., Auguste, E., & Menelas, K. (2020). Together for hope and resilience: A humanistic experience by the vulnerability, trauma, resilience and culture lab members during the COVID-19 pandemic. *Journal of Loss and Trauma, 25*(8), 643–648. doi:10.1080/15325024.2020.1774704

Cicchetti, D. (2010). Resilience under conditions of extreme stress: A multilevel perspective. *World Psychiatry; Official Journal of the World Psychiatric Association (WPA), 9*(3), 145–154. doi:10.1002/j.2051-5545.2010.tb00297.x PMID:20975856

Cicha, K., Rizun, M., Rutecka, P., & Strzelecki, A. (2021). COVID-19 and higher education: First-year students' expectations toward distance learning. *Sustainability, 13*(1889), doi:10.3390/su13041889

Connor, K. M., & Davidson, J. R. (2003). Development of a new resilience scale: The Connor-Davidson resilience scale (CD-RISC). *Depression and Anxiety, 18*(2), 76–82. doi:10.1002/da.10113 PMID:12964174

De Backer, L., Keer, H. V., & Valcke, M. (2015). Promoting university students' metacognitive regulation through peer learning: The potential of reciprocal peer tutoring. *Higher Education, 70*(3), 469–486. doi:10.100710734-014-9849-3

Earley, P. C. (1994). Self or group? Cultural effects of training on self-efficacy and performance. *Administrative Science Quarterly, 39*(1), 89–117. doi:10.2307/2393495

Eaton, M. J., & Dembo, M. H. (1997). Differences in the motivational beliefs of Asian American and non-Asian students. *Journal of Educational Psychology, 89*(3), 433–440. doi:10.1037/0022-0663.89.3.433

Flavell, J. H. (1985). *Cognitive development* (2nd ed.). Prentice Hall.

Galla, B. M., Shulman, E. P., Plummer, B. D., Gardner, M., Hutt, S. J., Goyer, J. P., D'Mello, S. K., Finn, A. S., & Duckworth, A. L. (2019). Why high school grades are better predictors of on-time college graduation than are admissions test scores: The roles of self-regulation and cognitive ability. *American Educational Research Journal, 56*(6), 2077–2115. doi:10.3102/0002831219843292

Grotberg, E. H. (Ed.). (2003). *Resilience for today: Gaining strength from adversity*. Greenwood Publishing Group., doi:10.5860/CHOICE.41-5592

Gunnestad, A. (2006). Resilience in a cross-cultural perspective: How resilience is generated in different cultures. *Journal of Intercultural Communication*, 11.

Hadley, J., Mowbray, T., & Jacobs, N. (2017). Examining the mediating effect of self-efficacy on approval of aggression and proactive aggression. *Journal of School Violence, 16*(1), 86–103. doi:10.1080/15388220.2015.1116993

Hair, J. F. Jr, Black, W. C., Babin, B. J., & Anderson, R. E. (2009). *Multivariate data analysis* (7th ed.). Pearson.

Hambleton, R. K., & Patsula, L. (1998). Adapting tests for use in multiple languages and cultures. *Social Indicators Research, 45*(1), 153–171. doi:10.1023/A:1006941729637

Hernández, A. L., Escobar, S. G., Fuentes, N. I. G. A. L., & Eguiarte, B. E. B. (2019). Stress, self-efficacy, academic achievement and resilience in emerging adults. *Electronic Journal of Research in Educational Psychology, 17*(47), 129–148. https://core.ac.uk/download/pdf/286590307.pdf

Herrman, H., Stewart, D. E., Diaz-Granados, N., Berger, E. L., Jackson, B., & Yuen, T. (2011). What is resilience? *Canadian Journal of Psychiatry, 56*(5), 258–265. doi:10.1177/070674371105600504 PMID:21586191

Hilpert, J. C., Stempien, J., van der Hoeven Kraft, K. J., & Husman, J. (2013). Evidence for the latent factor structure of the MSLQ: A new conceptualization of an established questionnaire. *SAGE Open, 3*(4). Advance online publication. doi:10.1177/2158244013510305

Hjemdal, O., Friborg, O., Stiles, T. C., Rosenvinge, J. H., & Martinussen, M. (2006). Resilience predicting psychiatric symptoms: A prospective study of protective factors and their role in adjustment to stressful life events. *Clinical Psychology & Psychotherapy: An International Journal of Theory & Practice, 13*(3), 194–201. doi:10.1002/cpp.488

Hofstede, G. (1984). *Culture's consequences: International differences in work-related values* (Vol. 5). Sage.

Hromalik, C. D., & Koszalka, T. A. (2018). Self-regulation of the use of digital resources in an online language learning course improves learning outcomes. *Distance Education, 39*(4), 528–547. doi:10.1080/01587919.2018.1520044

Jenson, J. D. (2011). Promoting self-regulation and critical reflection through writing students' use of electronic portfolio. *International Journal of ePortfolio, 1*(1), 49-60.

Jose, P. E., & Bellamy, M. A. (2012). Relationships of parents' theories of intelligence with children's persistence/learned helplessness: A cross-cultural comparison. *Journal of Cross-Cultural Psychology, 43*(6), 999–1018. doi:10.1177/0022022111421633

Joseph, S., & Linley, P. A. (Eds.). (2008). *Trauma, recovery, and growth: Positive psychological perspectives on posttraumatic stress*. John Wiley & Sons. doi:10.1002/9781118269718

Kaufmann, R., & Vallade, J. I. (2020). Exploring connections in the online learning environment: Student perceptions of rapport, climate, and loneliness. *Interactive Learning Environments*, 1–15. Advance online publication. doi:10.1080/10494820.2020.1749670

King, R. B., & McInerney, D. M. (2016). Culture and motivation: The road travelled and the way ahead. In Handbook of motivation at school (pp. 275-279). Routledge.

Kizkapan, O., Bektas, O., & Saylan-Kimizigul, A. (2018). Examining self-regulation skills of elementary school students. *Cypriot Journal of Educational Science, 13*(4), 613–624. doi:10.18844/cjes.v13i4.3569

Klassen, R. M. (2004, December). A cross-cultural investigation of the efficacy beliefs of South Asian immigrant and Anglo Canadian nonimmigrant early adolescents. *Journal of Educational Psychology, 96*(4), 731–742. doi:10.1037/0022-0663.96.4.731

Klassen, R. M., & Kuzucu, E. (2009). Academic procrastination and motivation of adolescents in Turkey. *Educational Psychology, 29*(1), 69–81. doi:10.1080/01443410802478622

Komarraju, M., Karau, S. J., & Schmeck, R. R. (2009). Role of the Big Five personality traits in predicting college students' academic motivation and achievement. *Learning and Individual Differences, 19*(1), 47–52. doi:10.1016/j.lindif.2008.07.001

Kroeber, A. L., & Kluckhohn, C. (1952). *Culture: A critical review of concepts and definitions*. Vintage Books.

Leung, R. S., Floras, J. S., & Bradley, T. D. (2006). Respiratory modulation of the autonomic nervous system during CheyneStokes respiration. *Canadian Journal of Physiology and Pharmacology, 84*(1), 61–66. doi:10.1139/Y05-145 PMID:16845891

Loree, D. (2020). Building corporate resilience. *Ivey Business Journal*, 2–7.

Luong, G., & Charles, S. T. (2014). Age differences in affective and cardiovascular responses to a negative social interaction: The role of goals, appraisals, and emotion regulation. *Developmental Psychology, 50*(7), 1919–1930. doi:10.1037/a0036621 PMID:24773101

Luthar, S. S., & Cicchetti, D. (2000). The construct of resilience: Implications for interventions and social policies. *Development and Psychopathology, 12*(4), 857–885. doi:10.1017/S0954579400004156 PMID:11202047

Luthar, S. S., & Ziegler, E. (1991). Vulnerability and competence: A review of research on resilience in childhood. *The American Journal of Orthopsychiatry, 61*(1), 6–22. doi:10.1037/h0079218 PMID:2006679

Mackey, J., Gilmore, F., Dabner, N., Breeze, D., & Buckley, P. (2012). Blended learning for academic resilience in times of disaster or crisis. *Journal of Online Learning and Teaching, 8*(2), 122–135.

Mahat, G., Scoloveno, M., & Ayres, C. (2014). Comparison of HIV/AIDS peer education program across two cultures. *Journal of Cultural Diversity: An Interdisciplinary Journal, 21*(4), 152–200.

Masten, A. S., Best, K. M., & Garmezy, N. (1990). Resilience and development: Contributions from the study of children who overcome adversity. *Development and Psychopathology, 2*(4), 425–444. doi:10.1017/S0954579400005812

McClelland, M. M., John Geldhof, G., Cameron, C. E., & Wanless, S. B. (2015). *Handbook of child psychology and developmental science, socioemotional processes* (Vol. 1). John Wiley & Sons. doi:10.1002/9781118963418.childpsy114

McInerney, D. M., & King, R. B. (2018). Culture and self-regulation in educational contexts. In D. H. Schunk & J. A. Greene (Eds.), Educational psychology handbook series. Handbook of self-regulation of learning and performance (pp. 485–502). Routledge/Taylor & Francis Group.

Merriam, S. B., & Mohamad, M. (2000). How cultural values shape learning in older adulthood: The case of Malaysia. *Adult Education Quarterly, 51*(1), 45–63. doi:10.1177/074171360005100104

Minkov, M., Dutt, P., Schachner, M., Morales, O., Sanchez, G., Jandosova, J., Khassenbekov, Y., & Mudd, B. (2017). A revision of Hofstede's individualism-collectivism dimension: A new national index from a 56-country study. *Cross Cultural & Strategic Management, 24*(3), 386–404. doi:10.1108/CCSM-11-2016-0197

Moke, K., Chang, C. K. W., Prihadi, K., & Goh, C. L. (2018). Mediation effect of resilience on the relationship between self-efficacy and competitiveness among university students. *International Journal of Evaluation and Research in Education, 7*(4), 279–284. doi:10.11591/ijere.v7i4.15725

Oettingen, G. (1995). Cross-cultural perspectives on self-efficacy. In A. Bandura (Ed.), *Self-efficacy in changing societies* (pp. 149–176). Cambridge University Press. doi:10.1017/CBO9780511527692.007

Oettingen, G., & Zosuls, K. (2006). Culture and self-efficacy in adolescents. In F. Pajares & T. Urdan (Eds.), *Self-efficacy beliefs of adolescents* (Vol. 5, pp. 245–265). Information Age Publishing.

Panter-Brick, C. (2014). Health, risk, and resilience: Interdisciplinary concepts and applications. *Annual Review of Anthropology, 43*(1), 431–448. doi:10.1146/annurev-anthro-102313-025944

Pieloch, K. A., McCullough, M. B., & Marks, A. K. (2016). Resilience of children with refugee statuses: A research review. *Canadian Psychology, 57*(4), 330–339. doi:10.1037/cap0000073

Pintrich, P. R. (1989). The dynamic interplay of student motivation and cognition in the college classroom. *Advances in Motivation and Achievement: a Research Annual, 6*, 117–160.

Pintrich, P. R., Smith, D. A. F., Garcia, T., & McKeachie, W. J. (1991). *A manual for the use of the Motivated Strategies for Learning Questionnaire (MSLQ)*. Technical Report (No. 91-8-004). The Regents of The University of Michigan.

Rachmajanti, S., & Musthofiyah, U. (2017). The relationship between reading self-efficacy, reading attitude and EFL reading comprehension based on gender difference. *Journal of English Language, Literature, and Teaching, 1*(1), 20–26. doi:10.17977/um046v1i1p20-26

Rashid, S., & Yadav, S. S. (2020). Impact of the COVID-19 pandemic on higher education and research. *Indian Journal of Human Development, 14*(2), 340–343. doi:10.1177/0973703020946700

Reyna, J., Hanham, J., Vlachopoulos, P., & Meier, P. (2019). A systematic approach to designing, implementing, and evaluating learner-generated digital media (LGDM) assignments and its effect on self-regulation in tertiary science education. *Research in Science Education*, 1–27. doi:10.100711165-019-09885-x

Robertson, I. T., Cooper, C. L., Sarkar, M., & Curran, T. (2015). Resilience training in the workplace from 2003 to 2014: A systematic review. *Journal of Occupational and Organizational Psychology, 88*(3), 533–562. doi:10.1111/joop.12120

Salisbury-Glennon, J. D., Wang, C.-h., Dai, Y., Jang, H. S., Collins, T. M., & Durham, K. (2021, April 8-11). *The effects of parental relationships on college students' motivation, learning strategies and metacognition during the COVID-19 global pandemic*. Poster presented at the annual meeting of the American Educational Research Association, Virtual Conference.

Scholz, U., Doña, B. G., Sud, S., & Schwarzer, R. (2002). Is general self-efficacy a universal construct? Psychometric findings from 25 countries. *European Journal of Psychological Assessment, 18*(3), 242–251. doi:10.1027//1015-5759.18.3.242

Shen, J. J., Cheah, C. S. L., & Yu, J. (2018). Asian American and European American emerging adults' perceived parenting styles and self-regulation ability. *Asian American Journal of Psychology*, *9*(2), 140–148. doi:10.1037/aap0000099

Shunk, D. H. (2008). Metacognition, self-regulation, and self-regulated learning: Research recommendations. *Educational Psychology Review*, *20*(4), 463–467. doi:10.100710648-008-9086-3

Steel, Z., Marnane, C., Iranpour, C., Chey, T., Jackson, J. W., Patel, V., & Silove, D. (2014). The global prevalence of common mental disorders: A systematic review and meta-analysis 1980–2013. *International Journal of Epidemiology*, *43*(2), 476–493. doi:10.1093/ije/dyu038 PMID:24648481

Strunk, K. K., & Mwavita, M. (2020). *Design and analysis in educational research: ANOVA designs in SPSS*. Routledge. doi:10.4324/9780429432798

Stutman, S., Baruch, R., Grotberg, E., & Rathore, Z. (2002). *Resilience in Latino youth*. Working Paper, Institute for Mental Health Initiatives. The George Washington University.

Takano, Y., & Osaka, E. (2018). Comparing Japan and the United States on individualism/collectivism: A follow-up review. *Asian Journal of Social Psychology*, *21*(4), 301–316. doi:10.1111/ajsp.12322

Taras, V., Steel, P., & Kirkman, B. L. (2016). Does country equate with culture? Beyond geography in the search for cultural boundaries. *Management International Review*, *56*(4), 455–487. doi:10.100711575-016-0283-x

Tope-Banjoko, T., Davis, V., Morrison, K., Fife, J., Hill, O., & Talley, C. (2020). Academic resilience in college students: Relationship between coping and GPA. *Anatolian Journal of Education*, *5*(2), 109–120. doi:10.29333/aje.2020.529a

Torun, E. D. (2020). Online distance learning in higher education: E-learning readiness as a predictor of academic achievement. *Open Praxis*, *12*(2), 191–208. doi:10.5944/openpraxis.12.2.1092

Travis, J., & Bunde, J. (2020). Self-regulation in college: The influence of self-efficacy, need satisfaction, and stress on GPA, persistence, and satisfaction. *Current Psychology (New Brunswick, N.J.)*. Advance online publication. doi:10.100712144-020-01091-7

Trommsdorff, G. (2009). Teaching and learning guide for: Culture and development of self-regulation. *Social and Personality Psychology Compass*, *3*(5), 687–701. doi:10.1111/j.1751-9004.2009.00209.x

Trumbull, E., & Rothstein-Fisch, C. (2011). The intersection of culture and achievement motivation. *School Community Journal*, *21*(2), 25–53.

Ungar, M. (Ed.). (2005). *Handbook for working with children and youth: Pathways to resilience across cultures and contexts*. Sage Publications.

Ungar, M. (2006). Nurturing hidden resilience in at-risk youth in different cultures. *Journal of the Canadian Academy of Child and Adolescent Psychiatry*, *15*(2), 53–58. PMID:18392194

Ungar, M. (2008). Resilience across cultures. *British Journal of Social Work*, *38*(2), 218–235. doi:10.1093/bjsw/bcl343

Ungar, M. (2013). Resilience, trauma, context, and culture. *Trauma, Violence & Abuse, 14*(3), 255–266. doi:10.1177/1524838013487805 PMID:23645297

United Nations Educational, Scientific and Cultural Organization. (2015). *Rethinking education: Towards a global common good?* https://unevoc.unesco.org/e-forum/RethinkingEducation.pdf

van der Meer, C. A., Te Brake, H., van der Aa, N., Dashtgard, P., Bakker, A., & Olff, M. (2018). Assessing psychological resilience: Development and psychometric properties of the English and Dutch version of the resilience evaluation scale (RES). *Frontiers in Psychiatry, 9,* 169. doi:10.3389/fpsyt.2018.00169 PMID:29867601

Wagnild, G. M., & Young, H. M. (1993). Development and psychometric evaluation of the Resilience Scale. *Journal of Nursing Measurement*. Advance online publication. doi:10.1037/t07521-000 PMID:7850498

Wang, Y.-L., Liang, J., & Tsai, C.-C. (2018). Cross-cultural comparisons of university students' science learning self-efficacy: Structural relationships among factors within science learning self-efficacy. *International Journal of Science Education, 40*(6), 579–594. doi:10.1080/09500693.2017.1315780

Welzel, C. (2013). *Freedom rising: Human empowerment and the quest for emancipation*. Cambridge University Press. doi:10.1017/CBO9781139540919

Wood, E. M. (1972). *Mind and politics*. University of California Press. doi:10.1525/9780520332485

Wu, Y. J., Carstensen, C. H., & Lee, J. (2020). A new perspective on memorization practices among East Asian students based on PISA 2012. *Educational Psychology, 40*(5), 643–662. doi:10.1080/01443410.2019.1648766

Zainuddin, M., Yasin, I. M., Arif, I., & Hamid, A. B. A. (2018, December 30-31). Alternative cross-cultural theories: Why still Hofstede? *Proceedings of International Conference on Economics, Management and Social Study*.

Zhang, J., Norvilitis, J. M., & Ingersoll, T. S. (2007). Idiocentrism, allocentrism, psychological well being and suicidal ideation: A cross cultural study. *Omega, 55*(2), 131–144. doi:10.2190/OM.55.2.c PMID:17944311

Zheng, P., Gray, M. J., Duan, W. J., Ho, S. M., Xia, M., & Clapp, J. D. (2020). Cultural variations in resilience capacity and posttraumatic stress: A tri-cultural comparison. *Cross-Cultural Research, 54*(2-3), 273–295. doi:10.1177/1069397119887669

Zimmerman, B. J. (2002). Becoming a self-regulated learner: An overview. *Theory into Practice, 41*(2), 64–70. doi:10.120715430421tip4102_2

ADDITIONAL READING

Bandura, A., & McClelland, D. C. (1977). *Social learning theory* (Vol. 1). Prentice Hall., doi:10.1177/105960117700200317

Herrman, H., Stewart, D. E., Diaz-Granados, N., Berger, E. L., Jackson, B., & Yuen, T. (2011). What is resilience? *Canadian Journal of Psychiatry, 56*(5), 258–265. doi:10.1177/070674371105600504 PMID:21586191

King, R. B., & McInerney, D. M. (2016). Culture and motivation: The road travelled and the way ahead. In K. R. Wentzel & D. B. Miele, Handbook of motivation at school (pp. 275-279). Routledge.

McInerney, D. M., & King, R. B. (2018). Culture and self-regulation in educational contexts. In D. H. Schunk & J. A. Greene (Eds.), Educational psychology handbook series. Handbook of self-regulation of learning and performance (pp. 485–502). Routledge/Taylor & Francis Group.

Oettingen, G. (1995). Cross-cultural perspectives on self-efficacy. In A. Bandura (Ed.), *Self-efficacy in changing societies* (pp. 149–176). Cambridge University Press. doi:10.1017/CBO9780511527692.007

Rashid, S., & Yadav, S. S. (2020). Impact of the COVID-19 pandemic on higher education and research. *Indian Journal of Human Development, 14*(2), 34043. doi:10.1177/0973703020946700

Shunk, D. H. (2008). Metacognition, self-regulation, and self-regulated learning: Research recommendations. *Educational Psychology Review, 20*(4), 463–467. doi:10.100710648-008-9086-3

Ungar, M. (2008). Resilience across cultures. *British Journal of Social Work, 38*(2), 218–235. doi:10.1093/bjsw/bcl343

Ungar, M. (2013). Resilience, trauma, context, and culture. *Trauma, Violence & Abuse, 14*(3), 255–266. doi:10.1177/1524838013487805 PMID:23645297

Zimmerman, B. J. (2002). Becoming a self-regulated learner: An overview. *Theory into Practice, 41*(2), 64–70. doi:10.120715430421tip4102_2

KEY TERMS AND DEFINITIONS

College Student: A student enrolled at a college or university.

COVID-19 Global Pandemic: A global pandemic of coronavirus disease 2019 (COVID-19) caused by severe acute respiratory syndrome coronavirus 2 (SARS-CoV-2). It broke out in December 2019 and is still going on by the time this chapter was written.

Cross-Cultural Comparison: A Comparison of two or more different cultural factors to assess the psychological, sociological, or cultural similarities or diversities in various cultures or societies.

Resilience: The capacity to cope with adversity and bounce back.

Self-Efficacy: Beliefs in one's capabilities to organize and execute to produce the attainments in a specific domain.

Self-Regulation: An individual's ability to control, adjust, and regulate their feelings, thoughts, and behaviors.

Chapter 3
Due to COVID-19, Food Insecurity and Access to Healthy Food Have Become Significant Public Health Problems

Darrell Norman Burrell
https://orcid.org/0000-0002-4675-9544
The Florida Institute of Technology, USA & Capitol Technology University, USA

Anton Shufutinsky
https://orcid.org/0000-0003-3819-0623
Cabrini University, USA

Jorja B. Wright
https://orcid.org/0000-0002-7028-995X
University Charleston, USA

Seleste Bowers
University of Phoenix, USA

ABSTRACT

Since the onset of COVID-19, food insecurity and access to healthy food have become significant public health problems. Inequalities in dietary behaviors have been unambiguously correlated to the food environment, including access to healthy and fresh foods. The Coronavirus Disease, also known as the COVID-19 pandemic, has led to significant fluctuations in the distribution, sale, purchase, preparation, and food consumption in the United States (U.S.). In addition, in the United States (U.S.), substantial socioeconomic and racial disparities exist in dietary behaviors. Limited access to fresh food, coupled with a greater prevalence of fast-food outlets in lower-income and minority neighborhoods, is partially responsible for sub-optimal eating patterns among residents. The purpose of this research is to highlight the factors and influences concerning childhood obesity, food education, community gardening, and healthy eating.

DOI: 10.4018/978-1-7998-8996-0.ch003

Due to COVID-19, Food Insecurity and Access to Healthy Food Have Become Significant Public Health

INTRODUCTION

Since the onset of COVID-19, food insecurity and access to healthy food have become a significant public health problem (Leone et al., 2020). Inequalities in dietary behaviors have been unambiguously correlated to the food environment, including access to healthy and fresh foods (Leone et al., 2020). The Coronavirus Disease, also known as the COVID-19 pandemic, has led to significant fluctuations in the distribution, sale, purchase, preparation, and food consumption in the United States (U.S.) (Leone et al., 2020). In addition, in the United States (U.S.), substantial socioeconomic and racial disparities exist in dietary behaviors (Leone et al., 2020). Limited access to fresh food, coupled with a greater prevalence of fast food outlets in lower-income and minority neighborhoods, is partially responsible for sub-optimal eating patterns among residents (Leone et al., 2020).

Those that are quarantined and not engaged in regular exercise can be susceptible to weight gain and obesity. Obesity is a global issue with significant health and social consequences (Lake, 2011). More specifically, childhood obesity has continued to grow as a problem in the United States. Obesity is defined as a complex disorder affected by many interacting genetic and non-genetic factors (Lake, 2011). Childhood obesity falls under this definition as well but with a focus on a younger demographic. The tool used to aid in indicating high body fat and screen different weight categories is Body Mass Index (BMI) (Centers for Disease Control, 2019). For adults, having a BMI of greater than or equal to 30 is considered obese; however, body mass index for children and adolescents is age and sex-specific (Anderson & Butcher, 2006). The prevalence of obesity in the U.S. is 18.5% and affects about 13.7 million children and adolescents (Centers for Disease Control, 2019). Hispanics (25.8%) and non-Hispanic blacks (22.0%) have a higher prevalence than non-Hispanic whites (14.1%) (Centers for Disease Control, 2019). There is a correlation between childhood obesity and adult obesity, where children that are obese tend to grow to become obese adults (Anderson & Butcher, 2006). According to the World Health Organization (2019), most of the world's population lives in nations plagued with high death rates from overweight and obesity. In 2016, 41 million children under five were overweight (World Health Organization, 2019).

Child obesity has attained an epidemic level not only in the U.S. but all over the world. The Centers for Disease Control identify overweight as "a BMI at or above the 85th percentile and below the 95th percentile for children and teens of the same age and sex" (Centers for Disease Control, 2018). Children and teens who have a BMI above the 95th percentile of their peers of the same age and sex are considered obese (Centers for Disease Control, 2018). In 2016, the number of overweight children globally had reached over 41 million (World Health Organization, 2019). Childhood obesity remains a critical concern in the U.S., as indicated by the number of affected children has tripled. According to 2015 and 2016 statistics, 1 in 5 school-aged children is considered obese (Centers for Disease Control, 2018). It is widely believed that obesity and overweight stem from caloric input exceeding caloric output. However, existing literature indicates excessive consumption of sugar through soft drinks, increased portion intake, and continuous decline in physical activity contribute significantly to the increased rates of obesity in the world (Sahoo et al., 2015).

The Object of Research

The purpose of this research is to highlight the factors and influences concerning childhood obesity, food education, community gardening, and healthy eating.

The Goal of the Research

This research is an in-depth review of the existing literature to explore childhood obesity and explore an innovative approach that has emerged during COVID-19 concerning community gardening and healthy eating education.

LITERATURE AND PREVIOUS RESEARCH

Childhood obesity is influenced by genetics, high sugar consumption, unhealthy snack food, portion size, activity level, environment, socio-culture, family, and psychological factors (Sahoo et al., 2015). Each area plays a significant role in shaping the lives of young children. According to Sahoo et al. (2015), genetics is one of the leading factors for developing obesity; however, it does not contribute to its increase entirely. Physical activity plays a significant role in personal and preventative health in which exercising could reduce chronic diseases and premature mortality by 6 to 10 percent (Lee et al., 2012). The World Health Organization mandates health guidelines and recommends that children and young people in the age range from 5-17 years should participate in "moderate- to vigorous-intensity physical activity daily" (World Health Organization, 2010).

Obesity has an even higher impact on low-income communities. In some cases, children lack adequate facilities and outdoor places to engage in exercises such as playing. Another growing phenomenon is the high consumption of fast food rather than fresh food because fast food lacks proper nutrition and is loaded with unhealthy ingredients. An essential element is "where families live, work, play, and attend school; all have a major impact on the choices they are able to make" (Easterling et al., 2018). Social disparities are predominant in these communities and contribute to the overweight and obesity epidemic.

Some epidemiologists classify obesity as a non-communicable disease; however, it is just as deadly as a biological virus. Numerous factors contribute to non-communicable health conditions (McKenzie et al., 2018). The cause of being overweight and obese is a lot more complicated and is influenced by (a) diet and insufficient physical activity, (b) heredity and genetics, (c) family and social factors, (d) behavioral and cultural factors, (e) environmental and socioeconomic status, and (f) media marketing (Easterling et al., 2018). Children who are overweight and obese are likely to remain unhealthy into adulthood and develop other non-communicable diseases (Sahoo et al., 2015). The long term effect of obesity and overweight puts the younger generations at an increased risk of the following health outcomes (Easterling et al., 2018):

1. high blood pressure and high cholesterol (cardiovascular disease);
2. breathing problems such as asthma and sleep apnea;
3. type 2 diabetes, impaired glucose tolerance, insulin resistance;
4. fatty liver disease, gallstones, gastroesophageal reflux;
5. psychological issues such as anxiety and depression;
6. joint and musculoskeletal disorders;
7. social problems such as bullying; and some cancers.

Researchers are continuously seeking methods to reduce childhood obesity, which includes leveraging technology and develop innovation. For example, telemedicine uses "interactive synchronous video" to deliver medical care to patients (or communities) that lack the accessibility to healthcare services (Davis et al., 2016, p. 87). Healthcare professionals and scientists have concluded that telemedicine is a viable delivery platform for behavioral healthcare services to rural areas (Davis et al., 2016). These technologies have become invaluable during the COVID-19 pandemic, where social distancing has become very important. This 8-week long study (Davis et al., 2016) focused on eight measures:

1. Feasibility – includes attendance and retention, and satisfaction.
2. Child Body Mass Index (BMIz) – height and weight measurements
3. Parent BMI – Parent height and weight
4. 24-hour dietary recall – U.S. Department of Agricultural national nutritional surveillance
5. Accelerometers – participant wears a small device to measure physical activity.
6. Child behavior checklist (CBCL) – standardized measurement tool to assess the parental report of child competencies, behavioral, and emotional problems.
7. Behavioral pediatrics feeding assessment scale (BPFAS) – 35-item measurement tool to evaluate mealtime behavior problems.
8. Obesity-related quality of life is collected via child self-report and parent-proxy reports (Davis et al., 2016, p. 91-92).

Their claims were substantiated with their attrition rate of study participants; this specific study's attrition rate was below the range of previous studies (0-42%) at six months and (12-52%) at 12 months (Davis et al., 2016). Moreover, telemedicine as a modality of healthcare treatment showed a slight decrease in child BMIz (during active treatment – from baseline to eight weeks) in the results (Davis et al., 2016; Alencar et al., 2017). This is significant in that even though the BMIz change may be considered "small" (Davis et al., 2016, p. 95), the "slowing of weight gain, weight maintenance, and weight loss should all be considered 'successful'" (Alencar et al., 2017) outcomes in pediatric weight management.

To combat obesity, nutrition alone is not enough. Physical activity is a crucial part of any dietary and health program. Guidelines established by the U.S. and the WHO recommend at least 60 minutes of moderate-to-vigorous physical activity daily, including "muscle and bone strengthening three days a week" (Katzmarzyk et al., 2016). However, only about 25% of children and youth participate in the required physical activity (Fakhouri, 2014). A few theories can be used in understanding the behaviors and what it takes to implement a healthy change.

Social Cognitive Theory

As mentioned earlier, the most widely used theory for nutritional education is the SCT (Hall, 2016). The SCT implies that an individual's behavior is determined by the ability to regulate their behavior and shape their environment (Knol, 2016). Therefore, understanding the connection between knowledge, self-efficacy, and behavior among children could help create or improve nutritional programs (Hall, 2016).

The article *"Impacting Dietary Behaviors of Children from Low-Income Communities"* has set out to evaluate the effectiveness of SCT interventions of the nutritional programs aimed at children in low-income communities (Branscum, 2013). The Food Fit Program was initially tested in 5 schools with children in 3rd through 4th grade. The principals of the program were structured around behaviors like "choosing lower-calorie snack foods, choosing beverages low in sugar, and eating fruits and vegetables in which all are thought to be associated with the prevention of childhood obesity" (Branscum, 2013).

The curriculum consisted of 14 individual programs that allowed children to participate regardless of routines absences. Each lesson was delivered between 30 to 45 minutes of periods of instruction. All sections followed the same format (a) introduction, (b) benefits, and consequences, (c) modeling and taste testing, (d) role-playing, and (e) wrap up (Branscum, 2013). Researchers used activities to show the effects of healthy behaviors or modeled that behavior themselves for the children. In addition, Role-playing was used to reinforce targeted behaviors. The study gauged the effectiveness of BMI and self-efficacy through measuring before and after the program (Branscum, 2013). Eighty-five children participated in the study, ranging in ages from 8 to 13 years old. Approximately half of the children were overweight or obese (Branscum, 2013). Based on the data obtained, the results suggested that the Food Fit Program effectively modified most children's behaviors.

Based on Bandura's Social Cognitive Theory, "repeated exposure to modeling stimuli "produce[s] enduring, retrievable images of modeled performances" (Branscum, 2013). The Food Fit Program mainly focused on the repetition of the intended behaviors for children to learn and practice every day. Every child was asked to demonstrate those behaviors as well. Research indicated that children remember better if they observed and mimic the desired behavior (Branscum, 2013).

The application of SCT intervention in this study was a success. Even though the children from low-income families did not duplicate all the pilot study results, the children showed encouraging results once their behavioral capabilities improved. In addition, this type of intervention can be easily accomplished in schools because it does not require an extensive amount of time to introduce the concepts (Branscum, 2013).

As much as the school environment is considered a perfect ground to teach children knowledge and behaviors, the SCT demonstrated that repetitive behavior is an essential factor in reinforcing the desired outcome in children. Therefore, the parents need to continue fortifying behaviors taught in schools; otherwise, the results will be minimal or non-existent.

Health Belief Model

Researchers of the "Conceptual Application of the Adapted Health Belief Model to Parental Understanding of Child Weight" proposed a concept that can help identify factors and strategies for future intervention and prevention of obesity (Woods, 2018).

Another commonly used study associated with a person's ability to change is the Health Belief Model (HBM). The HBM is a social-psychological theory that addresses an individual's readiness to change health behavior based on beliefs. The model consists of the following five components (Woods, 2018): (a) benefits, (b) barriers, (c) severity, (d) susceptibility, and (e) health value. The HBM states that "an individual must be devoted to the change, which means the person feels susceptible to the condition given that this occurrence could have serious consequences" (Woods, 2018). Additionally, there needs to be an advantage that reduces the susceptibility to the condition, which is higher than the psychological and actual costs. The HBM explains that the desired action will result in a perception of how severe the illness appears to an individual. The authors propose a model that uses HBM to "evaluate parental weight classification, recognition of a problem, and behavior change" (Woods, 2018). For that, 18 different studies were evaluated to determine which components of HBM had the most influence. The main drivers of change were identified to be severity, barriers, and benefits. Woods (2018) suggested that the parents who correctly understood the perceived barriers, perceived susceptibility, and perceived severity could accurately determine the weight and realize when it was a problem (Woods, 2018). Hence, it would lead to health behavior changes. The depth of knowledge determines the parent's understanding of perceived health threats that obesity creates. For change to happen, HBM indicates that individuals must understand the actual situation, which will allow individuals to make that change because benefits outweigh the psychological or physical costs (Woods, 2018). The lack of knowledge downgrades the severity of the health condition and impedes changes.

A study reviewed a meta-analysis of 15 different experiments and determined that 26% of parents of overweight children were concerned about the health risks associated with the condition (Woods, 2018). Furthermore, some studies have demonstrated that parents do not understand the ramifications of their children being obese, but they also shield their children from the negativity associated with it (Woods, 2018). According to Woods (2018), a change in knowledge could affect weight and weight loss. As far as perceived susceptibility, some of the studies suggest that parents who have overweight and obese children and underestimate their weight lacked concern for unhealthy children (Woods, 2018). And it was also demonstrated that self-efficacy plays an important part in prevention efforts. Parents with high self-efficacy affect their child's behavior, translating into improved sleep and less media time (Woods, 2018). From an intervention point of view, prevention is a lot more cost-efficient and has better outcomes. A 3-year study concluded that parental self-efficacy contributes to a positive home environment that facilitates healthy child development (Woods, 2018).

The researchers efficiently applied the HBM model to show the importance of knowledge for parents on determining their child's weight. Once the correct determination is made, appropriate behaviors would be established to prevent or remediate potential health issues (Woods, 2018). However, future action depends on the perceived severity of the problem. Because of these stipulations, the Health Belief Model might be harder to apply to communities challenged by various disparities. First, the cost of living is a lot more imminent versus a perceived health problem in the future. Second, healthy habits are not a priority for families that are in survival mode. Third, the best determinant of whether an individual can progress towards an increased self-efficacy and the actual ability to attain that level is Maslow's Hierarchy of Needs (Liken, 2018). Finally, the socioeconomic status of any family determines the ability to achieve their full potential. "Even education and a family's perception of the critical nature of the problem may not provide an adequate solution to the issues of childhood obesity because of the barriers in their daily lives" (Liken, 2018).

Integrated Theory of Health Behavior Change

The Integrated Theory of Health Behavior change states that health behavior change can be enhanced by fostering knowledge and beliefs, increasing self-regulation skills, abilities, and enhancing social facilitation (Ryan, 2009). According to Ryan (2009), healthy persons and those with chronic diseases have opportunities to improve their health by regularly engaging in health promotion activities. Some health promotion activities consist of exercise, diet, and dealing with a significant mental aspect. Researchers have suggested that more than 50% of all illnesses stem from personal behaviors (Ryan, 2009). In addition, data has shown that adolescents and children within the defined weight standards that participated in physical education decreased their chances of becoming obese by 5 percent (Story et al., 2009).

Church and Community Gardens can Address this Issue

Four families were interviewed to explore the impacts of these gardens on them and their families.

Question 1- In what do you see is the impact of the church garden on the community?

The mother in family 1 said, "Churches typically have the people and the land to take on this type of project. As a result, they can feed those in need fresh and healthy food options during the pandemic. The community church garden has been important. So many food pantries have closed on our community because many of the workers and volunteers at these pantries were senior citizens who were at high risk during the pandemic."

The father in family 4 said, "I had lost my job. We did not have the same income for food. The church garden allowed me to feed my family and maintain my dignity because I could work, participate, and learn about growing my own food with my kid by my side, learning and helping too. My family was one of many in need in the community. So many families were facing issues with hunger and food in our community."

The mother in family 3 said, "the church garden helped all the family participants have increase access to fresh foods, increase physical activity through garden maintenance activities, improve dietary habits through education, increase fruit and vegetable intake, and improve mental health and promote relaxation."

Question -2- What do you see as the impact of participating in the church garden on your family?

A child in family 2 said, "I learned about growing and eating vegetables and fruits. I had fun knowing that I was eating food that I had grown on my own. Going to the garden and working was a fun time with my mom, my dad, and brothers."

The mother in family 3 said, "We were stuck in the house during the pandemic. I was watching T.V., and my kids were playing a lot of video games. Working on the church farm allowed us to get more regular exercise. However, before working on the church garden, we were not exercising at all, and we were not eating healthy foods."

The father in family 4 said, "I was out of work, but working on the garden allowed me to develop some new skills that led to a job working at the farmer's market. This job allowed me to earn additional income to take care of my family."

Question 3- In what ways did participating in the church garden influence your eating habits?

The mother in family 4 said, "I had never really been taught about eating healthy or the importance of fresh foods. Working at the church garden, I learned about healthy eating and healthy cooking too. I started to pay more attention to fresh foods for my kids and me over fast food. Working at the garden influenced that change greatly."

The mother in family 2 said, "I am giving my kids fresh fruit as snacks when I always used to give them cookies, candy, and chips all the time. My kids seem excited about the fact they are eating food that was grown in their church garden."

CONCLUSION

The concept of community gardens and how it benefits the health of children and families is rooted in the theory of experiential learning. Experiential learning is "learning by experience and doing, followed by reflection," (Baker, Hagedorn, Hendricks, Clegg, Jospeh, McGowan, & Olfert, 2018, p.130). It is through the process of thoughtfully caring for a garden, through the seasons of planting and harvesting, that an individual learns the value of the food they are purposefully cultivating for consumption. The research regarding the benefits of community gardens has led may agencies and local governments to promote community gardens as a way to access nutritious food and increase physical activity (Castro, Samuels, & Harman, 2013).

In a study that looked at pre and post BMI measures of primarily low socio-economic status Hispanic families after participating in various activities including a tending to a community garden, children diagnosed as obese and overweight saw a 13% and 23% decrease in weight, respectively (Castro, Samuels, & Harman, 2013). Additionally, there was an increase of the reported fruits and vegetables available at home and consumed at post-measures (Castro, Samuels, & Harman, 2013).

Experiential learning has been shown to increase health behaviors, including health knowledge. Baker, Hagedorn, Hendricks, Clegg, Joseph, McGowan, and Olfter (2018) found that when two Appalachian schools utilized Katalyst curriculum, there was knowledge increase from 4.1% to 11.1% in both schools. Katalyst is a pilot program focused on experiential learning in physiology and anatomy as a foundation for health and lifestyle choices. These results indicate an increased health knowledge as well as an interest in a healthy lifestyle for children who participated (Hagedorn, Baker, DeJarnett, Hendricks, McGowan, Jospeh, & Olfert, 2018).

In another pilot program focusing on addressing obesity, *iCook 4H*, that targeted low-income youth and adult primary meal preparer similar benefits were noted (Franzen-Castle, Colby, Kettelmann, Olfert, Mathews, Yerxa, Baker, Krehbiel, Lehrke, Wilson, Flanaga, Ford, Aguirre, & White, 2019). Unlike previous studies that focused on family based or child only experiential learning, this pilot program focused on one main meal preparer and the youth. The program *iCook 4H*, focused on four primary objectives; promoting culinary skills, family meals and communication, physical activity, and goal setting (Franzen-Castle et al., 2019). The Experiential Learning Model was defined as: 1) Experience 2) Share 3) Process 4) Generalize 5) Apply (Franzen-Castle et al, 2019). This study provides a new variation of experiential learning being used to focus the primary meal preparer as a catalyst for change in childhood health patterns.

Increasing access to and consumption of fresh vegetables is an important public health goal. Gardening can contribute to food security at all income levels by providing access to fresh, culturally acceptable produce and encouraging a more nutritious diet. Food security is defined as "access by all people at all times to enough food for an active and healthy life" (Coleman-Jensen et al., 2012). It is a concept that encompasses food's quantity, quality, and cultural acceptability.

Many families in the United States have increasing rates of food insecurity since the emergence of COVID-19 (Mercado, 2021; Leone et al., 2020). "Feeding America, the largest hunger-relief organization in the U.S., estimates that more than 54 million people in the country, including 18 million children, are currently experiencing food insecurity" (Mercado, 2021). Household food insecurity has excessively impacted African-American and Latinx households at nearly twice the rate of Caucasian families (Leone et al., 2020). As many urban residents struggle with access to fresh fruits and vegetables and continue to face food insecurity, community gardens have helped alleviate these nutritional gaps (Algert et al., 2014; Mercado, 2021).

Public health practitioners, for years, have promoted participation in community gardens given their outcomes of increased physical activity and vegetable intake (Algert et al., 2014). A study among urban adults in Michigan revealed that community gardeners consumed, on average, 1.4 times more fruit and vegetables than non-gardeners and were 3.5 times more likely to consume fruits and vegetables at least five times daily (Mercado, 2021). Exposing communities to gardens and offering access to healthy produce has the potential for significant improvements in physical and social health outcomes (Algert et al., 2014).

Due to COVID-19, Food Insecurity and Access to Healthy Food Have Become Significant Public Health

Inhabitants in the U.S. face a range of threats to health and well-being, which could theoretically be adopted by proposals such as community gardening. These hazards incorporate non-communicable diseases and their causative risk considerations, such as minimal physical activity levels and poor diet (Lovell et al., 2014; Mercado, 2021). Thus, neighborhood gardening is a multifaceted multi-factorial endeavor, likely to have numerous influences (direct and indirect) on the health and well-being of those taking part (Lovell et al., 2014).

Community gardening has been contended to have the promise to enhance the nutritional status of those participating (Lovell et al., 2014; Mercado, 2021). For example, where community gardeners focus on fruit and vegetable production, there is the potential that participants could improve their diets through more positive perceptions towards, awareness of, and access to these fresh foods (Lovell et al., 2014; Mercado, 2021).

Some have contended that community gardening may have a role in decreasing stress and fostering better mental health (Lovell et al., 2014). Gardening as an activity is thought to be therapeutic (Lovell et al., 2014). Constructive engagement in meaningful actions, such as volunteering for community benefit, may encourage a sense of value and accomplishment; both are considerations that contribute to a greater sense of the quality of life (QOL) (Lovell et al., 2014).

Some of the most innovative programs have been developed by churches and faith-based organizations. Churches have used the ability to collect food for communities and developed gardening programs to offer healthy and fresh food options for those in need. Because of the pandemic, church members off work have become volunteers to plant crops and feed those in need. Local farmers with expertise and church members with expertise have volunteered their time to educate church members. Families have used these opportunities as supplements to school learning that is taking place online by allowing their children to learn about farming, fresh food, and healthy eating by social distancing outside while they work on the farm. The church gardens have also become outdoor activities that have allowed parents and children to learn about farming, fresh foods, and healthy eating. Tending these community gardens has also provided a needed outlet for exercise. Churches have seen the potential for improving environmental stewardship by turning underutilized land into tracts for raising vegetable crops and fruit trees. This level of community engagement has become an effective learning tool in helping children and families become more active and healthier as they learn about farming and healthy food choices. By expanding gardens, churches are tapping into a national trend fueled by Americans staying home, seeking healthy outlets, attending to food security issues, and addressing childhood obesity issues.

Future Research

Future research is needed to determine the different pathways towards decreasing childhood obesity. Experiential learning has been shown to be effective in increasing family patterns of food choices (Castro, Samuels, & Harman, 2013). Further research is needed to determine how to sustain these patters in the wake of current sociological factors; global pandemic, increased access and proximity to fast-food/high density foods, loss or low income, and cultural factors.

Additional research is needed to focus on the pathways between child and family education on health knowledge and lifestyle and action. Baker, Hagedorn, Hendricks, Clegg, Joseph, McGowan, and Olfter (2018) indicated that there is a need to research the impact of health knowledge over time on food and lifestyle choices including activity level. These long-term studies could deepen the understanding of how pilot programs aimed at children may impact the health of the child over time.

REFERENCES

Alencar, M. K., Johnson, K., Mullur, R., Gray, V., Gutierrez, E., & Korosteleva, O. (2017). The efficacy of a telemedicine-based weight loss program with video conference health coaching support. *Journal of Telemedicine and Telecare*, *25*(3), 151–157. doi:10.1177/1357633X17745471 PMID:29199544

Algert, S. J., Baameur, A., & Renvall, M. J. (2014). Vegetable output and cost savings of community gardens in San Jose, CA. *Journal of the Academy of Nutrition and Dietetics*, *114*(7), 1072–1076. doi:10.1016/j.jand.2014.02.030 PMID:24751664

Anderson, P. M., & Butcher, K. F. (2006). Childhood obesity: Trends and potential causes. *The Future of Children*, *16*(1), 19–45. doi:10.1353/foc.2006.0001 PMID:16532657

Baker, K., Hagedorn, R. L., Hendricks, T., Clegg, E. N., Joseph, L., McGowan, M., & Olfert, M. D. (2018). Katalyst: Development of a fifth-grade novel approach to health and science experiential learning. *Science Activities*, *55*(3-4), 127–139. doi:10.1080/00368121.2018.1561406 PMID:31723307

Behavioral Economics in Child Nutrition Programs (BEN). (2018). *Smarter Lunchroom Movement*. The Cornell Center for Behavioral Economics in Child Nutrition Programs. Cornell University. Retrieved from: http://www.ben.cornell.edu/index.html

Branscum, P., Kaye, G., & Warner, J. (2013). Impacting dietary behaviors of children from low-income communities: An evaluation of a theory-based Nutrition Education Program. *Californian Journal of Health Promotion*, *11*(2), 43–52. doi:10.32398/cjhp.v11i2.1530

Carlson, S., Rosenbaum, D., Keith-Jennings, B., & Nchako, C. (2016). *SNAP Works for America's Children*. Center on Budget and Policy Priorities. Retrieved from: https://www.cbpp.org/research/food-assistance/snap-works-for-americas-children

Carter, R. (2002). The impact of Public Schools on Childhood Obesity. Published: November 6, 2002. *Journal of the American Medical Association*, *288*(17), 2180. doi:10.1001/jama.288.17.2180-JMS1106-6-1 PMID:12413386

Castro, D.C., Samuels, M., & Harman, A.E. (2013). Growing healthy kids: A community garden-based obesity prevention program. *American Journal of Preventive Medicine*, *44*(3S3), S193-199. doi:10.1016/j.amepre.2012.11.024

Center for Disease Control and Prevention. (2019). *Childhood obesity*. Retrieved from https://www.cdc.gov/obesity/data/childhood.html

Centers for Disease Control. (2018). *Obesity. CDC Healthy Schools*. Centers for Disease Control and Prevention. Retrieved from: https://www.cdc.gov/healthyschools/obesity/index.htm

Coleman-Jensen, A., Nord, M., Andrews, M., & Carlson, S. (2012). *Household Food Security in the United States in 2011. ERR141*. U.S. Department of Agriculture, Economic Research Service.

Cornell. (2019). *Agriculture and Food Systems*. Cornell Cooperative Extension. Retrieved from: https://cce.cornell.edu/program/agriculture

Davis, A., Sampilo, M., Gallagher, K., Dean, K., Saroja, M., Ma, Q., He, J., Sporn, N., & Befort, C. (2016). Treating rural pediatric obesity through telemedicine vs. telephone: Outcomes from a cluster randomized controlled trial. *Journal of Telemedicine and Telecare*, *22*(2), 86–95. doi:10.1177/1357633X15586642 PMID:26026186

Easterling, T., Kerley, K., & Wright, J. (2018). *Overweight and obesity in children and adolescents in schools – The role of school nurse.* Retrieved from: https://www.nasn.org/advocacy/professional-practice-documents/position-statements/ps-overweight

Fakhouri, T., Hughes, J., Burt, V., Song, M., Fulton, J., & Ogden, C. (2014). *Physical Activity in U.S. Youth Aged 12-15 Years, 2012.* NCHS Data Brief. Retrieved from: https://permanent.access.gpo.gov/gpo77970/db141.pdf

Franzen-Castle, L., Colby, S. E., Kattelmann, K. K., Olfert, M. D., Mathews, D. R., Yerxa, K., Baker, B., Krehibiel, M., Lehrke, T., Wilson, K., Flanagan, S. M., Ford, A., Aguirre, T., & White, A. A. (2019). Development of the *iCook* 4-H Curriculum for youth and adults: Cooking, eating, and playing together for childhood obesity prevention. *Journal of Nutrition Education and Behavior*, *51*(3, 3S), S60–S68. doi:10.1016/j.jneb.2018.11.006 PMID:30851862

Gatto, N., Martinez, L., Spruijt-Metz, D., & Davis, J. (2015). L.A. Sprouts randomized controlled nutrition, cooking, and gardening programme reduces obesity and metabolic risk in Hispanic/Latino youth. *Pediatric Obesity*. Retrieved from: https://onlinelibrary-wiley-com.portal.lib.fit.edu/doi/epdf/10.1111/ijpo.12102

Greene, K., Gabrielyan, G., Just, D., & Wansink, B. (2017). Fruit-Promoting Smarter Lunchrooms Interventions: Results From a Cluster RCT. *American Journal of Preventive Medicine*, *52*(4), 451–458. doi:10.1016/j.amepre.2016.12.015 PMID:28214248

Hagedorn, R. L., Baker, K., DeJarnett, S. E., Hendricks, T., McGowan, M., Joseph, L., & Olfert, M. D. (2018). Katalyst Pilot Study: Using Interactive Activities in Anatomy and Physiology to Teach Children the Scientific Foundation of Healthy Lifestyles. *Children (Basel, Switzerland)*, *5*(12), 162. doi:10.3390/children5120162 PMID:30487474

Hall, E., Chai, W., & Albrecht, J. (2016). Relationships between nutrition-related knowledge, self-efficacy, and behavior for fifth-grade students attending Title I and non-Title I schools. *Science Direct*, *96*, 245-253. Retrieved from: https://www-sciencedirect-com.portal.lib.fit.edu/science/article/pii/S0195666315300441

Katzmarzyk, P. T., Denstel, K. D., Beals, K., Bolling, C., Wright, C., Crouter, S. E., McKenzie, T. L., Pate, R. R., Saelens, B. E., Staiano, A. E., Stanish, H. I., & Sisson, S. B. (2016). Results From the United States of America's 2016 Report Card on Physical Activity for Children and Youth. *Journal of Physical Activity & Health*, *13*(11, Suppl 2), S307–S313. doi:10.1123/jpah.2016-0321 PMID:27848726

Knol, L., Myers, H., Black, S., Robinson, D., Awololo, Y., Clark, D., & Higginbotham, J. C. (2016). Development and Feasibility of a Childhood Obesity Prevention Program for Rural Families: Application of the Social Cognitive Theory. *American Journal of Health Education*, *47*(4), 204–214. doi:10.1080/19325037.2016.1179607 PMID:28392882

Lake, A. A. (2011). Obesity. *Perspectives in Public Health, 131*(4), 154. doi:10.1177/1757913911413188 PMID:21888112

Lee, I. M., Shiroma, E. J., Lobelo, F., Puska, P., Blair, S. N., Katzmarzyk, P. T., & the Lancet Physical Activity Series Working Group. (2012). Effect of physical inactivity on major non-communicable diseases worldwide: an analysis of burden of disease and life expectancy. *Lancet (London, England), 380*(9838), 219–229. Retrieved from: https://www.ncbi.nlm.nih.gov/pmc/articles/PMC3645500/ doi:10.1016/S0140-6736(12)61031-9

Leone, L. A., Fleischhacker, S., Anderson-Steeves, B., Harper, K., Winkler, M., Racine, E., Baquero, B., & Gittelsohn, J. (2020). Healthy Food Retail during the COVID-19 Pandemic: Challenges and Future Directions. *International Journal of Environmental Research and Public Health, 17*(20), 7397. doi:10.3390/ijerph17207397 PMID:33050600

Liken, M. (2018). *How Teachers and Schools Can Address Childhood Obesity*. Concordia University-Portland. Retrieved from: https://education.cu-portland.edu/blog/classroom-resources/teachers-schools-childhood-obesity/

Lovell, R., Husk, K., Bethel, A., & Garside, R. (2014). What are the health and well-being impacts of community gardening for adults and children: A mixed-method systematic review protocol. *Environmental Evidence, 3*(1), 20. doi:10.1186/2047-2382-3-20

McKenzie, J. F., Pinger, R. R., & Seabert, D. (2018). An introduction to community & public health. Jones & Bartlett Learning.

Mercado, L. (2021). *The Role of Community Gardens During the COVID-19 Pandemic*. Columbia University School of Public Health. Retrieved from: https://www.publichealth.columbia.edu/public-health-now/news/role-community-gardens-during-covid-19-pandemic

Morris, J., Briggs, M., & Zidenberg-Cherr, S. (2000). School-based gardens can teach kids healthier eating habits. *California Agriculture, 54*(5), 40–46. doi:10.3733/ca.v054n05p40

Nutrition Education Strategies & Initiatives. (n.d.). Retrieved 2020, from https://hungerandhealth.feedingamerica.org/explore-our-work/nutrition-education-initiatives/

Pfleger, P. (2015). *Healthy eaters, strong minds: What school gardens teach kids*. Retrieved from https://www.npr.org/sections/thesalt/2015/08/10/426741473/healthy-eaters-strong-minds-what-school-gardens-teach-kids

Ryan, P. (2009). Integrated theory of health behavior change: Background and intervention development. *Clinical Nurse Specialist CNS, 23*(3), 161–172. doi:10.1097/NUR.0b013e3181a42373 PMID:19395894

Sahoo, K., Sahoo, B., Choudhury, A. K., Sofi, N. Y., Kumar, R., & Bhadoria, A. S. (2015). Childhood obesity: causes and consequences. *Journal of Family Medicine and Primary Care, 4*(2), 187–192. Retrieved from: https://www.ncbi.nlm.nih.gov/pmc/articles/PMC4408699/ doi:10.4103/2249-4863.154628

Story, M., Nanney, M. S., & Schwartz, M. B. (2009). Schools and obesity prevention: Creating school environments and policies to promote healthy eating and physical activity. *The Milbank Quarterly, 87*(1), 71–100. doi:10.1111/j.1468-0009.2009.00548.x PMID:19298416

Tsukayama, H. (2015). Teens spend nearly nine hours every day consuming media. *The Washington Post*. Retrieved from: https://www.washingtonpost.com/news/the-switch/wp/2015/11/03/teens-spend-nearly-nine-hours-every-day-consuming-media/

Woods, T., & Nies, M. (2018). Conceptual Application of the Adapted Health Belief Model to Parental Understanding of Child Weight. *Journal of Health Science & Education*, 2(4), 1-6. Retrieved from: https://www.researchgate.net/publication/327230594_Conceptual_Application_of_the_Adapted_Health_Belief_Model_to_Parental_Understanding_of_Child_Weight

World Health Organization. (2010). *Global recommendations on Physical Activity for Health*. Retrieved from: https://www.who.int/dietphysicalactivity/global-PA-recs-2010.pdf

World Health Organization. (2019). *Childhood overweight and obesity*. World Health Organization. Retrieved from: https://www.who.int/dietphysicalactivity/childhood/en/

Chapter 4
Ionization, Gadget Radiation Analysis, and Disease Control by Yajna:
An Ancient Vedic Wisdom for Human Health Relevant Amidst Pandemic Threats

Rohit Rastogi
https://orcid.org/0000-0002-6402-7638
Dayalbagh Educational Institute, India & ABES Engineering College, India

Mamta Saxena
Government of India, Delhi, India

T. Rajeshwari
Gayatri Chetna Kendra, Kolkata, India

Sheelu Sagar
Amity University, Noida, India

Bhavna Singh
G. S. Ayurved Medical College and Hospital, Pilkhuwa, India

Neeti Tandon
Vikram University, Ujjain, India

ABSTRACT

The use of electronic items like computers, laptops, tablets, television, LED lights, mobile phones, microwaves, etc. are mandatory necessity of lifestyle today. Electro-magnetic radiation is emitted from the electronic devices and are very harmful to human beings its excessive use leads to growth of cancer cells. Therefore, we need to find a way out to prevent ourselves from the harmful effect EMR level at workplace and homes. It is time to adopt modern way from traditional techniques and forward a model that involves the community, with a stakeholder-focused approach. Ancient Indian scriptures have described Yagya to absorb the harmful effect of cosmic waves. Hence, in the present study, the authors have done test to find the impact of Yagya on effect of radiation on human beings emitted from electronic devices. Results of the experiment showed significant decrease in EMR with Yagya, indicating Yagya can be one of the useful solutions as non-conventional method for reducing indoor EMR level.

DOI: 10.4018/978-1-7998-8996-0.ch004

Table 1. Different types of ionizing radiation and levels of penetration with shielding features

Type of radiation	Penetrating energy	Penetrating capacity in human body	Shielding capacity
Alpha (α)	Low	Epidermis	Dissipates in air
Beta (β)	Intermediate	Soft tissue	Sheet of paper
Gamma (γ)	High	Bones and organs	Lead

INTRODUCTION

The modern lifestyle is the victim of hazards transmitted from the usage of electronic devices and gadgets yet, most of the people are ignorant of the fact that how harmful are the Electromagnetic Radiation emitted from essential appliances & gadgets use frequently. Few unavoidable applications of EMR are for medical diagnostic instruments, security scanning at airports and shopping malls for radars, for microwave ovens and so on. Additionally, EMR (Infra-red waves) are used in, remote controls of television, goggles for night vision etc. Moreover, radio-waves are used in radio and television broadcasts. The harmful effects of EMR over longer exposure of electronic devices are hazardous according to International Commission on Radiological Protection (Rastogi, R. et al., 2020d).

Harmful Effects of Radiation on Human Body

Low-frequency electric fields when passes through human body as on conducting materials, they interrupt the electrically charged sphere of different organs of the body causing harmful effects. It is seen that circulating currents are induced when low-frequency magnetic fields passes in the human body, (Blettner, M., et al., 2009; Rastogi, R. et al., 2020e). The power of current depends on the intensity of the external magnetic field. If the field is large, these currents can affect and stimulate muscles and nerves. The main biological effect of the electromagnetic fields is heating. In microwave ovens users are exposed to the high radiations emitted from the device (Ghoneim, F. M., et al., 2016; Alers, A., et al., 2019; Rastogi, R. et al., 2020f).

Many researches have done study to investigate whether cellular phone use is connected with an increased risk for intracranial tumours gliomas. However, the results are still not decisive. A study analysis on two case-control done by (Alexiou, G. A., et al 2015) on malignant brain tumours, that comprised 1498 cases and 3530 controls, revealed that mobile phone use increased the risk of glioma. The result analysis showed that there was increased risk of meningioma or glioma with using mobile phones for more than 10 years. IARC then classified electromagnetic radiofrequency fields as possibly carcinogenic to humans, as per the report of World Health Organization (Dongre, A. S., et al., 2017; Rastogi, R. et al., 2020g; Rastogi, R. et al., 2020l).

The measurement unit for absorbed radiation is given in sievert (Sv). Since one sievert is quite large quantity hence radiation doses normally met are expressed in millisievert (mSv) or micro-sievert (μSv) which are one-thousandth or one millionth of a sievert. For example, one chest X-ray will give about 0.2 mSv of radiation dose (Pl. refer figure 1), (Rastogi, R. et al., 2018b; (Rastogi, R. et al., 2020k).

The radiation exposure caused due to all natural sources amounts to about 2.4 mSv in a year. In residential buildings, there are radioactive elements in the air. These radioactive elements are radon

Figure 1. The radiation exposure level measured in millisieverts (mSv) and associated biological indices. Source (Alers, A., et al., 2019)

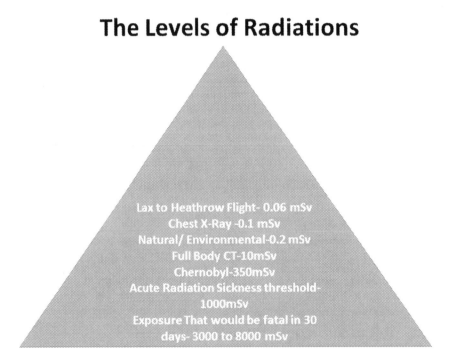

(Radon 222), thoron (Radon 220) and by products formed by the decay of radium (Radium 226) and thorium present in many sorts of rocks, other building materials and in the soil. Very large source of natural radiation exposure comes from changing amounts of uranium and thorium in the soil around the world. Our body absorbs the infra-red rays present in sunlight however infra-red rays do not produce ionization in body tissue. The amount of energy essential to cause significant biological effects through ionization is so little that our body cannot feel this energy as in the case of infra-red rays which produce heat (Radiation in Everyday Life | IAEAhttps://www.iaea.org; Rastogi, R. et al., 2020h).

LITERATURE SURVEY

Surya Namaskar, a Yogic Exercise

Surya Namaskar is an ancient scientific method in which we infuse the infinite energy of the Sun within us through some simple yoga postures. By practicing yogic postures, breathing process and chanting Omkar mantra, while the energy centers located in the body are activated, it also purifies the person's aura. Its various activities lead to the circulation of prana in all parts of the body and long-term practice further develops different powers (Rastogi, R. et al., 2018c; Rastogi, R. et al., 2020m).

By doing Surya Namaskar, our lungs, heart and heartbeat are free from disorder. While practicing this, our attention should be on the seven chakras located on the sushumna nadi. Since ages, Sun has

Figure 2. Effect of Yajna activity on diabetes control and diabetic patients

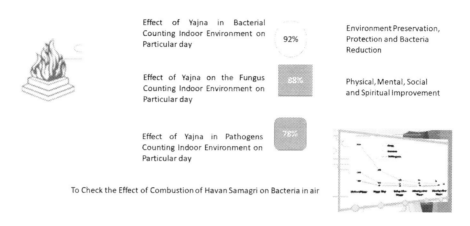

been worshiped as the basis of life. The sun not only gives us the energy and spiritual power of life, but many beneficial nectar-like elements present in its rays make our body disease free. When the balance of chemicals present in the body deteriorates, many diseases and ailments start growing in our body (Rastogi, R. et al., 2019e).

Consuming the rays of the sun fills us with positive energy and all negativity gets out. The imbalance of chemicals is removed and the body becomes disease free. The best time to get energy from the sun is at 6, 7 am, when there are no harmful ultraviolet rays in the sun. At that time it is beneficial to look towards the sun and walk barefoot on the grass.

The sun gives power to the whole world, hence it is called Shaktipunj. It has seven power centers and five fire centers. In our body also there are 7 Prana affected centers and 5 fire glands. Which is affected by the 12 positions of Surya Namaskar including the living nerves and energizes the whole body? (Rastogi, R. et al., 2018d; Rastogi, R. et al., 2020n; Rastogi, R. et al., 2018e; Rastogi, R. et al., 2018f; Rastogi, R. et al., 2020o).

Scientifically there is an atomic reactor in our body which activates the various glands of our body by the energy received from the sun. Due to this, the circulation of blood occurs smoothly throughout the body, due to which the person remains happy (Rastogi, R. et al., 2019b; Saxena, M. et al., 2018; Rastogi, R. et al., 2019c; Rastogi, R. et al., 2019d).

Mantra Can Heal the Radiated Atmosphere

What is a Mantra? A mantra is a sound which is generated with repeated recitation of a phrase or words in consistent flow of sound, it is used to control body and mind frequency. The definition of the word Mantra can simply be compared with the oar of the boat; meaning it is the instrument which practitioner uses to move ahead and cross restless mind, with its unending waves of thoughts. A mantra can be said to cure the mental depression and used for calming the mind. Among the most popular and prevailing mantra which is practiced among Indian Hindu population is *Gayatri Mantra, Mahamritunjay Mantra* and *Maha Mantra* (Rastogi, R. et al., 2017; Rastogi, R. et al., 2020i).

According to Sridhar (2020) every human body has Aura Human bio energy field which works as a repellent for the electromagnetic radiation from the objects because the human skin is porous. Healthy human biofield the normal frequency range is considered to be 62MHz to 68MHz. The frequency generated within human body is directly proportional to the emission of electromagnetic energy. Human body frequency gets energized positively whenever human beings listens to mantra, prayers or music (S. Sundaravadivelu., et al., 2015) hence the voice vibrations can easily get converted into electromagnetic radiation or waves through antennas which passes through the skin of human body (Rastogi, R. et al., 2018a; Rastogi, R. et al., 2020j, Pl. refer Fig. 2).

EXPERIMENTAL SETUP AND METHODOLOGY

The following Mudras were used as a protocol for the different subjects under study (Pl. refer Figure 3, Fig. 4 and Fig. 5).

Mudrā Science

Hands and fingers are capable to do some extra ordinary things besides assisting in holding, eating and doing physical work. Hands are the instrument to everything. They are like the control panel to everything. In science of yog and meditation there are hundreds of Mudrās, some are used for health, some for wellbeing, some Mudrās are done for creating processes. In fact, different features of life can be denoted with the Mudrās. For example, in yoga a particular asana has a unique Mudrā, and a specific kind of breathing another Mudrā is useful, to derive the best result from within the human body (Rastogi, R. et al., 2019f).

As per figure 4, the Mudrā are connected with Yogic Sciences and are very easy to perform. They have no side effects. These Mudrās can be practiced in any easy position. For those who wish to go beyond the physical health benefits and calming effects of meditation, may go for higher stage of meditation with the practice of yog Mudrā. There are 24 Mudrā associated with each word of the Gayatri Mantra, if performed in a correct way it can help to transform an ordinary man to a super human being. The mudrās can be performed simply while meditating in a lotus position or seated in a straight-backed chair. Before each Mudrā session washing of hands is mandatory then rub both the hands each other for 5-7 times, then hold the hands before the Navel this helps to flow energy in the hands. To perform Dhyana Mudrā, place both hands like bowls in your lap, with the left hand on top and two thumb-tips touching. Please refer below figures 1 to 10 for detailed description of Mudrās.

In Hinduism a spiritual gesture performed by the fingers and hands are called mudrā it represents seal of energy of the body. muːˈdra means seal, mark, or gestures. Since ancient times in Indian religions and traditions, Mudrās are being practiced spiritually to assist in meditation and /or healing. There are many types of Mudrā which can be performed with the hands and fingers. In an Indian dance form, sculpture and painting iconography (Buddha) variety of Mudrās are portrayed.

In yoga, different gestures of fingers and hand (mudrās) are used in conjunction with pranayama (the yogic breathing exercises) and are generally done while seated in the pose of Padmasana or Vajrasana. Each mudrās formations stimulate and activates different organs and body parts. Mudrās when done with breathing exercise it affect the flow of energy and also help to change the mood of an individual. Each hand gestures and its positions during Mudrā act as locks it guide energy flows and reflexes to the brain. During Mudrā making crossing, curling, pressing, stretching or touching thumb with different fingers of the hand we can help to manipulate the mind body. Mudrās allows a physical connection with an intangible wish this is possible because each area of the hand corresponds to a certain part of the mind or body. There are different mudrās formation however by meditating on a specific Mudrā helps manifest certain hopes, energies, or devotions into your life. At a higher spiritual level, practicing on specific mudrās shows the outward representation of one's inward intentions. Mudrās show what a practitioners' desires and what he intends to be!. Please refer annex for more details and related contents (Rastogi, R. et al., 2019g).

Meditation for Personality and Spiritual Growth

The primary purpose of meditation practice is to facilitate awakened spiritual consciousness. The benefits which contribute to our well-being and improved functioning are several few as cited by various practitioners in the text are given below:

1. Meditation helps in mental transformations and thinking processes become more organized as the result of meditative calmness and the influence of refined states of consciousness.
2. Practice of meditation boosts the immune system, physiological functions organs are strengthened and encouraged to be more balanced and efficient.
3. Meditation enables to slow down the biological ageing processes. The meditators are mentally and physically younger than their calendar years' age.
4. With the practice of meditation, stress symptoms are reduced. The nervous system is refreshed and enlivened, allowing awareness to be more easily processed through it.
5. Regenerative energies are awakened with meditation they are directed by innate intelligence, vitalize the body, empower the mind, and have restorative and healing influences (Rastogi, R. et al., 2019h).

RESULTS AND DISCUSSIONS

The Experiments Related to health Protection and Improvement

A. Disease-Diabetes, Place - Noida Chetna Kendra

The first Yagyopathy camp was organized in Gayatri Chetna Kendra Noida, on 11 subjects from 25th April 2019 to 20 may 2019, conducted by Sh. R.N. Singh and Sh. U.S. Gupta. A round shaped Havan Kunda of grounded soil with CowDung based Samidha was used and oblations were given with special Havan Samagri of diabetes.

B. Disease-Diabetes, Place - Noida Chetna Kendra

- Yagyopathy treatment was given for an hour as per pre-decided protocol as below:

Figure 3. Different Mudra of hands for health cure – Part1

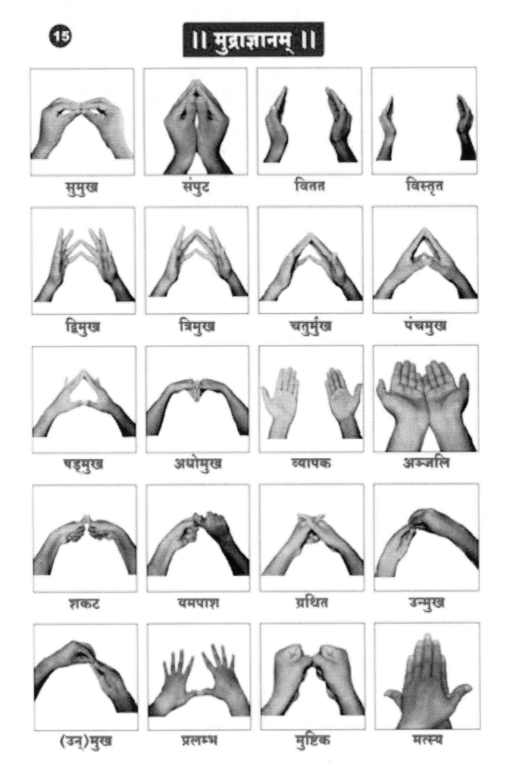

Figure 4. Different Mudra of hands for health cure – Part 2

Figure 5. Different Mudra of hands for health cure – Part 3

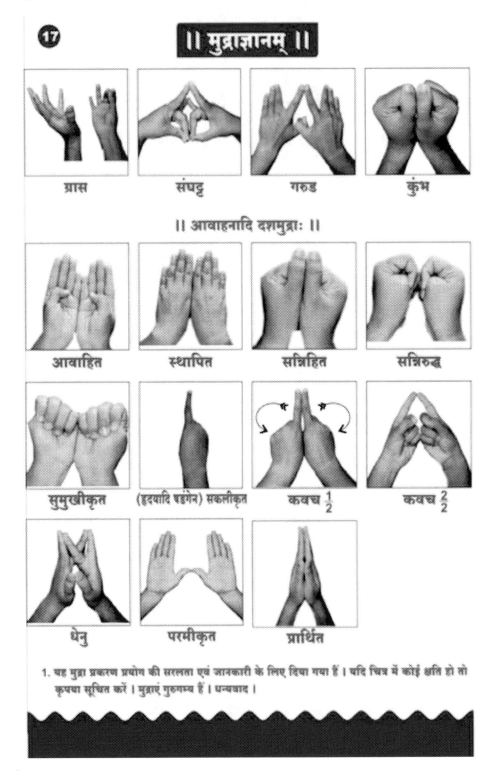

Table 2. Yagyopathy experiments tabular summary at GCK, Noida, NCR, Delhi, India (11th -20th May 2019)

S.NO	NAME OF PATIENTS	GENDER / WEIGHT	CHETNA KENDRA NOIDA EVALUATION DONE ON 11TH MAY 2019				IMPROVEMENT IN OTHER SYMPTOMS
			FASTING BLOOD SUGAR		FBST PRANDALBLOOD SUGAR		
			B.T	A.T	B.T	A.T	
1	Mr. Raman Singh	Gents/71 yrs	205	93	405-455	266	Improvements in all sections
2	Smt. Meera Sharma	Lady/59 yrs	305	188	405	277	improvement in knee pain and body weight
3	Mrs. Revati Gupta	Lady/56yrs	RBS-165	117.3	RBS-165	107.3	Improvement in energy level
4	Smt. Rajbala Yadav	Lady/41yrs	RBS-329	218.7	RBS-329	280.4	Improvement in body weight from 65.3 to 64.1
5	Smt. Rekha	Lady/73 Yrs	RBS-159	111	RBS-159	130	positive thinking has increased
6	Shri. Ghanshyam	Gents/57	RBS-139	122	RBS-139	132	165/90-135/80

- 30 Minute Yajna with herbal Havan Samgri
- 10 minute mental Jap (chanting)
- 20 minutes Pranayam
- 10 Minutes Asan
- Subjects were also informed about exile tap and were asked their secret issues.
- Besides all above, the dietary plan was decided and patients were asked to follow them strictly.

C. The Results Obtained from Above Session

- Total subjects were 11 out of them 10 experienced drastic reduction of 5% to 56% in blood sugar in duration of one month.
- All reported that they felt surprisingly improvement in their health.
- All reported that they are feeling more energetic and vital than earlier.
- Blessed with good and sound sleep.
- They achieve a series of positive thoughts throughout the day.

Pl.Refer Table 2 for Tabular summary of GCK Noida experiments.
    Jaipur Gayatri Chentna Kendra, Durgapura, Jaipur, rajasthan, India
    Third Yagyopathy camp on the Artheritis and muscle pain was conducted from 20 may 2019 to 30 may 2019.
    5 patients participated
    Mrs. Chandrakala Sharma, Mrs. Geeta Goyal, Mrs. Yashodhara Bhatia, Mrs. Radha Ballabh Khuteta, Mr. Pannalal Soni. (Pl. refer Table 3 to Table 5 for detailed health summary.)

Table 3. Yagyopathy experiments tabular summary at GCK, Jaipur, Rajashthan, India (20-30 May 2019). Subject Details – Part 1

Name of patient	Age	Disease / Problems Particulars	Pre - Treatment	Post Treatment	Improvement in Percentage (%)
Mrs Chandrakala Sharma	71 Years	a. Gyaene Problem	15	8	a. 70%
		b. BP			b. 50%
		c. Acidity	15	10	c. 50%
		d. Knee Pain	15	10	d. 50%
		e. Sleeping Trouble	15	10	e. 50%
		f. Over Weight (83 Kg)	88 kg	85 kg	f. 85Kg (-5 Kgs)
		g. Toe Swelling	15	05	g. 95% Relief

Table 4. Yagyopathy experiments tabular summary at GCK, Jaipur, Rajashthan, India (20-30 may 2019). Subject Details – Part 2

Name of patient	Age	Disease / Problems Particulars	Pre - Treatment	Post Treatment	Improvement in Percentage (%)
Suneeta Lahri	62 Years	a) Severe Backpain	15	7	a) During the Camp, patient got relief of 80% in back pain.
		(Long treatment taken at EHCC hospital, Narayana hospital and Fortis hospital but No Relief)			b) Relief by 20% in Knee pain
		b) Knee Pain	15	13	
Rama Singh	67 yrs	a) Back pain: (Treatment taken from Metro Mass Hospital for about 18 months but no relief)	15	9	a) 60% relief in Backpain
		b) Burning Sensation on Lower Feet	10	9.5	b) 10% relief in Burning Sensation on Lower feet

Biowell Aura Scanner Instrument (Russia)

The Yagyopathy research team obtained the high techno and advanced instrument to measure the human bioelectricity Biowell and scanner on 1st Sept. 2019 and it's training was provided in Lodhi colony, Delhi, India where 10 trainers were imparted training to use it.

In one month experiment, many annals were collected from this instrument where the effect of Yajna on the physical, mental status and energy of internal organs of body was recorded.

Total 16 subjects were chosen where the following parameters were taken care of

Human Energy and Bioelectricity, Anxiety, Mental Stress, Mental Balance, Mis/ Dis balance in internal organs of body, Change in the energy of internal organs, Effect on the seven Chakras of Body.

It was obtained in most of the people that Yajna therapy and effect were causing the energy, enthu and positivity level of an individual.

A case study:

Table 5. Yagyopathy experiments tabular summary at GCK, Jaipur, Rajashthan, India (20-30 May 2019). Subject Details – Part 3

Name of patient	Age	Disease / Problems Particulars	Pre - Treatment	Post Treatment	Improvement in Percentage (%)
Janki nath	78 Yrs	a) Swelling on Feet for about 10 years after bypass surgery.	15	7	a) 80% relief in Swelling
		b) Joint Pain	15	7	b) 80% relief in Joint Pain
		c) Cramps	15	7	c) 80% relief in cramps
Sahi Ram Sharma	67	a) Problem in deep breathing (Heart problem Underwent 3 heart attacks)	15	10	a) Now very much comfortable in deep breathing.
		b) Heart Effeciency 25%			b) Feeling 80% relief & Energetic

The result of the study of physical energy parameters and others on the subject Sh. Raj Kumar Sain, Vikaspuri Delhi are as below.

- The whole vital power and physical energy was increased up to 13% in one time Yajna therapy.
- Balance of whole body was 92%.
- An increase of 53% in left hemisphere and 20% increase in right hemisphere was recorded and it meant that the internal organs with low energy were recorded with higher amount.

Effects on Ions

Alpha lab USA instrument provided by research lab of Shantikunj Haridwar, India, the effect of negative ions produced by Yajna was measured.

The experiments were done in 5 to 6 different areas and it was found that Yajna is responsible for increasing the negative ions.

The negative ions increase in starting from the lightening the fire and the growth continue till the end-phases of the process (Pl. refer Table 6).

Pollutions Created by Radiations

a. Electromagnetic radiation is resulted due to current modern westernized life style. Mobile, Laptop, Microwave, Television and all electronic gadgets emit the radiations. Long term exposure of these instruments can cause the tumor at neck or head parts of body. IARC (International Agency for Research on Cancer) has done analysis and research that whether there is a correlation of head or neck cancer with useage of phones by adults.
b. The data was collected and calculated after analysis which was recorded from 13 countries and it was found that more than 10 years usage of mobiles increases the risk of brain or nervous cancers.
c. It was observed that the high radiations were decreased up to zero as soon as oblations were started in Yajna in Vipin Garden Extension, New Delhi, India.
d. The pakces or homes where the Yajna is conducted on daily basis, radiations are diminished up to distance of 3 to 5 inches only (Pl. refer Fig. 6, Fig. 7 and Fig. 8 and Table 7).

Table 6. Counting of negative (-) ions at different area

Sr	Address	Yagya Size	Date	-ve ION Counts per CM³	
				Before Yagya	During Yagya
1	Mr. JP Sharma, 181, Surya Nagar, taro ki Koot, Near Radha Govind Temple, Jaipur	1 Kunidya	6-Oct-19	1290	16600
2	Gayatri Chetna Kendra, Durgapura, Jaipur, 302010	5 Kundiya Yagya	8-Oct-19	190	10780
3	108 Kundeeya Yagya, Kalwad Road, Vatika, Jaipur	108 Kundiya	13-Oct-19	430	4370
4	Mr. SK Aggarwal, 111, Sriji Nagar, Durgapura, Jaipur	1 Kunidya	26-Oct-19	80	6870
5	Mr. GL Sharma, Z9A, Street No. 2 Vetesta Enclave, Papravat Road, Nazafgadh, New Delhi, 110043	1 Kunidya	27-Oct-19	260	5730
6	112, Sriji Nagar, Durgapura, Jaipur, 302018	1 Kunidya	20-Nov-19	2520	7140

RECOMMENDATIONS

As well as on our body a result oriented research based work just asking for medicine is not going to cure, buying a medicine is not going to cure, even worshipping and praising is not going to cure. Only by consuming it can cure. So just like that doing Yagya in right way with right things. At right time with right mindset can give assured results. So many times people demand to put videos and ask questions but before suggesting what is our input we never judge it as it's others job (Rastogi, R. et al., 2019i).

Figure 6. Effect of Agnihotra on ions

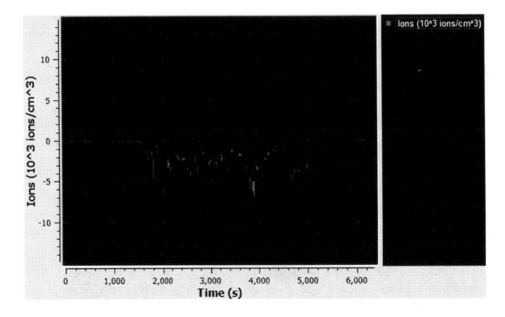

Figure 7. Effect of Yajna on electromagnetic radiations, Gautam Nagar, Delhi, India

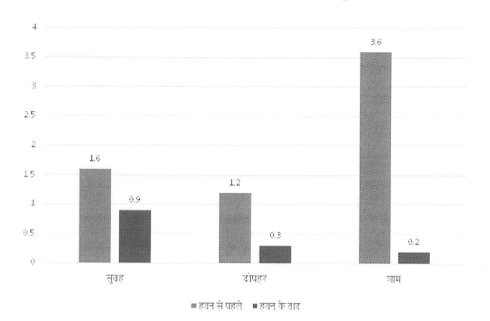

The practice of Yoga, Pranayama Meditation and Mudrā practices develops positive psychology with mental and physical well-being, personality development with fulfilment of joyous living can be attained with its basic practice as propounded by Ved Murti Pt. Sri Ram Sharma Acharya. It is recommended that Yoga Practice may be prescribed by the doctors as an additional therapy to common people who have suffered health loss due to Covid 19 pandemic or due any physiological disorder of the body system. It is also recommended to consider theclear instruction on breath work, postures, relaxation techniques,

Figure 8. Effect of Yajna on electromagnetic radiations, Vikas Puri, Delhi, India

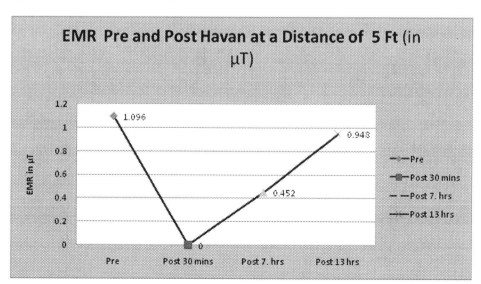

Table 7. Effect of Yajna on electromagnetic radiations, Vikas Puri, Delhi, India

	Before Yajna	After Yajna
Distance in Ft.	5 "	5 "
Magnetic flux in μT	0.33	0
	1.43	0
	0.99	0
	1.2	0
	1.53	0

and meditation on different methods of Hatha Yoga, Ashtanga yoga, Iyengar yoga and Bikram yoga and meditation techniques (Rastogi, R. et al., 2019j).

NOVELTIES

At the workplace there is huge work pressure besides personal tension of employees hence alternative interventions is required for sound physical and mental health of employees. The author team has tried to give an insight through this review paper to check out the effect of Yoga, Pranayama Meditation and Mudrā practices which are simple, workable and can be practiced without much stress and strain. It provides appropriate ways to improve the health and quality of life of employee's further yoga may establish spiritual essence in common man, this may be considered as major novelty of this manuscript (Rastogi, R. et al., 2020a).

FUTURE RESEARCH DIRECTIONS

This research design is developed for need for holistic development of corporate workers in order to reduce the severe loss of skilled workforce due to psychological disorders like stress, anxiety, distress etc., and causing hinderance for human race to flourish however thereis scope of future research in this area. The Corporate Yoga as atool can be customized in future for a specific organization to cope up with stress, anxiety, distress etc. The study canbe undertakenseparately for physicalhealth, physiological benefits andmental health benefits with practice of yoga asanas, meditation, pranayama and Mudrā formation.

For future scope there are lot of possibilities to explore more on mind-body synchronization through Yoga asana and meditation. The intervention can be done on group of individuals with different age group and with different rank of employees who may have mutual goals.

For correct evaluation of effects of yoga on a particular population, methodology adopted should be supportive, statistical test should be error free sample size should be scientifically proven and systematic randomization of sample is essential for establishing results with high degree of variability between intervention methods (Rastogi, R. et al., 2020b; Rastogi, R. et al., 2020c).

CONCLUSIONS

Effects of Radiations

Radiation are either non-ionizing or ionizing depending on the radiated particle's energy. Radioactive materials that emit α, β, or γ r Radiofrequency (RF) radiation used in many broadcast and communications applications. Common sources of ionizing radiation are Microwaves oven used in the home kitchen, Infrared radiation used in heat lamps, Ultraviolet (UV) radiation from the sun and tanning beds. Both types of radiation are harmful to health however they have few advantages also. Various types of ionizing radiation have different levels of penetration and shielding features.

These electromagnetic radiations may have more positive vibrations and energy than speech signal (which are yet to be studied), In the ancient Indian scriptures there are numerous mantras, slokas, prayers, Islamic- dua, music which are helpful for curing deficiencies and diseases. The science behind this is these mantras, dua or music work as an input to the antenna (Isotropic or Directive antenna) and the output of antenna is electromagnetic wave radiations which can have equal or more positive energy than the sound vibrations. Absorption of electromagnetic emissions by the human body by the antenna reduces the deficiency or diseases.

In above preented experuiemnts in manuscripts, it has been clearly established that the radiation effects were higly ciurtailed in Yajna atmosphere. The effect of Radiations was nullified in spiritual environment.

ACKNOWLEDGMENT

The Team of authors would love to pay our deep sense of gratitude to the ABES Engineering College, Ghaziabad & Amity International Business School, Amity University, and Noida for arranging us all the facilities, the direct-indirect supporters for their timely help and valuable suggestions and the almighty for blessing us throughout. We would also like to extend the vote of thanks to IIT Delhi, IIT Roorkee, Dev Sanskriti Vishwavidyalaya, Haridwar, Patanjali Foundation and Ayurveda Institute, Dehradun for their support and guidance in accomplishing our research paper.

REFERENCES

Alers, A., Salen, P., Yellapu, V., Garg, M., Bendas, C., Cardiges, N., Domer, G., Oskin, T., Fisher, J., & Stawicki, S. (2019). *Fundamentals of Medical Radiation Safety: Focus on Reducing Short-Term and Long-Term Harmful Exposures*. doi:10.5772/intechopen.85689

Blettner, M., Schlehofer, B., Breckenkamp, J., Kowall, B., Schmiedel, S., Reis, U., Potthoff, P., Schuz, J., & Berg-Beckhoff, G. (2008, September 19). Mobile phone base stations and adverse health effects: Phase 1 of a population-based, cross-sectional study in Germany. *Occupational and Environmental Medicine*, 66(2), 118–123. https://www.ncbi.nlm.nih.gov/pubmed/19017702. doi:10.1136/oem.2007.037721 PMID:19017702

Dongre, A. S., Inamdar, I. F., & Gattani, P. L. (2017). Nomophobia: A study to evaluate mobile phone dependence and impact of cell phone on health. *National Journal of Community Medicine*, 8(11), 688–693.

Ghoneim, F. M., & Arafat, E. A. (2016). Histological and histochemical study of the protective role of rosemary extract against harmful effect of cell phone electromagnetic radiation on the parotid glands. *Acta Histochemica, 118*(5), 478–485. doi:10.1016/j.acthis.2016.04.010 PMID:27155802

Rastogi, R. (2020f). Intelligent Mental Health Analyzer by Biofeedback: App and Analysis. *Handbook of Research on Optimizing Healthcare Management Techniques.* doi:10.4018/978-1-7998-1371-2.ch009

Rastogi, R. (2020i). Exhibiting App and Analysis for Biofeedback Based Mental Health Analyzer. *Handbook of Research on Advancements of Artificial Intelligence in Healthcare Engineering.* Doi: doi:10.4018/978-1-7998-2120-5

Rastogi, R. (2020j). Computational Approach for Personality Detection on Attributes: An IoT-MMBD Enabled Environment. *Handbook of Research on Advancements of Artificial Intelligence in Healthcare Engineering.* Doi: doi:10.4018/978-1-7998-2120-5

Rastogi, R. (2020k). Tension Type Headache: IOT and FOG Applications in Healthcare Using Different Biofeedback. *Handbook of Research on Advancements of Artificial Intelligence in Healthcare Engineering.* Doi: doi:10.4018/978-1-7998-2120-5

Rastogi, R. (2020m). Yajna and Mantra Science Bringing Health and Comfort to Indo-Asian Public: A Healthcare 4.0 Approach and Computational Study. *Learning and Analytics in Intelligent Systems, 13.* https://link.springer.com/chapter/10.1007%2F978-3-030-40850-3_15 doi:10.1007/978-3-030-40850-3_15

Rastogi, R., & Chaturvedi, D. K. (2020d). Intelligent Personality Analysis on Indicators in IoT-MMBD Enabled Environment. In Multimedia Big Data Computing for IoT Applications: Concepts, Paradigms, and Solutions. Springer Nature Singapore. doi:10.1007/978-981-13-8759-3_7

Rastogi, R., & Chaturvedi, D. K. (2020g). Surveillance of Type –I & II Diabetic Subjects on Physical Characteristics: IoT and Big Data Perspective in Healthcare @NCR, India. Internet of Things (IoT). doi:10.1007/978-3-030-37468-6_23

Rastogi, R., & Chaturvedi, D. K. (2020l). Tension Type Headache: IOT Applications to Cure TTH Using Different Biofeedback: A statistical Approach in Healthcare. In Biopsychosocial Perspectives and Practices for Addressing Communicable and Non-Communicable Diseases. IGI Global. doi:10.4018/978-1-7998-2139-7

Rastogi, R., Chaturvedi, D. K., Satya, S., Arora, N., Sirohi, H., Singh, M., Verma, P., & Singh, V. (2018b). Which One is Best: Electromyography Biofeedback Efficacy Analysis on Audio, Visual and Audio-Visual Modes for Chronic TTH on Different Characteristics. *Proceedings of International Conference on Computational Intelligence &IoT (ICCIIoT).*

Rastogi, R., Chaturvedi, D. K., Arora, N., Trivedi, P., & Singh, P. (2017). Role and efficacy of Positive Thinking on Stress Management and Creative Problem Solving for Adolescents, *International Journal of Computational Intelligence. Biotechnology and Biochemical Engineering By Mantech Publications, 2*(2), 1–27.

Rastogi, R., Chaturvedi, D. K., Arora, N., Trivedi, P., Singh, P., & Vyas, P. (2018e). Study on Efficacy of Electromyography and Electroencephalography Biofeedback with Mindful Meditation on Mental health of Youths. *Proceedings of the 12th INDIACom,* 84-89.

Rastogi, R., Chaturvedi, D. K., Gupta, M., Sirohi, H., Gulati, M., & Pratyusha. (2020h). Analytical Observations Between Subjects' Medications Movement and Medication Scores Correlation Based on Their Gender and Age Using GSR Biofeedback. In *Pattern Recognition Applications in Engineering* (pp. 229-257). IGI Global. . doi:10.4018/978-1-7998-1839-7.ch010

Rastogi, R., Chaturvedi, D. K., & Satya, S. (2019e). Comparative Study of Trends Observed During Different Medications by Subjects under EMG & GSR Biofeedback. *IJITEE, 8*(6S), 748-756. https://www.ijitee.org/download/volume-8-issue-6S/

Rastogi, R., Chaturvedi, D. K., Satya, S., & Arora, N. (2020n). Intelligent Heart Disease Prediction on Physical and Mental Parameters: A ML Based IoT and Big Data Application and Analysis. Learning and Analytics in Intelligent Systems, 13, 199-236. doi:10.1007/978-3-030-40850-3_10

Rastogi, R., Chaturvedi, D. K., Satya, S., Arora, N., Gupta, M., Saini, H., Mahelyan, K. S., & Verma, H. (2019g). Comparative Efficacy Analysis of Electromyography and Galvanic Skin Resistance Biofeedback on Audio Mode for Chronic TTH on Various Indicators. *International Journal of Computational Intelligence & IoT, 1*(1), 18–24. https://ssrn.com/abstract=3354371

Rastogi, R., Chaturvedi, D. K., Satya, S., Arora, N., Gupta, M., Singhal, P., & Gulati, M. (2019f). Statistical Analysis of Exponential and Polynomial Models of EMG & GSR Biofeedback for Correlation between Subjects' Medications Movement & Medication Scores. *IJITEE, 8*(6S), 625–635.

RastogiR.ChaturvediD. K.SatyaS.AroraN.GuptaM.SirohiH.SinghM.VermaP.SinghV.(2019h). Which one is Best: Electromyography Biofeedback, Efficacy Analysis on Audio, Visual and Audio-Visual Modes for Chronic TTH on Different Characteristics. *International Journal of Computational Intelligence & IoT, 1*(1), 25-31. Available at SSRN: https://ssrn.com/abstract=3354375

Rastogi, R., Chaturvedi, D. K., Satya, S., Arora, N., Gupta, M., Verma, H., & Saini, H. (2020c). An Optimized Biofeedback EMG and GSR Biofeedback Therapy for Chronic TTH on SF-36 Scores of Different MMBD Modes on Various Medical Symptoms. Studies Comp. Intelligence, 841. doi:10.1007/978-981-13-8930-6_8

Rastogi, R., Chaturvedi, D. K., Satya, S., Arora, N., Gupta, M., Yadav, V., Chauhan, S., & Sharma, P. (2019i). Chronic TTH Analysis by EMG & GSR Biofeedback on Various Modes and Various Medical Symptoms Using IoT. In Big Data Analytics for Intelligent Healthcare Management. Academic Press. doi:10.1016/B978-0-12-818146-1.00005-2

Rastogi, R., Chaturvedi, D. K., Satya, S., Arora, N., Saini, H., Verma, H., & Mehlyan, K. (2018c). Comparative Efficacy Analysis of Electromyography and Galvanic Skin Resistance Biofeedback on Audio Mode for Chronic TTH on Various Indicators. *Proceedings of International Conference on Computational Intelligence &IoT (ICCIIoT).*

Rastogi, R., Chaturvedi, D. K., Satya, S., Arora, N., Saini, H., Verma, H., Mehlyan, K., & Varshney, Y. (2018f). Statistical Analysis of EMG and GSR Therapy on Visual Mode and SF-36 Scores for Chronic TTH. *Proceedings of international Conference on 5th IEEE Uttar Pradesh Section International Conference.* 10.1109/UPCON.2018.8596851

Rastogi, R., Chaturvedi, D. K., Satya, S., Arora, N., Singh, P., & Vyas, P. (2018d). Statistical Analysis for Effect of Positive Thinking on Stress Management and Creative Problem Solving for Adolescents. *Proceedings of the 12thINDIACom,* 245-251.

Rastogi, R., Chaturvedi, D. K., Satya, S., Arora, N., Trivedi, P. M., Gupta, M., Singhal, P., & Gulati, M. (2020e). MM Big Data Applications: Statistical Resultant Analysis of Psychosomatic Survey on Various Human Personality Indicators. *Proceedings of Second International Conference on Computational Intelligence 2018.* 10.1007/978-981-13-8222-2_25

Rastogi, R., Chaturvedi, D.K., Satya, S., Arora, N., Yadav, V., Yadav, V., Sharma, P., & Chauhan, S. (2019d). Statistical Analysis of EMG & GSR Biofeedback Efficacy on Different Modes for Chronic TTH on Various Indicators. *Int. J. Advanced Intelligence Paradigms.* . doi:10.1504/IJAIP.2019.10021825

Rastogi, R., Chaturvedi, D. K., Sharma, P., Yadav, V., Chauhan, S., Gulati, M., Gupta, M., & Singhal, P. (2019j). Statistical Resultant Analysis of Psychosomatic Survey on Various Human Personality Indicators: Statistical Survey to Map Stress and Mental Health. In Handbook of Research on Learning in the Age of Transhumanism (pp. 363-383). IGI Global. doi:10.4018/978-1-5225-8431-5.ch022

Rastogi, R., Chaturvedi, D. K., Sharma, S., Bansal, A., & Agrawal, A. (2018a). Audio Visual EMG & GSR Biofeedback Analysis for Effect of Spiritual Techniques on Human Behaviour and Psychic Challenges. *Proceedings of the 12th INDIACom,* 252-258.

Rastogi, R., Chaturvedi, D. K., Singhal, P., & Gupta, M. (2020o). Investigating Diabetic Subjects on Their Correlation with TTH and CAD: A Statistical Approach on Experimental Results. In *Opportunities and Challenges in Digital Healthcare Innovation.* . doi:10.4018/978-1-7998-3274-4

Rastogi, R., Chaturvedi, D. K., Singhal, P., & Gupta, M. (2020p). Investigating Correlation of Tension Type Headache and Diabetes: IoT Perspective in Health care. In C. Chakerborty (Ed.), *IoTHT: Internet of Things for Healthcare Technologies.* doi:10.1007/978-981-15-4112-4_4

Rastogi, R., Chaturvedi, D. K., Verma, H., Mishra, Y., & Gupta, M. (2020a). Identifying Better? Analytical Trends to Check Subjects' Medications Using Biofeedback Therapies. *International Journal of Applied Research on Public Health Management,* 5(1), Article 2. https://www.igi-global.com/article/identifying-better/240753 doi:10.4018/IJARPHM.2020010102

Rastogi, R., Gupta, M., & Chaturvedi, D.K. (2020b). Efficacy of Study for Correlation of TTH vs Age and Gender Factors using EMG Biofeedback Technique. *International Journal of Applied Research on Public Health Management,* 5(1), Article 4. . doi:10.4018/IJARPHM.2020010104

Rastogi, R., Saxena, M., Gupta, U. S., Sharma, S., Chaturvedi, D. K., Singhal, P., Gupta, M., Garg, P., Gupta, M., & Maheshwari, M. (2019b). Yajna and Mantra Therapy Applications on Diabetic Subjects: Computational Intelligence Based Experimental Approach. *Proceedings of the 2nd edition of International Conference on Industry Interactive Innovations in Science, Engineering and Technology (I3SET2K19)*. https://papers.ssrn.com/sol3/papers.cfm?abstract_id=3515800

Rastogi, R., Saxena, M., Sharma, S. K., Muralidharan, S., Beriwal, V. K., Singhal, P., Rastogi, M., & Shrivastava, R. (2019a). Evaluation of efficacy of yagya therapy ont2- diabetes mellitus patients. *Proceedings of the 2nd edition of International Conference on Industry Interactive Innovations in Science, Engineering and Technology (I3SET2K19)*. https://papers.ssrn.com/sol3/papers.cfm?abstract_id=3514326

Rastogi, R., Saxena, M., Sharma, S. K., Murlidharan, S., Berival, V. K., Jaiswal, D., Sharma, A., & Mishra, A. (2019c). Statistical Analysis on Efficacy of Yagya Therapy for Type-2 Diabetic Mellitus Patients through Various Parameters. Advs in Intelligent Syst., Computing, 1120. doi:10.1007/978-981-15-2449-3_15

Saxena, M., Kumar, B., &Matharu, S. (2018). Impact of Yagya on Particulate Matters. *Interdisciplinary Journal of Yagya Research, 1,* 1-8. doi:10.36018/ijyr.v1i1.5

Sridhar, N. (2020). Effect of Chanting, Recitation of Mantras, Slokas, Duas, Music on Human Beings using EMF Radiation A Study. *Test Engineering and Management,* 83. https://testmagzine.biz/index.php/testmagzine/article/view/9212.11476-11480

Sundaravadivelu, S., & Suresh, R. (2015). Study of Physical, Mental, Intellectual andSpiritual Health of a Human Being Living in ADwelling Place Constructed According toThe Vastu Principle. *International Journal of Innovative Research in Computerand Communication Engineering, 3*(7).

KEY TERMS AND DEFINITIONS

Ayurveda: Ayurveda system of medicine with historical roots in the Indian subcontinent. Globalized and modernized practices derived from Ayurveda traditions are a type of alternative medicine. In countries beyond India, Aurvedic therapies and practices have been integrated in general wellness applications and in some cases in medical use. The main classical Ayurveda texts begin with accounts of the transmission of medical knowledge from the Gods to sages, and then to human physicians. In SushrutaSamhita (Sushruta's Compendium), Sushruta wrote that Dhanvantari, Hindu god of Ayurveda.

Energy Measurements: There are various kind of units used to measure the quantity of energy sources. The Standard unit of Energy is known to be Joule(J). Also, other mostly used energy unit is kilowatt /hour (kWh) which is basically used in electricity bills. Large measurements may also go up to terawatt/hour (TWh) or also said as billion kW/h. Other units used for measuring heat include BTU (British Thermal Unit), kilogram calorie (kg-cal) and most commonly Tonne of Oil Equivalent. Actually it represents the quantity of heat which can be obtained from a tonne of oil. Energy is also measured in some other units such as British Thermal Unit(BTU), calorie, therm, etc. which varies generally according to their area of use.

Jap: Jap is the meditative repetition of a mantra or a divine name. It is a practice found in Hinduism, Jainism, Sikhism, Buddhism, and Shintoism. The mantra or name may be spoken softly, enough for the practitioner to hear it, or it may be spoken within the reciter's mind. Jap may be performed while sitting in a meditation posture, while performing other activities, or as part of formal worship in group settings.

Machine Learning: Machine learning (ML) is the study of computer algorithms that improve automatically through experience. It is seen as a subset of artificial intelligence. Machine learning algorithms build a mathematical model based on sample data, known as "training data", in order to make predictions or decisions without being explicitly programmed to do so. Machine learning algorithms are used in a wide variety of applications, such as email filtering and computer vision, where it is difficult or infeasible to develop conventional algorithms to perform the needed tasks.

Mantra: A mantra is a sacred utterance, a numinous sound, a syllable, word or phonemes, or group of words in Sanskrit believed by practitioners to have psychological and/or spiritual powers. Some mantras have a syntactic structure and literal meaning, while others do not.

Pollution: Pollution is the introduction of contaminants into the natural environment that cause adverse change. Pollution can take the form of chemical substances or energy, such as noise, heat or light. Pollutants, the components of pollution, can be either foreign substances/energies or naturally occurring contaminants. Pollution is often classed as point source or nonpoint source pollution. In 2015, pollution killed 9 million people in the world. The major kinds of pollution, usually classified by environment, are air pollution, water pollution, and land pollution. Modern society is also concerned about specific types of pollutants, such as noise pollution, light pollution, and plastic pollution. Pollution of all kinds can have negative effects on the environment and wildlife and often impacts human health and well-being.

Sanskrit: Sanskrit is an Indo-Aryan language of the ancient Indian subcontinent with a 3,500-year history. It is the primary liturgical language of Hinduism and the predominant language of most works of Hindu philosophy as well as some of the principal texts of Buddhism and Jainism. Sanskrit, in its variants and numerous dialects, was the lingua franca of ancient and medieval India. In the early 1st millennium AD, along with Buddhism and Hinduism, Sanskrit migrated to Southeast Asia, parts of East Asia and Central Asia, emerging as a language of high culture and of local ruling elites in these regions.

Sensor and IoT: The internet of things (IoT) is a system of interrelated computing devices, mechanical and digital machines provided with unique identifiers (UIDs) and the ability to transfer data over a network without requiring human-to-human or human-to-computer interaction. Sensors are devices that detect and respond to changes in an environment. Inputs can come from a variety of sources such as light, temperature, motion and pressure. Sensors output valuable information and if they are connected to a network, they can share data with other connected devices and management systems. They are an integral part of the Internet of Things (IoT).There are many types of IoT sensors and an even greater number of applications and use cases.

Vedic: The Vedic period or Vedic age (c. 1500 – c. 500 BCE), is the period in the history of the northern Indian subcontinent between the end of the urban Indus Valley Civilization and a second urbanization which began in the central Indo-Gangetic Plain c. 600 BCE. It gets its name from the Vedas, which are liturgical texts containing details of life during this period that have been interpreted to be historical and constitute the primary sources for understanding the period. These documents, alongside the corresponding archaeological record, allow for the evolution of the Vedic culture to be traced and inferred.

Yajna: Yajna literally means "sacrifice, devotion, worship, offering", and refers in Hinduism to any ritual done in front of a sacred fire, often with mantras. Yajna has been a Vedic tradition, described in a layer of Vedic literature called Brahmanas, as well as Yajurveda. The tradition has evolved from offering oblations and libations into sacred fire to symbolic offerings in the presence of sacred fire (Agni).

Chapter 5
The Need for Adaptive Organizational Systems Concerning Proactive Health Literacy Approaches in the Misinformation State of COVID-19

Darrell Norman Burrell
https://orcid.org/0000-0002-4675-9544
The Florida Institute of Technology, USA & Capitol Technology University, USA

ABSTRACT

When it comes to COVID-19 in America, the country represents four percent of the global population but accounts for 22% of global COVID-19 deaths. The convergence of misrepresentation and rapid growth contagious are considered interrelated. Social media has played a significant role in the spread of myths and misconceptions concerning COVID-19, and as a result, health literacy has become critical to fighting the virus. Misinformation has come to define COVID-19 due to unrelenting public fables misinformation on everything from the virus being a hoax, untested cures, and the uselessness of wearing facemasks. Health literacy is the extent to which the public and patients can acquire and understand essential health knowledge required to make proper health choices and decisions. The inquiry employs a content analysis of current literature and qualitative interviews to explore practical organizational adaptive approaches that promote COVID-19 health literacy.

OBJECTIVES, METHODS, AND RESULTS

The objective of this study is to shed light on the importance of adaptive organizational systems change concerning health literacy in the age of COVID 19. As for the method, this study employs a content analysis

DOI: 10.4018/978-1-7998-8996-0.ch005

of current literature and qualitative interviews of 12 accomplished researchers and subject matter experts on health literacy. The results classify the barriers to adaptive organizational change concerning health literacy in medical organizations, the best practices for literacy, and the new approaches needed because of COVID 19. Recommendations are outlined for medical providers to promote adaptive organizational systems by incorporating health literacy programs to identify patients with low health literacy, improve health literacy, and impact health outcomes concerning disease and health condition management.

OVERVIEW

Low health literacy is a public health travesty. Health information and health literacy around COVID 19 is a miscalculated public health conundrum. Zarocostas (2020) referred to the COVID 19 not as a pandemic but an info-demic because of the need for patients to be more health literate when they are being bombarded by inaccurate or misleading information from social media, public officials, and family. During a global pandemic, the need to understand and explore health literacy's nuances has never been more pressing. This qualitative exploratory study uses the expertise of subject matter experts on health literacy to classify the barriers to health information literacy, the best practices for improving health information literacy, and the additional measures are taken by medical providers during the COVID 19 outbreak ensure that patients have the most accurate and useful health information. Health literacy is an area in need of significant attention in health information management and health services delivery because it is often a critical factor in disease risk management. Health literacy is essential with the outbreak of COVID 19, especially in an age when so much inaccurate health information is readily available.

Paakkari and Okan (2020) outlined that health literacy concerning COVID 19, also known as the Coronavirus, is an underestimated public health challenge. Zarocostas (2020) referred to the COVID 19 not as a pandemic but an infodemic because of the need for patients to be more health literate at a time when they are being bombarded by inaccurate or misleading information from social media. COVID 19 has created two significant public health paradoxes (Paakkari & Okan, 2020). One has to do with the importance of health literacy as a critical aspect of risk management in contagious diseases (Paakkari & Okan, 2020). The second has to do with the need for accurate information for everyone regarding pandemic planning and risk (Paakkari & Okan, 2020). High levels of health literacy and compliance depend on reliable and readily available information on the nature of threats, disease transmission, risk safety protocols, and protective measures (Paakkari and Okan, 2020; Zarocostas, 2020). With COVID 19, a significant number of people lack accurate information on the symptoms, proper risk management strategies and believe in fictitious conspiracy theories concerning the existence, emergence, and risks of the disease (Frieden, 2020). According to Spring (2020), since the outbreak of COVID 19, social media and the Internet have burst with a significant amount of false news and information about the disease, which has hampered health literacy. Incorrect Social media stories, citizens, and politicians have distributed conflicting messages about the symptoms of COVID 19, how it is transmitted, and the effectiveness of gloves and face masks (Spring, 2020; Frieden, 2020).

HEALTH LITERACY

Health literacy is an individual's capacity to obtain, interpret, and understand the necessary health information and services to improve their health (Andrews, 2014). The supposition is that for patients to accomplish health literacy duties, they must be acquainted with health-related terms, comprehend discharge instructions, understand medication instructions, and have some actionable knowledge of how a health care system works so they can navigate it to access the care they need (Grace, 2016; Smith, 2020; Andrews, 2014; Jean, 2017).

Health literacy is conditional on an individual's capability to manage health information given to them to help them manage their conditions (Andrews, 2014). Health literacy also concerns the ability to comprehend information in forms, discharge instructions, brochures, and information concerning symptoms and side effects (Alberti, 2014). The inability to become health literate can put patients at risk for harm and can lead to longer recovery times (Drake, 2015). A strong hope to change the conversation on leadership practices concerning health literacy can revolutionize healthcare services and open the door to repair the damage-causing inadequate patient care and healthcare disparities (Smith, 2020; Carlton, 2016). If patients are not health literate then this could provent them from becoming effective at the management of their illness, the prevention of disease, and the change in risky health behaivors (Sarfo, 2018). For example, taking a prescription necessitates a patient how to take a medication, when to take the prescription, the dosage, and even the specialized instructions including taking the prescripton with food or not, or the side effects like do not drive cause it could cause drowsiness (Sarfo, 2018; Smith, 2020).

Impact of Low Health Literacy

Patients will often mask their lack of comprehension of instructions, directions, or information to evade the embarrassment not being health literate (Sarfo, 2018). Patients with low literacy skills have a 50% increased risk of hospitalization than patients with adequate literacy skills (Sarfo, 2018). Low health literacy leads to poor illness management skills including improper management of medications and inappropriate prevention activities (Sarfo, 2018). Research indicates that patients with low health literacy are less likely to follow treatment protocols, are less effective at following medical direction, have higher risks of hospitalizations, and have more prescription miscalculations (Sarfo, 2018).

Health literacy affects all individuals but is more frequently identified in older adults with limited English language command, individuals of lower socioeconomic status, and lower educational level (Grace, 2016; Smith, 2020; Andrews, 2014; Jean, 2017). Low health literacy significantly correlates with poorer health outcomes and more inferior use of health resources (Grace, 2016; Smith, 2020; Andrews, 2014; Jean, 2017). The yearly price of low health literacy to the U.S. economy was $106 billion to $238 billion (Vernon, Trujillo, & Rosenbaum, 2007). Patients with low health literacy have a lesser probability of getting flu shots, comprehending medical labels and guidelines, and a greater likelihood of taking medicines improperly compared to adults with superior health literacy. (Bennett, 2008; Sarfo, 2018). Patients with inadequate health literacy reported inferior health conditions and were less probable to use preventative care (Andrews, 2014). Patients with low levels of health literacy are more likely to be hospitalized and have poorer disease management outcomes (Sarfo, 2018). Low health literacy often leads to worse health outcomes, and the causal relationship between health literacy and health outcomes is not entirely (Grace, 2016; Smith, 2020; Andrews, 2014; Jean, 2017). Limited health literacy is recognized to have strong associations with age, socioeconomic status, educational level, race, ethnic origin, and poorer health outcomes (Grace, 2016; Smith, 2020; Andrews, 2014; Jean, 2017). Health literacy echelons are influenced by linguistic variances which are connected to health inequalities for those where English is not a first language, immigrants, and those of minority groups (Grace, 2016; Smith, 2020; Andrews, 2014; Jean, 2017).

The Absence of Knowledge and Engagement

Nearly one-half of the United States residents are touched by low health literacy, yet health care clinicians are often not trained with the tools to identify patients with limited health literacy (Sarfo, 2018; Smith, 2020). Skillful health communication requires the health care provider and the patient to engage in a reciprocal dialogue (Andrews, 2014). This clinician-patient engagement is essential when communicating health and treatment material with patients who have minimal health literacy proficiencies (Grace, 2016). A clinician's limited understanding of patient behaviors or attributes correlated with deficient health literacy may impact their capacity to converse successfully (Grace, 2016). Their deficiency of expertise can drastically change how health information is communicated to patients (Smith, 2020). Research has shown that health care providers overestimate a patient's literacy skills (Alberti, 2014). Research outlines that over 40% of physicians misjudge the level of patient's literacy (Alberti, 2014).

Nurses and doctors are often unmindful that a patient has poor health literacy and often do not have the tools or the training to diagnose a patient's degree of health literacy or improve a patient's health literacy level (Grace, 2016; Jean, 2017). Strategies for addressing the issue are often low-priority or absent in medical organizations (Grace, 2016; Jean, 2017). Research has outlined that frequently nursing and other clinicians have limited understanding of health literacy, a limited understanding of how increasing health literacy can improve health outcomes and that health literacy is a low priority in patients' treatment protocols (Grace, 2016; Jean, 2017). The nurse plays a vital role in direct patient care and delivering health services (Grace, 2016; Jean, 2017). Educating nurses, doctors, physician assistants, and medical center office staff on the issue and reaching them better communications approach is critical to increasing health literacy among patients (Grace, 2016; Jean, 2017).

Provider-patient interactions are inherent in any health care delivery model (Carlton, 2016). Suppose the current healthcare leadership conversations reveal a vast chasm of confounding outcomes stemming from limited health literacy, a lack of interprofessional partnerships, and mishandling of cross-cultural engagement (Andrews, 2014). Barriers in communication continue to be a significant concern for disparities interest groups hoping to transform patient care through healthcare leadership communication (Smith, 2020). Leaders face challenges in adopting changes to improve healthcare conditions for patients. Miscommunication between healthcare professionals is a leading cause of poor conditions and serious medical errors (Freeman, Holderbery-Fox, & Houspian, 2015). Dysfunction in a clinician's communication competency causes distrust among patients. Disparaging interpersonal communication barriers insinuate that further discussions are necessary to address patient care (2015).

Miscommunication of Health Information Leads to Issues

Common health information miscommunication problems reveal how leadership conversations become problematic (Andrews, 2014). Fostering collaborative capital, connecting disjointed interprofessional teams, and understanding cultural sensitivity is crucial to healthcare leadership development around health literacy (Grace, 2016; Andrews, 2014). Operating within confined parameters will divide subcultural networks with an authority gradient. Mitigating the consequences of hierarchy prevent fluidity in interprofessional communication and cause patients to mismanage or misunderstand their care and treatment (Morris & Mathews, 2014).

Health information miscommunication can often inflate barriers to a sufficient understanding of treatment and care (Marx, 2014). Improving cross-functional workplace communication dysfunction pinpoints silos as an area of concern (Marx, 2014). Barriers to streamline interprofessional communication present ineffective methods to disseminate information (Howard, 2016). Leaders who do not seek partnerships, ownership of outcomes, integration, and inclusion strengthen barriers restricting the exchange of useful information concerning health literacy (Andrews, 2014). Disparities are inevitable with limited healthcare literacy resources, and it demonstrates a lack of cultural sensitivity in practice (Andrews, 2014).

Adaptive Organizational Systems

The clinical microsystem provides a conceptual and practical framework for approaching organizational learning and delivery of care healthcare organizations are, in some sense, conglomerates of smaller systems, not coherent monolithic organizations (Burrell, 2020). Adaptive performance refers to a performance dimension that does not fit into either of the typically considered task and contextual performance domains (Allworth & Hesketh, 1999). The task performance domain refers to the necessary behaviors to complete the tasks required of one's position and contribute to its success (Borman & Motowidlo, 1993). In contrast, contextual performance refers to the behaviors that contribute to creating a thriving work environment (Burrell, 2020). These behaviors are valuable to the organization in that they can promote a positive effect out of others, improve interpersonal communication, and promote cohesiveness and teamwork (Cheung-Judge & Holbeche, 2015). At its core, adaptive performance is the ability of people to manage and succeed in unfamiliar situations (Cheung-Judge & Holbeche, 2015)

The ability to adapt is becoming more of a necessity and less of a luxury, especially with the world of work changing rapidly (Koenigsbauer, 2018). Frequently referred to as adaptive performance, viewing performance is more than merely an achievement of outcomes. Still, it includes applying learning from one task to the next, maintaining composure when things get hard, and moving between contexts and cultures efficiently (Koenigsbauer, 2018).

Cultural Adjustment and Adaptation

Culture refers to how those in an organization interact with the workplace environment around them through observation and experiences and how they make sense of a changing environment (Cheung-Judge & Holbeche, 2015). Being put in these ambiguous and new situations can be a significant source of work and non-work-related stress (Cheung-Judge & Holbeche, 2015). It should be no surprise that this is an essential dimension of adaptive performance. Within the context of adaptive performance, cultural adaptability is the ability of an individual to perform at a high level in different cultures and adjusting one's interpersonal style to continue to achieve goals when working with new teams and groups of individuals (Cheung-Judge & Holbeche, 2015). As the workplace continues to change and evolve, there will be a growing interest in how leaders can be adaptive and continue to perform at a high level (Burrell, 2020). Moreover, it will become critical that leaders are adaptive and encourage those they lead to striving to be the same (Burrell, 2020).

FUTURE IMPACT OF CHANGING THE HEALTH LITERACY CONVERSATION

Creating healthcare organizational cultures that can adapt and employ new engagement approaches around health information and literacy includes restructuring teamwork and educating both patients and clinicians (Smith, 2020). Healthcare leaders who seek reform will adapt to modified communication strategies that encourage leadership development in health literacy (Grace, 2016). Effective communication channels to share information will validate leadership sentiments to develop a greater interconnectivity sense (Andrews, 2014). Creating subcultural networks will legitimize partnerships and shared outcomes concerning patient care education (Andrews, 2014). Incorporating multiple diverse methods of communication, such as face-to-face contact, e-mails, and video conferencing will increase rates of contact (LeBreton, 2015).

As a result, improved clinical performance and cross-training will advance operations to procure productivity and proficiency concerning information sharing and information accuracy (Kic-Drgas, 2015). A useful method to health literacy necessitates the nurse, doctor, or physician assistant to determinedly engage the patient by drawing pictures, using videos, using the teach-back method for comprehension, and using everyday language to help the patient find clarity about how to manage their discharge best (LeBreton, 2015). Research shows that patients want to know what is wrong, what they need to do about it, and why, and they want to understand the benefits of the treatment as it applies to them (Howard, 2016). The teach-back method, teach-to-goal, and using plain language are examples of communication skills that promote health literacy and independent decision-making, integral to patient-centered care (LeBreton, 2015).

Pollio (2018) outlined that when patients are encouraged to increase health literacy, their correlated hazards for healthcare-associated mistakes are decreased, thereby enhancing patient safety and disease management and health outcomes. Smith (2020) outlined that a higher level of health literacy can increase knowledge about the importance of access to health services and treatment in a timely or more appropriate manner with the correct medical provider. The challenge health providers must address is measuring staff and patients' competency in solving all the issues related to health literacy (Grace, 2016). Drake's (2015) health literacy research asserted that a patient's high education level and profession of higher socioeconomic status does always equal a high level of health literacy. Bewilderment, the lack of comprehension, or both, is often the result of poor communication, leading to errors with medication usage, execution of discharge instructions, or the management of health conditions (Carlton, 2015). Suppose individuals do not have the health literacy concerning access to health services when needed (Howard, 2016). In that case, they do not promptly receive the latest treatments and the appropriate care by the right medical provider (Andrews, 2014).

Health care providers expect patients to have the skills to read medication labels, appointment slips, consent documents, and health education materials (Sarfo, 2018). When patients cannot read or are not able to read well, they are more likely to withhold their literacy limitations from the health care provider because of shame and embarrassment (Sarfo, 2018). Patients with low performing health literacy have the propensity to suffer humiliation, feelings of insufficiency, worry, and minimal self-esteem (Sarfo, 2018). Patient cultural norms and practices impact health literacy. Research in psychiatry, psychology, sociology, and anthropology document substantial differences in how people experience, understand, and discuss illness as well as their willingness to seek help (Sarfo, 2018).

RESEARCH METHOD

Interviews were conducted with 12 researchers with expertise and research on health literacy. Interviews were conducted using ZOOM video conferencing software due to COVID 19 social distancing restrictions. All participants had a doctorate degree with more than five post-doctorate years of academic research. All participants also had to have a minimum of 5 years of professional healthcare experience. Six participants were male, and six were female. They were selected based on peer-reviewed research studies indexed in Google Scholar, ResearchGate, and Academia.edu. All participants had over 300 citations on Google Scholar. They were asked questions about their perceptions of health literacy barriers and the best practices to improve health literacy by patients with COVID-19.

Data Results

Research Question 1 - **What do you see as the barriers to adaptive performance around better COVID-19 health communication and health literacy at medical practices, hospitals, and medical facilities?**

The following were themed responses to this question:

- Many healthcare clinicians have limited information about the issues and impacts of low health literacy.
- A lack of understanding of how much health literacy would improve health outcomes
- The belief that health literacy is not a significant problem
- Lack of time to screen patients
- Health literacy is a low priority.
- A perception that a health literacy program would too difficult to implement because staff members are already too busy, and there was a concern as to who would have ownership and responsibility for the program.
- A lack of leadership support
- A lack of understanding that everyone in the medical office plays a role in health literacy.

Research Question 2 - **Based on your expertise and experiences, what do you see as the best practices for adaptive performance in implementing COVID- 19 health literacy programs in healthcare facilities?**

The following were themed responses to this question:

- Staff training – All staff needs to be fully trained in health literacy's importance to disease management and improved health outcomes for patients. Staff also need to have tools and an understanding of how to use those tools to help patients.
- Health literacy screening tools/questionnaires – Medical facilities needed to implement protocols to address and identify patients with low health literacy levels.
- Repeat back exercises- This is when patients are asked to repeat back treatment information, medication dosage directions, and health instructions to ensure that they understand what to do after leaving the medical office. A unanimous consensus regarding the preferred method to confirm a patient's understanding is to have the patient repeat back the information in their own words.

- Use patient education material (Fliers, Brochures, letters, videotapes)- Medical facilities need to invest in educational material development to understand better their role and steps in managing their conditions.
- Training for all medical office professionals on communicating about health conditions in plain language or using plain terms.
- Follow-up survey to see if the patient has any questions or needs additional information from the hospital's medical office.
- Follow up letter and e-mail with discharge instructions, medication directions, or self-care information even after discussing it with a patient in the medical office.
- Follow-up texts with discharge instructions, medication directions, or self-care information even after it is discussed with the patient in the medical office.

Because there was so much misinformation on social media about COVID-19, what do you recommend as additional practices that should be explicitly implemented to promote more accurate health literacy around COVID 19?

The following were themed responses to this question:

- Physician-led webinars for patients that are live and taped are intended to educate patients with accurate health information. The rationale would be that a person would be more likely to trust the information provided by their doctor over information shared through social media.
- Ask all patients that have appointments for other conditions if they wish to be tested for COVID 19.
- Medical offices should send E-mailed updates about testing policies, procedures, and safety precautions for patients directly around COVID 19.
- Health literacy screening tools/questionnaires explicitly designed for COVID 19
- Repeat back exercises- This is when patients are asked to repeat back treatment information, medication dosage directions, and health instructions to ensure that they understand what to do when they leave the medical office concerning COVID 19. There was a unanimous consensus regarding the preferred method to confirm a patient's understanding is to have the patient repeat back the information in their own words.
- Create a COVID 19 website for the medical facility where patients can get accurate content and up to date information.
- Use educational blogs to provide information specifically about COVID 19.
- The use of handouts and brochures with accurate information on COVID 19 is given to every patient that visits the medical facility.

DISCUSSIONS AND CONCLUSIONS

Successfully countering the misinformation about the impact of wearing masks, proper treatments, and risks surrounding the COVID-19 pandemic will play a significant role in the reduction of new infections, increased hospitalizations, and deaths (Bagherpour & Nouri, 2020). Research shows that honest and proactive communications and messaging are critical in educating the public about the precautions needed to keep everyone safe (Bagherpour & Nouri, 2020). Social media has played a significant role in the spread of myths and misconceptions concerning COVID-19, and as a result, health literacy has become critical to fighting the virus (Bagherpour & Nouri, 2020).

Healthcare leaders can change the conversation to diminish miscommunication through engagement in activities that support improving patient care through health literacy, which is critical as people continue to lose their lives and become hospitalized due to COVID 19 (Paakkari and Okan, 2020; Zarocostas, 2020). All too often, stagnation in adaptive organizational systems provides barriers to health literacy (Andrews, 2014). Process solutions may include the following effective resolutions:

- Utilize health literacy screening tools.
- Oversee the effectiveness of training with open dialogue that responds to patients' and providers' feedback concerning health literacy.
- Train staff on cultural competency issues around health literacy.
- Create interprofessional teams are driving cooperation and positive engagement around health literacy.
- Implement health literacy programs that include both staff and patient education.
- Create on-going patient communications strategies that include verbal, mailed, e-mailed, and texted to patients.

Healthcare organizational systems will experience better patient care outcomes cultivating health literacy leadership programs (Andrews, 2014). These programs can result in a progressive stance to reduce health disparities (Redden, 2017). Health literacy programs expand cross-cultural disciplinary techniques that inhibit participatory relationships that change the nature and utility of conversations in the healthcare system (Smith, 2020). Changing, increasing, and improving health literacy conversations provide higher quality patient care, give hope to patients in recovery, and bring faith to a system designed to save lives (Jean, 2017).

REFERENCES

Alberti, T. L. (2014). *Health literacy and health information-seeking behaviors are associated with adherence to discharge instructions (Order No. 3580089)*. Available from ProQuest Dissertations & Theses Global.

Allworth, E., & Hesketh, B. (1999). Construct-oriented biodata: Capturing change-related and contextually relevant future performance. *International Journal of Selection and Assessment, 7*(2), 97–111. doi:10.1111/1468-2389.00110

Andrews, M. (2014). *Health literacy competencies for health professionals: A Delphi study (Order No. 3648821)*. Available from ProQuest Dissertations & Theses Global.

Bagherpour, A., & Nouri, A. (2020, October 11). COVID Misinformation Is Killing People: This "infodemic" has to stop. *Scientific American*.

Borman, W. C., & Motowidlo, S. J. (1993). Expanding the criterion domain to include elements of contextual performance. In N. Schmitt & W. C. Borman (Eds.), *Personnel selection in organizations*. Jossey-Bass.

Burrell, D. N. (2020). Management consulting intervention case study in a complex and toxic hospital organizational culture. *Holistica Journal of Business and Public Administration, 11*(2), 100–114. doi:10.2478/hjbpa-2020-0022

Carlton, C. E. (2016). *Evaluation of health literacy as a predictor of the need for additional medical care (Order No. 10111908)*. Available from ProQuest Dissertations & Theses Global.

Cheung-Judge, M. Y., & Holbeche, L. (2015). *Organization development: A practitioner's guide for OD and HR*. Kogan Page Limited.

Donaldson, L. (2001). *The contingency theory of organizations*. Sage. doi:10.4135/9781452229249

Drake, G. (2015). *Health literacy: The knowledge, experience, and education of advanced practice registered nurses in Arizona (Order No. 3710735)*. Available from ProQuest Dissertations & Theses Global.

Formosa, C. (2015). Understanding power and communication relationships in health settings. British Journal of Healthcare Management, 21(9), 420-424.

Freeman, D., Holderby-Fox, L. R., & Housepian, G. (2015). Best practices and cost controls: Improving healthcare access through innovation and communication. *Tennessee Journal Of Law & Policy, 10*(3), 108–144.

Frieden, J. (2020, June 10). *Lack of Health Literacy a Barrier to Grasping COVID-19*. MedPage. Retrieved from: https://www.medpagetoday.com/infectiousdisease/covid19/87002

Glymph, D. C., Olenick, M., Barbera, S., Brown, E. L., Prestianni, L., & Miller, C. (2015). Healthcare Utilizing Deliberate Discussion Linking Events (HUDDLE): A Systematic Review. AANA Journal, 83(3), 183-188.

Grace, S. O. (2016). *Nursing assessment of health literacy (Order No. 10012950)*. Available from ProQuest Dissertations & Theses Global.

Haustein, E. (2014). *Management control systems in innovation companies: A contingency theory study* (Order No. 28197618). Available from ProQuest Dissertations & Theses Global. (2440376463).

Hellriegel, D., & Slocum, J. W. Jr. (1973). Organizational design: A contingency approach. *Business Horizons, 16*(2), 59–68. doi:10.1016/S0007-6813(73)80011-4

Howard, S. N. (2016). *Health literacy program proposal for health care workers (Order No. 10145339)*. Available from ProQuest Dissertations & Theses Global.

Jean, A. L. (2017). *Evaluation of nurses patient engagement strategies and perceived effectiveness: Implications for health literacy (Order No. 10260578)*. Available from ProQuest Dissertations & Theses Global.

Kic-Drgas, J. (2015). Communication Conflicts in an International Environment. *Global Management Journal, 7*(1/2), 73–80.

Koewnigsbauer, K. (2018). The workplace evolution. Harvard Business Review Analytic Services.

Lawrence, P. R., & Lorsch, J. W. (1967a). Differentiation and integration in complex organizations. *Administrative Science Quarterly, 12*(1), 1–47. doi:10.2307/2391211

Lawrence, P. R., & Lorsch, J. W. (1967b). *Organization and environment: Managing differentiation and integration.* Division of Research, Graduate School of Business Administration, Harvard University.

LeBreton, M. (2015). *Implementation of a validated health literacy tool with teach-back education in a super utilizer patient population (Order No. 3700719).* Available from ProQuest Dissertations & Theses Global.

Marx, M. (2014). Examining the structural challenges to communication as experienced by nurse managers in two U.S. hospital settings. Journal of Nursing Management, 22(8), 964-973. doi:10.1111/jonm.12091

McCaskey, M. B. (1974). An introduction to organizational design. *California Management Review, 17*(1), 13–20. doi:10.2307/41164556

Mohr, J., Batalden, P., & Barach, P. (2004). Integrating patient safety into the clinical microsystem. *Quality & Safety in Health Care, 13*(suppl 2), ii34–ii38. doi:10.1136/qshc.2003.009571 PMID:15576690

Morris, D., & Matthews, J. (2014). Communication, Respect, and Leadership: Interprofessional Collaboration in Hospitals of Rural Ontario. *Canadian Journal of Dietetic Practice & Research, 75*(4), 173-179. doi:10.3148/cjdpr-2014-020

Nadler, D. A., & Tushman, M. (1988). *Strategic organization design: Concepts, tools & processes.* Scott, Foresman.

Nadler, D. A., & Tushman, M. L. (1990). Beyond the charismatic leader: Leadership and organizational change. *California Management Review, 32*(2), 77–97. doi:10.2307/41166606

Paakkari, L., & Okan, O. (2020). COVID-19: Health literacy is an underestimated problem. *The Lancet. Public Health, 5*(5), e249–e250. https://doi.org/10.1016/S2468-2667(20)30086-4

Pille, R. O. (2016). *Assessing the relationship between health promotion-related health literacy and health psychology's sense of coherence in young adults (Order No. 10130915).* Available from ProQuest Dissertations & Theses Global.

Pollio, E. W. (2018). *Health education materials: Where are the patients? (Order No. 10743845).* Available from ProQuest Dissertations & Theses Global.

Redden, G. M. (2017). *Ambulatory registered nurses' perspectives on health literacy roles and patient communication (Order No. 10257434).* Available from ProQuest Dissertations & Theses Global.

Sarfo, R. (2018). *Relationships among health literacy, self-care, and hospital readmission status in African American adults with heart failure (Order No. 10821653).* Available from ProQuest Dissertations & Theses Global.

Schein, E. H. (1985). Defining organizational culture. *Classics of Organization Theory, 3*, 490-502.

Schein, E. H. (2006). *Organizational culture and leadership* (Vol. 356). John Wiley & Sons.

Smith, H. M. (2020). *Educating medical-surgical nurses to improve nursing knowledge and understanding of health literacy (Order No. 13810361)*. Available from ProQuest Dissertations & Theses Global.

Spring, H. (2020, July). Health literacy and COVID-19. *Health Information and Libraries Journal, 37*(3), 171–172. Advance online publication. doi:10.1111/hir.12322 PMID:32672399

Zajac, E. J., Kraatz, M. S., & Bresser, R. K. (2000). Modeling the dynamics of strategic fit: A normative approach to strategic change. *Strategic Management Journal, 21*(4), 429–453.

Zarocostas, J. (2020). How to fight an infodemic. *Lancet, 395*(10225), 676.

Chapter 6
A Review of the Healthcare System in the State of Punjab, India

Mandeep Kaur
https://orcid.org/0000-0001-5044-8581
Punjabi University, Patiala, India

Baljit Singh
Sri Guru Teg Bahadur Khalsa College, Sri Anandpur Sahib, India

ABSTRACT

This study attempted to analyse the healthcare system in the state of Punjab at a community level, village level, and district level. In the chapter, an attempt is made to review the literature concerned with different aspects such as organizational structure, institutions and infrastructure, service delivery, and healthcare expenditure. It will enable the reader to have a look at the past trends and present functioning of healthcare system of the state and give the reader a direction for further research in the potential areas. This review accounts for various studies conducted in the healthcare in the state of Punjab, India. A thematic comprehensive presentation of literature review is done in this chapter.

INTRODUCTION

Health and Healthcare System in India

"Health is Wealth" and good health is a valuable asset for the nation. The human resource of any country is productive only when it has good health otherwise it is a burden on the growth and development of the country. The World Health Organisation (WHO) defines health as a complete state of physical, mental and social well-being and not merely an absence of infirmity and disease (Arya, 2012; Svalastog et al., 2017). In the Constitution of India, health is given due consideration under different parts of it. The Preamble of the Constitution gives direction to the State for ensuring social, economic & political

DOI: 10.4018/978-1-7998-8996-0.ch006

justice and health sector falls under the term social justice. Article 21 under fundamental rights guarantees protection of life and personal liberty to every citizen. Under the Directive Principles of State Policy (DPSP), Clause No.38 gives direction to the State for the promotion of the welfare of the people and Clause No.47 says that the State shall record the level of nutrition, standard of living of its people and improvement in the public health as its primary duty. Clause 51A of the Fundamental Duties states that there is joint responsibility of State and citizens to ensure maintenance of human and animal health (Mathiharan, 2003; Arya, 2012). The United Nation General Assembly in 2015 gave a collection of 17 Sustainable Development Goals (SDGs) for 2030 Agenda (Transforming our World: the 2030 agenda for sustainable development). The Goal 3 namely, Good health and well-being, ensures universal access to healthcare services, quality & affordable medicines and family planning etc. (Aftab et al., 2020).

In Indian healthcare system, services are delivered through a decentralised approach and organized by a complex network of public and private healthcare providers of states. Public sector includes Ministry of Health and Family Welfare (MoH&FW), state owned Directorate of Health Services and Department of Health and Family Welfare, and after that district-level health services which are providing a link between each state and primary healthcare services. There is lack of information for clear understanding about regulating the private sector in India as there are multiple agencies to regulate under different ministries (Thomson et al., 2013).

The review chapter is divided into sections as mentioned here: Role of Union and state government in framing health policies, Healthcare organizational structure at national level and in Punjab, Healthcare Institutions &Infrastructure, Service Delivery and Healthcare Expenditure.

ROLE OF UNION AND STATE GOVERNMENT IN FRAMING HEALTH POLICIES

The Central government is concerned with assisting the state activities, promoting research and professional education for health and States are responsible for providing health services to all citizens (Patel & Patel, 2017). In 1943, Bhore Committee was appointed by Government of India (GOI) to review the health and medical needs of India and its recommendations were given due consideration during the Five Year Plans. It recommended for controlling communicable diseases and developing health institutions for better health services to the people. In 1962 Mudaliar Committee was appointed to evaluate the performance of health sector. It found that conditions in Primary Health Centres (PHCs) were unsatisfactory and committee recommended to strengthen the existing PHCs before establishing new ones (Arya, 2012). Health was given priority also in the First Five Year Plan (1951-56) by mentioning that nothing can be considered more important than the health of the people and it was an essential factor for the efficiency of industry and of agriculture. At the time of independence, the healthcare infrastructure was very poor in rural areas and on 2 October, 1952, rural health services were launched by establishing Primary Health Centres (PHCs) in each block having a population of 66000. At the end of Third Five Year Plan (1961-66) the country became successful to lay the foundation of basic health services. The Sixth Five Year Plan (1980-85) has focused on "Health For All" (HFA 2000 AD). In Seventh Five Year Plan (1985-90), focus was given on consolidating the health infrastructure that has already been developed. The Ninth Five Year Plan has identified the factors responsible for the poor functioning of the public health institutions and focused to rectify the gaps (Suthanthiraveeran, 2011). The first National Health Policy (NHP) was made in 1983 by the Parliament of India. It was a response to Alma Ata Declaration to achieve Health For All by 2000. The NHP 1983 mentioned the failures of the government in health sector in India. It focused on the provision of universal and comprehensive primary healthcare services. It suggested for integration with private & voluntary organisations and also for a decentralised health care system. It was updated in 2002 and NHP 2002 focused on the improved funding, health infrastructure and equitable access for health care services (Arya, 2012). To reform the healthcare sector, NRHM (National Rural Health Mission) is launched in 2005 which has an objective to improve the healthcare for the poor in rural. The aim of RSBY (Rashtriya Swasthya Bima Yojana) is to provide financial protection from OOP expenditure and it is providing insurance coverage for selected hospital expenses to people below poverty line. It is analysed that reform should address the requirement of increased public expenditure on healthcare & its distribution should be just and fair also and greater focus should be given to low-income states (Rao and Choudhury, 2012).

The Union Government has enacted The Clinical Establishments Act, 2010 to register and regulate, prescribe the minimum standards for facilities and services provided by the all type of clinical establishments in the country. Till now, this act has been implemented by 11 states and 6 UTs. It is applicable on both public and private sector establishments (including single doctor clinics) except those run by armed forces.

Recently in March 2017, Union Cabinet, GOI approved the NHP 2017, which is India's 3rd National Health Policy. The policy concentrates on providing free drugs, free diagnosis, free emergency and essential healthcare services in all public health institutions for an accessible and well-equipped healthcare system. The policy aims to make comprehensive primary health care by establishing 'Health & Wellness Centres'(Gupta & Kumari, 2017). Some other health initiatives taken by Punjab Health Systems Corporation (PHSC), in healthcare sector are as mentioned here. Pardhan Mantri Janaushadi Pariyojana is a govt. of India campaign, started in December 2008 under which it was decided to provide cheaper and non-branded generic medicines through the janaushadi outlets inall districts of Punjab. In every civil hospital of Punjab except those in Fatehgarh Sahib and Ropar, the Jan Aushadi Kendras are operational. Telemedicine Project was launched in 2005 on a pilot basis in 3 hospitals of Punjab with the aid of ISRO and PGIMER. After the successful implementation at first stage it was extended and there are currently 27 nodes in total under this project. Till Aug 2016, total 6,109 consultations were done by using the telemedicine in these different nodes. Punjab Nirogi Society is a scheme to provide financial assistance to poor patients who are living below poverty line and suffering from major life threatening disease to receive medical treatment at any of the hospital under government. Ayushman Bharat Sarbat Sehat Bima Yojana is flagship scheme of Government of India that was recommended by National health Policy 2017 and launched to achieve the universal health coverage. The scheme was designed to meet the Sustainable Development Goals (SDGs) set to be achieved by 2030. Punjab government has implemented this scheme by providing an entitlement based cashless health insurance cover of Rs.5 lakhs per family per year. There are government and empanelled private hospitals to avail the cashless treatment. The cost is shared by central and state government in 60:40 ratio under this scheme.

Punjab government has signed a MOU with union government on June 15, 2006 for National Rural Health Mission (NRHM), the aim of which is to fill the gaps in the healthcare delivery in rural areas. This focuses on investing on basic health services at existing facilities instead of creating the new ones. Janani Suraksha Yojana (JSY) is not strongly implemented in Punjab as there is only 2.7% women in state who received financial assistance under JSY whereas national average is 13.3%. Rashtriya Swasthya Bima Yojana (RSBY) is implemented in Punjab on July 2008 and it covered all districts by 2010 in the state. Out of those patients who are availing the benefits of RSBY, 58.14% are females and average age of these patients is 47 years and patients are commonly hospitalized for either 1, 3 or 5 days (Asfaw et al., 2014). According to *Economic Survey 2019-2020* of Punjab, the state is at rank 5th on the public health aspect of Good Governance Index of Ministry of Statistics. Health is a state subject but even though, Punjab does not have its own health policy and it is also continuing the policies of central government. It reveals that during five year plans the focus is given on health infrastructure & health Sub-centres and a Public Health System Corporation (PHSC) is set up in 1996-97 covering 150 hospitals (Planning Commission, 2002).

Recently in October-2020, Government of Punjab has enacted its own Punjab Clinical Establishments (Registration and regulation) Act, 2020 on the lines of Union Government Clinical Establishment Act, 2010.

In Table 1, the studies regarding the healthcare policies, initiatives and other schemes are shown up. National health policy by the union government is only the policy that is followed by the states too in framing their health related programmes. A state specific health policy is suggested to ensure proper utilization of allocated resources, qualitative improvement in health services for the common people, vulnerable groups, women and children, for regulating both private and public sector and there is urgent need for large public investment in health sector that should be in favour of vulnerable & weaker sections of the society.

Table 1. Studies regarding the union/state government healthcare policies and other initiatives

Author/s and Year	Location	Objective	Results
Arya, 2012	Mumbai	To comparatively analyse the public and private health services, availability and utilization pattern.	Discussed about committees and commissions formed in India for healthcare and their recommendations.
Suthanthiraveeran, 2011	India	To describe the implementation of health policy in India in the Five year plans period.	Reviewed and discussed in detail all the five year plans, their targets and achievements.
Rao and Choudhury, 2012	India	To review the salient features of healthcare system, health status and recent healthcare financing reforms.	Discussed National Health Policies, National Rural Health Mission and Rashtriya Suraksha Bima Yojana; Low levels of public spending i.e, only 1% of GDP.
Gupta & Kumari, 2017	India	To review the National Health Policy, 2017.	Thoroughly discussed the priority areas under NHP 2017, role of state in implementation and challenges faced.
Asfaw et al., 2014	Punjab	To review the healthcare service delivery in state.	Explored about Janani Suraksha Yojana and Rashtriya Suraksha Bima Yojana, their programme implementation and structure, scheme successes and challenges in Punjab.

ORGANIZATIONAL STRUCTURE OF HEALTHCARE SYSTEM

At National Level

India's healthcare sector has federal structure and federal-state divisions and state governments are responsible for providing and organizing health services in their respective states. The central government is responsible for health related treaties, national disease control, framing national health policies and regulating the healthcare system.

A Review of the Healthcare System in the State of Punjab, India

The health system at national level is comprised of 3 institutions i.e., Ministry of Health and Family Welfare, The Directorate General of Health services and The Central council of Health and Family Welfare. The healthcare sector organisation in the country extends from national level to village level and it can be studied differently at national, state, district, community, primary health centres and sub-centres levels (PGCHSM, 2013). The synoptic view of health sector in India is shown. (See Diagram 1)

Figure 1. Organisational structure of health system in India
Source: http://www.iapsmgc.org/userfiles/file/MODULES%20OF%20PGCHSM/Mod2_Ch6A_Organisation%20of%20 health%20care%20in%20India.pdf

The Indian healthcare system is comprised of public sector, private sector, NGOs and firms. The public actors in healthcare system of India include the Ministry of Health and Family Welfare, then state governments and municipal and local bodies. Each state in country has its own Directorate of Health services and Department of Health and Family Welfare. In public sector there is 3-tier structure i.e., primary, secondary and tertiary facilities. In public sector there is network of sub-centres, PHCs and CHCs (Chokshi et al., 2016).

The Directorate of Health Services is principal adviser to the union government in matters of public health and medical both.

The Central Council of Health considers and recommends broad outlines for the policies of remedial and preventive care, environment hygiene, health education and promotion of facilities for training and research.

Private sector in the country is not well regulated and most of the facilities are not registered with the concerned medical council and about 40% of the private care is provided by unqualified providers. The government sponsored schemes in the country are also relying on private sector hospitals as part

Table 2. Public healthcare system under ministry of health & family welfare

Sr. No.	Level	Infrastructure	Facilities	Population Served
1.	**Sub-Centre (SHC):** First point of contact between primary health care system and community	Own building, 1 male and 1 female health worker.	For maternal health and health counselling.	Around 3000 in Tribal and hilly areas, 5000 in plains.
2.	**Primary Health Centre:** Providing link between village community and a medical officer	Comprises of 6 sub-centres having 4-6 beds for patients.	For curative & preventive services.	20,000 – 30,000 people
3.	**Community Health Centre:**	Managed and controlled by state government having 4 medical specialists, 21 paramedical and other staff, 30 beds, laboratory, X-ray	Provide referral as well as specialist health care to the rural population	Cover 80,000-1,20,000 people load
4.	**Sub-Divisional hospitals**	31-100 beds or more. **Category 1:** 31-50 beds. **Category 2:** 51-100 beds. Fully operationalized	Round the clock emergency care and blood storage is available.	5-6 lakhs people
5.	**District Level**	75-500 beds	Provides effective, affordable health care services (curative including specialist services, preventive and promotive); Function as a secondary level referral centre for the public health institutions; provide wide ranging technical and administrative support and education and training for primary health care.	Varies from 35,000 to 30 lakhs in big districts.

Source: Indian Public Health Standards, 2012

of public-private partnerships. There is lack of clarity about the fact that which councils or entities are responsible for the regulation of private sector (Thomson et al., 2013). Approximately 70% of population in country is availing services from private health sector. The private sector is comprised of single clinic, multi-speciality clinic, single hospital, multi-speciality hospital, super-speciality hospital, trust hospital, corporate hospital and medical colleges (PGCHSM, 2013).

At State Level

Punjab is a prosperous state and has growing economy also. The Punjab Health System Corporation (PHSC), Department of Health & Family Welfare, Government of Punjab is responsible for providing preventive, promotive and curative health services to the people of state through a 3-tier structure. PHSC functions under the DOH&FW and it monitors and coordinates public hospitals in implementation of various schemes. At village level, department is playing very crucial role in facilitating program delivery and spreading awareness in rural areas. It consists of Subsidiary-Health Centres (SHCs) at below providing basic healthcare services, above it there are Primary Health centres (PHCs). To support PHCs there is secondary level healthcare system which spread over the district through civil hospitals, sub-divisional and district hospitals. Above all there is tertiary level health care system, which provides services of

Table 3. Studies regarding organizational structure of healthcare system

Author/s or Reports and Year	Location	Objective	Results
Chokshi et al., 2016	India	To describe the public health structure in the country and trace the evolution of major health programmes and initiatives.	Discussed about the Indian public health system at primary, secondary & tertiary level, NRHM and National programmes and initiatives for new-born health.
IPHS, 2012	India	To explain detailed guidelines and standards for PHCs, CHCs, district and sub district hospitals in the country.	Presented the detailed guidelines for standards for infrastructure, personnel, facilities and population served at all levels.
Thomson et al., 2013	India	To study the health care systems of countries at international level.	Explained in detail about the role of government, healthcare delivery system, financing, key entities for health system governance, organizational structure, strategies to ensure quality of care, status of electronic health records, Major innovations and reforms in healthcare sector.
DOH&FW, Punjab	Punjab	To describe organizational structure of healthcare system in the state.	Discussed about the role of Punjab Health System Corporation, Department of Health & Family Welfare and implementation of their schemes, role of SHCs, PHCs, District and sub district hospitals in healthcare delivery.

specialised hospitals & medical colleges. The medical colleges are expected to conduct research & development for health services of the state (DOH&FW, Punjab).

HEALTHCARE INSTITUTIONS AND INFRASTRUCTURE IN PUNJAB

Infrastructure includes the number of public and private health institutions, beds, doctors/nurses in both areas: rural and urban. State public heath institutions include district and sub-district hospitals, CHCs, PHCs and SHCs (Dispensaries of Rural Development and Panchayats). There are total 4,069 subsidiary health centres, 566 PHCs, 369 CHCs, 55 Sub-districts and 31 district hospitals in the state(*Punjab: Land of Five Rivers; IBEF, December 2019*). India's health achievements are very low as compared to the country's income level. Out of 6,28,708 government beds, 1,96,182 beds are in rural areas. The doctor –population ratio in India is 1:1,674 and as per WHO guidelines it must be 1:1000 .

According to the website of *Open Government Data (OGD) Platform India (A Digital India Initiative by Govt. of India)* there are total 1060 private hospitals in the state of Punjab. Private sector has created 63% of total hospital beds in the country from the year 2002 to 2010 and currently providing 80% of outpatient care and 60% of inpatient care (Rao & Choudhury, 2012; Thomson et al., 2013)

There is high rate of vacancies and absenteeism at public health facilities and it is the major reason for difficulty in improvement of healthcare. Either the public clinics are not open or are understaffed. Despite having high income relative to others, Punjab has a vacancy rate of around 20%. There is high rate of absenteeism by health workers and there is almost 15% of absences without any reason. The predominant factor behind the absenteeism is whether a health worker lives close to the facility or not.

In 2005, only 41% of PHCs in Punjab have properly functioned labour rooms and out of these just 35% offered 24-hour facility (Asfaw et al., 2014). According to Statistical Abstract of Punjab 2019 the public medical institutions in the state are hospitals, CHCs, PHCs and dispensaries/SHCs. Amritsar has maximum number of hospitals across all districts & Pathankot and Moga has the least. There are 13 CHCs in Gurdaspur i.e., maximum among all districts and SBS Nagar has only 3 CHCs. The maximum number of dispensaries are in Ludhiana i.e., 286 and minimum is in Pathankot. If we make a look at the special medical institutions in the state, then Jalandhar, Ludhiana and Patiala are on top in this list whereas Moga and Mansa are on bottom. In year 2019 in all over Punjab, 8,08,559 indoor patients and 1,71,54,104 outdoor patients were served. In the year, 2018 there are 495 Ayurveda, 34 Unani and 111 Homeopathic institutions in the state and maximum out of these are in Hoshiarpur and Ludhiana i.e., 51 and 48 respectively. The sanctioned bed capacity in public medical institutions is maximum in Amritsar and Patiala and minimum is in Pathankot. In SAS Nagar, the population served per institution is highest among all districts of Punjab i.e. 11,336 and lowest in SBS Nagar i.e. 5,150 in the year 2019 and population served per bed is highest in Ludhiana i.e. 3,244 individuals. The ratio of beds per '000 population is 1.06 in Amritsar that is highest and 0.30 in Ludhiana that is lowest among the all. The *Economic Survey 2019-20 of Punjab* states that, on an average a medical institution in the state serves a radius of 2.68 kms. The population served per doctor has improved in the state and in 2019 it is 585 individuals per doctor as compared to 1083 in 2015. Government of Punjab is converting all the 2650 sub-centres into Health and Wellness Centres (HWCs) in a phased manner and till now 1365 HWCS have been operationalized in the state.

There is slow increase in number of medical institutions as well as beds in Punjab during last 3 decades which is insufficient to meet the demand of growing population of state. There is also a gap in allocation of health institutions among the districts within Punjab and majority are in 7 districts namely, Ludhiana, Gurdaspur, Jalandhar, Amritsar, Hoshiarpur, Firozpur and Patiala. The population served per institution is highest in Ludhiana i.e., 16247 and lowest in SBS Nagar i.e., 8148. Population served per bed is lowest in Amritsar i.e., 688 and highest in SAS Nagar (1775). Kapurthala, Ropar and newly created districts like Barnala, Fatehgarh Sahib, Mansa, Moga, Muktsar, SAS Nagar, SBS Nagar and Tarntaran lag far behind for the other districts in health infrastructure. Approximately 64% population have confidence in medical institutions of Punjab and 80%-95% of times people in Punjab visit private facilities without considering the fact that whether they live in urban or rural areas and also whether they are suffering from short term or long term illness. Individuals most oftenly seek treatment from a licensed doctor or nurse in state (Asfaw *et al.*, 2014). Infrastructure of the government hospitals is always insufficient for its patients and private hospitals have advance amenities more than that of govt. hospitals as they get many corporate & private investments. Although private hospitals have best equipment, advanced technology, high bed-patients ratio, but these hospitals provide services only to those patients who can afford the treatment costs (Banerjee, 2013).

In Table 4 the studies and reports related to healthcare infrastructure are shown up. There should be greater focus on improving the level of confidence of beneficiaries so that PHCs can perform their functions effectively, efforts should be taken by medical authorities to ensure that staff services are adequate, Women doctors need to be employed at PHCs and there was need for improved public spending to finance infrastructure in rural sub-centres, PHCs, CHCs and district-hospitals (Sreenu, 2012).

Table 4. Studies regarding healthcare infrastructure

Author/s or Reports and Year	Location	Objective	Results
Punjab: Land of Five Rivers, IBEF, 2019	Punjab	To discuss the physical, social and industrial infrastructure of key sectors of state of Punjab.	Discussed thoroughly about economic status of state, health infrastructure and health indicators.
Asfaw et al., 2014	Punjab	To review the healthcare service delivery in state.	Mentioned about the absenteeism and vacancies in public health facilities of state.
Rao & Choudhury, 2012	India	Review of salient features of healthcare system, health status and recent healthcare financing reforms.	Low per-capita GSDP and low expenditure on health sector by states, large vacancies for doctors and other paramedical staff in healthcare facilities.
Banerjee, 2013	Kolkata	To compare the public and private owned healthcare facilities in Kolkata.	In government hospitals, doctors and nurses are well qualified but number of trained employees is not sufficient in these hospitals. On the other hand private facilities offer best services but their employees are not highly qualified and trained.

SERVICE DELIVERY OF PUBLIC AND PRIVATE HEALTH INSTITUTIONS

There are more negative responses than positive ones for the effectiveness of any medical centre which depends upon the service delivery. Analysis showed that beneficiaries are mostly dependent upon the facilities available at the rural health care centres (Sreenu, 2012). At the time of independence, private sector was accountable for just 8% of healthcare services in India but it increased to 60% by the 1990s. *National Sample Survey 1995-96* records that by 1996, private sector was providing 54% rural hospitalization and 70% urban hospitalization. Private sector consists for-profit and not-for-profit organisations (including non-governmental organisations & charitable hospitals), private pharmacies and also unqualified informal service providers. Some of these service providers are registered and some are not. Private sector is providing a large share of primary healthcare. It is easily accessible at convenient timings, provides huge coverage, high quality but it is costly, located in urban areas and poor population finds it unaffordable. The biggest problem in private health sector is that it is growing without any regulation from public sector. *Punjab Human development Report, 2004* mentions that Punjab is one of the highest per-capita income states of India and it is at advanced stage in human development than many other states of India. There is a lack of information about the private medical institutions and in many cases these institutions operates without following the regulations. In rural areas, public sector provides only 7% non-hospitalized treatment & remaining 93% by others (private sector, charitable hospitals and NGOs) and in urban areas it is 6% & 91% respectively. Private facilities cover 90% of cases of non-hospitalized care and over 66% of hospitalized care. Despite heavier costs, the poor strata of Punjab is inclined towards private health service providers. Even though they have the option of free public health services they prefer private ones either due to enough resources or they lack faith in public health facilities. Most of the public health facilities have low capacity, weak administration & supervision, inadequate human resource, vacant post (26% to 38%), acute shortage of specialists because of which all beds available were not utilized (Punjab Governance Reform Commission, 2013). About half

(53%) of the participants access public health facilities; 56.5% for outpatient & 48.4% for inpatient care and among BPL households, 50.6% have been treated in public health sector for outpatient and 51.3% for inpatient healthcare, private services are being utilized more for healthcare related to accidents and non-communicable diseases and public services are being accessed for infections, respiratory problems etc. (Singh et al., 2018).

The satisfaction level of patients for services delivered by hospitals under PHSC, is high on most of the parameters. Both OPD and IPD patients find the location, diagnostic facilities and quality of medical care of public hospitals satisfactory, but still there are difficulties regarding availability of medicines from within the hospitals, delay in obtaining reports of diagnostic tests, and laxity in emergency cases. (Sharma, 2008). Punjab health system is plagued with high absenteeism, low satisfaction with quality care, low quality in clinical care, and with rampant corruption, there are 3 key challenges: cost-incurred, equitable distribution of financial burden of ill-health and ensuring better quality of medical care. In Punjab no. of health institutions in rural areas are growing at a lower rate than that in urban areas, lack of state support and improper utilization of funds, no community participation and only private sector is bearing entire burden of critically ill patients (Kapoor, 2011). According to the economic theory, rise in income level led to higher standard of living and better health indicators but actual analysis reveals that there is still a large gap in health amenities, sanitation and water supply in Punjab, there is a mismatch between the disease prevention & control programmes and medicine supplied in the state. There is no increase in the no. of health institutions in rural areas which consists of 60% of total population and private healthcare is operating in the state without following the regulations and it is a barrier to make healthcare services accessible to all (Rana, 2013). Cost is found to be most important criteria for selecting a hospital and distance to be travelled in order to access a dispensary or hospital. Most of the poor people avoid treatment because of loss of subsistence as most of them are employed in unorganised sector and earning daily wages. Most of the slum dwellers prefer private clinics over govt. dispensaries just because these clinics are located within their locality and open till late in the evening. Govt. hospitals are preferred by 96% of the slum dwellers due to affordability (Arya, 2012). Admissions of patients are high in govt. hospitals than private hospitals because of differences in cost or payment structure and higher catchment area of govt. hospitals. There is overburden of patients in case of govt. hospitals due to differences of expenditure or cost of treatment in private hospitals because the latter ones are operating from the view point of earning more and more profit (Banerjee, 2013). Private sector seems to be much more efficient in effecting policy making, satisfying the public at local and national levels than the public sector. Private hospitals are focusing on their patients' demand and developing themselves to provide maximum healthcare facilities. Public health care is satisfactory in terms of space and operational equipment but services to patients are inadequate. The reasons for poor quality services are lack of government funding, lack of govt. interest and overburdened public hospitals due to rapid growth in population. Cost of treatment is a major deciding factor and it is significant for both poor and affordable class of people (Khan & Fatima, 2014).

Table 5 has description of studies regarding the service delivery of the healthcare institutions. The service of public healthcare institutions is not satisfactory in terms of availability of medicines, timely reports, absenteeism, utilization of funds and in handling emergency cases (Sharma, 2008; Kapoor, 2011). The healthcare workforce in rural areas is not sufficient and majority is working in non-government sector (Rana, 2013). There is overburden of patients in public hospitals and private sector is charging very high to provide quality services on time (Banerjee, 2013; Khan & Fatima, 2014).

Table 5. Studies regarding service delivery by public/private healthcare institutions

Author/s or Reports and Year	Location	Objective	Results
Sreenu, 2012	Andhra Pradesh	To study the management of rural healthcare in Andhra Pradesh.	More negative responses than positive ones for the effectiveness of any medical centre; Beneficiaries are mostly dependent upon the facilities available at the rural health care centres.
Sharma, 2008	Punjab	To explore about the healthcare services in Punjab.	Patients find the location, diagnostic facilities and quality of medical care of public hospitals satisfactory, but still there are difficulties regarding availability of medicines from within the hospitals, delay in obtaining reports of diagnostic tests, and laxity in emergency cases.
Kapoor, 2011	Punjab	To Analyse the Health & Healthcare sevices in Punjab.	High absenteeism, low satisfaction with quality care, low quality in clinical care, and with rampant corruption; 3 key challenges: cost-incurred, equitable distribution of financial burden of ill-health and ensuring better quality of medical care; lack of state support and improper utilization of funds; no community participation and only private sector is bearing entire burden of critically ill patients.
Rana, 2013	Punjab	To explore the factors affecting job satisfaction of healthcare employees in public and private hospitals.	Quality of healthcare depends upon the size, commitment, and skill of the health workforce, In India, the distribution of health workers is heavily skewed towards urban areas and majority of the health workers are working in non-government sector, shortage of public health infrastructure and health workers at various levels of healthcare system of the country.
Arya, 2012	Mumbai	To analyse comparatively the public and private health services, availability and utilization pattern.	Cost is the most important criterion for the patients to select a dispensary/hospital and most of them preferred private clinics in their vicinity to save time and commuting charges. Waiting time in private clinics is very less than the government ones and doctors report on time. On the other hand patients refrain from availing services at government hospitals due to long waiting hours and high commuting charges.
Khan & Fatima, 2014	Hyderabad	To compare the private and government hospitals in Hyderabad.	Private sector seems to be much more efficient in effecting policy making, satisfying the public at local and national levels than the public sector. They are focusing on their patients' demand and developing themselves to provide maximum healthcare facilities. Public health care is satisfactory in terms of space and operational equipment but services to patients are inadequate. Reasons for poor quality services are lack of government funding, overburdened public hospitals.
Banerjee, 2013	Kolkata	To compare the public and private owned healthcare facilities in Kolkata.	Overburden of patients in government hospitals and monetary problems leads to the poor infrastructure in these hospitals. A major portion of the population is not able to avail careful treatment in private hospitals due to their costly services.
Singh et al., 2018	Punjab	To explore about the health-care utilization and expenditure patterns in the rural areas of Punjab.	About half (53%) of the participants access public health facilities; 56.5% for outpatient & 48.4% for inpatient care and among BPL households, 50.6% have been treated in public health sector for outpatient and 51.3% for inpatient healthcare, private services are being utilized more for healthcare related to accidents and non-communicable diseases and public services are being accessed for infections, respiratory problems etc.

HEALTHCARE EXPENDITURE PATTERN

There is high variation in the health expenditure among countries and the high income countries' per-capita health expenditure is above 3000 US $, while in poor countries, it is just 30 US $. Some countries are spending more than 12% of GDP on health while others spend less than 3% on health. An increase in GDP also leads to increased government expenditure and an increase in OOP (Xu et al., 2010). The major industrial countries of the world like United States, Switzerland, United Kingdom and Australia spend a large portion (14%-20%) of government expenditure on health. The Asian countries like Bhutan. Thailand, Sri Lanka, Maldives and Malaysia spend 6%-10%, but India spends very low amount, around 1.5% of its total expenditure on healthcare sector. Government spent only 1.02% of its GDP on health sector in 2015-16, in which the centre-state share was in the ratio of 69:31. The large proportion of total health expenditure is being financed by the private sources. Punjab government is spending very little share of GSDP on healthcare sector. During all five year plans, Punjab government spent between 1.9%-

4.5% of the total outlay on medical and Public Heath (MPH). According to National Health Accounts of 2014-15, it is only 0.7% whereas total expenditure on health is 4.1% of GSDP. The remaining health expenditure is out-of-pocket (OOP) which is a burden on the poor and middle income population. The gap is being filled by the private sector. The total health expenditure in India was about 6% of GDP, out of which private health expenditure was 75% (Planning Commission, 2002). OOP should be lower in poorer countries but in actual opposite occurred in the low-income countries and the average OOP share is high (20-80% of all health spending). In India, health needs of households are financed by selling assets or borrowing cash (Musgrove et al., 2002).

Govt. pays a little of its GDP (1.1%) on public healthcare & additional is privately financed. So, in the absence of contribution by govt., private hospital sector seems to offer best healthcare facilities (Banerjee, 2013). From the year 2005-06 to 2014-15, India has spent only 1.41% of GDP on health in 2005-06, which is increased to 1.62% in 2010-11 and then reduced again to 1.40% in 2014-15. In 2014-15, less-populated, small and hilly states spent between Rs.2289 and Rs.7409 per person. The states which have better health outcomes show high health expenditure and vice-versa. Centrally sponsored schemes have substituted the state's own health expenditure. In the year 2005-06, Punjab has Rs.519 per-capita expenditure on health and allied fields and it has increased to Rs.1,095 in 2015-16. The public expenditure on health by Punjab is decreasing year by year. In 2005-06, it was 1.24% of GSDP, by the year 2014-15 it was 0.90%. Till the FY 2015-16 it was 0.87%, not even 1% of GSDP in all previous financial years (Pavan Srinath, Pranay Kotasthane, Devika Kher, 2018).

One of the major causes of ill-state of healthcare in Punjab is decreasing state-govt. expenditure on health which leads to other problems like lack of medicines, limited doctor salaries and poor infrastructure. The private healthcare is dominating the delivery of primary and secondary healthcare system; state expenditure on public health decreased because of centrally sponsored NRHM, which is to fill gaps in the delivery of rural healthcare services; the expenditure on health & family welfare for Punjab has increased at a lower speed than its GSDP for past years. The reasons which affected the delivery of healthcare services in public sector are absenteeism and unfilled vacancies in Punjab Public Health System. Punjab has performed better in institutional deliveries & antenatal care as per DLHS-3 due to JSY (Janani Suraksha Yojana) (Asfaw *et al.*, 2014). The OOP expenditure for inpatient and outpatient care is 4 times to 15 times higher, in private facilities compared to the public facilities for almost all diseases. The outpatient services are mostly paid through current income and about 21% of the patients have to arrange money from borrowings, and nearly 4.9% from other sources such as sale of household items and insurance. For inpatient services, more than half the households (61.5%) had to borrow money (Singh *et al.*, 2018).

Even though private sector is operating for just profits but they have all latest machinery & technology as compared to public healthcare institutions. Although private medical care in Punjab is highly expensive yet even the poor are inclined towards it and households in Punjab are dependent upon Out-of-Pocket (OOP) expenditure due to low public spending on health sector and Punjab government is itself giving support to corporate sector by providing them lands at subsidized rates (Rana, 2013).

The list of studies reviewed for healthcare expenditure in the state is shown up in Table 6. Public health spending is inadequate in state to meet healthcare demands of population and as per the NHP 2017 and other policy documents it should be at least 2.5% of GDP whereas government spends only 1.1% of its GDP on health (Banerjee, 2013). The OOP expenditure is very high for both inpatient and out-patient services and health needs of Indian population are financed by borrowing or selling assets (Musgrove et al., 2002; Singh et al., 2018).

Table 6. Studies regarding healthcare expenditure

Author/s or Reports and Year	Location	Objective	Results
Xu et al., 2010	143 OECD Member countries	To explore the determinants of health expenditure.	High variation in the health expenditure among countries. Some countries are spending more than 12% of GDP on health while others spend less than 3% on health. An increase in GDP also leads to increased government expenditure and an increase in OOP. But income is not the sole factor that leads to high health expenditure.
Musgrove et al., 2002	191 WHO member countries	To describe the basic patterns in national health expenditure.	In India, health needs of households are financed by selling assets or borrowing cash. OOP should be lower in poorer countries but in actual opposite occurred in the low-income countries and the average OOP share is high (20-80% of all health spending).
Srinath et al., 2018	India	To analyse the public health expenditure in the country from 2005-06 to 2014-15.	The states which have better health outcomes show high health expenditure and vice-versa. Centrally sponsored schemes have substituted the state's own health expenditure; the public expenditure on health by Punjab is decreasing year by year. In 2005-06, it was 1.24% of GSDP, by the year 2014-15 it was 0.90%. Till the FY 2015-16 it was 0.87%, not even 1% of GSDP in all previous financial years
Singh et al., 2018	Punjab	To explore about the health-care utilization and expenditure patterns in the rural areas of Punjab.	The OOP expenditure for inpatient and outpatient care is 4 times to 15 times higher, in private facilities compared to the public facilities for almost all diseases; Outpatient services are mostly paid through current income (72.9%) and 21% have to arrange money from borrowings, and nearly 4.9% from other sources such as sale of household items and insurance; For inpatient services, more than half the households (61.5%) had to borrow money.
Rana, 2013	Punjab	To explore the factors affecting job satisfaction of healthcare employees in public and private hospitals.	Private medical care in Punjab is highly expensive yet even the poor are inclined towards it, households are dependent upon Out-of-Pocket (OOP) expenditure due to low public spending on health sector and government is itself giving support to corporate sector by providing them lands at subsidized rates.
Banerjee, 2013	Kolkata	To compare the public and private owned healthcare facilities in Kolkata.	Govt. pays a little of its GDP (1.1%) on public healthcare & additional it is privately financed. In the absence of contribution by govt., private hospital sector seems to offer best healthcare facilities.

MAJOR FINDINGS AND SUGGESTIONS

Characteristics of Punjab Healthcare System

From the above discussion, it is found that the Punjab healthcare system has characterised with

- No state- specific public health policy.
- The IPHS (Indian Public health Standards) guidelines, 2012 have not been adopted properly in the state.
- Lack efficient implementation of social awareness programmes.
- Insufficient public investment in health sector.
- Ad-hoc appointments of healthcare service providers in the state.
- Absenteeism and vacancies of doctors and other Para-medical staff in public healthcare facilities.
- In government hospitals, doctors and nurses are well qualified but number of trained employees is not sufficient in number.
- Overburden of patients in public hospitals and private sector is charging very high to provide quality services on time.
- The public expenditure on health by Punjab government is decreasing year by year. In 2005-06, it was 1.24% of GSDP, by the year 2014-15 it was 0.90%. Till the FY 2015-16 it was 0.87%, not even 1% of GSDP in all previous financial years.

There urgent need of social awareness programmes was suggested along with community level education campaigns. There should be collaborative activities with private sector, NGOs and public sector to improve the health services. There is an immediate need of attractive incentive system that motivates the private medical personnel to go to rural areas and also in public hospitals. Ad-hoc appointment method should be removed and permanent appointments with better pay-scale should be made (Patel & Patel, 2017).

CHALLENGES AND SCOPE FOR FURTHER RESEARCH IN HEALTHCARE SYSTEM OF PUNJAB

The major challenge faced by policy makers is to allocate and utilize efficiently the limited resources to the welfare of the citizens. The government should increase the budgetary allocation to the health sector, private sector should be encouraged to contribute in healthcare services as their social responsibility, affordable and qualitative healthcare infrastructure and a well-established system to determine the impact of public spending on the health performances (Maiwada, 2016). The high rate of population growth has an adverse effect on quality of healthcare and there is lack of required nutrition level, safe drinking water, clean environment and sanitation etc. Hospitals should concentrate on improving medical care and better health schemes for age group of 40 and above, should focus on strategies for illiterate segment and population with income below Rs.1,00,000, the structure and architecture of hospitals should be negotiable by patients and name of wards must be mentioned in regional languages (Subbarao, 2012).

The previous studies related to healthcare systems have concentrated on other states than Punjab and even in Punjab also very limited area (maximum 3 districts) has been considered for the research studies. The low income rural & urban population have been ignored while evaluating the accessibility and affordability of health services. The reasons for accessing healthcare institutions by the rural population in urban areas, reduced per-capita expenditure in the state and beds-shortage in public healthcare institutions have not identified also.

By considering these gaps of research in the area of healthcare system, it is necessary to review the policy making strategies and the implementation programmes of these policies. There is a requirement to study the healthcare system in Punjab from the view-point of low income population of the state and also the perceptions of the service providers must be considered for a proper assessment of the public & private healthcare performance.

Further, more districts or areas in a state can be evaluated to know the ground realities of a state. It is required to compare the public and private health care units to know the reasons for their good or worst working situations as well as for their performances. Job satisfaction of doctors, nurses and other staff plays a major role in the performance and service quality of the hospitals, so job satisfaction of employees can also be studied with the performance of the hospitals.

CONCLUSION

The more detailed data is required district wise to understand proper functioning of public health and then for suggesting a state-specific health policy. The officials should prioritize the measurement of quality care in public facilities. There is need to understand the linkage of public and private health sector. The data quality should be focused which would be helpful in further health analysis and awareness campaigns should be promoted more to increase the low utilization rates of various schemes. There should be increased budget allocation to health sector by government and effort should be made to recognise the unproductive expenditure so that relief can be provided to the poor population by reducing their out-of-pocket expenditure, rational human resource employment policy should be adopted and specialists must be paid more than the general doctors. There should be external monitoring and evaluation of performance of the public health institutions in the state of Punjab. The greater investments should be made for the needy, poor segments and under-privileged sections and role of public sector in Indian context should not be missed. A state specific health policy is suggested to ensure proper utilization of allocated resources, qualitative improvement in health services for the common people, vulnerable groups, women and children, for regulating both private and public sector and there is urgent need for large public investment in health sector that should be in favour of vulnerable & weaker sections of the society. To improve the public health, physical infrastructure along with healthcare personnel are must be given importance. Govt. should improve the availability of essential drug and the state must take adequate measures to regulate the private sector, state must design a healthcare system and increase its budget allocations towards health sector.

REFERENCES

Aftab, W., Siddiqui, F. J., Tasic, H., Perveen, S., Siddiqi, S., & Bhutta, Z. A. (2020). Implementation of health and health-related sustainable development goals: Progress, challenges and opportunities-a systematic literature review. *BMJ Global Health*, *5*(8), 1–10. doi:10.1136/bmjgh-2019-002273 PMID:32847825

Arya, B. S. (2012). *A Comparative Study of Public and Private Health Services in Mumbai Region-Availability and Utilization Pattern* [Thesis]. S.N.D.T. Women's University, Department of Economics.

Asfaw, K., Bumpus, M., Coen, T., Edelstein, C., Rojas, A. L., Mendieta, C., . . . Vidarte, R. (n.d.). Health Service Delivery in Punjab, India. Woodrow Wilson School of Public and International Affairs.

Bahuguna, P., Mukhopadhyay, I., Chauhan, A. S., Rana, S. K., Selvaraj, S., & Prinja, S. (2018). Subnational health accounts: Experience from Punjab State in India. *PLoS One*, *13*(12), e0208298. Advance online publication. doi:10.1371/journal.pone.0208298 PMID:30532271

Banerjee, E. (2013). Comparative Study on Healthcare facilities produced by Government and Privately Owned Hospitals in Kolkata Municipal Corporation. *Asian Journal of Multidisciplinary Studies*, *1*(3), 7–16.

Chokshi, M., Patil, B., Khanna, R., Neogi, S. B., Sharma, J., Paul, V. K., & Zodpey, S. (2016). Health systems in India. *Journal of Perinatology*, *36*(S3, s3), S9–S12. doi:10.1038/jp.2016.184 PMID:27924110

Faimunissa Ahmed Khan, A. F. (2014, December). Comparative Study on Private and Government Hospitals working in Hyderabad. *New Man International Journal of Multidisciplinary Studies*, *1*(12).

Govinda Rao, M. M. C. (2012). Health Care Financing Reforms in India. National Institute of Public Finance and Policy.

Gupta, R. K., & Kumari, R. (2017). National health policy 2017: An overview. *JK Science*, *19*(3), 135–136.

Kapoor, B. (2011). *Analysis of Health & Healthcare sevices in Punjab* [Thesis]. Punjabi University, Patiala, Department of Economics.

Kavitha, R., D. (2012). A Comparative Study on Patients' Satisfaction in Health care Services. *European Journal of Business and Management, 4*(13).

Maiwada, Y., & Phd, B. (2016). An Assessment of the Impact of Government Expenditure on Infrastructures: Evidence from Nigerian Health Sector Performance. *European Journal of Business and Management, 8*(14), 2222–2839. https://iiste.org/Journals/index.php/EJBM/article/viewFile/30542/31385

Mathiharan, K. (2003). The fundamental right to health care. *Issues in Medical Ethics, 11*(4), 123. PMID:16335519

Mehta, A. K. (n.d.). *Gender Responsive Budgeting: Issues related to the Health Sector in Punjab*. Retrieved December 28, 2018, from pbplanning.gov.in:http://pbplanning.gov.in/HDR/Gender%20Responsive%20Budgeting%20in%20Health%20in%20Punjab%20sent_pending.pdf

Musgrove, P., Zeramdini, R., & Carrin, G. (2002). Basic patterns in national health expenditure. *Bulletin of the World Health Organization, 80*(2), 134–142. doi:10.1590/S0042-96862002000200009 PMID:11953792

Patel, R., & Patel, H. R. (2017). A study on waiting time and out-patient satisfaction at Gujarat medical education research society hospital, Valsad, Gujarat, India. *International Journal of Community Medicine and Public Health, 4*(3), 857. doi:10.18203/2394-6040.ijcmph20170772

Pavan Srinath, P. K. (2018). *A Qualitative and Quantitative Analysis of Public Health Expenditure in India: 2005-06 to 2014-15*. The Takshila Institution.

Pawan Kumar Sharma, S. I. (2008, September). Health Care Services in Punjab: Findings of a Patient Satisfaction Survey. *Social Change, 38*(3), 458–477. doi:10.1177/004908570803800304

Philip Musgrove, R. Z. (2002). Basic Patterns in National Health Expenditure. *Bulletin of the World Health Organization, 80*(2). PMID:11953792

Rana, A. (2013). *Job Satisfaction among Healthcare Employees in Public & Private Sector Hospitals in Punjab*. Academic Press.

Rao, M. G., & Choudhury, M. (2012). Health Care Financing Reforms in India. *Nipfp, 100*, 34.

Sanjay Basu, J. A. (2012). Comparative Performance of Private and Public Healthcar Systems in Low and Middle-Income Countries: A Systematic review. *PLoS Medicine, 9*(6). PMID:22723748

Sreenu, N. (2012). *A study on management of rural healthcare in Andhra Pradesh* [Thesis]. University of Hyderabad, School of Management Studies.

Suthanthiraveeran, S. (2018). The five year plans in India: Overview of Public Health Policies. *The Five Year Plans in India: Overview*.

Svalastog, A. L., Donev, D., Kristoffersen, N. J., & Gajović, S. (2017). Concepts and definitions of health and health-related values in the knowledge landscapes of the digital society. *Croatian Medical Journal, 58*(6), 431–435. doi:10.3325/cmj.2017.58.431 PMID:29308835

Tarundeep Singh, N. B. (2018, December 8). Health-care Utilization and Expenditure Patterns in the Rural Areas of Punjab, India. *Journal of Family Medicine and Primary Care, 7*(1), 39–44. doi:10.4103/jfmpc.jfmpc_291_17 PMID:29915731

Thomson, S., Osborn, R., Squires, D., & Jun, M. (2013). *International Profiles of Health Care Systems.* Commonwealth Fund Pub. No. 1717. http://www.commonwealthfund.org/~/media/files/publications/fund-report/2013/nov/1717_thomson_intl_profiles_hlt_care_sys_2013_v2.pdf

WanjohiA. M. (2014). Social Research Methods Series: Proposal Writing Guide. https://ssrn.com/abstract=2378204

Chapter 7
Theoretical and Empirical Approaches and Typologies Into Failures and Enhancement of Organizational Resilience Analysis

José G. Vargas-Hernández
https://orcid.org/0000-0003-0938-4197
Instituto Tecnológico José Mario Molina Pasquel y Henríquez, Mexico

ABSTRACT

The aim of this chapter is to analyze the implications of theoretical, empirical, and typologies into failures and enhancement of organizational resilience. It is assumed that the application of conceptual, theoretical, and empirical knowledge base to specific knowledge and practice integrated into organizational resilience will help, but it is unclear to what extent it can be designed and supported because of lack of empirical evidence. The method employed is the analytical reflection sustained in the review of theoretical and empirical literature and observation. It is concluded that each organizational system transformation needs different and specific conceptual, theoretical, and empirical knowledge bases to take advantage of failures and enhance organizational resilience.

INTRODUCTION

The concept of resilience become relevant after 9/11 (Linnenluecke, 2017). The ongoing pandemics provide the opportunity to apply this concept and develop it further. Organizational resilience is active and purposeful to cope with unknown unexpected events. Organizational resilience is the capacity to maintain positive adjustment, bounce back and maintain desirable functions and outcomes under challenging conditions, from untoward events during strain. Organizational resilience is the system property that confers the ability to remain functional despite the threats. Organizational resilience is the ability to bounce back from unanticipated events with adverse effects.

People have positive contributions towards resilience (Hollnagel, Woods and Leveson, 2006). Organizational resilience should get the right people in the right positions and roles to achieve the organization's success. The dynamic nature of resilience provides the foundation for the development of organizational resilience.

To address each of these types of resilience requirement areas, this chapter highlights key terms and concepts in the literature, along with several empirical studies, that demonstrate general wisdom and lessons learned for each case. Descriptive and outcome focused analysis of organizational resilience after a threatening situation is required (Lengnick-Hall et al. 2011; Linnenluecke and Griffiths 2012).

The analysis begins by conceptualizing and defining the notion of organizational resilience, to develop a framework for a theoretical and empirical knowledge base. After doing so, it is necessary to analyze the more general typologies of organizational resilience to concentrate on failures and tools of enhancement. Finally, some concluding remarks are offered.

CONCEPT AND DEFINITION OF ORGANIZATIONAL RESILIENCE

The concept of resilience is criticized (Carpenter and Brock, 2008) because the conceptual and hypothetical organizational resilience constructs can be confusing as pseudo-multi-dimensional construct as being interrelated (Hirsch and Levin, 1999; Wong *et al.* 2008). There is not any agreement on a formal and uniform definition of organizational resilience (Linnenluecke, 2017).

There is little consensus on the concept of organizational resilience (Kendra and Wachtendorf, 2003; Linnenluecke, 2017). Organizational resilience as a broad concept comprises multiple and divergent themes used loosely for a set of diverse phenomena (Hirsch and Levin, 1999, p. 200). The concept of organizational resilience is fuzzy and lacks of consistency (Amann and Jaussaud 2012; Brand and Jax, 2007; Burnard and Bhamra, 2011; Linnenluecke, 2017). The absence of resilience and the attributes attached to the concept are assessable *ex-post*.

Organizational resilience is an emergent concept (Paul et al., 2016, King et al., 2016). The term resilience comes from the Latin resilience which means 'to recoil or rebound' and it is being used since the 1620's. It has evolved sin then to include the notion of sense in the 19th century (MacMillan, 2017). The concept of resilience is derived from the Latin word *resilio* (*resilire*), which means to rebound, spring back (Klein *et al.* 2003; van der Vegt *et al.* 2015). A conceptual definition of organizational resilience identifies attributes that are common to the phenomenon (Podsakoff *et al.* 2016, p. 165).

Conceptualizations of organizational resilience focuses on the detection on variables. The conceptualization of resilience is related to several events (Linnenluecke, 2017), among which the nature of change described as a specific phenomenon, is the most crucial (Koslowski, *et al.* 2013). Organizational resilience is the ability to absorb and recover from shocks (Williams and Shepherd, 2016). Organizational resilience is the ability to develop effective plans for both short-term resuming and long-term restoration following disruptive events (Sahebjamnia *et al.*, 2015).

Organizational resilience is the ability to withstand stress and bounce back or recover from traumatic events (van der Vegt *et al.* 2015). Organizational resilience is the ability to bounce back from adverse effects of unanticipated events (Lampel, *et al.* 2014). Organizational resilience is the ability of affected parties to communicate and reorganize across periods of rapid change or chaos (Chewning *et al.* 2013).

Organizational resilience is the capacity to absorb the impact and recover from the occurrence of extreme weather events (Linnenluecke *et al.*, 2012). Organizational resilience is the characteristic to deal with unexpected abrupt and or extreme change (Linnenluecke and Griffiths, 2012). Organizational resilience is the capacity to maintain positive adjustment, bounce back and maintain desirable functions and outcomes under challenging conditions, outward events and during strain (Salanova, *et al* 2012). Organizational resilience is the organizational ability to absorb, develop situation-specific responses to engage in transformative activities and capitalize on disruptive surprises that potentially threaten survival of the organization (Lengnick-Hall *et al.* 2011, p. 244).

Organizational resilience is the capacity for resisting, absorbing, responding, reinventing to disruptive change (McCann *et al.* 2009). Organizational resilience as preventative control protects the organization by bounce back from threats and disruptions to restore the stable state. The essential domain of organizational resilience is stability. Resilience is the ability to forestall chaos from disruptions by bouncing back, recovering control, and maintaining a sense of comfort.

Organizational resilience is the ability to cope with crisis due to relational and financial reserves (Gittell *et al.* 2006). Financial crisis hit resilience of organizations. Organizational resilience is the capacity to be robust under enormous stress and change (Coutu, 2002). Resilience starts with the awareness of people who feel engaged with the organization built in preparedness to cope with unpredicted events. The concept of organizational resilience incorporates the notion of anticipation (Rerup, 2001; McManus et al. 2008; Somers, 2009) defined as the prediction and prevention of potential danger for damage in contrast to resilience is a feasible alternative to prevent crisis defined as the capacity to cope with unknown dangers and bounce back (Wildavsky, 1991).

Resilience is the capacity to adjust timely the organization confronted by dramatic changes. Resilience is an attribute of a system that indicates the ability to maintain critical operations during the adverse disruptions. Resilience determines the systemic relationships measuring the ability to absorb changes of state and driving variables. The organizational resilience is based on its capacity to carry on organizational operations regardless of the contexts and circumstances. As a cross-level concept, organizational resilience is a whole system response to significant change that disrupts the expected pattern of events without engaging in an extended period of regressive behavior (Horne & Orr, 1998, p. 31).

The concept of organizational resilience is based on the ability of organizations to cope with turbulent changes in business economics (King et al., 2016). The *ability to cope* is an attribute of organizational resilience (Duchek, 2014; Gittell *et al.* 2006; Sutcliffe and Vogus 2003) including development of feasible solutions and related to bricolage as the ability to make whatever is at hand such as improvising (Acquaah *et al.* 2011; Mallak, 1998a; Weick, 1993; Coutu, 2002; Mallak, 1998b; Ray, *et al.* 2011). Organizational resilience is the ability of maintaining a positive mindset in the organization (Salanova *et al.* 2012; Sutcliffe and Vogus, 2003), the *ability to bounce back* or *recover from* a situation (Freeman *et al.* 2004; Lampel, *et al.* 2014).

In another perspective, organizational resilience is the ability to absorb, develop situation-specific responses and engage in transformative actions to capitalize on disruptive events that threaten organization survival (Lengnick-Hall et al. 2011; p. 244). Organizational resilience is the capacity to maintain positive adjustment, bounce back, maintain desirable functions and outcomes from under challenging conditions, from untoward events and during strain (Salanova *et al.* 2012). Resilience is defined as the ability of the system to retain and recover a stable condition, enabling a normal functioning during, and after any unexpected disruptions.

Organizational resilience is defined by Lengnick-Hall et al. (2011) as the ability of the organization to absorb and develop responses to specific situations, engage in transformative activities to capitalize on disruptive events threatening the survival of the organization. Organizational resilience is the capacity to improvise, bounce back from organizational setbacks (Ray *et al.* 2011). Organizational resilience is the function of accumulation of vulnerability and coping capacity (Wedawattaa *et al.* 2010).

Organizational resilience is the capacity to maintain and restore an acceptable level of functioning during and after failures and perturbations (Robert 2010, p. 13). Organizational resilience is the ability to repair old practices or develop new practices (Mark, Al-Ani, & Semaan, 2009, p. 690, 2008). Organizational resilience is the ability to resist being affected by an incident (Elwood, 2009). Organizational resilience is a blend of cognitive, behavioral, and contextual properties that increase understand its current situation, develop customized responses (Lengnick-Hall and Beck, 2005).

Resilience is defined from different and varied perspectives, focuses and scopes (Bruneau et al., 2002; Horne & Orr, 1998; Kendra, 2001; Weick, 1993). The phenomena of organizational resilience are being treated as the power of organizational units to adjust, resume, and rebound back untoward events. Organizational resilience is the power phenomenon that the organizational units must resume, rebound, bounce back, and adjust untoward events (Sutcliffe and Vogus, 2003). Organizational resilience is after-the-fact- intervention to overcome unexpected problems and limitations (Marcus and Nichols, 1999. Organizational resilience is the ability to excel amidst chaos, tap the power liberated by change (Kiuchi and Shireman, 1999).

Organizational resilience is the fundamental quality of an individual, group or organization to respond productively to significant change that disrupts the expected pattern of events without engaging in an extended period of regressive behavior (Horne and Orr, 1998). Resilience is defined by Rutter (1993) as the way of being able to deal with and remove stressful circumstances. Organizational resilience means the anticipation, preparation, dealing and coping with unanticipated and unknown dangers and hazards after they become manifest (Wildavsky, 1991, p. 77).

THEORETICAL AND EMPIRICAL APPROACHES

Resilience research lacks empirical, theoreticak and conceptual measurability and validity (Aleksić et al. 2013; Linnenluecke 2017; Mafabi et al. 2012), which considers is a fuzziness, fragmented and disjoint concept (Burnard and Bhamra 2011; Martin-Breen and Anderies 2011; Koslowski et al. 2013). There is not any specific knowledge and practice to achieve organizational resilience and it is unclear to what extent can be designed (Duit, 2016).

Application of theoretical concepts to resilience are integrated to other theories guiding empirical research (King et al., 2016). The knowledge base of organizational resilience supports the analysis of resilience within essential service organizations, although is lacking empirical evidence. Annarelli & Nonino (2016) investigated the domains of organizational resilience to trace its development without analyzing the different concepts. Linnenluecke (2017) studied the evolution of organizational resilience theory to find that there is not one theory. The organizational literature is more conceptual than empirical studies (Bhamra et al., 2011).

The sources of resilience were explored by Weick (1996), and the principles of resilience were addressed by Mallak (1998). Organizational resilience is the result of collective actions at collective level (Gittell *et al.* 2006; Powley, 2013; Salanova *et al.* 2012; Sutcliffe and Vogus 2003). Collective behaviors are sources of organizational resilience (Weick, 1993; Horne, 1997; Horne and Orr, 1998). The potential sources of resilience principles identified by Weick (1993) are the improvisation and bricolage, virtual role systems, attitude of wisdom, and respectful interaction that facilitate sensemaking to avoid the consequences of unexpected events (Mallak, 1998; Weick et al. 1999; Kendra and Wachtendorf, 2003). These approaches of organizational resilience are operationalized and measured (Mallak, 1998; Somers, 2009).

The organizational resilience emerges in the conjunction of cognition and behavior to generate alternatives of actions to respond to crisis situations (Fiol and Lyles 1985). Organizational resilience brings a duality, from advancing out of crisis while taking advantage of opportunities (Colse et al., 2020). Building organizational resilience is affected by history, activity, size and characteristics of leadership and history (Alesi 2008 and Biggs 2011). The historical development of organizational resilience is developed by Linnenluecke (2017).

Research on organizational resilience has increased (Linnenluecke, 2017). Research in organizational resilience experiences on issues such as business model, organizational behavior, and supply chain. Other studies on organizational resilience provide insights on what and how must be resilience. For psychology, organizational resilience is a specific process of action and orientation and not a feature.

From the perspective of psychology and organizational behavior, Weick (1993) considers that organizational resilience can improvise, wisdom, virtual role systems, individual and social interactions. Social relationships influence the way people work together shaping the organizational resilience outcomes (Gittell *et al.* 2006). From the same perspective, Lengnick-Hall et al. (2011) organizational resilience must express resilience into cognitive, behavior and context dimensions.

A conceptual orientation of cognitive resilience enables an organization to notice, interpret, analyze, and formulate responses beyond a survival. Survival is the most relevant consequence to organizational resilience (Freeman *et al.* 2004; Gao *et al.* 2017; Limnios *et al.* 2014; Ortiz-de-Mandojana and Bansal, 2016). Another consequence is the reduction of failure and decline (Carmeli and Markman, 2011; Farjoun, 2010; Marwa and Zairi, 2008).

Social and behavioral sciences are the origin of personal resilience whereas natural sciences and organizational systems created the organizational resilience (Le Coze, 2015). The facets of resilience as career, trait, psychological and ego resilience (Paul et al. 2016) with implications in individual and organizational contexts. Individual interactions and contacts in the organizational context create the conditions for the enactment of organizational resilience. Individuals subject to stress require resilience as the capacity to recover. Individuals emerging from adverse experiences can improve their psychological strength and emotional well-being, attitude related and often more subjective. Organizational resilience is a recovery ability rather than a resistance after destruction by unexpected events.

The general approach to resilience discusses important features of each approach separately. Organizational resilience can use more global approaches and methods focusing on the concept of general resilience to address the threats already know and to accrue the unknown (Sheffi, 2005). Organizational resilience is conceptualized as the latent type of higher-order construct. Organizational resilience is conceptualized as latent, embedded, higher-order construct, and inherent quality that can be assessed with some degree of accuracy. The conceptual model of organizational resilience aimed to resolve a crisis include several domains (Powley, 2013).

Organizational resilience research and theory-building analyses the responses of organizations threatened by severe adverse conditions. The theory-building of organizational resilience requires more consistency from its given antecedents to yield outcomes. The existing theoretical and empirical studies of organizational resilience have not uncovered all the factors and variables involved including in the context-dependency. Therefore, the organizational resilience is path-dependent and idiosyncratic (Ortiz-de-Mandojana and Bansal, 2016).

Organizational systems transformation needs different applications of organizational resilience theory from the application to natural systems. A normative perspective of organizational resilience focus on indicators such as awareness, commitment preparedness. The organizational resilience indicators should correspond to the theoretical aspects of resilience being considered such as impact resistance (Carpenter et al. 2005)

A process perspective of organizational resilience explains what have to do the surviving organizations and the good outcomes not necessarily define resilience (Sutcliffe and Vogus, 2003).The different approached of resilience processes vary in types and definitions. There are types of organizational resilience such as basic and reflexive resilience (Bonß, 2015), defensive and offensive organizational resilience (Mamouni-Limnios & Mazzarol, 2011) active and passiveresi-lience (Somers, 2009). Resilience as a process of successive stages respond to the past in reactive action, to the current events in concurrent action and to the future as anticipatory action (Pearson and Clair, 1998; James and Wooten, 2005; Boin et al. 2005).

The empirical and operational assessment of resilience concept have used retrospective analysis for data interpretation (Somers, 2009). However, one difficulty lies in the predictive impacts and contributed factors to be anticipated for future resilience (Carpenter et al. 2005). Organizational resilience is the reaction to threats by responding to challenging situations. Organizational resilience interactions and stages are interrelated overlapping, linking and depending on each other as in the case of anticipation of change and coping stages by a broad range of actions (Weick et al. 1999).

The first stage of the resilience process is to anticipate and be prepared to critical developments and potential threats (Somers, 2009; Boin and van Eeten 2013). The response options enhance resilience. An offensive response can cope during critical situations (Wildavsky, 1991; Weick et al. 1999; Rerup 2001). The balanced relational systems are the initial point to develop theory about organizational resilience capacity because they can recover (Kahn et al. 2013).

An organizational collaborative approach towards anticipation of risks to respond more effectively to any threats coming from unknow events and disruptions. Theoretical and empirical factors of organizational resilience and their effects on climate change and extreme weather are limited and sparse.

There are two schools of thought regarding the organizational resilience (Sutcliffe & Vogus 2003). From a sociological perspective, the findings of Richardson (2002) support correlations among self-efficacy, personal resilience, psychological empowerment, and leadership style with organizational resilience. The sociological organizational resilience theory. The sociological resilience theory assumes that may be multiple possible equilibriums in each organizational system (Gunderson, 2000). In organizational theory, organizational resilience incorporates insights from contingency and coping theories. Organizational resilience is contextually specific to a certain situation. Contextual organizational resilience is situational or oriented toward specific situations.

The empirical research is difficult to conduct. Resilience is a source of sustainable advantage for organizations (Hamel and Vaelikangas, 2003; Sheffi, 2007). Preliminary results of empirical research indicates that resilience indicators including awareness issues and stakeholders' responsibilities in organizational recovery priorities contribute to enhance the overall organizational resilience.

Another outcome of organizational resilience is competitive advantage. (Acquaah *et al*. 2011; Kiuchi and Shireman 1999; Marwa and Milner 2013; Reeves and Deimler 2009; Stephenson, 2010). A construct on organizational resilience contribute to theory building and testing, must be approached from a validity police perspective (Brahma, 2009; Suddaby, 2010). The asset-based approach draws on the theory of resilience (Barnard, 1994)

Conceptual and empirical studies are more concerned with the identification and assessment of vulnerabilities and risks, strengthen the resistance of organizations in the face of potential unforeseen threats and avoiding crises before they happen and planning capacities to mitigate in the case these crises occur (Aigbogun, Ghazali, & Razali, 2014; Albrito, 2012; Aldrich & Meyer, 2014; Edgeman & Williams, 2014; Jaaron & Backhouse, 2014; Lee, Vargo, & Seville, 2013; Mallak,1998; McManus, Seville, Vargo, & Brunsdon, 2008; Norris et al., 2008). The empirical approach for assessing organizational resilience is more case-focused research (e.g., Gittell et al. 2006; Meyer, 1982).

TYPOLOGY OF ORGANIZATIONAL RESILIENCE

A typology of organizational resilience is developed by Limnios (2014). The assessment of resilience requires clarification of the type of resilience. Organizational resilience is expressed and divided into cognitive, behavior and context dimensions (Lengnick-Hall et al. 2011). Cognitive resilience enables the orientation of the organization to notice, analyze, interpret, and respond beyond survival. Contextual resilience integrates and uses cognitive resilience and behavioral resilience in specific setting. There are three main types of resilience related to the construct: Resilience as bounce back from shocks where the system rebounds to pre-shock state. The engineering resilience (Martin & Sunley, 2015:4).

Psychology classifies the different types of disorganizations required to build resilience that may respond to specific threats. When there is little or no disorganization caused by threats, the type or organizational resilience used and deploys may be routinized responses to maximize efficiency (Flach, 1997).

Organizational resilience arises from the interplay of multi-factors and multi-levels (Lengnick-Hall et al. 2011, and Cunha et al. (2013). Organizational resilience is multifactorial influenced by attributes, behaviors, collective leadership, and contextual and external forces. The multi-levels are the individual, group and organizational and the factors are different in each level. The evolution of organizational resilience must be monitored as a multilevel system to detect the categories and identify the individual contributions by repeating the assessments over time, if the organizational context develops local and global properties of the whole system (van der Vorm, van der Beek, Bos, Steijger, Gallis, 2011).

Only having resilience individuals, they do not make organizational resilience (Horne and Orr 1998) and they do not develop a shared vision. There are some factors that influence organizational resilience by defining the hierarchy of abilities with organizational resilience lying at the top, and other categories at intermediate and lowest level and at the bottom the final questions.

There are 4 types of resilience: personal, organizational, sectoral, and societal (Sawalha 2015). Organizational resilience is deconstructed in individual, group, and organizational level (Cunha et al. 2013). Organizational resilience is deconstructed from the main source of individual resilience, group, and organizational levels (Cunha et al. 2013). Because the individual has resilience, the groups, and organizations he belongs not necessarily possess it. Resilience is defined depending about every organizational group. A fundamental quality of an individual or group to responded productively to significant change that disrupts the pattern events without engaging in regressive behavior (Horne and Orr, 1998). The resilience of an occupational group does not necessarily implicate organizational resilience.

Individual resilience is the source of organizational resilience although the resilience of an individual may have different characteristics that the group and organizational resilience. The identities, power relations and positions of the interdependent working groups influence the organizational resilience. Individual resilience is formed by the personal character, confidence, faith, optimism, and belongingness (Luthans et al., 2006; Cunha et al., 2013). An individual possessing solidified resilience in childhood may have little chance of modification during his adulthood (Benard 1991, Garmezy 1991, Masten 1998, 2011, Rutter 1993, 2012, and Werner 1997). Individual resilience and leadership self-efficacy are reciprocally reinforced (Bandura, 1988; Vogus & Sutcliffe, 2007).

Grant et al. (2009) differentiated between individual resilience work-related resilience. Personal attributes and behaviors affect organizational resilience (Lee, Vargo, & Seville, 2013; Masten, 2011; Windle, 2011). Resilience as a personal trait includes a sense of self, a social attitude and determination (Dyer & McGuinness, 1996).

Individual resilience is linked to organizational resilience and they are reciprocally influenced each other (Riolli and Savicki, 2003). An organizational resilience system exhibits personal resilience at micro level, leadership style and psychological empowerment at meso level and interactions between the organization and the community at macro level. The resilience of the system may be specific but not general, besides increasing specific resilience may not increase general resilience (Baral, 2013; Baral et al., 2013).

Any type of organization needs to increase its organizational resilience which may contribute to play a vital role in community resilience and recovery (Dalziell, 2005) in such a way that the vulnerability of organizations is linked to the resilience of communities.

FAILURES

Resilience is the ability to learn from failure, and still pursue goals (Wright et al. 2009). Resilience avoids failures linked to anticipate, recognize, avoid, neutralize, and adapt to pressures (Moran and Mallak 2016). Organizational resilience prevents survival and decline or failure (Farjoun 2010; Marwa and Zairi 2008)

The existing literature on organizational development fails to inform about the actions to enhance resilience and how to prevent and confront a collapse. Organizations can learn resilience and survive any type of collapse by making the appropriate choices in decisions and avoid the high rates of entrepreneurial organizations failures (Bhidé, 2000). Commitment to resilience is a micro-foundation to organizational resilience that enable the identification of failure and making corrections (Wofford et al. 2011)

Personal and organizational resilience cannot be separated in an entrepreneurial setting to recover from failure (Corey and Deitch, 2011; Doern, 2016; Doyle Corner, Singh, and Pavlovich 2017). Organizational resilience relies on the development of general capacities. Organizations with unexpected events and catastrophic consequences for failure may have different behavioral calculus than tolerable disruptions to address resilience. Organizational resilience has also different features between family and non-family firms (Acquaah *et al.* 2011; Amann and Jaussaud, 2012; Danes, *et al.* 2009).

The origin of the term resilience is used in physics and mathematics to indicate the energy that a material holds under strain just before failing (Castleden, McKee, Murray, & Leonardi, 2011). Organizational failures, testing and learn are a way to enhance resilience (Weick, Sutcliffe, and Obstfeld, 1999). The resilience manifestation of an undesirable system state may lead to a dysfunctional system rigidity (Miller and Friesen, 1980). Counter poles to resilience are brittleness (Vogus and Sutcliffe, 2007) and rigidity (Parker and Ameen, 2018; Sutcliffe and Vogus, 2003).

Building and maintaining organizational resilience in several specific cases may reflect a significant trend to approach and identify successes and failures. Organizations enhance resilience by sharing balanced information among personnel with different roles, appropriate designations, and levels of decision-making authority. Organizations must evaluate the required information available to decision making. A flood of information out of balance, could damage organizational resilience efforts. The collected information demonstrates key features of successful methods for ensuring mission success in each.

Organizations enact resilience not necessarily with the efforts of ICT but supplemented by community interactions and relationships. Virtual communities of practices can support and enhance organizational resilience (Gimenez et al. 2017). Currently, one of the major threats of important consideration to organizational resilience is data security. The interconnectedness of a supply chains makes resilience a critical concern. Making decisions based on partial or unneeded information may have a negative impact on operations and decrease resilience. The different levels of communication between individuals and organizations are blurred by the lack of information. Exploration of organizational resilience theoretically developed in crisis communication.

Different organizations require different indicators of organizational resilience. Comparison of resilience across organizations identified commonalities (McCann *et al*. 2009; Seville *et al*. 2007; Stephenson, 2010).

TOOLS FOR ENHANCEMENT OF ORGANIZATIONAL RESILIENCE

Resilient organizations require assessment tools (Stephenson 2010). Organizational resilience ensures the survival and growth of the organizational competitive advantage through the development and enhancement of resilience in times of disruptive turbulence (Kiuchi and Shireman 1999; Marwa and Milner 2013; Reeves and Deimler 2009). Organizational resilience benchmark research based on grounded theory is oriented to the development of tools (Lee et al., 2013). Enhancement of organizational resilience is relevant to prevent and control abrupt disruptions through a sequential interconnection between others individual, group, communities, organizations, societies, and nations.

Therefore, organizational resilience is dependent of individuals and organizational staff, related directly to other stakeholders of the organizations, suppliers, customers, competitor, governments, neighborhoods, industry sector, etc. Resilience benefits the organizations by upgrading the capacity to recognize, anticipate and respond to vulnerabilities and threats. Participants in organizations in the context of a community may determine the transferability of results to build the capacity to enhance organizational resilience.

There are methods for ensuring operations, recover and avoid risks. The advantage resilience-based methods signal on failures (Øien 2013). People involved in the development of the organizations must built the critical social skills to keep organizational resilience. Organizational skills are the skills in managing the unexpected (Weick & Sutcliff, 2001). Organizations need to build and develop resilience capacities enabling to react and face unexpected and unknown events that threaten the organization's survival (Lengnick-Hall et al. 2011). Organizational resilience is the ability to develop new skills in disruptive events and to restore to the original state.

Organizational resilience improves with the factors of psychological capital self-efficacy, optimism, resiliency, and hope (Sutcliffe and Vogus, 2003; Youssef, Luthans and Youssef, 2007). Organizational work-related resilience derives its ability to create organizational meaning and purpose and their affiliated members aimed to enhance employee self-reliance (Wagnild & Young, 1990).

Organizational resilience requires of commitment, control and compliance that can be enhanced by experience, training, and development of knowledge (Coutu, 2002). The concept of absorptive capacity is linked to the concept of organizational resilience but different (Richtnér and Löfsten 2014) considered as the ability to appreciate, transform and exploit knowledge (Zahra and George, 2002). Also, effective organizational communication as a soft management practice enhances the organizational resilience (Seville et al. 2008).

The variable self-efficacy is a motivational and planning drive to act for effecting an outcome (Bandura, 1997, 2001). Planning may enhance resilience through formal systems approaches (Coates et al. 2016; Blundel, 2013; Herbane, 2015; Mikušová, 2013; Musgrave and Woodman, 2013). Some organizations formalize resilience planning activities while others place relationships with others choosing their locations to enhance their potential of organizational resilience. Non-material approaches may be effective to enhance organizational approaches. Organizations must strike a balance between efficiency and resilience ensuring the development of an ability to operate through disruptive events to achieve longevity and viability.

Resilience as a personality trait has an impact on leadership ability. A critical issue of organizational resilience is the leadership leveraging organizational tensions and enabling virtuous cycles (Lewis and Smith, 2014; Farjoun, 2010). The tensions in Organizational Resilience can be balanced by leadership (Uhl-Bien, Marion and McKelvey, 2007). Leadership in complex organizational resilience possesses a transformational style, psychological empowerment, and self-efficacy. Individual resilience is enhanced by leaderships intellectual stimulation and inspirational motivation (Sutcliffe & Vogus, 2003).

Personal resilience strengthened by transformational leadership style supports psychologically and intellectually professional growth (Hannah et al., 2008). Leaders may hold a perception of personal resilience and contribute to the resilience of the organization. Organizations may select and cultivate leadership attributes and behaviors that contribute to organizational resilience. Organizations may develop leaders in possession of high levels of resilience (Harvey & Martinko, 2009). To achieve high levels of organizational resilience is necessary high potential and abilities to realize it. There are several abilities of resilience such as forward planning, perception, and reaction to variations (Hollnagel, Leveson & Woods, 2006).

Collective leadership attributes and behaviors are associated with organizational resilience (Richardson, 2002). Collective leadership resilience impacts personal wellness and productivity toward sustaining the organizational mission (European Agency for Health and Safety at Work, 2014). Collective leadership attributes and behaviors are modifiers for personal resilience and organizational resilience.

There are several models to assess resilience that provide a set of indicators and sub indicators of different integrated components of the resilience model (Supply Chain Risk Leadership Council, 2013). The indicators for organizational resilience are required to improve and enhance the abilities of resilience in essential services organizations. The development of an organizational resilience approach aimed to assess and enhance the organizational mission is critical in organizational development.

Organizational resilience includes system interdependencies high and low correlated risk events. Organizations may have a high tolerance for risk and operate in consistent demand of resilience. The notion of organizational resilience is linked to risk control depending on the capacity to account on irregular, variations, disruptions, and degradation of working conditions (Hollnagel, Leveson & Woods, 2006: 347). An insurance policy that takes much of the risks away through cost-effective and pragmatic procedures and taking steps towards ensuring the organizational resilience.

Organizational resilience is related to the assessment of the system's purpose in domain-specific context. The compact way to rate the abilities in a specific time represents a snapshot of organizational resilience. Hollnagel developed the questionnaire RAG to monitoring resilience intended to question more specifically for the system under analysis (Wreathall, 2009; Hollnagel, 2011).

CONCLUSIONS

Resilience is an organizational characteristic. The definitions of organizational resilience provide explicit attributes and components related to the change phenomenon.

This study analyzes the conceptual, theoretical, and empirical knowledge base of organizational resilience to find some implications of its typologies into failures and enhancement of organizational of organizational resilience. Despite the limited empirical evidence of knowledge base of organizational resilience, it can be integrated into practice in specific organizational systems. Therefore, each organizational systems transformation needs different and specific conceptual, theoretical, and empirical knowledge base to take advantage of failures and enhance organizational resilience.

Organizational resilience incorporates both coping and contingency theories. Resilience is a source of knowledge for sustainable competitive advantage based on the organizational ability directed toward organizational development and advancement.

The organizational resilience has an impact across the interactions among the organizational levels including individuals, groups, and the whole organization. Researchers and practitioners must collaborate to theory building and practical skills to enhance organizational resilience of specific organizations and to solve problems in real time and to withstanding future shocks.

REFERENCES

Acquaah, M., Amoako-Gyampah, K., & Jayaram, J. (2011). Resilience in family and nonfamily firms: An examination of the relationships between manufacturing strategy, competitive strategy, and firm performance. *International Journal of Production Research*, *49*(18), 5527–5544. doi:10.1080/00207543.2011.563834

Aigbogun, O., Ghazali, Z., & Razali, R. (2014). A framework to enhancesupply chain resilience the case of Malaysian pharmaceutical industry. *Global Business and Management Research*, *6*(3), 219–225.

Albrito, P. (2012). Making cities resilient: Increasing resilience to disastersat the local level. *Journal of Business Continuity & Emergency Planning*, *5*(4), 291–297.

Aldrich, D. P., & Meyer, M. A. (2014). Social capital and community resilience. *The American Behavioral Scientist*, *59*(2), 254–269. doi:10.1177/0002764214550299

Aleksić, A., Stefanović, M., Arsovski, S., & Tadić, D. (2013). An assessment of organizational resilience potential in SMEs of the process industry, a fuzzy approach. *J Loss Prevent Proc*, *26*, 1238–1245. doi:10.1016/j.jlp.2013.06.004

Alesi, P. (2008). Building enterprise-wide resilience by integrating business continuity capability into day-to-day business culture and technology. *Journal of Business Continuity & Emergency Planning, 2*, 214–220.

Amann, B., & Jaussaud, J. (2012). Family and non-family business resilience in an economic downturn. *Asia Pacific Business Review, 18*, 203–223.

Annarelli, A., & Nonino, F. (2016). Strategic and operational management of organizational resilience: Current state of research and future directions. *Omega, 62*, 1–18.

Bandura, A. (1988). Organizational applications of social cognitive theory. *Australian Journal of Management, 13*, 275–302. doi:10.1177/031289628801300210

Bandura, A. (1997). *Self-efficacy*. Freeman and Company.

Baral, N. (2013, March). What Makes Grassroots Conservation Organizations Resilient? An Empirical Analysis of Diversity, Organizational Memory, and the Number of Leaders. *Environmental Management, 51*(3), 738–749.

Baral, S., Logie, C. H., Grosso, A., Wirtz, A. L., & Beyrer, C. (2013). Modified social ecological model: A tool to guide the assessment of the risks and risk contexts of HIV epidemics. *BMC Public Health, 13*, S293. doi:10.1186/1471-2458-13-482

Barnard, C. P. (1994). Resiliency: A shift in our perception? *The American Journal of Family Therapy, 22*, 135–144.

Benard, B. (1991). *Fostering resiliency in kids: Protective factors in the family, school, and community*. Department of Education.

Bhamra, R., Dani, S., & Burnard, K. (2011). Resilience: The Concept, a Literature Review and Future Directions. *International Journal of Production Research, 49*(18), 5375–5393.

Bhidé, A. V. (2000). *The Origin and Evolution of New Businesses*. Oxford University Press.

Blundel, R. (2013). *Quarterly Survey of Small Business in Britain Special Topic: Resilience and Recovery*. Open University. (Original work published 2013)

Boin, A., Hart, P., Stern, E., & Sundelius, B. (2005). *The politics of crisis management: Public leadership under pressure*. Cambridge University Press.

Bonß, W. (2015). Karriere und sozialwissenschaftliche Potenziale des Resilienzbegriffs. In M. Endreß & A. Maurer (Eds.), *Resilienz im Sozialen. Theoretische und empirische Analysen* (pp. 15–31). Springer VS.

Brahma, S. S. (2009). Assessment of construct validity in management research. *Journal of Management Research, 9*, 59–71.

Brand, F. S., & Jax, K. (2007). Focusing the meaning(s) of resilience: Resilience as a descriptive concept and a boundary object. *Ecology and Society, 12*, 23–39.

Bruneau, M., Chang, S., Eguchi, R. T., Lee, G. C., O'Rourke, T. D., Reinhorn, A. M., & von Winterfeldt, D. (2002). *A framework to quantitatively assess and enhance seismic resilience of communities.* Multidisciplinary Center for Earthquake Engineering Research, State University of New York at Buffalo.

Burnard, K., & Bhamra, R. (2011). Organisational resilience: Development of a conceptual framework for organisational responses. *International Journal of Production Research, 49*(18), 5581–5599.

Carmeli, A., & Markman, G. D. (2011). Capture, governance, and resilience: Strategy implications from the history of Rome. *Strategic Management Journal, 32,* 322–341.

Carpenter, S. R., & Brock, W. A. (2008). Adaptive capacity and traps. *Ecology and Society, 13*(2), 40. doi:10.5751/ES-02716-130240

Carpenter, S. R., Westley, F., & Turner, M. G. (2005). Surrogates for resilience of social-ecological systems. *Ecosystems (New York, N.Y.), 8,* 941–944.

Castleden, M., McKee, M., Murray, V., & Leonardi, G. (2011). Resilience thinking in health protection. *Journal of Public Health, 33*(3), 369–377. doi:10.1093/pubmed/fdr027

Chewning, L. V., Lai, C.-H., & Doerfel, M. L. (2013). Organizational resilience and using information and communication technologies to rebuild communication structures. *Management Communication Quarterly, 27,* 237–263. doi:10.1177/08933 18912 46581 5

Coates, G., McGuinness, M., Wright, N. G., Guan, D., Harries, T., & McEwen, L. (2016). SESAME: Improving Small and Medium Enterprises' Operational Response and Preparedness to Flood Events. In Management of Natural Disasters (pp. 107 – 116). WIT Press.

Corey, C. M., & Deitch, E. A. (2011). Factors Affecting Business Recovery Immediately after Hurricane Katrina. *Journal of Contingencies and Crisis Management, 19*(3), 170–181. doi:10.1111/j.1468-5973.2011.00642

Coutu, D. L. (2002). How resilience works. *Harvard Business Review, 80*(5), 46–55.

Cunha, E. M. P., Castanheira, F., Neves, P., Story, J., Rego, A., & Clegg, S. (2013). *Resilience in organizations.* Working paper.

Dalziell, E. P. (2005). Understanding the vulnerability of organizations. *Proc., 1855 Wairarapa Earthquake Symp.,* 130–135.

Danes, S. M., Lee, J., Amarapurkar, S., Stafford, K., Haynes, G., & Brewton, K. E. (2009). Determinants of family business resilience after a natural disaster by gender of business owner. *Journal of Developmental Entrepreneurship, 14*(4), 333–354. doi:10.1142/S1084946709001351

Doern, R. (2016). Entrepreneurship and Crisis Management: The Experiences of Small Business during the London 2011 Riots. *International Small Business Journal, 34*(3), 276–302. doi:10.1177/0266242614553863

Doyle Corner, P., Singh, S., & Pavlovich, K. (2017). Entrepreneurial Resilience and Venture Failure. *International Small Business Journal.* Advance online publication. doi:10.1177/0266242616685604

Duchek, S. (2014). Growth in the face of crisis: The role of organizational resilience capabilities. *Academy of Management Proceedings, 2014,* 13487.

Duit, A. (2016). Resilience thinking: Lessons for Public Administration. *Public Administration, 94*, 364–380.

Dyer, J. G., & McGuiness, T. M. (1996). Resilience: Analysis of the concept. *Archives of Psychiatric Nursing, 10*, 2760–282. doi:10.1016/S0883-9417(96)80036-7

Edgeman, R., & Williams, J. A. (2014). Enterprise self-assessment analytics for sustainability, resilience, and robustness. *The TQM Journal, 26*(4), 368–381.https://doi.org/10.1108/TQM-01-2014-0012

Elwood, A. (2009). Using the disaster crunch/release model in building organisational resilience. *Journal of Business Continuity & Emergency Planning, 3*, 241–247.

European Agency for Health and Safety at Work. (2014). *Calculating the costs of work-related stress and psychosocial risks: A literature review*. Publications Office of the European Union.

Farjoun, M. (2010). Beyond dualism: Stability and change as a duality. *Academy of Management Review, 35*(2), 202–225.

Fiol, C. M., & Lyles, M. A. (1985). Organizational learning. *Academy of Management Review, 10*, 803–813.

Flach, F. F. (1997). *Resilience: How to Bounce Back When the Going Gets Tough!* Hatherleigh Press.

Freeman, S. F., Hirschhorn, L., & Maltz, M. (2004). *Organizational resilience and moral purpose: Sandler O'Neill & Partners in the aftermath of 9/11/01*. Paper presented at the Annual Meeting of the Academy of Management, New Orleans, LA.

Gao, C., Zuzul, T., Jones, G., & Khanna, T. (2017). Over-coming institutional voids: A reputation-based view of long-run survival. *Strategic Management Journal, 38*, 2147–2167.

Garmezy, N. (1991). Resiliency and vulnerability to adverse developmental outcomes associated with poverty. *The American Behavioral Scientist, 34*, 416–430. doi:10.1177/0002764291034004003

Gimenez, R., Hernantes, J., Labaka, L., Hiltz, S. R., & Turoff, M. (2017). Improving the resilience of disaster management organizations through virtual communities of practice: A Delphi study. *Journal of Contingencies and Crisis Management, 25*, 160–170. doi:10.1111/1468-5973.12181

Gittell, J. H., Cameron, K., Lim, S., & Rivas, V. (2006). Relationships, layoffs, and organizational resilience: Airline industry responses to September 11. *The Journal of Applied Behavioral Science, 42*, 300–329.

Grant, A. M., Curtayne, L., & Burton, G. (2009). Executive coaching enhances goal attainment, resilience, and workplace well-being: A randomized controlled study. *The Journal of Positive Psychology, 4*, 396–407. doi:10.1080/17439760902992456

Gunderson, L. H. (2000). Ecological resilience: In theory and application. *Annual Review of Ecology and Systematics, 31*, 425–439.

Hamel, G., & Välikangas, L. (2003). The quest for resilience. *Harvard Business Review, 81*(9), 52–63.

Hannah, S. T., Avolio, B. J., Luthans, F., & Harms, P. D. (2008). Leadership efficacy: Review and future directions. *The Leadership Quarterly, 19*, 669–692. doi:10.1016/j.leaquea.2008.09.007

Harvey, P., & Martinko, M. J. (2009). Attribution theory and motivation. In N. Borkowski (Ed.), *Organizational behavior, theory, and design in health care* (pp. 143–158). Jones, and Bartlett Publishers.

Herbane, B. (2015). Threat Orientation in Small and Medium-Sized Enterprises: Understanding Differences toward Acute Interruptions. *Disaster Prevention and Management*, *24*(5), 570–582. doi:10.1108/DPM-12-2014-0272

Hirsch, P. M., & Levin, D. Z. (1999). Umbrella advocates versus validity police: A life-cycle model. *Organization Science*, *10*, 199–212.

Hollnagel, E. (2011). Epilogue: RAG – the resilience analysis grid. In Resil. Eng. Pract. Ashgate Publishing, Ltd.

Hollnagel, E., Woods, D. D., & Leveson, N. (Eds.). (2006). *Resilience engineering: Concepts and precepts*. Ashgate Publishing Company.

Horne, J., & Orr, J. (1998). Assessing behaviors that create resilient organizations. *Employment Relations Today*, *24*, 29–39.

Jaaron, A. A. M., & Backhouse, C. J. (2014). Service organisations resilience through the application of the vanguard method of systems thinking: A case study approach. *International Journal of Production Research*, *52*, 2026–2041.

James, E. H., & Wooten, L. P. (2005). Leadership as (un)usual: How to display competence in times of crisis. *Organizational Dynamics*, *34*, 141–152.

Kahn, W. A., Barton, M. A., & Fellows, S. (2013). Organizational crises and the disturbance of relational systems. *Academy of Management Review*, *38*, 377–396. doi:10.5465/amr.2011.0363

Kendra, J. M. (2001). *Resilience*. Internal working paper. Disaster Research Center, University of Delaware.

Kendra, J. M., & Wachtendorf, T. (2003). Elements of Resilience after the World Trade Center Disaster: Reconstituting New York City's Emergency Operations Center. *Disasters*, *27*(1), 37–53.

King, D. D., Newman, A., & Luthans, F. (2016). Not if, but when we need resilience in the workplace. *Journal of Organizational Behavior*, *37*(5), 782–786. doi:10.1002/job.2063

Kiuchi, T., & Shireman, B. (1999). Metrics for business in the new economy: An economic change of seasons creates demands for new business metrics. *Environmental Quality Management*, *9*, 79–90.

Klein, R. J. T., Nicholls, R. J., & Thomalla, F. (2003). Resilience to natural hazards: How useful is this concept. *Environmental Hazards*, *5*, 35–45.

Koslowski, T. G., Geoghegan, W., & Longstaff, P. H. (2013). *Organizational Resilience: A Review and Reconceptualization*. In 33rd annual international conference of the strategic management society, Atlanta, GA.

Lampel, J., Bhalla, A., & Jha, P. P. (2014). Does governance confer organisational resilience? Evidence from UK employee-owned businesses. *European Management Journal*, *32*, 66–72.

Le Coze, J. C. (2015). *Vive la diversite! High reliability organization and resilience engineering.* doi:10.1016/j.ssci.2016.04.006

Lee, A. V., Vargo, J., & Seville, E. (2013). Developing a tool to measure and compare organizations'' resilience. *Natural Hazards Review, 14,* 29–41. doi:10.1061/(ASCH)NH.1527-6996.0000075

Lengnick-Hall, Beck, & Lengnick-Hall. (2011). Developing a capacity for organizational resilience through strategic human resource management. *Human Resource Management Review, 21,* 243–255.

Lengnick-Hall, C. A., & Beck, T. E. (2005). Adaptive fit versus robust transformation: How organizations respond to environmental change. *Journal of Management, 31,* 738–757.

Lewis, M. W., & Smith, W. K. (2014). Paradox as a Metatheoretical Perspective: Sharpening the Focus and Widening the Scope. *The Journal of Applied Behavioral Science, 50*(2), 127–149.

Limnios, A. M., Mazzarol, T., Ghadouani, A., & Schilizzi, S. G. M. (2014). The Resilience Architecture Framework: Four Organizational Archetypes. *European Management Journal, 32*(1), 104–116.

Linnenluecke, M. K. (2017). Resilience in business and management research: A review of influential publications and a research agenda. *International Journal of Management Reviews, 19*(1), 4–30.

Linnenluecke, M. K., & Griffiths, A. (2012). Assessing organizational resilience to climate and weather extremes: Complexities and methodological pathways. *Climatic Change, 113,* 933–947.

Luthans, F., Avey, J. B., Avolio, B. J., Norman, S. M., & Combs, G. M. (2006). Psychological capital development: Toward a micro-intervention. *Journal of Organizational Behavior, 27*(3), 387–393.

MacMillian. (2017). *Word of the Day – Resilient.* http://www.macmillandictionaryblog.com/resilient

Mafabi, S., Munene, J., & Ntayi, J. (2012). Knowledge management and organisational resilience: Organizational innovation as a mediator in Uganda parastatals. *J Strategy Manag, 5,* 57–80. doi:10.1108/17554 25121 12004 55

Mallak, L. (1998). Putting organizational resilience to work. *Industrial Management (Des Plaines), 40*(6), 8–13.

Mamouni Limnios, E. (2011). Resilient organizations: Offense versus Defense. *25th Annual ANZAM Conference,* 7–9.

Marcus, A. A., & Nichols, M. L. (1999). On the edge: Heeding the warnings of unusual events. *Organization Science, 10,* 482–499.

Mark, G., Al-Ani, B., & Semaan, B. (2009). Resilience through technology adoption: Merging the old and the new in Iraq. In *Proceedings of the 27th international conference on Human factors in computing systems,* (pp. 689-698). ACM Press.

Mark, G., & Semaan, B. (2008). Resilience in collaboration: Technology as a resource for new patterns of action. In *Proceedings of the CSCW Conference* (pp. 137-146). ACM Press.

Martin, R., & Sunley, P. (2015). On the notion of regional economic resilience: Conceptualization and explanation. *Journal of Economic Geography, 15,* 1–42.

Martin-Breen, P., & Anderies, J. M. (2011). *Resilience: A literature review*. https://opendocs.ids.ac.uk/opend ocs/handl e/20.500.12413 /3692

Marwa, S., & Zairi, M. (2008). An exploratory study of the reasons for the collapse of contemporary companies and their link with the concept of quality. *Management Decision, 46*, 1342–1370. doi:10.1108/00251 74081 09119 84

Masten, A. S. (2011). Resilience in children threatened by extreme adversity: Frameworks for research, practice, and translational synergy. *Development and Psychopathology, 23*, 493–506. doi:10.1017/S0954579411000198

Masten, A. S., & Coatsworth, J. D. (1998). The development of competence in favorable and unfavorable environments: Lessons from research on successful children. *The American Psychologist, 53*, 205–220. http://psycnet.apa.org/journals/amp/53/2/

McCann, J., Selsky, J., & Lee, J. (2009). Building agility, resilience, and performance in turbulent environments. *People & Strategy, 32*, 44–51.

McManus, S., Seville, E., Vargo, J., & Brunsdon, D. (2008). Facilitated process for improving organizational resilience. *Natural Hazards Review, 9*, 81–90. doi:10.1061/(ASCE)1527-6988(2008)9:2(81)

Meyer, A. D. (1982). Adapting to environmental jolts. *Administrative Science Quarterly, 27*(4), 515–537.

Mikušová, M. (2013). Do Small Organizations Have an Effort to Survive? Survey from Small Czech Organizations. *Economic Research-Ekonomska Istraživanja, 264*, 59–76. doi:10.1080/1331677X.2013.11517630

Miller, D., & Friesen, P. H. (1980). Momentum and revolution in organizational adaptation. *Academy of Management Journal, 23*, 591–614.

Moran, K. A., & Mallak, L. A. (2016). Organizational resilience: Sustained institutional effectiveness among smaller, private, non-profit US higher education institutions experiencing organizational decline. *WOR, 54*, 267–281. doi:10.3233/WOR-16229 9

Musgrave & Woodman. (2013). *Weathering the Storm – The 2013 Business Continuity Management Survey*. London: Chartered Management Institute.

Norris, F. H., Stevens, S. P., Pfefferbaum, B., Wyche, K. F., & Pfeffer-baum, R. L. (2008). Community resilience as a metaphor, theory, set of capacities, and strategy for disaster readiness. *American Journal of Community Psychology, 41*(1–2), 127–150. doi:10.100710464-007-9156-6

Øien, K. (2013). Remote operation in environmentally sensitive areas: Development of early warning indicators. *Journal of Risk Research, 16*, 323–336.

Ortiz-de-Mandojana, N., & Bansal, P. (2016). The long-term benefits of organizational resilience through sustainable business practices. *Strategic Management Journal, 37*(8), 1615–1631. https://EconPapers.repec.org/RePEc:bla:stratm:v:37:y:2016:i:8:p:1615-1631

Parker, H., & Ameen, K. (2018). The role of resilience capabilities in shaping how firms respond to disruptions. *J Bus Res, 88*, 535–541. https ://doi.org/ es.2017.12.022 doi:10.1016/j.jbusr

Paul, H., Bamel, U. K., & Garg, P. (2016). Employee resilience and OCB: Mediating effects of organizational commitment. *Vikalpa, 41*(4), 308–324.

Pearson, Ch. M., & Clair, J. A. (1998). Reframing crisis management. *Academy of Management Review, 23*, 59–76.

Podsakoff, P. M., MacKenzie, S. B., & Podsakoff, N. P. (2016). Recommendations for creating better concept definitions in the organizational, behavioral, and social sciences. *Organizational Research Methods, 19*, 159–203. doi:10.1177/10944 28115 62496 5

Powley, E. H. (2013). The process and mechanisms of organizational healing. *The Journal of Applied Behavioral Science, 49*, 42–68. doi:10.1177/00218 86312 47119 2

Ray, J. L., Baker, L. T., & Plowman, D. A. (2011). Organizational mindfulness in business schools. *Academy of Management Learning & Education, 10*, 188–203. doi:10.5465/AMLE.2011.62798 929

Reeves, M., & Deimler, M. S. (2009). Strategies for winning in the current and post-recession environment. *Strat Leader, 37*, 10–17. doi:10.1108/10878 57091 10014 44

Rerup, C. (2001). Houston, we have a problem: Anticipation and improvisation as sources of organizational resilience. *Comportamento Organizacional e Gestão, 7*, 27–44.

Richardson, G. E. (2002). The metatheory of resilience and resiliency. *Journal of Clinical Psychology, 58*, 307–321. doi:10.1002/jclp.10020

Richtnér, A., & Löfsten, H. (2014). Managing in turbulence: How the capacity for resilience influences creativity. *R & D Management, 44*, 137–151.

Riolli, L., & Savicki, V. (2003). Optimism and Coping as Moderators of the Relation Between Work Resources and Burnout in Information Service Workers. *International Journal of Stress Management, 10*(3), 235–252. doi:10.1037/1072-5245.10.3.235

Rutter, M. (1993). Resilience: Some conceptual considerations. *The Journal of Adolescent Health, 14*, 626–631. https://www.jahonline.org/issue/S1054-139X(00)X0125-5

Sahebjamniaa, N., Torabia, S. A., & Mansourib, S. A. (2015). Integrated Business Continuity and Disaster Recovery Planning: Towards Organizational Resilience. *European Journal of Operational Research, 242*(1), 261–273. doi:10.1016/j.ejor.2014.09.055

Salanova, M., Llorens, S., Cifre, E., & Martínez, I. M. (2012). We need a hero! Toward a validation of the healthy and resilient organization (HERO) model. *Group & Organization Management, 37*, 785–822.

Sawalha, I. H. S. (2015). Managing adversity: Understanding some dimensions of organizational resilience. *Management Research Review, 38*(4), 346–366.

Seville, E., Brunsdon, D., Dantas, A., Le Masurier, J., Wilkinson, S., & Vargo, J. (2007). Organisational resilience: Researching the reality of New Zealand organisations. *Journal of Business Continuity & Emergency Planning, 2*, 258.

Seville, E., Brunsdon, D., Dantas, A., Masurier, J. L., Wilkinson, S., & Vargo, J. (2008). Organisational resilience: Researching the reality of New Zealand organisations. *Journal of Business Continuity & Emergency Planning, 2*, 258–266.

Sheffi, Y. (2005). Preparing for the big one. *Supply Chain Management, 84*(5), 12 – 15. Doi:10.1049/me:20050503

Sheffi, Y. (2007). *The resilient enterprise: Overcoming vulnerability for competitive advantage.* MIT Press.

Somers, S. (2009). Measuring resilience potential: An adaptive strategy for organizational crisis planning. *Journal of Contingencies and Crisis Management, 17*(1), 12–23. doi:10.1111/j.1468-5973.2009.00558.x

Stephenson, A. (2010). *Benchmarking the Resilience of Organizations* [Unpublished PhD Thesis]. Civil and Natural Resources Engineering Department, University of Canterbury.

Suddaby, R. (2010). Editor's comments: Construct clarity in theories of management and organization. *Academy of Management Review, 35*(3), 346–357. doi:10.5465/AMR.2010.51141319

Supply Chain Risk Leadership Council. (2013). *SCRLC Emerging Risks in the Supply Chain 2013.* White paper.

Sutcliffe, K. M., & Vogus, T. J. (2003). Organizing for resilience. In K. S. Cameron, J. E. Dutton, & R. E. Quinn (Eds.), *Positive organizational scholarship: Foundations of a new discipline* (pp. 94–110). Berrett-Koehler.

Uhl-Bien, M., Marion, R., & McKelvey, B. (2007). Complexity leadership theory: Shifting leadership from the industrial age to the knowledge era. *The Leadership Quarterly, 18*(4), 298–318.

van der Vegt, G. S., Essens, P., Wahlstrom, M., & George, G. (2015). Managing risk and resilience. *Academy of Management Journal, 58*, 971–980.

Vogus, T. J., & Sutcliffe, K. M. (2007). *Organizational resilience: Towardsa theory and research agenda.* Paper presented at the Systems, Manand Cybernetics, 2007. ISIC. IEEE International Conference.

Wagnild, G., & Young, H. (1990). Resilience among older women. *Journal of Nursing Scholarship, 22*(4), 252–255.

Wedawattaa, G., Ingirige, B., & Amaratunga, D. (2010). Building up resilience of construction sector SMEs and their supply chains to extreme weather events. *International Journal of Strategic Property Management, 14*, 362–375. doi:10.3846/ijspm. 2010.27

Weick, K. (1993). The collapse of sensemaking in organizations: The Mann Gulch disaster. *Administrative Science Quarterly, 38*, 628–652.

Weick, K. (1996). Prepare your organization for fight fires. *Harvard Business Review, 74*, 143–148.

Weick, K. E., & Sutcliffe, K. M. (2001). *Managing the unexpected: resilient performance in an age of uncertainty.* Jossey-Bass Inc.

Weick, K. E., Sutcliffe, K. M., & Obstfeld, D. (1999). Organizing for High Reliability: Processes of Collective Mindfulness. In R. S. Sutton & B. M. Staw (Eds.), *Research in Organizational Behavior* (Vol. 1, pp. 81–123). Jai Press.

Werner, E. E. (1997). Vulnerable but invincible: High-risk children from birth to adulthood. *Acta Paedictric Supplement, 422,* 103-105. doi:.1997.tb.18356.x doi:10.1111/j.1651-2227

Wildavsky, A. B. (1991). *Searching for Safety*. Transaction.

Windle, G. (2011). What is resilience? A review and concept analysis. *Reviews in Clinical Gerontology, 21,* 152–169. doi:10.1017/S0959259810000420

Wofford, L., Troilo, M., & Dorchester, A. (2011). Point of View: Cognitive Risk and Real Estate Portfolio Management. *Journal of Real Estate Portfolio Management, 17*(1), 69–73. doi:10.1080/10835547.2011.12089891

Wong, C.-S., Law, K. S., & Huang, G.-H. (2008). On the importance of conducting construct-level analysis for multidimensional constructs in theory development and testing. *Journal of Management, 34,* 744–764.

Wreathall, J. (2009). Measuring resilience. Resil. Eng. Perspect., 2, 95-114.

Wright, Suh, & Leggett. (2009). If at first you don't succeed: Globalized production and organizational learning at the Hyundai Motor Company. *Asia Pacific Business Review, 15,* 163–180. doi:10.1080/13602 38070 16984 18

Youssef, C. M., Luthans, F., & Youssef, C. M. (2007). Emerging Positive Organizational Behavior. *Journal of Management, 33*(3), 321–349.

Zahra, S. A., & George, G. (2002a). Absorptive Capacity: A Review, Reconceptualization, and Extension. *Academy of Management Review, 27*(2), 185–203.

Chapter 8
Organizational Resilience Capability and Capacity Building

José G. Vargas-Hernández
https://orcid.org/0000-0003-0938-4197
Instituto Tecnológico José Mario Molina Pasquel y Henríquez, Mexico

ABSTRACT

The objective of this chapter is to analyze the implications of organizational resilience capability and capacity building and development processes and the posed challenges to its design and implementation. It is based on the conceptual and theoretical assumptions underpinning the capabilities of resilience that can be learned and designed by organizations to be implemented and applied to adverse conditions. These underlying assumptions affect the organizational resilience capabilities building. It is concluded that building and development organizational resilience capabilities processes has increased the research agenda on the theoretical and conceptual literature and the notions, factors, elements, and challenges.

INTRODUCTION

Organizations are subject to complex, uncertain, ever changing, and diverse environment which require to develop resilience capabilities to manage and recover from disruptions. Resilience remains a problem in practice as the organizational capability to alleviate the effects of disruptions and to bounce back from a crisis (Hamel and Välikangas 2003; Salwan and Gada 2018).

Many organizational threats require different types of resilience of the system by making decisions on the best resilience way to approach the operational environment depending on the mission characteristics. To achieve this requires balancing all the specific elements of organizational resilience such as the objective, the mission capability, and the operational environment to avoid, mitigate and recover from the impact. Resilience capabilities avoid and limit the impacts of adverse events (Sheffi and Rice 2005; Jüttner and Maklan 2011).

Unfortunately, the organization science has developed a lot of inadequate conceptual assumptions and frameworks that fail to contribute to find solutions. Organizational resilience can be studied as a capacity and capability-based concept (Duchek, 2020; Williams *et al.* 2017). This processual perspective

DOI: 10.4018/978-1-7998-8996-0.ch008

concerns the phases of crises as an integral model of organizational resilience that acknowledges the inherent uncertainty (Williams et al., 2017). Organizational resilience is being studied by the resilience capabilities and processual approaches. At the organizational level, organizational resilience derives from a set of organizational capabilities, processes, practices, routines orienting the organization and acting forward to create a setting of diversity and adjustable integration (Lengnick-Hall *et al*. 2011, p. 246).

Organizational resilience may be considered the ability, capability, and property which can be improved over time despite the difficulties to find the right elements that may contribute to handle disruptive events. Organizational resilience is a desirable property, an ability, capacity, and capability to deal with changes, jolts, and risks. Some characteristics of organizational resilience are the potential capability and capacity under emergent, disruptive, and discontinuous internal and external environment not always perceived in operational activities. Some characteristics of organizational resilience are the development of potential capabilities that take advantage under emergent and discontinuous, emergent, and disruptive environment. The essence of organizational resilience capabilities is the dealing with change, risks, and environmental jolts.

Organizational resilience behaviors are explained by the resilience capabilities, practices, and routines to cope with unexpected threats and events. Behavioral resilience enables the organization to learn about the situation, use resources and capabilities in collaborative actions.

CONCEPTUALIZATION

The conceptualization of organizational resilience considers capabilities, awareness, perceptions, planning, etc. (De Florio, 2013). There is little consensus about the meaning of organizational resilience, what are its elements, what are the organizational capabilities and conditions needed and how they are composed. The conceptualization of organizational capabilities to develop resilience are required despite the existing inconsistencies in the literature. The organizational resilience literature is based on turnaround the resources and capabilities advancing from different disciplines such as psychology, ecology, engineering, and organization science, etc., for building new theory.

Resilience is conceptualized as a meta-capability formed by a set of organizational capabilities and routines. The organizational capabilities and meta-capability that underlie resilience are complex, embedded, and dependent on social context factors. Resilience capabilities become effective when leveraged on complexity (Birkie et al. 2017).

The integral and capability-based resilience model provides a frame of reference structure to ongoing debate. The capability-based perspective contributes to organizational resilience capabilities for the organization for survival and prosperity despite the adversity and turbulence. Resilience based on the perspective of capabilities that become effective in situations of complexity of risks contributes with applying stability while addressing the disruptions through incorporating non-linearity quantum thinking replacing the Newtonian thinking (Pellissier 2011, 2012). Organizational resilience capability building is context-dependent on the specific exposure to desirable characteristic dealing with unexpected, abrupt, and extreme change (Linnenluecke and Griffiths 2012).

The conceptual development of organizational resilience remains underdeveloped based on assumptions about the nature of capabilities (Limnios et al., 2014), which can incorporate other dimensions used in disciplines that have adopted the resilience construct as it applies within each domain in psychology, engineering, ecology, management sciences, etc., with an intention to further developing organizational applicability. The conceptual analysis of the organizational resilience construct is a cognitive frame on development of resilience capabilities.

Assumptions of an integrated model supported by managerial cognitions lead to organizational resilience capability building of a specific type of resilience to apply actions, as the heuristics-based capability model. An integrative resilience framework for uncertain environments is the capability for turning adverse conditions into organizational opportunities, bouncing back in an agile deportment without being stuck by an unexpected event (Kantur and İşeri-Say, 2012)

Resilience is the ability and the capability of any system to return and recover to a stable state after displacement (Bhamra, Dani, & Burnard, 2011; Norris et al., 2008). Organizational resilience is determined by the capabilities designed to cope with environmental shifts (Lengnick-Hall & Beck, 2009). Resilience is the system´s capability to maintain its structure and function in the face of internal and external changes and to degrade when it must (Weick & Sutcliffe, 2007: 69). Organizational resilience is the function of specific capabilities and abilities (Erol *et al.*, 2009; Gunasekaran, Rai, Griffin, 2011; McManus, Seville, Vargo, Brunsdon, 2008).

The concept of resilience based on integral, and capabilities support the conceptual and empirical studies for the recovery of organizational activities and the capacity to operate (van der Vegt et al., 2015). Most of the studies have been conducted on qualitative research (Bansal & Corley, 2011; Eisenhardt & Graebner, 2007; Gephart, 2004). The empirical evidence of organizational resilience is more than restoration to include the building of new capabilities to expand abilities to keep pace and create opportunities (Lengnick-Hall et al., 2011).

Organizational resilience is the capability to alleviate and bounce back adverse effects of disruptions and from crisis situations (Salwan and Gada, 2018). Organizational resilience is the actor´s process by which builds and uses its capability endowments to interact with the environment adjusting and maintaining the functioning prior to, during and following adversity (Williams *et al.* 2017). Organizational resilience is an emergent property to lean to adjust and strengthen its capability to overcome adversity and future challenges (Teo *et al.* 2017).

Organizational resilience is a latent attribute characterized by a set of capabilities that are path-dependent and developed by organizations coping unexpected events (Ortiz-de-Mandojana and Bansal, 2016). Resilience is an ability and capability for the organizations, which may be desirable depending on the state of the organization and system (Mamouni Limnios, 2011; Mamouni Limnios *et al.*, 2014). Resilience is a characteristic of an organization development of resources and capabilities.

A resilience capability means having both ability and capacity for resilience that need to be transformed into action (Richtnér and Löfsten, 2014, p. 138) becoming an organizational resilience capability. A systemic organizational resilience refers to a proactively mitigating risks in different contexts balancing mitigation and reactive capabilities (Marchese and O'Dwyer, 2014; Sáenz and Revilla, 2014; Deloitte Development LLC, 2013; Sheffi, 2005). Organizational resilience is the ability and capability to accommodate and absorb change without shocks, without catastrophic failure and gracefully (Boin and van Eten, 2013). Organizational resilience is the capability to maintain operations under the spectrum of potential breakdowns (Aleksić et al. 2013)

Organizational resilience is a capability for turning adverse conditions into an opportunity, a positive attitude of bouncing back, agile deportment an unexpected and disruptive event in an inertia stages (Kantur and Iseri-Say 2012). Organizational resilience is the capability for turning adverse conditions into the organizational opportunity, the positive attitude of bouncing back and relative agile deportment brought by an expected and disruptive event or a series of them without being stuck too long in the stagnation and inertia stage.

Organizational resilience is the set of specific organizational capabilities, routines, practices, and processes to conceptually orient itself, act to move forward and create a setting of diversity and adjustable integration (Lengnick-Hall et al. 2011). Organizational resilience is the capability to maintain operations under a wide spectrum of potential breakdowns (Antunes, 2011). Organizational resilience is the capability to meet current market demands that consider alternative options for growth to capitalize upon anticipated trend in the Marketplace (Ismail et al. 2011). Organizational resilience is the capability to anticipate periods of chaos and crisis by reacting to disruptions and shocks to achieve adjustments.

Organizational resilience is an ability of a system to meet operating, maintaining, and recovering critical capabilities under pressures, tensions and stressors of disasters and unexpected events. Specific resilience is the capability to maintain functions during and after specific threat or unexpected event. Organizational resilience is the emergent capability to investigate, learn, act, and improve and those overall capabilities without knowing in advance what one will be called to act upon (Wildavsky, 1988).

The integral capability-based organizational resilience expands the theoretical concept leads to cope with crises and to enact practices and their interplay occurring during, before and after the crises. This integration is not considering the recovery of the crises and disasters conceptualized as bouncing back to achieve a new normal. This temporal differentiation of crisis is the bases to develop an integral capability-based organizational resilience that allows to plan the resistance and the containing crisis approach. This approach is being regarded as the conceptual umbrella to cover all the capabilities associated to the different phases of crisis (Masten & Obradović, 2007: 14).

The capability-based theory of organizational resilience is supported by Duchek, (2014); Parker and Ameen, 2018; Williams et al. 2017). A capability-based conceptualization of organizational resilience is done by Lengnick-Hall, Beck, & Lengnick-Hall (2011), as shown in figure 1.

The organizational context of resilience is relevant for the anticipation in coping with unexpected events by the understanding of the environment and acceptance of reality of existing problems (Coutu 2002; Catalan and Robert, 2011). The anticipation stage in the resilience process comprises important and specific capabilities such as the abilities to analyze internal and external organizational developments, to identify potential threats and critical developments and, and to prepare for unexpected and unknown events (Kendra and Wachtendorf, 2003; Somers, 2009; Burnard and Bhamra, 2011).

Organizational resilience accepts the overlapping elements of anticipation capabilities by understanding the environment and the reference of its operational system and the awareness of accepting failures (Catalan and Robert, 2011). Resilience capabilities inherent to the system are the homeostasis, morphostasis and morphogenesis (Chan 2011). The resilience potential is defined as the one not presently evident and realized built by the anticipation capabilities (Somers, 2009, p. 13) as the foundations to respond to critical situations and provide control and undertake actions, decisions and adjustments (Schulman, 2004, p. 43) and coping capabilities.

The organizational development of resilience capabilities potential, not evident and realized, needs the anticipation capabilities, although they are not sufficient. The organizational resilience evolves from one level to another based on the improvement of capabilities to deal with shocks and disturbances and survive to environmental changes. High levels of resilience needs the development require to focus on several resilience stages and capabilities forming the meta-capabilities mixing anticipation and coping capabilities (Somers, 2009).

Figure 1. A capability-based conceptualization of organizational resilience
Source: Lengnick-Hall, Beck, & Lengnick-Hall (2011).

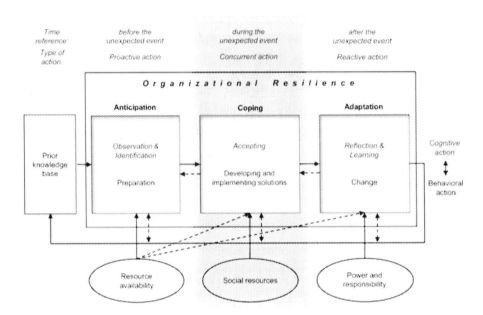

Organizations strengthen resilience as the ability to recover basic and critical capabilities from threat events and natural disasters to facilitate recovery efforts, prevent system collapse and reduce economic impacts (Bernstein, Bienstock, Hay, Uzunoglu, Zussman, 2004). Resilience is the set of attitudes and development of new capabilities of organizational representatives about desirable actions (Kendra and Wachtendorf 2003).

The most recognized categorizations of the concept of organizational resilience are the resilience as an outcome, as a process and resilience capabilities. The conceptualization of resilience as an outcome considers that organizations performs well during periods of crisis and bounce back due to different factors (Horne and Orr 1998) or attributes that are adequate resources (Kendra and Wachtendorf, 2003; Gittell et al. 2006; Vaelikangas and Romme, 2013) such as positive relationships (Gittell et al. 2006) or redundancy (Kendra and Wachtendorf 2003). Self-awareness is an attribute of organizational resilience that requires the ability to understand real time activities and capabilities, mindset, and tools to monitor the environmental vulnerabilities, and risks across the organization and in its value chain.

THEORETICAL FRAMEWORK

The theory of organizational resilience may help to build resilience capabilities to overcome the challenges of adversity, no continuous and disruptive environment, manage disasters and crisis. Organizational resilience has a diversity of responses to adversity using functional resources and capabilities to respond in a specific context and operate under several conditions. Organizational resources and capabilities facilitate resilience.

An interdisciplinary approach to organizational resilience theory is useful to expand the conceptualization to include transformative changing levels of ecological adversity to develop resources and capabilities aimed to mitigate the negative impacts. Conceptual advancements of organizational resilience combine the ecological, psychological, and economic perspective linked to the capability building as a formative construct. The functional dimensions of biodiversity aids ecological resilience leading organizations to prepare resources and building capability redundancies to anticipate adversities (Folke et al., 2004: 570)

A general organizational resilience theoretical framework provides the identification and assessment of the appropriate measures to address, enhance and optimize the capabilities of a resilience approach based on risk tolerance, threat environment and the organizational mission needs and goals (McLeod et al., 2016; Dreyer, P., Langeland, K. S., Manheim, D. McLeod, G. and Nacouzi, G. 2016). The organizational resilience framework based on transdisciplinary, interdisciplinary, and multidisciplinary contributions that support activities and actions of the different organizational actors and stakeholders sharing resources, capabilities, methods, and tools aimed to identify unforeseen crisis and face catastrophic events.

Organizational resilience and adaptation depend on the assessment that organizational actors and agents do evaluating their sensemaking processes, the access to their resources and capabilities in relation to anomalous weather variabilities and conditions. The alternative sensemaking focus on the organizational resilience in exploring the emerging capabilities required for the survival of an adverse collapse and rebuild growth performance.

An empirical framework may give grounded basis to resilience capabilities to be applied to a range of organizational conditions. Organizational resilience framework supports the capability development to deal with unexpected events and disruptions-based risks.

A framework of organizational resilience uses the key concepts and their relationships and interactions of resilience capabilities to organize an heterogenous field as the basis for the operationalization. Relational resilience activation model emerges when the organization learns to adjust to adversity strengthening its capability to overcome future risks and disruptions (Mallak 1998; Teo et al. 2017).

A framework related to crisis and organizational resilience is developed by Williams, et al (2017), to define capabilities for organizing, durability and adjusting to disturbances. The crisis and disaster management theoretical and empirical framework provide limited knowledge and insights aimed to strengthen organizational capabilities in organizational resilience to deal with impacts (Boin & McConnell, 2007; Rosenthal & Kouzmin, 1996). The resilience management model defines areas to include asset management, risk management, people management and resilience development to be used as a benchmark of organizational capability (Caralli *et al.* 2010). Resilience is a process that includes the development a broader store of capabilities (Limnios et al. 2014).

Organizational resilience has the dimensions of impact resistance and rapidity. There are two dominating organizational resilience approaches: the resistance, and the containing approaches that have shown limitations. These limitations are overcome by the development of an integral capability-based model of organizational resilience. This model integrates the elements and components of the organizational resilience and focuses more on the recovery phase of resilience.

By integrating the resistance and containing crisis approaches into an integral and capability-based model of organizational resilience, there is a reference to the long-term oriented recovery resilience that requires analytic, evaluative response measures and policymaking to identify the best practices to improve mitigation and preparedness (Boin and van Eeten 2013: 431; Boin et al., 2010: 4; National Governors' Association, 1979: xv).

Elements of organizational resilience is the mobilization of resources and capabilities during the crisis (Doern, 2016). Organizational actors and agents can have access through improvising and mobilize resources and capabilities of resilience for recovery (Weick et al., 2005). Resources and capabilities for organizational resilience contribute to growth opportunities.

The impact resistance is the capacity to withstand damaging effects and rapidity is an organizational capability to recover and restore the previous state of disturbance and to improved state after the damaging impact (Linnenluecke & Griffiths, 2010; McDaniels et al., 2008).

Organizational resilience has the possession of cognitive and behavioral resilience capabilities that give support to the realization and reactive resilience capabilities and of the potential and proactive resilience capabilities. Despite the differentiation of cognitive, behavioral, and contextual dimensions of resilience (Lengnick-Hall and Beck 2005, 2009; Lengnick-Hall et al. 2011), they are always in interplay between behavioral and cognitive capabilities.

The interplay of cognitive and behavioral elements of organizational resilience, the contextual factors such as power, resources, social capital, etc. are necessary to develop the resilience capabilities and successfull resilience processes. The behavioral resilience enables to learn the situation, to use the resources and capabilities and to move the organization forward through collaborative actions.

Resilience capabilities in organizations are complex, socially embedded and path-dependent to be analyzed by the use of observational and conversational methods of analysis on environments, developments and competitive advantages management (Teixeira and Werther, 2013). Prior organizational knowledge based on the capabilities as the basic drivers for organizational resilience is the source of power, the main social resources, and responsibilities. Social resources have a positive influence on the development of coping capabilities for organizational resilience.

BUILDING AND DEVELOPMENT ORGANIZATIONAL RESILIENCE CAPABILITIES PROCESSES

Theoretical assumptions underpinning the capabilities of resilience can be learned by organizations to be applied to adverse conditions. The underlying assumptions affect the organizational resilience capabilities building. Organizations build resilience capabilities based on a range of antecedents, organizational internal factors, and outcomes, all of which affect the make-up of capabilities development. Organizations must balance internal resilience capabilities and external influences (Erol et al. 2010) A model of organizational resilience should outline the factors and antecedents to adversity and the internal capabilities of organizations to react to adversities with a positive reintegration.

The transformational perspective of organizational resilience is based on the interpersonal factors that lead to organizational capacity of individual resilience used to generate, managed, and employ resources and capabilities to create a supportive environment and overcome challenges. Organizational resilience capabilities are learned according to environmental changes outside the organizations. Building the capability in resilience based on the processes of sensing, seizing, and transforming, corresponding to before, during and after adversity. Organizational resilience is achieved in practice of organizational capabilities that provide support for the internal workings and conditions although they are required by the different phases of the process.

The concept of resilience from human resources management perspective is based on training considering that the organizational capacity for the development of resilience derives from specific organizational capabilities, conceptualizations, processes, routines, practices creating a diverse and adjustable integration (Lengnick-Hall et al. 2011)

Organizations build the resilience capability considering the contextual factors of the actor's decisions. Constraints and opportunities in the decision context have effects in the way actors in organizations build the organizational resilience capabilities. Adversity has an impact on the resilience capabilities in different contexts which may require theory-building to understand the building capabilities.

The organizational resilience capability loop embraces both adverse and advantage orientations of performance and growth. The resilience capability loop is repeatable and secure. The organizational resilience loop model extends to routines and heuristic based capabilities which can be built and applied at any time in anticipation of adverse events and in any organization adopting the resilience perspective, rather than assuming a favorable environment. Organizational resilience capabilities are built to cope the adverse conditions arising from the orientation addressed on the antecedent conditions of the environment.

Building capabilities in organizational resilience to remain capable may lead to the collapse trap when the capabilities are gone. Building the organizational resilience capabilities enable to cope with any kind of shocks.

Resilience in organizational settings is a process of capability building than as a trait requires innate orientations (Taleb, 2012). Building organizational resilience capability is a process model developed from a construct across all domains with emphasis in the psychology domain (Luthar, 2006; Masten, 2007, 2014; Richardson, 2002). Building an organizational resilience capability is based on higher order constructs to identify the critical parameters.

The resilience-as-a-process perspective that blends with organizational routines and capabilities. The process model thrives adversity by resilience and agility by differentiating routine-based capabilities and heuristics (Lengnick-Hall & Beck, 2009). If key resources and assets remain intact in less severe adversity, then heuristics and routines are part of the make-up of organizational resilience capability. Organizational resilience capabilities are built based on routines and heuristics affected by salient antecedents, internal factor governing and the outcomes. The combination of different practices of both heuristics and routines are needed to build organizational resilience capabilities.

The heuristics and processes built in organizational resilience are based on the anatomy and types of threats and disorganizations experienced by the organization and the learned knowledge and skills. Organizational resilience capability building considers the anatomy of capabilities and how the actor's knowledge and skills cohere into processes that are more collective.

Resilience collective capacities building is an inclusive process that involves the individuals, organizations, and communities' actors to interact, use and build its capability endowments adjusted with the environments to maintain functioning prior to, during and after any adversity. These endowment capabilities are cognitive, behavioral, emotion and relational. The response capabilities are cognitive, behavioral, and contextual (Williams et al. 2017). An inclusive perspective of organizational resilience must integrate knowledge from risks and crisis as pre-adversity capabilities, crisis organizing and adjusting and post crisis response (Williams et al. 2017). The organizational response capabilities are the vulnerability considered as the acceptance of crisis and resilience representing the level of tolerance to cope with adversity (Gaillard 2007).

Heuristics is part of the make-up of the organizational resilience capability development if resources are decimated and deploying routines become unavailable. The sequence heuristic-based capabilities are the critical element of building organizational resilience based on individual skills (Miller, Eisenstat, &

Foote, 2002). Heuristics is part of the makeup of resilience capability in circumstances when there are limited key resources and assets.

Routine based capabilities achieve efficiency but lacks flexibility to respond to adverse conditions while heuristics or simple rules conserve cognitive and operating resources have an impact on capabilities required to navigate through uncertainty and survive any disruption (Felin, Foss, Heimeriks, & Madsen, 2012; Winter, 2013; Bingham & Haleblian, 2012; Mousavi & Gigerenzer, 2014). The organizational resilience capacity derives from a set of organizational capabilities, processes, practices, routines aiming to create a setting diversity and adjustable integration (Lengnick-Hall and Beck 2005, p. 245). The knowledge of building the resilience capability can be passed to early-stage ventures.

Organizational resilience capabilities building can follow different patterns based on simple rules to enable decisions to apply to uncertain adversities. Building capabilities in organizational resilience and leading into a selection method of heuristics when resources uncertain, unstable and collapse and the routines are unreliable. Heuristics based organizational resilience capability model functions across operating conditions (Bingham & Eisenhardt, 2011).

The theoretical model of resilience capability building based on heuristics behavior-action of individuals in the organizations and their attitudes of recovery from collapse considered as a resilience capability. An organization that can apply its capabilities in actions enhances resilience to confront further adversities that may have an impact upon it. Practices of organizational resilience are evidence of actions that may render reintegration into different organizational capabilities.

Organizational resilience is achieved through preparation and development of capabilities and functions necessary to deal with unexpected events (Kendra and Wachtendorf, 2003). Preparedness for formalization of organizational resilience activities may result in an enhanced capability to respond to disruptions, although strong orientation does not necessarily correspond to resilience formalization.

After a disruption, resilient capabilities can be reintegrated aimed to regain the performance levels (Richardson, 2002). Resilience reintegration intends to exceed the previous performance levels existing before the adversity and the declining results. Resilience reintegration orientation is part of the resilience theory that affects the development of capability and the intended ends.

Organizational capabilities form stages of the organizational resilience process. Each resilience stage requires different capabilities for resilience-enhancing practices. Organizational resilience focus on general capabilities and routines (Lengnick-Hall and Beck, 2005, 2009; Lengnick-Hall et al. 2011).

In organizational environments of high uncertainty, fluency in organizational routines becomes essential to improve the capability of organizational resilience. The organizational resilience framework improves the capabilities and abilities to anticipate, prevent, manage, and respond to any disruption-related risks, ensuring continuity of normal operations.

The essence of organizational resilience capabilities is the dealing with change, risks, and environmental jolts. Organizational resilience is the perpetual adjustment and anticipation to develop proactively the capabilities and capacities to change before any disruption-based risks. The organizational capabilities and processes to develop resilience organizations remains as a black box. The capacity of an organization to develop resilience derives from a set of capabilities, practices, routines, and processes (Lengnick-Hall et al. 2011) used to move forward.

Organizational resilience is dependent on the individual resilience capacities and consists of organizational process capabilities emerging from coping with unexpected events to generate resilience outcomes expressed in organizational routines (Nelson & Winter, 1982). Individual resilience is the starting point as an additive composite for organizational resilience of capabilities and actions (Lengnick-Hall *et al.*

2011). Equifinality of organizational resilience-related capabilities is different for small and medium sized companies than for large companies (Aleksić *et al.* 2013; Burnard and Bhamra, 2011; Chan, 2011; Dewald and Bowen, 2010; Gunasekaran, *et al.* 2011; Ismail *et al.* 2011; Pal *et al.* 2014; Sullivan-Taylor and Branicki 2011).

The foundations of organizational resilience capabilities can be applied to dismantling and rebuilding processes while navigating through uncertainty (Weick & Sutcliffe, 2007). Organizational decline offers some insights in skill building for resilience but may not incorporate the combination of both resilience and capabilities. Decline and rebuilding phases of organizational resilience require different set heuristic capabilities separated by the operational stability threshold on access to a determined level of resources.

Organizations build resilience capabilities subject to below or above their level of stability. The organizational decline, collapse, and rebuilding heuristics, enhance the organizational resilience capability. The foundations of organizational resilience capabilities can be applied to dismantling and rebuilding processes while navigating through uncertainty (Weick & Sutcliffe, 2007).

Disorganization is an opportunity for the organizational resilience capabilities repertoire to respond, cope and growth. The disorganization and collapse of resources deprive the organization of building resilience capabilities and handling adversity (Cheng & Kesner, 1997). Adopted organizational resilience is supported by the built and developed capabilities to manage the resources available. Management of organizational resilience must be bi-focal consciously nurturing the capabilities and capacities to function during disorganization.

Resilience requires an ability to withstand a disruption with high degradation and failure, without reduction of capabilities and without representing a safety hazard. Non-material factors have the potential to enhance resilience in an environment of budget and fiscal constraints and technological capabilities. An organization must invest in organizational resilience capability building and development leading to better incarnations of the core business and to remain committed subject to the specific conditions for a period before exit (Peteraf et al., 2013; Dew, Goldfarb, & Sarasvathy, 2006; Watts & Paciga, 2011). Organizational resilience capability building needs specific development to suit specific circumstances.

The resilience capabilities of flexibility, reaction speed and velocity, access to timely information, and collaborations in the supply chain resilience during the financial crisis limited the negative impacts on costs, revenues, and targets (Juettner and Maklan, 2011).

CHALLENGES

Organizations as societies are facing increasing number of major challenges, adverse events, and disasters (UNISDR, 2015, vander Vegt, Essens, Wahlström, & George, 2015; Tierney, 2014: 238). High-reliable organizations accept uncertainty as the condition of their current operations (Leveson et al., 2009; Sutcliffe & Vogus, 2003) despite there are disparities between organizational reliability and organizational resilience, facing some theoretical and empirical challenges (La Porte, 1996; Leveson et al., 2009; Rijpma, 2003).

Organizational resilience has increased the research agenda on the theoretical and conceptual literature on the notions and factors, the elements, the challenges. The theoretical concept of resilience and methods to improve operational resilience remain as challenges for academics, researchers, and practitioners (Klein et al. 2003). The development of a multi-level resilience concepts and constructs have methodological challenges (Chen *et al.* 2005) and needs further consideration, such as the measures presented by McCann and Selsky (2012) at the levels of employee, team, organization and industry. Measurement of resilience challenges the use of a required empirical and context dependent measurement tool. Organizational resilience is the ability to withstand challenging and unexpected shocks through the firm's response to prior challenges (Gao *et al.* 2017).

Organizational resilience is the ability to weather and withstand crisis-associates challenges (Fleming, 2012). An organizational resilience is the ability that result from a complex process to match internal and external challenges with the capacity to shift them into opportunities (Witmer & Mellinger 2016). Resilience is the development of inner robustness in the ability to anticipate challenges using the available resources reacting appropriately (Welter-Enderlin & Hildenbrand, 2006).

Resilience becomes a priority for the new challenges posed by potential cyber security threats. With many organizations sleepwalking into chaos and disaster depending on the nature of the challenges, resilience in organizations is difficult to recognize, identify, implement, and sustain. Individual resilience starts accepting the reality of unexpected events to be able to cope with them (Coutu, 2002). This phenomenon is discussed as "the cognitive challenge" in organizational resilience (Hamel and Vaelikangas 2003, p. 54). It requires a shift in mind and servant leadership. Organizational resilience requires a servant leadership agenda to mobilize people to meet the challenges.

Organizational resilience requires leadership to coordinate and direct from the bottom up the visions and targets to identify and implement solutions to the emerging challenges. However, tensions emerge between a supportive leadership during times of change and demanding leadership required to sustain the organization in balance between consistency and flexibility, and defense and progression.

Organizational resilience is an expression of capability growth after trauma. Organizational resilience (Denyer, 2017) and high reliability organizations (Roberts, 1990) are a capability approach that challenges the planning approach. The incorporation process of a trauma into the organizational resilience capabilities repertoire enable to build tools to manage a strong resistance for adverse events. Each one of the organizational missions has unique demands of resilience but there are several features and challenges that are common such as awareness and information sharing, flexible balance between distributed and centralized decision making, structures and cultures, and environmental risks.

Long-term organizational resilience requires holistic capabilities enabling to hold and strive for continual organizational resilience, which may be drawn as a feedback loop and linked to the organizational culture. Organizational resilience is the capability that link culture and resilience (Parsons 2010). Building an organizational resilience capability in a holistic management framework to identify threats and their impacts might cause to the interests of stakeholders, their reputation and value creation (British Standards Institution, 2006). A holistic approach of organizational resilience balances the internal capabilities and the external influences.

The mechanisms for specific resilience and general resilience challenge the flexible response capabilities. Insights on organizational resilience are gained from analyzing mechanisms that foster the resilience capabilities. Assuring the development of organizational resilience against specific and general unprepared threats that make the organization potentially more vulnerable and rigid, has several challenges related to the risks, needs and capabilities required for an optimal solution. Resilience is the ability of a system to respond with the required capabilities to the environmental system failures and challenges (Sheton, 2013). The indicators of resilience are categorized as specific, general, and universal presenting some challenges.

Organizational resilience challenges the best practices to find guidance as a defensive, preventative control and mindful action or progressive perspectives. Organizational resilience is challenged by the multilevel variability for assessing the indicators and the integration of the whole system. Communities facing similar challenges may have relevant approaches of striving toward resilience.

CONCLUSIONS

It is an imperative to study the interdependencies and interactions to capture resilience capabilities in different organizational contexts to build a strong theoretical framework for more effective organizational resilience management. It is urgently needed to find more robust conceptual foundations of organizational resilience and its underlying assumptions about capabilities building to cope with disruptions and threats.

Organizational resilience adopts the best practice to deliver continual organizational improvement, competence, and capabilities. Organizational resilience requires to adopt best habits and practices to deliver improvement by embedding capabilities and competences, from vision, values, behaviors, and culture. The improvement of organizational resilience is challenged by their inability to rely on trial and error (Weick, Sutcliffe, and Obstfeld, 1999)

Individuals like organizations can build capabilities and abilities in resilience to become more competent and confident, create a growing positive organizational culture able to face organizational change as a less stressful opportunity while achieving more control over the trends of the environment in the future.

Organizational resilience is a measure of the combination of abilities, capacities, and capabilities that allows the organization to withstand disturbances and survive. Organizational capabilities to overcome vulnerabilities is one of the best measures of organizational resilience (Pettit et al. 2010, 2013).

Building organizational resilience requires investments on resources and capabilities to ensure the analysis of alternative and options of operations to face disruptions based on risks. Investments on resilience resources and capability building to respond to turbulence. Organizations can deploy resources and capabilities to implement resilience mechanisms aimed to deal with crisis responses and temporal and spatial discontinuities, disasters, and crisis. The temporal dimension of an organizational resilience capabilities building is related to the re-building process to accomplish outcomes that affects the organizations.

Every organization has its own way to achieve its organizational resilience which has a certain degree of heterogeneity inherent to different organizations and depending on its resources and capabilities. Organizational resilience requires activated, combined, and recombined resources to face challenges (Sutcliffe and Vogus, 2003).

Organizational resilience as a capability-based may have common paths, may be equifinal to the organization or both aspects. The integral and capability-based concept of organizational resilience bridges the gap with a processual notion with the capabilities to prepare for and respond to breakdowns.

Organizations must manage resilience to climate changes and extreme weather by using efficiently organizational resources, capabilities, and ideologies through the transferable and underlying mechanisms and processes to different contexts and sectors. The entrepreneurial and resilience mindset as an organizational capability can emerge from the identification and recognition that organizations are vulnerable and organizational crisis events are part of the normal life.

REFERENCES

Aleksić, A., Stefanović, M., Arsovski, S., & Tadić, D. (2013). An assessment of organizational resilience potential in SMEs of the process industry, a fuzzy approach. *J Loss Prevent Proc*, *26*, 1238–1245. doi:10.1016/j.jlp.2013.06.004

Antunes, P. (2011). BPM and exception handling: Focus on organizational resilience. *IEEE Transactions on Systems, Man, and Cybernetics*, *41*, 383–392. doi:10.1109/TSMCC. 2010.20625 04

Bansal, P. T., & Corley, K. (2011). From the editors: The coming of age for qualitative research: Embracing the diversity of qualitative methods. Academy of Management Journal, 54(2), 233–237. https://doi.org/ doi:10.5465/amj.2011.60262792

Bernstein, A., Bienstock, D., Hay, D., Uzunoglu, M., Zussman, G. (2004). Power Grid Vulnerability to Geographically Correlated Failures—Analysis and Control Implications. *IEEE INFOCOM 2014 Proceedings*, 2634–2642.

Bhamra, R., Dani, S., & Burnard, K. (2011). Resilience: The Concept, a Literature Review and Future Directions. *International Journal of Production Research*, *49*(18), 5375–5393. doi:10.1080/00207543.2011.563826

Bingham, C. B., & Eisenhardt, K. M. (2011). Rational Heuristics: The 'Simple Rules' that Strategists Learn from Process Experience. *Strategic Management Journal*, *32*(13), 1437–1464.

Bingham, C. B., & Haleblian, J. (2012). How Firms Learn Heuristics: Uncovering Missing Components of Organizational Learning. *Strategic Entrepreneurship Journal*, *6*(2), 152–177.

Birkie, S. E., Trucco, P., & Kaulio, M. (2017). Sustaining performance under operational turbulence: The role of Lean in engineer-to-order operations. *International Journal of Lean Six Sigma*, *8*(4), 457–481.

Boin, A., & McConnell, A. (2007). Preparing for critical infrastructure breakdowns: The limits of crisis management and the need for resilience. *Journal of Contingencies and Crisis Management*, *15*(1), 50–59.

Boin, A., & van Eeten, M. J. B. (2013). The Resilient Organization—A critical appraisal. *Public Management Review*, *15*, 429–445.

British Standards Institution. (2006). *BS 25999-1 Code of Practice for Business Continuity Management*. British Standards Institution.

Burnard, K., & Bhamra, R. (2011). Organisational resilience: Development of a conceptual framework for organisational responses. *International Journal of Production Research*, *49*, 5581–5599.

Caralli, R. A., Curtis, P. D., Allen, J. H., White, D. W., & Young, L. R. (2010). Improving operational resilience processes: The CERT® resilience management model. Proceedings - SocialCom 2010: 2nd IEEE International Conference on Social Computing, PASSAT 2010: 2nd IEEE International Conference on Privacy, Security, Risk and Trust, 1165–1170. https://doi.org/10.1109/SocialCom.2010.173

Catalan, C., & Robert, B. (2011). *Evaluation of organizational resilience: application in Quebec*. Centre risque & performance, École Polytechnique de Montréal.

Chan, J. K. (2011). Enhancing Organisational Resilience: Application of Viable System Model and MCDA in a Small Hong Kong Company. *International Journal of Production Research, 49*(18), 5545–5563. doi:10.1080/00207543.2011.563829

Cheng, J. L. C., & Kesner, I. F. (1997). Organizational Slack and Response to Environmental Shifts: The Impact of Resource Allocation Patterns. *Journal of Management, 23*(1), 1–18.

Coutu, D. L. (2002). How resilience works. *Harvard Business Review, 80*(5), 46–55.

De Florio, V. (2013). On the Constituent Attributes of Software and Organizational Resilience. *Interdisciplinary Science Reviews, 38*(2), 122–148. doi:10.1179/0308018813Z.00000000040

Denyer, D. (2017). *Organizational Resilience: A summary of academic evidence, business insights and new thinking.* BSI and Cranfield School of Management.

Dew, N., Goldfarb, B., & Sarasvathy, S. D. (2006). Optimal Inertia: When Organizations Should Fail. *Advances in Strategic Management, 23*, 73-99.

Dewald, J., & Bowen, F. (2010). Storm clouds and silver linings: Responding to disruptive innovations through cognitive resilience. *Entrepreneurship Theory and Practice, 34*(1), 197–218. doi:10.1111/j.1540-6520.2009.00312.x

Doern, R. (2016). Entrepreneurship and Crisis Management: The Experiences of Small Business during the London 2011 Riots. *International Small Business Journal, 34*(3), 276–302. doi:10.1177/0266242614553863

Dreyer, P., Langeland, K. S., Manheim, D., McLeod, G., & Nacouzi, G. (2016). RAPAPORT (Resilience Assessment Process and Portfolio Option Reporting Tool): Background and Method. RR-1169-AF. RAND Corporation, RR-1169-AF.

Duchek, S. (2014). Growth in the face of crisis: The role of organizational resilience capabilities. *Academy of Management Proceedings, 2014*, 13487.

Duchek, S. (2020). Organizational resilience: A capability-based conceptualization. *Bus Res, 13*, 215–246. doi:10.100740685-019-0085-7

Eisenhardt, K. M., & Graebner, M. E. (2007). Theory building from cases: Opportunities and challenges. *Academy of Management Journal, 50*(1), 25–32. doi:10.5465/amj.2007.24160888

Erol, O., Mansouri, M., & Sauser, B. (2009). A framework for enterprise resilience using service-oriented architecture approach. 2009 IEEE International Systems Conference Proceedings, 127–132. https://doi.org/10.1109/SYSTEMS.2009.4815785

Erol, O., Sauser, B. J., & Mansouri, M. (2010). A framework for investigation into extended enterprise resilience. *Enterprise Information Systems, 4*(2), 111–136. doi:10.1080/17517570903474304

Felin, T., Foss, N. J., Heimeriks, K. H., & Madsen, T. L. (2012). Microfoundations of Routines and Capabilities: Individuals, Processes and Structure. *Journal of Management Studies, 49*(8), 1351–1374.

Fleming, R. S. (2012). Ensuring organizational resilience in times of crisis. *J Glob Bus Issues, 6*, 31–34.

Folke C, Carpenter S, Walker B, Scheffer M, Elmqvist T, Gunderson L, Holling CS (2004) Regime shifts, resilience, and biodiversity in ecosystem management. Annu Rev Ecol Evol Syst, 35, 557–581. https://doi.org/ ys.35.02110 3.105711 doi:10.1146/annurev.ecols

Gaillard, J. (2007). Resilience of traditional societies in facing natural hazards. *Disaster Prevention and Management*, *16*(4), 522–544.

Gao, C., Zuzul, T., Jones, G., & Khanna, T. (2017). Overcoming institutional voids: A reputation-based view of long-run survival. *Strategic Management Journal*, *38*, 2147–2167. doi:10.1002mj.2649

Gephart, R. P. (2004). Qualitative research and the Academy of Management Journal. *Academy of Management Journal*, *47*(4), 454–462. doi:10.5465/amj.2004.14438580

Gittell, J. H., Cameron, K., Lim, S., & Rivas, V. (2006). Relationships, layoffs, and organizational resilience: Airline industry responses to September 11. *The Journal of Applied Behavioral Science*, *42*, 300–329.

Gunasekaran, A., Rai, B. K., & Griffin, M. (2011). Resilience and Competitiveness of Small and Medium Size Enterprises: An Empirical Research. *International Journal of Production Research*, *49*(18), 5489–5509. doi:10.1080/00207543.2011.563831

Hamel, G., & Välikangas, L. (2003). The quest for resilience. *Harvard Business Review*, *81*(9), 52–63.

Horne, J., & Orr, J. (1998). Assessing behaviors that create resilient organizations. *Employment Relations Today*, *24*, 29–39.

Ismail, H. S., Poolton, J., & Sharifi, H. (2011). The role of agile strategic capabilities in achieving resilience in manufacturing-based small companies. *International Journal of Production Research*, *49*(18), 5469–5487. doi:10.1080/00207543.2011.563833

Juettner, U., & Maklan, S. (2011). Supply chain resilience in the global financial crisis: An empirical study. *Supply Chain Management*, *16*, 246–259.

Jüttner, U., & Maklan, S. (2011). Supply Chain Resilience in the Global Financial Crisis: An Empirical Study. *Supply Chain Management*, *16*(4), 246–259. doi:10.1108/13598541111139062

Kantur, D., & İşeri-Say, A. (2012). Organizational resilience: A conceptual integrative framework. *Journal of Management & Organization*, *18*(6), 762–773.

Kendra, J., & Wachtendorf, T. (2003). Elements of resilience after the World Trade Center disaster: Reconstituting New York City's Emergency Operations Centre. *Disasters*, *27*(1), 37–53.

Klein, R. J. T., Nicholls, R. J., & Thomalla, F. (2003). Resilience to natural hazards: How useful is this concept. *Environmental Hazards*, *5*, 35–45.

La Porte, T. R. (1996). High reliability organizations: Unlikely, demanding and at risk. *Journal of Contingencies and Crisis Management*, *4*(2), 60–71. doi:10.1111/j.1468-5973.1996.tb00078.x

Lengnick-Hall, C. A., & Beck, T. E. (2005). Adaptive fit versus robust transformation: How organizations respond to environmental change. *Journal of Management*, *31*, 738–757.

Lengnick-Hall, C. A., & Beck, T. E. (2009). Resilience capacity and strategic agility: Prerequisites for thriving in a dynamic environment. In Resilience engineering perspectives, Volume 2. Preparation and restoration. Ashgate Publishing.

Lengnick-Hall, C. A., Beck, T. E., & Lengnick-Hall, M. L. (2011). Developing a capacity for organizational resilience through strategic human resource management. *Human Resource Management Review*, *21*, 243–255.

Leveson, N., Dulac, N., Marais, K., & Carroll, J. (2009). Moving Beyond Normal Accidents and High Reliability Organizations: A Systems Approach to Safety in Complex Systems. *Organization Studies*, *30*(2–3), 227–249.

Limnios, E. A. M., Mazzarol, T., Ghadouani, A., & Schilizzi, S. G. M. (2014). The resilience architecture framework: Four organizational archetypes. *European Management Journal*, *32*, 104–116.

Linnenluecke, M. K., & Griffiths, A. (2010). Beyond adaptation: Resilience for business considering climate change and weather extremes. *Business & Society*, *49*(3), 477–511.

Linnenluecke, M. K., & Griffiths, A. (2012). Assessing organizational resilience to climate and weather extremes: Complexities and methodological pathways. *Climatic Change*, *113*, 933–947.

Luthar, S. S. (2006). Resilience in Development: A Synthesis of Research across Five Decades. Developmental Psychopathology: Vol. 3. *Risk, Disorder and Adaptation, 739-795*.

Mallak, L. A. (1998). Measuring resilience in health care provider organizations. *Manpower Management*, *24*(4), 148–152. doi:10.1108/09552069810215755

Mamouni Limnios, E. (2011). Resilient organizations: Offense versus Defense. *25th Annual ANZAM Conference*, 7–9.

Mamouni Limnios, E., Mazzarol, T., Ghadouani, A., & Schilizzi, S. G. (2014). The resilience architecture framework: Four organizational archetypes. *European Management Journal*, *32*(1), 104–116. doi:10.1016/j.emj.2012.11.007

Marchese, K., & O'Dwyer, J. (2014). From Risk to Resilience: Using Analytics and Visualization to Reduce Supply Chain Vulnerability. *Deloitte Review*. http://dupress.com/articles/dr14-risk-to-resilience

Masten, A. S., & Obradović, J. (2007). Competence and resilience indevelopment. *Annals of the New York Academy of Sciences*, *1094*(1), 13–27.

McCann, J. E., & Selsky, J. W. (2012). *Mastering turbulence: the essential capabilities of agile and resilient individuals, teams, and organizations* (1st ed.). Jossey-Bass.

McDaniels, T., Chang, S., Cole, D., Mikawoz, J., & Longstaff, H. (2008). Fostering resilience to extreme events within infrastructure systems: Characterizing decision contexts for mitigation and adaptation. *Global Environmental Change*, *18*(2), 310–318.

McLeod, G., & Nacouzi, G. (2016). Enhancing Space Resilience Through Non-Materiel Means. RAND Corporation, RR-1067-AF.

McManus, S., Seville, E., Vargo, J., & Brunsdon, D. (2008). A facilitated process for improving organizational resilience. *Natural Hazards Review*, *9*, 81–90.

Miller, D., Eisenstat, R., & Foote, N. (2002). Strategy from the Inside Out: Building Capability-Creating Organizations. *California Management Review*, *44*(3), 37–54.

Mousavi, S., & Gigerenzer, G. (2014). Risk, Uncertainty and Heuristics. *Journal of Business Research*, *67*(8), 1671–1678.

Nelson, R. R., & Winter, S. G. (1982). *An evolutionary theory of economic change*. Harvard University Press.

Norris, F. H., Stevens, S. P., Pfefferbaum, B., Wyche, K. F., & Pfeffer-baum, R. L. (2008). Community resilience as a metaphor, theory, set of capacities, and strategy for disaster readiness. *American Journal of Community Psychology*, *41*(1–2), 127–150. doi:10.100710464-007-9156-6

Ortiz-de-Mandojana, N., & Bansal, P. (2016). The long-term benefits of organizational resilience through sustainable business practices. *Strategic Management Journal*, *37*, 1615–1631.

Pal, Torstensson, & Mattila. (2014). Antecedents of Organizational Resilience in Economic Crises – an Empirical Study of Swedish Textile and Clothing SMEs. *International Journal of Production Economics*, *147*(Part B), 410–428. doi: . doi:10.1016/j.ijpe.2013.02.031

Parker, H., & Ameen, K. (2018). The role of resilience capabilities in shaping how firms respond to disruptions. J Bus Res, 88, 535–541. https ://doi.org/ es.2017.12.022 doi:10.1016/j.jbusr

Parsons, D. (2010). Organizational resilience. *Australian Journal of Emergency Management*, 25(2), 18–20.

Pellissier, R. (2011). The Implementation of Resilience Engineering to Enhance Organizational Innovation in a Complex Environment. *International Journal of Business and Management*, *6*(1), 145–164.

Pellissier, R. (2012). Innovation in a complex environment. SA Journal of Information Management, 14(1).

Peteraf, M., Di Stefano, G., & Verona, G. (2013). The Elephant in the Room of Dynamic Capabilities: Bringing Two Diverging Conversations Together. *Strategic Management Journal*, *34*(12), 1389–1410.

Pettit, T. J., Croxton, K. L., & Fiksel, J. (2013). Ensuring supply chain resilience: Development and implementation of an assessment tool. *Journal of Business Logistics*, *34*(1), 46–76.

Richardson, G. E. (2002). The Metatheory of Resilience and Resiliency. *Journal of Clinical Psychology*, *58*(3), 307–321.

Richtnér, A., & Löfsten, H. (2014). Managing in turbulence: How the capacity for resilience influences creativity. *R & D Management*, *44*, 137–151.

Rijpma, J. A. (2003). From deadlock to dead end: The normal accidents-high reliability debate revisited. *Journal of Contingencies and Crisis Management*, *11*(1), 37–45. doi:10.1111/1468-5973.1101007

Roberts, K. H. (1990). Some Characteristics of One Type of High Reliability Organization. *Organization Science*, *1*(2), 160.

Rosenthal, U., & Kouzmin, A. (1996). Crisis management and institutional resilience: An editorial statement. *Journal of Contingencies and Crisis Management, 4*(3), 119–124.

Sáenz, M. J., & Revilla, E. (2014). Creating More Resilient Supply Chains. *MIT Sloan Management Review*. https://sloanreview.mit.edu/article/creating-more-resilient-supply-chains

Salwan, P., & Gada, V. P. (2018). Antecedents of resilience: An investigation into bharat forge. *Indian Journal of Industrial Relations, 53*, 449–461.

Schulman, P. R. (2004). General attributes of safe organizations. *Quality & Safety in Health Care, 13*, ii39–ii44.

Sheffi, Y. (2005). Building a Resilient Supply Chain. *Harvard Business Review Supply Chain Strategy Newsletter, 1*(8). https://sheffi.mit.edu/sites/default/files/genmedia.buildingresilientsupplychain.pdf

Sheffi, Y., & Rice, J. B. (2005). A supply chain view of the resilient enterprise. *MIT Sloan Management Review, 47*, 41–48.

Sheton, G. W. (2013). *Resiliency and Disaggregated Space Architectures*. White paper, Peterson AFB.

Somers, S. (2009). Measuring Resilience Potential: An Adaptive Strategy for Organizational Crisis Planning. *Journal of Contingencies and Crisis Management, 17*(1), 12–23.

Sullivan-Taylor, B., & Branicki, L. (2011). Creating resilient SMEs: Why one size might not fit all. *International Journal of Production Research, 49*(18), 5565–5579.

Sutcliffe, K. M., & Vogus, T. J. (2003). Organizing for resilience. *Positive Organizational Scholarship*, 94-110.

Taleb, N. N. (2012). *Antifragile: Things that Gain from Disorder* (Vol. 3). Random House.

Teixeira, E. de O., & Werther, W. B. (2013). Resilience: Continuous renewal of competitive advantages. *Business Horizons, 56*, 333–342.

Teo, W. L., Lee, M., & Lim, W.-S. (2017). The relational activation of resilience model: How leadership activates resilience in an organizational crisis. *Journal of Contingencies and Crisis Management, 25*, 136–147. doi:10.1111/1468-5973.12179

Tierney, K. (2014). *The social roots of risk: Producing disasters, promoting resilience*. Stanford University Press.

UNISDR. (2015). *Making development sustainable: the future of disaster risk management. global assessment report on disaster risk reduction 2015—making development sustainable: the future of disaster risk management*. United Nations Office for Disaster Risk Reduction. Retrieved fromhttps://www.preventionweb.net/english/hyogo/gar/2015/en/gar-pdf/GAR2015_EN.pdf

Vaelikangas, L., & Romme, A. G. L. (2013). How to design for strategic resilience: A case study in retailing. *Journal of Organization Design, 2*, 44–53.

Van Der Vegt, G. S., Essens, P., Wahlström, M., & George, G. (2015). Managing risk and resilience. *Academy of Management Journal, 58*(4), 971-980.

Watts, G., & Paciga, J. J. (2011). Conscious Adaptation: Building Resilient Organizations. In T. Carmichael (Ed.), *Complex Adaptive Systems: Energy, Information, and Intelligence*. Arlington VA: AAAI Fall Symposium Series.

Weick, K. E., & Sutcliffe, K. M. (2007). Managing the unexpected: Resilient performance in an age of uncertainty (2nd ed.). San Francisco, CA: Jossey-Bass.

Weick, K. E., Sutcliffe, K. M., & Obstfeld, D. (1999). Organizing for High Reliability: Processes of Collective Mindfulness. In R. S. Sutton & B. M. Staw (Eds.), *Research in Organizational Behavior* (Vol. 1, pp. 81–123). Jai Press.

Weick, K. E., Sutcliffe, K. M., & Obstfeld, D. (2005). Organizing and the process of sensemaking. *Organization Science*, *16*(4), 409–421.

Welter-Enderlin, R., & Hildenbrand, B. (2006). *Resilienz. Gedeihen trotz widriger Umstände*. Carl Auer Verlag GmbH.

Wildavsky, A. (1988). *Searching for Safety*. Transaction Press.

Williams, T. A., Gruber, D. A., Sutcliffe, K. M., Shepherd, D. A., & Zhao, E. Y. (2017). Organizational response to adversity: Fusing crisis management and resilience research streams. *The Academy of Management Annals*, *11*, 733–769.

Winter, S. G. (2013). Habit, Deliberation and Action: Strengthening the Micro foundations of Routines and Capabilities. *The Academy of Management Perspectives*, *27*(2), 120–137.

Witmer, H., & Mellinger, M. S. (2016). Organizational resilience: Nonprofit organizations' response to change. *Work (Reading, Mass.)*, *54*, 255–265.

Chapter 9
Implications of Implementing Operational Multi-Levels:
Individual, Organizational, Community, and Societal Resilience

José G. Vargas-Hernández
https://orcid.org/0000-0003-0938-4197
Instituto Tecnológico José Mario Molina Pasquel y Henríquez, Mexico

ABSTRACT

The purpose of this study is to analyze the operational implications of implementing resilience at the multi-levels of individual, organizational, community, and societal resilience. It is assumed that the implementation of resilience requires identifying the concepts, antecedents, fundaments, principles regarding the nature, processes, orientations, and outcomes. The method employed is the analytical-reflective based on conceptual, theoretical, and empirical literature review and observation of specific situations. This chapter considers a wide range of research related to resilience to be comprehensive. It is concluded that resilience is critically relevant at multi-level for individuals, organizations, communities, and society that must remain capable and strong even when all the events are adverse and seem incapable and consider ad hoc responses based on the nature of experienced major incidents. Neither academic research nor the practitioners are fully considering the implementation of resilience to solve problems.

INTRODUCTION

Organizational resilience is a new organizational paradigm (Johnson and Elliott, 2011). The concept of resilience is polysemous (Chmutina, Lizzarralde, Dainty and Bosher, 2016). Resilience has been defined and described in different ways in the literature. For that reason, this paper considers a wide range of research related to resilience to be comprehensive.

The term resilience is used in any academic field and discipline, the main reason why there are so many conceptualizations and definitions. There is a conceptual variety and disciplinary perspective of

DOI: 10.4018/978-1-7998-8996-0.ch009

organizational resilience inferred from the differences of patterns found on the ontology, need for resilience and solutions (Krippendorff, 2004). The concept of organizational resilience is related to other concepts that lead to the conceptual domain of resilience (Podsakoff et al., 2016).

The concept of resilience as bouncing back opens opportunities. Resilience is the ability rebound and recover with speed. Resilience is an emergent organizational property (Burnard & Bhamra, 2011; Hilton, Wright, Kiparoglou, 2012). Resilience is a process to achieve responses of positive outcomes in times of turbulent events (Sutcliffe and Vogus, 2003). Resilience building is a process of detection of turbulent events and activation (Burnard and Bhamra, 2011). Several features must be considered for the process of developing organizational resilience.

Resilience deals with turbulence as the capacity to absorbing, resisting, responding, and reinventing from disruptive change (McCann et al., 2009). Resilience is the vulnerability as the capacity to resist damage (Gaillard, 2007; Moore and Lakha, 2004). Resilience is the ability of people, households, communities, countries, and systems to mitigate and recover from shocks and stresses to reduce chronic vulnerability and facilitates inclusive growth (USAID, 2012).

Resilience is generated in different ways and forms. Resilience is context specific (Boin and van Eeten, 2013). Resilience is dependent on organizational communicative and mindset processes aimed to facilitate organizational resilience (Ishak and Williams, 2018). Resilience is the quality of responding to change (Horne III & Orr, 1998). Resilience requires high quality data. Resilience demands real-time high-quality data.

Resilience is the capacity to become robust under conditions of stress and change (Coutu, 2002). Resilience has the capacity to cope with decay and to slow down, it may decelerate and stop corporate demise (Marwa and Zairi, 2008). Resilience refers to expected and unexpected events (Hilton *et al.*, 2012; Hollnagel, 2010; Wright *et al.*, 2012). Resilience is a formative construct. Resilience deals with stretch goals benefiting from the cognitive, affective, and behavioral capacities (Sitkin et al., 2011).

The concept of resilience is being used more directly to bounce back and to bounce forward (Hamel & Välikangas, 2003; Hayward, Forster, Sarasvarthy, & Fredrickson, 2010; Limnios, Mazzarol, Ghadouani, & Schilizzi, 2014; Sutcliffe & Vogus, 2003). The original concept of resilience has evolved through its application on other academic and scientific fields. In science, resilience is the ability of materials to recover from deformation and return to their original state and form (Sheffi, 2006). Resilience is the process to recover from any disruption (van Breda, 2016). Resilience is a latent capacity (Powley 2009). Non-novelty and quantity emphasize resilience as normal organizational phenomenon (Rudolph and Repenning, 2002).

Resilience is intrinsic to the organization (Manyena 2006; and Hollnagel, 2010). An organization is "an organized group of people with a particular purpose, such as business or government department" (Oxford University Press, 2017). Resilience is an organizational attribute to deal with unexpected, abrupt, and extreme changes (Weick and Sutcliffe, 2007). Resilience is an organizational relational system (Kahn et al., 2013). Resilience can be opportunities to be taken by organizations (Ates & Bititci, 2011; Bhamidipaty *et al.*, 2007; Dewald & Bowen, 2010). Organizations must seek resilience more than achieve it. Organizations have differences in resilience (Ishak and Williams, 2018). The organization must reflect social and human factors considered as the ability to resist being affected by incidents (Elwood, 2009). Organizations resist to crises as a way of enhancing resilience.

Organizations are becoming increasingly aware of real risks, and they are underpinning resilience. The resilience is the capacity to absorb and recover from the occurrence of extreme weather events. Potential and resilience grow in the reorganization phase while internal regulation and connectedness are low giving the possibility for the creation of a new system (Gotts 2007; Holling, 2001). Resilience is high with connectedness and potential in the exploitation phase; however, resilience decreases in the conservation phase, but other values increase (Holling, 2001). Organizations under Cournot duopoly increasing the costs of production may not be willing to bounce back to previous costs and exhibit resilience (Lambertini & Marattin, 2016).

Organizational resilience is a new concept that is being explored in other fields (Lengnick-Hall & Beck, 2005; Linnenluecke & Griffiths, 2013; Vogus & Sutcliffe, 2007; Yang, Bansal, & DesJardine, 2014). Organizational resilience is the ability to effectively absorb, develop situation specific responses to, and engage in transformative activities aimed to capitalize on disruptive surprises that threaten organizational survival (Lengnick-Hall, Beck, & Lengnick-Hall, 2011: 244).

It is considered not to be practical assessment of organizational resilience when survivors live for a short period before any collapse (Gielnik et al., 2015). Organizational resilience is the ability to maintain, recover and improve functioning despite the adverse conditions (Sutcliffe & Vogus, 2003; Weick & Sutcliffe, 2001). Organizational growth is different than organizational resilience which is positively related to organizational creativity (Lengnick-Hall and Beck, 2005; Powley, 2013; Sutcliffe and Vogus, 2003; Richtnér and Löfsten, 2014). Creativity is linked to organizational resilience (Marwa and Milner, 2013). Organizational growth and resilience are supported in meeting challenges.

Some relevant literature reviews of resilience are detailed and discussed by Klein et al. (2003); Folke, (2006), and Hollnagel et al. (2006). A longitudinal approach to study the emergent and organic resilience (Macpherson, Herbane, and Jones, 2015). There are several disciplines that offer contributions to organizational resilience considered as developing generic characteristic. Several disciplines influence the development and application of the organizational resilience concept. Each one of this discipline is related to organizational resilience, providing disciplinary perspectives with its own ontologies, making important contributions in applications.

Disciplines have their own ontologies and methodologies leading to a debate between different concepts of organizational resilience without any systematic perspective and out of that, one is chosen from the multitude to be used by any author to focus on its application situated in the existing perspectives. The interdisciplinary approach of organizational resilience supported by communication leads to new perspectives. Resilience is the ability to communicate and reorganize across periods of change and chaos (Chewning et al., 2013). Organizational resilience is studied by Grande & Trucco (2008) using Fuzzy Cognitive Maps (FCM) to analyze the relations between the variables that contribute to resilience. A Fuzzy-JESS Expert System developed by Asgary *et al.* (2009) determine the level of organizational resilience.

The fragmented notion of resilience requires a more general cepted processual concept (Masten & Obradović, 2007: 14; Norris, Stevens, Pfefferbaum, Wyche, & Pfefferbaum, 2008: 130). Operational resilience depends upon an analysis of outputs and inputs of people, processes, and products. The contribution of the state like and open development perspective, like the resilience engineering, the focus is on individuals, teams, groups, and organizational resilience.

INDIVIDUAL RESILIENCE

Resilience is an individual or organizational trait that needs the means for developing to be explicit (Lissack & Letiche, 2002). Resilience is the property state-like substance that can be developed in individuals, teams and organizations and improve them at different levels. Resilience is described from different personal, team, organizational, sectoral, and societal (Whitehorn, 2010).

Organizational resilience is enacted at the levels of individual and collective relationships in times of crisis (Horne and Orr, 1998; Gittell et al., 2006). The response capabilities are cognitive, behavioral, and contextual (Williams et al., 2017). Multi-level, individual and team resilience approach facilitates the organizational healthy capacity to maintain adjustments under challenging conditions and desirable functions, bounce back from undesired events and achieve outcomes during strain (Salanova et al., 2012). Resilience leads to all levels as the ability to withstand stress, bounce back and recover from traumatic events (van der Vegt et al., 2015)

The role of individuals and their relationships in organizational resilience. Human development is organized to facilitate organizational resilience. The individual contributions to overall resilience prevail on some specific categories. At personal resilience is the ability to absorb shocks and pressures with consistency to restore prior order with the notion of keep going on no matter what happens (Chang and Wong, 1998). Resilience in human beings makes more competent and confident with well-built skills to meet risks and challenges when they arise.

Resilience in organizations is the result of a developmental process, not just individual traits whit implications for organizational development. The organizational development perspective develops organizational resilience based on individual and team relationships. Organizational development contributes to analyze the organization level resilience at the individual and team roles as subsystems.

ORGANIZATIONAL RESILIENCE

The objective of organizational resilience is to accept any incident that may occur with negative consequences. Organizational resilience is what the organization does with what happens. Organizational resilience is a latent construct supporting family business resilience (Somers, 2009; Mallak, 1998; Amann and Jaussaud, 2012). A factor constructs of the resilience concept proposed to analyze resilience capacity by (Lengnick-Hall and Beck, 2005) is based on cognitive, behavioral, and contextual resilience.

Information, operational and supply resilience are domains of organizational resilience. Organizational resilience may occur through managing inter-organizational relationships such as in the case of supply chain resilience (Gimenez et al., 2017). Resilience is an alternative to face supply chain risks and disruptions (Pettit et al., 2010, 2013). Interpretations of the concept of organizational resilience aimed to prioritize risks and challenges to improve its objectives conceived as the maturity levels (Allenby and Roitz, 2005).

Every organization must develop and harness its own right resilience as a value driver underpinned by its values, brand, interactions, and practices in the face of growing threats. The components of organizational resilience are the behavioral, cognitive, and contextual (Lengnick-Hall & Beck, 2005). Organizational resilience blends behavioral, cognitive, and contextual properties to increase the ability to develop responses to deal with the current situation.

The organizational context entails the need of resilience. Organizational resilience focuses on organizational context (Burnard and Bhamra, 2011; Parsons, 2010; Somers, 2009; Madni, and Jackson, 2009; Crichton *et al.*, 2009; Cheng, 2007; Allenby and Roitz, 2005; Robb, 2000; Mallak, 1998).

The cognitive component enables the capacities of noticing, interpreting, analyzing, and formulating responses, supported by the elements to building cognitive resilience are the constructive sensemaking and the ideological identity. The sensemaking processes laid the foundations for organizational resilience.

Social ties in organizations facilitate sensemaking and leadership to determine organizational resilience (Gittell et al., 2006; Kahn et al., 2013; Powley, 2013; Williams and Shepherd, 2016; Teo et al., 2017). Organizational resilience requires caring and servant leadership whom followers want to follow. Localized leadership contributes to organizational resilience in times of change (Stewart and O'Donnell, 2007). Sensemaking in resilience have sources of improvisation, bricolage, virtual role systems, attitude of wisdom and respectful interaction (Weick, 1993). Resilience is essential in developing multiple sources of change for competitive advantage (Ates and Bititci, 2011; Reinmoeller and van Baardwijk, 2005).

Organizational resilience must be supported by information technology in connection, coordination, and creation of a context before, during and aftermaths of the recovery crisis (Chewning et al., 2013). The recovery level and time are relevant parameters to certify the quality of organizational resilience. The process of embedding and disembodying communication and information systems facilitate or reduce the organizational resilience. Information systems can be risk or enabling factors to organizational resilience (Ignatiadis and Nandhakumar, 2007). Resilience is likely to be improved using internet and enforcing internal security (Allenby and Roitz, 2005)

Organizational resilience can be tested when the potential for equilibrium states is realized and enabled during the occurrence of adverse events. Organizational resilience is reduced during the conservation phase characterized by a gradual expansion of the system. Equilibrium of the organizational system states have low potential, connectedness, and resilience, that is difficult to reverse (Gunderson and Holling, 2002; Walker, Abel, and Anderies, 2009). Organizational resilience is relevant in the creative destruction, renewal stage and the application of balanced score card to develop an index (Mistry et al., 2014). A renewal phase of organizational resilience is dependent on the life cycle considering the ability to tap the power liberated by change and excel amidst chaos (Kiuchi and Shireman, 1999)

An organizational system that has a persistent low potential for equilibrium states has also low resilience that is difficult to reverse (Gunderson & Holling, 2002; Walker et al., 2009). The resilience´s system determines the nature of the regime to reorganize itself if it possesses or rebuilds residual resilience. An organizational resilience orientation of returning to homeostasis to overcome the disruption and restore previous circumstances. Organizational sustainable includes resilience and greening issues (Ponomarov and Holcomb, 2009; Azevedo et al., 2012).

Organizational resilience integration pathways in a process-based model have positive outcomes when coping with disorganization events. In a dialectical process, coping techniques may determine organizational resilience (Riolli and Savicki, 2003). Each different disorganization due to specific threats can require specific resilience and can entail distinctive responses and remedial actions. Organizational resilience must be able to sense the troubles of threats and to take previous actions and responses seeking to minimize damage and return to homeostasis post disorganization.

An expanded concept of organizational resilience includes transformative change aimed to mitigate the mutual impact and dependence (Winn & Pogutz, 2013, p. 220). Organizational resilience can be more focused on improvement more than risk prevention and mitigation. Long-term resilience is more prevalent on some organizational higher-risk industries. Organizations could increase their resilience by implementing a risk assessment system tied to potential threats originated inside and outside leading to strengthen their resistance (Anheier & Moulton, 1999: 4; Beck & Holzer, 2007; Gephart et al., 2009; La Porte & Consolini, 1991).

The temporal and spatial aspects of organizational resilience are relevant to extreme weather events. While a systematic analysis benefit from multiple assessments, a single assessment of the resilience profile, may generate valuable insights of the organizational resilience profile. Organizations can use their scale of organizational resilience and maturity to create and develop market value and to compare to other organizations. Resilience mechanisms may be transferable to different contexts to extreme weather events. Organizational resilience is a mechanism that provides stability to the organization. However, for other authors (Bingham, Eisenhardt and Davis, 2007) organizational resilience is the outcome of stability and not a mechanism.

Mechanisms developed to facilitate resilience (Dalgaard-Nielsen, 2017) such as delegation and experimentation become organizational values and risky factors. Organizational resilience building is influenced by many factors such as the human, social and financial capital in different ways for female and male owned organizations. Organizational resilience building creates value as a source of competitive advantages (Sullivan-Taylor and Branicki, 2011). Organizational resilience ensures the survival, growth, and generates a competitive advantage in turbulent times through developing and enhancing resilience for the organization (Kiuchi and Shireman, 1999)

Organizational resilience is the capacity to absorb the impacts and recover from current weather extreme. Organizational resilience is an active and reactive capacity (Gilly *et al.,* 2014). Organizational resilience is considered as a reactive functional approach to operate close to instability overcoming unexpected problems and limitations (Marcus and Nichols, 1999). Resilience is a concept linked to climate change and vulnerability (Timmerman, 1981). Organizational resilience during the recovery and restoration to the same previous level prior to exposure to the climate change vulnerabilities and weather extreme. Several challenges emerge in the assessment of organizational resilience and its impact on climate and weather extremes.

Assessments of organizational resilience can identify some aspects of the stakeholders involved in certain contexts and identified through experts and workshops. Organizational resilience monitors the ability to cope with the variabilities (Carvalho et al., 2012). Organizations have similar characteristics and attributes related to organizational resilience, but they are affected by climate variability and weather extremes with different impact. The appropriate organizational resilience analysis considers the exposure to climate and weather extremes and its direct and indirect impact on the organizations.

Organizations have an impact on the resilience of the climate system. The scenarios of organizational resilience to changes in climate vulnerabilities and weather extremes provide an approach to interconnections in its factors and coping range with non-climate related factors at different temporal and spatial scales (Wilbanks et al., 2007). Organizational resilience has the characteristic of variability to climate conditions and weather extremes as the interannual variability can be in the coping range of circumstances that the organization can tolerate (Smit et al., 2000; Yohe and Tol, 2002).

Organizational resilience assessed used to identify actions to alter climate and weather extremes (Cumming et al., 2005) is under methodological inquiry and interpretation. Linnenluecke & Griffiths (2010) suggest some approaches and methodologies intended to enhance organizational resilience. The assessment of organizational resilience to climate variability and weather extremes needs to identify the factors of organizational resilience and the physical variabilities of climate and weather extremes. The physical aspect of resilience is a biological survival and implies the ability to grow and prosper (Reich, 2006).

Regional climate projections may be able to provide quantitative information for organizational resilience assessments while for some classes of extremes may only provide qualitative data (Barros et al.,

2009). To estimate resulting organizational resilience losses needs specific data of the event. Exceeding the coping range does not mean that the critical organizational resilience threshold has passed, although it is difficult to define.

The resilience assessment has come methodological implications subject to the goal, timeframe, frequency changes, plausibility, estimate losses, develop indicators, identify thresholds, evaluate future events, build scenarios, etc. (Barros et al., 2009). Estimations of organizational losses and resilience are difficult when the information on future changes in the frequency and intensity is limited. The notion of resilience is linked to future studies (Pasteur, 2011; Smith and Fischbacher, 2009; Alesi, 2008).

The assessment methodology for organizational resilience and its impact on future climate variabilities and weather extremes is still a challenge. It is being suggested to identify properties and factors of future climate and weather extremes based on some approaches such as climate projections, analogues, and impacts. Property loss estimations are used for assessing monetary losses rather than for estimating resilience. Retrospective analysis of organizational development, decline and recovery do not provide useful information, insights and impacts into organizational resilience to future climate variabilities and weather extremes (Linnenluecke and Griffiths, 2010).

Models of organizational resilience can be used to gain insights into some potential factors considering that they are simplified of reality, have different weaknesses and strengths, and reduced to some indicators and parameters (Jentsch et al., 2006). A process research model of organizational resilience sheds light on antecedents, methods, processes, orientations which can lead to different outcomes (Langley, 1999). Engineering resilience concerns with the boundary conditions of the model for competence to accommodate the changing demands (Woods, 2006).

The models assume that the reduction of organizational resilience is the loss that results from a particular event. The models to assess the loss of organizational resilience provide only rough estimates based on assumptions of which factors must be included in the model, besides the difficulties to gather the input data.

Organizational interruption losses can be modelled under some hypothetical events and circumstances to estimate the effects on the adjustments of organizational resilience (Rose and Liao, 2005; Rose et al., 2007). The organizational interruption loss model has been developed to assess the resistance as an impact in organizational resilience of the difference between direct output losses that results from extreme events (Rose, 2004). The organizational interruption impacts determine the losses from current events and limited insights on the future resilience (Rose and Lim, 2002).

Organizational resilience indicators are context-dependent and should be complementary to address multiple issues of resilience, assessed and validated in their relationship once the adverse events have occurred (Carpenter et al., 2005). The relationships of organizational contribute to their organizational resilience.

SOCIETAL AND COMMUNITY RESILIENCE

Resilience is survivability, resumption, restoration and optimize support to the community resilience (Coullahan and Shepherd, 2008). Resilience focuses on local community and social perspectives (Cox, 2012; Graugaard, 2012; Coaffee, 2008; Sapountzaki, 2007; Boin and McConnell, 2007; Reich, 2006; Pelling, 2003; Paton et al., 2001; Adger, 2000) and sectorial and industry perspective (Biggs, 2011; McCullough, 2008). Resilience collective capacities building is an inclusive process that involves the individuals, organizations, and communities' actors to interact, use and build its capability endowments. These endowment capabilities are cognitive, behavioral, emotion and relational.

Societal resilience can be proactive and reactive (Dovers and Handmer, 1992). A proactive resilience response is questioned due to the bounded rationality of individuals. A proactive resilience response is questioned due to the bounded rationality of individuals (Handmer and Dovers, 1996). Organizational resilience is a critical component of community resilience which are very interrelated and interdependent to provide a systematic approach in an ability to plan, respond and recover from crisis and emergencies (Lee et al., 2013) as well as actions to strengthen resilience (Pasteur, 2011).

Organizational resilience thrives in the context of a community. Resilience contextual transformation and changing conditions are guided in the manipulation of variables time and space or location. The greater the time needed for recovery indicates the lower resilience at the same level of vulnerability. Resilience degrades is unaltered if the variables change slow with impact only on routines (Walker & Salt, 2012: 161, 193). Routine and heuristic-based responses to disruption make the distinction between organizational and personal resilience. The organizational resilience orientation affects the outcomes. Organizational resilience requires a buffer to maximize the potential to regenerate.

Location is a factor in resilience in determining and shaping vulnerability and its role in resilience at the organizational level. Locational characteristics are relevant to organizational resilience with the potential to benefit from locations and community vulnerabilities (Chamlee-Wright, 2010; Chewning, Lai, and Doerfel, 2012; Coates et al., 2016; de Vries and Hamilton, 2017; Westhead and Batstone, 1998). Geographical proximity leads to recombine know-how and development of cognitive capital to absorb, anticipate, resist, and sustain the capacities of resistance and adaptation by creating new technological solutions and pathways (Gilly et al., 2014). Location influences organizational resilience and vulnerability.

IMPLEMENTATION AND OPERATION OF RESILIENCE

Resilience is deliberately nurtured (Johnson, Elliott, and Drake, 2013). Organizational resilience seeking can be transferred to organizational activities (Roberts and Bea, 2001; Rudolph and Repenning, 2002). Organizational resilience is related to the design of organizations and systems to anticipate risk (Jackson, Firtko, and Edenborough, 2007; Fiksel, 2003). Resilience is considered as an anticipation approach. Organizational resilience is an outcome of entrepreneurial decisions and activities processes associated to recovery following a crisis.

Organizations become more resilience capable because of responding to disruptive shocks (Lengnick-Hall & Beck, 2009: 43). Organizational mistakes offer an opportunity to learn through processes of feedback for resilience capacity building. Resilience is precursor and recovery resilience (Boin and van Eeten, 2013). One of the precursors for organizational resilience is exploratory patience as not giving up in the face of insensitivity to negative feedback and discouragement (Välikangas, 2007). Precursor resilience is a priori, as the ability to accommodate change and the capacity to absorb shocks and recovery resilience is and ex post assessment (Boin and van Eeten, 2013).

Resilience can be reinforced by complementary actions including spreading the financial risks (Hoffmann et al., 2009), enhancing knowledge (Berrang-Ford et al., 2011) and developing partnerships and collaborations (Berkhout et al., 2006; Hertin, Berkhout, Gann, & Barlow, 2003). Organizational resilience results from relationships supported by financial reserves in coping with crisis (Horne and Orr, 1998 and Gittell et al., 2006). Organizational experiences of its own crisis or in proximity, has an influence on its perceptions and actions in associated relation to the different levels of resilience activities. The collective action in the organization determines organizational resilience (Horne and Orr, 1998)

Prevention and influence are findings in shaping organizational resilience (Corey and Deitch, 2011; Vargo and Seville, 2011). Organizations with the ability to intervene, prevent and reduce the impact of severe interruptions may have higher level of resilience planning formalization. The existing distance between a current state to a threshold of change into another regime is resilience (Walker & Salt, 2006: 74). Organizational resilience can be enhanced by diverse loosely and tightly-couple feedback.

Resilience changes with circumstances, times and locations as new vulnerabilities emerge in a developmental progressive path (Luthar, 2006). Organizations can leverage radical shifts to rebuild resilience and capable outfit emerging. The level of organizational resilience possessed by an organization is demonstrated by the time to recover from damage. The essential factors of organizational resilience are needed in the face of an unexpected negative event.

Surrogates for resilience or vulnerability are the planning and formal processes (Corey and Deitch, 2011; Spillan and Hough, 2003). The all-hazards approach for organizational resilience and organizational contingency planning. Increased resilience as an expected return based on the level of investment. Reciprocal adjustments and monitoring, sharing knowledge, information, and feedback lead to organizational resilience. Organizations intendedly to be rational, they frequently behave on incomplete and incorrect information without being aware of all alternatives (March & Olsen, 1975: 148)

Organizations build a facilitation process of organizational resilience supported by the psychological factors for a rapid recovery after an unexpected negative event. The psychological resilience model is based on process research in response to disorganizations and other threats posed by adverse conditions (Richardson, 2002). Organizational resilience is the result of evolutionary psychological traits and processes development and growth. A combination of both ergonomics and psychology resilience enables a broad approach regarding organization resilience as the one retained that enables recovery from an unexpected disruption and catastrophe caused by a negative event. This concept of resilience is different from the individual resilience concept.

Organizational resilience improves the organizational commitment. Organizational commitment to resilience is factor of mindfulness scale and the capacity to improvise and bounce back from organizational setbacks (Ray et al., 2011). A proactive posture committed to organizational resilience is a mindful engagement in self-evaluation (Stephenson, 2010). Building resilience requires to be based on trust, engagement, and commitment. The evaluation of the organizational resilience evaluated by the employees is a relevant factor supported for confidence and belief in the ability to recover which may results in greater commitment. Resilience evaluation based on organizational capacities to respond, monitor, and anticipate threats and opportunities and learn from past events (Rigaud *et al.,* 2013).

Organizational resilience may result from effective commitment, sharing of knowledge and information and interpersonal consideration and intentionality. Organizational resilience enhances employee strength (Mallak, 1998). Employees well treated are more connected to the organization to be able to facilitate the organizational resilience (McCoy and Elwood, 2009). High levels of organizational commitment among the employees are a critical factor at any contingency event. Employee's treatment influences resilience. Building organizational resilience in the face of threatening events helps employees to handle stressful effects. Treatment to employees more connected to the organization may facilitate organizational resilience (McCoy and Elwood, 2009). Organizational resilience is strengthened by the employees and team's resilience.

Teamwork processes establish organizational commitment after the recognition and identification of organizational resilience. Teamwork commitment is relevant to improve the organizational resilience evaluation of employees which in turn facilitates organizational commitment. Involvement of employees in governance decisions is considered as the ability to bounce back after dealing with adverse effects of unanticipated events (Lampel et al., 2014).

Reputation is linked to organizational resilience (Gao et al., 2017). Resilience as a subset of reputation is the ability to withstand unexpected shocks, built through the organization's response to prior challenges (Linnenluecke et al., 2012; Gao et al., 2017). Corporate reputation strengthens the organizational resilience and increases the positive effects on marketing, operations, and activities (Wartick, 2002).

The potential of organizational resilience of SMEs. Resilience is relevant for SMEs in the construction sector (Wedawattaa et al., 2010). Resilience as the capacity for coping affects MNEs that stay in war country or flee (Dai et al., 2017). The enterprise age, size and experience and the owners' lifestyle values are significantly related to resilience levels (Biggs, 2011). Family and non-family organizations build resilience through different mechanisms, such as equal efforts of renewal and optimization (Demmer et al., 2011). Organizational resilience building is different for family and non-family business (Amann and Jaussaud, 2012)

Organizational resilience building is a challenge in public organizations (Dalgaard-Nielsen, 2017).

CONCLUSION

The objective of the organizational resilience is to accept that incidents may occur with negative consequences. The analysis of organizational resilience must have a relative tendency towards more objective and rational implementation taking into consideration the reactive and proactive approaches.

Neither academic research nor the practitioners are considering the organizational resilience to solve problems. Conventional thinking and problem-solving do not facilitate organizational resilience. Organizational resilience requires to identify the concepts, antecedents, fundaments, assumptions regarding the nature, processes, orientations, and outcomes. Resilience is critically relevant for organizations that must remain capable because it shows the strength even when all the events are adverse and seem incapable. Organizations may consider resilience as ad hoc responses based on the nature of experienced major incidents.

Resilience is the ability to respond according to the societal needs and rebound from crisis. Resilience is the ability to be able return to original shape after being stretched, bent, and pressed. Organizational resilience is the harmonious integration of the functions of risk, compliance, and governance to enable proactive organizational decision making. Ensuring an appropriate level of organizational resilience, compliance on development effectiveness and sustainability and transparency outcomes define the required balance by involving personnel in the operational process of the organization. Organizations must develop the ability to deal with stress derived from disruptions based on risks applied to the different levels of organizational resilience.

Organizational resilience drives benefits by the anticipation of existing and creating new market needs and in response to the corporate environments. Organizational resilience applies principles that should resonate with all sectors and stakeholders. Accepting to assume lower level of organizational resilience gives an opportunity to speak up and share feelings and thoughts about the situation and how to get away and advance.

Committing the same mistake several times reduces the level of resilience and increases the operational costs and risk treatment. Coordinated collaboration among organizational actors and stakeholders improves resilience facilitates support and response to provide relief and recovery to meet the needs of communities. Social ties determine organizational resilience facilitating leadership and sensemaking.

Resilience organizations must be prepared to face disruptions to be able to survive. Development of organizational resilience should identify antifragile organizations. The organizations can recover and takes advantage of opportunities and threats to become stronger.

The coexistent dimensions to evaluate organizational resilience provide an estimation of the potential and after a disruptive event. The attributes of organizational resilience must be measurable to provide an estimate the potential. Measuring organizational resilience after the occurrence of a disruptive event provides the potential to make corrections. The analysis of resilience leading to values of the organizational resilience indexes are insufficient to explain the quality of the affected services. The concept of organizational resilience correlated with service quality preservation show concentration of competitiveness in organizations.

REFERENCES

Adger, W. (2000). Social and ecological resilience: Are they related? *Progress in Human Geography*, *24*(3), 347–364.

Allenby, B., & Roitz, J. (2005). Building the resilient firm: The new challenge to EHS organizations. *Environmental Quality Management*, *15*(2), 27–36.

Amann, B., & Jaussaud, J. (2012). Family and non-family business resilience in an economic downturn. *Asia Pacific Business Review*, *18*, 203–223.

Anheier, H. K., & Moulton, L. (1999). Organizational failures, breakdowns, and bankruptcies: An introduction. In H. K. Anheier (Ed.), *When things go wrong: Organizational failures and breakdowns* (pp. 3–16). Sage Publications.

Asgary, A., Kong, A., & Levy, J. (2009). Fuzzy-Jess expert system for indexing business resiliency. TIC-STH'09: 2009 IEEE Toronto International Conference - Science and Technology for Humanity, 153-158. https://doi.org/10.1109/TIC-STH.2009.5444516

Ates, A., & Bititci, U. (2011). Change process: A key enabler for building resilient SMEs. *International Journal of Production Research*, *49*(18), 5601–5618. doi:10.1080/00207543.2011.563825

Azevedo, J. S., de Souza-Sarkis, J. E., Oliveira, T. A., & Ulrich, T. (2012). Tissue-specific mercury concentrations in two catfish species from the Brazilian coast. *Brazilian Journal of Oceanography*, *60*, 211–219.

Barros, V., Abdulla, A., & Boncheva, A. I. (Eds.). (2009). *Scoping meeting for an IPCC special report on extreme events and disasters: managing the risks*. WGII Technical Support Unit.

Beck, U., & Holzer, B. (2007). Organizations in world risk society. In C. M. Pearson, C. Roux-Dufort, & J. A. Clair (Eds.), *International Handbook of Organizational Crisis Management* (pp. 3–21). Sage Publications Inc.

Berkhout, F., Hertin, J., & Gann, D. (2006). Learning to adapt: Organizational adaptation to climate change impacts. *Climatic Change, 78*, 135–156.

Berrang-Ford, L., Ford, J. D., & Paterson, J. (2011). Are we adapting to climate change? *Global Environmental Change, 21*, 25–33.

Bhamidipaty, A., Lotlikar, R., & Banavar, G. (2007). RMI: a framework for modeling and evaluating the resiliency maturity of IT service organizations. IEEE International Conference on Services Computing (SCC 2007), 300–307. https://doi.org/10.1109/SCC.2007.94

Biggs, D. (2011). Understanding resilience in a vulnerable industry: The case of reef tourism in Australia. *Ecology and Society, 16*(1), 30.

Bingham, C. B., Eisenhardt, K. M., & Davis, J. P. (2007). *Opening the black box of organizational expertise: understanding what firms learn from their process experience and how that learning unfolds over time*. University of Maryland Working Paper.

Boin, A., & McConnell, A. (2007). Preparing for critical infrastructure breakdowns: The limits of crisis management and the need for resilience. *Contingencies and Crisis Management, 15*(1), 50–59.

Boin, A., & van Eeten, M. (2013). The resilient organization. *Public Management Review, 15*(3), 429-445.

Burnard, K., & Bhamra, R. (2011). Organisational resilience: Development of a conceptual framework for organisational responses. *International Journal of Production Research, 49*(18), 5581–5599.

Carpenter, S. R., Westley, F., & Turner, M. G. (2005). Surrogates for resilience of social-ecological systems. *Ecosystems (New York, N.Y.), 8*, 941–944.

Carvalho, H., Barroso, A., Machado, V., Azevedo, S., & Cruz-Machado, V. (2012). Supply chain redesign for resilience using simulation. *Computers & Industrial Engineering, 62*(1), 329–341.

Chamlee-Wright, E. (2010). *The Cultural and Political Economy of Recovery: Social Learning in a Post-Disaster Environment* (Vol. 12). Routledge.

Chang, W., & Wong, W. (1998), Rational traditionalism: Chinese values in Singapore. In Values and Development. Centre for Advanced Studies, Faculty of Arts and Social Sciences, National University of Singapore.

Cheng, P. (2007). The cultural value of resilience: The Singapore case study. *Cross Cultural Management, 14*(2), 136–149.

Chewning, L. V., Lai, C. H., & Doerfel, M. (2012). Organizational Resilience following Disaster: A Longitudinal View of Information and Communication Technologies Use to Rebuild Communication Structure. *Management Communication Quarterly, 27*(2), 237–263. doi:10.1177/0893318912465815

Chewning, L. V., Lai, C.-H., & Doerfel, M. L. (2013). Organizational resilience and using information and communication technologies to rebuild communication structures. *Management Communication Quarterly, 27*, 237–263. doi:10.1177/08933 18912 46581 5

Chmutina, K., Lizarralde, G., Bosher, L., & Dainty, A. (2016). Unpacking Resilience Policy Discourse. *Cities (London, England), 58*, 70–79. doi:10.1016/j.cities.2016.05.017

Coaffee, J. (2008). Risk, resilience and environmentally sustainable cities. *Energy Policy*, *36*(12), 4633–4638.

Coates, G., McGuinness, M., Wright, N. G., Guan, D., Harries, T., & McEwen, L. (2016). SESAME: Improving Small and Medium Enterprises' Operational Response and Preparedness to Flood Events. In Management of Natural Disasters. WIT Press.

Corey, C. M., & Deitch, E. A. (2011). Factors Affecting Business Recovery Immediately after Hurricane Katrina. *Journal of Contingencies and Crisis Management*, *19*(3), 170–181. doi:10.1111/j.1468-5973.2011.00642

Coullahan, R.; Shepherd, C. (2008). Enhancing enterprise resilience in the commercial facilities sector. *Journal of Business Continuity & Emergency Planning*, *3*(1), 5-18.

Coutu, D. L. (2002). How resilience works. *Harvard Business Review*, *80*(5), 46–55.

Cox, L. (2012). Community resilience and decision theory challenges for catastrophic events. *Risk Analysis*, *32*(11), 1919–1934.

Crichton, M., Ramsay, C., & Kelly, T. (2009). Enhancing organizational resilience through emergency planning: Learnings from cross-sectoral lessons. *Journal of Contingencies and Crisis Management*, *17*(1), 24–37.

Cumming, G. S., Barnes, G., & Perz, S. (2005). An exploratory framework for the empirical measurement of resilience. *Ecosystems (New York, N.Y.)*, *8*, 975–987.

Dai, W., Peterson, A., & Kenney, T. (2017). Quantitative microscopy of the *Drosophila* ovary shows multiple niche signals specify progenitor cell fate. *Nature Communications*, *8*, 1244. doi:10.103841467-017-01322-9

Dalgaard-Nielsen, A. (2017). Organizational resilience in national security bureaucracies: Realistic and practicable? *Journal of Contingencies and Crisis Management*, *25*(4), 341–349. doi:10.1111/1468-5973.12164

de Vries, H. P., & Hamilton, R. T. (2017). Why Stay? In Business and Post-Disaster Management - Business, Organisational and Consumer Resilience and the Christchurch Earthquakes. London: Routledge.

Demmer, W. A., Vickery, S. K., & Calantone, R. (2011). Engendering resilience in small-and medium-sized enterprises (SMEs): A case study of Demmer Corporation. *International Journal of Production Research*, *49*, 5395–5413.

Dewald, J., & Bowen, F. (2010). Storm clouds and silver linings: Responding to disruptive innovations through cognitive resilience. *Entrepreneurship Theory and Practice*, *34*(1), 197–218. doi:10.1111/j.1540-6520.2009.00312.x

Elwood, A. (2009). Using the disaster crunch/release model in building organisational resilience. *Journal of Business Continuity & Emergency Planning*, *3*(3), 241–247.

Fiksel, J. (2003). Designing Resilient, Sustainable Systems. *Environmental Science & Technology*, *37*(23), 5330–5339. doi:10.1021/es0344819

Folke, C. (2006). Resilience: The emergence of a perspective for social–ecological systems analyses. *Global Environmental Change, 16*(3), 253–267. doi:10.1016/j.gloenvcha.2006.04.002

Gaillard, J. (2007). Resilience of traditional societies in facing natural hazards. *Disaster Prevention and Management, 16*(4), 522–544.

Gao, Ch., Zuzul, T., Jones, G., & Khanna, T. (2017). Overcoming Institutional Voids: A Reputation-Based View of Long-Run Survival. *Strategic Management Journal, 38*(11), 2147–2167.

Gephart, R. P., Van Maanen, J., & Oberlechner, T. (2009). Organizations and risk in late modernity. *Organization Studies, 30*(2–3), 141–155. doi:10.1177/0170840608101474

Gielnik, M. M., Spitzmuller, M., Schmitt, A., Klemann, D. K., & Frese, M. (2015). I Put in Effort, Therefore I am Passionate: Investigating the Path from Effort to Passion in Entrepreneurship. *Academy of Management Journal, 58*(4), 1012–1031.

Gilly, J. P., Kechidi, M., & Talbot, D. (2014). Resilience of organisations and territories: The role of pivot firms. *European Management Journal, 32*(4), 596–602. doi:10.1016/j.emj.2013.09.004

Gimenez, R., Hernantes, J., Labaka, L., Hiltz, S. R., & Turoff, M. (2017). Improving the resilience of disaster management organizations through virtual communities of practice: A Delphi study. *Journal of Contingencies and Crisis Management, 25*, 160–170. doi:10.1111/1468-5973.12181

Gittell, J. H., Cameron, K., Lim, S., & Rivas, V. (2006). Relationships, layoffs, and organizational resilience: Airline industry responses to September 11. *The Journal of Applied Behavioral Science, 42*, 300–329.

Gotts, N. M. (2007). Resilience, panarchy, and world-systems analysis. *Ecology and Society, 12*, 24–38.

Grande, O., & Trucco, P. (2008). Resilience analysis of civil defence organization: A fuzzy cognitive Map based approach. *9th International Conference on Probabilistic Safety Assessment and Management 2008, 2*, 1542–1549.

Graugaard, J. (2012). A tool for building community resilience? A case study of the lewes pound. *Local Environment, 17*(2), 243–260.

Gunderson, L. H., & Holling, C. S. (2002). *Panarchy: Understanding transformations in human and natural systems.* Island Press.

Hamel, G. & Välikangas, L. (2003). The quest for resilience. *Harvard Business Review, 81*(9), 52–63.

Handmer, J. W., & Dovers, S. R. (1996). A typology of resilience: Rethinking institutions for sustainable development. *Organization & Environment, 9*, 482–511. doi:10.1177/10860 26696 00900

Hayward, M. L. A., Forster, W. R., Sarasvarthy, S. D., & Fredrickson, B. L. (2010). Beyond Hubris: How Highly Confident Entrepreneurs Rebound to Venture Again. *Journal of Business Venturing, 25*(6), 569–578.

Hertin, J., Berkhout, F., Gann, D., & Barlow, J. (2003). Climate change and the UK house building sector: Perceptions, impacts and adaptive capacity. *Building Research and Information, 31*, 278.

Hilton, J., Wright, C., & Kiparoglou, V. (2012). Building resilience into systems. In SysCon 2012 - 2012 IEEE International Systems Conference, Proceedings, 638–645. https://doi.org/10.1109/SysCon.2012.6189449

Hoffmann, V. H., Sprengel, D. C., Ziegler, A., Kolb, M., & Abegg, B. (2009). Determinants of corporate adaptation to climate change in winter tourism: An econometric analysis. *Global Environmental Change, 19*, 256–264.

Holling, C. S. (2001). Understanding the complexity of economic, ecological, and social systems. *Ecosystems (New York, N.Y.), 4*, 390–405.

Hollnagel, E. (2010). How Resilient Is Your Organisation? An Introduction to the Resilience Analysis Grid (RAG). Sustainable Transformation: Building a Resilient Organization.

Hollnagel, E., Woods, D. D., & Leveson, N. (2006). *Resilience engineering: Concepts and precepts*. Ashgate.

Horne, J. F. III, & Orr, J. E. (1998). Assessing behaviors that create resilient organizations. *Employment Relations Today, 24*(4), 29–39.

Ignatiadis, I. & Nandhakumar, J. (2007). The Impact of Enterprise Systems on Organizational Control and Drift: A Human-Machine Agency Perspective. *International Journal of Enterprise Information Systems, 3*(3), 36-51. DOI: doi:10.1057/palgrave.jit.2000087

Ishak, A. W., & Williams, E. A. (2018). A dynamic model of organizational resilience: Adaptive and anchored approaches. *Corporate Communications, 23*, 180–196.

Jackson, D., Firtko, A., & Edenborough, M. (2007). Personal resilience as a strategy for surviving and thriving in the face of workplace adversity: A literature review. *Journal of Advanced Nursing, 60*(1), 1–9. doi:10.1111/j.1365-2648.2007.04412.x

Jentsch, V., Kantz, H., & Albeverio, S. (2006). Extreme events: magic, mysteries, and challenges. In S. Albeverio, V. Jentsch, & H. Kantz (Eds.), *Extreme events in nature and society*. Springer.

Johnson, N., & Elliott, D. (2011). Using Social Capital to Organise for Success? A Case Study of Public–Private Interface in the UK Highways Agency. *Policy and Society, 30*, 101–113. doi:10.1016/j.polsoc.2011.03.005

Johnson, N., Elliott, D., & Drake, P. (2013). Exploring the Role of Social Capital in Facilitating Supply Chain Resilience. *Supply Chain Management, 18*(3), 324–336. doi:10.1108/SCM-06-2012-0203

Kahn, W. A., Barton, M. A., & Fellows, S. (2013). Organizational crises and the disturbance of relational systems. *Academy of Management Review, 38*(3), 377–396. doi:10.5465/amr.2011.0363

Kiuchi, T., & Shireman, B. (1999). Metrics for business in the new economy: An economic change of seasons creates demands for new business metrics. *Environmental Quality Management, 9*, 79–90.

Klein, R. J. T., Nicholls, R. J., & Thomalla, F. (2003). Resilience to natural hazards: How useful is this concept. *Environmental Hazards, 5*, 35–45.

Krippendorff, K. (2004). *Content Analysis: An Introduction to Its Methodology* (2nd ed.). Sage.

La Porte, T. R., & Consolini, P. M. (1991). Working in practice but not in theory: Theoretical challenges of "high-reliability organizations". *Journal of Public Administration Research and Theory. J-PART, 1*(1), 19–48.

Lambertini, L., & Marattin, L. (2016). To adjust or not to adjust after a cost-push shock? A simple duopoly model with (and without) resilience. *Economics of Innovation and New Technology, 25*(2), 172–181. doi:10.1080/10438599.2015.1031344

Lampel, J., Bhalla, A., & Jha, P. P. (2014). Does governance confer organisational resilience? Evidence from UK employee-owned businesses. *European Management Journal, 32*, 66–72.

Langley, A. (1999). Strategies for Theorizing from Process Data. *Academy of Management Review, 24*(4), 691–710.

Lee, A., Vargo, J., & Seville, E. (2013). Developing a tool to measure and compare organizations' resilience. *Natural Hazards Review, 14*(1), 29–41.

Lengnick-Hall, C. A., & Beck, T. E. (2005). Adaptive fit versus robust transformation: How organizations respond to environmental change. *Journal of Management, 31*, 738–757.

Lengnick-Hall, C. A., & Beck, T. E. (2009). Resilience capacity and strategic agility: Prerequisites for thriving in a dynamic environment. In Resilience engineering perspectives, Volume 2. Preparation and restoration. Ashgate Publishing.

Lengnick-Hall, C. A., Beck, T. E., & Lengnick-Hall, M. L. (2011). Developing a Capacity for Organizational Resilience through Strategic Human Resource Management. *Human Resource Management Review, 21*(3), 243–255.

Linnenluecke, M. K., & Griffiths, A. (2010). Beyond adaptation: Resilience for business considering climate change and weather extremes. *Business & Society, 49*, 477–511.

Linnenluecke, M. K., & Griffiths, A. (2012). Assessing organizational resilience to climate and weather extremes: Complexities and methodological pathways. *Climatic Change, 113*, 933–947.

Linnenluecke, M. K., Griffiths, A., & Winn, M. I. (2013). Firm and industry adaptation to climate change: A review of climate adaptation studies in the business and management field. *Wiley Interdisciplinary Reviews: Climate Change, 4*, 397–416.

Lissack, M. R., & Letiche, H. (2002). Complexity, Emergence, Resilience and Coherence: Gaining Perspective on Organizations and their Study. *Emergence, 4*(3), 72–94.

Luthar, S. S. (2006). Resilience in Development: A Synthesis of Research across Five Decades. Developmental Psychopathology: Vol. 3. *Risk, Disorder and Adaptation, 739-795*.

Macpherson, A., Herbane, B., & Jones, B. (2015). Developing Dynamic Capabilities through Resource Accretion: Expanding the Entrepreneurial Solution Space. *Entrepreneurship and Regional Development, 27*(5–6), 259–291. doi:10.1080/08985626.2015.1038598

Madni, A. & Jackson, S. (2009), Towards a conceptual framework for resilience engineering. *IEEE, 3*(2), 181-191.

Mallak, L. (1998). Putting organizational resilience to work. *Industrial Management (Des Plaines)*, *40*(6), 8–13.

Manyena, S. B. (2006). The Concept of Resilience Revisited. *Disasters*, *30*(4), 433–450. doi:10.1111/j.0361-3666.2006.00331.x

Manyena, S. B., O'Brien, G., O'Keefe, P., & Rose, J. (2011). Disaster resilience: A bounce back or bounce forward ability? *Local Environment*, *16*(5), 417–424.

March, J. G., & Olsen, J. P. (1975). The Uncertainty of the Past: Organizational Learning Under Ambiguity. *European Journal of Political Research*, *3*(2), 147–171.

Marcus, A. A., & Nichols, M. L. (1999). On the edge: Heeding the warnings of unusual events. *Organization Science*, *10*, 482–499.

Marwa, S., & Zairi, M. (2008). An exploratory study of the reasons for the collapse of contemporary companies and their link with the concept of quality. *Management Decision*, *46*, 1342–1370. doi:10.1108/00251 74081 09119 84

Marwa, S. M., & Milner, C. D. (2013). Underwriting corporate resilience via creativity: The pliability model. *Total Qual Manag Bus*, *24*, 835–846. doi:10.1080/14783 363.2013.79111 0

Masten, A. S., & Obradović, J. (2007). Competence and resilience in development. *Annals of the New York Academy of Sciences*, *1094*(1), 13–27.

McCann, J., Selsky, J., & Lee, J. (2009). Building agility, resilience, and performance in turbulent environments. *People & Strategy*, *32*, 44–51.

McCoy, J., & Elwood, A. (2009). Human factors in organisational resilience: Implications of breaking the psychological contract. *Journal of Business Continuity & Emergency Planning*, *3*, 368–375.

McCullough, T. (2008, May 12). The industry's strength is its resilience. Money Management Executive, p. 7.

Mistry, V., Sharma, U., & Low, M. (2014). Management accountants 'perceptions of their role in accounting for sustainable development: An exploratory study. *Pacific Accounting Review*, *26*(1/2), 112–133.

Moore, T., & Lakha, R. (2004). *Tolley's Handbook of Disaster and Emergency Management: Principles and Practice*. Lexis Nexis.

Norris, F. H., Stevens, S. P., Pfefferbaum, B., Wyche, K. F., & Pfeffer-Baum, R. L. (2008). Community resilience as a metaphor, theory, set of capacities, and strategy for disaster readiness. *American Journal of Community Psychology*, *41*(1–2), 127–150. doi:10.100710464-007-9156-6

Oxford University Press. (2017). *Oxford Dictionaries*. Retrieved November 17, 2017, from https://en.oxforddictionaries.com/definition/organization

Parsons, D. (2010). Organizational resilience. *Australian Journal of Emergency Management*, *25*(2), 18–20.

Pasteur, K. (2011). *From Vulnerability to Resilience: A Framework for Analysis and Action to Build Community Resilience*. Practical Action Publishing.

Paton, D., Millar, M., & Johnston, D. (2001). Community resilience to volcanic hazard consequences. *Natural Hazards*, *24*(2), 157–169.

Pelling, M. (2003). *The Vulnerabilities of Cities: Natural Disasters and Social Resilience*. Earthscan.

Pettit, T., Fiksel, J., & Croxton, K. (2010). Ensuring Supply Chain Resilience: Development of a Conceptual Framework. *Journal of Business Logistics*, *31*(1), 1–21.

Pettit, T. J., Croxton, K. L., & Fiksel, J. (2013). Ensuring Supply Chain Resilience: Development and Implementation of an Assessment Tool. *Journal of Business Logistics*, *34*(1), 46–76.

Podsakoff, P. M., MacKenzie, S. B., Lee, J. Y., & Podsakoff, N. P. (2003). Common method biases in behavioral research: A critical review of the literature and recommended remedies. *The Journal of Applied Psychology*, *88*(5), 879–903.

Ponomarov, S. Y., & Holcomb, M. C. (2009). Understanding the concept of supply chain resilience. *International Journal of Logistics Management*, *20*, 124–143. doi:10.1108/09574090910954873

Powley, E. H. (2013). The process and mechanisms of organizational healing. *The Journal of Applied Behavioral Science*, *49*, 42–68. doi:10.1177/0021886312471192

Ray, J. L., Baker, L. T., & Plowman, D. A. (2011). Organizational mindfulness in business schools. *Academy of Management Learning & Education*, *10*, 188–203. doi:10.5465/AMLE.2011.62798929

Reich, J. (2006). Three psychological principles of resilience in natural disasters. *Disaster Prevention and Management*, *15*(5), 793–798.

Reinmoeller, P., & Baardwijk, N. v. (2005). The link between diversity and resilience. *MIT Sloan Management Review*, *46*, 61–65.

Richardson, G. E. (2016). The applied metatheory of resilience and resiliency. In U. Kumar (Ed.), *The Routledge International Handbook of Psychological Resilience* (pp. 124–135). Routledge.

Richtnér, A., & Löfsten, H. (2014). Managing in turbulence: How the capacity for resilience influences creativity. *R & D Management*, *44*, 137–151.

Rigaud, E., Neveu, C., Duvenci-Langa, S., Obrist, M.-N., & Rigaud, S. (2013). Proposition of an organisational resilience assessment framework dedicated to railway traffic management. In *Rail Human Factors* (pp. 727–732). Supporting Reliability, Safety and Cost Reduction. doi:10.1201/b13827-97

Riolli, L., & Savicki, V. (2003). Optimism and Coping as Moderators of the Relation Between Work Resources and Burnout in Information Service Workers. *International Journal of Stress Management*, *10*(3), 235–252. doi:10.1037/1072-5245.10.3.235

Robb, D. (2000). Building resilient organizations. *OD Practitioner*, *32*(3), 27–32.

Roberts, K. H., & Bea, R. (2001). When systems fail. *Organizational Dynamics*, *29*, 179–191.

Rose, A. (2004). Defining and measuring economic resilience to disasters. *Disaster Prevention and Management*, *13*, 307–314.

Rose, A., & Liao, S. Y. (2005). Modeling regional economic resilience to disasters: A computable general equilibrium analysis of water service disruptions. *Journal of Regional Science, 45*, 75–112.

Rose, A., & Lim, D. (2002). Business interruption losses from natural hazards: Conceptual and methodological issues in the case of the Northridge earthquake. *Global Environmental Change, 4*, 1–14.

Rose, A., Oladosu, G., & Liao, S. Y. (2007). Business interruption impacts of a terrorist attack on the electric power system of Los Angeles: Customer resilience to a total blackout. *Risk Analysis, 27*, 513–531.

Rudolph, J. W., & Repenning, N. P. (2002). Disaster dynamics: Understanding the role of quantity in organizational collapse. *Administrative Science Quarterly, 47*, 1–30.

Salanova, M., Llorens, S., Cifre, E., & Martínez, I. M. (2012). We need a hero! Toward a validation of the healthy and resilient organization (HERO) model. *Group & Organization Management, 37*, 785–822.

Sapountzaki, K. (2007). Social resilience to environmental risks: A mechanism of vulnerability transfer? *Management of Environmental Quality, 18*(3), 274–297.

Sheffi, Y. (2006). Manage risk through resilience. *Chief Executive, 214*, 28–29.

Sitkin, S. B., See, K. E., & Miller, C. C. (2011). The paradox of stretch goals: Organizations in pursuit of the seemingly impossible. *Academy of Management Review, 36*(3), 544–566.

Smit, B., Burton, I., Klein, R. J. T., & Wandel, J. (2000). An anatomy of adaptation to climate change and variability. *Climatic Change, 45*, 223–251.

Somers, S. (2009). Measuring resilience potential: An adaptive strategy for organizational crisis planning. *Journal of Contingencies and Crisis Management, 17*(1), 12–23. doi:10.1111/j.1468-5973.2009.00558.x

Spillan, J., & Hough, M. (2003). Crisis Planning in Small Businesses: Importance, Impetus, and Indifference. *European Management Journal, 21*(3), 398–407. doi:10.1016/S0263-2373(03)00046-X

Stephenson, A. (2010). *Benchmarking the Resilience of Organizations* [Unpublished PhD Thesis]. Civil and Natural Resources Engineering Department, University of Canterbury.

Stewart, J., & O'Donnell, M. (2007). Implementing change in a public agency. *International Journal of Public Sector Management, 20*(3), 239–251. doi:10.1108/09513550710740634

Sullivan-Taylor, B., & Branicki, L. (2011). Creating resilient SMEs: Why one size might not fit all. *International Journal of Production Research, 49*(18), 5565–5579.

Sutcliffe, K. M., & Vogus, T. J. (2003). Organizing for resilience. In K. Cameron, J. E. Dutton, & R. E. Quinn (Eds.), *Positive organizational scholarship* (pp. 94–110). Berrett-Koehler.

Teo, W. L., Lee, M., & Lim, W.-S. (2017). The relational activation of resilience model: How leadership activates resilience in an organizational crisis. *Journal of Contingencies and Crisis Management, 25*, 136–147. doi:10.1111/1468-5973.12179

Timmerman, P. (1981). *Vulnerability, Resilience, and the Collapse of Society: A Review of Models and Possible Climatic Application, Institute for Environmental Studies*. University of Toronto.

USAID. (2012). *Building resilience to recurrent crisis*. Available at: www.usaid.gov/sites/default/files/documents/1870/USAIDResiliencePolicyGuidanceDocument.pdf

Välikangas, L. (2007). Rigidity, exploratory patience, and the ecological resilience of organizations. *Scandinavian Journal of Management, 23*(2), 206–213.

van Breda, A. D. (2016). Building Resilient Human Service Organizations. *Human Service Organizations, Management, Leadership & Governance, 40*(1), 62–73. doi:10.1080/23303131.2015.1093571

van der Vegt, G. S., Essens, P., Wahlstrom, M., & George, G. (2015). From the editors: Managing risk and resilience. Academy of Management Journal, 58, 3. https://doi.org/ doi:10.1163/18770703-00503003

Vargo, J., & Seville, E. (2011). Crisis strategic planning for SMEs: Finding the silver lining. *International Journal of Production Research, 49*, 5619–5635.

Walker, B. H., Abel, N., & Anderies, J. M. (2009). Resilience, adaptability, and transformability in the Goulburn-Broken catchment. Australia. *Ecology and Society, 14*(1), 12.

Walker, B. H., & Salt, D. A. (2012). *Resilience Practice: Building Capacity to Absorb Disturbance and Maintain Function*. Island Press.

Wartick, S. (2002). Measuring corporate reputation: Definition and data. *Business & Society, 41*(4), 371–392.

Wedawattaa, G., Ingirige, B., & Amaratunga, D. (2010). Building up resilience of construction sector SMEs and their supply chains to extreme weather events. *International Journal of Strategic Property Management, 14*, 362–375. doi:10.3846/ijspm. 2010.27

Weick, K. E. (1993). The collapse of sensemaking in organizations: The Mann Gulch disaster. *Administrative Science Quarterly, 38*(4), 628–652.

Weick, K. E., & Sutcliffe, K. M. (2001). *Managing the unexpected: Assuring high performance in an age of complexity*. Jossey-Bass.

Weick, K. E., & Sutcliffe, K. M. (2007). *Managing the unexpected: resilient performance in an age of uncertainty* (2nd ed.). Jossey-Bass.

Westhead, P., & Batstone, S. (1998). Independent Technology-Based Firms: The Perceived Benefits of a Science Park Location. *Urban Studies (Edinburgh, Scotland), 35*(12), 2197–2219. doi:10.1080/0042098983845

Wilbanks, T. J., & Romero Lankao, P. (2007) Industry, settlement, and society. In Climate change 2007: impacts, adaptation, and vulnerability: contribution of Working Group II to the Fourth Assessment Report of the Intergovernmental Panel on Climate Change. Cambridge University Press.

Williams, T., & Shepherd, D. (2016). Building resilience or providing sustenance: Different paths of emergent ventures in the aftermath of the Haiti earthquake. *Academy of Management Journal*. Advance online publication. doi:10.5465/amj.2015.0682

Williams, T. A., Gruber, D. A., Sutcliffe, K. M., Shepherd, D. A., & Zhao, E. Y. (2017). Organizational response to adversity: Fusing crisis management and resilience research streams. *The Academy of Management Annals, 11*, 733–769.

Winn, M. I., & Pogutz, S. (2013). Business, ecosystems, and biodiversity: New horizons for management research. *Organization & Environment, 26*, 203–229.

Woods, D. D. (2006). Essential Characteristics of Resilience. In E. Hollnagel, D. D. Woods, & N. Leveson (Eds.), *Resilience Engineering: Concepts and Precepts* (pp. 21–34). Ashgate.

Wright, C., Kiparoglou, V., & Williams, M. J. (2012). A framework for resilience thinking. *Procedia Computer Science, 8*, 45–52. doi:10.1016/j.procs.2012.01.012

Yang, W., Bansal, P., & DesJardine, M. R. (2014). What doesn't kill you makes you stronger: A multi-level process theory of organizational resilience. *Academy of Management Proceedings, 2014*(1), 13934.

Yohe, G., & Tol, R. S. (2002). Indicators for social and economic coping capacity: Moving toward a working definition of adaptive capacity. *Global Environmental Change, 12*, 25–40.

Chapter 10
Renewable Energies and the Urban Environment in Spain

Maria Jesus Garcia Garcia
University of Valencia, Spain

ABSTRACT

Sustainable development is a type of development that advocates first of all the harmonization between economic development and environmental protection. Adding social progress, it would therefore be development in which high and stable growth in the production of goods and services is compatible with widespread social progress, environmental protection, and prudent and efficient use of natural resources. It is therefore a delicate building supported by three main pillars—social, economic, and environmental—in which none of them prevails over the other. Accordingly, sustainability has an integrated character, preceded as it is by the objectives of economic recovery, environmental sustainability, and social cohesion. It is a general principle with transversal or horizontal projection capable of crossing different and varied sectoral areas, as many as are relevant to achieve its integrating objectives.

INTRODUCTION

The idea of sustainable development has to relate to other concepts and ideas within the framework of which it finds its justification and its content. We cannot talk about sustainable development without first placing it in a broader context from which it owes. In this sense, a reference to the principle of sustainable development, energy efficiency and the idea of urban renovation is necessary. These are generic concepts within the framework of which energy renovation is framed and which also lend its justification and reason for being.

The first term to which it is necessary to allude to explain the idea of energy renovation has to do with the concept of sustainable development, which for some time now has been used in our domestic legislation and whose legal implementation has been carried out mainly through Law 2/2011, of 4 March, on Sustainable Economy.

Sustainable development is a concept that combines three interrelated elements and has traditionally been treated differently in Spanish legislation. Perhaps that is why it can be said that in our legal system

DOI: 10.4018/978-1-7998-8996-0.ch010

the concept is relatively new in that it interrelates different objectives that converge in the different sectoral areas, emphasizing the interdependence between them rather than in their singular treatment (Chu, Steven, and Arun Majumdar 2012). These three elements or pillars that converge in the concept of sustainable development are: social, economic and environmental. "Sustainable development is a type of development that advocates first of all the harmonization between economic development and environmental protection, adding social progress; it would therefore be development in which high and stable growth in the production of goods and services is compatible with widespread social progress, environmental protection and prudent and efficient use of natural resources."; it is therefore a delicate building supported by three main pillars: social, economic and environmental in which none of them prevails over the others ".

Accordingly, sustainability has an integrated character, preceded as it is by the objectives of economic recovery, environmental sustainability and social cohesion. It is a general principle with transversal or horizontal projection, capable of crossing different and varied sectoral areas, as many as are relevant to achieve its integrating objectives (Curry, Nathan, and Pragasen Pillay, 2012).

Among the different sectoral areas transferred by the idea of sustainable development is undoubtedly the field of urban planning and housing. The activity generated in cities has an important environmental impact, so it is necessary to orient urban structures, homes and buildings under premises that are as respectful as possible with the environment, also taking advantage of its economic potential and its effect on the social fabric that inhabits it. It is about promoting integrated actions in the urban environment that are in tune with the objectives also integrating sustainable development.

Since sustainable development is an integrative concept, its influence on the urban and housing sector could not fail to have these same connotations, insofar as sustainable urbanism is nothing but a projection of sustained development in a specific area. Urban planning must respond to the requirements of sustainable development, minimizing its commitment to growth and betting on the regeneration of the existing city in order to achieve a sustainable and inclusive urban model, environmentally, socially and economically that improves the quality of life of citizens in urban spaces. In short, we are talking about the integrated objectives of sustainability applied to urban planning, in which the duty of conservation plays a fundamental role.

Spanish Constitution is devoid of explicit references to sustainable development, since it is a relatively new concept in our domestic law. However, the relationship between this principle and certain constitutional rights is evident, since the idea of sustainable urbanism advocates the preservation of urban spaces and buildings in which the constitutional right to decent housing and an adequate environment can be realized. From the perspective of the principle of sustainability, urban planning must be oriented towards renovation in order to comply with article 45 of the Constitution, since renovation does not consume land and makes it possible to exploit and use, rather to reuse, the existing heritage. In this sense, the implications between sustainable development and protection and the right to an adequate environment that guarantees the quality of life are fully established. Sustainable urban development would comply with article 45 of the Constitution in its two aspects: as a requirement imposed on the public authorities to ensure their protection and as the right of citizens to enjoy an adequate environment in order to ensure a certain quality of life. The observation that the urban environment is also the environment, or in other words, that the environment is also integrated by the urban environment, is clearly deduced from this and other recently adopted laws in our legal system. Thus, article 1 of Royal Legislative Decree 7/2015, of 30 October, approving the revised text of the Land Law, when defining its object, shows that the actions that are carried out try to ensure citizens an adequate quality of life, and the effectiveness of their right to enjoy a decent and adequate housing. Article 5 of the Act also establishes the rights of the citizen to whose satisfaction the act is subject, including the right to enjoy a decent, adequate and accessible home that is free of noise or other polluting emissions, as well as the right to enjoy an environment and a suitable landscape (Droege, Peter, ed., 2008)).

On the other hand, Law 7/85 of 2 April, regulating the bases of local regime, in its most recent amendment, also highlighted this point when it speaks in its article 25 of the competence of the municipalities in matters relating to the urban environment.

The connections with the constitutional right to housing are also clear in the extent maintaining the housing in proper condition for use, ensuring the maintenance of the existing population in a way that promotes the social and economic texture of this urban area.

In short, this is indicative that the actions of renovation, renewal and regeneration referred to from the point of view of sustainable development has its legal basis in articles 45 and 46 of the Constitution, without denying the implications that such a treatment of environmental protection will have on the economic and social aspects, such as the revival of economic activity, among others.

And precisely with this integrative purpose, the Law on renovation, renovation and urban regeneration is enacted, which combines the treatment of urban development actions in the urban environment and actions on housing and the architectural park from the point of view of the umbrella of sustainability. The point of view from which this Law rushing to the processing of such sectoral domains was certainly novel, as if, until then, we were accustomed to witness the treatment sector of the subjects on the basis of its consideration of the substantive, that is, as a sectoral domains where the material determined the content of the Law, in the case of the mentioned norm, the unifying element of the different precepts contained in it is not the substantive scope or material one, but the principle under which this treatment acted as an element of cohesion of the different precepts. We refer to the principle of sustainability, which justified that we found regulated under the umbrella of the same law sectoral areas as varied as urban legislation, precepts on urban renovation, urban leasing legislation or horizontal property. Nothing new if we take into account Law 2/2011 of 4 March, Sustainable Economy. The Real Decreto Legislativo 7/2015, de 30 October, approving the revised text of the Land Law and Urban Renovation serves now to a more specific, as it regulates subjects with a greater connection to each other that are all grouped under the generic concept of "urban", or more accurately, "urban environment". The content of this Law seems to consider the regulation of urban planning, as it affects consolidated urban land, susceptible to renovation, regeneration or renovation actions or new urbanization actions. But the truth is that the Law seems to be aimed at regulating urban development actions based on the principle of sustainable development.

BACKGROUND

Obviously, within this perspective of environmental sustainability present in the idea of sustainable urbanism one of the most relevant aspects from the point of view of its impact on the environment is that it has to do with the use and exploitation of energy and the use of certain forms of energy that maximize their consumption causing the minimum environmental impact. And focused as sustainable urbanism is on the idea of maintenance and conservation of the already made city and the existing buildings, this objective is to accommodate the buildings and the existing real estate park to these new energy demands. That is why we talk about energy renovation, meaning a set of actions in the urban environment and in existing buildings and homes that try to adapt the pre-existing elements (housing, but not only this, but also endowments, services and equipment) to the principles of efficiency and energy saving in accordance with the legal framework provided by Law 38/1999, of 5 November, on Building Planning and Royal Decree 314/2006, of 17 March, Technical Building Code.

Directive 2012/27 / EU states that buildings represent 40% of energy consumption in the European Union, so it becomes clear the need to influence the building sector and improve its energy performance (Lund, Peter, 2012).

These objectives, we find in article 3 of Royal Legislative Decree 7/2015, of 30 October, consolidated text of the Law of Soil and Urban Renovation, which speaks of minimizing polluting emissions and greenhouse gases, water and energy consumption and waste production. Also in paragraph i) of the same article these objectives are highlighted, when the Law refers to the need to prioritize renewable energies over the use of fossil energy sources and combat energy poverty with measures in favor of efficiency and energy saving. And finally, subparagraph (h) refers to the need to promote the protection of the atmosphere and the use of clean materials, products and technologies that reduce pollutant emissions and greenhouse gases from the construction sector, as well as reused and recycled materials that contribute to improving resource efficiency.

Energy efficiency is therefore one of the goals to be achieved in the urban environment aimed at achieving the objectives of environmental sustainability that underlie the generic concept of sustainable urban development. Thus, when article 3 of Royal Legislative Decree 7/2015, of 30 October, refers to the purposes to which public policies will tend in the urban environment, it bets on a concept of sustainability from the economic, social, environmental point of view that promotes the rational use of natural resources and energy efficiency. The Law seems to understand that energy efficiency is capable of promoting sustainable environmental conditions by itself and contributing to economic sustainability by generating jobs and employment, which is why its treatment is singled out as an emerging sector with great potential, not only environmental, but also economic.

To this end, energy efficiency must also be accompanied by a policy of diversifying the sources used in energy production, which opens the door to the use, promotion and use of renewable energies. The much discussed energy efficiency cannot consist only of measures aimed at saving and containing demand, but also requires the regulation and management of supply that promotes the introduction of renewable energy sources, which is in turn clean energy given its low level of emissions into the atmosphere (Purohit, Ishan, Pallav Purohit, and Sashaank Shekhar,2013).

In accordance with the above, energy renovation, based on the principle of energy efficiency, would be aimed at:

- Prioritize renewable energies.
- Promote energy savings.
- Reduce pollutant emissions and waste production.

ENERGY EFFICIENCY IN THE CONTEXT OF EUROPEAN UNION REGULATIONS

It should not be forgotten that European legislation sets specific targets for energy efficiency and emission reductions. In this sense it is necessary to make reference to the Directive 2010/31/EU of the European Parliament and of the Council of 19 may 2010 on the energy performance of buildings (object transposition part in the Royal Decree 235/2013 of April 5) and Directive 2012/27/EU of the European Parliament and of the Council of 25 October 2012 on energy efficiency, which aims to update the community legal order in the context of the general objective of the Europe 2020 Strategy, this implies the objectives of a 20% reduction in greenhouse gas emissions, an increase in the contribution of renewable energies by 20% and a 20% improvement in energy efficiency. The Directive also sets more ambitious targets for 2050 aimed at reducing the level of CO_2 emissions by 80-90% compared with 1990 levels. The measures identified by the said Directive concern key areas and sectors for achieving energy efficiency targets, such as building renovation. In this context, the Directive requires not only a significant percentage of central Government buildings to be renovated annually in order to improve their energy efficiency, but also that Member States also establish a strategy to mobilize investment in the renovation of residential buildings in order to improve the energy efficiency of the entire housing stock. The formulas to achieve these objectives are through the control of demand, promoting actions aimed at ensuring savings measures, but also through actions of management and regulation of supply, which includes its diversification, prioritizing the use of renewable energies for energy production over the use of fossil energies.

In this context, the Renewable Energy Plan (PER) 2011-2020 has been approved by resolution of the Council of Ministers of November 11, 2011, setting objectives that are in line with Directive 2009/28/EC of the European Parliament and of the Council of 23 April 2009 on the promotion of the use of energy from renewable sources, and in response to the mandates of the Royal Decree 661/2007, which regulates the activity of electricity production under the special regime and the Law 2/2011 of 4 march, Sustainable Economy. The PER has the objective of achieving, as indicated by the Community Directive, that in the year 2020 at least 20% of the gross final consumption of energy in Spain comes from the use of renewable sources.

Law 8/2013 of 26 June on urban renovation, regeneration and renewal served these purposes by partially transposing Directive 2012/27/EU, on energy efficiency, so that the principle of energy rationality is one of the pillars of the standard. The aforementioned standard established among its objectives those of minimizing the consumption of energy in homes constituting habitual residence and prioritizing renewable energies with measures in favor of efficiency and energy saving. This applies not only to new buildings and installations, but also to existing ones that are the subject of intervention, as we shall see below. As we already know, the content of this rule has become part of the Royal Legislative Decree 7/2015, of 30 October, consolidated text of the Land and Urban Renovation Law. In this context, the urban duty of conservation is considered as an instrument at the service of energy renovation, to the extent that its content is divided into a series of strata that support actions aimed at adapting the existing real estate to the demands of energy efficiency that the rules that regulate the building are demanding.

Some Clarifications on the Concept of Renovation in the Current Regulations

Law 8/2013, of 26 June, established a new nomenclature when formulating actions in the urban environment that differs from the nomenclature used in previous legislation, where the concept of urban renovation was comprehensive of a set of isolated or integrated actions that could even involve the demolition of buildings and urban elements incompatible with actions of sanitation or urban regeneration. Thus, two types of renovation were distinguished: isolated renovation and integrated renovation. The first considered the real estate in its own individuality, without implications or connections with the surrounding elements. On the contrary, integrated renovation considered the affected heritage as part of a larger space in which it was integrated. Integrated renovation consisted of the renovation of urban spaces, which without dispensing with the renovation of individual elements, transcended their effects to project on other elements of the environment, considering it as a whole.

According to the new nomenclature introduced by Law 8/2013, of 26 June, renovation is the term that refers to singular actions in buildings, while those that affect the urban fabric is called regeneration or urban renewal, according to entail the demolition of any of the elements of urban pre-existing. Based on this distinction, article 2 of Royal Legislative Decree 7/2015 of 30 October, establishes possible actions to be carried out in the urban environment, differentiating between renovation of buildings and regeneration and urban renewal. According to the cited article, performances on the urban environment are those that are intended to perform renovation work, when there are situations of failure or degradation of the basic requirements of functionality, safety and habitability of buildings, and the regeneration and urban renewal will be those that affect, both buildings as urban structure, including works of new building in the replacement of buildings previously demolished.

With reference to the basic requirements of functionality, safety, and livability, the idea of renovation of building is spacious and accommodates works and activities related to energy efficiency of the buildings, which introduces the concept of energy renovation, which involves performing actions on the real estate existing in a situation of failure or degradation in relation to the basic requirements of the building to adapt it to the demands of efficiency and energy savings.

Efficiency and Energy Renovation within the Framework of the Urban Duty of Conservation and the Use of Renewable Energies

Both the renovation of buildings and the integrated actions of urban renewal and regeneration are actions of urban significance, so on these actions must be projected the urban instruments and techniques that affect the situation of buildings and homes. So what sets the Real Decreto legislativo 7/2015, de 30 October, which in its article 2.1 states that all of these actions will apply to the statutory scheme basic duties and charges to which they are entitled in accordance with the performance of urban transformation or building that behave, in accordance with the provisions of article 7.

One of these duties is the duty of urban conservation, whose content is integrated by reference to Law 38/1999, of 5 November, on Building Planning, which in turn refers to Royal Decree 314/2006, of 17 March, which approves the Technical Building Code. The requirements of energy efficiency are incorporated into the duty of conservation through the regulation made in the Technical Building Code in its reference to living conditions, since they are applicable not only to new buildings, but also to existing ones when they are the subject of some intervention. Among these requirements are those related to the use of renewable energies.

But in addition, the Building Planning Law configures the duty of conservation in open terms by reference to the regulations that may be applicable in each case. The Act points to the Technical Building Code may be supplemented with the requirements of other regulations issued by the competent Authorities and is regularly updated according to the evolution of technology and the demand of the society, which emphasizes the open-ended character of the setting of the duty of conservation.

The Content of the Duty of Conservation: The Three Levels

The duty of urban conservation is regulated in article 15 of the consolidated text of the Law on Land and Urban Renovation, article that reformulates the wording of the duty of conservation established by

Royal Legislative Decree 2/2008, of 20 June in the terms in which it was drafted after Law 8/2013, of 26 June of urban renovation, regeneration and renewal.

The aforementioned precept establishes different duties and burdens that configure the urban content of the property right, among which is, as we say, the duty of conservation. According to the statement of reasons of the Law on urban renovation, regeneration and renovation, of which the aforementioned article 15 brings cause, the duty of conservation is articulated in three levels depending on the content that results from it for the owner.

At its basic level, the duty of conservation entails the duty to allocate the buildings to uses compatible with territorial and urban planning and the need to guarantee the safety, health, accessibility and decoration of the real estate. In this way, the duty of conservation includes the three basic requirements of the building, referring to functionality, safety and habitability. So far the duty of conservation coincides with its traditional formulation. However, the Law of renovation, regeneration and renewing urban added to article 9 of the Consolidated Text of the Land Act, Royal legislative Decree 2/2008 20 June, a new section under which the duty of conservation also includes the realization of the work and the necessary works in order to satisfy, in general, the basic requirements of the building set forth in article 3.1 of the Law 38/1999, de 5 de November on building renovation. This explicit reference to the previous Law is no longer included in article 15 of Royal Legislative Decree 7/2015 of 30 October, but is implicit in said article insofar as the aforementioned precept establishes the duty to preserve buildings in the legal conditions of safety, health, universal accessibility, ornament and the others required by the laws to serve as support for the uses for which they are intended and are compatible with territorial and urban planning, from which an implicit reference to the Building Planning Law and the Technical Building Code is inferred.

A second level, in which the duty of conservation includes the works and works necessary to adapt and progressively update the buildings, in particular the facilities, to the legal norms that are explicitly required at all times. Law 8/2013, of June 26, started from the consideration of an open conservation duty, whose content was not delimited by article 9 of Royal Legislative Decree 2/2008, of June 20, consolidated text of the Land Law, but subject to variations or extensions from other subsequent laws. Thus, Article 9, paragraph 2, established the competent administration could impose at any time the realization of works to comply with the legal duty of conservation in accordance with the provisions of the applicable state and autonomous community legislation. This provision, due to its obviousness, is also absent in article 15 of Royal Legislative Decree 7/2015 of 30 October, which does not prevent considering the duty of conservation as a duty of an evolutionary nature and subject to the variation of the technical requirements that are foreseen in the different applicable regulations. In this way, the duty of conservation will also include the necessary works to adapt the buildings and update their facilities to the legal norms that are required at any time, as the regulations of the sector introduce modifications in order to maintain the conditions of use of the buildings. The duty of conservation is thus in open terms, by reference to the regulations that may be applicable in each case.

Finally, a third level includes additional works, carried out for reasons of general interest, in respect of which the Law distinguishes two cases:

- those carried out for tourist or cultural reasons that constitute an assumption already included in the previous legislation, although under the consideration of improvement and forced renovation works.

- those carried out for the improvement of the quality and sustainability of the urban environment, assumption that now introduces Law of renovation, regeneration and urban renewal in the modification that makes of the Consolidated Text of the Law of the Land.

Energy Efficiency, Duty of Conservation and Renovation

The Initial Content of the Duty of Conservation: Energy Saving and the Use of Renewable Energy

The preservation of buildings in conditions of safety, health and public decoration constitutes a legal duty imposed on the owner on the basis of the social function of the property in accordance with article 33 of the Constitution. To the duty of the owner to maintain the buildings in the aforementioned conditions, it is now also added that of universal accessibility, and in addition, it is implicitly integrated into the duty of conservation the realization of the works and the works necessary to satisfy in general, the basic requirements of the building established in article 3.1 of Law 38/1999, of 5 November, of Building Planning.

Article 3.1 of the Building Planning Act establishes three basic requirements for buildings aimed at ensuring the safety of people, the welfare of society and the protection of the environment. These are requirements relating to functionality, safety and habitability. And precisely in this last section the measures relating to energy saving and thermal insulation are established so that a rational use of the energy necessary for the proper use of the building is achieved. The efficiency and energy savings are part of the duty of conservation to the extent that this duty entails keeping the buildings in terms of serving to its use, which leads to the need to satisfy the basic requirements of the building, within which are located relative to energy savings, thermal insulation and rational use of energy, and that is conducive to the simultaneous execution of conservation work directed to maintain the buildings in terms of safety, sanitation and beautification works and aimed to enhance the energy efficiency of the same. Therefore, we wanted to take advantage of the realization of conservation works in the most traditional sense of the term to promote the realization of actions related to energy renovation, which are now integrated into the duty of conservation.

The requirements of energy efficiency have been incorporated into the duty of conservation through the regulation carried out by the Technical Building Code, Royal Decree 314/2006, of 17 March. and are applicable not only to newly constructed buildings, but also to those undergoing repair or renovation. The aforementioned Royal Decree is issued in implementation of Law 38/1999 of 5 November, on Building Planning, whose second provision empowers the Government to approve a regulatory norm that establishes the basic requirements that buildings must meet in relation to the requirements relating to safety and habitability listed in paragraphs b) and c) of article 3.1 of the Building Planning Law.

Among the requirements relating to habitability, Article 15 of the said Code regulates the basic requirements of energy saving. These basic requirements apply and must be met both by new buildings and by existing buildings that are subject to modification, reform, extension or renovation and are basic, so that their requirements are mandatory throughout the national territory. The eleventh Final Provision of the Law 8/2013, of June 26, has widened the scope of application of Technical Building Code to modify its article 1 that the basic requirements must be met, as established by the regulations set in the project, the construction, the maintenance, preservation and use of buildings and facilities, as well as in interventions in existing buildings. Likewise, the aforementioned rule has modified Article 2 of the

Technical Code, so that its basic requirements will be required not only to new buildings but also to all those existing buildings that are the subject of intervention.

The basic requirements for energy savings set out in the Technical Code are five, namely: limitation of energy demand, performance of thermal installations, energy efficiency of lighting installations, minimum solar contribution of domestic hot water and minimum photovoltaic contribution of electrical energy. The purpose for which it is intended with this energy saving enters into what was formerly defined as energy efficiency, as it is to get a rational and sustainable use of the energy used in the building or home, and also enhance the consumption comes from renewable energy sources.

For this reason, among these basic requirements we must highlight those that refer to solar contributions, and above all, those that refer to the production of domestic hot water, which " have the character of minimums, and can be extended as a result of additional provisions issued by the competent administrations"

And this raises the question of which Administration is competent to regulate this question. Some autonomous communities have adopted their own regulations on renewable energy. This is the case of the Autonomous Community of Andalusia and its Law 2/2007, on the promotion of renewable energies and energy savings and efficiency in Andalusia. The aforementioned Law is developed by Decree 169/2011, of 31 May, whose Chapter II " Basic requirements for the use of renewable energies, savings and energy efficiency", complies with the provisions of the Technical Building Code by adapting these requirements to the energy needs and climatic characteristics of Andalusia. However, the Andalusian regulations do not establish additional requirements of contribution to the minimum contributions of thermal energy required in the state regulations through the Technical Building Code.

By applying the principle of linking negative in the interpretation of the principle of legality, the judgments of the Supreme Court of 22 may 2015 (RJ 2015/2620 and 2015/2016) consider such other competent authorities are, in addition to the autonomous communities, local authorities and that the criteria listed in the Technical Building Code constitute minimum values that the local authorities have to respect, but that can increase.

According to the jurisprudential criterion established after the judgments of the Supreme Court of May 22, 2015 (RJ 2015/2620 and 2015/2016), this reference to the competent administrations, also includes local entities that can thus adapt the state provisions to their own peculiarities and the needs that conform their specific local interests.

Thus, some municipalities, in the context of sustainable urbanism, have adopted ordinances aimed at promoting energy savings and promoting the use of renewable energies such as solar energy based on the competences that local legislation recognizes them in matters such as urbanism and the environment. Such is the case of the municipal Ordinance on the collection and use of solar thermal energy in buildings, of the City of Burgos . Also the Ordinance of the same name of the City of Pamplona as well as the municipal Ordinance of eco-energy efficiency and use of renewable energy in buildings and their facilities, of the City of Zaragoza among others.

The approval of the Technical Building Code, Royal Decree 314/2006, of 17 March, has come to provide the legal authorization whose absence motivated the challenge of the local ordinances on energy use to understand that the Law of Bases of Local Regime did not provide sufficient legal authorization for municipalities to approve ordinances in this sense. The judgments of the Supreme Court of May 22, 2015 (RJ 2015/2620 and 2015/2016) indicate that from the approval of the Technical Building Code the normative coverage of the ordinances relating to the use of solar energy is accommodated in the aforementioned legal text, which has the character of basic legislation

Energy Efficiency as an Additional Content to the Duty of Conservation: The Improvement of Energy Efficiency and the Use of Renewable Energy Sources

The duty of conservation will also include the adaptation of the building to the use of renewable energies indirectly when renovation actions are carried out that update the duty of conservation.

The duty to initial conservation is added to the duty to perform additional work for tourism or cultural, or to improve the quality and sustainability of the urban environment, since the distinction between the duty of conservation based on the fulfillment of the social function of property and the duty of conservation based on reasons of general interest has been a constant in the planning legislation that the different laws have been addressed in a different way, but always on the basis of their recognition . The content of these additional works is defined by reference to the Technical Building Code, and may consist of partial or complete adaptation to all or some of the basic requirements established therein. In accordance with this article, the Administration may order the owners to carry out works aimed at improving the quality or sustainability of the urban environment, including works to improve energy efficiency and including those aimed at encouraging the installation of renewable energy sources in buildings.

The attention to renewable energies is framed by both in the works additional ordering the administration to improve the quality and sustainability of the urban environment imposed by reasons of general interest, and is justified in the community legislation and in particular Directive 2012/27/EU, noting that buildings represent 40% of energy consumption in the European Union compels the member states to develop strategies that include the realization of investment in the renovation of residential and commercial buildings . The Directive requires not only the annual renovation of a percentage of public buildings of the central State Administration (thus underlining the exemplary nature of public actions), but also the mobilization of investments aimed at the renovation of buildings for commercial or residential uses with the aim of improving their energy efficiency.

The characteristic of these actions is that the law empowers the public administrations to impose them for reasons of general interest beyond the limits that govern the duty of conservation, in which case, the Law indicates, the ordering Administration will be responsible for the works that exceed this limit to obtain improvements of general interest. We are talking about additional conservation, which involves carrying out additional works and financing measures to improve the energy efficiency of buildings. This implies the renovation of buildings through internal strategies of mobilization of real estate investments where the legal limit for the owner is that of the duty of conservation and the administration has to contribute to the financing of the rest, since they are improvements of general interest. In this case, the duty of conservation goes beyond the particular objective of adaptation of the building in question to identify with a broader objective of general interest focused on the consolidated urban environment where it is located and on the fulfillment of energy efficiency objectives that are deduced from European policies, for which the mobilization of investments aimed at the renovation of residential and commercial buildings is foreseen. The additional content of the duty of conservation must be framed within integral actions and policies of economic, social, environmental regeneration and cohesion of the city as a whole, perspective from which the duty of conservation transcends the individual level to achieve improvements of general interest. And from this perspective, not only building renovation actions are imposed, but also actions that include actions to implement renewable energy not only at the building level, but also through urban development actions in urban fabrics that involve urban regeneration or renewal.

However, article 15 of Royal Legislative Decree 7/2015, of 30 October, does not seem to require any additional requirements for the imposition of such additional conservation works. Since it is an additional duty that transcends the individual plan of the property to which it refers to have an impact on the urban environment, it could be considered consubstantial to the general interest alleged that the property was included in some type of legal instrument of renovation. Well established, for example in the article 111 of the Law of Sustainable Economy, repealed by the Law 8/2013, of June 26, in which it is stated that the competent authority could command, in the form, terms and deadlines set by the applicable law, the execution of works of improvement up to the maximum amount of statutory duty, in addition to for reasons cultural and tourist collected by the applicable legislation, in the course of the construction or the building that were to become affected by a program, plan or any other legal instrument for the renovation of housing approved and in force, and refers to works designed to guarantee the rights recognized by law to individuals, or to be imposed by legal norms supervened for reasons of safety, adequacy of facilities and minimum services, reduction of polluting emissions and emissions of any kind and those necessary to reduce water and energy consumption.

Energy Renovation and the Limit of the Duty of Conservation

The Quantitative Limits Of The Duty Of Conservation

Law 8/2013, of 26 June, introduced some modifications regarding the limits of the duty of conservation and that were fixed by reference to quantitative criteria. These amendments are now incorporated in article 15 of the consolidated text of the Law on Land and Urban Renovation. In this sense, the limit of the duty of conservation is established at half of the current construction value of a new plant property, equivalent to the original in relation to the constructive characteristics and the useful surface, carried out in the necessary conditions so that its occupation is authorized, or where appropriate, is in a position to be legally destined for its own use. By establishing this limit, the state legislation configures the content of the duty of conservation by reference to an objective criterion, thus preventing the autonomous legislation from establishing its own limits with respect to that duty. Law 8/2013, of June 26, introduced an important novelty in the duty of urban conservation and in the regulation that until now had been carried out of it by the Consolidated Text of the Land Law of 2008, by quantifying the limit of the duty of conservation, which were doing the autonomous regulations in some cases. This modification should be subject to positive evaluation, as in this way, the limit is set up with basic character and binding on the legislator autonomous, so that in accordance with the provisions of article 149.1.1 of the Constitution, defines the legal positions of the owners in relation to their duty of conservation, and imposes rules equal and uniform to all property owners of buildings.

The duty of conservation is thus established by reference to an objective limit and individualized by reference to each particular property, which is fixed by reference to a percentage applied on the current value of a new construction of similar functional and structural characteristics and equal useful surface. In short, the Law addresses the value or cost of replacement by taking into account not the value of the damaged building (current value of the building), but a new building whose valuation will serve to contrast the cost of repair works and set the limit of the duty of conservation. The valuation system deals exclusively with the replacement value, that is, the hypothetical value of a construction of the same structure and building typology that allows a use of similar characteristics to that of the construction with respect to which the declaration of ruin is intended. The evaluation of these repairs will have to be carried out based on current techniques and materials that allow to maintain or return to the construction the original functionality. The legislation takes into account the economic profitability of the extension of the useful life of the constructions through the conservation or renovation of the same ones. In this sense, the limit of the profitability of the conservation of the buildings is fixed in the disbursement by the owner of expenses that remain below half of the cost of a new construction with characteristics similar to the existing one.

But the limit of the duty of conservation is solved based on economic criteria where the cost of replacement works is only one of the terms of the equation. The second is related to the content and extent of the works to be made to understand fulfilled the aforementioned duty. In this sense, it should be noted that the conservation works are not merely the works necessary to maintain the property in conditions of safety, health and ornament. We have already indicated in the previous section that the duty of conservation also involves the realization of works necessary to ensure universal accessibility, as well as those others that are necessary to meet the basic requirements of the building established in article 3.1 of Law 38/1999 of 5 November on Building Planning, where interventions related to energy efficiency are registered, including both those that are deduced from the current regulations and those others that are explicitly required to adapt and update their facilities to the standards. In short, this means going to the Technical Building Code, in which the basic requirements of the building are specified, which in terms of energy saving also implies the need to include among these works, those relating to the installation of collection systems, transformation, storage and use of solar energy. In addition, the values derived from this basic requirement will be considered minimum, without prejudice to stricter values that may be established by the competent administrations and that contribute to sustainability according to the characteristics of their location and territorial scope.

It could be thought that since one of the terms of the equation expands with respect to what was the traditional duty of conservation, the logical consequence will be that the limit of the duty of conservation will be easily exceeded by including more demanding actions in the maintenance of buildings that also meet criteria of saving and energy efficiency. However, this possible consequence is remedied if we take into account that the second comparative term focuses on the replacement cost of the property. This clarification is important, since urban planning legislation has not always made use of this criterion to delimit the cessation of the duty of conservation. Thus, for example, article 247 of the Consolidated Text of the Land Act of 1992, when referring to the declaration of ruin (which implied the cessation of the duty of conservation), referred to the present value of the building or plants concerned, excluding the value of the land. This meant taking as a reference the value of the building at the time when it was planned to carry out the repair works on it, which implied valuing the building applying criteria indicative of the depreciation suffered by the property depending on age and state of conservation among others. Obviously, this means that the building is quantified at a lower magnitude easily exceeded by the cost of maintenance and renovation works carried out in it. As we said, the option to include the replacement cost of a similar building of new plant allows to increase quantitatively the second term of the equation.

CONCLUSIONS

The Law 8/2013 introduced within the duty of urban conservation the realization of additional works that had as a common denominator the fact that its imposition is based on reasons of general interest, and that the Consolidated Text of the Land Law of 2008 considered as works of improvement. Royal Legislative Decree 7/2015, of 30 October, refers to them in article 15.1 c). These additional works include those carried out for tourism and cultural reasons, to which are added those focused on improving the quality and sustainability of the urban environment, introduced by Law 2/2011 of 4 March on Sustainable Economy and where those actions related to energy efficiency are framed. The content of these additional works for the improvement of quality and sustainability is determined as we have indicated, by reference to the Technical Building Code

Well, these works additional to the duty of conservation which now also include those related to the improvement of the quality and sustainability of the urban environment, has a particular legal regime, since the law establishes the possibility for the administration to force the landlord to the realization of the same, even once exceeded the limit of the duty of conservation. In this case, the administration that orders or imposes the realization of such works must pay the economic excess that entails the realization of the same. And this economic excess is fixed by reference to the limit of the duty of conservation referred to above. In this way, the limit of the duty of conservation (half of the current value of construction of a building of a new plant, equivalent to the original in connection with the construction features and the useful surface, taken with the conditions necessary for their occupation is approvable or, in your case is in a position to be legally intended for use by own) it is also the limit of the works to be executed at the expense of the owners when the Administration of the order to the improvement of the quality or sustainability of the urban environment. The Law assumes the criterion of the joint participation of the owner and the Administration in the maintenance of the property, as deduced from article 9.1 of the Land Law after the wording given to it by the Law on urban renovation, regeneration and renovation.

Royal Legislative Decree 7/2015, of 30 October, considers the importance of these renovation actions in the urban environment and the need to adapt them to the limits of the legal duty of conservation through the economic viability report, regulated in article 22. This memory, it is expected not only in cases in which they carry out activities of regeneration and renewal, but also in the case of actions of renovation of building, isolated or included in a scope of work (by areas or spaces), establishing as one of its aims to ensure the least possible impact on the personal wealth of the individuals, adjusted in any case the limits of the duty to bequeath conservation.

REFERENCES

Ahuja, D., & Tatsutani, M. (2009). Sustainable energy for developing countries. *S.A.P.I.EN.S, 2*(1). https://journals.openedition.org/sapiens/823

Chu, S., & Majumdar, A. (2012). Opportunities and challenges for a sustainable energy future. *Nature, 488*(August), 294–303. doi:10.1038/nature11475 PMID:22895334

Curry, N., & Pillay, P. (2012). Biogas prediction and design of a food waste to energy system for the urban environment. *Renewable Energy, 41*(May), 200–209. doi:10.1016/j.renene.2011.10.019

Droege, P. (Ed.). (2008). *Urban Energy Transition: From Fossil Fuels to Renewable Power*. Elsevier Ltd. doi:10.1016/B978-0-08-045341-5.00029-3

Lund, P. (2012). Large-scale urban renewable electricity schemes—Integration and interfacing aspects. *Energy Conversion and Management, 63*(November), 162–172. doi:10.1016/j.enconman.2012.01.037

Purohit, I., Purohit, P., & Shekhar, S. (2013). Evaluating the potential of concentrating solar power generation in North-western India. *Energy Policy, 62*, 157–175. doi:10.1016/j.enpol.2013.06.069

UN-HABITAT, Local Governments for Sustainability, and the United Nations Environment Programme. (2009). *Sustainable Urban Energy Planning: A handbook for cities and towns in developing countries*. UNEP.

Chapter 11
Welfare State, Income, and Public Debt:
Their Implications for Latin American Life Satisfaction

Jessica Dávalos-Aceves
https://orcid.org/0000-0002-7031-879X
Escuela de Ciencias Económicas y Empresariales, Universidad Panamericana, México

José G. Vargas-Hernández
https://orcid.org/0000-0003-0938-4197
Instituto Tecnológico José Mario Molina Pasquel y Henríquez, Mexico

ABSTRACT

The effect of economics on the subjective well-being of people has been studied by treating country information in the same way as data from individuals. The objective of this chapter is to analyze 17 Latin American countries with data from 2016 by including both effects handled into two different levels. This work contributes to extend the current debate regarding the impact of economics on subjective well-being of people by applying the multilevel method. Some of the findings revealed that both the individual economic situation as well as the welfare state and the rule of law of a country generate effects on subjective well-being. Similarly, the effect of interaction between some variables was analyzed, and it was concluded that people with great economic difficulties have a stronger relationship with subjective well-being in areas of higher government spending and higher tax burden.

INTRODUCTION

The present pandemic has changed the perspective of people regarding well-being, by increasing the value that is given to it. Individuals are appreciating all the time more their physical, as well as mental and psychological condition, after two years of living with the presence of a virus that has threatened

DOI: 10.4018/978-1-7998-8996-0.ch011

the survival of mankind and has modified life styles and human interactions and with no end in sight for the mutating COVID 19.

For this reason, it is of utmost importance to analyze the effects that economic variables have had in well-being. Among the studies that link economy to the subjective well-being of people, several researchers have been interested in how the latter is affected by people's income (Lea, Webley & Levine, 1993; Easterlin, 2001; Frey & Stutzer, 2002; Schyns, 2002; Helliwell, 2003; Alesina, Di Tella & MacCulloch, 2004; Gasper, 2005; Binswanger, 2006).

On the other hand, several other authors have focused on analyzing the effect of variables at the country level on subjective well-being, such as Hayo and Seifert (2003); Alesina et al. (2004); Sanfey and Teksoz (2007); Bjørnskov, Dreher and Fischer (2007); Di Tella and MacCulloch (2008); Shahbaz and Aamir (2008); Dluhosch and Horgos (2013); Powdthavee, Burkhauser and De Neve (2017); Brzezinski (2019) to name a few. That is, economically speaking there are influences at the individual level and at the country level. However, the vast majority of jobs use single-level methodologies, and disaggregate macroeconomic data at an individual unit level. Or, the authors carry out the analysis at the individual level and omit the context in which mentioned individuals live. The first case may present problems of self-correlation, and the second case of omission of important contextual effects. And both options lead to argumentation errors based on the misinterpretation of statistical results.

Objective and Contributions

The objective of this work is to analyze the subjective well-being in Latin America, by considering the repercussions that the individual economic condition, diverse macroeconomic variables and the effect of the interaction between them could have on it.

The novel finding of the current work aims to contribute by taking into account variables at the individual level and context level, as well as their interaction effect, by using a model that considers in an adequate way the nature and level of every variable. Additionally, studies of Latin America regarding subjective well-being are scarce. As well, these countries are interesting since they have the peculiarity of keeping a certain cultural similarity, and at the same time they can show marked differences in terms of political and economic indicators.

The models that will be used in the present work will be multilevel, since they allow to involve different independent variables at more than one level. This is important because it offers a way to evaluate the effect on well-being in a more adequate way that takes into consideration the structure of data, and in consequence it turns out to be a more robust measurement. Therefore it will have results that reflect more closely what happens in reality, what could be useful in terms of creating public policy more accurate for bringing well-being to citizens in general.

Firstly, the antecedents of subjective well-being and its link with the welfare state are described, in order to then review the empirical literature. Subsequently, the multilevel technique is explained, then a description of the data is made, followed by the presentation and analysis of the results. Finally, the conclusions and limitations of the study are shown.

BACKGROUND

Subjective well-being

For the purposes of this work, the concept of subjective well-being will be understood in the same way as the Organization for Economic Cooperation and Development (OECD) does. Definition taken from Diener (2006): "Good mental state, which includes all the different evaluations, both positive and negative that people make of their lives, as well as the affective reactions of people to their experiences" (p.152).

With respect to subjective well-being in Latin America, it was found that socio-demographic variables maintain a relationship with subjective well-being not very different from that of industrialized economies (Graham & Pettinato, 2001). However, as economies, the Latin American ones are more heterogeneous among them than they could be, for example, the European ones. So the context could have an even more important role for the Latin case. As an example, Graham and Felton (2006) found greater and more consistent effects of wage inequality on subjective well-being in Latin America in relation to the United States and Europe. A more recent study, identified a slightly positive association between income inequality and subjective well-being in Latin America, contrary to the negative association in other regions (Ngamaba, Panagioti & Armitage, 2018).

Welfare State and Subjective Well-Being

Bryson (1992) defined the welfare state as "the institutionalized provision of the State to cover the basic economic and social requirements of its citizens" (p.36). While Spicker (1995) referred to it as "the delivery of social services by the State and the strategy of developing inter-related services to address a wide range of social problems" (p.274).

In the beginning, studies were carried out whose purpose was to analyze the living conditions that favored the objective well-being. This gave rise to the term "standard of living", referring to conditions that initially were limited to the economic. This expression was within the frame of reference of the welfare state. This orientation introduced the term *quality of life*. This, in a progressive way, was incorporating more subjective components such as perceptions and social evaluations related to the living conditions of people. This differentiation between the level of individual versus social analysis, managed to distinguish well-being in its subjective dimension apart from the objective one, studying human welfare from the point of view of the individual (Martín, 2002). This is how there is a link between the welfare state and the subjective well-being of people.

According to the neo-classical theory, the government takes the role of a benevolent dictator, which seeks to achieve maximum social welfare, in turn resolving market failures and misallocations as a consequence of market processes (Pareto, 1906). This takes place through the provision of public goods (Musgrave, 1959) and corrective taxes (Pigou, 1947). Authors such as Ribeiro and Marinho (2017) asserted that "government has the relevant attribution to offer society those factors that grant more satisfactory conditions of life" (p.157).

Next, an empirical review of the literature will be made. The way in which it is organized is by topic of interest. It will begin with studies related to the effect of government spending on subjective well-being, followed by the effect on it by the application of taxes or tax burden.

EMPIRICAL REVIEW

Several authors have studied empirically the way in which the subjective well-being of people is affected by the welfare state, generally using government spending as a variable that represents it (Veenhoven, 2000; Bjørnskov, Gupta & Pedersen, 2008; Hessami, 2010; Kotakorpi & Laamanen, 2010).

Bjørnskov, Dreher and Fischer (2007) concluded that satisfaction with life decreases at higher government spending. In another study conducted in countries in transition, it was found rather that there was a positive correlation with happiness (Perovic & Golem, 2010). Same result in the study of Ram (2009). Hessami (2010) concluded that the effect of government spending on people's happiness depends on the level of co-ownership in the government, its effectiveness and federalism. While other authors did not find any correlation (Kacapyr, 2008; Ribeiro & Marinho, 2017).

On the other hand, spending on social security was not correlated with well-being in a group of countries (Veenhoven, 2000), and it did have a positive correlation in another study for the case of Finland (Kotakorpi & Laamanen, 2010). As well, Peru and Brazil, which showed the largest increases in delivery quality of governance, presented, additionally, a positive relationship with life evaluations (Helliwell, et al., 2018).

Also, Macchia and Plagnol (2019), through their analysis, found a significant upward trend between 2009 and 2016 in South America, due to the participation of citizens in democratic elections during this period of time. However, confidence in financial institutions, the honesty of elections, the judicial system and the national government displayed a significant overall downward trend because of liberal governments involved in corruption.

For government to meet the needs of citizens through the provision of public services, solving social problems, and others, it is necessary to obtain an income from the collection of taxes of population.

There are different theoretical frameworks related to the behavior of taxpayers and their link with well-being.

Feld and Frey (2002) established that the relationship that exists between the State and taxpayers can be modeled through a relational contract, which involves strong emotional ties and where trust plays a very important role. This psychological contract takes more force when a constitution is presented that provides participation rights to citizens to freely and democratically choose their government. In this type of relationship, both the taxpayers and government are seen as partners.

Alm, McClelland and Schulze (1992) stated that if taxpayers were to be assumed as rational beings from the point of view of purely economic analysis then most of them would evade taxes since the probability of being caught and penalized is low. Other authors argued that a rational choice model of subjective probabilities is the one that fits best (Quintanilla, Martin & Pardo, 2005). In this type of models, the rational agent maximizes its utility by weighing the utility of each of the results that can be given by the subjective probability that they occur. This probability is estimated according to their own beliefs (Abitbol & Botero, 2005).

Guilt, social disapproval and the uncertainty of being caught should also be considered as negative emotions that are generated if the person fails to pay taxes (Erard & Feinstein, 1994).

In other works, it has been commented that the effect of taxes on taxpayers depends on issues such as the sense of perceived justice, that is, that people receive what they deserve. Where hard work and proper behavior are rewarded (Alesina & Angeletos, 2005). There are works that show positive correlations between the perceptions of inequity in the matter of tax payments and tax evasion (Spicer, 1974; Song & Yarbrough, 1978). On the other hand, these elements of equity and justice are also based on the degree to which citizens perceive that their taxes are reinvested in society in the form of public services and social protection, which also entails a third element that involves the perceived reciprocity (Pommerehne, 1984; Torgler, 2003; Quintanilla et al., 2005). "Population is prepared to tolerate a high tax burden if they beieve that certain public goods and services, provided by government, will substantially increase their quality of life, and ultimately, their happiness," commented Perovic and Golem (2010, p.10).

The low provision of public goods has a negative effect in relation to the subjective well-being of people as observed in the works of Frey, Luechinger and Stutzer (2009); Levinson (2012). In turn, Smith (1991); Alm, Jackson and McKee (1992) found in their respective works that legitimacy, justice, reciprocity, and being able to appreciate benefits from the payment of their taxes reflected in the society used to increase the intention to cover with fiscal obligations.

Another important aspect is the satisfaction of fulfilling the duty. Lubian and Zarri (2011) conducted a study based on the Survey of Income and Welfare of Italian Households in 2004 with a two-stage analysis in which the authors concluded that people who pay their taxes are happier than those who do not. The authors argued that this is consistent with the perspective of Aristotle's eudimonist school, in which virtuous behavior leads to an increase in happiness. Similarly, Harbaugh, Mayr and Burghart (2007) conducted an experiment in which the authors scanned subjects while performing two types of transfers from their bank accounts, one voluntary and one compulsory imitating what would be a tax. Concluding that even mandatory transfers had an effect on the brain's reward system. Scholz and Pinney (1995) found that taxpayers resort to the "heuristic of duty", under a rationality approach with little information, to gauge their perception of risk of being caught in case of not paying taxes. Likewise, in another study, the results showed that duty and fear diminished by increasing the level of taxes and vice versa (Scholz & Lubell, 1998).

On the other hand, Frey and Stutzer (2000), with the objective of testing whether participation in direct democracy and institutional factors increased subjective well-being, analyzed data on more than 6000 inhabitants of Switzerland in 1992. Within their findings the authors found no significant correlation between tax burden and happiness.

Torgler (2005) conducted a study in Latin countries based on the World Values Survey from 1981 to 1987, as well as the 1998 Latinobarometer survey through a multivariate regression analysis and weighted estimates of ordered probit. The author concluded that tax burden, lack of honesty and corruption are the most important factors for people to decide to evade taxes. Also that trust in the president and the authorities, the belief that other people comply with the law and an attitude in favor of democracy are elements that generate a positive effect on tax morale.

Akay et al. (2012) subsequently made an empirical application with data from the German Socio-Economic Panel survey from 1985 to 2010 applying an ordered probit analysis. The results showed that, after controlling for socio-demographic variables and for net income, taxes have a significant positive effect on the subjective well-being of people.

METHOD USED: MULTILEVEL MODELING AND ITS THEORETICAL AND STATISTICAL SUBSTANTIATION

In the modeling of human behavior, context takes a relevant role. Individual action may be influenced by independent variables operating at different levels, from the micro to the macro.

Figure 1. Illustration adapted from Bronfenbrenner's ecological framework (Bronfenbrenner, 1977)
Source: Prepared by the authors with information of social ecological model of Bronfenbrenner

Macrosystem
GDP, Gov. expense & integrity,
Public debt, Fiscal burden
Exosystem
Mesosystem
Mycrosystem
Religion, Educational level,
Marital status, Employment status, Econ. situation
Individual
Gender, Age, Race

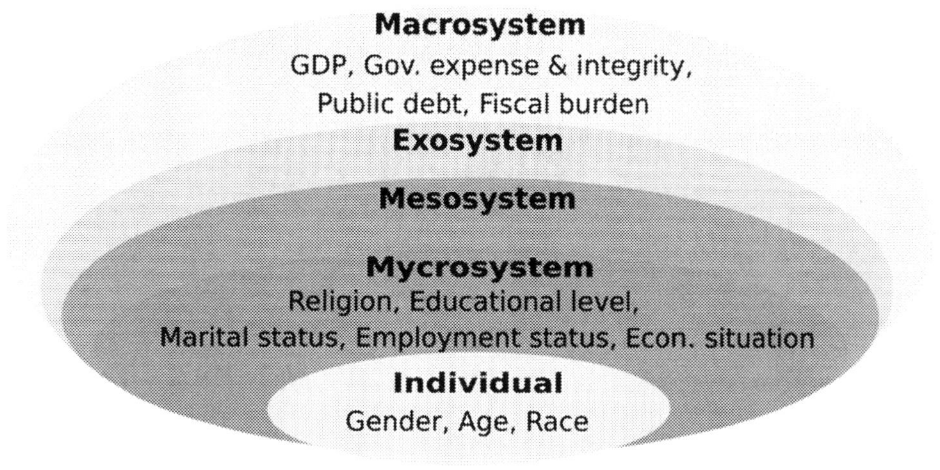

For example, let is mention the case where the level of learning of a student is evaluated. This variable is influenced by characteristics proper of the child, like the amount of time the student dedicates to study or his/her skills. As well, as characteristics of the classroom where the child belongs it can be taken into account the size of the classroom, the quality of installations, to mention some. These characteristics occurring at a higher level of analysis are influencing processes at a lower level. In this example, it can be considered the child to be measured and modeled at level 1, and the classroom at level 2.

Bronfenbrenner (1977) proposed the Ecological Systems Theory, which consists of an environmental focus about the development of the individual through the different contexts where this one participates. According to this theory, the contexts where the person interacts affect the way their cognitive, relational and moral development takes place. The ecological model of Bronfenbrenner posited an integral and systemic vision of psychological development. The author identifies in life of people five environmental systems with which an individual interacts: Individual, Microsystem, Mesosystem, Exosystem and Macrosystem. This model can be appreciated in Figure 1 with the variables of the current work.

According to the Office of Behavioral and Social Science (OBSSR): "Social ecological models emphasize multiple levels of influence and the idea that behaviors both shape and are shaped by the social environment" (Glanz, 2018, p.18).

With this in mind, it can be considered that subjective well-being of a person is as well a result of the combination of factors that can be situated at different levels, and in this way they should be treated.

Now, let is talk from a statistical perspective. When the hypothesized relations between different constructs operate across different levels, an ordinary least square (OLS) regression model might be applied. However, in the presence of multilevel effects, it can be difficult for OLS to meet the classical regression assumptions (Luke, 2004).

For the analysis of the effect of economics on subjective well-being of population across countries, the vast majority of works use single-level methodologies such as least squares, data panels or probabilistic. Some authors have chosen to dis-aggregate macroeconomic data at an individual unit level. However, this will cause the non-modeled contextual information to end up being grouped within the same model error term (Duncan, Jones & Moon, 1998). That is, people belonging to the same country could have

Table 1. Dependent variable and individual independent economic variables

Type of variable	Question	Options
Yo Satisfaction with life	In general terms, would you say that you are satisfied with your life? Would you say you are...?	1- Very satisfied 2- Quite satisfied 3- Not very satisfied 4- No satisfied at all
Xo_1 Personal economic situation	Does the salary you earn and the total family income allow you to satisfactorily cover your needs? In which of these situations are you?	1-Great difficulties to cover needs 2-Difficulties to cover needs 3-Barely cover needs 4-Save and cover needs

Source: Prepared by the authors with data from the 2016 Latinobarometer Survey

correlated errors, violating the assumption of uncorrelated errors. Furthermore, if a single-level analysis is used at the group level and it is assumed that the results apply to individuals, it would result into an ecological fallacy problem (Freedman, 1999).

If, on the other hand, the analysis is carried out at the individual level and the context is ignored, important effects could be missing at the group level, or what is known as the atomistic fallacy (Hox, Moerbeek & Van de Schoot, 2017). And by ignoring the context, the model will assume that the regression coefficients apply in the same way in all contexts (Duncan et al., 1998).

One partial solution to these statistical problems is to include a grouping of the individuals effect in the model. That would be an ANOVA or ANCOVA modeling. However a power reduction and parsimony can occur in the case of the inclusion of many groups. In the same way, the random variability associated at group-level would be ignored and also this kind of methods no offer much flexibility in handling missing data or greatly unbalanced designs. This circumstance requires multilevel modeling with maximum likelihood estimation (MLE). "The objective of a multilevel model is to predict values of some dependent variable based on the function of predictor variables at more than one level" (Luke, 2004, p.9).

An additional advantage of this type of technique is that it is feasible to explicitly model differences in the variance in each level (Schyns, 2002).

DATA

The present work is based on data from the Latinobarometer survey for 2016. Data for this year were taken since it was the most recent by the time the work started. The analyzes are based on 18,915 individual respondents in 17 countries in Latin America. The countries that make up the sample are: Argentina, Bolivia, Brazil, Chile, Colombia, Costa Rica, Dominican Republic, Ecuador, Guatemala, Honduras, Mexico, Nicaragua, Panama, Peru, Paraguay, El Salvador and Uruguay. The program used to develop the multi-level model was MlwiN.

The dependent variable is life satisfaction, which can be used as a measure of subjective well-being (Easterlin, 2001). As an individual predictive variable, the economic situation was included. Table 1 shows the questions that were asked of the respondents and the response options.

The advantage of using the personal economic situation variable classified in this way is that it reflects the degree to which the perceived income is sufficient or not to cover the needs, so it gives a better idea about the economic circumstances of the person. For example, if instead of this, the household income would be provided, it would not be possible to know if that amount of money is enough for that person to face their economic needs and commitments. On the other hand, there was a sample of 85 macroeconomic data corresponding to the total number of countries. Table 2 shows relevant information on the economic variables at the country level that were included.

Table 2. Macroeconomic independent variables

Variable	Dimensions	Indicators	Source
Xo_2 Gross domestic product per capita	Gross domestic product per capita based on purchasing power parity.	Gross domestic product converted into international dollars using purchasing power parity rates at constant 2011 prices divided by 1000.	World Development Indicators
Xo_3 Well-being state	Government expense	State consumption at all levels as % of GDP.	The Heritage Foundation
Xo_4 Well-being state	Tax burden	Marginal tax rate of personal and corporate income.	The Heritage Foundation
Xo_5 Rule of law	Integrity of government	Index that assesses the level of trust in politicians, perception of corruption and transparency of the government.	The Heritage Foundation
Xo_6 Well-being state	Public debt	Balance of public debt of the central government as % of GDP.	Economic Commission for Latin America and the Caribbean

Source: Prepared by the authors with data from World Development Indicators, The Heritage Foundation and Economic Commission for Latin America and the Caribbean

MODEL

The model will include as level-one variables factors related to personal characteristics. The life satisfaction of the individual i in the nation j is a function of a series of individual variables: marital status, age, religion, employment situation, race, educational level and economic situation.

Followed by country-level or level-2 variables, such as GDP per capita, government spending, government integrity, and public debt or fiscal burden. There will be two variants of the model, one that includes public debt to finance public spending and another that includes fiscal burden.

The model in its two variants also includes terms of interaction between the variables at the country level and the individual economic situation variable. This with the intention of discovering the way each macro-economic variable influences population well-being according to their particular economic condition. The last part ($\mu_j X_{ij} + \mu_{0j} + \varepsilon_{ij}$) represents the residual error term resulting from both levels.

- Model with public debt:

$$\text{LIFE SATISFACTION}_{ij} = {}^2\beta_0 + {}^2\beta_1 x_{ij}\text{indivvariables} + {}^2\beta_2 X_j \text{gdppercapita} + {}^2\beta_3 X_j \text{govexpense} \quad (1)$$

$+²\,_4X_j\text{govintegrity}+²\,_5X_j\text{pubdebt}+²\,_1x_{ij}\text{econ.sit.}*X_j+\left(\mu_jX_{ij}+\mathcal{V}_{0j}+\mu_{ij}\right)$

- Model with fiscal burden:

$$\text{LIFE SATISFACTION}_{ij}=²\,_0+²\,_1x_{ij}\text{indivvariables}+²\,_2X_j\text{gdppercapita}+²\,_3X_j\text{govexpense} \quad (2)$$

$+²\,_4X_j\text{govintegrity}+²\,_5X_j\text{fiscalburden}+²\,_1x_{ij}\text{econ.sit.}*X_j+\left(\mu_jX_{ij}+\mathcal{V}_{0j}+\mu_{ij}\right)$

RESULTS

The results will be presented as follows. In the first place, the variance partition coefficients are shown, that is, the explanatory weight of the individual variables and that corresponding to the context variables. Subsequently, the results for each of the models will be presented, in which the variables will accumulate. From Model 4, the macroeconomic variables will be added one by one with their interaction with the individual economic situation. In each subsequent model the previous interaction variable will be removed in order to obtain results of the next interaction.

Partition coefficient of variance at country level:

$$\frac{\sigma^2 u}{\sigma^2 u + \tilde{A}^2 e} = \frac{0.048}{0.048 + 0.638} = 0.069 \quad (3)$$

Partition coefficient of variance at the individual level:

$$\frac{\sigma^2 e}{\sigma^2 u + \tilde{A}^2 e} = \frac{0.638}{0.048 + 0.638} = 0.93 \quad (4)$$

The 7% of the happiness score variation is explained between countries (3). This indicates that the total variation without explaining 7% of happiness levels is due to the country of residence, while 93% is attributable to individual characteristics (4).

Model 1 (null)

The Model 1 in Table 7 of results shows an Akaike Information Criterion (AIC) of 45263.204 and a Bayesian Information Criterion (BIC) of 45271.052, which are lower than those presented by a single-level model of 46533.82 and 46541.668 respectively (results no presented). The previous results favor a multilevel structure.

Model 2 (Fixed part)

Next the explanatory fixed variables of the lower level are added to the model: age, religion, educational level, race, marital status, employment status and economic situation. Neither gender nor age in their quadratic form were significant, so they were not included. By adding the individual variables, the differences in happiness between the diverse categories of each variable are modeled. It is the fixed part of the model. The results are shown in Table 7 (part A) Model 2. The AIC was 37478.261 and the BIC 37486.109, that is, this model is preferred to the previous one.

Starting with the variable of marital status, compared to single people, married people are more satisfied with their lives, and less so if they are widowed or separated. In relation to race, where the mestizos were the reference group. There were no significant differences of these with the whites, Asian and mulattos. However, African-Americans, indigenous people and people belonging to *other races* category were significantly less happy. Regarding education, illiterate people, people with complete secondary education, and individuals with incomplete, and complete higher education were happier than people with complete primary education. Also, non-religious people turned out to be statistically less happy than those who are. On the other hand, there is a negative correlation with age, that is, at younger age people are happier. People with employment have a greater satisfaction with life than those who do not.

And finally, with regard to economic situation, all the groups were significantly happier than those who face great difficulties in meeting their needs. Here a phenomenon is observed, as it rises from the reference group (Great difficulties to cover needs) to the highest (Save and cover needs), the difference between the coefficients increases and then decreases in the category of (Barely covers their needs). That is, there will be a positive effect on happiness as economic situation improves, but this effect after a point begins to decrease since the needs are at least met. People who have the possibility of saving is happier, but the effect is in smaller proportion.

Another relevant aspect that can be seen is that when adding the personal variables, the variance coefficient was reduced at the individual level.

The change of R^2 from the model to the individual level is (0.638-0.596) /0.638=6.58%

The change of R^2 from the country-level model is (0.048-0.056) /0.048) = - 0.16 = -16%

The fact that the variance is increased without explaining at the group level after introducing personal variables usually indicates that there is an omission of explanatory variables at the country level, which is not uncommon in this type of analysis (Schyns, 2002).

Model 3 (Random Effects)

Random effects are introduced for economic situation. Again the AIC and the BIC turn out to be smaller than the previous model, as shown in Table 7 (part B) Model 3, so it is favored. In this model, the coefficients of *Difficulties to cover needs*, *Barely cover needs* and *Save and cover needs* have a fixed component representing contrast with the reference category: *Great difficulties to cover needs* on average, and a specific component for each country. After considering the fixed demographic effects of the past model, people with difficulties in meeting their needs living in country j are expected to have a happiness score of 0.178 + u + e higher than people who face great difficulties in the same country.

People who barely cover their needs expect a score of 0.383 + u + e over those in great difficulty, and people who can also save a score of 0.512 + u + e is expected over people living in great difficulties in the same country. In Figure 2, the random effects model of happiness, we can visualize the variation in

Figure 2. Variation in happiness of countries: 17 lines of regression between economic situation and happiness
Source: Prepared by the authors with data from the 2016 Latinobarometer Survey

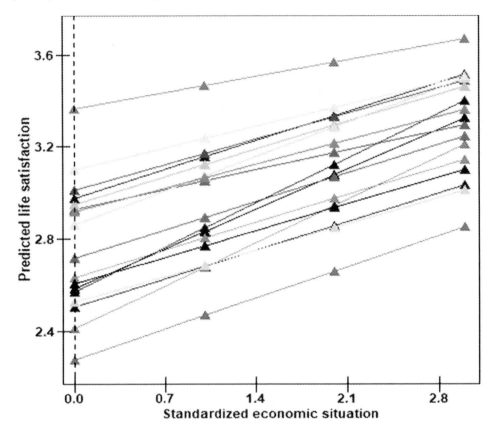

happiness according to the economic situation by plotting the regression lines of each of the 17 countries standardizing the independent variable as Schyns (2002) does. The graph shows convergences of lines, that is, there is greater variability in the categories of more precarious economic condition and there is more consistency in the higher categories. The same is reflected in Figure 3 where the variation in happiness is plotted with respect to the economic situation, both at the individual level and at the nation level.

Models 4 and 5 (GDP per Capita and Interaction Term)

The variable turns out to be significant as seen in Table 7 (part C). Once again, the AIC and BIC indicators favor this new model. Consecutively, another model is generated (Model 5) in which the interaction term between the economic situation and GDP per capita is included. Only the interaction between GDP per capita and people with the possibility of saving was statistically significant. That is, a person with the possibility of saving is even happier if he/she also lives in a country with a high GDP per capita.

Figure 3. Variation of happiness in economic situation at the individual level and at the country level
Source: Prepared by the authors with data from the 2016 Latinobarometer Survey

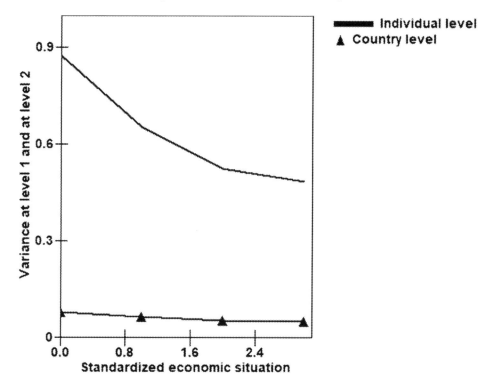

Models 6 and 7 (Government Expenditure and Interaction Term)

The interaction term between GDP per capita and economic situation is removed. Now the government spending variable is integrated. The AIC and the BIC of this model should be compared with Model 4 of GDP without the interaction term, which turns out to be smaller. The variable shows to be significantly positive for happiness. On the other hand, the rate of change in the opportunity to be happy for people with capacity to save is slightly lower in areas of higher government spending compared to those who have great difficulties in meeting their needs. To explain this better, in Table 3, happiness estimates are presented for each category of economic situation within the nation with the lowest government spending, with respect to a country with average government spending, and another with the highest value of it. Here we can see that the differences of happiness scores between the category of *Great difficulties to cover needs* and S*ave and cover needs* is greater within the country that allocates lower percentage of GDP to government spending. While this difference is much smaller in the country with the highest government spending. However, the differences between one category and another begin to be greater in the country scenario with maximum government spending compared to the minimum expenditure level up to the category of *Barely covers needs*. Subsequently, for the category of *Save and cover needs* the increase in happiness is lower in the scenario of maximum government spending, as explained by the model. Tables 4, 5 and 6 are read the same as Table 3.

Table 3. Estimated values of life satisfaction as a function of economic situation of each category and government expenditure of nations

Economic situation category	Minimum government expense	Average government expense	Maximum government expense
Great difficulties to cover needs	2.806	2.752	2.921
Difficulties to cover needs	2.856	2.939	3.073
Barely cover needs	3.004	3.167	3.331
Save and cover needs	3.389	3.327	3.461

Source: Prepared by the authors with data from the Latinobarometer Survey 2016 and The Heritage Foundation

Model 8 and 9 (Integrity of Government and Interaction Term)

The government integrity variable is included and the interaction term between economic situation and government spending is removed. When comparing the values of AIC and BIC, it is observed that they are smaller with respect to Model 6, so it is preferred. When adding the variable it is not significant. However, in the model of interaction, Model 9, it is observed the relationship of the economic situation of people and their happiness can vary as a function of the degree of integrity of the country's government. The relationship of the three levels with life satisfaction will be stronger within countries with greater integrity compared to the reference group.

Table 4. Estimated values of satisfaction with life, as a function of economic situation of each category and integrity of government

Economic situation category	Minimum government integrity	Average government integrity	Maximum government integrity
Great difficulties to cover needs	2.717	2.738	2.315
Difficulties to cover needs	2.639	2.926	2.730
Barely cover needs	2.945	3.138	3.078
Save and cover needs	2.968	3.305	3.325

Source: Prepared by the authors with data from the Latinobarometer Survey 2016 and The Heritage Foundation

Model 10A and 11A (Public Debt and Interaction Term)

When adding public debt, it turned out to significantly affect negatively the dependent variable. When the interaction term, Model 11A, is added, the relationship between economic situation and happiness of the population is moderated by the level of public debt that the country has. People within the three levels of higher economic status have a higher rate of change in the opportunity to be happy in countries with higher public debt, in relation to the lowest level.

Table 5. Estimated values of satisfaction with life, as a function of economic situation of each category and public debt

Economic situation category	Minimum public debt	Average public debt	Maximum public debt
Great difficulties to cover needs	2.806	2.752	2.245
Difficulties to cover needs	2.856	2.939	2.470
Barely cover needs	3.004	3.223	2.734
Save and cover needs	3.389	3.120	2.827

Source: Prepared by the authors with data from the 2016 Latinobarometer Survey and Economic Commission for Latin America and the Caribbean

Model 10B and 11B (Tax Burden and Interaction Term)

The tax burden variable is not significant, however, by integrating the interaction term in Model 11B, it can be seen that people in the three highest levels of economic condition maintain a more superficial relationship with happiness in countries with a higher tax burden, compared to the most precarious economic situation group. This can be seen graphically in Table 6. People with great difficulty in meeting basic needs increase their happiness in countries with greater fiscal burden. While the rest of the

Table 6. Estimated values of satisfaction with life, as a function of economic situation of each category and tax burden

Economic situation category	Minimum tax burden	Average tax burden	Maximum tax burden
Great difficulties to cover needs	2.481	2.743	2.717
Difficulties to cover needs	2.862	2.932	2.639
Barely cover needs	3.101	3.158	2.945
Save and cover needs	3.342	3.328	2.968

Source: Prepared by the authors with data from the Latinobarometer Survey 2016 and The Heritage Foundation

categories tend to decrease in areas where taxes are higher.

In Figures 4 and 5 a construct is shown presenting the main results of this work in order to have them in a clearer and more structured way.

CONCLUSIONS AND LIMITATIONS

Among the findings of this study it was observed that both, the characteristics of individuals and the economic conditions of the context in which they operate are relevant to model the subjective well-being of people in Latin America. Due to the difference in the nature of data, using a multilevel model turned out to be an adequate strategy to carry it out.

Figure 4. Results construct (part A)
Source: Prepared by the authors with data from the Latinobarometer Survey 2016, The World Development Indicators, The Economic Commission for Latin America and the Caribbean and The Heritage Foundation

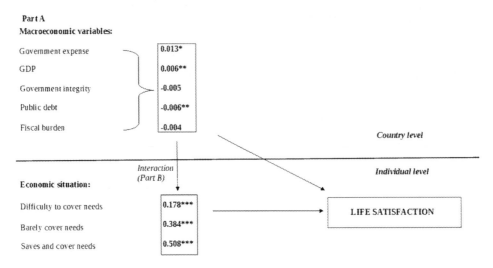

The Latinobarometer survey allowed to include more demographic variables such as race and educational level. These factors were significant for subjective well-being.

Figure 5. Results construct (part B)
Source: Prepared by the authors with data from the Latinobarometer Survey 2016, The World Development Indicators, The Economic Commission for Latin America and the Caribbean and The Heritage Foundation

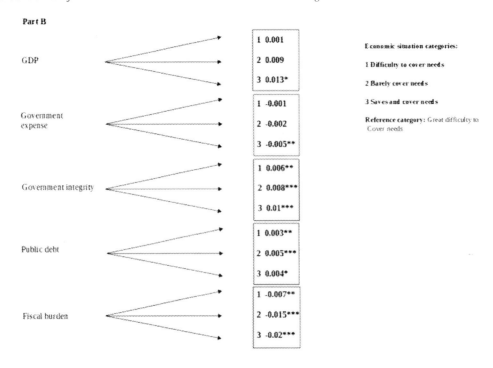

Regarding the impact caused by personal economic situation, there is a curvilinear effect of growth at decreasing rates. After people are able to meet their needs the positive effect begins to decrease.

Regarding the second-level variables, it was found that GDP per capita PPP and government spending have a significant positive impact on the variable of interest. When the interaction term is included with the individual economic situation, two phenomena were observed. People with the ability to save tend to have a stronger relationship with subjective well-being when their country's GDP per capita PPP was higher than the reference group, and slightly lower when the country's government spending was sumptuous. Since government expense frequently is directed to social programs, this could explain such result.

In relation to public debt, it was found that it generates a negative effect on subjective well-being. However, the three highest economic strata resulted with a positive interaction effect in areas of higher public debt. As is known, as part of public debt government emits certificates and other instruments in order to obtain financing support from citizens in return of an interest rate chargeable at the end of the established period. This could explain the fact that people who is able to invest in this promissory notes which offer profit and safety, maintain a positive relation with public debt.

Integrity of government and fiscal burden were not significant. However, they showed to have a moderating effect for the individual economic situation. People with difficulties to cover needs onward showed a stronger relationship with subjective well-being in areas of greater government integrity. While the same three highest social strata maintained a more superficial relationship with happiness in countries with higher tax burdens. Probably this could be explained by the fact that people who belongs to the lowest strata is more likely to work in the informal economy, and therefore are not affected by tax increases. According to the report of the International Labour Organization (ILO) in 2013, 46.8% of jobs were informal in Latin America. The poorest quintile had an informal employment rate of 72.5%, while the richest quintile had 29.8% of participation (ILO, 2014).

Through this analysis it was notorious that Economics indeed have an effect on subjective well-being of population, and multilevel technique helped to organize and consider these factors apart from the ones proper of the individual in an adequate way.

Regarding the limitations of the present analysis, there is no consensus on the size of the sample of countries for this type of analysis. Authors have used 8, 10, 30, and even 100 groups (Afshartous 2011; Kreft 1996; Rabe-Hesketh & Skrondal, 2008). In the current work, information was available from 17 countries, assuming that the results would be more accurate with a larger sample.

In future research a global sample of countries could be included and the results compared with those of the present analysis. Other idea could be to take information for more years and include time variable as a third level in the analysis, in order to observe if the same results persist in time.

From 2018, diverse Latin American countries have been facing government and regime changes, mainly left-oriented, with the exception of Brazil, which has an extreme right-wing government. The common denominator between them are the presence of populist presidents. Future research works could study this in an attempt to identify if these type of transformations has led to significant differences in well-being terms among populations. Within countries, as is the case in Mexico, there is not always a union of ideologies between the president and state governors, which could imply changes in fiscal policy within the republic.

Another factor that could be of interest could be the way the different countries, through their governments, have decided to manage the present pandemic, a new variable that is having collateral effects not only in health terms, but in job positions, business survival and tax application.

Table 7. Results (part A)

	Model 1		Model 2		Model 3		Model 4		Model 5		Model 6		Model 7	
FIXED PART	Coefficient	SE	Coefficient	SE	Coefficient	SE	Coefficient	SE	Coefficient	SE	Coefficient	SE	Coefficient	SE
Individual effect														
Constant	3.064***	0.053	2.754***	0.064	2.756***	0.77	2.758***	0.082	2.755***	0.077	2.753***	0.73	2.75***	0.7
Married			0.038***	0.014	0.041***	0.014	0.041***	0.014	0.04***	0.014	0.041***	0.014	0.041***	0.014
Separated/widowed			-0.066***	0.023	-0.068***	0.023	-0.068***	0.023	-0.067***	0.023	-0.068***	0.023	-0.068***	0.023
Unemployed			-0.033***	0.014	-0.031***	0.013	-0.031***	0.013	-0.031***	0.013	-0.031***	0.013	-0.031***	0.013
Asian			0.102	0.082	0.088	0.081	0.089	0.081	0.086	0.081	0.088*	0.051	0.089	0.081
Afro-American			-0.064**	0.028	-0.068**	0.028	-0.068**	0.028	-0.068**	0.028	-0.068**	0.028	-0.068**	0.028
Indigenous			-0.077***	0.023	-0.076***	0.023	-0.077***	0.023	-0.076***	0.023	-0.077***	0.023	-0.077***	0.023
Mulatto			-0.031	0.029	-0.025	0.029	-0.026	0.029	-0.026	0.029	-0.026	0.029	-0.026	0.029
White			-0.001	0.017	-0.001	0.017	-0.001	0.017	-0.002	0.017	-0.001	0.017	-0.001	0.017
Other race			0.096**	0.051	0.088**	0.051	0.088**	0.051	0.09**	0.051	0.088*	0.051	0.089*	0.051
Illiterate			0.051**	0.028	0.052**	0.029	0.052**	0.029	0.051**	0.029	0.052**	0.029	0.052**	0.029
Education Basic incomplete			0.006	0.022	-0.003	0.022	-0.003	0.022	-0.003	0.022	-0.003	0.022	-0.003	0.022
Education Sec. Incomplete			0	0.023	-0.004	0.023	-0.004	0.023	-0.003	0.023	-0.004	0.023	-0.004	0.023
Education Sec. Complete			0.058***	0.021	0.051***	0.02	0.051***	0.02	0.051***	0.02	0.051***	0.02	0.051***	0.02
Education Sup. Incomplete			0.101***	0.026	0.1***	0.026	0.1***	0.026	0.1***	0.026	0.1***	0.026	0.1***	0.026
Education Sup. Complete			0.137***	0.025	0.131***	0.024	0.131***	0.024	0.129***	0.024	0.13***	0.024	0.131***	0.024
Not religious			-0.033**	0.017	-0.035**	0.017	-0.035**	0.017	-0.034**	0.017	-0.035**	0.017	-0.035**	0.017
Difficulty to cover needs			0.178***	0.022	0.178***	0.038	0.179***	0.038	0.177***	0.038	0.178***	0.038	0.179***	0.035
Barely cover needs			0.384***	0.022	0.383***	0.044	0.382***	0.044	0.384***	0.042	0.382***	0.044	0.384***	0.044
Saves and cover needs			0.508***	0.027	0.512***	0.051	0.511***	0.051	0.511***	0.048	0.512***	0.052	0.515***	0.048
Centered age			-0.003***	0	-0.003***	0	-0.003***	0	-0.003***	0	-0.003***	0	-0.003***	0
AIC		45263		37797		37502		37479		37468		37478		37472
BIC		45271		37954		37596		37487		37476		37486		37480

Significance levels are denoted by ***p<0.01;**p<0.05;*p<0.1

Table 8. Results (part B)

	Model 8		Model 9		Model 10-A		Model 11-A		Model 10-B		Model 11-B	
FIXED PART	Coefficient	SE	Coefficient	SE	Coefficient	SE	Coefficient	SE	Coefficient	SE	Coefficient	SE
Individual effect												
Constant	2.754***	0.065	2.749***	0.059	2.757***	0.064	2.759***	0.062	2.756***	0.066	2.753***	0.73
Married	0.041***	0.014	0.038***	0.014	0.041***	0.014	0.041***	0.014	0.04***	0.014	0.041***	0.014
Separated/widowed	-0.068***	0.023	-0.066***	0.023	-0.068***	0.023	-0.068***	0.023	-0.067***	0.023	-0.068***	0.023
Unemployed	-0.03***	0.013	-0.033***	0.014	-0.031***	0.013	-0.031***	0.013	-0.031***	0.013	-0.031***	0.013
Asian	0.088	0.081	0.088	0.081	0.089	0.081	0.088	0.081	0.088	0.081	0.09	0.081
Afro-American	-0.068**	0.028	-0.067**	0.028	-0.068**	0.028	-0.067**	0.028	-0.068**	0.028	-0.067**	0.028
Indigenous	-0.077***	0.023	-0.076***	0.023	-0.076***	0.023	-0.076***	0.023	-0.076***	0.023	-0.076***	0.023
Mulatto	-0.025	0.029	-0.025	0.029	-0.025	0.029	-0.025	0.029	-0.025	0.029	-0.025	0.029
White	-0.001	0.017	-0.001	0.017	-0.001	0.017	-0.001	0.017	-0.001	0.017	-0.001	0.017
Other race	0.088*	0.051	0.087*	0.051	0.088*	0.051	0.088*	0.051	0.088*	0.051	0.087*	0.051
Illiterate	0.052**	0.029	0.05***	0.029	0.052**	0.029	0.052**	0.029	0.052**	0.029	0.052**	0.029
Education Basic incomplete	-0.003	0.022	-0.004	0.022	-0.003	0.022	-0.002	0.022	-0.003	0.022	-0.002	0.022
Education Sec. Incomplete	-0.004	0.023	-0.004	0.023	-0.004	0.023	-0.004	0.023	-0.004	0.023	-0.004	0.023
Education Sec. Complete	0.051***	0.02	0.051***	0.02	0.051***	0.02	0.051***	0.02	0.051***	0.02	0.051***	0.02
Education Sup. Incomplete	0.1***	0.026	0.1***	0.026	0.1***	0.026	0.1***	0.026	0.1***	0.026	0.101***	0.026
Education Sup. Complete	0.13***	0.024	0.13***	0.024	0.130***	0.024	0.129***	0.024	0.13***	0.024	0.129***	0.024
Not religious	-0.035**	0.017	-0.035**	0.017	-0.035**	0.017	-0.034**	0.017	-0.035**	0.017	-0.034**	0.017
Difficulty to cover needs	0.176***	0.038	0.179***	0.035	0.0174***	0.038	0.173***	0.036	0.175***	0.038	0.172***	0.033
Barely cover needs	0.38***	0.044	0.385***	0.036	0.378***	0.044	0.377***	0.041	0.379***	0.044	0.376***	0.038
Saves and cover needs	0.51***	0.052	0.513***	0.041	0.507***	0.052	0.508***	0.05	0.509***	0.052	0.508***	0.044
Centered age	-0.003***	0	-0.003***	0	-0.003***	0	-0.003***	0	-0.003***	0	-0.003***	0
AIC		37475		37465		37473		37470		0.117		7.479
BIC		37483		37472		37481		37477		37481		37473

Significance levels are denoted by ***p<0.01;**p<0.05;*p<0.1

Table 9. Results (part C)

FIXED PART	Model 1		Model 2		Model 3		Model 4		Model 5		Model 6		Model 7	
	Coefficient	SE	Coefficient	SE	Coefficient	SE	Coefficient	SE	Coefficient	SE	Coefficient	SE	Coefficient	SE
Group effect														
Gross domestic product per /1000							0.013*	0.009	-0.007	0.013	0.009	0.008	0.008	0.008
Difficulty to cover needs									0.001	0.007				
Barely cover needs									0.009	0.007				
Saves and cover needs									0.012*	0.009				
Government spending											0.006**	0.003	0.01	0.005
Difficulty to cover needs													-0.001	0.003
Barely cover needs													-0.002	0.003
Saves and cover needs													-0.005**	0.003
Government integrity														
Difficulty to cover needs														
Barely cover needs														
Saves and cover needs														
Public debt														
Difficulty to cover needs														
Barely cover needs														
Saves and cover needs														
Tax burden														
Difficulty to cover needs														
Barely cover needs														
Saves and cover needs														
AIC		45263		37797		37502		37479		37468		37478		37472
BIC		45271		37954		37596		37487		37476		37486		37480

Significance levels are denoted by ***p<0.01;**p<0.05;*p<0.1

Table 10. Results (part D)

	Model 8		Model 9		Model 10-A		Model 11-A		Model 10-B		Model 11-B	
FIXED PART	Coefficient	SE	Coefficient	SE	Coefficient	SE	Coefficient	SE	Coefficient	SE	Coefficient	SE
Group effect												
Gross Domestic Product/1000	0.016*	0.011	0.016*	0.011	0.024***	0.01	0.026***	0.01	0.021***	0.01	0.027***	0.007
Difficulty to cover needs												
Barely cover needs												
Saves and cover needs												
Government spending	0.007***	0.003	0.007***	0.003	0.005**	0.003	0.005**	0.003	0.005**	0.003	0.005**	0.003
Difficulty to cover needs												
Barely cover needs												
Saves and cover needs												
Government integrity	-0.005	0.004	-0.015***	0.005	-0.006*	0.004	-0.006*	0.004	-0.005	0.004	-0.007**	0.004
Difficulty to cover needs			0.006**	0.003								
Barely cover needs			0.008***	0.003								
Saves and cover needs			0.01***	0.003								
Public debt					-0.006**	0.003	-0.008**	0.004	-0.006**	0.003	-0.006**	0.003
Difficulty to cover needs							0.003*	0.002				
Barely cover needs							0.005***	0.002				
Saves and cover needs							0.004*	0.003				
Tax burden									-0.004	0.009	0.013	0.011
Difficulty to cover needs											-0.015***	0.005
Barely cover needs											-0.015***	0.006
Saves and cover needs											-0.02***	0.007
AIC		37475		37465		37473		37470		0.117		7.7479
BIC		37483		37472		37481		37477		37481		37473

Significance levels are denoted by ***p<0.01;**p<0.05;*p<0.1

Table 11. Results (part E)

RANDOM PART	Model 1		Model 2		Model 3		Model 4		Model 5		Model 6		Model 7	
	Coefficient	SE	Coefficient	SE	Coefficient	SE	Coefficient	SE	Coefficient	SE	Coefficient	SE	Coefficient	SE
Level 2														
Var Cons	0.048	0.017	0.056	0.019	0.085	0.033	0.096	0.036	0.084	0.032	0.073	0.028	0.067	0.026
Cov Cons-Difficulty to c/needs					-0.019	0.014	-0.02	0.014	-0.019	0.014	-0.018	0.013	-0.016	0.012
Var Difficulty to c/needs					0.012	0.008	0.012	0.008	0.012	0.008	0.012	0.008	0.012	0.008
Cov Cons-Barely c/needs					-0.026	0.016	-0.03	0.017	-0.023	0.015	-0.026	0.015	-0.023	0.014
Cov Difficulty to c/needs-Barely c/needs					0.016	0.009	0.016	0.009	0.015	0.009	0.016	0.009	0.015	0.009
Var Barely c/needs					0.022	0.011	0.022	0.011	0.018	0.01	0.022	0.011	0.021	0.011
Cov Cons-Saves and c/needs					-0.037	0.019	-0.041	0.021	-0.034	0.018	-0.035	0.018	-0.028	0.016
Cov Difficulty to c/needs-Saves and c/needs					0.018	0.01	0.018	0.01	0.017	0.01	0.019	0.01	0.017	0.01
Cov Barely c/needs-Saves and c/needs					0.024	0.012	0.024	0.012	0.019	0.011	0.024	0.012	0.021	0.011
Var Saves and c/needs					0.03	0.015	0.03	0.015	0.025	0.013	0.03	0.015	0.025	0.013
Level 1														
Var Cons	0.638	0.007	0.596	0.007	0.841	0.03	0.841	0.03	0.842	0.032	0.841	0.03	0.841	0.03
"Cov" Cons-Difficulty to c/needs					-0.091	0.016	-0.091	0.016	-0.091	0.016	-0.091	0.016	-0.091	0.016
"Cov" Cons-Barely to c/needs					-0.161	0.015	-0.161	0.15	-0.161	0.15	-0.161	0.15	-0.161	0.15
"Cov" Cons-Saves and c/needs					-0.179	0.017	-0.179	0.017	-0.179	0.017	-0.179	0.017	-0.18	0.017

Table 12. Results (part F)

RANDOM PART	Model 8 Coefficient	SE	Model 9 Coefficient	SE	Model 10-A Coefficient	SE	Model 11-A Coefficient	SE	Model 10-B Coefficient	SE	Model 11-B Coefficient	SE
Level 2												
Var Cons	0.056	0.022	0.042	0.018	0.053	0.021	0.049	0.02	0.056	0.021	0.042	0.017
Cov Cons-Difficulty to c/ needs	-0.013	0.011	-0.004	0.008	-0.008	0.01	-0.005	0.009	-0.01	0.011	0.001	0.008
Var Difficulty to c/needs	0.013	0.008	0.009	0.007	0.013	0.008	0.011	0.008	0.013	0.008	0.007	0.006
Cov Cons-Barely c/ needs	-0.019	0.013	-0.007	0.009	-0.015	0.012	-0.011	0.011	-0.017	0.013	-0.005	0.009
Cov Difficulty to c/needs-Barely c/needs	0.016	0.009	0.009	0.007	0.017	0.009	0.013	0.008	0.016	0.009	0.01	0.007
Var Barely c/ needs	0.022	0.011	0.011	0.007	0.022	0.008	0.017	0.009	0.022	0.011	0.014	0.008
Cov Cons-Saves and c/ needs	-0.026	0.016	-0.012	0.01	-0.025	0.015	-0.022	0.014	-0.028	0.016	-0.014	0.011
Cov Difficulty to c/needs-Saves and c/ needs	0.019	0.011	0.01	0.007	0.019	0.011	0.017	0.01	0.019	0.011	0.01	0.007
Cov Barely c/ needs-Saves and c/needs	0.024	0.012	0.01	0.008	0.024	0.012	0.02	0.011	0.024	0.012	0.014	0.009
Var Saves and c/ needs	0.031	0.015	0.013	0.009	0.031	0.015	0.028	0.014	0.03	0.015	0.017	0.011
Level 1												
Var Cons	0.841	0.03	0.841	0.03	0.841	0.03	0.841	0.03	0.841	0.03	0.841	0.03
"Cov" Cons-Difficulty to c/ needs	-0.09	0.016	-0.091	0.016	-0.091	0.016	-0.091	0.016	-0.091	0.016	-0.091	0.016
"Cov" Cons-Barely to c/ needs	-0.161	0.15	-0.161	0.15	-0.161	0.15	-0.16	0.15	-0.161	0.15	-0.161	0.15
"Cov" Cons-Saves and c/ needs	-0.179	0.017	-0.179	0.017	-0.179	0.017	-0.179	0.017	-0.179	0.017	-0.179	0.017

Source: Prepared by the authors with data from the Latinobarometer Survey 2016, The World Development Indicators, and The Heritage Foundation

REFERENCES

Abitbol, P., & Botero, F. (2005). Teoría de elección racional: estructura conceptual y evolución reciente. *Colombia internacional*, (62), 132-145.

Afshartous, D. (2011). *Determination of sample size for multilevel model design*. Department of Statistics, UCLA. Retrieved from https://escholarship.org/uc/item/4cg0k6g0

Akay, A., Bargain, O., Dolls, M., Neumann, D., Peichl, A., & Siegloch, S. (2012). Happy taxpayers? Income taxation and well-being. *Income Taxation and Well-Being*, (526), 1–34.

Alesina, A., & Angeletos, G. M. (2005). Fairness and redistribution. *The American Economic Review*, *95*(4), 960–980. doi:10.1257/0002828054825655

Alesina, A., Di Tella, R., & MacCulloch, R. (2004). Inequality and happiness: Are Europeans and Americans different? *Journal of Public Economics*, *88*(9-10), 2009–2042. doi:10.1016/j.jpubeco.2003.07.006

Alm, J., Jackson, B. R., & McKee, M. (1992). Estimating the determinants of taxpayer compliance with experimental data. *National Tax Journal*, *45*(1), 107–114. doi:10.1086/NTJ41788949

Alm, J., McClelland, G. H., & Schulze, W. D. (1992). Why do people pay taxes? *Journal of Public Economics*, *48*(1), 21–38. doi:10.1016/0047-2727(92)90040-M

Binswanger, M. (2006). Why does income growth fail to make us happier?: Searching for the treadmills behind the paradox of happiness. *Journal of Socio-Economics*, *35*(2), 366–381. doi:10.1016/j.socec.2005.11.040

Bjørnskov, C., Dreher, A., & Fischer, J. A. (2007). The bigger the better? Evidence of the effect of government size on life satisfaction around the world. *Public Choice*, *130*(3-4), 267–292. doi:10.100711127-006-9081-5

Bjørnskov, C., Gupta, N. D., & Pedersen, P. J. (2008). Analysing trends in subjective well-being in 15 European countries, 1973–2002. *Journal of Happiness Studies*, *9*(2), 317–330. doi:10.100710902-007-9055-4

Bronfenbrenner, U. (1977). Toward an experimental ecology of human development. *The American Psychologist*, *32*(7), 513–531. doi:10.1037/0003-066X.32.7.513

Bryson, L. (1992). *Welfare and the State: Who Benefits?: Who Benefits?* Macmillan International Higher Education.

Brzezinski, M. (2019). Top incomes and subjective well-being. *Journal of Economic Psychology*, *73*, 60–65. doi:10.1016/j.joep.2019.05.003

Di Tella, R., & MacCulloch, R. (2008). Gross national happiness as an answer to the Easterlin Paradox? *Journal of Development Economics*, *86*(1), 22–42. doi:10.1016/j.jdeveco.2007.06.008

Diener, E. (2006). Guidelines for national indicators of subjective well-being and ill-being. *Applied Research in Quality of Life*, *1*(2), 151–157. doi:10.100711482-006-9007-x

Dluhosch, B., & Horgos, D. (2013). Trading up the happiness ladder. *Social Indicators Research*, *113*(3), 973–990. doi:10.100711205-012-0122-9

Duncan, C., Jones, K., & Moon, G. (1998). Context, composition and heterogeneity: Using multilevel models in health research. *Social Science & Medicine*, *46*(1), 97–117. doi:10.1016/S0277-9536(97)00148-2 PMID:9464672

Easterlin, R. A. (2001). Income and happiness: Towards a unified theory. *Economic Journal (London)*, *111*(473), 465–484. doi:10.1111/1468-0297.00646

Erard, B., & Feinstein, J. (1994). The role of moral sentiments and audit perceptions in tax compliance (No. 94-03). Carleton University, Department of Economics.

Feld, L. P., & Frey, B. S. (2002). Trust breeds trust: How taxpayers are treated. *Economics of Governance*, *3*(2), 87–99. doi:10.1007101010100032

Freedman, D. A. (1999). Ecological inference and the ecological fallacy. *International Encyclopedia of the social &. Behavioral Science*, *6*(4027-4030), 1–7.

Frey, B. S., Luechinger, S., & Stutzer, A. (2009). The life satisfaction approach to valuing public goods: The case of terrorism. *Public Choice*, *138*(3-4), 317–345. doi:10.100711127-008-9361-3

Frey, B. S., & Stutzer, A. (2000). Happiness, economy and institutions. *Economic Journal (London)*, *110*(466), 918–938. doi:10.1111/1468-0297.00570

Frey, B. S., & Stutzer, A. (2002). What can economists learn from happiness research? *Journal of Economic Literature*, *40*(2), 402–435. doi:10.1257/jel.40.2.402

Gasper, D. (2005). Subjective and objective well-being in relation to economic inputs: Puzzles and responses. *Review of Social Economy*, *63*(2), 177–206. doi:10.1080/00346760500130309

Glanz, K. (2018). *Social and Behavioral Theories* (pp. 1-40, Rep. No. 1). Bethesda, MD: Office of Behavioral and Social Science.

Graham, C., & Felton, A. (2006). Inequality and happiness: Insights from Latin America. *The Journal of Economic Inequality*, *4*(1), 107–122. doi:10.100710888-005-9009-1

Graham, C., & Pettinato, S. (2001). Happiness, markets, and democracy: Latin America in comparative perspective. *Journal of Happiness Studies*, *2*(3), 237–268. doi:10.1023/A:1011860027447

Harbaugh, W. T., Mayr, U., & Burghart, D. R. (2007). Neural responses to taxation and voluntary giving reveal motives for charitable donations. *Science*, *316*(5831), 1622–1625. doi:10.1126cience.1140738 PMID:17569866

Hayo, B., & Seifert, W. (2003). Subjective economic well-being in Eastern Europe. *Journal of Economic Psychology*, *24*(3), 329–348. doi:10.1016/S0167-4870(02)00173-3

Helliwell, J. F. (2003). How's life? Combining individual and national variables to explain subjective well-being. *Economic Modelling*, *20*(2), 331–360. doi:10.1016/S0264-9993(02)00057-3

Helliwell, J. F., Huang, H., Grover, S., & Wang, S. (2018). Empirical linkages between good governance and national well-being. *Journal of Comparative Economics*, *46*(4), 1332–1346. doi:10.1016/j.jce.2018.01.004

Hessami, Z. (2010). The size and composition of government spending in Europe and its impact on well-being. *Kyklos*, *63*(3), 346–382. doi:10.1111/j.1467-6435.2010.00478.x

Hox, J. J., Moerbeek, M., & Van de Schoot, R. (2017). *Multilevel analysis: Techniques and applications*. Routledge. doi:10.4324/9781315650982

ILO. (2014). Thematic Labour Overview 1: Transition to Formality in Latin America and the Caribbean (2014 ed., Thematic labour overview, pp. 1-79, Rep. No. I). Lima: International Labor Organization.

Kacapyr, E. (2008). Cross-country determinants of satisfaction with life. *International Journal of Social Economics, 35*(6), 400–416. doi:10.1108/03068290810873384

Kotakorpi, K., & Laamanen, J. P. (2010). Welfare state and life satisfaction: Evidence from public health care. *Economica, 77*(307), 565–583.

Kreft, I. G. (1996). *Are multilevel techniques necessary? An overview, including simulation studies.* Unpublished manuscript, California State University, Los Angeles.

Lea, S. E., Webley, P., & Levine, R. M. (1993). The economic psychology of consumer debt. *Journal of Economic Psychology, 14*(1), 85–119. doi:10.1016/0167-4870(93)90041-I

Levinson, A. (2012). Valuing public goods using happiness data: The case of air quality. *Journal of Public Economics, 96*(9-10), 869–880. doi:10.1016/j.jpubeco.2012.06.007

Lubian, D., & Zarri, L. (2011). Happiness and tax morale: An empirical analysis. *Journal of Economic Behavior & Organization, 80*(1), 223–243. doi:10.1016/j.jebo.2011.03.009

Luke, D. A. (2004). *Multilevel modeling.* Sage. doi:10.4135/9781412985147

Macchia, L., & Plagnol, A. C. (2019). Life satisfaction and confidence in national institutions: Evidence from South America. *Applied Research in Quality of Life, 14*(3), 721–736. doi:10.100711482-018-9606-3

Martín, M. Á. G. (2002). El bienestar subjetivo. *Escritos de Psicologia,* (6), 18–39. doi:10.24310/espsiescpsi.vi6.13409

Musgrave, R. A. (1959). *Theory of public finance; a study in public economy.* Academic Press.

Ngamaba, K. H., Panagioti, M., & Armitage, C. J. (2018). Income inequality and subjective well-being: A systematic review and meta-analysis. *Quality of Life Research: An International Journal of Quality of Life Aspects of Treatment, Care and Rehabilitation, 27*(3), 577–596. doi:10.100711136-017-1719-x PMID:29067589

Pareto, V. (1906). *Manuale di economia politica.* Societa Editrice.

Perovic, L. M., & Golem, S. (2010). Investigating macroeconomic determinants of happiness in transition countries: How important is government expenditure? *Eastern European Economics, 48*(4), 59–75. doi:10.2753/EEE0012-8775480403

Pigou, A. C. (1947). *A study in public finance.* Read Books Ltd.

Pommerehne, W. W. (1984). Was wissen wir eigentlich über Steuerhinterziehung? *International Review of Economics and Business, 32,* 1155–1186.

Powdthavee, N., Burkhauser, R. V., & De Neve, J. E. (2017). Top incomes and human well-being: Evidence from the Gallup World Poll. *Journal of Economic Psychology, 62,* 246–257. doi:10.1016/j.joep.2017.07.006

Quintanilla, I., Martín, T. B., & Pardo, I. Q. (2005). *Psicología y economía.* Universitat de València.

Rabe-Hesketh, S., & Skrondal, A. (2008). *Multilevel and longitudinal modeling using Stata.* STATA press.

Ram, R. (2009). Government spending and happiness of the population: Additional evidence from large cross-country samples. *Public Choice, 138*(3-4), 483–490. doi:10.100711127-008-9372-0

Ribeiro, L. L., & Marinho, E. L. L. (2017). Gross National Happiness in Brazil: An analysis of its determinants. *Economía, 18*(2), 156–167. doi:10.1016/j.econ.2016.07.002

Sanfey, P., & Teksoz, U. (2007). Does transition make you happy? 1. *Economics of Transition, 15*(4), 707–731. doi:10.1111/j.1468-0351.2007.00309.x

Scholz, J. T., & Lubell, M. (1998). Adaptive political attitudes: Duty, trust, and fear as monitors of tax policy. *American Journal of Political Science, 42*(3), 903. doi:10.2307/2991734

Scholz, J. T., & Pinney, N. (1995). Duty, fear, and tax compliance: The heuristic basis of citizenship behavior. *American Journal of Political Science, 39*(2), 490–512. doi:10.2307/2111622

Schyns, P. (2002). Wealth Of Nations, Individual Income andLife Satisfaction in 42 Countries: A Multilevel Approach. *Social Indicators Research, 60*(1-3), 5–40. doi:10.1023/A:1021244511064

Shahbaz, M., & Aamir, N. (2008). Macroeconomic Determinants of the Happiness of the Poor: A Case Study of Pakistan. *Journal of Economic and Social Policy, 5*, 9–27.

Smith, K. W., & Stalans, L. J. (1991). Encouraging tax compliance with positive incentives: A conceptual framework and research directions. *Law & Policy, 13*(1), 35–53. doi:10.1111/j.1467-9930.1991.tb00056.x

Song, Y. D., & Yarbrough, T. E. (1978). Tax ethics and taxpayer attitudes: A survey. *Public Administration Review, 38*(5), 442–452. doi:10.2307/975503

Spicer, M. W. (1974). *A behavioral model of income tax evasion* (Doctoral dissertation). The Ohio State University.

Spicker, P. (1995). *Social policy: Themes and approaches*. Prentice Hall.

Torgler, B. (2003). *Tax morale: Theory and empirical analysis of tax compliance* (Doctoral dissertation). University of Basel.

Torgler, B. (2005). Tax morale in latin america. *Public Choice, 122*(1-2), 133–157. doi:10.100711127-005-5790-4

Veenhoven, R. (2000). Well-being in the welfare state: Level not higher, distribution not more equitable. *Journal of Comparative Policy Analysis, 2*(1), 91–125. doi:10.1080/13876980008412637

Chapter 12
US Dependance on Chinese Pharma in the Pandemic Era and the Nationalization of the US System

Paolo Bongarzoni
Swiss School of Management, Italy

Adriano Ferri
Swiss School of Management, Italy

ABSTRACT

The severe impact of the coronavirus pandemic has indeed prompted several questions about economic and social security. Among them is placed the current concern about the possible nationalization of the U.S. pharmaceutical industry due to the fear of a possible generic drug shortages. More importantly, since the United States imports most of its drugs from other countries (e.g., China), is the impact of Covid-19 on the pharmaceutical industry the catalyst for a future nationalization for the U.S. pharmaceutical industry? Are there real reasons to support this prospect, or is it an old argument renewed by fear?

INTRODUCTION

The impact of the new coronavirus pandemic has been nothing short of severe for both the economies of the United States and China. Not only has the Covid-19 pandemic brought serious damages to the economies of both countries, but it has also disrupted the livelihoods of millions of people across the world (even more so in countries as severely afflicted by the pandemic as the United States). Regarding how the pandemic impacted the U.S.A., the Congressional Budget Office (C.B.O.) has released in May a report that provided for a summary of the current and expected economic consequences. The C.B.O. reported that between the months of February and April, the unemployment rate went from 3.5% to 14.7% (Congressional Budget Office, 2020). The wild fluctuations caused by the Covid-19 have continued to

DOI: 10.4018/978-1-7998-8996-0.ch012

impact labor markets both in the United States and globally. As a matter of fact, the business sectors that were mostly hit by layoffs were the ones to be the most dependent on human interaction (e.g. hospitality, education, retail, etc.). The severity of the situation can be further seen in how the ongoing pandemic has affected the labor force participation rate. As a matter of fact, in the months between February and April the labor force participation rate went down 3.2%, amounting to 60.2% in April (which is the lowest this rate has ever been since 1948, when the CBO officially started collecting and analyzing data). Such a substantial decrease in labor force participation is the direct result of the pandemic's ongoing effects on the demand and supply of labor. Consequently, along with unemployment also consumer's spending fell during the pandemic. Indeed, the C.B.O. reported that consumer spending would decline at an annual rate of 39%, in particular caused by households decreasing their spending as the consequences of the pandemic became more severe. On a different note, the ongoing covid-19 pandemic has also negatively affected the U.S. federal budget. According to a forecast conducted by the C.B.O., for the fiscal year 2020 the federal budget deficit would amount to $3.7 trillion, which constitutes about 17.9% of the U.S. GDP. In addition, the covid-19's pandemic has severely impacted the U.S. in terms of imports and exports. Indeed, the CBO reported that between the first two quarters of 2020, the imports went from - 4.1% in the first quarter to -16.4% in the second. Likewise, the exports have decreased during the first two quarters of 2020, resulting in a -2.2% decrease in the first quarter and in a -21.2% decrease in the second quarter. To sum up, the CBO reported that as an annual rate in 2020, the exports and imports are expected to amount respectively -8.3% and -11.9% (specifically, these statistics reflect a positive outlook held by the CBO regarding the effects and efficiency of the policies adopted by the U.S. government in order to tackle the pandemic). In a similar manner, China's economy has also been severely affected by the ongoing pandemic.

According to estimates provided for by the National Bureau of Statistics of China (the Bureau), China's GDP for the first quarter of 2020 amounted to 20,650.4 Yuan, which is resulting from a year-on-year projected decrease of about 6.8% (National Bureau of Statistics of China, 2020). On the same note, the National Bureau of Statistics of China reported that in terms of industry performance, the added value provided by the primary industry was about 1,018.6 billion Yuan, 7,363.8 billion yuan for the secondary industry and 12,268.0 billion Yuan for the tertiary industry. Respectively, the added value for each of said industries is underperforming by 3.2%, 9.6% and 5.2%. However, on a different note compared to the U.S., the ongoing pandemic has not led to substantial increases to China's unemployment rate. According to the Bureau, during the first quarter of 2020 the unemployment rate in urban areas was about 5.9%, with the total employed people in said areas to be about 2.29 million. Compared to the February estimate, the unemployment rate only decreased by 0.3%. More specifically, the unemployment rate in 31 major cities surveyed by the Bureau amounted to 5.7%, remaining unchanged from February. This said, it is also important to consider how the pandemic has impacted China's economy in terms of nationwide disposable income. As reported by the Bureau, the disposable income per capita of China's residents saw a real decrease of 3.9% and a nominal increase of 0.8%, which corresponds to about 8,561 Yuan. In rural areas and households, the disposable income per capita saw a real decrease of 4.7% and a nominal increase of 0.9%, which corresponds to 4,641 Yuan. In terms of sources of income, the Bureau stated that nationwide the net property income increased by 2.7%, the net transfer income increased by 6.8% and that the capital wage income increased by 1.2%. Regarding how the pandemic has affected China's balance of trade, the Bureau reported that in the first quarter of 2020, the total value of both exports and imports of good amounted to 6,574.2 billion Yuan (which would correspond to a year-on-year decrease of 6.4%). In addition, the report provided for by the Bureau stated that as of March of 2020, the total value of exports and imports amounted to about 2,445.9 billion Yuan (of which 1,297.7 billion Yuan of exports and 1,153.2 billion Yuan of imports), with the general trade of imports increasing of 4% and exports decreasing of 3.5%. Furthermore, during the first quarter of 2020 the export delivery value of industrial enterprises amounted to 2,408.2 billion Yuan (which corresponds to a year-on-year decrease of 10.3%); whereas during the month of March, the Bureau reported it to have reached 1,030.7 billion Yuan.

THE ORIGINS OF MANUFACTURING OUTSOURCING

An interesting study published in March 2020 by the University of Indiana (Kota S. and Mahoney T.) focuses on the US Manufacturing Policies and outsourcing initiatives. The authors describe the concerns on U.S. global economic competitiveness between the 70's and the 80's, leading to the change of U.S. manufacturing policies. In particular, while during the 70's it was accepted that labor and management would join forces to share "the fruits of domestic production", in the following decade a shift occurred, pushed by shareholders, more and more relevant in the firm's decision making and more and more focused on efficiency. In this case, efficiency was elementarily met by cutting costs and maximizing profits (cutting jobs and outsourcing the manufacturing process); it is indeed during these decades that American industries (in particular those with low-skill workers) began to move their manufacturing plants to other parts of the world (mainly Latin America and Asia). Outsourcing was particularly present in those industries at the time deemed to be "mature", where innovation was not playing an important role for competition.

The first major consequence of outsourcing could be identified in the progressive loss of "innovation capacity"; countries which have been the biggest recipients for outsourcing (e.g. China) became attractive destinations for R&D (since also R&D is now becoming an "hindrance" cost). In fact, U.S. became "most aggressive in moving R&D to China", with an investment of $18 billion in 2015 (40% of the total R&D Investments in China). The loss of innovation capacity is reflected in the fact that the U.S. are getting worse in International measures of innovation (e.g. the U.S. were ranked 7th in 2000 and 12th in 2017 by Harvard University's Atlas of Economic Complexity). In addition, the U.S.' Global Innovation Index rank went from 1st in 2009 to 11th in 2019 (Kota & Mahoney, 2020).

The second consequence of outsourcing identified is the increase in foreign dependency. As a matter of fact, United States completely over relies on China for drug supplies and telecommunication equipment and lost engineering, R&D, industrial commons and manufacturing facilities. In conclusion, several studies confirmed that decades of outsourcing left the United States incapable of innovating, of producing products independently and, more importantly, strategically vulnerable.

CHALLENGES IN THE SUPPLY CHAIN OF PHARMA MANUFACTURERS

In their research, authors Aasiye Moosivand, Ali Rajabzadeh Ghatari and Hamid Resa Rasekh have elaborated a qualitative analysis (acquired also over interviews of pharmaceutical supply chain managers) over the challenges that are currently impacting the supply chain of pharmaceutical manufacturers. Their research adopted the Supply Chain Operations Reference model (SCOR model) in order to assess the different problems and variables related to pharmaceutical supply chains, using qualitative system dynamics modeling. More specifically, the focus of the research is divided between supply chain performance (in terms of supply chain capabilities and supply chain efficiency) and the SCOR model (in terms of reliability, flexibility and responsiveness for the supply chain capabilities and in terms of costs and asset management for the supply chain efficiency). Along with this methodology, the authors recurred to a qualitative analysis through the usage of causal loop diagrams which helped visualize the effects of decisions and activities on the firm's goals. Due to the extension of the methodology, this research is limited in the pharmaceutical industry and, as claimed by its authors, cannot be used as a comparative example for other industries. Another limit is the lack of quantitative analysis which leaves out of the picture the financial variables that can play a major role in the industry. The major problems that were found related to the supply chain capabilities are several. First, inventory and sales problems (for instance, destocking, high backorders, inventory oscillation) which often manifest as possible inaccurate forecasts and result in the substantial decrease of supply orders. Second, the high amount of time needed to complete both the manufacturing and the R&D cycle. Consequently, another problem identified to be affecting the supply chain capabilities is the limited quantity of time available for tackling unpredictable events. On the other hand, the problems identified to be affecting pharmaceutical supply chains in terms of efficiency are: higher average inventory costs, higher average time of "inactive" inventory and longer cash-to-cash cycles. Within their research, Moosivand, Ghatari and Rasekh have also elaborated on different strategies that pharmaceutical firms can adopt in order to tackle supply chain challenges. First, strategic supplier relationships can allow pharmaceutical firms to better face the instability of the markets (and other negative occurrences such as the "bullwhip effect") by sharing information and pursuing joint decisions. Furthermore, the research documents how strategic supplier relationships result in: increased capability of responding to demand, increased market share, increased customer satisfaction, increased profitability and the reduction of costs. Second, it is of most importance that pharmaceutical companies should focus their investments into new technologies, in order to improve production processes and R&D and in order to decrease the amount of wasted materials and reworks (Moosivand, Ghatari & Rasekh, 2020). By adopting new technologies into the manufacturing process, firms can in fact become more flexible and more competitive. The final suggestion provided by the authors consists in the establishment of improved information technologies. Indeed, with an improved IT firms can achieve more accurate forecastings, decreasing the risks related to inventory mismanagement and to the instability of the markets. All of these suggestions combined create what the authors referred to as "Collaborative Planning, Forecasting and Replenishment".

COVID 19 AND THE GLOBAL VALUE CHAINS

In an article published in the *Journal of International Business Policy*, author Gary Gereffi provides commentary over what the Covid-19's pandemic has taught the scientific community about the global value chain and how the pandemic has affected global medical supplies. The author elaborates on this topic by discussing current relevant academic literature while focusing on three main aspects: the global value chain research framework, the trade interdependencies of essential medical goods before the pandemic, how the U.S.'s supply chain reacted to the pandemic and suggestions for better post-crisis policymaking and more "resilient" supply chains. With global value chain the literature refers to the growth that happened between 1990 and 2010 of the global economy with the ever-increasing decision taken by western companies to outsource their manufacturing processes abroad, establishing a "cross-border production network". These "global networks" allowed firms to achieve the advantages of superior production scales with lower costs (Gereffi, 2020). Furthermore, said networks granted firms the capability to achieve spatial flexibility through: increased efficiency of logistic providers, access to a greater pool of low-cost workers, and overall betterment of innovation and ease to access to natural resources. As elaborated by the author, the global value chain framework is built over different aspects. First, the global industries present governance structures; specifically, the major firms in the global value chain strategize the performance requirements for the various suppliers. Second, the global supply chains present "specialized divisions of labor" with specific products and components being manufactured in determined locations. This characteristic allows the global supply chain to be more efficient; yet, the eventual disruption of the supply chain in one location can endanger the efficiency of the whole chain. Third, the global supply chain's geographical distribution is subject to change over time (for example, this is possibly due to government policies and technology shifts); however, "global sourcing patterns" exist in several industries. Fourth, value is not evenly distributed across the global supply chain. And lastly, governmental policies can be the catalyst of extensive pressure to both suppliers and lead firms. Regarding the international commerce of medical supplies before the pandemic, the author focuses this aspect of the analysis on the medical supplies that are now needed for the treatment of covid-19. The author's findings can be summarized as follows. The global commerce for medical devices and personal protective equipment more than doubled in value. Moreover, considering covid-19 related medical goods, the major exporters before the pandemic were "Germany (15%), the U.S. (11%), Switzerland (9%), China (8%) and Ireland (7%)". On the other hand, the two major importers of the same goods before the pandemic were the U.S. (18%) and Germany (about 9%) (Gereffi, 2020). In fact, the author elaborates that before the pandemic what characterized the commerce of the aforementioned goods were "trade interdependencies". Regarding how the U.S. supply chain reacted to the Covid-19 pandemic, the authors based his analysis on 3M's (a company which manufactures personal protective equipment) supply capacity of N95 masks in front of the sudden U.S. demand growth for respirators after the pandemic. In his analysis, the author identified two main factors that contributed to 3M not meeting the rising demand for N95 masks in the American market. First, the dominant practice of "just in time" inventory management in the American healthcare industry, which for years prioritized across the supply chain low inventories and low production. And second, the liability waivers needed for the shift from industrial to medical N95 masks. However, the author clarifies that the shortage of N95 seemed to be caused more by policy rather than by the market inefficiency. Specifically, the author recognized that the U.S. governance did not recognize the seriousness of the problem before it was too late, resulting in "lack of testing, bureaucratic in-fighting, and unwillingness to confront the health risks posed by the looming pandemic" (Gereffi, 2020). Finally, the author provides some strategic options and considerations that need to be taken in consideration for the post-covid-19 world. First, countries need to improve their local capability to "address security concerns for products deemed essential" (Gereffi, 2020). Second, countries ought to become less dependent on the supply chains of fewer locations by increasing international production sites. Third, firms need to pursue partnerships in terms of research, marketing and production. Along with these suggestions, the author concludes with another consideration. In the post covid-19 world it will be of most importance that regulatory policies that are planned with worst-case scenarios in mind shall be essential.

HOW DRUG SHORTAGES IMPACT PATIENT CARE

In a research published in May 2020 by the *Elsevier Public Health Emergency* Collection, authors Hisham A. Baldredin and Bassam Atallah discuss how the drug shortages caused by the Covid-19 pandemic have impacted patient care. The research methodology focuses on the qualitative analysis of primary data related to patient care and the role of both policy makers and pharmacists during the pandemic. The research also includes the discussion of possible impact mitigation strategies. The focal limit of this research is that it does not include a quantitative analysis of "hard data" that could have been useful in order to complement the conclusive findings. Another limitation that affects the research is the difficulty in properly quantifying (and most importantly, predict) the occurrence and scope of drug shortages: For this reason; mostly, researchers who discuss similar topics focus on qualitative analysis. This said, the research begins with an assessment of the possible consequences of drug shortages over the quality of patient care. For instance, in order to gain access to drugs in shortage some patients may be transferred to other medical facilities, causing discomfort. Another important consequence mentioned by the author is the increase in medical errors, between "drug omission, dispensing and administration". This is mostly due to the fact that in order to substitute a drug in shortage with its non-listed substitute "involves creating a new computerized physician order entry build", which consequently requires to familiarize pharmacists, nurses and physicians with the new entry. Moreover, the drug substitute could be "less effective or may place the patient at a higher risk of developing unwarranted adverse effects" (Baldredin & Atallah, 2020). On the same note, drug shortages would result in possible changes of drug concentrations which then would cause possible drug overdoses. Furthermore, the author rightly points out that the more extended the time-frame of the shortage the more it will interrupt other public health emergencies (for example, the author refers to the possibility of influenza vaccines scarcity). Moreover, the longer the shortage will be protracted the likelier the possibility of "the risk of patient deterioration, worsen the acuity of patient illness, postpone or cancel crucial surgical procedures, prolong the hospital stay, and increase the rate of mortality". In short, drug shortages would result in the "increase the patient's levels of distress, frustration, and confusion" (Baldredin & Atallah, 2020). The authors then proceed to discuss their findings over the role of the pharmacist during the covid-19 pandemic. First, Pharmacists communicate regularly with health-related authorities while "granting institutional review board approvals, and submitting the necessary related paperwork". And obviously, pharmacists focus on securing the largest possible amount of "evidence-based Covid-19 medications" for the sake of the patients (Baldredin & Atallah, 2020). However, the authors elaborate on more characteristics related to critical roles of pharmacists. Pharmacists are *de facto* "entrusted with advocating for appropriate prescribing" and "helping in setting institutional and community pharmacy policies on appropriate prescribing and dispensing of medications" (Baldredin & Atallah, 2020). Furthermore, due to the sudden surge in demand for medications, the authors of the study argue that pharmacists are "expected to be involved in strategies to deal with these shortages" by "evaluating and switching to alternative generic medications and switching between therapeutic options. Indeed, due to the shortages of medications and raw materials which are only manufactured in selected locations (e.g. China and India), the pharmacist needs to be "able to navigate alongside other members of the healthcare team alternative therapeutic options until the shortages are resolved" while following the "general guidelines to mitigate shortages such as those published by the American Society of Health-System Pharmacists" (Baldredin & Atallah, 2020). Concluding on the role of the pharmacist during the covid-19 pandemic, the authors argue that it is of most importance to world pharmacists to be open on a global-scale collaboration in order to better tackle the consequences of the pandemic. This said, the authors provide for different examples of the role of policymakers during the covid-19 pandemic. Most importantly, policymakers should be focusing on proactively mitigating the issue of drug supply shortages on both the national and institutional level. The authors suggest that this can be achieved by, for instance, efficiently creating and monitoring a list of drugs that are at risk of facing a shortage (specifically those drugs which are not manufactured locally). Furthermore, policymakers ought to mandate manufacturers full public disclosure of drug manufacturing facilities locations. By doing so, the authors conclude that policymakers can grant more time to drug purchases in order to assess the situation and look for alternatives if needed. In addition, policymakers ought to create incentives for their local manufacturers "to optimize their supply to meet the demand without contravening the good manufacturing practices" (Baldredin & Atallah, 2020). Simply put, policymakers must bring more focus over the implementation of policies which will allow for the creation of mitigation plans of drug shortages. On a side note, the authors also provide for a short explanation of what role will institutional policy makers assume during the pandemic. First, these policymakers "should institute and implement several internal policies and procedures to ensure the wise utilization of all drugs". Second, institutional policymakers "should establish a step-wise approach to transition patients to alternative bioequivalent generics that could be nationally manufactured" (Baldredin & Atallah, 2020). This said, the authors concluded their research by reinforcing the notion that "communication is key" and that any task forces involved in facing drug shortages "should aim to provide regular updates to all involved entities".

US MANUFACTURING POLICIES

In issue 20 of the Manufacturing Policy Initiative published in March 2020 by the University of Indiana, authors Sridhar Kota and Thomas C. Mahoney discuss insights on the U.S. manufacturing policies and the consequences led by outsourcing. The issue follows both a qualitative and a quantitative methodology; however, the issue leaves a gap when it comes to comparing economic performances of companies involved in similar sectors discussed during the analysis. The authors track the origin of the concerns regarding the U.S. global economic competitiveness between the 70's and the 80's. According to Kota and Mahoney, what led to the change of U.S. manufacturing policy was the mere evolution of management theories and how they were performed. During the 70's, it was accepted that labor and management would join forces to share "the fruits of domestic production". However, the following decade a paradigm shift occurred, during which shareholders (which began to become more relevant in the firm's decision making) demanded efficiency. In this case, efficiency was elementarily met by cutting costs and maximizing profits. This process, as pointed out by the authors, was met by cutting jobs and outsourcing the manufacturing process. It is indeed during these decades that American industries (in particular those with low-skill workers) began to move their manufacturing plants to other parts of the world (mainly Latin America and Asia). The authors also mention that outsourcing was particularly present in those industries at the time deemed to be "mature", where innovation was not playing an important role for competition. The first major consequence of outsourcing can be identified in the progressive loss of "innovation capacity". With this terminology the authors refer to the fact that countries which have been the biggest recipients for outsourcing (e.g. China) have become attractive destinations for R&D (since also R&D is now becoming an "hindrance" cost). In fact, the authors mention that the U.S. have become "most aggressive in moving R&D to China", with an investment of $18 billion in 2015 (40% of the total R&D Investments in China). The loss of innovation capacity can be seen, according to the authors, in the fact that the U.S. are getting worse in International measures of innovation (e.g. the U.S. were ranked 7th in 2000 and 12th in 2017 by Harvard University's Atlas of Economic Complexity). In addition, the U.S.' Global Innovation Index rank went from 1st in 2009 to 11th in 2019 (Kota & Mahoney, 2020). The second consequence of outsourcing identified by the authors is the increase in foreign dependency. As a matter of fact, the authors mention in this regard the complete overreliance of the United States on China for drug supplies and telecommunication equipment. More importantly, the authors note that the U.S. have lost engineering, R&D, industrial commons and manufacturing facilities. In short, the study concludes that decades of outsourcing have left the United States incapable of innovating and producing products independently; and more importantly, strategically vulnerable.

GEOGRAPHICAL ORIGINS OF US PHARMACEUTICAL SUPPLIES

In their research paper published in December 2019 by the National bureau of economic research, authors Neriman Beste Kaygisiz, Yashna Shivdasani, Rena M. Conti and Ernst R. Berndt elaborate on the geography of drug manufacturing that include very commonly used and prescribed drugs in the U.S.. In order to do so, the authors referred to quantitative data that is now publicly available in order to further discuss the implications of foreign supply chain dependency for U.S. foreign and domestic policies. More specifically, this paper elaborated on pre-existing research (that compared data from 2013 to 2017 about U.S. and foreign manufacturing sources of pharmaceutical generics) with a more expansive geographical analysis and more recent data reports. In this research, the authors focused on "off-patent generic prescription drugs" for a plethora of reasons. First, the authors identified that the U.S. is the world's biggest drug market in terms of consumption: about 70% of Americans are taking at least one prescription drug (a 15% increase over the seven years of analysis). Second, the last few decades saw a substantial increase for generics demand in the U.S.; indeed, *de facto* 90% of U.S. drug prescriptions are recorded as pharmaceutical generics (Kaygisis, Shivdasani, Conti & Berndt, 2020). This said, the research paper initially divides its focus on the four main geographies of particular importance for the U.S. supply chain: India, China, Puerto Rico and Ireland. However, it is important to specify that the findings reported in the research have then highlighted the importance of China and India which resulted to be the two most important geographical locations for the U.S. pharmaceutical supply. For instance, the market share of APIs manufactured to be sold in the U.S. market amounts to 87%, of which China and India held the largest shares (respectively 18% and 26% over a global production scale). On the other hand, the U.S. remained the largest world supply source of Finished Dosage Forms (FDF) counting for almost 41% of the World's manufacturing sites; only to be followed by India and China (respectively about 21% and 8%) (Kaygisis, Shivdasani, Conti & Berndt, 2020). In terms of manufacturing plants, the number of U.S. FDF plants remained stable between 2013 and 2019. However, during the years concerning the research analysis, U.S. API plants have decreased in number for about 10%. The South-East region of the United States lost nine sites, whereas the Central region lost ten (Kaygisis, Shivdasani, Conti & Berndt, 2020). The authors have also specified that these regions were already susceptible to possible supply chain interruptions due to either belonging to the so-called "rust belt" (which refers to regions with declining birth-rates and industrial development) or environmental hazards (e.g. hurricanes, floods, etc.). Within their research, Kaygisiz, Shivdasani, Conti and Bernt have highlighted how limited is the information currently available about where exactly do certain drugs come from (an information limit that also has impacted the FDA during the last ten years) due to both the now common practice of outsourcing pharmaceutical manufacturing and the firm's inadequacy to promptly notify the public or the FDA about product discontinuation or possible quality issues.

US OVER-DEPENDANCE ON CHINA

The covid-19 pandemic seems to be teaching the United States a valuable lesson about economic independence. Indeed, the pandemic has highlighted the fact that everything that the American people, white and blue collars alike, use commonly every day and may need the most in dire times is coming from manufacturing plants in China. For example, the telecommunications industry is increasingly becoming more dependent towards China for equipment. In fact, Huawei is the current largest supplier and owner of 5G equipment patents (Repoza, 2020). However, the seriousness of how dangerously the U.S. economy relies on China can be seen in the context of the pharmaceutical industry. Indeed, it is estimated that about 70% of active pharmaceutical ingredients (API) present in the U.S. are coming from other countries; and more specifically, almost the whole quantity of Ibuprofen consumed in the United States comes from China (Repoza, 2020). In addition, China is responsible for the manufacturing of medical devices, surgical masks (which became even more relevant as the demand for masks drastically increased during the pandemic), antibiotics, painkillers and penicillin. It is important to mention that the United States are extremely dependent on foreign production of penicillin because the last U.S. manufacturing plant dedicated to the production of the active ingredients used for penicillin was closed in 2004. U.S.'s dependence on China for drugs has also been highlighted by Yanzhong Huang, senior fellow for global health at the Council on Foreign Relations, who stated that Chinese pharmaceutical firms have supplied the U.S. market with about more than 90% of ibuprofen, vitamin C, hydrocortisone and antibiotics, about 45% of heparin and almost 70% of acetaminophen (Swanson, 2020). This said, what would be the ultimate price for U.S. dependency on China?

As it is easy to understand, the U.S.' overreliance on Chinese drug manufacture would result in severe consequences in the event of a possible conflict between the two nations, due to the fact that China can use its supply chain as a political leverage to bring a quicker end to the conflict. In a war scenario, it is not hard to imagine that China may logically block any distribution of medical supplies to the U.S., affecting the lives and morale of millions of Americans. As stated by the senior advisor of the Hasting Center Rosemary Gibson, in the possible event that China may block the exports of APIs it is to be expected that "within months our pharmacy shelves would become bare and our healthcare system would cease to function" (Swanson, 2020). In addition, Gibson has also argued that the U.S. will face similar consequences in case of pandemics and natural disasters, during which the U.S. will be forced to "wait in line with every other country for essential medicines". As a matter of fact, the restrictions to transportation followed by the closure of factories in China during the first stages of the pandemic have indeed affected the supply chains for drugs. However, although some shortages may already have happened because of the pandemic (as of February 28 the FDA was monitoring a list of 20 drugs which may have been in potential shortage), the worst-case scenario remains plausible yet unlikely. Indeed, as the pandemic went on China did not seem to actually enforce a blockage on drug exports (although during the first quarter of 2020 they stopped mask exports); and yet, the U.S. vulnerability to this foreign dependence remains the same. For instance, this year has seen what Rosemary Gibson warned about in her book "China RX: Exposing America's dependence on China for medicine" through the actions of other nations. India accounts for one-fifth of the world's generics export by volume and in March the

Indian authorities mandated their local drug manufacturers to stop exporting 26 drugs and APIs (the majority of which resulted to be antibiotics) (Goel, 2020). Consequently, as the Coronavirus pandemic is exposing the global supply chains' weaknesses, this topic has sparked political discussion in the United States. As a matter of fact, it can be expected that similar decisions taken by the Indian authorities may as well be similarly adopted by China eventually. For this reason, American politicians are becoming more interested in tackling this over-dependence on China for drug supplies. For example, in March during a meeting with the chief officers of the bigger pharmaceutical companies, Donald Trump stated "The coronavirus shows the importance of bringing all of that manufacturing back to America, and we will have that started". In addition, U.S. senator Marco Rubio similarly stated that "The coronavirus outbreak has made clear we must combat America's supply chain vulnerabilities and dependence on China in critical sectors of our economy" (Swanson, 2020). On the same note, these circumstances anteceding the pandemic obviously represent an issue in terms of U.S. national security. Indeed, U.S. defense officials are worrying about the possibility that China might not only take advantage over the United States for its economic dependence but also for acquiring stakes in businesses that have endured severe losses of capital because of the pandemic. According to undersecretary of defense for acquisition and sustainment Ellen Lord, the U.S. needs to be "very careful about the focused efforts some of our adversaries have to really undergo sort of economic warfare with us, which has been going on for some time". These arguments only help the political call for a more economically "independent" U.S. and a more independent and especially local pharmaceutical supply chain. However, do these arguments come exclusively from rational thought, or are they a reflection of fear? Is there real concern for a nationalized U.S. pharmaceutical industry or is it a mere consequence of media-fueled fear mongering?

BUILDING A RESILIENT SUPPLY CHAIN

Based on these fears, the main Pharmaceutical companies are taking advantage of all the Pharma 4.0 new technologies and tools to predict supply chain disruptions, to respond quickly and to increase their resilience during this pandemic crisis.

First of all, Pharma 4.0 helps company leaders to assess the level of supply chain risk by mapping production sites, distribution centers/material flows and by identifying all the potential events affecting supply/demand and leading to drugs shortage.

After this first risk assessment these tools are useful to draw the supply chain strategy by reducing the risk exposure and increase the company resilience.

In particular, this activities are aimed at reducing redundancy by creating capacity buffers to increase and decrease production volume (safety stock, flexible production lines and shift models). In this phase it's fundamental to adopt flexible contracts with suppliers and manufacturers in order to shift production volumes and locations.

Digitalization and automation of the production lines help companies to takes quick decisions and actions to cope with disruption (e.g. shifting production sites, changing production plans etc.).

Artificial intelligence gives visibility on the entire network and helps to predict demand fluctuation and risks. With these tools, visibility on stock levels and demand is also offered to other stakeholders (suppliers and customers), together with the possibility to simulate scenarios and take quick actions in order to mitigate the risk of disruption.

Finally, the above-described process could work better through the empowerment of company organization; in particular, at production site level, it should be possible to take independent and quick decisions in order to protect business continuity.

NATIONALIZING US PHARMA

Many eminent authors have so far contributed to this important topic. In a research paper published by the *"Robert H. McKinney School of Law"*, author of the study Fran Quigley discusses the contributing factors leading to the "path to Nationalizing the U.S. Pharmaceutical Industry". The author's methodology is based on both a quantitative and qualitative analysis of data that the author used in order to elaborate over the primary causes that are leading to the possible nationalization of the American pharmaceutical industry. Although the rationalization of all of the contributing factors provided by the author is sound, one of the limits of the study is its focus on the legislative aspects of the research problem, which leaves out of focus ulterior hard data that could be used to support the author's argument. Moreover, the author focuses on how the drug pricing strategies of pharmaceutical supplies have negatively impacted the lives of middle- and lower-class Americans. In this regard, the author uses as an example the pricing of insulin. Allegedly it costs pharmaceutical firms only $6 per insulin vial; yet, this product registered an increase in price of "more than 1,000%" now being priced about $300. Moreover, the author mentions how Americans affected with type 1 diabetes pay on average $1300 a month over medicines (Quigley, 2020). This notion is also important because in 2020, this situation worsened during the ongoing covid-19 pandemic and the related shortages. This said, the literature content can be broken down into three main arguments.

First, pharmaceutical patent development does not necessarily lead to innovation. Indeed, despite the $39 billion of annual budget granted by the National Institute of Health to fund early-stage R&D of new medicines, only 5% of the novel drugs approved by the FDA between 2005 and 2016 addressed a "new medical need" or helped improve patient care (the remaining percentage of said drugs consists in the so-called "me-too" drugs). It is also important to mention that in fact pharmaceutical firms still fund the majority of clinical trials, however, these firms are also eligible to at-most 50% tax credits. More specifically, the author mentions that also 25% of drugs get Government funding support during the later stages of development (Quigley, 2020). The major consequence of this business-government economic relationship is that there is no incentive for R&D which meets, as pointed out by the author, "the needs of the poor". Indeed, between 1975 and 2004 only 21 (out of 1,556) "new chemical entities" were destined for the treatment of either neglected or tropical diseases (Quigley, 2020). Moreover, the author argues that patents are *de facto* "artificially-imposed zones of exclusivity, acting as an "anticommons" by blocking the use of information that could lead to further innovation" which consequently become barriers to "follow-on discoveries". In fact, these consequences are partially caused by the side-effect of the creation of "patent thickets" (Quigley, 2020). For instance, the research mentions the results of a 2018 report published by *Initiative for Medicines, Access and Knowledge* which "revealed that the twelve top-selling drugs in the U.S. average a remarkable 125 patent applications per drug, many of them frivolous" (Quigley, 2020). These results suggest that, as pointed out by the author, "each drug carries an average thirty-eight years of attempted patent protections—far beyond the baseline 20-year patent life" a *de facto* form of protectionism. This protectionism is harmful according to the author, and it is in direct opposition with the various practices that resulted in breakthrough discoveries in the healthcare scientific field (e.g. open source software and journals, commons licenses, etc.).

Second, medical goods should be managed as public goods. This argument is, as mentioned by the author, consistent "with both economic theory and the multi-century, global legacy of preventing private entities from monopolizing and price-gouging drugs that are essential for life and health" (Quigley, 2020). For instance, in the literature the author explains how economists' consensus over the definition of public goods consists in "public goods as being non-rivalrous, meaning any person can benefit from the good without reducing others' opportunity to benefit" and "non-excludable, meaning a person cannot be prevented from consuming the good in question" (Quigley, 2020). Consequently, the author explains that said notion is indeed applicable to medicines: "although an individual pill is available to only one person, the formula for creating it can be widely shared". Moreover, the author provides for another reasoning that supports this notion. Medicines de facto generate positive externalities "such as vaccines halting the spread of disease or effective treatment leading to greater productivity" (Quigley, 2020).

The third main argument of this literature is focused on discussing the historical legacy of the nationalization of industries in the United States. In the research literature it is indeed often cited the historical pattern that dates back to World War I, during the nationalization of the railroad industry. Moreover, the same railroad nationalization happened in the U.S. during world war 2 and, as mentioned by the author, "World War II-era nationalizations were so voluminous that for a period in 1945, the government was taking over on average one industrial plant per week" (Quigley, 2020). More importantly, the nationalization of several industries in the U.S. continued even after the war. Primarily thanks to the implementation of the "Defense Production Act of 1950, which gives the President broad authority to take action within the domestic industrial base in response to military or disaster response needs" (Quigley, 2020). To summarize, the author proceeded to discuss three main historical examples of successful nationalization of U.S. industries. First, the creation of the Tennessee Valley Authority in 1993, a federal corporation which provided "electricity, flood control, and agricultural and economic development to a struggling region" (Tennessee Valley was particularly marred by the Great Depression) (Quigley, 2020). Second, the creation of the National Railroad Passenger Corporation (Amtrak) in 1970. And finally, the nationalization of airport security signed by George W. Bush after 9/11. All of these examples demonstrate how, according to the author, the U.S. government is indeed capable of nationalizing an industry "when public safety and attendant political pressures are in play" (Quigley, 2020). This said, in the final section of the research the author suggests a "four-step plan" for the nationalization of the U.S. pharmaceutical industry.

For the sake of brevity, the "four-step plan" suggested by the author can be summarized as follows. The first step consists in Congress passing a legislation which creates a "U.S. Medicines Agency (USMA)". The second step consists in the executive branch of the U.S. government issuing "compulsory licenses for the USMA to manufacture patented medicines". The third step consists in the USMA executing "seizures that are exempt from the 5th Amendment's compensation requirement". And the final step consists in the USMA seizing and compensating "private industries for the remaining assets that trigger the just compensation requirement" (Quigley, 2020).

CONCLUSION

As of 2022, the United States has become increasingly more dependent on foreign nations for its pharmaceutical supply. As discussed in this chapter, and as observed in several other studies, China is responsible for the production of a vast majority of generic pharmaceuticals destined for consumption in the United States. Such phenomena have the potential for catastrophic consequences for the American public, as the Chinese pharmaceutical supply chain has already faced disruptions during the Covid-19 pandemic. Furthermore, the United States could even be deprived of their generic drugs supply during a possible future conflict with China. As Americans have a history of putting the interest of their community before the interests of the few, the current vulnerabilities of their pharmaceutical supply chain (as exposed by the impact of the Covid-19 pandemic) should lay down the foundation for a nationalized American pharmaceutical supply chain.

REFERENCES

Badreldin, H. A., & Atallah, B. (2020). Global drug shortages due to COVID-19: Impact on patient care and mitigation strategies. *Research in Social & Administrative Pharmacy*. Advance online publication. doi:10.1016/j.sapharm.2020.05.017

Congressional Budget Office. (2020). *Interim Economic Projections for 2020 and 2021*. Author.

Deng, Y., & Pan, F. (2019). Dependence analysis of Sino-US trade. *Journal of Physics: Conference Series*, *1176*(4), 042093. Advance online publication. doi:10.1088/1742-6596/1176/4/042093

Desmet, B. (2018). *Supply chain strategy and financial metrics* (1st ed.). Kogan Page.

Gao, L., & Wang, X. (2019). Healthcare Supply Chain Network Coordination Through Medical Insurance Strategies with Reference Price Effect. *International Journal of Environmental Research and Public Health*, *16*(18), 3479. doi:10.3390/ijerph16183479 PMID:31540517

Gaouette, N., Starr, B., & Salama, V. (2020). *Pentagon warns China is exploiting the coronavirus pandemic to wage 'economic warfare' on the US*. Retrieved 31 August 2020, from https://edition.cnn.com/2020/06/16/politics/pentagon-china-economic-warfare/index.html

Gereffi, G. (2020). What does the COVID-19 pandemic teach us about global value chains? The case of medical supplies. *Journal Of International Business Policy*, *3*(3), 287–301. doi:10.105742214-020-00062-w

Goel, V. (2020). *As Coronavirus Disrupts Factories, India Curbs Exports of Key Drugs*. Retrieved 31 August 2020, from https://www.nytimes.com/2020/03/03/business/coronavirus-india-drugs.html

Gurvich, V. J., & Hussain, A. S. (2020). In and Beyond COVID-19: US Academic Pharmaceutical Science and Engineering Community Must Engage to Meet Critical National Needs. *AAPS PharmSciTech*, *21*(5), 153. doi:10.120812249-020-01718-9 PMID:32449007

Huang, L., Lin, Y., Ieromonachou, P., Zhou, L., & Luo, J. (2015). Drivers and Patterns of Supply Chain Collaboration in the Pharmaceutical Industry: A Case Study on SMEs in China. *Open Journal Of Social Sciences*, *03*(3), 23–29. doi:10.4236/jss.2015.37004

Huang, N., Huang, N., & Wang, Y. (2020). US economic policy uncertainty on Chinese economy: Industry level analysis. *Applied Economics Letters*, *27*(10), 789–802. doi:10.1080/13504851.2019.1645942

Jiang, S., Chen, Z., Wu, T., & Wang, H. (2020). Collective pharmaceutical procurement in China may have unintended consequences in supply and pricing. *Journal of Global Health*, *10*(1), 010314. doi:10.7189/jogh.10.010314 PMID:32566150

Kancharla, S., & Hegde, V. (2016). Inferences about supply chain practices using financial ratios. *Journal of Supply Chain and Operations Management*, *14*(1).

Kaygisiz, N., Shivdasani, Y., Conti, R., & Berndt, E. (2019). *The geography of prescription pharmaceuticals supplied to the U.S.: levels, trends and implications*. NBER Working Paper Series, (26524).

Kota, S., & Mahoney, T. (2020). *Invent Here, Manufacture There*. Manufacturing Policy Initiative At O'neill, (20).

Layne, C. (2018, January). The US–Chinese power shift and the end of the Pax Americana. *International Affairs*, *94*(1), 89–111. doi:10.1093/ia/iix249

Li, C., He, C., & Lin, C. (2018). Economic Impacts of the Possible China–US Trade War. *Emerging Markets Finance & Trade*, *54*(7), 1557–1577. doi:10.1080/1540496X.2018.1446131

Lloyd, R. (2018). *Successful integrated planning for supply chain* (1st ed.). Kogan Page.

Mikic, M., Puutio, T. A., & Gallagher, J. G. (2020). *Healthcare products trade and external shocks: The US-China trade war and COVID-19 pandemics*. ARTNeT Working Paper Series, No. 190, Asia-Pacific Research and Training Network on Trade (ARTNeT), Bangkok.

Miller, H. I., & Cohrssen, J. J. (2020). China's Coronavirus-Induced Paralysis Threatens U.S. Drug Supply Chain. *Missouri Medicine*, *117*(2), 86–88. PMID:32308220

Momtazmanesh, S., Ochs, H. D., Uddin, L. Q., Perc, M., Routes, J. M., Vieira, D. N., Al-Herz, W., Baris, S., Prando, C., Rosivall, L., Abdul Latiff, A. H., Ulrichs, T., Roudenok, V., Aldave Becerra, J. C., Salunke, D. B., Goudouris, E., Condino-Neto, A., Stashchak, A., Kryvenko, O., ... Rezaei, N. (2020). All together to Fight COVID-19. *The American Journal of Tropical Medicine and Hygiene*, *102*(6), 1181–1183. doi:10.4269/ajtmh.20-0281 PMID:32323644

Moosivand, A., Rajabzadeh Ghatari, A., & Rasekh, H. R. (2019). Supply Chain Challenges in Pharmaceutical Manufacturing Companies: Using Qualitative System Dynamics Methodology. Iranian journal of pharmaceutical research. *IJPR*, *18*(2), 1103–1116. doi:10.22037/ijpr.2019.2389 PMID:31531092

National Bureau of Statistics of China. (2020). *Decline of Major Economic Indicators Significantly Narrowed Down in March*. Author.

Quigley, F., & Ends, T. M. H. I. (2019). The Path to Nationalizing the U.S. Pharmaceutical Industry. *University of Michigan Journal of Law Reform*. https://ssrn.com/abstract=3496795 doi:10.2139/ssrn.3496795

Repoza, K. (2020). *Why Is The U.S. So Ridiculously Dependent On China?* Retrieved 31 August 2020, from https://www.forbes.com/sites/kenrapoza/2020/04/30/why-is-the-us-is-so-ridiculously-dependent-on-china/#1b8e436b56b5

Serhan, Y., & Gilsinan, K. (2020). *Can the West Actually Ditch China?* Retrieved 31 August 2020, from https://www.theatlantic.com/politics/archive/2020/04/us-britain-dependence-china-trade/610615/

Sharma, A., Gupta, P., & Jha, R. (2020). COVID-19: Impact on Health Supply Chain and Lessons to Be Learnt. *Journal of Health Management, 22*(2), 248–261. doi:10.1177/0972063420935653

Swanson, A. (2020). *Coronavirus Spurs U.S. Efforts to End China's Chokehold on Drugs*. Retrieved 31 August 2020, from https://www.nytimes.com/2020/03/11/business/economy/coronavirus-china-trump-drugs.html

Taylor, D. (2020). *A Timeline of the Coronavirus Pandemic*. Retrieved 31 August 2020, from https://www.nytimes.com/article/coronavirus-timeline.html

Taylor, G. (2020). *'Wake-up call': Chinese control of U.S. pharmaceutical supplies sparks growing concern*. Retrieved 31 August 2020, from https://www.washingtontimes.com/news/2020/mar/17/china-threatens-restrict-critical-drug-exports-us/

U.S. Food & Drug Administration. (2019). *Safeguarding Pharmaceutical Supply Chains in a Global Economy*. https://www.fda.gov/news-events/congressional-testimony/safeguarding-pharmaceutical-supply-chains-global-economy-10302019

Chapter 13
Does It Hold Water?
An Empirical Investigation on the Usefulness of Filtering Tap Water to Treat Health Complaints

Rainer Schneider
https://orcid.org/0000-0002-5943-647X
RECON, Germany

ABSTRACT

Recently, it was shown that regular consumption of a standardized amount of filtered tap water over a period of three weeks improved self-reported physical complaints. However, since individuals were fully aware of the type of water they consumed, it was unclear to what extent this effect was ascribable to placebo effects. This chapter tests the effectiveness of an in-home water filter system (AcalaQuell®) by comparing it with a sham water filter containing no significant filter ingredients. Both filters were concealed, and participants knew that the probability to receive the clinically proven filter was 50%. There were large differences with regard to symptom reduction between the two groups. For individual-specific complaints, the reduction was 38% for the filtered water group while the reduction in the placebo group was about 8%. Subjective health complaints are considerably reduced after daily intake of AcalaQuell®-filtered tap water during a three-week administration period. This effect is specific and independent from placebo effects.

INTRODUCTION

Health is critically dependent on the quality of drinking water (Chowdhury et al., 2019; Clasen et al., 2014; Daughton, 2018; Koopaei and Abdollah, 2017), but many health care professionals tend to somewhat reduce its significance to maintaining physiological functions, e.g., blood pressure, pH, and body temperature (Armstrong and Johnson, 2018; Perrier, 2019). Yet, throughout recorded human history the preventive and curative power of water was well known and part of various therapeutic approaches (Moss, 2010). Even if one disregards or questions the healing properties of water, many entertain a widespread

DOI: 10.4018/978-1-7998-8996-0.ch013

misconception with regard to the quality of drinking water. The rapidly rising number of toxic substances contaminating municipal surface and groundwater impacts all wastewater treatment works (Petrie et al, 2015). Flowing waters used as municipal water supplies also show high concentrations of contaminants which act as vectors for waterborne contaminants or pathogens (Lechner, 2020). However, there is a discrepancy in the understanding of the situation and its implication for public health. A recent American survey of perceptions about water showed that while 60 percent of the experts recognize that pathogens, fertilizers or pesticides pose a risk to public water systems in the U.S., the majority still rated the water supply as normal or good (Eck et al., 2019). This contradiction could stem from a subjective probability bias or a defense mechanism (Ferrer and Klein, 2015), which is even more accentuated if one takes into account additional factors that may corrupt tap water quality. Apart from microbiological and biochemical concerns, water treatment and transportation are additional potential harmful factors. It has been argued that the intake of 'stressed' water disrupts the water between and within cells in the human body and may prompt pathological macromolecular changes (Davidson et al., 2013). Among such stressors are, e.g., water disinfection (e.g. chlorine or ozone), supplementation (e.g. fluoride), and compression of water through pipe transportation from the supplier to the household. Bottled water, which some regard as a viable alternative, is also contaminated, regardless of whether the bottle is made of plastic or glass. For instance, in a recent study testing 259 bottles from 19 different countries, 93 per cent showed some sign of microplastic contamination (fragments and fibers), which stemmed from both packaging and bottling (Mason et al., 2018). In a large study conducted in Germany, the country with the highest number of bottled mineral water brands, about one third failed to meet the drinking water regulations defined by the EU (Birke et al., 2010). A recent systematic review selecting studies that used procedural blank samples and a validated method for particle composition analysis found that the high-quality studies confirmed strong microplastic contamination of drinking water with the maximum reported contamination of 628 MPs/L for tap water and 4889 MPs/L for bottled water (Danopoulos et al., 2020).

These findings are cause for concern both from the point of view of ecological damage and the burden caused for the health care system. They also suggest that the definition of healthy or 'vital' water warrants reconsideration over and above current regulation policies and recommendations established by national and international health organizations. For example, Pollack (2001) showed that water in the human cell is found in a state of structured aggregation, which he dubbed EZ-water (exclusion zone water). In this state, water homogenously organizes against a hydrophilic surface to form a crystalline structure, 'forcing' other molecules beyond the EZ. Experimental evidence indicates that EZ-water has a negative electric charge which improves its functions for biochemical and structural processes (e.g. by improving the phase angle of tissue, cf. Emilee and Wilhelm-Leen, 2014). Additionally, it also contains higher levels of oxygen, which may help to improve wound healing (Ladizinsky and Roe, 2010), enhance lactate clearance kinetics (Fleming et al., 2017), protect against muscle fatigue (Ivannikov et al., 2017), and boost the immune status and liver function (Grubera et al., 2005). This suggests that there are factors beyond mere contaminants threshold values that influence the quality of the water.

In fact, epidemiological studies support the notion that less-than-optimal household water quality has adverse effects over time, as do natural water sources due to the increase of environmental contamination (Vörösmarty et al., 2010). Health-conscious consumers seek alternative sources, for instance by resorting to point-of-use (POU) water treatment systems which may improve tap water quality, especially with regard to filtering out some of the most commonly known contaminants (Brown et al., 2017). However, there is a general lack of studies investigating such POUs in actual use (i.e. in real life). Recently, the effectiveness of one such POU system, an in-home water filter system, was tested in a pre-clinical sample of adults suffering from various health complaints (Schneider, 2021). According to several chemical analyses this filter system significantly reduces pesticides, bacteria, light-, heavy-, and semi-metals, pharmaceuticals and other major contaminants. The device also aims to revitalize tap water by restoring its original (hexagonal) structure, which is thought to improve the water's bioavailability and biophysiological properties. This claim has not yet been tested empirically, but Schneider (2021) found large health improvement rates after daily consumption of filtered water for three weeks. On average, both physical and mental complaints decreased considerably ($1.0 < d < 1.4$), with individuals suffering from a higher complaint burden at the onset of the study experiencing stronger symptom relief. However, one methodological caveat concerning the generalizability of this result was the type of control employed. Since the filtered water was tested against a natural control treatment (i.e., unfiltered tap water consumption) placebo effects were not controlled for. Hence, the present study was conducted to test (a) if the effect can be replicated and (b) to what extent it is specific (i.e. ascribable to the consumption of filtered water).

MATERIALS AND METHOD

Sample

A total of fifty participants were enrolled in the study (cf. figure 1). Seven individuals met the exclusion criteria, i.e. current intake of pharmacologic agents (n = 4), concurrent medical treatment for the symptoms tested in the study (n = 2), and complaints existing for less than three months (n = 1). Two individuals did not meet the inclusion criteria (i.e., their primary physical complaints did not involve cardiovascular, gastrointestinal, musculoskeletal pain or fatigue symptoms). One participant withdrew from participation after enrollment without specifying further reasons. Based on the effect size found by Schneider (2021), the minimum sample size needed to obtain a power of $1-\beta = .95$ was n = 24 (Faul et al., 2009). Thus, the sample size of n = 40 (22 females and 18 men) was sufficiently large to replicate the effect and to determine whether it was specific. The mean age was 46.6 years (SD = 12.1). The average body weight was 75.1 kilos (SD = 13.9). All participants provided written informed consent and were remunerated with € 20. The study's protocol was run following the Ethical Principles for Medical Research Involving Human Subjects of the World Medical Association and in accordance with the CONSORT guidelines for nonpharmacologic treatments (Bautron and Ravaud, 2014).

Questionnaires

The Complaints List Revised (CLR)

The CLR is a German self-assessment form to determine subjective impairment caused by physical or general complaints, covering the entire spectrum from absence of complaints to severe impairment (von Zerssen and Petermann, 2011). It consists of 20 items (e.g., fatigue, sleeplessness, nausea, tension) which all load on one general complaint factor. The item format comprises the anchors 'strong' (3), 'moderate' (2), 'barely' (1), and 'not at all' (0). The instrument is used across a wide range of patient groups, i.e. both patients with physical (especially chronic) and mental illnesses or disorders, and in the fields of somatic medicine, medical rehabilitation, clinical psychology, and psychiatry. The internal consistency (Cronbach's alpha) of the CLR is $\alpha = .94$.

Figure 1.

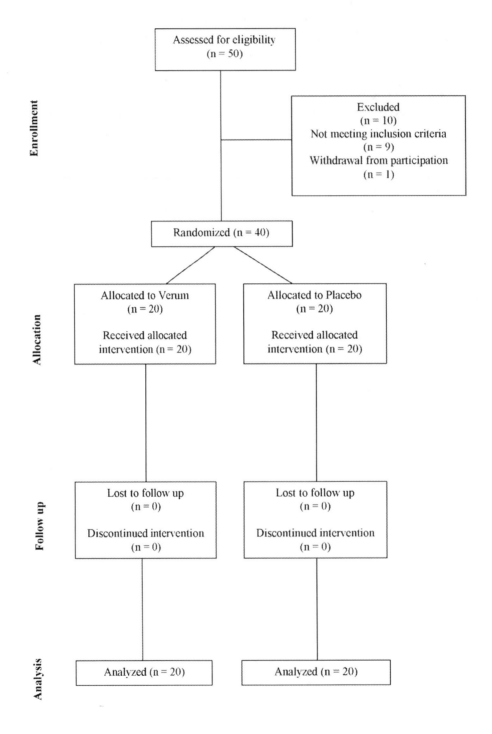

Giessen Subjective Complaints List (GSCL)

The GSCL is a questionnaire for assessing the psychosomatic or co-conditioned nature of physical complaints (Brähler et al., 2006). In the clinical realm, it is used to validate medically-caused and subjectively reported symptoms. The 24 items with the anchors 'not' (0), 'barely' (1), 'somewhat' (2), 'considerably' (3), and 'strongly' (4) cover the following complaints: exhaustion (e.g., weariness, excessive need for sleep), gastro-intestinal problems (e.g., stomach aches, nausea), musculoskeletal pain (e.g., pains in joints or limbs, backache), and heart problems (e.g., irregular heart-throbbing, dizziness). The four scales can be aggregated to obtain an overall complaint burden index. Internal consistency of the scales ranges from $\alpha = .82$ (gastro-intestinal complaints) to $\alpha = .94$ (complaint burden).

Individual-specific symptoms

Since most participants primarily suffered from one predominant medical condition, an individual-specific complaint score was calculated which was derived from one of the GSCL scales. It represented participants' prevalent ailment and thus best reflected any significant changes observed for the treatment. This was also done to minimize the impact of non-relevant complaints that would otherwise lower the complaint burden. In accordance with the first study, this variable was deemed the primary outcome parameter.

Treatment/Intervention

Water filter

Participants in this condition consumed 35 ml of filtered tap water per kg of body weight per day, following the recommendations of the German Society for Nutrition (DGE) for optimal daily water intake. The amount of water was consumed in small portions throughout the day. Beyond the required amount of water intake, participants were free to consume additional beverages. The filter used (AcalaQuell®) was a jug sized container consisting of a refill unit of 1 liter, a containing unit of 1.3 liters, a pre-filter-unit (microsponge), and a filter cartridge. The filter is non-pressurized and lets the water permeate a 1 µm pore sized microsponge impenetrable to dust, rust, microplastic or other floating particles. Then, it enters the filter cartridge consisting of three different compartments, where (a) an ion exchanger reduces lime, nitrate, and heavy metals, (b) a high-tech activated carbon removes additional potentially harmful substances, like pesticides, or drug residues, and (c) several materials like ceramic-fired tourmaline, calcium, magnesium, magnets, and quartz sand mineralize, structuralize and mildly alkalize the water. The water filter has been tested by several independent microbiological laboratories and has been certified to reduce pesticides. For the purpose of this study the filter was opaque and could not be opened without being physically tampered with. This constituted a safeguard to check participants' adherence/blinding.

(Pseudo) placebo

Participants in this condition consumed the same amount of 'filtered' tap water. The opaque filter used the same microsponge, but otherwise contained ineffective ingredients, i.e. sand and gravel, which mimicked the water flow of the verum water filter and thus imparted the impression of an active filtering process.

Study Design and Procedure

This field study involved a randomized, placebo-controlled, double-blind design. Participants were contacted individually by the female experimenter who explained the measurement protocol, the questionnaires, and the water filter device. Additionally, participants were handed out the participation information, the operation manual, and the consent form. They were randomly assigned to the treatment conditions using a randomized block design containing five-digit random number sequences that were ranked in ascending succession and assigned to the experimental conditions. After that, the experimenter opened an envelope containing the treatment condition 1 (verum) or 2 (placebo). Participants were told that two types of filters were being tested, one that was proven to eliminate contaminants, and one that was a placebo, and that the probability to receive either was 50 percent. Data collection started on a Monday morning and ended on Sunday night of the third week. At the end of the study, participants were contacted for the second time to return the water filter and questionnaires. Additionally, they were unblinded and remunerated.

Data Analysis

To assess treatment effects, the effect size d (Cohen, 2008) and confidence intervals (95%) for between-group comparisons were calculated (Borenstein et al., 2009). Dependent variables were difference scores between pre-treatment and post-treatment measures. Calculation of effect sizes was in alignment with meta-analytical practice (Hunter and Schmidt, 2004), the statistics reported by Schneider (2021), and as a consequence of the highly problematic use of Null Hypothesis Significance Testing (Greenland et al., 2016).

RESULTS

Symptomatology

At the beginning of the study, twenty-two participants complained primarily about symptoms of fatigue (e.g. weakness, excessive need for sleep), eleven subjects reported stomach/intestinal problems (e.g. bloating, nausea) and seven suffered from of musculoskeletal pain (e.g. joint pain, back pain).

Water consumption

Compared to the amount of water usually consumed (2,487.5 ml), participants drank 2,628.5 ml of water during the study. This difference was statistically insignificant because it fell within positive and negative confidence interval limits ($d = 0.3$; CI: $-0.3 < d < 0.9$). Due to this the amount of water consumed was not included as a covariate in the analyses.

Complaints

The analyses of the individual-specific symptoms as the primary symptom measure showed that the complaints in both groups ranged on average between "somewhat" and "considerable" at the onset of the study. At the end of the study, there was a sizable reduction only in the verum group. It was reduced by about 38 percent after consuming the AcalaQuell® water, while the reduction after consumption of placebo-filtered water was about 8 percent. This difference was large (d = 1.2; CI: 0.5 < d < 1.8; M_{Verum} 0.78, SD = 0.59 vs. $M_{Placebo}$ = 0.19, SD = 0.42). The effectiveness of the AcalaQuell® filter was 4.9 times larger than the improvement after consumption of placebo filter (see Table 1).

The analysis for the global complaint measure CLR yielded a similar result. Upon using the AcalaQuell® filter, participants' symptoms decreased by about 36 percent, while the reduction after using the placebo filter was 14 percent. This effect was medium to large (d = 0.7; CI: 0.1 < d < 1.4; M_{Verum} 0.34, SD = 0.24 vs. $M_{Placebo}$ = 0.17, SD = 0.22). Likewise, the global burden score of the GBB-24 showed a comparable improvement in the verum group by approx. 38 percent while in the placebo condition it improved by approx. 12 percent. The differential effect, however, was higher (d = 1.3; CI: 0.6 < d < 2, M_{Verum} = 0.52, SD = 0.38 vs. $M_{Placebo}$ = 0.15, SD = 0.12).

With regard to the subscales of the GSCL, there was a larger symptom relief in the verum group than in the placebo group in all four dimensions. For musculoskeletal pain, this effect was very large (d = 2; CI: 1.2 < d < 2.6) and amounted to a relief in the verum group of about 35 percent, while in the placebo group it was about five percent. In absolute terms, pain improved by 0.51 scale points (SD = 0.38) after using the AcalaQuell® filter, and by 0.08 scale points (SD = 0.16) after consuming the placebo filtered water. For gastrointestinal complaints there was a large effect between the study arms (d = 1.2; CI: 0.5 < d < 1.9), such that in the verum group the symptoms were reduced by about 31 percent, and in the placebo condition by about 18 percent (M_{Verum} = 0.62; SD = 0.48 vs. $M_{Placebo}$ = 0.18; SD = 0.21). With regard to exhaustion, a medium to large effect of d = 0.7 (CI: 0.1 < d < 1.3) was found. The percentage changes were approx. 34 percent for verum and seven percent for placebo (M_{Verum} = 0.53; SD = 0.63 vs. $M_{Placebo}$ = 0.16; SD = 0.43). The differential effect for heart complaints was identical to exhaustion (d = 0.7; CI: 0.1 < d < 1.4), the respective changes from pretreatment to posttreatment were 44 percent for verum and 16 percent for placebo (M_{Verum} = 0.34; SD = 0.28 vs. $M_{Placebo}$ = 0.17; SD = 0.19. It should be noted, however, that this symptom complex was not reported as the primary complaint by any participant.

As suspected, the mean scores of both the global scales (CLR, GSCL) and the subscales of the GSCL were not particularly high. For example, at pretreatment the severity for the CLR scale and the total GSCL scale was relatively low (anchor scale "hardly"). As outlined above, this was due to the fact that only few persons suffered from multiple symptoms and therefore the scores in the scales were averaged out. Nonetheless, there were still large effects in symptom reductions after consumption of the AcalaQuell®

Table 1. Means and standard deviations of reported complaints

	Placebo Filter Water		AcalaQuell® Filter Water	
	Pre	Post	Pre	Post
Individual Specific Complaint [a]	2.2 (0.7)	2.1 (1)	2.1 (0.5)	1.3 (0.5)
Giessen Subjective Complaints List [a]	1.6 (0.6)	1.4 (0.6)	1.3 (0.5)	0.8 (0.4)
Exhaustion [a]	2.3 (0.8)	2.2 (1)	1.5 (0.9)	1 (0.7)
Gastro-intestinal Problems [a]	1 (0.6)	0.8 (0.6)	1.6 (0.7)	0.9 (0.4)
Musculoskeletal Pain [a]	1.9 (0.8)	1.8 (0.8)	1.4 (0.5)	0.9 (0.5)
Heart Problems [a]	1 (0.6)	0.8 (0.6)	0.8 (0.5)	0.4 (0.6)
Complaints List Revised [b]	1.4 (0.5)	1.2 (0.6)	1.1 (0.4)	0.7 (0.3)

⁺rounded values;[a] range = 0-4;; [b] range = 0-3;

filter water despite relatively low total symptom burden. This indicated that the water had an effect that was not caused by placebo or expectation effects (see Fig. 1).

Additional Analyses

The fact that the range of symptoms varied considerably in the sample suggests that the effectiveness of the AcalaQuell® water filter could have been underestimated. It was conceivable that participants with milder symptoms did not benefit to the same extent. Theoretically and statistically speaking reductions of mild symptoms are less prone to be detected than mitigations of strong ones, which could skew the results. To explore this assumption, the analyses for the differential effects were limited to those individuals who reported an individual complain burden of at least "somewhat" (scale anchor 2), which was the case for n = 21 participants (n_{Verum} = 10; $n_{Placebo}$ = 11). As a result, the mean improvement in the verum group was considerably larger with a reduction from 2.5 (SD = 0.2) to 1.3 (SD = 0.6), corresponding to a burden of "hardly". The results for the placebo group remained unchanged (scale value 2.8 (SD_{pre} = 0.5; SD_{post} = 0.6). The corresponding effect was very large (d = 2.5; CI: 1.7 <d <3.3).

The first study showed that the response rate of individuals consuming the AcalaQuell® filter was very high (90 percent). In this study, two test persons did not experience any change in their prevalent symptoms, which replicated the aforementioned response rate. The responders' improvement rate ranged between 12 and 87 percent. In contrast, five individuals in the placebo group experienced no changes, and three reported a deterioration of 6-13%. It should not be assumed that the consumption of tap water caused this deterioration however, and it could well be the result of natural fluctuations or the course of symptoms. It is noteworthy, that the three individuals already had a high level of complaints (fatigue) at the start of the study.

Figure 2.

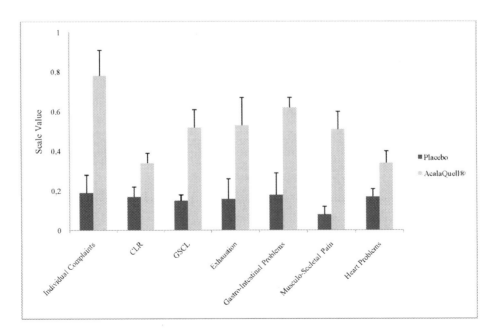

Figure 3.

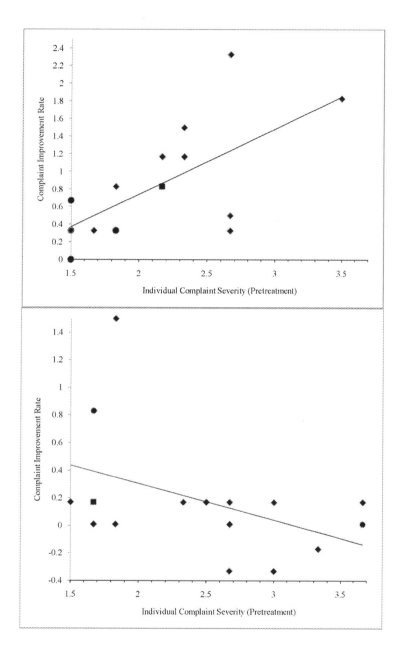

The first study revealed that the effectiveness of the AcalaQuell® water filter was higher, the higher the burden of complaints was at the beginning of the study. To explore this relationship, the same analysis was carried out for the present sample. Figure 2 shows the correlation pattern between individual symptom severity at the beginning of the study and symptom improvement at the end. As can be seen, the pattern was opposite for both study arms. While the correlation effect in the verum group was r = 0.67 (d = 1.8), it was r = -0.48 (d = 1.1) in the placebo group. Participants drinking the AcalaQuell® water benefited more the greater their symptoms were initially. In contrast, the symptoms of individuals who drank the placebo filtered water got worse the higher the degree of complaints at the onset of the study. The difference between the correlations was large (Cohen's q = 1.3).

DISCUSSION

The aim of this study was to test whether the effectiveness of the AcalaQuell® water filter system was due to mediating placebo effects or the direct result of consumption of filtered water. The results indicated both overall and individual-specific complaint reductions that were highly specific. The pattern of results in this study matched those of the first, both with regard to the effect size (d = 1.2 vs. d = 1.4) and the percentage decrease (30 percent vs. 26 percent). The size of the effect is demonstrated by the fact that 88.5 percent of the participants in the verum group had an improvement rate that was above the mean of the placebo group. As expected, there were distinct interindividual differences in response rate, with some individuals showing smaller improvements while others experienced greater symptom relief. As in the first study, there was a strong relationship between effectiveness of the AcalaQuell® filter system and symptom severity such that individuals suffering from stronger symptomatology benefitted to a stronger degree. Overall, the effectiveness of the AcalaQuell® water filter was replicated, and the effect was not mediated by placebo effects, which is corroborated by the fact that the specific effect exceeded the placebo effect by 275 percent.

The observation that the placebo filter only produced a small effect suggested that the microsponge exerted no notable effect on complaint symptomatology, as it was also part of the placebo filter. Thus, the improvement in the verum group must have been caused by the components of the filter, which, besides purifying, mineralizing, and alkalizing tap water, claims to "structure" it. The nature of this study did not allow investigation of this assertion. There are, however, orthodox explanations for the complaint-reducing effect. For instance, improved water quality enhances its cleansing properties by assisting the kidneys in removing waste products from the blood and eliminating toxic substances in the urine. Such effects have been shown to alleviate symptoms of fatigue (Pross et al., 2014). Likewise, gastro-intestinal disturbances may be improved by altering drinking water pH, which may affect the gut microbiota and glucose regulation (Sofi et al., 2014). However, as mentioned in the introduction there are a number of studies supporting the notion that there may be medical effects of structured water that, in principle, might have added to the beneficial effect of this water filter system.

The results of this work are potentially beneficial to both private health and the public health care system. Epidemiological data suggest that the continuous increase of contaminants in drinking water become increasingly resistant to metabolization or excretion. Their role in causing oxidative stress, which is symptomatic for numerous detrimental health effects, involving cancer, cardiovascular disease, diabetes, atherosclerosis, and neurological disorders, is well documented (Chowdhury et al., 2019; Jomova and Valko, 2011). Although there are many point-of-use (POU) water treatment systems, ranging e.g. from distillation, reverse osmosis, activated carbon filters, ultraviolet treatment, or cation exchange resin beads, the empirical evidence for their usefulness is scarce. The result of this study is in alignment with evidence suggesting that the use of an effective water filter is associated with reductions in health problems even when the quality of the sources is accounted for (Bain et al., 2012; Wolf et al., 2014). Thus, the regular use of filtered water from the AcalaQuell® system may promote health at least in subclinical populations and reduce long-term public health care costs caused by consumption of contaminated water.

There are several questions this work could not address. For instance, subjective health complaints and medical symptoms may or may not covary. Phenomenological (i.e. experienced) complaints may not have an actual clinical causation and therefore cannot be quantified organically or functionally (i.e. objectively). Rather, they may manifest as physical symptoms that are caused by psychological factors (e.g. life stress). Conversely, patients with a diagnosed illness may be symptom-free and thus do not experience complaints (e.g., hypertension). On average, subjective complaints and objective health issues only correlate moderately, and therefore the results of this study await confirmation beyond merely subjective health issues. Nonetheless, subjective complaints should not be dismissed as insignificant, as they exist even if they have no medical foundation. The fact that this study demonstrated a highly specific effect on subjective health complaints attests to that.

One aim of this study was to investigate a POU filter system in actual use and in a natural environment. As such, the results are externally valid. There are many factors, however, that could not be accounted for, for instance, adherence to the study protocol, water installations on site, or the supplier's water quality. Furthermore, only a relatively limited period of time was investigated and participants were not followed-up upon. Future studies should account for these factors and employ research designs that allow drawing conclusions for different types of ailments, outcome parameters (e.g. biomarkers, medical diagnoses), and samples (clinical vs. non-clinical).

With regard to the therapeutic use of the device future studies should shed more light on the filter's capacity to expedite or complement other treatments, e.g. during convalescence, recuperation and therapeutic treatment. Although the filter is not designed as a medical tool, its effectiveness could be utilized and extended to the clinical realm. Such studies should also employ techniques in more controlled environments that allow investigation of biomedical factors which act as mediating factors to restore health. In doing so, the questions if and how the filter actually structures water should be elucidated since this might substantially contribute to our understanding of the healing properties of water.

CONCLUSION

The AcalaQuell® water filter system substantially reduces subjective health complaints. The effect is large and shows already after three weeks of regular daily water intake. The consumption of filtered water may reduce individual health issues, potentially preventing ensuing organic and/or medical health problems and may thus be an effective tool to reduce public health costs associated with contaminated drinking water.

FUNDING

This research did not receive any specific grant from funding agencies in the public, commercial, or not-for-profit sectors.

CONFLICT OF INTEREST

The study was supported by Acala Inc., Germany. The company had no role in the collection, analysis and interpretation of data, in the writing of the report, and in the decision to submit the article for publication.

ACKNOWLEDGMENT

I thank Nick Singer for helpful comments regarding the paper's intelligibility.

REFERENCES

Armstrong, L. E., & Johnson, E. C. (2018). Water intake, water balance, and the elusive daily water requirement. *Nutrients, 10*. doi:10.3390/nu10121928 PMID:30563134

Bain, R., Gundry, S., Wright, J., Yang, H., Pedley, S., & Bartram, J. (2012). Accounting for water quality in monitoring access to safe drinking-water as part of the Millennium Development Goals: Lessons from five countries. *Bulletin of the World Health Organization, 90*(3), 228–235. doi:10.2471/BLT.11.094284 PMID:22461718

Bautron, I., & Ravaud, P. (2014). CONSORT for nonpharmacologic treatments. In D. Moher, D. G. Altman, K. F. Schulz, I. Simera, & E. Wager (Eds.), *Guidelines for reporting health research. A user's manual* (pp. 101–112). John Wiley and Sons.

Birke, M., Rauch, U., Harazim, H., Lorenz, H., & Glatte, W. (2010). Major and trace elements in German bottled water, their regional distribution, and accordance with national and international standards. *Journal of Geochemical Exploration, 107*(3), 245–271. doi:10.1016/j.gexplo.2010.06.002

Borenstein, M., Hedges, L. V., Higgins, J. P. T., & Rothstein, H. R. (2009). *Introduction to meta-analysis*. John Wiley & Sons. doi:10.1002/9780470743386

Brähler, E., Hinz, A., & Scheer, J. W. (2006). *GBB-24. Der Gießener Beschwerdebogen*. Huber.

Brown, K. W., Gessesse, B., Butler, L. J., & MacIntosh, D. L. (2017). Potential effectiveness of Point-of-Use filtration to address risks to drinking water in the United States. *Environmental Health Insights, 11*. Advance online publication. doi:10.1177/1178630217746997 PMID:29270018

Chowdhury, R., Ramond, A., O'Keeffe, L. M., & Shahzad, S. (2019). Environmental toxic metal contaminants and risk of cardiovascular disease: Systematic review and meta-analysis. *BMJ (Clinical Research Ed.), 362*, k3310. PMID:30158148

Clasen, T., Prüss-Üstun, A., Mathers, C. D., Cumming, O., Cairncross, S., & Colford, J. M. Jr. (2014). Estimating the impact of unsafe water, sanitation and hygiene on the global burden of disease: Evolving and alternative methods. *Tropical Medicine & International Health, 19*(8), 884–893. doi:10.1111/tmi.12330 PMID:24909205

Cohen, J. (2008). *Statistical power analysis for the behavioral sciences*. Laurence Erlbaum Associates.

Danopoulos, E., Twiddy, M., & Rotchell, J. M. (2020). Microplastic contamination of drinking water: A systematic review. *PLoS One, 15*(7), e0236838. doi:10.1371/journal.pone.0236838 PMID:32735575

Daughton, C. G. (2018). Monitoring wastewater for assessing community health: Sewage Chemical-Information Mining (SCIM). *The Science of the Total Environment, 619-620*, 748–764. doi:10.1016/j.scitotenv.2017.11.102 PMID:29161600

Davidson, R. M., Lauritzen, A., & Seneff, S. (2013). Biological water dynamics and entropy: A biophysical origin of cancer and other diseases. *Entropy (Basel, Switzerland), 15*(12), 3822–3876. doi:10.3390/e15093822

Eck, J. E., Wagner, K. L., Chapagain, B., & Joshi, O. (2019). A survey of perceptions and attitudes about water issues in Oklahoma: A comparative study. *Journal of Contemporary Water Research & Education, 168*(1), 66–77. doi:10.1111/j.1936-704X.2019.03321.x

Emilee, R., & Wilhelm-Leen, M. D. (2014). Phase angle, frailty and mortality in older adults. *Journal of General Internal Medicine, 29*(1), 147–154. doi:10.100711606-013-2585-z PMID:24002625

Faul, F., Erdfelder, E., Buchner, A., & Lang, A.-G. (2009). Statistical power analyses using G*Power 3.1: Tests for correlation and regression analyses. *Behavior Research Methods, 41*(4), 1149–1160. doi:10.3758/BRM.41.4.1149 PMID:19897823

Ferrer, R., & Klein, W. M. (2015). Risk perceptions and health behavior. *Current Opinion in Psychology, 5*, 85–89. doi:10.1016/j.copsyc.2015.03.012 PMID:26258160

Fleming, N., Vaughan, J., & Feeback, M. (2017). Ingestion of oxygenated water enhances lactate clearance kinetics in trained runners. *Journal of the International Society of Sports Nutrition, 14*(1), 9. doi:10.118612970-017-0166-y PMID:28360825

Greenland, S., Senn, S. J., Rothmann, K. J., Carlin, J. B., Poole, C., Goodman, S. N., & Altman, D. G. (2016). Statistical tests, P values, confidence intervals, and power: A guide to misinterpretations. *European Journal of Epidemiology, 31*(4), 337–350. doi:10.100710654-016-0149-3 PMID:27209009

Grubera, R., Axmann, S., & Schoenberg, M. H. (2005). The influence of oxygenated water in the immune status, liver enzymes, and the generation of oxygen radicals: A prospective, randomized, blinded clinical study. *Clinical Nutrition (Edinburgh, Lothian), 24*(3), 407–414. doi:10.1016/j.clnu.2004.12.007

Hunter, J. E., & Schmidt, F. (2004). *Methods of meta-analysis: Correcting error and bias in research findings*. Sage Publishers. doi:10.4135/9781412985031

Ivannikov, M. V., Sugimori, M., & Llinás, R. R. (2017). Neuromuscular transmission and muscle fatigue changes by nanostructured oxygen. *Muscle & Nerve, 55*(4), 555–563. doi:10.1002/mus.25248 PMID:27422738

Jomova, K., & Valko, M. (2011, May). Advances in metal-induced oxidative stress and human disease. *Toxicology, 283*(2-3), 65–87. doi:10.1016/j.tox.2011.03.001 PMID:21414382

Koopaei, N. N., & Abdollah, M. (2017). Health risks associated with the pharmaceuticals in wastewater. *DARU Journal of Pharmacological Sciences, 25*(1), 9. doi:10.118640199-017-0176-y PMID:28403898

Ladizinsky, D., & Roe, D. (2010). New insights into oxygen therapy for wound healing. *Wounds: a Compendium of Clinical Research and Practice, 12*, 294300. PMID:25901579

Lechner, A. (2020). "Down by the River": (Micro-)Plastic pollution of running freshwaters with special emphasis on the Austrian Danube. In M. Streit-Bianchi, M. Cimadevila, & W. Trettnak (Eds.), *Mare plasticum - The plastic sea* (pp. 141–185). Springer. doi:10.1007/978-3-030-38945-1_8

Mason, S. A., Welch, V. G., & Neratko, J. (2018). Synthetic polymer contamination in bottled water. *Frontiers in Chemistry*, *6*, 4017. doi:10.3389/fchem.2018.00407 PMID:30255015

Moss, G. A. (2010). Water and health: A forgotten connection? *Perspectives in Public Health*, *130*(5), 227–232. doi:10.1177/1757913910379192 PMID:21086819

Perrier, E. (2019). Hydration for Health: So what? Ten advances in recent hydration history. *Annals of Nutrition & Metabolism*, *74*(Suppl. 3), 4–10. doi:10.1159/000500343 PMID:31203297

Petrie, B., Barden, R., & Kasprzyk-Hordern, B. (2015). A review on emerging contaminants in wastewaters and the environment: Current knowledge, understudied areas and recommendations for future monitoring. *Water Research*, *72*, 3–27. doi:10.1016/j.watres.2014.08.053 PMID:25267363

Pollack, G. (2001). *Cells, gels and the engines of life*. Ebner and Sons.

Pross, N., Demazières, A., Girard, N., Barnouin, R., Metzger, D., Klein, A., Perrier, E., & Guelinckx, I. (2014). Effects of changes in water intake on mood of high and low drinkers. *PLoS One*, *9*(4), e94754. doi:10.1371/journal.pone.0094754 PMID:24728141

Schneider, R. (2021, October). Self-reported physical complaints are reduced upon regular use of an in-home water filter system (AcalaQuell®): A prospective, controlled, documentation study. *The Natural Products Journal*, *11*(5), 673–681. doi:10.2174/2210315510999200727204959

Sofi, M. H., Gudi, R., Karumuthil-Melethil, S., Perez, N., Johnson, B. M., & Vasu, C. (2014). pH of drinking water influences the composition of gut microbiome and Type 1 Diabetes incidence. *Diabetes*, *63*(2), 632–644. doi:10.2337/db13-0981 PMID:24194504

von Zerssen, D., & Petermann, F. (2011). *B-LR. Beschwerden-Liste*. Hogrefe.

Vörösmarty, C. J., McIntyre, P. B., Gessner, M. O., Dudgeon, D., Prusevich, A., Green, P., Glidden, S., Bunn, S. E., Sullivan, C. A., Liermann, C. R., & Davies, P. M. (2010). Global threats to human water security and river biodiversity. *Nature*, *2010*(7315), 555–561. Advance online publication. doi:10.1038/nature09440 PMID:20882010

Wolf, J., Prüss-Ustün, A., Cumming, O., Bartram, J., Bonjour, S., Cairncross, S., & ... . (2014). Assessing the impact of drinking water and sanitation on diarrheal disease in low- and middle-income settings: Systematic review and meta-regression. *Tropical Medicine & International Health*, *19*, 928–942. doi:10.1111/tmi.12331 PMID:24811732

Chapter 14
Assessing Differential Vulnerability to Health Risks Associated With Microbial Contamination of Vegetables

Emmanuel Kyeremeh
https://orcid.org/0000-0001-5312-6991
Berekum College of Education, Ghana

Dacosta Aboagye
Kwame Nkrumah University of Science and Technology, Ghana

Felix Asante
https://orcid.org/0000-0002-0601-6877
Kwame Nkrumah University of Science and Technology, Ghana

ABSTRACT

In the Sunyani Municipality, rapid population growth and uncertainties in rainfall have encouraged the use of untreated surface water for irrigating vegetables. However, microbial levels of ready-to-eat vegetables remain untested, and the differences in exposure unexplored. Further, there is a paucity of studies that compare the quality of local and exotic vegetables. A mixed method approach was used to collect and analyse primary data for the study. Forty-one farmers were sampled whilst 24 vegetable samples were used. The results showed on-farm vegetables in the municipality had microbial counts beyond the acceptable World Health Organization (WHO) threshold. Comparatively, the microbial counts of on-farm vegetables in rural and peri-urban locations differed, and the quality of local and exotic vegetables also differed. Also, vulnerability to on-farm microbial contamination differed across space and among producers. It is recommended that vegetable farmers should be educated on the safety of vegetables by the Agricultural Extension Officers in the municipality.

DOI: 10.4018/978-1-7998-8996-0.ch014

INTRODUCTION

Vegetables make up an essential component of the human diet because they contain minerals, carbohydrates, vitamins, proteins, and fibre. They are also a major supplier of nutrient and non-nutrient bioactive substances, that provide, minerals, dietary fibre, vitamins, and phytochemicals, especially antioxidants to the body (Slavin and Lloyd, 2012). Population growth and the quest to practice healthy eating and lifestyles has led to a sudden boost in the cultivation of vegetables for consumption by the teeming population in most urban areas creating an important livelihood activity for many people particularly in the developing world. Globally, an estimated 800 million people are said to be engaged in urban agriculture (FAO, 2016). Vegetable production is thus an important aspect of urban food production and contributes to the alleviation of food insecurity (Eigenbrod and Gruda, 2015).

However, in most growing urban areas in sub-Saharan Africa, uncertainties in rainfall and the difficulties associated with accessing clean water for irrigation purposes remains a perennial challenge. This has encouraged the resort to untreated surface water for the irrigation of vegetables to satisfy the ever increasing urban demand.

The microbial quality of vegetables in most parts of the world has raised major public health concerns due to contamination by pathogens, viruses and chemicals (Akinde *et al.*, 2016; Alamnie *et al.* 2018; Houngla *et al.*, 2019; Hussaini *et al.*, 2013; Sharma *et al.*, 2009). Alamnie *et al.* (2018) in their study in Ethiopia observed high contamination of vegetables by pathogenic bacteria, exceeding the recommended levels of 10 to 100 coliforms CFU/g by the International Commission on Microbiological Specifications for Food (ICMSF, 1998). Similarly, research in urban gardening at Porto-Novo, Benin by Houngla *et al.* (2019), reported high microbial contamination of three leafy vegetables - amaranth, nightshade, and lettuce. In Ghana, Sunyani is increasingly becoming an important vegetable producing area. Here, vegetables cultivated include cabbage, carrot, garden eggs (types of eggplant), tomatoes and okra for the increasing population in the Municipality taking advantage of the numerous surface water (streams) available to irrigate the vegetables but the Ministry of Food and Agriculture (MoFA, 2010) has cautioned that, use of untreated water may contaminate vegetables produced.

Earlier studies on vegetable production in urban and peri-urban Ghana have produced mixed results. For example, studies by Tiimub *et al.* (2012); Cobbina *et al.* (2013); Antwi-Agyei *et al.* (2015); and Aboagye *et al.*, (2018) all reported of poor quality of vegetables. Tiimub *et al.*, (2012) demonstrated that lettuce on selected farm sites in the Kumasi Metropolis were highly polluted above the WHO and ICMSF standards. In the Tamale Metropolis, Cobbina *et al.* (2013), observed that, lettuce, amarantus and cabbage produced were contaminated with high levels of total and faecal coliform bacteria. They further indicated that *E. coli* were recorded in lettuce and amarantus but traces were found in cabbages. A study by Antwi-Agyei *et al.* (2015), in Accra reported that, high *E. coli* concentrations found on farm produce was as a result of high levels of *E. coli* found in the soil or irrigation water used to water the crops. Their study showed that bacterial contamination levels varied across space and the difference was statistically significant. However, a similar study in the Kumasi Metropolis by Ackerson and Awuah (2012) did not observe any significant difference in the mean faecal coliform concentration on lettuce at different farm sites.

Generally, most of the studies on urban agriculture in Ghana have focused on exotic vegetables in urban or peri-urban areas to the neglect of local vegetables in rural areas. Thus, there is paucity of studies that compare the quality of on-farm vegetables in rural and peri-urban locations as well as compare the quality of local and exotic vegetables. Also, the literature is silent on differential vulnerability to microbial contamination risks in rural and peri-urban areas. This study sought to fill these gaps by assessing on-farm vegetable quality and farmers' differential exposure and susceptibility to contamination risks within the Sunyani Municipality. The study objectives were to compare microbial contamination levels of local and exotic on-farm vegetables in peri-urban and rural locations with the World Health Organization standards and assess differential vulnerability to microbial contamination.

The Concept of Vulnerability

There is no universally approved definition for the concept of vulnerability (Birkmann, 2007). The concept has been variedly defined depending on the context within which it is being used and the background of the researcher. Vulnerability in the context of climate change, is the ability of a system to endure, recover or bounce to its original state after being exposed to climate hazards (UNDP, 2014). According to the Inter-Governmental Panel on Climate Change, vulnerability is the extent to which a system is at risk to and unable to survive adverse effects of climate change (IPCC, 2010). Turner, *et al.* (2003), define vulnerability as the degree of harm experienced by a system, or system component arising from their exposure to a shock/stress or hazard. To Welle *et al.* (2014), vulnerability of any system is defined by the likelihood to suffer injury, loss, and disruption of livelihood caused by an extreme event and/or by the obstacles in recovering from the disturbance. In spite of the varied nature of the definition of vulnerability, for purposes of this study we adopt the definition of vulnerability as espoused by Balica *et al.* (2009). According to them, vulnerability is contingent upon the level of damage that can be expected under conditions of exposure, susceptibility and resilience.

The broader concept of vulnerability has been applied in numerous models. De Leon (2006) in the framework to conceptualize disaster risk, defines risk as a function of hazard, exposure, vulnerability and capacities. A profound limitation of this framework is that, exposure and capacity are not included as determinants of vulnerability (Birkmann, 2006). The Double Structure of Vulnerability, propounded by Bohle identifies exposure and coping capacities as determinants of vulnerability but did not include sensitivity, which addresses the impact side of the hazard (Birkmann, 2006). The Framework for Vulnerability Analysis in Sustainability Science (SUST Model), defines vulnerability in terms of exposure, sensitivity and resilience (Turner, *et al.*, 2003). This model seems to be a good model for assessing vulnerability. Nonetheless, it considers impacts as an important component of resilience (Birkmann, 2006). The MOVE (Method for the Improvement of Vulnerability in Europe) framework was developed to provide an improved conceptualization of the multi-faceted nature of vulnerability (Birkmann, 2013). This frameworks defines vulnerability as in relation to key causal factors such as exposure, susceptibility, and lack of resilience. Additionally, in the MOVE framework, vulnerability can be assessed along different dimensions such as physical, social, ecological, economic, cultural and institutional (Birkmann *et al.*, 2013). Since the social dimension includes the health of people, it therefore appears to be more useful than the previous ones in assessing vegetable farmers' vulnerability to on-farm vegetable contamination which is the focus of this study.

The MOVE framework

To understand farmers' vulnerability to microbial contamination risks the MOVE framework as espoused by Birkmann *et al.* (2013) is being applied. The authors intend the framework to be a tool to guide systematic assessments of vulnerability and to provide the foundation for comparative indicators

Figure 1. The MOVE conceptual framework
Source: Birkmann et al., (2013)

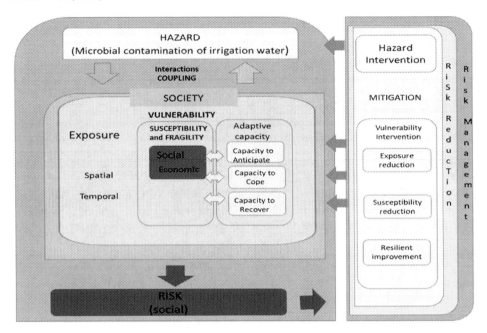

and develop the criteria to assess key factors and various components of vulnerability (Birkmann *et al.*, 2013). The framework provides an improved conceptualization of the multidimensional nature of vulnerability, responsible for key contributory causes such as exposure, susceptibility, lack of flexibility (lack of societal response capacities) as well as for the different magnitudes of vulnerability: physical, social, ecological, economic, cultural and institutional. The framework as shown in Figure. 1 is not dependent on hazards but recognizes hazards, which may be natural or socio-natural. The society, represented at different spatial scales, international-, national-, sub-national-, is recognized as an integral part of the environment (Birkmann *et al.* 2013).

Indicators of Vulnerability

The MOVE framework for purposes of this study, is being used as a yardstick to assess vegetable farmers' vulnerability to vegetable contamination risks. In the framework, exposure and susceptibility are the key factors of vulnerability. By exposure is meant the degree to which a unit of being assessed fits into the geographical reach of an event deemed hazardous (Birkmann *et al.*, 2013). It is defined geographically (spatial) as the social and material context in terms of people and ecosystems. In this study exposure was measured by the number of vegetable farmers in the Municipality differently exposed to vegetable contamination and the factors that amplify the severity of the hazard. Susceptibility (or fragility) within the framework "describes the predisposition of elements at risk to suffer harm" (Birkmann *et al.*, 2013, p. 200). Susceptibility in this study was measured by reported health conditions of the vegetable farmers, human behaviours and agronomic practices. Limitations in terms of access to, and mobilization of the resources of a community or a social-ecological system in responding to an identified hazard were used to illustrate lack of resilience and this includes pre-event risk reduction, in-time coping and post-event response measures (Birkmann *et al.*, 2013). In this study farmers' mitigation of the risk of bacterial contamination was assessed. Their resilience to pathogenic infection was gauged against their strategies to minimize exposure whilst their understanding of, and perception of the hazard, and measures to mitigate potential risk hinged on their level of education.

In the framework, the concept of hazard according to Birkmann, et al., (2013) describes the probable occurrence of events that are natural, human induced or socio-natural in nature that may manifest itself in a given area and over a period of time as physical, social, economic and environmental impact. In this study, hazards are represented by pathogenic microbial organisms such as faecal coliform and *E. coli*. These organisms contaminate on-farm vegetables and farmers become exposed through the consumption of contaminated vegetables.

MATERIALS AND METHODS

Study Area

The Sunyani Municipality (Figure 2) lies between Latitudes $7^0 20$"N and $7^0 05$'N and Longitudes $2^0 10$'W and $2^0 30$'W. Located in the wet semi-equatorial climatic zone of Ghana, the Municipality occupies an area measuring 829.3 km² (320.1 square miles) and experiences mean monthly minimum and maximum temperatures of 23°C (in August) and 33°C (in March and April) respectively. The rainy season spans from March till October with a clear break in August. November through to February mark the dry season (MoFA, 2010). The length of the rainy season allows for two cropping seasons in a year. The relative humidity in the Municipality averages between a high of 75 and 80% in the wet season and less than 70% in the dry season. The Municipality has a total of 9,752 households in agriculture representing 34.3% of the total households. Of this number, about 94 percent are engaged in crop farming and 0.3 percent practice fish farming (GSS, 2014). The area is also noted for vegetable farming. Vegetables produced in commercial quantities include cabbage, garden eggs, carrots, green pepper, tomatoes and pepper (MoFA, 2010).

Sampling and Data Collection

Abesim (peri-urban community) and Mensakrom (rural community) noted for vegetable cultivation were selected for the study on purpose. The selection of the broad study area and specific communities were based on the fact that studies of this nature were non-existent in the Municipality. Studies on vegetable contamination were scattered in the Accra, Tamale and Kumasi which are the major cities in Ghana. A mix of method approach was used in the collection, analysis and interpretation of the data. Primary data was obtained from a survey and the results of a laboratory test. Purposive sampling technique was used in selecting respondents for the survey due to the unavailability of a sample frame at the time of the study. Vegetable farmers who were engaged in the production of cabbage and tomato were sampled with the assistance of Agricultural Extension Officers from both communities for the survey. A total of forty-one farmers were interviewed in the survey. The interviews were conducted on farmers' field and participation was voluntary. Respondents' consent was sought before the interviews began. They were assured their anonymity. On average, an interview lasted between thirty-five and fifty minutes. Additional information was sourced using focus group discussions, involving a minimum of seven vegetable

Figure 2. Map of Sunyani Municipality showing the study areas
Source: *Sunyani Municipal Assembly (2017)*

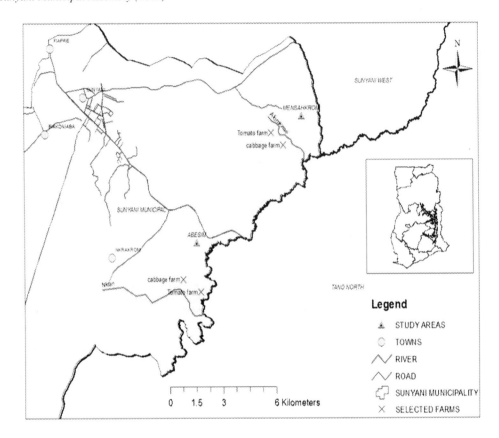

farmers in each community. The group comprises both males and females. The few female vegetable farmers in the communities were purposely selected to be part of the discussions.

A total of twenty-four (24) vegetable samples were collected and used in the laboratory analysis. They comprise twelve (12) cabbage samples for the exotic vegetable category and twelve (12) tomatoes for the local vegetable category. Two farm sites in each location, were selected. Two vegetables comprising one ready-to-harvest cabbage and tomato farms were selected for the study. Samples of ready-to-harvest cabbage and tomatoes were taken from different locations on each farm every week consecutively for three weeks in each community in October, 2017. Sampling was carefully done in order not to contaminate the samples. One sample each of cabbage and tomato from the selected farms in each community were collected, labelled and kept in zip bags. The zip bags containing the vegetables were kept in an ice chest with a temperature of about 4^0C. Ice cubes were placed on top of the samples before they were transported to the laboratory for analysis. Samples were labelled indicating the farm site and the community. All samples were collected between the hours of 7:00am and 9:00am and conveyed to the Biological Sciences laboratory at the Kwame Nkrumah University of Science and Technology, Kumasi within 5 hours for analysis.

Data Analysis

Quantitative data from the survey were analysed statistically, using descriptive and inferential statistics. The data was checked for errors and later entered into the SPSS software to summarise the data. The data were analysed using descriptive statistical techniques such as frequencies, percentages, averages and presented in tables. Results from the laboratory test were analysed quantitatively. Arithmetic means and standard deviations were calculated using Microsoft Excel. *E. coli* and faecal coliform loads of the vegetables were normalized by log transforming the raw data before it was analysed. The hypothesis was tested using the student t-test.

The three-tube most probable number method (MPN) as espoused by the APHA (1992) was used to estimate the quantum of faecal coliforms. Regardless of the nature of samples (liquid or solid), dilutions of 10-1 to 10-8 were prepared in maximum recovery diluent (peptone and sodium chloride) and 1ml of each dilution was inoculated into three tubes containing 5ml of MacConkey broth (Oxoid, CM0005). Three tubes from each dilution were incubated at 44°C for faecal coliform count. The presence of faecal coliforms, characterised by acid production (evident by colour change from red to yellow) and gas (CO_2) production, after incubation for 48 hours at 37°C was quantified and expressed as counts per 100ml from the most probable number table (Anon. 1994).

Estimation of *E. coli* in cabbage and tomato samples was done by sub culturing faecal coliform cultures that were positive unto eosin methylene blue agar (Levine) (Oxoid, CM0069) and incubated for 48hours at 37°C. Dark centred colonies with greenish metallic sheen were used to estimate the most probable number of E. coli per dilution and the results expressed as *E. coli* per 100ml (Anon. 1994).

RESULTS AND DISCUSSION

Bacterial Concentration Levels of Vegetables at Rural and Peri-urban Locations

Table 1 shows that all cabbage and tomato samples were highly contaminated with faecal coliform. The contamination levels of cabbage ranged from 6.65 ± 0.02mpn/g to 9.01 ± 0.05mpn/g whilst that of tomato was 3.37 ± 0.01mpn/g to 9.01 ± 0.05mpn/g.

The results of the concentration levels of faecal coliform and *E. coli* on vegetables tested indicate that both cabbage and tomato samples were highly contaminated exceeding the ICMSF recommended level of 10 to 100MPN/g but with slight variation from one locality to the other. This result corroborates the outcome of studies by Alamnie *et al.* (2018) and Tiimub *et al.* (2012) that reported high microbial levels in vegetables exceeding the ICMSF standard.

The results further showed that, tomato samples collected from both locations were contaminated with faecal coliform. The results indicate that maximum (9.01±0.05mpn/g) and minimum (3.23±0.02mpn/g) loads of faecal coliforms were recorded at Abesim (peri-urban). Also, all cabbage samples from both locations were contaminated with feacal coliform. Maximum (9.01±0.05mpn/g) loads of faecal coliform were recorded at the rural location (Mensakrom) whilst the minimum (6.65 ± 0.02mpn/g) loads were at the urban location (Abesim). Maximum loads of faecal coliform on cabbage and tomato samples recorded in the study area were the same (9.01±0.05mpn/g). This is the case since contaminated surface water (streams) constitute the major source of water for irrigation in the area. Again, the dominant method of irrigation used in the study area is water pump with hose which apply water directly unto the fruits and

Table 1. Assessment of the quality of vegetables at rural and peri-urban locations

Location	FAECAL COLIFORM (LOG 10 MPN/g)		E. COLI (LOG 10 MPN/g)	
	Cabbage	Tomato	Cabbage	Tomato
Abesim				
A1	6.65 ± 0.02	3.96 ± 0.01	2.37 ± 0.83	3.96 ± 0.01
A2	6.65 ± 0.02	9.01 ± 0.05	6.65 ± 0.02	4.37 ± 0.01
A3	8.18 ± 0.20	3.37 ± 0.01		6.23 ± 0.05
B1	7.20 ± 0.02	9.01 ± 0.01	3.86 ± 0.25	4.68 ± 0.20
B2	8.02 ± 0.72	4.76 ± 0.05	4.37 ± 0.02	4.56 ± 0.05
B3	6.16 ± 0.22	3.23 ± 0.02		
Mensakrom				
M1	8.01 ± 0.05	6.65 ± 0.02	4.98 ± 0.71	3.66 ± 0.42
M2	8.01 ± 0.05	8.37 ± 0.01		3.53 ± 0.82
M3	9.01 ± 0.05	4.77 ± 0.15		4.77 ± 0.16
N1	9.01 ± 0.05	4.53 ± 0.05	4.63 ± 0.20	3.96 ± 0.01
N2	8.01 ± 0.20	6.22 ± 0.15	6.22 ± 0.15	4.25 ± 0.05
N3	9.01 ± 0.05	6.23 ± 0.05		

Source: Authors' Fieldwork, (2017)

leaves of the vegetables. The microbiological quality of vegetable is dependent on the microorganisms in the soil, organic manure and on the type and quantity of the aquatic microorganisms within irrigation water (Amoah et al., 2005; Aboagye et al., 2018; Hasibur et al., 2016). Similarly, the contamination of vegetables in this study could be attributed to source of irrigation water and organic manure used by farmers to enhance the fertility of the soil.

This result suggests that vegetables from the farm sites were contaminated with faecal matter which might come from either humans or animals. Likewise, Weldezgina and Muleta, (2016) reported that cabbage and tomato samples from urban farms in Ethiopia were contaminated by both faecal coliform and E. *coli* bacteria. The result of this study is also consistent with a study in Ghana by Abass et al., (2016), which showed that vegetables produced in peri-urban Kumasi were highly contaminated with faecal coliform and E. *coli*. Another study by Cobbina et al. (2013) also reported that vegetables produced in the Tamale Metropolis were highly contaminated with faecal coliform.

E. *coli* were recorded in some of the samples from both locations. The results again indicated that, two of the three cabbage samples from the peri-urban location (Abesim) were contaminated with E. *coli* whereas E. *coli* was detected in one cabbage sample from Mensakrom, the rural location. Interestingly, both tomato and cabbage samples from Abesim in the third week were free of E. *coli* but not faecal coliform (A3 from farm A) but for Mensakrom the second and third week cabbage samples were free of E. *coli*. At least a sample of either cabbage or tomato from both locations tested positive for E. *coli*. The maximum (6.65±0.02mpn/g) loads of E. *coli* were observed at the peri-urban location (Abesim). All tomato samples collected from Mensakrom were contaminated with E. *coli* whereas two of the three samples from Abesim were contaminated. The presence of E. *coli* indicates that vegetables from both locations were contaminated with pathogenic organisms. The consumption of vegetables from both locations may be injurious to the health of consumers if uncooked or not properly decontaminated. Similar results were reported in Kumasi by Abass et al., (2016). They observed that cabbage samples were contaminated with high levels of E. *coli*. In contrast, Cobbina *et al.* (2013), did not find traces of E. *coli* in cabbage samples from the Tamale Metropolis. The results of the study shows that cabbages and tomatoes produced from both rural and peri-urban locations selected for the study were highly contaminated with pathogenic organisms and therefore unsafe for consumption without adequate decontamination processes especially if they are to be consumed uncooked.

An independent sample t-test was used to test the hypothesis: whether there was a statistically significant difference in the levels of bacterial contamination of on-farm vegetables between rural and peri-urban locations in the Sunyani Municipality. The results show that the difference in levels of faecal coliform concentration in cabbage was not statistically significant between rural and peri-urban locations ($p>0.05$). The same was true for tomatoes ($p>0.05$). The results suggest that bacterial contamination levels at both locations were generally the same. This could be attributed to similar agronomic practices - the method of irrigation and the use of organic manure - at both locations as observed by Amoah *et al.*, (2005 and Ndiaye *et al.*, (2011). Similar result was reported by Ackerson and Awuah (2012) in the Kumasi Metropolis. This study did observe that the difference in mean faecal coliform concentration in lettuce at different farm sites was not significant. This contrasts the findings of an earlier study in peri-urban Kumasi, Ghana by Tiimub *et al.* (2012), who observed significant differences in the faecal coliform counts in lettuce grown at different farm sites. Tiimub *et al.* (2012), contended that the differences in bacterial loads observed, could be attributed to different sources of irrigation water used to raise the respective vegetable farms at the different locations.

Exposure to Contaminated Vegetable Hazards

The study found that all (100%) the respondents consumed some of the vegetables they produced. The laboratory results also showed that contamination levels of faecal coliform bacteria on cabbage ranged from 6.65 ± 0.02mpn/g to 9.01 ± 0.05mpn/g whilst that of tomato was 3.23 ± 0.02mpn/g to 9.01 ± 0.05mpn/g. The implication of this is that, farmers' consumption of contaminated vegetables could potentially expose them to pathogenic microbial contamination. Table 2 shows that majority (61.0%) of the respondents were highly exposed to the hazard of microbial infection because they consumed on-farm vegetables more than four times in a week and in most instances in the uncooked or raw form. Also, it was observed during the field work that respondents hardly wore any protective clothing as they went about their daily activities. The results of the survey imply that, at least producers consumed some of the vegetables each day of the week which makes them highly exposed to possible health risks associated with the consumption of such contaminated vegetables.

During the focus group discussions, participants indicated that they consume some of the vegetables they produced. A discussant from Abesim had this to say:

I consume some of the vegetables I produce together with my families. At least I save some money because I do not buy from the market. (Male respondent, Abesim, Fieldwork, 2017)

Another indicated:

We do not only produce for the market, we also produce to feed our family, even though we sell much of what we produce. (Female respondent, Mensakrom)

Table 2. Location of respondents and frequency of vegetable consumption

Location of respondents	Frequency of vegetable consumption by farmers per week					Total
	Occasionally	Once	Two times	Three times	Four times and above	
Abesim	4.9%	4.9%	2.4%	14.6%	39.0%	65.9%
Mensakrom		2.4%	4.9%	4.9%	22.0%	34.1%
Total	4.9%	7.3%	7.3%	19.5%	61.0%	100.0%

Source: Authors' Fieldwork, (2017)

With regards to spatial variation of exposure to bacteria contamination, 39% of farmers from the peri-urban community (Abesim) and 22% of those at Mensakrom, the rural community, consumed some of their produce more than four times in a week respectively. This means that consumption of own produce was higher among the peri-urban farmers than among their rural counterparts. The implication of the results is that, majority of producers at the peri-urban community (Abesim) may be exposed to the risk of microbial infections than those at the rural community (Mensakrom).

Table 3 shows that, of all the respondents, majority (63.4%) of them were engaged in the production of exotic vegetables (cabbage) with the rest (36.6%) engaged in the production of traditional vegetables (tomatoes). Similarly, in terms of the spatial spread, majority (48.8%) engaged in the production of exotic vegetables, were located at the peri-urban community with 14.6% located in the rural community. However, in the rural community, there were more farmers (19.5%) engaged in the production of traditional vegetables than their counterparts (17%) in the peri-urban community.

The farmers claimed that, production of the local vegetable (tomato) is labour intensive as compared to the cultivation of cabbage. This could possibly account for the high number of farmers engaged in the production of exotic vegetables. With regards, to the spatial variation in producers, the large number of exotic vegetable farmers at the peri-urban area may be partly due to their proximity to Sunyani the regional capital, and the associated increasing demand for exotic vegetables especially, cabbage which is used mostly in the preparation of salad. It was also observed from the analysis that, all the respondents at Mensakrom were within the economically active population. This could also be responsible for the high number of farmers in that location that were engaged in the production of labour intensive traditional vegetables.

Table 3. Type of vegetables produced

Location of Respondents	Type of vegetables Produced	
	Exotic	Traditional
Abesim	(20) 74.1%	(7) 25.9%
Mensakrom	(6) 42.9%	(8) 57.1%
Total	(26) 63.4%	(15) 36.6%

Source: Authors' Fieldwork, (2017)

Table 4. Producers and the frequency of vegetable consumption

Type of Producers	Frequency of vegetable consumption by farmers					Total
	Occasionally	Once	Two times	Three times	Four times and above	
Exotic	2.4% (1)	4.9% (2)	4.9% (2)	12.2% (5)	39.0% (16)	63.4% (26)
Traditional	2.4% (1)	2.4% (1)	2.4% (1)	7.3% (3)	22.0% (9)	36.6% (15)
Total	4.9% (2)	7.3% (3)	7.3% (3)	19.5% (8)	61.0% (25)	100.0% (41)

Source: Authors' Fieldwork, (2017)

Table 4 shows that, majority of exotic producers (51.2%) consumed their own produce more than three times in a week whilst traditional vegetable producers who consumed same number of times of their own produce in a week, constituted 29.3%. This suggests more exotic vegetable farmers were exposed to microbial contamination than those who cultivated traditional vegetables.

From Table 1, the maximum faecal coliform recorded on both cabbage and tomato were the same (9.01 ± 0.05 mpn/g). However, the maximum E. *coli* bacteria was recorded on cabbage (6.65 ± 0.02/g). This result strengthens the findings that exotic vegetable farmers were much more exposed to pathogenic microbial hazards from contaminated on-farm vegetables through their consumption of the vegetables than their counterparts engaged in the production of traditional vegetables.

Susceptibility of On-Farm Vegetable Contamination

This study sought to examine farmers' perception on the bacterial quality of on-farm vegetables produced in rural and peri-urban areas in the Sunyani Municipality. The outcome of the survey (Table 5) shows that, 87.8% of the respondents disagreed that vegetables they produced were contaminated with bacteria. These were distributed as 63.4% and 24.4% in the peri-urban and rural locations respectively. A chi-square test of the association between the responses of farmers and their respective locations as shown in Table 5 indicates their response was statistically significant ($p<0.05$). Thus, farmers' perception of the bacteria quality of on-farm vegetables had an association with their location.

This survey outcome contrasts the results of the laboratory analysis of vegetables sampled from the study communities which indicates that farmers perception on the quality of vegetables were very low. Similarly, Antwi-Agyei *et al.* (2016) in their study of vegetable farmers in Accra observed that the farmer's perception on the health risks of contaminated vegetables were negative or low.

The laboratory analysis revealed that on-farm vegetables in the study areas were contaminated with both faecal coliform and E. *coli* bacteria. The contamination levels were higher and above the WHO and ICMSF recommended standards. This is evident from the The laboratory results showed that two cabbage samples from Abesim (peri-urban) tested positive for E. *coli* while only one sample from Mensakrom (rural) was positive for E. *coli* bacteria. Moreover, the maximum (6.65 ± 0.02/g) concentration level was recorded at Abesim. This results shows that farmers at the peri-urban community may be highly susceptible to pathogenic microbial infection from the consumption of cabbage than farmers at Mensakrom when consumed uncooked. Again, it is worthy to note that in terms of tomato, all samples

Table 5. Farmers perception of on-farm vegetable quality and chi-square test results

Statement	Farmers perception of on-farm vegetable quality			Total	Chi-square	Asymp. Sig. (2-sided)
	Response	Abesim (Peri-urban)	Mensakrom (Rural)			
The vegetables I produced are contaminated by bacteria	Agree	2.4% (1)	9.8% (4)	12.2% (5)	5.324	.021
	Disagree	63.4% (26)	24.4% (10)	87.8% (36)		

Source: Authors' Fieldwork, (2017)

from Mensakrom were positive for E. *coli* bacteria whiles two samples from Abesim tested positive. The maximum (4.77 ± 0.16/g) concentration levels was recorded at Mensakrom. This result suggests that consumers at the rural community may be more susceptible to pathogenic microbial hazards from tomato consumption than those from the peri-urban community when consume raw.

From the foregoing discussion, it can be concluded that, farmers in the study communities are susceptible to pathogenic microbial infection because of their low level of knowledge on the bacterial quality of vegetables they produced.

The outcome of the chi-square test (Table 6) shows that association between age and farmers' perception of bacterial quality of vegetables was not statistically significant ($p>0.05$).

The results suggest that age of farmers and their perception on bacterial quality of on-farm vegetables were independent of each other. This study's result contrasts that of Owusu *et al.* (2012), which reported that there was some relationship between age and the perception of farmers on health-related risks of untreated wastewater used for irrigation. The result of the chi-square test as presented in Table 7 shows that the relationship between educational level and farmers' perception on bacterial quality of on-farm vegetables was not statistically significant.

The result implies that educational level and farmers' perception were independent of each other. This result corroborates the findings of Okunlola and Ofuya (2010), who observed in their study of Nigeria that there was no statistically significant association between education of farmers and their use of plant extracts to control pests. It however, contrasts that of Kabir and Rainis (2012), whose study in Bangladesh found that education significantly influence farmers perceived effects of pesticide use on the environment.

Table 6. Age and farmers' perception on vegetable quality and chi-square test results

Age of Respondents	Farmers perception on vegetable consumption by bacteria		Chi-square value	Asymp. Sig. (2-sided)
	Disagree	Agree		
25 – 35	7	1		
36 – 45	16	1		
46 – 55	9	2	13.851a	0.310
55 and above	4	1		
Total	36	5		

Source: Authors' Fieldwork, (2017)

Table 7. Educational and farmers' perception on vegetable quality and chi-square results

Educational level of Respondents	Farmers perception on vegetable consumption by bacteria		Chi-square value	Asymp. Sig. (2-sided)
	Disagree	Agree		
None	4	0		
Basic	21	2		
Secondary	10	3	12.382a	0.416
Tertiary	1	0		
Total	36	5		

Source: Authors' Fieldwork, (2017)

With regards to the susceptibility of producers, exotic producers may be more susceptible to bacterial risks of contaminated vegetables than traditional producers. The analyses of the laboratory data showed that the level of faecal coliforms in cabbage samples tested were generally higher than that of tomatoes (Table 1). Even in situations where *E. coli* was detected in cabbage samples, their contamination levels were higher than levels recorded in tomatoes samples tested. The outcome of the focus group discussions indicates that, most of the respondents (16) ate some of the vegetables fresh without cooking and this could make them susceptible to pathogenic infections. A farmer said that:

We consume the tomatoes without cooking. The work on the farm is tedious and enormous and so less time is needed in preparing food. Sometimes we slice the tomatoes to make it faster. (Female respondent, Mensakrom, Fieldwork, 2017)

One of the parameters for assessing the susceptibility of farmers to bacterial contamination in the study was their health conditions. During the focus group discussions, farmers' health effects of consuming contaminated vegetables was explored. The objective was to assess whether farmers suffer diseases such as diarrhoea and typhoid fever due to their consumption of contaminated vegetables from their farms. Some of the farmers admitted that they suffer from these diseases occasionally. Interestingly, most of the participants from both the rural community (Mensakrom) and the peri-urban community (Abesim) said otherwise. A farmer remarked that:

We eat some of the vegetables we produce. Since we do not fall sick, it means they are of good quality. (Male respondent, Mensakrom)

Another respondent indicated:

I don't remember when I last went to the hospital. (Male respondent, Abesim)

This assertion by the farmers may be as a result of their low level of education which may affect their ability to access information on the risks of consuming contaminated vegetables and the lack of knowledge on the bacterial quality of on-farm vegetables in the study area. It may also imply that the farmers have built immunity to the diseases associated with vegetable contamination.

Mitigation of On-Farm Microbial Contamination Risks

Previous studies have reported high levels of microbial contamination of on-farm vegetables in Ghana (Abass *et al.*, 2016; Antwi-Agyei *et al.*, 2015; Tiimub *et al.*, 2012). It is therefore, important for farmers to be aware of the risks through regular testing of their vegetables and possibly the quality of water they use for irrigation. Unfortunately, all the respondents (100%) in the study communities do not conduct tests to check the quality of the vegetables they produced. The respondents had no knowledge of the microbial quality of vegetables they produced. This may be due to their lack of knowledge on bacterial contamination of on-farm vegetables or the non-availability of resources to conduct such tests. Judging by the low educational level of the farmers, they are unable to acquire information particularly from the print media which is usually in the English language.

Another means of mitigating on-farm microbial risk infection is to cease irrigation at least three days before harvesting is done. However, the respondents were of the view that, consumers demand vegetables which are fresh on the market. They therefore irrigate till the vegetables are harvested just to attract better prices. A discussant had this to say:

Consumers look out for fresh cabbages on sale. I therefore irrigated till the day I harvest my produce. When the vegetables are not fresh I do not get good price from the buyers (Male respondent, Abesim, Fieldwork, 2017)

The survey result suggests that farmers in both communities had no strategies to cope, adapt or mitigate the risk of bacterial infection from the consumption of contaminated vegetables. At the time of the study, an Agricultural Extension Officer was assigned to each of the broad farming area to assist farmers within the catchment area. They provided education on agronomic practices including the application of pesticides and insecticides. However, information on bacterial and microbial quality of vegetables produced was absent in their discussions with the farmers.

CONCLUSION AND RECOMMENDATIONS

This study sought to assess bacterial quality of on-farm vegetables in rural and peri-urban location and farmers' differential vulnerability to the risks of bacterial infections in rural and peri-urban locations within the Sunyani Municipality. Samples of cabbage and tomatoes were collected and analysed at the laboratory. A survey was also conducted to gather primary data from vegetable farmers in the Municipality. The outcome of the study showed that on-farm vegetables in the study area were contaminated above the WHO and ICMSF standards with slight variation from one location to the other. This poses great danger to both producers and consumers of vegetables without proper decontamination of the vegetables. Again, it was observed that farmers' vulnerability to bacterial contamination risks varied between rural and peri-urban locations within the Municipality. The results showed that, majority of producers at the peri-urban community frequently consume vegetables produced and may be more vulnerable to the risk of microbial infections than those at the rural community. In the same vein, exotic producers were may be vulnerable to the risks of bacterial contamination than traditional producers. It was also found that farmers perception on the bacterial quality of vegetables produces were negative. Age and the educational level of farmers had no association with their perceptions. The study recommends that the quality of both on-farm vegetables and the water used to irrigate them in the study area should be regularly monitored by the Crops Research Institute of the CSIR and the Environmental Protection Agency in order to assess their microbial contamination levels and initiate appropriate mitigation measures to deal with possible health risks and build the resilience of farmers. Also, vegetable farmers in the study area should also be educated on the health and safety of vegetables by the Agricultural Extension Officers in the Municipality

REFERENCES

Abass, K., Ganle, J. K., & Adaborna, E. (2015). Coliform contamination of peri-urban grown vegetables and potential public health risks: Evidence from Kumasi, Ghana. *Journal of Community Health*, *41*(2), 392–397. doi:10.100710900-015-0109-y PMID:26512013

Abass, K., Ganle, J. K., & Afriyie, K. (2016). The germs are not harmful: Health risk perceptions among consumers of peri-urban grown vegetables in Kumasi, Ghana. *GeoJournal*, *84*(4), 1–15. doi:10.100710708-016-9747-6

Abbam, T., Amoako, J. F., Dash, J., & Padmadas, S. S. (2018). Spatiotemporal variations in rainfall and temperature in Ghana over the twentieth century, 1900–2014. *Earth and Space Science (Hoboken, N.J.)*, *5*(4), 120–132. doi:10.1002/2017EA000327

Aboagye, D., Adu-Prah, S., & Dumedah, G. (2018). Assessing social vulnerability to biophysical hazards in the Kumasi metropolis, Ghana. *GeoJournal*, *83*(6), 1285–1299. doi:10.100710708-017-9833-4

Aboagye, D., Adu-Prah, S., & Owusu-Sekyere, E. (2019). Exposures to multiple biophysical stressors and response capacities of riparian communities in Ghana. *GeoJournal*, 1–14.

Ackerson, N. O. B., & Awuah, E. (2012). Microbial risk assessment of urban agricultural farming: A case study on Kwame Nkrumah University of Science and Technology campus, Kumasi, Ghana. *IACSIT International Journal of Engineering and Technology*, *2*(3), 356–363.

Adetunde, L. A., Sackey, I., Dombirl, D. D., & Mariama, Z. W. (2015). Potential links between irrigation water microbiological quality and fresh vegetables quality in Upper East Region of Ghana. *Annual Research & Review in Biology*, *6*(6), 347–354. doi:10.9734/ARRB/2015/8273

Akrong, M. O., Ampofo, J. A., & Danso, S. K. A. (2012). The quality and health implications of urban irrigation water used for vegetable production in the Accra Metropolis. *Journal of Environmental Protection*, *3*(11), 1509–1518. doi:10.4236/jep.2012.311167

American Public Health Association (APHA). (1992). *Standard Methods for the Examination of Water and Wastewater* (18th ed.). APHA.

Amoah, P., Drechsel, P., & Abaidoo, R. C. (2005). Irrigated urban vegetable production in Ghana: Sources of pathogen contamination and health risk elimination. *Irrigation and Drainage*, *54*(S1), 49–61. doi:10.1002/ird.185

Amoah, P., Drechsel, P., Abaidoo, R. C., & Henseler, M. (2007). Irrigated urban vegetable production in Ghana: Microbiological contamination in farms and markets and associated consumer risk groups. *Journal of Water and Health*, *5*(3), 455–466. doi:10.2166/wh.2007.041 PMID:17878560

Anon. (1994). The Microbiology of Water 1994: Part 1-Drinking Water. Reports on Public Health and Medical subjects, No. 71. Methods for the Examination of Water and Associated Materials. London: HMSO.

Antwi-Agyei, P., Cairncross, S., Peasey, A., Price, V., Bruce, J., Baker, K., Moe, C., Ampofo, J., Armah, G. and Ensink, J. (2015). A farm to fork risk assessment for the use of wastewater in agriculture in Accra, Ghana. *PLoS ONE*, *10*(11), 1-19. e0142346. doi:10.1371/journal.pone.0142346

Asiedu, B., Adetola, J., & Kissi, I. O. (2017). Aquaculture in troubled climate: Farmers' perception of climate change and their adaptation. *Cogent Food & Agriculture*, *3*(1), 1–16. doi:10.1080/23311932.2 017.1296400

Becker, M. H., & Maiman, L. A. (1975). Socio-behavioral determinants of compliance with health and medical care recommendations. *Medical Care*, *13*(1), 10–24. doi:10.1097/00005650-197501000-00002 PMID:1089182

Birkmann, J., Cardona, O. D., Carreño, M. L., Barbat, A. H., Pelling, M., Schneiderbauer, S., Kienberger, S., Keiler, M., Alexander, D., Zeil, P., & Welle, T. (2013). Framing vulnerability, risk and societal responses: The MOVE framework. *Natural Hazards*, *67*(2), 193–211. doi:10.100711069-013-0558-5

Cobbina, S. J., Kotochi, M. C., Korese, J. K., & Akrong, M. O. (2013). Microbial contamination in vegetables at the farm gate due to irrigation with wastewater in the Tamale Metropolis of Northern Ghana. *Journal of Environmental Protection*, *4*(07), 676–682. doi:10.4236/jep.2013.47078

Doe, E. O., Awua, A. K., & Larbi, D. K. (2016). Microbial quality monitoring of water from a lake associated with varying human activity. *International Journal of Health Sciences*, *4*(1), 160–165.

Eigenbrod, C., & Gruda, N. (2015). Urban vegetable for food security in cities. A review. *Agronomy for Sustainable Development*, *35*(2), 483–498. doi:10.100713593-014-0273-y

European Union (EU). (2015). *Final report summary - MOVE (methods for the improvement of vulnerability assessment in Europe)*. Retrieved on May, 19, 2017 from https://cordis.europa.eu/result/rcn/55194_en.html

FAO. (1997). Quality control of wastewater for irrigated crop production. FAO.

FAO. (2011). *Database collection of the Food and Agriculture Organization of the United Nations*. Retrieved on June 11 2017 from http://faostat.fao.org/site/354/default.aspx

Ghana Statistical Service. (2014). *2010 Population and Housing Census, District Analytical Report: Sunyani Municipality*. Available at: http://www.statsghana.gov.gh/docfiles/2010phc/2010_POPULATION_AND_HOUSING_CENSUS_FINAL_RESULSTS.pdf

Ghana Statistical Service (GSS), Noguchi Memorial Institute for Medical Research (NMIMR), and ORC Macro. (2004). *Ghana Demographic and Health Survey 2003*. GSS, NMIMR, and ORC Macro.

Hussaini, I. D., Aliyu, B., Bassi, A. A., Abubakar, S. I., & Aminu, M. (2013). Assessment of health risks associated with wastewater irrigation in Yola Adamawa State, Nigeria. *International Journal of Water Resources and Environmental Engineering*, *5*(1), 54–66.

Keraita & Cofie. (2014). Irrigation and Soil Fertility Management Practices. In Irrigated urban vegetable production in Ghana: Characteristics, benefits and risk mitigation (2nd ed.). International Water Management Institute (IWMI). doi:10.5337/2014.219

Mara, D., & Cairncross, S. (1989). *Guidelines for the Safe Use of Water and Excreta in Agriculture and Aquaculture Measures for Public Health Protection*. World Health Organization.

Ndiaye, M. L., Niang, S., Pfeifer, H. R., Peduzzi, R., Tonolla, M., & Dieng, Y. (2011). Effect of irrigation water and processing on the microbial quality of lettuces produced and sold on markets in Dakar (Senegal). *Irrigation and Drainage*, *60*(4), 509–517. doi:10.1002/ird.590

Ndunda, E. N., & Mungatana, E. D. (2013). Determinants of farmers' choice of innovative risk reduction interventions to wastewater-irrigated agriculture. *African Journal of Agricultural Research*, *8*(1), 119–128.

Sharma, S., & Prasad, F. M. (2009). Accumulation of lead and cadmium in soil and vegetable crops along major highways in Agra (India). *Journal of Chemistry*, *74*, 1174–1183.

Shuval, H. I. (1993). Investigation of typhoid fever and cholera transmission by raw wastewater irrigation in Santiago, Chile. *Water Science and Technology*, *27*(3/4), 167–174. doi:10.2166/wst.1993.0341

Silverman, A. I., Akrong, M. O., Amoah, P., Drechsel, P., & Nelson, K. L. (2013). Quantification of human norovirus GII, human adenovirus, and faecal indicator organisms in wastewater used for irrigation in Accra, Ghana. *Journal of Water and Health*, *11*(3), 473–488. doi:10.2166/wh.2013.025 PMID:23981876

Slavin, J. L., & Lloyd, B. (2012). Health benefits of fruits and vegetables. *Advances in Nutrition*, *3*(4), 506–516. doi:10.3945/an.112.002154 PMID:22797986

Tiimub, B. M., Kuffour, R. A., & Kwarteng, A. S. (2012). Bacterial contamination levels of lettuce irrigated with waste water in the Kumasi Metropolis. *Journal of Biology, Agriculture and Healthcare*, *2*(10), 116–127.

Valin, H., Sands, R. D., van der Mensbrugghe, D., Nelson, G. C., Ahammad, H., Blanc, E., Bodirsky, B., Fujimori, S., Hasegawa, T., Havlik, P., Heyhoe, E., Kyle, P., Mason-D'Croz, D., Paltsev, S., Rolinski, S., Tabeau, A., van Meijl, H., von Lampe, M., & Willenbockel, D. (2014). The future of food demand: Understanding differences in global economic models. *Journal of Agricultural Economics*, *45*(1), 51–67. doi:10.1111/agec.12089

Weldezgina, D., & Muleta, D. (2016). Bacteriological contaminants of some fresh vegetables irrigated with Awetu River in Jimma town, Southwestern Ethiopia. *Advances in Biology*, *20*(16), 1–11. doi:10.1155/2016/1526764

Winpenny, J., Heinz, I., Koo-Oshima, S., Salgot, M., Collado, J., Hernandex, F., & Torricelli, R. (2010). The Wealth of Waste: The Economics of Wastewater Use in Agriculture. Rome, Italy: Food and Agriculture Organization of the United Nations. *Water Reports*, *35*. Retrieved October 10, 2018, from https://www.fao.org/docrep/012/i1629e/i1629e.pdf

Chapter 15
Japanese Stone Gardens:
Diversity, Sustainability, and Consumerism

Simon Regin Paxton
Komazawa University, Japan

ABSTRACT

It has been suggested that the modern Japanese garden contains a wide variety of garden types. While some scholars have acknowledged the diversity of modern Japanese gardens, recent developments in Japanese stone gardens, known as karesansui, have gone largely unnoticed. Preconceived notions of karesansui do not encapsulate the true diversity which exists today. Moreover, the general public has tended to exoticize karesansui. Scholarly work on karesansui has, however, dispelled many of the myths and misrepresentations related to these gardens. In this chapter, the author will extend previous research and shed light on recent developments in karesansui and the myths that surround them. This chapter will examine karesansui from several perspectives: diversity, sustainability, and finally, from the perspective of consumerism.

INTRODUCTION

It has been suggested that the "modern Japanese garden contains a wide variety of garden types, from a 6.5 by 7 centimeter tabletop Zen gardening kit to large national park" (Watanabe, 2012, p. 340). While some scholars have acknowledged the diversity of modern Japanese gardens, recent developments in Japanese stone gardens, known as *karesansui*, have gone largely unnoticed. Preconceived notions of *karesansui* gardens do not encapsulate the true diversity which exists today.

Japanese gardens, including *karesansui*, have attracted a lot of attention from the general public, although, many generalist books have tended to exoticize the subject. In particular, the fascination with and romanticization of *karesansui* gardens has probably been the result of widespread interest in Japanese aesthetics, as well as the close association of *karesansui* gardens and Zen Buddhism, which has been glamorized in books such as Eugen Herrigel's, *Zen in the Art of Archery* (1978). Scholarly work on *karesansui* has, however, dispelled many of the myths and misrepresentations related to these gardens. For example, Yamada (2009) notes that Zen gardens were essentially reinvented during the post-war

DOI: 10.4018/978-1-7998-8996-0.ch015

period as a strategic means of restoring Japan's international credibility. In fact, Yamada (2009) also closely scrutinized the association with *karesansui* and Zen and argues that *karesansui* gardens such as *Ryōanji* illustrate the "magic mirror effect". That is, such gardens are a reflection of the ideal image of how Japanese people perceive themselves. In other words, Yamada views such gardens as symbolic of cultural nationalism.

In terms of modern designs of *karesansui* gardens, the work of *karesansui* garden designers such as Mirei Shigemori (1896—1975) and Shunmyō Masuno (1953—Present) has been well documented (See, for example Tschumi (2020); and Locher (2012), respectively). Given the immense popularity of these gardens, it is surprising that more recent developments in *karesansui* gardens have gone largely overlooked. However, as Girot (in Tschumi, 2020) notes, "we have ignored most developments in Japanese garden design over the past century" (p. 11). Indeed, this is particularly true in the case of *karesansui*.

In this chapter the author will seek to shed some light on recent developments in *karesansui* gardens by exploring different approaches to these gardens, and the motives which propel them. Contemporary *karesansui* gardens include a wide variety of garden designs, from avant-garde style *karesansui* gardens to digital *karesansui* gardens; from *karesansui* gardens designed with sustainability in mind to the adaptation of the easily recognizable patterns of *karesansui* gardens to a wide variety of consumer products. By examining some of the more recent developments in *karesansui* gardens, this chapter will show how more recent *karesansui* gardens overturn many preconceived ideas about these gardens.

This chapter will examine *karesansui* gardens from several perspectives: diversity, sustainability, and, finally, from the perspective of consumerism. This chapter is presented in three sections. The first section examines the history and characteristics of *karesansui*. Second, the development of new types of *karesansui* gardens are explored. Finally, *karesansui* are examined from the perspective of consumerism, and various modes of packaging *karesansui* for modern-day consumption are explored.

BACKGROUND

It is appropriate to begin with the most basic of all questions: What is a *karesansui* garden? The Oxford English dictionary defines a garden as, "a piece of ground, usually enclosed, where flowers, fruit, or vegetables are cultivated". Clearly, *karesansui* gardens, which are mostly comprised of rocks, gravel or sand, do not fit neatly within this definition. In fact, *karesansui* gardens have a number of characteristics which make them different from other types of gardens, even other types of Japanese gardens. The term *karesansui*, which is commonly used to describe Japanese stone gardens provides us with some idea of the history and nature of these style of gardens.

The term *karesansui* (枯山水) is comprised of the Chinese characters *kare* (枯) from the verb *kareru* (枯れる), which is typically translated as "wither", and *sansui* (山水), which comes from the Chinese term "*Shansui*", originally pronounced "*senzui*", and which literally means "mountain-water" but represents "nature" or "landscape" (Nakagawara, 2004). A term related to "*sansui*" is "*sansuiga*" (山水画), which refers to landscape paintings which were thought to have influenced the development of *karesansui*. An interesting discussion on *sansuiga* and their influence on *karesansui* can be found in Sekinishi (2006).

Rocks have been the objects of worship in a variety of cultures. In Japan, this has also been true, so much so that there is even a word for "rock worship" called *gansekisūhai* (岩石崇拝). The term *iwakura* (岩倉 or 磐座) is also used for specific rocks which are thought to have holy properties, and such rocks are often adorned by a *shimenawa* (しめ縄), a sacred type of rope. It is important to note that while separate to *karesansui* gardens, *suiseki* (水石), the art of stone appreciation, is a closely related art form. *Suiseki*, however, contrary to *karesansui* gardens, typically involves the displaying of a single rock in a similar manner to the way a *bonsai* plant is displayed. This respect and acknowledgement of rocks as elements of nature which possess a holy element suggests why *karesansui* gardens are not such an anomaly after all.

CHARACTERISTICS OF *KARESANSUI*

First, while many gardens are designed to be enjoyed by walking through them, *karesansui* gardens are enjoyed by viewing them from indoors, or from outside the garden itself. Ueda (1998), author of "The Inner Harmony of the Japanese House", notes that gardens are something to be seen, and not a places to exercise or relax in. While it is not a completely foreign concept to not walk in a garden, this idea of a garden which cannot be walked in is particularly evident in *karesansui* gardens because the act of walking in the garden will upset the carefully raked stones effectively reducing or destroying the beauty of the garden.

Second, water is a principal feature of many types of gardens, including Japanese gardens. In fact, including water as a feature in a garden requires tremendous planning and work to supply the garden with water. On the other hand, *karesansui* gardens avoid this difficulty by not using water at all. In this sense, these types of gardens are very different from the popular pond-based style of garden known as *chisen teien* (池泉庭園).

Third, unlike other types of gardens where plants and vegetation grow naturally, gravel and materials used in *karesansui* gardens will not experience such changes (Koren, 2000). While the background scenery, referred to as *shakkei* (借景), of *karesansui* gardens is important, the impact of seasonal changes on *karesansui* gardens is much more subtle, and therefore they are sometimes thought of as all-season gardens. Finally, Koren (2000) makes the interesting point that, every time a sand/gravel garden is re-raked it is "anew, yet not really different from how it was before" (p.31). Koren (2000) further notes that there are no exact guides for the raking of *karesansui* gardens making them unique each time, and over time the gardens are raked by different people making it a type of communal creation.

THE HISTORICAL ORIGINS OF *KARESANSUI*

Historical accounts of *karesansui* frequently cite the Muromachi era (1336-1573) as the starting point. However, reference to stone placement in gardens in Japan's seminal text on gardening *Sakuteiki* (作庭記), published in the latter part of the Heian era (794—1185), suggests that *karesansui* gardens were in existence much earlier (Matsumoto, 1980). *Sakuteiki* was a book of secret techniques for creating Japanese gardens and was only officially given its title in the Edo period (1603—1868), in which it was referred to as *senzaihishō* (前栽秘抄). In the "Anonymous Secret Teachings" section of Takei and Keane's translation of *Sakuteiki*, they provide the following translation of a section related to *karesansui*: "If there are stones that "flee," then there should be stones that "chase" after; if there are stones that lean, then there should be those that lend support; if some proceed then other should acquiesce; if some face up, then others should face down; and to balance with stones that stand upright there should also be those that recline" (p. 183). This is significant from a historical perspective, because it provides evidence of the existence of *karesansui* gardens in the Heian era, despite many scholars treating *karesansui* as a phenomenon of the Muromachi period.

Nevertheless, the Muromachi era is significant and remains the period most closely associated with *karesansui*. It is true that one of the main reasons that gardening skills developed so much during the Muromachi period was because of the rise of gardening specialists known as *niwamono* (庭者) and *sansui kawaramono* (山水河原者). Note that *kawaramono* was a discriminatory term used for the class known as *eta* or *burakumin*.

Ashikaga Yoshimasa (足利義政) (1436—1490), the eighth shogun during the Muromachi period, was a lover of rare gardens. He was particularly fond of the gardening philosophy of Musō Kokushi (夢窓国師) as well as one of Musō's companions Zenami (善阿弥), a member of the *kawaramono* class who had a significant impact on gardening culture of the time. Musō Soseki (夢窓疎石) (1275—1351), also known as Musō Kokushi, was a Rinzai Buddhist monk gardener who was active between the latter part of the Kamakura period through till early Muromachi era. For more on Musō Soseki and his gardens, see: Davidson (2006). He designed several gardens in Zen temples, including gardens at *Tenryūji* (天龍寺) and *Eihōji* (永保寺) and is believed to be the creator of what is regarded as the first *karesansui* garden in Japan, the *saihōjikôinzan* (西芳寺洪隠山). Thus, Musō Soseki is frequently referred to as the "father of Zen gardens".

In the Edo period (1604—1868), *karesansui* gardens spread beyond Zen Buddhist temples to a variety of different locations and residences of people from various classes, including the imperial Palace, samurai family residences, and townsfolk. The artist, tea ceremony master and garden designer, Kobori Enshū (小堀遠州) (1579—1647) is said to have contributed greatly to this spread of *karesansui* gardens during this period. Perhaps Kobori Enshū's greatest influence was on the Tea Ceremony in which his school was referred to as *Enshū ryū* (遠州流). It was during this period that *karesansui* gardens became more full scale in size, and, arguably, became more accepted by the general public.

The Meiji era (1868—1912) saw a decline in *karesansui* gardens. During this period, *Ueji ryū* (植治流) style gardens, which are a modern style of garden which emphasize the natural state of nature, became particularly popular during this time and continued through to the Shōwa period (1926—1989). While this period saw a decline in *karesansui* gardens, there was a revival of these gardens by the gardener Shigemori Mirei (1896-1975), who designed gardens such as the *karesansui* garden at *Tōfukuji* (東福寺). Shigemori strived to not only revive Japanese stone gardens but emphasized both the design of the garden as well as its conceptual elements.

Karesansui gardens are traditionally divided into two main categories: *zenkishiki* (前期式), which refers to *karesansui* gardens from the *Azuchimomoyama* period (安土桃山時代) (1573—1603); and, *kōkishiki* (後期式), which refers to *karesansui* gardens after that period. According to Miyamoto (1998), *zenshiki karesansui* gardens are constructed on the slope of a mountain, while *kōkishiki karesansui* gardens are constructed on the flat ground of temple premises. As we will see, however, these categories do not take into account more recent developments in design.

DIVERSITY OF *KARESANSUI*

Unfortunately, categorizing Japanese gardens does not encapsulate their true diversity. For example, Watanabe (2012) notes that public parks, many of which were daimyo gardens, are often neglected in discussions on Japanese gardens. Furthermore, Watanabe (2012) notes that there are many other types

Figure 1. Photo of karesansui garden at Ryōanji in Kyoto, Japan
Source: From author's collection

of gardens which tend to be overlooked, such as Isamu Noguchi's gardens, which incorporate sculptures and sculptural elements, and Japanese colonial gardens in Asia. The purpose here is not to suggest that more recent *karesansui* gardens are better. What is abundantly clear, however, is that *karesansui* gardens are far more diverse than most people realize, and their ability to easily adapt to any environment may make them a more significant feature in future living spaces and art work. This is an important point and one that merits further elucidation through an exploration of some *karesansui* gardens.

Ryōanji

The most acclaimed *karesansui* garden in the world is the UNESCO world heritage listed garden, *Daiunzan Ryōanji* (大雲山龍安寺) in Kyoto, which was established in 1450 by Hosokawa Katsumoto with the garden presumably being created around 1499. For most people, the image, as seen in Figure 1, is the image that first comes to mind when they think of *karesansui* gardens. It is representative of the quiet contemplative space that *karesansui* gardens have become so well known for.

However, there are a number of more modern style *karesansui* gardens that, while retaining some traditional elements, are distinctly different in appearance.

Kishiwada-jō teien

No discussion of contemporary *karesansui* gardens would be complete without considering the creative contributions of Mirei Shigemori (1896-1975). Shigemori was born in Yoshikawa in Okayama and studied painting at the Tokyo Fine Arts School. Shigemori was a prolific writer publishing on the history of *ikebana* as well as Japanese gardens and other topics. It was not until 1933 that Shigemori commenced designing gardens, and he is responsible for creating several gardens in the *karesansui* genre, including

Figure 2. Photo of Kishiwada-jō Teien
Source: Adobe Stock

the garden at Kishiwada castle in Osaka (See Figure 2). His gardens have an avant-garde flavor that make them distinctly different from traditional *karesansui* gardens. He achieved this by adding graphic elements such as lines, planes of colors, or shapes and fonts (Tschumi, 2003). Tschumi (2003) argues that Shigemori was strongly influenced by the work of the Russian painter Wassily Kadinsky (1866—1944), particularly his book "Point and Line to Plane," originally written in 1926.

Tschumi (2020), makes two significant observations about Shigemori. Firstly, Shigemori regarded garden design as art, and he was opposed to simply imitating past garden designs. Secondly, Shigemori believed that contemporary Japanese gardens lacked spirituality. His garden creations certainly seem to be consistent with this line of thinking. The *karesansui* garden at Kishiwada-jō in Osaka has fused elements of *karesansui* and modern art to create a modern looking *karesansui* garden. The sharp angles and straight lines of this garden are quite striking and are very different from *karesansui* gardens such as *Ryōanji*. The layout in this particular garden was inspired by the eight-fold battle camp strategic formation created by the Chinese strategy planner Zhuge Liang (181-234) from the Romance of the Three Kingdoms.

Canadian Embassy

Shunmyō Masuno (1953—Present) is an award-winning garden designer and Zen priest at Kenkōji temple in Yokohama city, Japan. He is a prolific author and designer having designed many gardens, including the dry landscape garden at the Canadian embassy (See Figure 3). According to Shunmyō Masuno's website, he is "a modern-day Zen priest who through this art form, strives to express his spiritual self."

Figure 3. Photo of dry landscape garden at Canadian Embassy in Tokyo
Source: Photo courtesy of John Lander Photography

Once again, here is a *karesansui* style garden which is in contrast to what most people envisage when they think of *karesansui* gardens. The use of rocks in this particular garden represents the grandeur of the Canadian landscape. The main idea behind this design was to create a space for people who visit or work at the embassy to contemplate their roles in connecting Canada and Japan.

There have been further developments in *karesansui* gardens, and perhaps one of the more recent and interesting developments is how *karesansui* gardens are being designed with sustainability in mind.

SUSTAINABILITY AND *KARESANSUI*

Given the ongoing fears of global warming and environmental degradation, as well as increased interest in creating sustainable living spaces, it is perhaps unsurprising that some recent developments in *karesansui* gardens have been motivated or influenced in some way by sustainable landscape design.

Sustainable landscape design strategies are becoming an important part of urban landscapes and many of the characteristics of *karesansui* gardens are compatible with the principles of sustainability. A sustainable garden is designed to be both attractive and in harmony with the environment.

Many of the features of *karesansui* gardens which are compatible with sustainability are self-evident. Perhaps the most obvious characteristic is that *karesansui* gardens conserve water. Moreover, they require very little maintenance. Gardens by their very nature change over time. Therefore, old gardens do not maintain their form over time. In the case of *karesansui* gardens, however, they do maintain their form to a much greater extent. Mental health has been included in the UN Sustainable Development Goals

(SDGs), and as *karesansui* gardens promote reflection and introspection, it could be argued that they are beneficial to mental health.

Vancouver International Airport

One recent example of a *karesansui* garden being motivated by sustainability is in Canada. The Vancouver Japanese Garden Association is building a *karesansui* garden at the West exit of the Vancouver International Airport. An article regarding this garden be found in the Vancouver *Shinpo*. The article discusses the difficulties associated with building a pond in a garden. For example, to create an artificial pond generally requires electricity to power a pump and may require chemicals to keep the water clean making it detrimental to the environment. On the other hand, a *karesansui* garden uses stones and sand to simulate the effect of water, making them much kinder to the environment. The article also mentions some other advantages, such as the low cost.

Nishinaka Glass *Karesansui*

Another example, and one which incorporates the use of recycled glass, is the glass *karesansui* garden "Eternal Affinity" (referred to as *Tsunagaru* in Japanese) at the entrance to the Honen-in Temple (法然院) in Kyoto, and created by the glass artist Nishinaka Yukito (西中千人) (1964—Present). Nishinaka has been influenced by *kintsugi* (金継ぎ) and *yobitsugi* (呼継ぎ) pottery work and adopted a similar approach to his glass work. He took this passion for glass and applied it to *karesansui* gardens. While sunlight on rocks used in *karesansui* gardens causes the rocks to glow and cast shadows, sunlight penetrates glass creating a very different effect. Nishinaka uses recycled glass in which remnants of the original piece of glass from bottles and so forth remain and are noticeable.

Another advantage of *karesansui* gardens is that they present an opportunity to engage with visual culture on a daily basis. Gardens function to sustain us aesthetically, but most of us do not have the good fortune to visit popular *karesansui* gardens on a regular basis. However, *karesansui* gardens can be made more accessible by incorporating them into our everyday environment. The author's interest in *karesansui* gardens from the perspective of everyday aesthetics has been influenced by the work of Saitō Yuriko, who defines everyday aesthetics as, aesthetics of objects, environments, and situations from our everyday life.

Entrance (*Genkan*)

While it is generally accepted that an aesthetic experience can be had with almost any object, discussions on aesthetics tend to focus on art. For example, in the case of *karesansui* gardens, gardens like *Ryōanji* are regarded as quintessential dry landscape gardens, and discussions of aesthetics tend to focus on them. However, it is possible for people even living in Japan to never visit *Ryōanji* or any of the other eminent *karesansui* gardens. As Victor Papanek said, "it is possible to avoid theatre and ballet, never to visit museums or galleries, to spurn poetry and literature and to switch off radio concerts. Buildings, settlements and the daily tools of living however, form a web of visual impressions that are inescapable" (Papanek, 1995, p.174).

The practical nature of *karesansui* gardens as well as their compatibility with sustainable design makes them particularly suitable for our everyday environment, and it could be argued that this can cre-

Figure 4. Photo of the glass karesansui garden Tsunagaru by Nishinaka Yukito
Source: Photo courtesy of Nishinaka Yukito

ate an aesthetic experience. Duncum exclaimed that, "ordinary everyday aesthetic experiences are more significant than experiences of high art in forming and informing one's identity and view of the world beyond personal experience" (Duncum, 1999, p. 246).

Once again, Nishinaka pushes boundaries with his glass *karesansui* garden, which has been used as an entrance (*genkan*) to a living space. It is arguably a symbiosis of contemporary and traditional garden design, and one which is a visible demonstration of the new as a tangible realization of innovation and change, while remaining representative of the past.

CONSUMERISM AND *KARESANSUI*

The distinct and iconic patterns used in *karesansui* gardens are immediately recognizable and identifiable as symbolic of traditional Japanese culture. Therefore, the popular swirls and patterns of *karesansui* gardens have been incorporated into a number of consumer products, including jigsaw puzzles, games, confectionary, and even desserts. Indeed, there are a number of consumer items which have been produced for that purpose. For example, miniature *karesansui* kits, which allow people to make small *karesansui* gardens and can be used as ornamentation, are available for purchase. These miniature kits can also be purchased in "capsules" from popular children's *gacha gacha* gift-dispensing machines. The close association between *karesansui* gardens and traditional Japan means that the *karesansui* patterns can be easily used to create a sense of "Japaneseness", which may be useful in marketing products to both domestic and foreign markets.

Figure 5. Photo of Nishinaka's glass Karesansui garden entrance
Source: Photo courtesy of Nishinaka Yukito

One interesting way in which *karesansui* has been packaged for consumers is in the form of a boardgame (See Figure 6). The *karesansui* boardgame is simply titled "枯山水"(*karesansui*) and was released in 2014 by the company New Games Order, LLC, and is the creation of the boardgame designer Yamada Kūta (山田空太). Japanese and English language versions of the game are available. The board game includes individual boards, which are used to create individual *karesansui* gardens; cards with different patterns of raked gravel and moss; cards with important historical figures related to *karesansui*, including *karesansui* garden designers Shigemori Mirei and Musō Soseki, and which can be used to acquire special privileges in the game; and, five different types of rocks which can be used to place on top of the cards to create their own *karesansui* gardens. The object of the game is to create the best *karesansui* garden by scoring the most points. There are several rules in relation to how one can acquire points. The release of new editions of this game and the difficulty of purchasing secondhand versions of the game suggests that the game is quite popular.

Why is this important? Is it another example of what Yamada termed the "magic mirror"? Is it a way for Japanese people to reaffirm their sense of identity? In what way does eating a dessert with a

Figure 6. Photo of karesansui boardgame
Source: From author's collection

pattern resembling something from a *karesansui* garden elevate the consumer's experience, particularly when this apparently has no impact on the taste. Is it in times of gastronomic bliss such as this when a Japanese consumer reaffirms to themselves that, *nihonjin ni umarete yokatta*. Literally, "I am glad I was born Japanese". It would be difficult to not concede that there is an element of that here, and one that savvy marketers are unashamedly exploiting.

As Cunningham (2016) acknowledged, *karesansui* gardens will have different meanings to different people. While the narrative which these gardens are built on has an unmistakable element of cultural nationalism, and one that scholarly criticism has aptly revealed, the multitude of forms in which these gardens appear suggests that they will continue to survive. Indeed, for the observer of *karesansui* gardens, in their many forms, these gardens may conjure up a feeling of nostalgic sentimentalism, reaffirm one's sense of cultural heritage, or simply provide a break from the grind of daily life. What is apparent is that, regardless of the various forms these gardens take and individual observer's experiences, these gardens are here to stay.

CONCLUSION

In this chapter, recent developments in *karesansui* gardens have been explored. Clearly, long-held preconceived notions of *karesansui* gardens no longer accurately depict the true diversity of these gardens. *Karesansui* gardens today are taking on greater meaning as they fit ideally within the context of sustainability, and present opportunities to utilize this form of garden as a practical means to engage with visual art in our everyday life.

This chapter contributes to our knowledge of these gardens and extends existing scholarship which questions previous attempts to categorize Japanese gardens. While traditional style *karesansui* gardens will no doubt continue to function as tourist destinations and glimpses into traditional Japanese culture, and while new approaches to these gardens may not reach similar heights of popularity as gardens such as at *Ryōanji*, these gardens will inevitably continue to evolve and appear in various forms in the future. That is to say, they will continue to function as a creative force in our society, and recent developments will continue to push the boundaries of garden design and create exciting possibilities for future living spaces.

REFERENCES

Cunningham, E. (2016). Cultivating enlightenment: The manifold meaning of Japanese Zen gardens. *Education about. Asia, 21*(3), 32–36.

Davidson, A. K. (2006). *A Zen life in nature: Musō Soseki in his gardens*. Center for Japanese Studies, University of Michigan.

Duncum, P. (1999). Case for an art education of everyday experiences. *Studies in Art Education, 40*(4), 295–311. doi:10.2307/1320551

Herrigel, E. (1978). *Zen in the art of archery*. Random House Inc.

Koren, L. (2000). *Gardens of gravel and sand*. Stone Bridge Press.

Locher, M. (2012). *Zen gardens: The complete works of Shunmyo Masuno, Japan's leading garden designer*. Tuttle publishing.

Mansfield, S. (2009). *Japanese stone gardens: Origins, meaning, form*. Tuttle Publishing.

Matsumoto. (1980). *Karesansui no hanashi: Mizu nakushite mizu wo tanoshimu niwa* [About *karesansui*: Enjoying gardens without water]. Heibonsha.

Miyamoto, K. (1998). *Zusetsu: Nihon teien no mikata* [Illustrated guide to Japanese gardens]. Gakugei Shuppansha.

Nakagawara, C. (2004). The Japanese garden for the mind: The 'Bliss' of paradise transcended. *Stanford Journal of East Asian Affairs., 4*(2), 83–102.

Papanek, V. (1995). *The green imperative: Natural design for the real world*. Thames and Hudson.

Saito, Y. (2007). *Everyday aesthetics*. Oxford University Press. doi:10.1093/acprof:oso/9780199278350.001.0001

Sekinishi, T. (2006). *Karesansui no haikan kôsei ni miru sansuiga no eikyô ni kansuru kōsatsu* [Investigation of the influence of *sansuiga* on *karesansui*]. Academic Press.

Slawson, D. A. (2013). *Secret techniques in the art of Japanese gardens*. Kodansha US Publishing.

Takei, J., & Keane, M. P. (2008). *Sakuteiki, visions of the Japanese garden: A modern translation of Japan's gardening classic*. Tuttle Publishing.

Tschumi, C. (2020). *Mirei Shigemori—rebel in the garden*. Birkhäuser. doi:10.1515/9783035621761

Ueda, A., Nitschke, G., & Suloway, S. (1998). *The inner harmony of the Japanese House*. Kodansha International.

Watanabe, T. (2012). The Modern Japanese Garden. In *Since Meiji: Perspectives on the Japanese Visual Arts, 1868-2000* (pp. 340-360). University of Hawai'i Press. Retrieved April 28, 2021, from https://www.jstor.org/stable/j.ctt6wqh84.19

Yamada, S., & Hartman, E. (2020). *Shots in the dark: Japan, Zen, and the west*. The University of Chicago Press.

Chapter 16
Art and Environment Seen Through the Lens of Politics in Japan

Mika Markus Merviö
https://orcid.org/0000-0001-7771-5280
Kibi International University, Japan

ABSTRACT

This chapter analyses the changing diversity of politically and socially relevant interpretations, ideas, and opinions concerning the environment in Japan with a special reference given to visual arts and how environment and environmental issues have been dealt with in Japanese art. Politics involves constant reinterpretation and rearranging of everything around us. Art and especially visual images allow endless opportunities for reconstruction and to be used, recomposed, and combined rhizomatically. The art world in Japan has been directly influenced by the changing political and social context, but within the art community in Japan, power relations have deeply influenced what ideas reach the public. Politicization of environment and art has a long history in Japan as environment and art both are an indispensable part of Japanese society and history. Shaping the interpretations for them has always had profound political and social significance. Moreover, the digitizing and internet together have made the spreading of images much easier and have made visual images more important than ever.

Rhizomatical Reconstruction of the World as a Method to Understand Better Japanese Art, Environment and Politics

This chapter analyses the changing diversity of politically and socially relevant interpretations, ideas and opinions concerning the environment in Japan with a special reference given to visual arts and how environment and environmental issues have been dealt with in Japanese art. Politics involves constant reinterpretation and rearranging of everything around us. Art and especially visual images allow endless

DOI: 10.4018/978-1-7998-8996-0.ch016

opportunities for reconstruction and to be used, recomposed and combined *rhizomatically*. Art world in Japan has been directly influenced by the changing political and social context, but within the art community in Japan power relations have deeply influenced what ideas reach the public.

Our understanding of the environment and art are always guided by our values. In short, environment and art play a highly political or ideological role in all parts of the world, although the exact nature and quality of that ideology is often rather evasive to the people themselves. Treating environment and art separately from their value- basis and great variety of histories and traditions have often meant compartmentalizing them as separate areas that can conveniently analysed as independent scholarly fields such as 'environmental science' for the environment or 'aesthetics' or 'art history' for the art. However, I firmly believe that understanding the close relationships between these areas of life is more important than ever if we want to alleviate the problems facing our societies and the environment. For instance, in the case of climate crisis the environmental issues and politics are closely linked and the understanding of the whole issue is related to visual and textual representation of this complex issue in science, media and art. Japan also provides very interesting case study due to its uniquely unique art scene and natural environment and rather unique political/ social system.

'Rhizomatic' itself is a philosophical (and botanics) concept nowadays associated especially with the work of Gilles Deleuze and Félix Guattari, used to describe theory and research that allows for multiple, non-hierarchical entry and exit points in data representation and interpretation. Rhizome comes originally from the Greek *rhizôma* (ρίζωμα) meaning "mass of roots" and from *rhizóō* (ριζόω) "cause to strike root" (Thesaurus Linguae Graecae online). Rhizome is often taken as being synonymous with "root." In botany, a rhizome is a plant structure that grows underground and has both roots (commonly, the part that grows down into the ground) and shoots (commonly, the part that grows up through the ground). In their book *A Thousand Plateaus: Capitalism and Schizophrenia* (in English 1987; original in French 1980: *Mille Plateaux*) Deleuze and Guattari use extensively the metaphor of trees and plants to illustrate the branching and natural growth taking place simultaniously in many places and often in ways that may appear surprising. They apply this metaphor to such fields as environment, culture, state machinery, language and mathematics. In their book of more than 600 pages they go through the long journey of history and culture and use plenty of references to philosophy and different natural sciences, but also to art, literature and phychoanalysis. They criticise heavily simple binary thinking that they claim to find easily in science and then proceed to develop something like an alternative theory that would be applicable to most areas of life. In the beginning of the book there are also references to postmodernism and it seems that the English translation of the book was first largely interpreted as a contribution to that discourse that at time was going strong. It did not help that the book was written for the French academic audience and the style did not open easily to those who expected more disciplined type of presentation of theory. In short, the book itself is contructed in a rather rhizomatic way and unfortunately has not been given much attention in recent years although its general approach could prove to be very useful to analyse in a more holistic manner what is going on in the world.

Furthermore, the development of Internet has provided one more example of rhizomatic growth that already requires a major effort to reinterpret the ways that knowledge is organised, distributed and dispersed in societies. A rhizome just like the Internet does not really start from anywhere or end anywhere; it grows from everywhere, and has no real center. Rhizomes may have some origin or seed if we want to trace back to the origin, but the 'seed' does not give very good idea what will be the future of growth in a constantly changing environment. Deleuze and Guattari also use rhizome to refer to a map that must be produced or constructed, is always detachable, connectable, reversable, and modifiable, with multiple entrances and exits, with its lines of flight. The tracings are what must be transferred onto the maps and not the reverse (Deleuze and Guattari 1987: 48-49). This certainly sounds like the Internet. The Internet already has proved to be very important for science, politics, art, economy and most everything and links and muddles issues in myriad of new ways. For instance, the digital currencies that consume huge volumes of energy through their 'mining' have become yet another environmental problem on the top of their social, cultural, political and economic consequences.

However, the concept of 'rhizomatic' was also used by Walter Bendix Schönflies Benjamin in the early 20th century to analyse the rapidly diversifying variety of art forms (such as cinema and photography) in modern society and how they connected with changing politics, ideology and society. He combined in innovative ways elements of German idealism, Romanticism. Frankfurt School Marxism and Jewish mysticism. In art theory the concept of 'rhizomatic' is still often associated with the thinking of Walter Benjamin and his key essays on the ways that art and the role of artists are changing in modern time. Walter Benjamin argued in his 'The Work of Art in the Age of Mechanical Reproduction' that the role of art in society was fundamentally changing because art had become modified through mechanical reproduction that changed the role of artists as well as other art professionals and museums and – most importantly – the role of public. Benjamin saw mostly in positive light and as a potentially liberating phenomenon the weakening of the 'aura' of the original art work. He was particularly happy to welcome the reproduction of works of art and the art of cinema and photography, all these developments making works of art widely available and introducing new ways of interpreting and appreciating art (Benjamin 1969).

In his words: "that which withers in the age of mechanical reproduction is the aura of the work of art. This is a symptomatic process whose significance points beyond the realm of art. One might generalize by saying: the technique of reproduction detaches the reproduced object from the domain of tradition. By making many reproductions it substitutes a plurality of copies for a unique existence. And in permitting the reproduction to meet the beholder or listener in his own particular situation, it reactivates the object reproduced. These two processes lead to a tremendous shattering of tradition" (Benjamin 1969).

Furthermore, Walter Benjamin believed that these changes taking place with the production and forms of art would help to bring art to public, to masses, and further weaken the elitist role that art had played when much of art had been created for private collections of wealthy patrons. Benjamin also analysed the 'cult-value' and 'exhibition-value' of art. For him the 'cult-value' was closely associated with the pre-modern societies but for him the 'exhibition-value' of art had plenty of liberating and potential and served as a power of demystification (Benjamin 1969).

Walter Benjamin believed that art would have a major social impact when it would reach in new innovative ways masses and in his later writings he comes often very close to the idea that politics will take the place of religion as a basis of aesthetics, if we see politics as an emencipatory force. This all would, of course, depend on the ability of artists to create art that would appeal to the masses and that the art would not be contaminated by such powers as advertising or economic dependence (for instance in movie industry). However, Walter Benjamin tried flee the Nazis and committed suicide in 1940 on the French-Spanish border and did not see how the potential of art was not used in ways that he had so much wished. The loss of the 'aura' of traditional art was something that Benjamin understood well but believed that the new art would replace it and people would start thinking about the authenticity of art and traditions as well as cultural values in new ways and that art would be far more important in the future societies. In his essay 'The Author as Producer' (1970 [written in 1934]) Walter Benjamin argued against well-meaning political correctness and was in favour of experimentation and technical innovation such as experimenting with form towards the functional transformation of the organization of production. Benjamin conceived a meltdown of forms, of machines and apparatuses into an molten steam or incandescent liquid mass from which the new forms will be cast', which can be read as his idea or technique how rhizomatic art can be created (Benjamin 1970).

Nowadays, Internet increasingly offers material and data in 'rhizomatic' manner and, in particular, has great potential for visual presentation and visual arts. My work largely uses interpretative methods to study art, politics and environment and, therefore, 'rhizomatic' appears to be a suitable term to make clear that in this kind of research there is need to organise research with multiple, non-hierarchical entry and exit points, reflected also in data representation and interpretation.

This chapter shows that politicization of environment and art has a long history in Japan as environment and art both are an indispensable part of Japanese society and history. Shaping the interpretations for them has always had profound political and social significance. Of course, the changing language relating to 'environment' and 'art' is just one area to analyse how they have been understood in Japan. Moreover, in the present social context the digitizing and Internet together have made the spreading of images much easier and have made visual images more important than ever as a tool to interpret and understand the world. However, the narrative of Japanese modernization and the history of Japanese nationalism and capitalism are quite unique since they are based on rather different preceding traditions and values that have continued to influence Japanese society. Especially in such areas as the environment and art it is very important to be able to analyse them in their specific social contexts and I believe that 'rhizomatic' and interpretative approaches provide some of the best tools to penetrate beyond the surface and catch something essential about the environment and art within the Japanese culture and society.

Art Influencing and Reflecting the Japanese Society and its Value Systems

Japanese society has created new ideas and representations of reality that reflect the actual environment and changes in society. Furthermore, both the environmental thinking and art have served agents of change. The environmental conditions in Japan are markedly varied and quite different from any other places and it is no wonder that the nature/environment as well as animals have frequently been understood and depicted in ways that are quite different from the other centres of global culture.

In particular, the Japanese art has been able to depict nature and animals with great sensitivity and warm humour. Sensitivity to nature plays a role in such key concepts of Japanese aesthetics as *wabi, sabi, yûgen* as well as *mononoaware*. These developments helped the Japanese visual art to diverge ever further from the Chinese models, where the symbols and political & philosophical ideas continued to play a far more important role. Meanwhile in China, the link between literature/ poetry and Chinese painting remained strong and the role of the Imperial Court continued to play a leading role in cultural sphere. However, in Japan the *bushi* (warrior class) were essentially soldiers rather than artists, historians or philosophers, which in many cases provided more freedom to the artists who largely represented other social classes. During the Edo period the Tokugawa bakufu (government) never established as effective censorship and control in terms of aesthetic and ideological ideas as the Chinese imperial court exerted on Chinese society and art scene.

On the other hand, the sophistication of the *bushi* varied a lot according to their individual talent and aptitude to cultural matters. There are also such cases as Kobori Enshū (小堀 遠州, 1579 – 1647) who was a notable Japanese artist and aristocrat during the reign of the founder of Tokugawa bakufu,Tokugawa Ieyasu. He was one of the leading artists of the time in arts ranging from painting to poetry, ikebana flower arrangement, tea ceremony, architecture and garden design. In his later career he was appointed to teach tea ceremony to the third shôgun of Tokugawa line, Tokugawa Iemitsu, and in this role his influence of designing tea houses became very important. The Enshû Sadô School of Tea Ceremony is still active and the present Grand Master in 13th generation is Kobori Sôjitsu (for more, the homepage of Enshûryû sadô), Kobori Enshū's own fief was in Ômi prefecture (present-day Shiga), but his major castle and garden works were in such places as the Katsura Imperial Villa (Kyôto), (Nijô Castle (Kyôto), Fushimi Castle (Kyôto), Sentô Imperial Castle (for retired emperors in Kyôto), Kôdaiji (Kyôto), Ôsaka Castle, Sunpu Castle (Shizuoka), Nagoya Castle, Bitchû Matsuyama Castle (Bitchû Takahashi) and Tôkoen garden (Okayama) (for more on Kobori Enshû, the homepage of Kobori Enshû kenshûkai/ Honoring Association). Most of these still survive but, for instance, the Tôkoen garden in Okayama that was created for the Ikeda daimyô clan during the time of Ikeda Tadakatsu (1602-1632) survived in its original form until 2014 when it demolished to make room to a condominium. The city or people of Okayama and Japanese state or media did next to nothing stop this brutal act of barbarism and today there is nothing reminding of this great garden that existed only few years ago. The family who owned the garden could not take care of the property and in the absence of authorities having any interest to save the aesthetically and historically very important site they sold it to real estate company. That tells a very sad story about the present value system in such places as Okayama city and Japan, in general. About the demise of this site there is very little information on Internet but in English there is small article by Casey Baseel with some photograps (Baseel 2014).

The freedom from overly dogmatic artistic traditions is particularly visible in Japanese animal art. The Chinese animal art focused in particular on phoenixes (or the Chinese firebird, hôô, 鳳凰), dragons, tigers and elegant horses. Japanese art borrowed all these themes and developed them further with often rather liberal interpretations of Chinese symbolism. The Chinese list of favoured animals is full of religious, cosmic and political symbolism and when the Chinese added new animals, such as monkeys and Mandarin ducks these were animals with clear references to the human world. On the contrary, Japanese art, including some of the early masterpieces has remarkable biodiversity present. For instance, there are very nice early Japanese works of humble bulls (or bullocks), which certainly were not high on the list of Chinese art themes. The bull art continued to flourish in Japan and especially in Edo period the bulls were increasingly accompanied by equally humble peasants. Similarly. Japanese artists had more freedom to experiment with animal art and observe real animal behaviour and such artists as Itō Jakuchū (伊藤 若冲, 1716 –1800) used that freedom well.

The symbolic values of animals can easily be manipulated for political purposes and in the Japanese case, just like in Europe with the family coat of arms, the symbolic value of any symbols related to families or individuals was not left unused in arts, as I will in this chapter illustrate with the case of tigers and Katô Kiyomasa ("Toranosuke"). In other words, there are artists that show a keen eye to observe and respect the beauty of nature. Then there are many others who do not care to study the nature more carefully and are content to follow the established conventions and symbolic representations without adding their own interpretations.

Matsuoka (2020) in his book 'Flowers, Birds, Wind, and Moon. The Phenomenology of Nature in Japanese Culture' is seeking a synthesis of the long narrative of Japanese culture and analyses different symbols of nature and the ways those have been used in Japanese culture. Matsuoka argues that the ancient Japanese seem to have contented themselves with brief excursions to pick a few grasses and flowers and never studied or described them closely. He goes on to say that there is no Japanese poetry that closely describes flowers in terms of how they look or how they grow. Japanese culture was not developing a rigorous examination of natural forms in a similar way with Europe and that certainly is reflected in Japanese arts (Matsuoka 2020: 166-169). However, Matsuoka in his book demonstrates that Japanese culture has created a wealth of narratives of natural phenomena that are not easily approachable by science. With cultural interpretations of natural world we are always dealing primarily with human perception and cognition of nature rather than nature itself and that science surely has its limits when it tries to approach natural phenomena.

As for the tigers, traditionally in China, the tiger was depicted among bamboo and was often paired with a dragon amidst swirling clouds. Together the two images represented opposite principles in nature. The much-feared tiger was associated with hunger, wind, and termination of life–symbolic of the autumn. In contrast, the dragon could create mist and rain, and was thus associated with spring and new beginnings. However, in Japan tiger gradually started to be depicted in different ways, and in increasingly realistic manner by different schools and individual artists when the artists finally had a chance to see real tigers instead of foreign depictions of tigers or tiger pelts. However, in Japan representations of tigers were first closely tied to the symbolism of Chinese origin while a shift to more realistic approach was triggered by the Japanese experiences of real tigers in Korea during the Hideyoshi's campaigns in Korea. The new symbolism where tiger hunting became associated with Japanese military campaigns in Korea was largely due to popular visual representations of tiger hunting in Korea personified by Katô Kiyomasa and legends about his tiger hunting in Korea and his military exploits at home and in Korea.

Kkachi horangi (까치호랑이) is a prominent Korean genre of *minhwa* (folk art) that depicts magpies and tigers. "Foolish tiger" represents authority and the aristocratic *yangban* class, while the dignified magpie represents the common people, the overwhelming majority of Korean people. This symbolism was never introduced to Japan where the whole idea of openly criticizing the military would have been a very brave act, indeed. Moreover, the magpies (Pica pica) that are very common in Korea can be found only in Saga prefecture in Japan and most Japanese people are not familiar with them or with their behavior unlike in Korea where in large cities they are still among the most visible birds to be seen. However, Korea was the place where the Japanese people discovered the real living tigers during the Japanese invasions of Korea (1592–1598) lauched by Toyotomi Hideyoshi (1537-1598). Hideyoshi planned to conquer not only Korean peninsula, but also the Ming China and then India and the Philippines. After the initial success in Korea the Ming China under emperor Wanli understood the existential threat and wanted to stop the Japanese attack before it would reach China. The all-out Ming support to Korean forces and the continued well-organized Korean naval operations turned the Hideyoshi's campaigns into a stalemate. However, Hideyoshi believed in final victory until his death in 1598 and only after his death the new governing Council of Five Elders decided to withdraw from Korea (Cf. Turnbull 2002).

The Japanese Korean campaign used largely *ashigaru* light infantry of mostly peasant origin to fight in European style by firing in formation their arquebuses (long guns). In command of the Japanese forces were Konishi Yukinaga, who relied more on diplomatic than military skills and Katô Kiyomasa, who was known in Japan as *Toranosuke* ("the young tiger", Toranosuke being his original name and meaning literally 'tiger's assistant') and to the Koreans as the "devil general" on the account of his brutality and ferocity. During the Korean campaigns, Katô Kiyomasa was widely known to have hunted tigers for sport, using just a spear, and later presented the pelts to Hideyoshi. Some versions of the story says he was in fact hunting tigers to catch them alive, in order to bring their meat to Hideyoshi, as he thought it would improve his lord's health, but later, the tigers were killed because of the lack of food for his men (NHK 2008). Japanese artists have immortalized Katô Kiyomasa's tiger hunt by an endless number of versions. Kakejiku scrolls on silk and paper were popular throughout the Edo period and well until the end of Pacific war. In the 19th century the theme became particularly popular in ukiyo-e and often the scene was depicted in triptychs with bright colours and action.

For his legendary fame it became important that Katō became remembered as one of the "Seven Spears of Shizugatake", a group of seven samurais serving as mounted bodyguards of Hideyoshi who distinguished themselves in the decisive combat that handed to Hideyoshi the succession of Oda Nobunaga at the Battle of Shizugatake in 1583, where samurai had fought one another, and where especially Katō demonstrated his skills with a cross-bladed spear with great effect by cutting so many men, whose severed and salted heads were thereafter tied to a stalk of green bamboo and carried by one of Katō's attendants into battle. After Hideyoshi gained control of Japan, most of the "Seven Spears" were promoted to Daimyô and Katô continued to serve Hideyoshi faithfully, but after Hideyoshi's dealth Katô would soon be betrayed by Hideypshi's son Toyotomi Hideyori with the effect that Katö would switch along five other of the "Seven Spears" to the Tokugawa side. To settle old scores Katô used the opportunity to invade Konishi Yukinaga's lands and annex them to his own lands in Higo. Konishi Yukinaga remained loyal to Toyotomi Hideyori and was executed after the battle of Sekigahara, that decided Japan's future for the next centuries. Tokugawa Ieyasu never trusted Katô Kiyomasa and their difficult relationship is well-recorded also in Japanese visual arts. Katô died in 1611 when he fell ill while being asked to negotiate between Toyotomi Hideyori and Tokugawa Ieyasu. The sudden death was widely believed to be caused by poisoning by Tokugawa Ieyasu. Of course, the death was never investigated but the theme became even the subject of a much later Kabuki play that premiered in 1807, but due to continued government censorship at the time, the main character's name was slightly modified to Satô Masakiyo. In the play, Masakiyo was summoned to the shoguns's castle in Kyôto and offered a cup of wine, which he knew was poisoned but drank out of loyalty and while the lethal mix was slowly starting to affect the Kabuki actor continues to stay up trough several dramatic scenes (Ruth Chandler Williamson Gallery, Scripps College).

His son Katô Tadahiro inherited his lands, but the lands were confiscated by Tokugawa Iemitsu and Katô Tadahiro was exiled in 1632 for being suspected of lack of loyalty (Cf. Turnbull 2002). Then the Hosokawa clan became the Daimyô clan of what would become the present Kumamoto Prefecture. The history of Hosokawas in Kumamoto has continued to contemporary times when in 1983 the direct descendant Hosokawa Morihiro was elected the governor of Kumamoto and then went on to become the Prime Minister of Japan (1993-94). Also Hosokawa Morihiro's maternal grandfather, Konoe Fumimaro, served as the Prime Minister (1937-39 and 1940-41) providing yet another example of long narratives of political influence and relationships in Japan.

Katô Kiyomasa was known as a devoted follower of Nichiren Buddhism, a type of Buddhism closely associated with militarism and ultra-nationalism in Japan. Nichiren was a 13th century monk who preached especially against the Pure Land and Zen sects of Buddhism claiming that their erroneous teachings had caused a series of recent earthquakes, plagues and famines. He told that all other forms of Buddhism except his new sect should be banished, for they were false and were misleading the people. Nichiren also tried to use the threat of Mongol invasion in 1258-60 as a means to convince people that Japanese people had to convert to Nichiren Buddhism and abandon all other religions. Due to his hostility and narrowmindedness he angered the de facto head of shogunate at the time, Hôjô Tokiyori and was in 1271 condemned to death, but at the last moment the sentence was commuted and he was forced into exile, first to Izu and then to Sadô Island, where he wrote in 1272 his main work *Kaimokushō* ("The Opening of the Eyes"). The shogunate pardoned Nichiren and let him leave the exile as a result of Mongol embassies threatening again an invasion. The last years of his life he lived on Mount Minobu focusing on writing and suffering from bad health, dying in 1282 most likely of cancer of intestinal tract. His main support base was among the lower ranks of samurais in Kantô region and in the coming centuries the Nichiren sect provided a nationalist and belligerent alternative to those Japanese who were disillusioned with other religious sects and believed that Japan was the one and only chosen country of true Buddhism (see e.g. del Campana 2021; Kawabata 2003).

Nichiren Buddhism not only provided an alternative vision in terms of religion and politics but also went on to influence Japanese arts for centuries. However, the modern art establishment and museums in Japan have often been rather hesitant to pay attention to the influences of Nichiren Buddhism in Japanese visual arts. The first ever major exhibition of art of Nichiren Buddhism was organised in 2003 at the Tokyo National Museum in Ueno. That exhibition included pieces by the founders of the Rimpa School, Hon'ami Kôetsu (1558-1637) and Tawaraya Sôtatsu (died ca. 1643). Also represented were the Ogata brothers, designer and calligrapher Kôrin (1658-1716) and potter and painter Kenzan (1663-1743) who established the style of Rimpa in Japanese arts and provided an alternative especially to the Kanô School. That exhibition also included artworks by the ukiyo-e masters Katsushika Hokusai (1760-1849), Totoya Hokkei (1780-1850) and Torii Kiyomitsu II (1787-1868). Furthermore, art objects made by artists who were influenced by or were known to be devout adherents of the Lotus Sutra were on show in the exhibition, together with portraits of well-known followers including Katô Kiyomasa (1562-1611) and Oman-no-kata, a concubine of Tokugawa Ieyasu. (Kawabata 2003).

In that particular exhihition, one of the organising principles seemed to be the influence of the Lotus Sutra on particular pieces of art and secondly a known connection with Nichiren temples. However, it is rather problematic to equate Lotus Sutra with Nichiren Buddhism as this early Mahâyâna Buddhist text first was associated in Japan with the Tendai sect and is open to be interpreted in myriad of ways as it consists of charms and mantras (sacred chants) venerating the mystical and wondrous powers of eternal Buddha. However, something similar can be argued about the influences of Zen Buddhism as Japanese aesthetic ideas have often turned to mystery and contemplation. In the art history narratives quite correctly Zen Buddhism is usually seen to provide the most important inspiration of Japanese art traditions with Shintô following behind but the artistic influences of Nichiren Buddhism are less frequently traced, apparently for the shadows of ethnonationalism and intolerance that many people associate with Nichiren Buddhism.

In Japan, the Lotus Sutra certainly has been strongly associated with Nichiren but is could also be argued that Nichiren successfully hijacked the Lotus Sutra to serve his ideology and attempts to show that all other Buddhist sects had failed to understand the true Buddhism. Nichiren also largely ignored the parts of Lotus Sutra (especially part 14) which focuses on peace, compassion, gentleness and wisdom (for a good collection of Mahâyâna Buddhist texts in many languages, International Dunhuang Project). There is also a larger issue that Mahâyâna Buddhist texts were largely interpreted both in Japan and in China to replace or abandon the teachings and goals of Hīnayāna Buddhism and the ways of the Buddhist Elders. Nichiren went much further with this rift and declared himself and his Japanese followers the true representatives of Buddhism. However, it would be wrong to treat all followers of Nichiren Buddhism or all people who have turned to Lotus Sutra as rabid supporters of ethnocentrism or violence. Katô Kiyomasa is just one more person on the list of people who have used religion to justify violence, which certainly goes against the beliefs of the overwhelming majority of people following Buddhism now or in the long history of Buddhism. As for the Lotus Sutra, it represents particularly strong and beautiful poetry that can easily influence powerful and mystical visions of art.

In Katô Kiyomasa's case Nichiren Buddhism became an excuse to treat with vicious cruelty anyone that Katô Kiyomasa regarded as enemies of Nichiren Buddhism. That would cover most people in Japan and all people elsewhere but Katô Kiyomasa is remembered in particular for his violence against Koreans and Christians. His relations with his colleague and peer the Catholic Konishi were extremely unfriendly, to the extent that the two men almost never met during the campaign in Korea. The subsequent role of Katô in the developments that led to the execution of Konishi and annexation of his lands contributed to a campaign of terror against Christianity in Kyûshû. What would be Katô Kiyomasa's primary motives will always remain open to different interpretations. Katō's battle standard was a white pennant which carried a message alleged to be have been written by Nichiren himself reading *Namu Myōhō Renge Kyō* ("Hail to the Lotus of the Divine Law"). At the battle of Hondo, Amakusa Islands, Katô Kiyomasa ordered his men to cut open the bellies of all pregnant Christian women and cut off their infant's heads. Katô Kiyomasa's brutality especially against Koreans and Christians demonstrated an unusual form of ethnic and religious intolerance by Japanese standards at that time. The continued popularity of Katô Kiyomasa during the rising militarism in Japan in popular arts shows that that he would under sufficient circumstances become a suitable icon of toxic nationalism and terror. In 1910, Katô Kiyomasa was posthumously promoted to junior 3rd court rank (*jusanmi*, 従三位) illustrating that the Japanese government was not blind to his popularity at that time.

In contemporary popular culture Katō Kiyomasa is a character in such popular video games as Sengoku Musou Chronicle 2nd, Sengoku Musou 3 Empires, Sengoku Musou Moushoden 3, Sengoku Musou 3Z, Warriors Orochi 3 (British game), *Kessen*, *Kessen III*, *Samurai Warriors 3*, *Samurai Warriors 4*, Mōri Motonari: Chikai no Sanshi and *Age of Empires III*. He is also a playable character in *Pokémon Conquest* (*Pokémon + Nobunaga's Ambition* in Japan). It is notable that the contemporary game and, for instance, such Internet pages as the Samurai Games Wiki do not tell anything about the Katô Kiyomasa's war crimes in Korea and, instead, glorify his military victories and sanitise or praise his brutality (Samurai Games Wiki). There is a long history in Japan to produce dolls of Katô Kiyomasa with cute cat-like tigers, but the merchandise has in recent years been significantly diversified and as a result there are nowadays *anime* toys depicting Katô Kiyomasa and ranging from figurines to key holders, blankets and money pouches (Cf. search result on Hobby Search). In the light of Katô Kiyomasa's well-documented war crimes in Japan and Korea as well as his legacy as a tiger-slayer he does not appear to be the most suitable role model for modern children in Japan and abroad. One should not underestimate the importance of popular culture contributing to values and interpretations of history. There is little controversy among professional historians concerning the actual deeds and exceptional brutality of Katô Kiyomasa even if we take into consideration the standards of his time. However, most of the children growing up with games and toys do not become professional historians or start looking for more trustworthy sources. Outside Japan there have been recent controversies regarding the reinterpretation of such historical figures as Cristoffa Corombo (a Genoese navigator known in Italian as Cristoforo Colombo, in Spanish as Cristóbal Colón and in English as Christopher Columbus) or various slave owners whose reputations have been questioned and statues have been removed from public view. Writing narratives of historical events always includes interpretation and selection. Rewriting or reinterpreting the history of any individual or any text such as the significance of a piece of art always takes place in a new social context and has always potential to question the existing status quo or established 'truths'.

Edo Period and its Value Systems, Art and Ideology

The new regime that was created by the Tokugawa clan in Japan interpreted the lessons of Korean campaigns in a manner that Japan should abandon the world conquest and instead isolate politically and control strictly the *bushi* within Japan and make impossible all attempts to turn against the authority of the Tokugawa bakufu by perfecting such methods as *sankin kôtai*, alternate residence duty, where the feudal lords (daimyô) had to reside several months each year in the Tokugawa capital at Edo. When the lords returned to their fiefs, they were required to leave their wives and families in Edo. The inhabitants of towns and villages throughout the country were required to form *gonin-gumi* ("five-household groups"), or neighbourhood associations, to foster joint responsibility for tax payment, to prevent offenses against the laws of their overlords (which included banning and confiscating weapons from peasants), to provide one another with mutual assistance, and to keep a general watch on one another by making people collectively responsible for offenses in their group. Economic controls over peasants were further strengthened. They were strictly prohibited from buying, selling, or abandoning their land or from changing their occupation; minute restrictions were also placed on their attire, food, and housing. This system became the foundation of social system that Tokugawa bakufu controlled until the Meiji Restoration in 1868 (Cf. Encyclopedia Britannica, Bakuhan system). This was the type of feudal system that influenced all values systems and cultural as well as social ideas in Japan during this long period and has left its traces to subsequent Japanese value systems.

The conservatism of Japanese visual art in Edo period is closely related to the social system that by definition was designed to be stable and conservative. The old cultural traditions of high culture enjoyed the patronage of the upper classes and, therefore, social status and arts were closely connected. The rigid social order of Edo Period was based on rather narrowminded control of the Tokugawa Bakufu. While the central government was rather undeveloped and did not even try to fullfil anything resembling the functions of modern state, the Bakufu nevertheless did not want to see any open challenge to social order. Social rank determined everything especially within the ruling samurai class: the shape and size of residences (and gardens alike) were closely regulated, so were the colour and designs of clothing and even many small but symbolically significant minute details were strictly regulated, such as the the borders of tatami straw mats reserved to various ranks of officials in Edo castle. In other words, the social order and control had also a very strong aspect of visual symbolism. This meant that there was very little room left for individual choice or more precisely, it was risky to appear as disrespectful or too individualistic. As Nishiyama Matsunosuke points out, "knowing one's place" in Japanese feudal system did not only require everyone from avoiding rising above their place but also banned them from falling below one's status (Nishiyama 1997: 32).

In other words, political discourse could not be openly exercised through the means of art or any other means of free expression of ideas and the relative isolation of Japan as an island nation also prevented new and especially potentially subversive ideas from spreading. The realm of politics and Orthodox political discourse was reserved to a very small class of samurai and its top echelon. This class covered less than 7 percent of the population while the peasants officially were regarded as the second most important class but were kept closely politically and economically controlled by the samurai. The artisans and merchants (and those falling outside classes) were in the lowest position and certainly knew better than openly raising their voices against the system. The samurai class itself was divided over such issues as hereditary or family support to Tokugawa rulers (*fudai* group) and plain subjugation to the strongest faction after the battle of Sekigahara (*tozama* group). In economic terms the fundamentally untrustworthy *tozama* group emerged as victors and destabilized the whole system towards the end of Edo Period.

Ideological foundation was provided by official recognition of a few simple tenets of Neo-Conficianism. Japan did have in the beginning of Edo Period learned scholars such as Hayashi Razan, Fujiwara Seika and Ogyû Sorai who understood well the Chinese thought and the possibilities for social thought. However, the Bakufu was able to hijack the Neo-Confucian thought and by appointing some of the leading scholars to official roles it effectively established an official simplified state ideology that also substituted Buddhist religious thought (and the role of Buddhish temples) by a thought system which appeared to be rational compared with previous thought systems and still competing effectively with all relevant religious doctrines (Cf. Ooms 1984, 27-61). However, the Bakufu support was a kiss of death in terms of free discussion and development of anything resembling 'rational thought'.

However, most existing Japanese traditions and institutions adapted to new political and social realities. The mainstream Buddhist temples served their social roles without challenging the political authority. Zen Buddhism continued to be important among the *bushi* while espcially the Pure Land sects served well the rest of the population. Neo-Confucianism was primarily an ideology to legitimise the rule of the Tokugawa bakufu. For Nichiren sect there was a need to lay lower during the Edo period and learn a way to avoid antagonising others. The Lotus Sutra certainly was acceptable for most everyone in Japan. The isolation of Japan also meant that the *bakufu* simply eradicated Christianity as completely as it could and controlled all the exchanges with the rest of the world by allowing only small closely watched trading posts for the Dutch, Koreans and the Chinese. This seclusion meant that the risk of foreigners or foreign ideas was removed from the minds of many people until the reach of colonialism started to come closer to Japan in the nineteenth century. Meanwhile, Japan was divided between different Daimyô domains and even domestic travel was strictly controlled with pilgrimages to famous temples providing the most important exception. In other words, for most people the idea of Japanese culture or a common Japanese ideology as a monolith did not make much sense. It was only in the nineteenth century that Japanese nationalism and ethnocentrism started to take a form that is similar to that in other modernising societies of that time. It is no wonder that such historical figures as Katô Kiyomasa and Nichiren could become popular again and interpreted to support new brand of Japanese nationalism and imperialism, both something that had little room after the establishment of Edo bakufu which stood for strict separation of social classes and blind loyalty to military rule and hierarchy. As for the imperialism, Tokugawa rule and rigid seclusion policies were directly influenced by the ultimately failed military campaigns during Hideyoshi's relatively short rule and the preceding long period of Warring States. The Tokugawa rulers understood well that they could never subjugate by military or any other means the rest of the world or Asia but they could do that in Japan and at least end the wars and stay themselves alive and in power. However, they never trusted much the other Samurai clans and looked down upon all lower classes. This kind of social order could not foster strong notions of national unity or common culture.

During the Edo period there was little room left for alternative ways of expression in hight arts while in cities and among the wealthier peasants new art forms started to take place and were not regarded as important and as such a direct threat by the bakufu. *Toba-e* (鳥羽絵) in particular was successful during Edo period by using long scrolls to combined humorous images and texts to create narratives with a sarcastic sense. The name, origin and style derives from the 12th century artist-monk Toba Sôjô, but the style proliferated in the mid-Edo period and nowadays is often understood as a major influence behind Japanese *manga* and *anime*. Many of the *Ukiyo-e* artists also created works that come close to this genre as they are based on similar kind of humour and intended for a similar kind of group of ordinary people in growing cities. In past years there has been a significant increased in the number of museum exhibitions presenting *Toba-e* and taking seriously this art form. Of course, art combining images and text in a hurorous manner is often more easy to explain/ present to modern audiences than, for instance, religious art in a society that has largely serered its relations with past religious teachings.

In visual art the refined realm of aesthetic pleasure was the escape that was left open for all artists, especially among the new rich groups among merchant class where their tastes were less stringently controlled. For instance, the extravagance or Rimpa school tells much about this splendid escapism and how it relatively quickly became part of the mainstream, and even (part of) the upper classes could enjoy all the glitter, fancy details and exquisite craftsmanship that Rimpa offered, while few seemed to notice or care that exquisite beauty and impeccable taste easily risks rising above one's place. Both art and social thought easily lead to dangerous directions and the Edo high culture was quite a mine-field, but, of course, the elite also acquired the survival skills to make the best of situation. However, there are also a good number of cases where learned men ended up becoming boiled alive, crucified or otherwise losing their lives for expressing their thoughts too freely. This kind of situation made it very difficult to spread culture or ideas to all segments of population and, therefore, Japanese nationalism and the whole idea of common Japanese culture starts from rather unique situation when Japanese modernisation started from the top with Meiji Restoration.

State, Art and Environment in Modern Japan

Older religious ideas (those that often are connected with different varieties or sects of Shintô and Buddhism) about sanctity of nature and life – and inspiration for arts - are often ignored when modern ideological constructions of environment are created and reinforced. In Japan the traditional ideas of nature as a venerated object of awe have been gradually replaced by turning environment into a reserve of resources for the nation, nation state and corporations. The intersubjective practices in Japan have been nurtured to benefit those institutions that evolved with the modern state. There has been only very slow shift in the ideology to a more sustainable society where the welfare of the citizens and environment is the primary goal and especially the political and administrative institutions have been very reluctant to change the course although a significant part of the population, especially the young people, are alienated or disinterested about politics and political participation.

Most political parties in Japan have more or less represented this social model, which explains that even changes in government or within the LDP have not fundamentally changed the policy approach to such issues as environment or culture. Japan has been particularly slow to change legislation that would potentially erode the collusive relationships between politics and business. All this is very much based on the social values that were created with the modern state. In the following I am creating a narrative that binds together the state (politics), art and environment in modern Japan.

While he political elite invented new institutions of modern Japan during the Meiji Period it also created at the same time narratives of Japanese history and culture to suit the uses of new state and nationalism that supported it – a process which is rather typical for nation-states everywhere. However, the invention of traditions or narratives does not mean that they are all false or invented from a scratch. Instead, in Japan the old cultural traditions of the samurai class provided a perfect arsenal from which the political elite could choose the most suitable ones for the whole nation. The refined tastes of upper classes have served as a basis for artistic traditions that have been/ are officially (in particular by the Ministry of Education, Culture, Sports, Science and Technology and its predecessors) associated with the essence of Japanese art and culture. The modern Japanese state has presented the Japanese authentic cultural traditions as a proof of Japanese cultural superiority and, therefore, there has all along been a tendency also to protect the Japanese cultural traditions from foreign influences if those influences appeared to be harmful for Japanese traditions or question their right to live and flourish. *Nihonga* (Japanese style painting on silk or paper) was seen by the policy makers as more Japanese than *yôga* (Western painting), regardless of the theme of painting and without much of critical discussion whether *nihonga* really is that uniquely Japanese. After all, both Japanese *nihonga* and Western painting *(yôga)* during Meiji Period and afterwards were both deeply influenced by former foreign and Japanese art and by each other. There is also the fundamental issue of profound Chinese influence in Japanese cultural traditions, including all aspects of visual art.

Such modern Japanese concepts as *bunka* (culture, 文化), *bunmei* (civilization, 文明), *bijutsu* (fine arts, 美術) and geijutsu (artworks, 芸術) all have evolved under the influence of foreign ideas but still carry quite different ideas of culture and arts than, for instance, the similar concepts in the English language. The original Chinese connotation of anything cultural is the opposite of anything military and the idea is to value learning and written word as well as mental cultivation. The Japanese culture, of course, is measured by different standards than is the case in other cultures that don't share the cultural values and history of Japanese culture. In fact, the term *nihon bunka* (Japanese culture) was seldom used before the 1920s. Tessa Morris-Suzuki (1998: 64) points out that the earliest case of use of word *bunka* to refer to specific cultures that she has discovered was in 1854 about the peculiar customs of the Ainu.

'Culture' and 'art' were not understood to be policy priorities of governance or social life, yet, culture with remarkable diversity did flourish in Japan, although cultural theory did not have much use in a society which, after all, did not encourage critical discourse. However, there is a long history of using cultivation and cultural capital as a means to earn respect and to improve one's social standing/ status – and this applies also to both Japanese society under feudalism and modern Japan. In both cases the 'culture' and 'cultivation' are by definition rather elitist. However, the modern Japanese canon for being 'cultured' is very elusive and has plenty of room for individual choice and freedom. Moreover, especially with arts it seems like the very human nature directs artists to experiment which promotes dynamism and originality in artistic expression, even if the society around tries to control that expression.

'Culture' (*bunka*) still refers much to cultivation of mind and, therefore, depends much on individual choice. The housing and life-styles continue to shape the ways that individual Japanese people enjoy/ consume art. The term '*Bunka jûtaku*' (cultured house) actually was used in the 1930s to refer to modern suburban houses that included the Western amenities and fancy modern details (see e.g. Ozawa & Mizunuma 2006: 311, 319). One benchmark of public recognition of culture and arts have been also the various kinds of cultural awards and titles to leading representatives of Japanese culture that have proliferated in Japan from the beginning of Shôwa era. In other words, 'culture' in Japanese context can mean very different things and is easy to manipulate according to different ideas and agendas.

As for the cultural instititions, it took a long time for Japan to build public museums for different kinds of art. The biggest boom was in the 1980s. However, nowadays the Japanese art market is much more dependent on museums and corporate customers than in countries where private citizens have helped to support the art scene. Of course, different groups of customers always tend to bring in their own interests. For instance, different museums and curators can have their own agenda. When the art education has increased and new art institutions have been built also a new art professional art establishment has created its own discourses and also networks/ power structures. However, one can still claim that espacially in Japan culture is where the people are expressing themselves artistically and that the dynamism in culture comes from the people. Against this background it can be claimed that the authorities have played a far smaller role in arts and culture than in many other 'cultures'.

In ethnographic studies and sociology Yanagita Kunio (1875-1962) is recognized as the respected academic pioneer who focused on the life and cultures of the majority of Japanese people, who still were largely living in rural communities, a long way from the elitist culture of the upper class. In postwar Japanese social sciences and anthropology many different varieties of past and present Japanese cultures and social practices have been studied and analyzed following and perfecting the methods established by such pioneers as Yanagita. In the meantime Japan has urbanized & modernized and has become a major hub of global technology and trade and early ethnographic studies now depict a bygone world that is very different from the modern Japan and also from the historical narratives that, for instance, the compulsory educational system is teaching to the nation.

There is a long list of Japanese thinkers who have identified modernization and Western culture as the sources of short-sighted development that endangers the more sustainable life-forms and 'cultures' that prevailed in Japan before. However, there still seem to be much confusion about using the basic concepts of culture when discussing Japan and other societies. Of course, Western cultures have even more diversity and much of the Japanese criticism of Western culture is directed towards the excesses of economy and technology, not the cultural values or cultural activities.

Do such sustainable Japanese traditions as *satoyama* (symbiotic relations between the traditional Japanese village and the natural envioronment in its vicinity*)*, *kyôsei* (symbiosis between Japanese people and the environment) and *mottainai* (frugality/ no waste) still characterize the Japanese value systems and a more sustainable relationship with nature, if so much destruction still goes on without real opposition? Both the Japanese academics and artists have at least raised the issues of sustainability and received inspiration from the Japanese culture and environment. However, these ideas often seem to have little impact when the forces of destruction decide to strike. It can be argued that the economic rationality would force the capitalism to go green everywhere sooner or later and that presently we are in the middle of period when the capitalists are divided on this score as some of them still want to collect the profits as long as possible while others are already wakening to the reality of nearing collapse (Cf. Plumwood 2002: 7). However, in Japan this very debate is difficult to find among the political = business elites. Small technical fixes are no substitute to real and fundamental cultural changes that are needed to stop the destruction of environment.

As a good example of a prominent contemporary Japanese artist mixing art, environment and politics I introduce Aida Makoto. His art touches every aspect of Japanese cultural tradition, high and low and most everything in between, and by doing so demonstrates his originality and ability to renew himself while also reinterpreting Japanese traditions of art. His art also is quite social in its character as it is not made to fall into some easily definable, sellable or exportable brand. When Mori Art Museum curator Kataoka Mami introduced Aida's exhibition in 2012 she characterised Aida as an artist of chaos and disorder and confinued to argue that Western rational worldview refutes ambiquity and paradox whereas Japanese society is based on contradiction and incomprehensibility. Kataoka certainly has a point about Aida's ability to show how in Japan art, politics, economy and society are interwoven in a complex way. However, the Western art can hardly be claimed to be dominated by the Western rational worldview only and the power of artistic expression everywhere and at most times has been associated very closely with the ability of art to express ideas in ways that are different from other modes of expression. Furthermore, paradoxes (word derives from Greek *paradoxos*, "contrary to expectations/ opinions") have a long history as a source of art and philosophy in Europe. It may be better to look directly Aida's works of art and their relationship with environment. For instance, his own words about the titled 'Electric Poles, Crows and Others' are: "I have always been interested in animals that thrive in disaster," and that "I have drawn cockroaches before, but I had always wanted to do something about crows. It just sort of gives a hint of the mood that might come after a disaster." Aida is also famous for depicting in massive paintings the realities of modern Japanese society. His 'Ash color mountains' monumental painting depicts the dead salarymen in grey suits and 'Human blenders' have both male and female versions where humans are simply processed as material. Some of his works simply make fun of the politicians and political institutions or make open references to Japanese history, usually taking a rather sarcastic view (for Aida Makoto's art, Mori Art Museum solo exhibition catalogue 2013 with Kataoka's commentary, Favell 2018, Dehart 2013 and Mizuma Art Gallery 2021).

REFERENCES

Baseel, C. (2014). Beautiful 400-year-old garden in Okayama about to be replaced with condominium complex. *Sora News 24*. https://soranews24.com/2014/07/22/beautiful-400-year-old-garden-in-okayama-about-to-be-replaced-with-condominium-complex/

Benjamin, W. (1969). The Work of Art in the Age of Mechanical Reproduction. In *Illuminations*. Schocken Books. Available online: https://web.mit.edu/allanmc/www/benjamin.pdf

Benjamin, W. (1970). The Author as Producer. *New Left Review*, *1*(62). Available online: https://www.marxists.org/reference/archive/benjamin/1970/author-producer.htm

DeHart, J. (2013). Aida Makoto: Far-Sighted Visions of Near-Sighted Japan. *The Diplomat*. https://thediplomat.com/2013/05/aida-makoto-far-sighted-visions-of-near-sighted-japan

del Campana, P. (2021). *Nichiren. Japanese Buddhist monk*. Encyclopedia Britannica. https://www.britannica.com/biography/Nichiren

Deleuze, G., & Guattari, F. (1987). A Thousand Plateaus: Capitalism and Schizophrenia. University of Minnesota Press.

Encyclopedia Britannica. (n.d.). *Bakuhan system*. https://www.britannica.com/place/Japan/The-bakuhan-system

Enshûryû sadô. (n.d.). http://www.enshuryu.com

Favell, A. (2018). Aida Makoto: Notes from an Apathetic Continent. In *Introducing Japanese Popular Culture*. Routledge. Available online: https://eprints.whiterose.ac.uk/116906/1/Aida-Routledge-Final-AAM.pdf

Hobby Search. (n.d.). *Japanese commercial site for toys*. https://www.1999.co.jp

International Dunhuang Project. (n.d.). http://idp.bl.uk

Kawabata, T. (2003). Nichiren. When the art of the Lotus blossomed. *Japan Times*. https://www.japantimes.co.jp/culture/2003/01/22/arts/when-the-art-of-the-lotus-blossomed/

Kobori Enshû kenshûkai [Kobori Enshû Honoring Association]. (n.d.). https://www.koborienshu.org

Matsuoka, S. (2020). Flowers, Birds, Wind, and Moon. The Phenomenology of Nature in Japanese Culture. Japan Publishing Industry Foundation for Culture.

Mizuma Art Gallery. (2021). *I can't stop the patriotism.* Aikoku ga tomararenai. https://mizuma-art.co.jp/en/exhibitions/2107_aidamakoto/

Mori Art Museum. (2013). Aida Makoto. Monument for Nothing. Aida Makoto. Tensai de gomen nasai. Solo exhibition catalogue. Kyôto Seigensha.

Morris-Suzuki, T. (1998). *Re-inventing Japan. Nation, Culture, Identity*. Routledge.

NHK (Nippon Hôsô Kyôkai). (2008). *Sono toki. Rekishi ga ugoita. Part 315* [Television documentary program]. https://web.archive.org/web/20081007132147/http://www.nhk.or.jp/sonotoki/2008_02.html

Nishiyama, M. (1997). *Edo Culture. Daily Life and Diversions in Urban Japan, 1600-1868* (G. Groemer, Ed. & Trans.). University of Hawai'i Press. doi:10.1515/9780824862299

Ooms, H. (1984). Early Tokugawa Ideology. In P. Nosco (Ed.), *Confucianism and Tokugawa Culture* (pp. 27–61). University of Hawai'i Press.

Ozawa, A., & Mizunuma, Y. (2006). *Nihon jûkyoshi*. Yoshikawa.

Plumwood, V. (2002). *Environmental Culture. The ecological crisis of reason*. Routledge.

Ruth Chandler Williamson Gallery, Scripps College. (1886). *Description of Woodblock print artwork by Chikanobu in the collection of Ruth Chandler Williamson Gallery*. https://ccdl.claremont.edu/digital/collection/cyw/id/21

Samurai Games Wiki. (n.d.). https://samuraigames.fandom.com/wiki/Kiyomasa_Kato

Thesaurus Linguae Graecae Online. (n.d.). http://www.tlg.uci.edu/lbg

Turnbull, S. (2002). *Samurai Invasion: Japan's Korean War, 1592-98*. Cassell & Company.

Chapter 17
Japanese Visual Arts:
Representation and Perfectioning of Reality – Mimesis and Understanding of Japanese Visual Arts

Mika Markus Merviö
https://orcid.org/0000-0001-7771-5280
Kibi International University, Japan

ABSTRACT

In this chapter, the author has analysed the Japanese visual traditions in the context of changing social, cultural, and political environment. He has provided detailed discussions about different phases of Japanese art history, and towards the end of the chapter, he has focused especially on the present situation of Japanese visual art scene. In addition, he has tried to add something new to the analysis by applying the concept of mimēsis in the sense that the human beings are mimetic beings and feeling an urge to create texts and art that reflect and represent reality. The Japanese visual art does much more than just copies the reality: it represents the reality and perfections it, and by accomplishing these acts, Japanese art remains dynamic and provides a means for artists in Japan to express themselves and the society around them.

Mimesis as a Tool of Understanding Japanese Visual Arts

I use here the concept of *Mimêsis* (representation 模写 *(mosha)*, depiction 描写 *(byôsha)*; Ancient Greek: μίμησις *(mimēsis)* to analyze the special characteristics of Japanese visual arts tradition, both social and aesthetic. In my other chapter in this volume I am linking Japanese art, environment and politics ant trying to analyse them in a *rhizomatically* composed whole. However, in this chapter I am taking a closer look at the arts themselves and using the old Greek ideas related to the concept of *Mimêsis* to understand the long tradition of Japanese visual arts. *Mimêsis* suits the purpose as the human beings are mimetic

DOI: 10.4018/978-1-7998-8996-0.ch017

beings and feeling an urge to create texts and art that reflect and represent reality. The Japanese visual art does much more than just creating copies of the reality: it represents the reality and perfections it and by accomplishing these acts Japanese art remains dynamic and provides a means for artists in Japan to express themselves and the society around them.

Aristotle in his *'Poetics'* focuses on *mimēsis* claiming that the human beings are mimetic beings, feeling an urge to create texts and art that reflect and represent reality. He is the one who defined *mimêsis* as the perfection and imitation of nature (Aristotle 1996). However, art for him was never only imitation but it also searches for the perfect and the timeless. In other words, the original concept is far from the idea of meekly copying the reality and I use it to find out what the Japanese tradition of visual arts tells about Japanese society and its position in the world. Unfortunately in many languages the translation *mimēsis* is based on ideas of other Greek philosophers, especially Plato, whose ideas about artistic expression and creativity were rather pessimistic and who simply did not value art work in the same manner as Aristotle did. The real damage was done by narrow-minded people who much later projected their ideas of art to Greek art and used the narrow/ twisted concept of *mimêsis* to legitimise their own idea about art. After all, the present ideas of classical Greek art are largely a product of 18th and 19th century Western European scholarship, that was rather constricted when it came to understanding possibilities of artistic expression. In short, *mimêsis* should not be understood as simply as 'copying' but there simply is much more to the picture. In this chapter I use the concept of *mimêsis* to analyse Japanese visual arts to understand better the concept of *mimêsis* as well as the Japanese visual arts.

Visual representation and verbal representation surely influence each other but visual arts have an ability to cross many borders of language and culture far more easily than modes of representation that use natural languages. Furthermore, interpreting visual arts is a very special case of 'textual interpretation' as the text here contains, first of all, visual clues to other works of visual arts. In addition, visual arts contain references to everything that the observer sees in them and, at least I see a lot when I observe Japanese art and place in the context of world art, history and politics. However, writing about visual arts brings back the issue of using written language to convey ideas of visual representation to a chosen group of people in a chosen language (this book chapter being in English). The vast array of possible interpretations obviously has turned away many researchers from using visual arts to analyze social reality or when art is used it has been given the subsidiary role of illustrating the author's message rather than being the message itself.

The International Nature of Japanese Visual Traditions and the Problems of Categorization

The tradition of Japanese visual arts has developed in close interaction with Asian and Western arts. However, Japanese visual arts have created a new tradition of re-presentation of reality that represents and reflects the changes in society and by doing so has served as an agent of change itself.   However, even the use of basic terminology of visual arts in Japanese reveals that there are different ideas about how "Japanese" different traditions of artistic expression are. The terms of 洋画 (*yôga*, literally Western painting, oil painting) and 絵画 (*kaiga*, picture, painting and increasingly, movies and animations) both refer primarily to art that is seen to fall under the category of Western art, while Asian art forms (東洋美術, primarily Chinese, Korean, "Silkroad" and Indian art traditions) and Japanese art forms are normally addressed by more specific names such as 絵巻物 (*emakimono*, picture scroll) 日本画 (*nihonga*) or 浮世絵 (*ukiyoe*). Many Japanese art forms have been labelled outside Japan as crafts or are not understood as arts that would easily fit the hierarchy of artistic expression, that had been developed primarily on the basis of European tradition. Ernest Fenollosa, the first foreigner with a good understanding of many different art traditions who seriously tried to understand the whole variety of Japanese art forms, already complained about the tendency to analyze and classify Japanese art by the technique or material rather than power of the imagination (Fenollosa 1912/2007: xxxii-xxxiii.). By focusing on that power of imagination and creativity Fenollosa was far more successful than most of his contemporaries, either Western or Japanese, to see how Japanese art clearly differed from Chinese art and who were the most interesting representatives of Japanese tradition, although also Fenollosa quite often also explicitly compared to the European tradition and with his deep knowledge of European arts was, indeed, able to detect faraway influences and parallels. Although Fenollosa complained about the other scholars' insensitive framework of analysis, he did not really try to cover the whole field of Japanese artistic expression, regardless of the technique or material. In fact, that task has not been completed by anyone and the lack of trying means that we do not have a good theoretical foundation that would easily accommodate Japanese artistic tradition and serve as a basis of further discussion.

One might easily assume that things have changed totally with modern art and a more liberal attitude towards a great diversity of techniques and ideas about art would have made it easier to analyze the whole range of Japanese artistic expression. However, when it comes to basic writing on Japanese art history both in Japan and elsewhere the concerns that Fenollosa raised are still very much with us. Among the many Japanese attempts to cover the long narrative of Japanese visual arts is a book by Tsuji Nobuo, the director of Miho Museum, *'Nihon bijutsu no rekishi. Jômon kara manga-anime made'* [The history of Japanese Arts. From Jômon period to Manga and Anime]. However, the short theoretical parts of the books simply discuss the awkwardness of translating 美術 *(bijutsu)* into "fine arts" and pointing out to Fenollosa's ideas. The book follows very much the traditional descriptive mode and gets to *manga & anime* and the really contemporary art (that is promised in the subtitle) appears only on page 428. The remaining 12 pages of the book fails to tell much how the contemporary Japanese art connects with all the preceding Japanese art. This kind of treatment of contemporary art is very common in art history everywhere: it is difficult to sum up the latest developments in art and say something meaningful about the contemporary art against the long tradition of arts. Tsuji's conclusion concludes with idea taken from Langdon Warner's The Enduring Art of Japan (1952) that Japanese art keeps on enduring and continuing its history while going through changes (Tsuji 2005: 440, Warner 1952). The book serves well its role of following the narrative of "fine arts" in Japan from Jômon Period to present, but it does not analyze the special character of Japanese arts, nor the selection of art pieces in the book or analyze how the art reflects all the changes in society since the Jômon Period. Of course, it is better not to dishonestly claim that there is an unbroken tradition of distinctly Japanese art starting from the Haniwa clay figures and continuing to the most original contemporary Japanese art, unless someone wants to write a history of Japanese art that selects only works that are unmistakably different from any other traditions. Therefore, the Japanese art history, as it is usually understood in Japan and elsewhere, is very much part of the global history of art, and making sense out of it requires that both the global and Japanese cultural context is taken into account. Easy to say but this is not the easiest task to accomplish as it requires both a good knowledge of the both and an open to include art in all forms, shapes and manifestations. In my other chapter in this volume I am also linking Japanese arts more deeply to the politics, society and environment of Japan, but in this chapter the primary goal is to understand the Japanese tradition of visual arts.

There is also another way to analyse the past and present of Japanese art. In *Furu/ima. Kurabete wakaru nippon bijutsu nyûmon* (Wada ed. 2010) such very basic ideas as composition, space, allusion, diorama, animism, jest and nothingness in Japanese visual arts are illustrated by showing one selected contemporary piece of art next to one old piece of art. In some cases it is obvious that the artist has been using a classic work as a source of inspiration or copied some part of it whereas in some cases the parallels are more general but work well enough to serve the purpose of the book to illustrate how much contemporary Japanese art owes to past Japanese art. In her introductory chapter Wada Kyôko argues that the distinguishing character of the Japanese art is that the tradition and present, foreign and domestic influences are all combined and adjusted to the natural features *(fûdo)* of Japan. Wada herself describes her method as seeking analogies *(anarojî)* between past and present works and art and then using them to illustrate some of the most basic conceptual ideas of Japanese art, such as the *wabisabi* and simplicity (Wada 2010: 18-19).

The book makes good reading, the selections are thought-evoking and provide interesting comparisons. Of course, the idea of analogy (Greek: ἀναλογία) is something that the classical philosophers already discussed at length. Analogies as shared abstractions are closely related to metaphors, allegories and other kinds of comparisons. In short, analogies make thinking and understanding of abstractions easier. Although Wada does not go any deeper to analyse her use of a term that is very much part of classical art theory, it is worth noticing that her approach is very close to the idea of classical art education in Europe where artists were closely studying past art and becoming skillful in using visual clues and references in interesting ways to enrich the meaning of their work and showing their knowledge. Furthermore, such vocabulary as allegories, metaphors and analogies are something that any classical European painter would have felt very familiar with. Of course, the idea of analogy can be used analogically with *mimêsis* to point out that both comparison and representation include both aspects of finding similarities and contrasting or new features. The danger of this approach is that the same method could easily be used to demonstrate that the Japanese artists often base their work on past foreign works of art, which, of course, is what the artists do in all parts of the world.

One of the most bizarre episodes of the history of contemporary Japanese painting involves the case of Wada Yoshihiko, who befriended Italian painter Alberto Sughi (1928-2012) by introducing himself as a fan of his art. He photographed Sughi's paintings and copied them with altering only small details and after that presented them as his own without making clear his debt to Sughi. After Wada had won the Ministry Education's art prize in 2006 the Agency for Cultural Affairs received an anonymous tip questioning whether Wada's paintings are plagiarized from Sughi, who, after all, was a well-known painter with major retrospective exhibitions at many European museums and whose works could easily be found also from the Internet. Sughi was shocked to learn that Wada was a painter and had systematically copied his work. The screening judges who had awarded Wada the prize examined again Wada's and Sughi's work and decided to strip Wada's prize, the first such case ever involving a major art prize in Japan. Even after Wada had lost his prize he was unapologetic. "I borrow others' compositions and add my own ideas," he insisted. "Only artists who've studied abroad can understand the subtle differences in nuance." (Hogg 2006). The story received major media attention in Japan and was also reported briefly by international media; Sughi uploaded many links to his homepage and also included photographs of some of his works that had been copied by Wada (Sughi 2006a); http://www.albertosughi.com/f_prima_pagina/2006_05_30.asp.

Sughi also made sure that he was not going to sue Wada, taking the view that Wada was already going to suffer enough due to social backlash. Furthermore, Sughi told on his (English language) blog that he had been contacted by many Japanese who wanted to "take advantage of the popularity of my name" and exhibit his work. Sughi told that he "would prefer to exhibit my work when this scandal has died down. My painting, I hope, deserves cultural attention, and not merely curiosity spawned by a scandal of this magnitude" (Sughi 2006b). It turns out that Sughi was correct about the reasons why the Japanese museums wanted to exhibit his work in 2006: after the scandal died down the Japanese museums and public soon lost interest in his art. An Internet search with Aruberuto Sûgi (and Sugi) in Japanese reveals that in June 2006 there were many articles about the scandal, but afterwards there is almost nothing, even his death seems to have gone largely unnoticed in Japan.

What is interesting in the Sughi case is that the Italian artist was fluent in English and could get his side of the story and dignity reported to the rest of the world simply by the use of his homepage and blog whereas Wada and the Japanese Ministry both continued to demonstrate their ignorance and parochialism throughout the story. Wada clearly tried to deceive the Japanese audience by presenting himself as someone who understood the European tradition and "subtle differences", whereas he had presented himself as an art lover in Italy and hid his professional background. The fact that these double standards actually worked tells a sad story about some blind spots in the globalization of Japanese arts. It can be argued that Wada took literally the unfortunate Japanese (mis-)translation of *mimesis* as 模写 *(mosha)* meaning a copy or honestly believed that his way of 'copying' was fine. After the Sughi scandal Wada continued to work as a Professor of Nagoya Art Museum (1985-2002) and has remained active as a painter, for instance, having his own exhibition at Tôkyô Central Museum in 2008 and painting the portrait of the King and Queen of Bhutan in 2012 in addition to his May 2013 exhibition of paintings about Bhutan, the happy country *(Shiawase no kuni bûtan)* at a Ginza rental gallery. What strikes on his partly bilingual (Japanese/English) homepage in 2013 was that he had studied seven years in Rome but he spells in English "Italian" as "Itarian" and "professor" as "professer". Subtle differences, indeed. (Wada homepage). His homepage presently in 2021 includes only information of online casinos. Internet searches do not show traces of recent exhibitions, which during the time of COVID 19 does not necessarily tell much. Anyway, his works have continued to show in sales and auctions in Japan. Private collectors may not shy away from his works even after the controversy.

Part of the problem with authenticity in Japanese art concerning so called Western art may relate to the rigid categories created to distinquish Japanese and Western art. The Japanese language still distinguishes the art forms largely on the basis of technique and material, and shows great concern to "foreign" origins of techniques – after about 150 years of very mixed traditions. Furthermore, both Western and Japanese art communities still find it problematic to locate, for instance, such important parts of Japanese artistic tradition as garden design or tea ceremony within the tradition of global arts. Nowadays it is quite difficult to decide what should be included within the Western art tradition as the borders of expression are all the time deliberately crossed and when the whole idea of 'Western art' looks increasingly anachronistic. Furthermore, the often quite rigid categorization used in Japanese language, art education and museums looks rather unusual from a European perspective. Furthermore, it is commonplace in Japan to find generalizations about rational world view being the basis of Western arts in a direct contrast to the less dogmatic and less naturalistic world view that defines the Japanese traditions of art, especially *nihonga*. Sometimes the Japanese art philosophy is extended to cover also the Chinese and Indian traditions (See e.g. Hatanaka 1986: 176-177). Of course, the reality is far more complex and interesting and has always been. Both Western and Japanese (or Asian) art traditions are impossible to capture by neat definitions as the whole idea of modern and contemporary art rests on the strive to seek new ways to create art and constant reinterpretation of all traditions, often in interesting cross-fertilized mixes. Anyway, Japanese tradition of art also has strong roots in realism. Curator Sherman E. Lee wrote many books and curated several splendid exhibitions focusing on realism in Japanese art. His point was that in Japanese art there is a strong tradition of boldness and pragmatic and frank realism. Someone reading only Lee's books would certainly reach the conclusion that Japanese tradition of visual art is particularly realist in its orientation and that artists focused primarily on depicting the human foibles and personalities with candor (Lee 1983).

The labels and names have not stopped the Japanese artists from adopting influences from everywhere and from mixing techniques. With art it is not only important what is being created but it also matters how works of art are received. Japan has developed its own way of appreciating art and artists and this relationship is constantly changing. It is a serious problem if the tastes and lifestyles of people do not have room for art in their lives, as art often makes people to think and feel more deeply about everything: life, society, environment, politics, people themselves and the meaning of everything. Culture tells much about the nation and its people. In political science culture is increasingly seen in the context of soft power, which is based on the attractiveness and admiration of the values on which the culture rests (Nye 2004). However, the idea of "getting others to want the outcomes you want" (Ibid: 5) is a bit naive in the complicated modern societies, when most people and nations are at loss to think what they really want. Culture may be the ultimate tool of influence, but it can not be easily used in a manipulated way, although Joseph Nye and a long list of Japanese Prime Ministers seem to think so after Japan copied the idea of Cool Britain and has kept the idea alive by changing the content of promoted Japanese culture accoding to changing political needs and personal likes and dislikes of politicians and bureaucrats. However, in culture there is always present an element of honesty and widely shared values and views, but it certainly does matter who selects the culture that is claimed to represent a nation. What is exactly that the Japanese state wants to show to the rest of the world by promoting the export of *manga* and *anime* and the idea that Japan is cool? Most likely the result is just fine, but there is no telling what will be the reception and whether it is anywhere near what the policymakers wanted.

The Abe administration presented its new Cool Japan agenda in May 2013. *Manga* and *anime* were still there but the new addition was the Japanese food culture and the idea that Japan will send its cultural missionaries to convert the rest of the world. One new aspect was that the government wanted support the Japanese creators to contribute internationally. The overall purpose seems to tell to the Japanese public that the TPP treaty (that later was watered down when the United States became strong again and stopped signing multilateral trade treaties) would also create new opportunities to Japanese agriculture and that Japanese culture can be exploited as a cash cow with little investment. The way the agenda was presented to the public made the whole idea appear as a business and marketing event rather than a serious attempt to change Japanese image and do something to facilitate that change. The whole campaign seems to be at least as much aimed to the domestic audience than to the world. The Abe version of Cool Japan included such bizarre elements as sending Japanese food missionaries to teach the virtues of tea ceremony and Japanese sake to the dignitaries of the world. Someone must have seen a great untapped global market for *macha* that would solve all the problems caused by the liberalization of farm trade (Mainichi Shimbun 28 May 2013).

Japanese politicians introduced the whole idea of Cool Japan after Japan started to cut its ODA and seemed to abandon many of the goals of its foreign policy of the 1990s. Japan will never be admitted to the UN Security Council as long as it depends on China and Russia and the UN diplomacy has little to offer to help with the acute problems of Japanese international relations. Heng Yee-Kuan has compared the soft power competition between Japan and China and puts forward the argument that Japanese popular cultural efforts are 'decentered' and often present the non-dogmatic and non-nationalist side of Japan.

Hello Kitty, for instance, is surnamed White, her parents are called George and Mary and they live in London (Heng 2010: 275-304).

The decentered Japanese cultural products surely did find a market and positive reception abroad. However, business-wise translating Japanese *manga* is not a big business for anyone and even potentially most of the profits would go to the foreign publishers. The Japanese manga artists have in most cases not received much of fame or forture. Hello Kitty apparently was not the first thing in the mind of Joseph Nye when he thought about using culture to influence others. The Cool Japan policy is presented primarily as a sales pitch to the Japanese audience and one should not think that Japanese diplomacy will be outsourced to Hello Kitty and Totoro anytime soon as a shrewd effort to win the hearts and minds of everyone.

However, the ongoing COVID 19 Pandemic means that Japanese government among many other governments has lost interest to trying to reach the minds of people elsewhere. After all, Japan is strictly isolated and already for several years it has been virtually impossible for foreigners to enter Japan and situation does not seem to change anytime soon. There are similaties with the present situation and the long Edo period and once the Pandemic is over there will many people saying that they do not want to foreigners back, a line that is nowadays often heard in larger cities that used to have larger numbers of foreigners, especially tourists, before the Pandemic. In this situation it is no wonder that the Suga and Kishida administrations have found it easy to close the borders and scale down all connections with the rest of the world. If foreigners are only wanted/appreciated as tourists that contribute to travel industry, they can easily be cut off. Moreover, the world is turning into a hostile place with confrontations between the major powers (Japan is not among them while the United States, China and Russia act like they are) and in the meantime the world is steadily moving towards an environmental collapse. It is not wonder that Japanese society in this situation could find the Galápagos or Edo model of international and cultural relations tempting.

My point of discussing the visual art of people and art that the political establishment promotes is that cultural values should be shared by a large segment of the society to become socially relevant and to really matter and having a lasting impact. Style in art can cover both individual style and the styles of groups of artists, schools of art or national or international style. As art becomes labelled and placed into these boxes, it also becomes evaluated by different specialist communities and by the larger society, whose tastes are often guided from above, but not nearly always. In fact, the Japanese art provides ample evidence of the constant interplay between the high art and popular art, and the popular art is often winning. Very often the reason is that the state actually does not seem to care that much about art and culture and mercifully it is left alone.

The Japanese modern lifestyles leave little room for traditional visual arts in the narrow sense of tradition. The number of households that have space to exhibit properly traditional Japanese art, especially *kakejiku* scrolls and *nihonga* are increasingly rare. Small sized Western paintings would be easier to hang on the walls of modern Japanese houses, but unlike with proper bourgeois households in Europe there are not so many ordinary people who have oil paintings covering all the walls. The European bureaucrat who used the expression *'cage à lapin'* (rabbit hutch) to describe Japanese modern houses and invited the anger of the Japanese nation and created an immortal description of the reality of modern Japanese living by simply comparing the life style of his own social class to that of the wealthy Japanese in Japanese urban centres. Even the most luxurious and spacious rabbit hutches are not ideal for art collecting and there have not that many art missionaries in Japan to teach how to beautify the walls of their dwellings from ceiling to floor with art. The Japanese basic ideas of aesthetics (such as *yûgen*, 'mysterious elegance') do not guide people to fill their homes with art and those who still are open to these ideas tend to show good taste when selecting the pieces of art that they would like to live with. The Japanese art market is much more dependent on museums and corporate customers, but as I will later discuss these customers tend to have somewhat narrow interests.

From a broader perspective, the Japanese tradition of visual arts is doing just fine: Japanese artists use every available opportunity to make use of the new wealthy consumer society and its rapidly shifting tastes. After all, there are not anymore enough wealthy connoisseurs of art available for the artists and, instead, there is a new much bigger target audience. The potential visual arts audience is everyone with their varying possessions of wealth and, at least, some knowledge of Japanese artistic traditions, sometimes simply as a result of school education, but even more from the exposure to popular culture. Graphic art is everywhere in Japan and the upper end of graphic art is just very good by any comparison, with an eye to detail, clarity and beauty. Some of the best known and commercially most successful Japanese painters have blended their art and careers with commercial graphic design, such as Yokoo Tadanori, Tanaami Kei'ichi, Ôtake Shinrô and Hibino Katsuhiko. The contemporary art after them owes much to the success of these artists in the 1970s and the 1980s. The internationally recognized artists, Murakami, Nara and Aida have went further with the elements of graphic design and commentary of contemporary society, as well as branding and marketing their own art. In recent years one of the most original, popular and representative graphic artists in Japan has been Higuchi Yûko who has published her art work especially as book illustratrions but has also collaborated with such fashion labels as Gcci and Uniqlo. In 2022 her art is exhibited in several museums in Japan (for her art, Higuchi 2019).

The visual environment of modern Japan is different from the Western traditions largely because of commercial aesthetics, which range from subdued and sensitive colours and forms derived from old traditions to the most blatant disrespect to harmony and good manners, which is the essence of visual culture using simple messages or images of sex and violence simply to make people stop and take notice. The presence of *kanji* characters, of course, brings a special visual effect everywhere. Some Westerns observers seem to be confused with the *kanji* and what they tell about Japanese society. One prominent example is Roland Barthes who interpreted the whole Japanese culture as an extraordinary case of an empire of signs (without much of focus or clear significance if we believe Barthes, who attempted to understand Japanese culture without any knowledge of Japanese culture and only marginally more knowledge about its art traditions) (Barthes 1982).

The other end of Japanese popular culture and its visual aesthetics, the one of unmistakably and often decidedly bad taste, is the one that has not been frequently analyzed. Much of *manga* falls into this category. During the Edo Period many artists started to produce so called toba-e (鳥羽絵) comical and satirizing coloured prints produced by woodblocks the same way as *ukiyoe*. The common people kept buying these cheap and funny works and many more ambitious *ukiyoe* artists produced also these works as a sidejob. In other words, the artists often had an open mind about producing very different kind of art to different audiences. *Manga* was used sometimes in the meaning of a sketch, but Imaizumi Ippyô used it in the Newspaper Jiji Shinpô in 1890 to translate Italian *caricatura* with the result that *toba-e* gradually was renamed to *manga* (Shimizu 2013: 9-10). During the 20th century the *manga* artists were quick to adopt ideas from Europe, such as Art Deco. A significant new development was a creation of mass market of childrens' *manga*. Meanwhile, many older art forms were in decline and manga artists were mostly professionals, who now could make their living with manga. Nowadays Japan has too many *mangaka* (*manga* artists), who struggle to get their work published and to survive in a market where the rules are made by the publishers. The result is that it does not pay to produce quality and to survive one needs to produce vast amounts of substandard work. Many artists also also know very well the dark attics of their audience and society and by their art create a "more balanced" picture of the Japanese traditions and culture. The Japanese artists who show the ugly condition of modern society with the occasional beauty in ugliness (Cf. Bacon) are often using the medium of commercial art, *anime* or *manga*. Also the big names of Japanese contemporary art sometimes have no worries to mix their art with images that would be branded as glorifying pedophilia, violence, racism or religious/ cultural insensitivity outside Japan. The rest of the world simply often has different set of rules concerning hypocrisy or political correctness than Japan and some Japanese art may end up being a bit too much for art lovers elsewhere, while in Japan it is just interpreted against the reality of the other end of popular culture.

The art of Aida Makoto is a good example of a contemporary artist who touches every aspect of Japanese cultural tradition and by doing so demonstrates his originality and ability to renew himself. His art also is far more social in its character as it is not made to fall into some easily definable, sellable or exportable brand (for discussion of Aida's art, see the end of my other chapter in this book and Mori Art Museum solo exhibition catalogue 2013 with Kataoka's commentary, Favell 2018, Dehart 2013 and Mizuma Art Gallery 2021).

In Japan art, politics, economy and society are interwoven in a complex way. However, the Western art can hardly be claimed to be dominated by the Western rational worldview only and the power of artistic expression everywhere and at most times has been associated very closely with the ability of art to express ideas in ways that are different from other modes of expression. Contemporary Japanese society has a wealth of examples of both rather rigid categorization of cultural tradition and very open and playful approach to high and low culture and everything between them. The best way to define popular culture is to note that it is popular and that alone is no reason to suspect low standards. Japan does have a mass market for popular culture and many artists want to navigate the both worlds. Such issues as former stereotypes, either Japanese or foreign, or narrow ideas about culture based on social class, gender or social convention can also seen as an opportunity to make art or make fun. Historically many genres of Japanese culture have travelled from rather humble origins to the top category and general respect, such as the journey of Kabuki from Edo period bourgeois pastime to an icon of Japanese traditional culture. Some of the most famous Kabuki stars have occasionally wanted to bring more dynamism and new tricks to keep the interest of the audience (for a discussion on the special characteristics of Japanese popular culture, Treat 1996).

Art Establishment and Art Market in Japan

The art museums were rather late to be established due to their "Western" image and because visual culture was not very high on the list of policy priorities. The first Japanese modern museums, national and regional, were built to preserve and sometimes to glorify Japanese past and material culture. The first Japanese museum that was devoted to Western Art was the private Ôhara Museum of Art in Kurashiki, Okayama. The national collections in Tôkyô were only gradually separated first into historical and science collections and then into different art collections following the usual Japanese classifications. The National Museum of Modern Art (東京国立近代美術館, *Tōkyō kokuritsu kindai Bijutsukan)* was opened in 1952 in Takebashi next to the Imperial Palace and it includes contemporary art, both Japanese Western Art and *Nihonga* Japanese painting, and also has a modest foreign collection. However, the museum often has major foreign exhibitions as foreign museums are glad to show their art in such a central place where it also is easier to find sponsors, foreign and Japanese alike. However, the art museum with the most important Western Art collection and exhibitions in Japan is the National Museum of Western Art (国立西洋美術館 Kokuritsu Seiyō Bijutsukan), which was built in 1959 around Matsukata Kôjirô's (1865-1950) collections that the French state had confiscated after the war but were partly donated by France to Japan as the French authorities valued much more the Matsukata's wish to establish his museum in Japan than the Japanese authorities ever did. Matsukata, who had made a fortune in shipbuilding knew well European art and artists, had wanted to bring his collection to Japan before the war, but the 100% import tax had made it impossible at the time when his businesses were already suffering. His collections in Japan and Britain were mostly burned during the war and the collections in France were cherry-picked by the French who first sent the best paintings to the French national collections. The remaining 370 works form the core of the most important Japanese Western Art collection, which has kept growing due to donations and acquisitions (for Matsukata Kôjirô's art collecting, Miyashita 2006).

In the 1960s several new private museums were established for Western Art and, again, many were built around private collections, such as the Idemitsu and Yamatane museums of art. However, in the 1970s and the 1980s there was a boom of new art museums. The bubble years of the 1980s were particularly beneficial for museums of contemporary art. Adrian Favell dismisses most of these museums as little more than an extension of "log-rolling and pork-barreling construction schemes" that cities and private patrons used to "put somewhere their wickedly expensive bubble period acquisitions, which were mostly Western modern classics". Favell also casts a doubt over the authenticity of Japanese museum acquisitions of Western art (Favell 2011: 163). I find Favells tone overly mean. Public construction in Japan is a highly political activity, but the same money could easily have been wasted for something truly wasteful, such as sports or defense. In particular, the Prefectural Art Museums have done a great job in educating people about different forms of art and broadened the world view of the public in the process.

The Japanese museum audience is one of the best anyone can hope for an exhibition, regardless of the content. C.B. Liddell, the art critic of the Japan Times, has a somewhat different opinion, as he noted that he got an impression that the Fancis Bacon exhibition at Takebashi museum had a more sophisticated art audience than normal since there was not the usual wall-hugging conveyer belt of viewers and, instead, the visitors moved around more freely and considered works more intensely – and there were more men (Liddell: 2013). The "conveyer belt" is a result of such factors, that the Japanese museum visitors really try to read most of the written information available and that many consider it to bad manners to move around more freely like Mr Liddell (and I often) do. I would not go as far to generalize too much about the sophistication of museum visitors on the basis of their gender, height or respect to Japanese manners. One should also note that the big Japanese exhibitions have enormous numbers of visitors and sometimes you really need to join the conveyer belt to see anything (unless one has Masai background and can easily find ways to look over the conveyer belt). In the global museum and art museum attendance surveys the global top places are regularly reserved to Japanese museums. The high attendance numbers and by European standards the rather expensive entry fees explain why the Japanese museums can afford to continue bringing big international exhibitions to Japan. Mr Liddell is not totally wrong saying that Tôkyô is a city that prefers its art on the pretty side – and the same could be said most large museums in Japan – but not only in Japan. However, this particular art critique involved Francis Bacon exhibition and it had indeed, found its way to the National Museum of Modern Art, as the first retrospective of Bacon in Asia. The Japanese museums and the Japanese audience have room for a very diverse art experience. The people in Britain and Japan who decided to bring Bacon to Japan were not thinking along the line of simple cultural propaganda of *utsukushii Igirisu* (beautiful Britain; Cf. prime Minister Abe's ideas and book about beautiful Japan *(utsukushii nihon)* as his trademark political ideology) and understood that the Japanese audience can stomach something like Bacon and end up having an increased respect and warm thoughts of Britain.

In 2012 the Tokyo Metropolitan Art Museum held the world record with 10,573 visitors a day seeing the Dutch Golden Age paintings including Vermeer's Girl with the Pearl Earring. However, the Shôsô-in treasure house (established in 756 A.D.) belonging to the Tôdaiji temple in Nara took once again home the museum category world record with its annual showing of its treasures: 14,240 visitors a day. To put these figures into a context: the US record in 2012 went to the MoMA (New York) when 5,700 visitors a day went to see the Cindy Sherman exhibition (Pes & Sharpe: 2013). Meanwhile, the current figures of the Art Newspaper annual survey reveals that in 2020 overall attendance of the world's 100 most- visited art museums dropped by a staggering 77% in 2020—from 230 million in 2019 to just 54 million as museums worldwide were forced to close. However, Japan fares very badly on this list although the museums in Japan actually had less days when they were closed than many other world art museums. In 2020 the top museum in Japan in terms of visitors was was the 21st Century Museum of Art in Kanazawa with 971,256 annual visitors, making it number 10 in the world. Tokyo Metropolitan Art Museum was number 38. On this list of 100 musems there were in 2020 five museums from both South Korea and Japan telling that Japan in these days faces a healthy competition in visual culture in East Asia, if measured by world class art museums. When the Chinese museums will fully open after the Pandemic the situation will still change substantially. The popular museums in Sao Paolo, Mexico City and Abu Dhabi have also greatly globalised the world art scene and left their mark on this list (The Art Newspaper 2020).

In Japan, many museums have struggled to stay open and the first exhibitions the be ditched are the foreign ones as planning has become difficult or even impossible. Moreover, the whole idea for bringing famous foreign art to Japan was that in Japan museums can easily charge high entrance fees and the world class exhibitions would be also commercially easy to organize when in addition to ticket sales there would be sponsors available. This equation stopped functioning with the COVID-19. Now most Japanese museums show Japanese art, if they manage to stay open. With Japanese art it is easier to postpone the exhibitions and hope for the best. In some cases the COVID-19 may end up creating more opportunities for local living artists to get exhibitions in museums.

The municipalities and private & corporate collectors have changed the Japanese art scene with a large number of art museums, each having a different profile. However, the Japanese public has proved to be interested especially in high-profile well-publizised exhibitions. This means that the Japanese public has an access to the world masterpieces. This is helped by the increasing willingness of European museums to loan their art to Japanese, Chinese and Taiwanese museums as they are struggling with drying public support and relatively low attendance even with ridiculously low ticket prices. For instance, in Britain the local council cuts have already for some time been forcing many galleries and museums to reduce staff and opening hours and there are many who believe that income from foreign tours would be the only way for them to replace public funding. If the foreigners don't come this equation will change. The British museums for some time saw that their biggest opportunities lie in China where new huge museums were built and where the British paintings are well received (Youngs 2013). Of course, part of the recipe is that there is also significant corporate and government support to make these tours possible and to improve the British (or German/French/Finnish/US/whatever) image(s) abroad. From the British point of view the large galleries have already cooperated with their Japanese counterparts for decades and know well the importance (and monetary rewards) of this reciprocal art exchange. They also know that the Japanese art audience is, indeed, sophisticated and curious enough to stomach British exhibits that do not likely directly contribute to the Anglo-Japanese trade and/or tourism. Another phenomenon is that the smaller museums work alone or in a group of museums to find new art audiences anywhere where there are decent museums and financial resources available. Basically the world is full of museums that would not mind sharing their art with the rest of the world and this kind of grass-roots internationalisation in art was spreading steadily until the Pandemic hit. There is no telling what happens next. Maybe art moves online, but if this happens it will be very different kind of art and art audience.

Art exhibitions, especially ones focusing on classic masterpieces attract the kind of audience that also is the target audience of many businesses, from travel industry to cuisine and design. For instance, in 2012-2013 there was a tour of Finnish design and art exhibition "The Essence of Finnish Design and Culture: Mythology, Moomin, and People in the Intimate Wilderness" visiting four Japanese Prefectural Art Museums and attracting good attendance everywhere. From a Finnish perspective the selection of paintings was very conservative focusing mostly on the era of national romanticism and its romantic view of Finnish nature while the modern era was represented almost entirely by Tove Jansson. In short, the exhibition mythologized the Finnish art and made it look very nationalistic, indeed. In short, there was no attempt to introduce a more diverse view of Finnish culture, especially visual arts. The design component and huge souvenir shop made no excuse about the objective of advertising contemporary Finnish design brands to the Japanese consumers, who already are familiar with these brands. However, the record has later been balanced by several major exhibitions in Japanese museums focusing on Finnish female painters. In 2015 the Miyagi Museum of Art held the first retrospective exhibition to be held in Japan for the Finnish painter Helene Schjerfbeck (1862-1946), who is widely recognised in Finland as the most imporant Finnish visual artist ever. That exhibition consisted works from the Finnish National Gallery, the Ateneum Art Museum. In 2019 to celebrate 100 years of diplomatic relations the Ateneum Art Museum, sent the exhibition 'The Modern Woman' to be presented at the National Museum of Western Art in Tokyo. That exhibition included works by Helene Schjerfbeck, Maria Wiik, Ellen Thesleff, Sigrid Schauman, Sigrid af Forselles, Elga Sesemann and Hilda Flodin. The same exhibition was shown in addition to Helsinki in Oulu, New York and Stockholm (Ateneum Art Museum 2019). Here we see two very different kind of concepts of international art exhibitions involving Japan and Finland and all these three exhibitions involve the Finnish National Gallery. The other approach makes no secret of an agenda of trade and tourism promotion and appears to be taking a rather while the other one focuses on art itself. It would be difficult to image that Finnish National Gallery or Finnish government would send an exhibition focusing on "The Essence of Finnish Design and Culture: Mythology, Moomin, and People in the Intimate Wilderness" to any European country. I do not know how much these exhibitions reflected the wishes of the Japanese side, but it is not very good idea for foreign governments to promote rather parochial views of their own country and culture in the name of trade promotion especially if they believe that the particular audience is not ready to receive exhibitions that reflect the contemporary ideas of art and society.

China seems to be following the Japanese path of establishing large museums and gradually educating its population about the marvels of foreign art by bringing the foreign masterpieces to the people to see them. At the same time the art history of China will be reconstructed and it will be very interesting to see what will be the end result. In China's case the Chinese government has shown its support to high culture and the government has become also much more sophisticated in the control and promotion of art. The purpose obviously is to prepare the Chinese people to the new global status of China. Financially the Chinese public sector is in a good position to establish fancy large museums if they wish to do so. In the Chinese case the history of ideological and political guidance and censorship makes the new more global approach to art very delicate. It remains to be seen how drastic the change will be and what kind of art the Chinese people will continue see in their new museums and what kind of difference this will make to the Chinese artists and the rapidly developed Chinese contemporary art market.

Part of the public art collections is that collectors and public collections often focus on the same big names and the existence of art investors have made art by popular artists very expenseive while most living artists struggle to make their living. Much of good art is never 'discovered' by the art establishment and, therefore, does not receive the recognition that it would deserve. The rather secluded nature of Japanese art scene means that it is often difficult to Japanese contemporary artists to find their place. Collectors are small in number and museums often want to show art that people already know or are part of famous collections, domestic or foreign. It is also often true that the Japanese museums and collectors have paid and continue to pay far too much for their acquisitions. The cost issue is due to art market conditions, where most people find it difficult to have a direct access to transparent art and antiquities auctions. The middle-men control much of the trade even with Japanese art, but with European art the middle-men add costs and do not always even quarantee authenticity. Art is a field where prices always fluctuate and it takes some effort to locate good pieces of art with reasonable prices. However, the European traders and collectors have an access to much more liquid market and good data of previous sales. The European-style art auctions with broad participation simply never made it to Japan and the Japanese art market lacks in transparency. This is made worse by such factors as the cultural, psychological and linguistic reasons favouring the use of middle-men. The middle-men use to their advantage the image of (Western) art being a luxury and something that is not to be haggled over the price. Furthermore, Japan happens to be geographically far away from most Western art auctions, which may explain some costs. The Internet should have removed many of the obstacles for distance buying in auctions. However, old habits often die hard and there are many other examples of middle-men making foreign purchases expensive in Japan. Part of the problem is that some Japanese organizations are used to deal with Japanese counterparts and they end up paying dearly for their inflexibility and willingness to trust Japanese dealers instead of learning to buy directly. In any case, it is unfair to dismiss the professional standards of all Japanese museums and professionals as there are also people with very high standards.

The issue of paying too much for foreign masterpieces is one of the least important problems of the Japanese art market and the most bizarre examples were seen during the bubble years that will not come back – at least in Japan. The real problem in Japan is that the Japanese artists receive very little support from the public sector and that the art market is even more unfavourable to them than in most other affluent societies. The big museums are interested mostly in the big names and in order to make it to major exhibitions one needs to have the right contacts, luck and prior exhibitions, and, of course, talent. The Japanese gallery system since the 1960s until recently was dominated by the so called *kashi garô* (rental galleries), where anyone with about 300 000 yen a week can rent a gallery from posh areas, especially Ginza in Tôkyô and hope that it will make a splash. Similar galleries exist in larger cities, although the rents may be a bit more reasonable. Most of the time very few people show up and the artist will end up paying most of the costs (rent and wining) and will get only some help with advertising, mostly by postcard mailing to people who are on the mailing list. Most art critics and media do not even bother with these unscreened exhibitions. However, artists need exhibitions on their CV and occasionally they get something sold by this method, too. The realities of young artists in Japan tend to be very harsh.

The other major method is the *kikaku garô* (*kikaku* having the meanings of planned and event), which are run by professional art dealers. These are based on commissions and the levels tend to be rather high by European standards, often around 50%. To get one's work there usually means that there must be good connections, such as support of teachers at art schools or other influential people whose words are taken seriously. Art magazines (there are many) pay attention to this group of artists, but it is still tough to proceed to the next level of major museum exhibitions and collections. However, in Japan also such factors as local roots can be important in helping artists to secure support in their career. The personal story is important and so are the personal contacts.

All these factors make it difficult also for foreign artists to enter Japanese art world unless they are already well established and their works have found their way to Japanese and foreign museums. The result is that the Japanese tend to see foreign art works mostly in high profile museum exhibitions and there is relatively little interaction between Japanese and foreign artists, except when Japanese artists go to study abroad or in those rare cases when foreign artists study or live in Japan and learn to play by the Japanese rules. There are only a few cases like Clifton Karhu, a Finnish-American who lived in Japan from 1955 to his death in 2007 and who ended up as a respected artist producing wood-block prints in Kyôto, often depicting the old wooden houses of Kyôto.

Yet another venue are the department store commercial galleries. They too tend to charge high commissions. In fact, many department stores have traditionally treated their suppliers in a similar way: the goods belong to the manufacturer or dealer unless they are sold. The good part with department stores is that there are many people visiting them and they certainly add visibility to artists. Some department stores have upgraded their galleries and have started to compete with museums by organizing more ambitious exhibitions and by publishing better quality exhibition catalogues.

Recently there are more independent galleries in larger cities that are not located in the most expensive areas and which often have more diversified business idea, serving food, for instance. However, here we get back to the problem I mentioned before that there is a fundamental shortage of art byers in Japan, especially collectors of reasonably priced contemporary art for private pleasure. Of course, it is exactly this kind of collections that universally serve as the basis of future museum collections as serious collections tend to be donated or otherwise find their way to museums. Furthermore, private collectors often have different interests and tastes from those people who are in charge of museum acquisitions. The public and private collections do complement each other. In the Japanese case the private collectors tend to be people with substantial financial resources and in many cases they can also afford to have their own museums. After the bubble years there have not been around that many people in Japan with money to spend freely on arts. There is no Japanese equivalent to Charles Saatchi. Nevertheless, another rather popular museum type in Japan is a museum centred around the atelier of a deceased artist and his/her work. In these cases it is usually the local network of people who recognize the importance of a (in Japan) famous local artist and see also the opportunies for domestic tourism promotion. What ever the background, the private museums can be found everywhere in Japan and especially in small communities they play an important role as providing a place for art lovers to meet. Very often these art museums also serve as a place for concerts and for all kinds of art workshops and being largely run by volunteers they are very flexible and have a quite different role than the public museums, which have more professional approach in the sense of following the ideas and examples set by the national art establishment. It needs to be added that also the public museums often try to build networks among supporters and professionals. By American standards the fundraising activities and volunteer work may appear modest, but by the Japanese standards art is one of the few fields where people are willing to give their time and financial support.

The archaic art market mechanisms in Japan have helped to isolate the Japanese art market from the world and the most obvious result is that Japanese contemporary art is relatively unknown outside Japan and the interest focuses on few individuals who have been lucky or energetic enough to win an access to present their work outside Japan and in major Japanese exhibitions in Japan. Among the international big names of contemporary Japanese artists Kusama Yayoi, Murakami Takashi and Nara Yoshitomo have made much of their art for the foreign audience and understand very well the American and European art market and its tastes. In their case, their Japanese success came after they had been recognized abroad. Kusama Yayoi is even a US citizen and her art is a rare case of high profile US-Japanese art, that blends nicely both art scenes. Aida Makoto is a prolific artist who has made his career largely in Japan and who clearly works for the Japanese audience, but whose work has been recognized also abroad, especially for those art works that touch a raw nerve due to their political or social content. Something like the air raid over New York is bound to attract at least some kind of reaction among the American audience and helps to diversify the image of contemporary Japanese art, as it is clearly not part of the wave of cute and superficial art emerging from Japan.

The Japan Society (New York) exhibitions of 2005 and 2011 tried to introduce the latest developments of Japanese art to the Amrican audience. The 2005 exhibition was curated by Murakami Takashi and it surely got through the message of cuteness and superflat quality of Japanese contemporary art, based on the flattened spaces of traditional art and many subsequent Japanese art genres as well as the empty or flat feeling accompanying consumerism in Japan. The 2011 exhibition was already titled Bye Bye Kitty and demonstrated that Japanese art was growing up and that there was, instead, lot of hybridity and struggle between extremes in contemporary Japanese art (Elliott 2010). Some works, like those of Aida, surely were not cute, but there was still some continuity: Nara Yoshitomo's work actually included a C type print of a pet cemetery with two Hello Kitty statues. The superflat art art was the first time that Japanese contemporary art established itself as just another global art tradition that was very much targeted to the foreign (buying) audience. However, it seems like especially during the Pandemic years the internationalization of Japanese art scenes has not moved much forward and Japanese art may appear to be very much isolated from the world. However, art nowadays does not exists only in museums or international art auctions and the Internet in principle makes it easy to reach a global audience and the artists certainly are exchanging ideas and influences globally across geographical, linguistic and mental borders, even if people are not able to move. After all, the COVID-19 has stopped the foreign travel for years almost entirely and there is no hope in sight for opening the Japanese borders for travel.

Representation of Japanese Art and Politics

As the previous discussion shows the Japanese state was slow to realize how important visual arts are for Japanese the Japanese society and culture and that visual arts have a huge potential to make Japan and Japanese ideas known abroad, in addition, to contributing to global culture. The idea of state being responsible for promoting the cultured life of people or the idea of cultural rights of people are rather foreign to Japanese society. However, the whole idea of 'being Japanese' is very much a cultural reconstruction and the Japanese state has been actively encaged in shaping that reconstruction together with other pillars of establishment in Japan, such as the educational and economic institutions. While the political elite invented traditions of modern Japan it also created at the same time narratives of Japanese history and culture to suit the uses of new state and nationalism that supported it – a process which is rather typical for nation-states everywhere (Cf. Vlastos (ed) 1998, which analyzes the project of Japanese modernization and invented traditions with a great diversity of examples).

However, the invention of tradition does not mean that they are all false or invented from a scratch. Instead, in Japan the old cultural traditions of the samurai class provided a perfect arsenal from which the political elite could choose the most suitable ones for the whole nation. The refined tastes of upper classes served as a basis for artistic traditions that are officially associated with the essence of Japanese art and culture. The modern Japanese state presented the Japanese cultural traditions as a proof of Japanese cultural superiority and, therefore, there has all along been a tendency also to protect the Japanese cultural traditions from foreign influences if those influences appear to be harmful for Japanese traditions or question their right to live and flourish. As we have seen *nihonga* was seen by the policy makers as more Japanese than *yôga*, regardless of the theme of painting and without much of critical discussion whether *nihonga* really is that uniquely Japanese. After all, both Japanese *nihonga* and *yôga* are deeply influenced by former foreign and Japanese art and by each other.

The conservatism of Japanese old visual art traditions has also another dimension. The old cultural traditions of high culture enjoyed the patronage of the upper classes and, therefore, social status and arts were (/are) closely connected. Japan had a very different social development leading to modernization than most European countries: in Europe it was the middle class which created a mass market for arts (starting in the Netherlands) and served as a basis for new political and intellectual elite, The European middle class was also early to develop a vast array of political and cultural ideologies, many of which directly challenged old political leadership and cultural traditions. The meaning of visual arts and arts in general were reinvented and reinterpreted in Europe especially in the 19th century, a process that also created the foundation for modern art from the beginning of the 20th century. The artists, especially painters and writers, poets and novelists, were particularly active politically. In all these developments Japan was late, but its political, social and economic modernization meant that the new invented cultural traditions were from the beginning influenced by European cultural traditions that influenced those who were determined enough to learn about them, even if and when the state was not always too eager to support that kind of modernizations.

In visual arts the most important new development was the introduction of Western painting *(yôga)* to Japan. During the Edo Period Western painting was effectively prevented by the bakufu policies from spreading although the use of pespective in Japanese arts obviously benefited from the sporadic contacts with Western art. However, the during the Bakumatsu years the pioneers of Japanese *yôga* such as Takahashi Yûichi trained seriously and learned the Western methods – to be mixed with their profound knowledge of Japanese painting, *nihonga* methods. In early Meiji Period there was a brief period when Western painting had a chance to be fully introduced to Japan. *Kôbu bijutsu gakkô* (Technical Art School 工部美術学校, 1876-1883) was established by the Meiji government and it employed Italian artists to teach western methods. Also Takahashi Yûichi was hired as a professor (For more about Takahashi, Hashimoto 2007: 28-40). However, the political currents soon turned against *yôga* and *nihonga* soon gained dominance and official support. Many *nihonga* artists adopted western techniques and practices, for instance, with perspective, shading, themes or composition. Western painting continued in Japan, but Western painters could not count on official support or even popular support and understanding. Against all odds many *yôga* artists persevered in Japan and many of these artists went to study in Europe as Japan lacked opportunities. While some Japanese artists developed quite international outlook and taste, the Japanese *yôga* community as a whole shifted towards Japanization *(nihonka)* already during the Meiji Period and during the early Shôwa Period *yôga* was actively supporting militarism in Japan and was seen primarily as a tool of war propaganda (Tsuruya 2007: 69-100).

In other words, the Japanese *yôga* artists were seldom testing the limits of freedom of expression and, instead, many of the *yôga* artists were quick to discover that *yôga* offered far better means for dramatic battlefield panorama paintings and realistic bloodshed than *nihonga*. Lucky for *nihonga* most of the *nihonga* artists saw no reason to abandon their traditional themes. It is also likely that at least some officers knew better *nihonga* and had more respect for its artistic tradition. Moreover, no one suspected the Japanese pedigree of *nihonga* and, therefore, there was no need to prove anything. On the contrary, *yôga* was something that had to be Japanized first in order to show its value to the new Japanese regime. In fact, the military leaders gave very precise instructions what kind of *yôga* they wanted, and that was what they got: they wanted realistic and accurate paintings, which recorded the bravery and suffering of the soldiers. Accuracy meant that such details as those of weaponry and uniforms as well as details relating to geography and foreign places had to be right and this kind of ideas do not really fit easily with the long traditions of Japanese aesthetic ideas and elegance achieved through simplicity. Interestingly, it was the military that was criticizing the weakness of a distinct Japanese style of *yôga*. They wanted *yôga* to surpass the western tradition (without even knowing much about the western tradition) and also record the establishment of a new Japanese imperial culture and saw no problem in the idea of instructing from above what the artists should do to achieve that artistic greatness. Of course, propaganda painting was something of a global trend at the same time with Nazi Germany, Italy and Soviet Union all pioneering and polishing that *genre,* while battlefield panoramas have a proud tradition within western tradition especially during the Renaissance and Baroque art. In modern warfare photojournalism is continuing that tradition and most armed forces still expect to see themselves being depicted in more or less heroic manner by those who accompany them or cooperate with them.

In Japan the ideas of modernism in visual arts could not easily develop as the authorities were actively trying to destroy everything that was distantly connected with anarchism or socialism. Suspicious ideas often included democracy and Christianity, meaning that there was little room for anything directly connected with the western tradition, except for technical skills. This does not mean that the authorities could successfully weed out everything they wanted as Japan did already have its small communities of people who had gained a deep knowledge about all the forbidden fruits, from anarchism to communism and from Christianity to democracy. Taishô Period, after all, is strongly associated with the ultimately failed attempt to develop a functioning multiparty democracy and a pluralistic society – and a cultural renewal. Visual arts in Taishô democracy reflect some of those attempts to bring new ideas to Japan. Especially in the less ideological niches of popular culture Western ideas and techniques were wholeheartedly embraced, often in a delightful mixture with Japanese traditions. The Japanese illustrations and graphic design, as well as fashion of this era show that the Japanese had no problem turning away from Japanese traditions to adopt Western styles or mixed styles. The influences of *Art Nouveau* and *Art Deco* can easily be detected in Japanese styles of the late Meiji to early Shôwa, but in Japan it was difficult to raise this art to the level of high art as that position was already reserved to *nihonga*.

For instance, *Art Nouveau* never attained the political significance of cultural awakening and national romanticism that it had in many parts of Europe. In Japan, *Art Nouveau* was mostly a harmless decorative element and had little to do with new representation of Japanese culture. Meanwhile the modern styles of painting or symbolism in Japanese *yôga* could not hope to gain acceptance in the ideological climate of the time – and they also were far more difficult to utilize in commercial ways or turn to fancy decorative novelties. That left the artistically more ambitious and more internationally minded artists with the only choice of finding their supporters among the small community of people who fell under the radar of the military and who knew well enough the Western art world and its currents. Taishô democracy did nurture a small group of internationally minded people, some with considerable wealth to spend on art. The Japanese modernization also did, indeed, create a new middle class, but the rise of militarism soon made life very difficult for anyone who did not fully support the aims and dominance of the military. It seems that most *yôga* artists were quick to choose the side of the military and the works defying the new political order were quite rare in visual arts. However, in literature it is easier to find examples of artists who clearly shared different values and understood the value of their own art (see e.g. Tanizaki Jun'ichirô and Yosano Akiko).

Revisionism and Japanese Culture Revisited

'Utsukushii kuni e' (toward a beautiful nation) is the title of Prime Minister Abe Shinzô's bestseller book in July 2006 just before Abe became first time chosen the Prime Minister. The main message of the book is that the Japanese should be proud of their country, its history and culture. The most controversial parts of the book deal with Japanese war history and the book, for instance, puts forward the argument that the convicted Japanese A Class war criminals were not war criminals according to Japanese law or understanding (Abe 2006). During his terms as Prime Minister Abe administrations have shown understanding to the need to promote Japanese culture abroad. Asô Tarô (Prime Minister from 2008 to 2009), the Foreign Minister during Abe's first administration is well known for his personal support for Japanse *manga* and *anime*, and Asô and Abe ended up giving a face to Japanese governments attempt to use contemporary Japanese culture to appeal to both Japanese younger generations and to soften and diversity Japanese image abroad. Abe and Asô both have a history of revisionistic interpretations of Japanese history (especially war history) and the statements by Abe in 2013 and afterwards are very much the root of present absence of working relations between Japan and South Korea. The concept of *'utsukushii'* is very much a concept of aesthetics. In the context of conservative Japanese political ideology it is, however, quite removed from the actual beauty of Japanese nature, people or artistic traditions. Instead, the message is that nationalism and patriotism should be the established norm and that they must be taught to every citizen. Although Abe and Asô apparently have had every opportunity to see real Japanese art, if one studies their writings and speeches, there is very little connected with art and culture to be found and in those cases culture is predominantly treated as a tool to advance business interests. Towards to end of his long stay as Prime Minister Abe used less frequently references to Japanese aesthetics or Japanese history. However, he has not done anything to soften his previous views. His successors, Prime Minister Suga and most recently Prime Minister Kishida (4 October 2021–) are politically very close or dependent on former Prime Minister Abe (due to the nature of Japanese party factions). Ther role of party factions or more precisely, Abe faction, has increased with Prime Minister Kishida strongly favouring the members of this faction. It is too early to tell about his views on culture or arts except that he has revealed himself to be a Demon Slayer fan and pledged to support manga and anime during his term (Liu 2021).

Where Does Japan Fit in the Theory of Art and Art Discourses?

The idea of art being a window to another culture and to the minds of people has been often put forward in art theory. John Dewey in his *Art as Experience* (1934) was treating art primarily as a universal language that makes it possible to achieve the internal experience of another language without knowing much about culture or studying such annoying "external facts" as history, geography, religion or natural languages. Dewey also argued that the aesthetic quality is the same for Greeks, Chinese and Americans (Dewey 1934). In short, Dewey was very much a democrat and a product of the American society of his time. However, he must known his Kant, as Kant's thought was the subject of his now lost Ph.D. dissertation. By the time when Dewey wrote about his art theory he had also spent his sabbatical leave in Japan and two more years in China (1919-1921) and should have known about the special qualities of East Asian arts. Dewey's idea apparently was to encourage people to have a direct emotional experience or encounter with art rather than first filtering the experience through everything that has been taught to them. With global culture that advise is still worth keeping in mind as open mind is still very good tool when approaching different cultures and societies. However, knowledge of cultural and social context is not always harmful and, instead, may help us understand and appreciate far more the piece of art.

Knowing nothing about the cultural and social context leads people to interpret the culture from their own cultural Tradition (using the term of Hans-Georg Gadamer; Gadamer 1995: 238). We really can not escape our own past when we make judgments about the world. With Japanese culture the issue of interpretation across traditions and cultures is a very important issue as the process has been going on for centuries and both ways. With modern art the focus is very much with the interaction between Japan and the West, whereas the older layer of far more one-sided Japanese interaction with China is still part of Japanese cultural traditions. My position with the need to learn the cultural context is that it really helps to know something about Christian religion and ancient Greek and Roman art to understand Renaissance arts or Christianity and Western traditions of music to appreciate Bach, Carmina Burana or Gospel music. Similarly, it helps to know about the Zen Buddhism, Shintô and a variety of Japanese life styles to have a basic understanding why particular types of art traditions have thrived in Japan. Furthermore, to understand contemporary Japanese arts it is not enough to know about great Japanese cultural traditions themselves, but it is often equally important to know about Japanese popular culture and social issues. Not every piece of art is connected with *manga*, Fukushima, 3-11, Senkaku Islands, Abenomics or Abenomasks, but quite a few are, although – luckily – not in the most straightforward way. Paying attention to all the trifle meanings and cues while viewing visual arts easily runs the risk of killing much of the direct emotional experience. Dewey certainly was ahead of his time when he was talking about universal language of arts and the need to ignore much of the insignificant boring realities. Indeed, he seems to be still ahead of our time, too, if we take a look at what has happened to the arts and art theory after him. In spite of all the globalization and post-post-modernity art is still viewed very much within the context of national and local culture rather than some universal standard.

Modern art theory very much owes to theorists like Michel Foucault who shifted the focus away from the intentions of the artist to more general interpretations of art. In short, the viewers interpret the pieces of art by trying to find what is meaningful in it, and by doing so work within the cultural and social context of their time. While agreeing with Foucault on the idea of futility to trace the artist's original thinking, I find it also unnecessary and unfair to treat piece of art as texts with meanings that are to be explained with self-assured voice, especially by the chosen few who dare to claim to possess the key to understand and explain someone else's (visual) art. The idea of a cultural debate and discourse is also very much related to specific cultures and time. It is also a human social activity within a highly hierarchical community. In France, cultural discourses are different from Japan or the United States and the participation has different rules and patterns, and in all these countries all these phenomena are subject to change. Art writing and critique themselves are worth taking a critical look when saying anything about art. The Japanese art establishment often seems to be very well informed about the latest developments in art elsewhere while their discourse about art may well be quite disconnected from the thinking of their fellow citizens. While the Japanese art professionals may know a lot about the art elsewhere, Japanese art itself may still often be hidden from the rest of the world behind a language barrier and other barriers, such as the ones created by the peculiar mechanisms of Japanese art market. Art writing in Japanese is not followed nearly as often by professionals abroad as is the case with writings in Indo-languages. After all, in arts and humanities there is a long tradition requiring professionals to be well-versed in different languages and cultural traditions. However, with Japanese or Chinese it simply takes much more effort, even if the significance of that expertise is acknowledged in the first place. Any talk about universal language of arts takes place within a landscape where the knowledge of some traditions is still all too often taken more or less as granted while some other traditions are regarded as exotic, primitive, worthless or cumbersome and the domain of specialists who know their own speciality. The absence of real communication is too often replaced by stereotypes and reinforced images. The phenomena of Japanese colorful and cute Superflat art and the *otaku* obsessions brought to museum space in the 1990s and after is at least partly an example of Japanese artists producing art that they have found to be well-received both home and abroad. It seems that there is a limit how much diversity is expected from Japanese art. Of course, the result of this "branding" of Japanese art is produced both by the foreign art establishments and by the Japanese art establishment/artists.

One way to counter the hype of officially recognized representatives of any particular period in art, there has been an attempt within the art community to look for outsider art that provides new fresh ways create art. For instance, the Venice Biannale has given increasing weight to art that can be seen as being created by artists who are in some way "outsiders". In many coutries, including Japan there have been attempts to recognise and promote "outsider" art. For instance, some social welfare institutions across Japan have organised exhibitions covering art in different forms: ceramics, textiles, paintings, sculpture and drawings. Very often the quality of that art can be very good but the whole point is that artistic expression itself is important for both the artists and to many people who have an opportunity to see it. Moreover, the life experiences of artists often make their way to their art. Being self-taught and being at the margins of the society are both reasons that normally condemn art and artists to oblivion. The rest of the world never sees much of the Japanese art and the same applies much to the Japanese domestic art scene in Japan. There would be a lot of Japanese visual art that would deserve a chance to be seen by far larger audiences, in Japan and elsewhere – and much of that art is created by artists who are somehow "outside". In short, the Japanese visual art tradition can not be easily defined or studied as there is nowhere a consensus what it covers and what would be meaningful. However, starting from the latest museum exhibitions would be a good start. For most people that already is quite a bit of art to be seen, felt, consumed and analysed.

What is Art, Anyway?

The issue of understanding and appreciating art is a very old one, as I have illustrated with my references to some Greek ideas. However, the modern writing on art is very much indebted to Immanuel Kant, who fixed much of the vocabulary for the next centuries of the discourse. His *Critik der Urtheilskraft* defined what art is and especially what is good art, as well introduced very influential/persistent ideas about such issues as artistic genius (1799, Kritik der Urteilskraft in modern German and Critique of Judgment in English. Kant 1799/1954). Kant, too, was a product of his times and his treatment of aesthetics in connection with ethics and his ideas about the importance to finding distance from the too worldly matters in order to attain morally, ethically and aesthetically superior and lasting art tells much about the mindset of the most progressive artists and thinkers of his time. No wonder that he soon found many followers (a proof that he was not too original?). Kant is often credited for finally raising Genius, the old Roman guiding spirit (of individuals, families, groups or nations) to the rank of extraordinary, almost non-human. The genius *(Genie)* artist of Kant was a Renaissance man who could do anything and did it without learning it from books or from others, but simply discovering it through genius, something like a mix of innate smartness, unbound imagination and energy, on the top of all the other qualities that distinguish the good art from the bad one. After this characterization nothing normal would never again serve as the ideal for an artist.

When Kant write his book visual arts were commonly regarded as inferior to arts requiring the use of language as medium, a tradition that may be extended to the ancient Greeks, who also distinguished a hierarchy of forms of literary and artistic expression. However, visual expression is far older than literature and, in fact, is practiced by many other species, such as apes, elephants and some species of birds. There are also studies indicating that the visual perception of domestic dogs is very similar with humans when the dogs are shown digital images on monitors. The dogs voluntarily focus their gaze in face areas of dog and human images very much the same way as humans – but do prefer dog images (Somppi et al 2010, Kujala et al 2013). The universality of visual art as a language is far more fundamental than Dewey ever thought. Moreover, the lofty ideals that Kant set for arts appear hypocritical and dishonest in our times when people are used to say things without any attempt to embellish them. The beauty of art lies much deeper. Nowadays it is increasingly difficult to even find art theorists who openly talk about the beauty of art or experiencing the beauty of art. The boundaries of visual art have been broadened and at the same time it has become more difficult to find simple explanations to such issues like what art is. That does not diminish the importance of art, quite the contrary, art can show new directions for thinking and interpretation for the simple reason that it is not limited by the same restrictions that natural languages and written languages are.

In this chapter I have analysed the Japanese visual traditions in the context of changing social, cultural and political environment. In addition, I have tried to add something new to the analysis by applying the concept of *mimēsis* in the sense that the human beings are mimetic beings and feeling an urge to create texts and art that reflect, perfection and represent reality (occasionally this might also involve copying). The Japanese visual art does much more than just copy the reality: it, indeed, represents the reality and perfections it. One book chapter obviously can not accomplish the aim of telling everything there is worth telling about the Japanese arts, culture and society – and relations with the rest of the world. Instead, I hope to have demonstrated a somewhat new way to analyse Japanese arts, society and its place in the world. That includes plenty of looking backward, in order to start moving forward. Moreover, *mimêsis* has been used here as a tool for understanding Japanese art and, hopefully, that will stimulate similar research with other art traditions.

REFERENCES

Aristotle. (1996). *Poetics*. Penguin Books.

Barthes, R. (1982). The Empire of Signs. Hill & Wang.

DeHart, J. (2013). Aida Makoto: Far-Sighted Visions of Near-Sighted Japan. *The Diplomat*. https://thediplomat.com/2013/05/aida-makoto-far-sighted-visions-of-near-sighted-japan

Dewey, J. (1934). *Art as Experience*. Minton, Balch & Company.

Elliott, D. (2010). Bye Bye Kitty. In *Bye Bye Kitty. Between Heaven and Hell in Contemporary Japanese Art* (pp. 1–45). Japan Society and the Yale University Press.

Favell, A. (2011). *Before and After Superflat. A Short History of Japanese Contemporary Art 1990-2011*. Blue Kingfisher Limited.

Favell, A. (2018). Aida Makoto: Notes from an Apathetic Continent. In A. Freedman & T. Slade (Eds.), *Introducing Japanese Popular Culture*. Routledge. Available online https://eprints.whiterose.ac.uk/116906/1/Aida-Routledge-Final-AAM.pdf doi:10.4324/9781315723761-39

Fenellosa, E. F. (2007). *Epochs of Chinese and Japanese Art. An Outline History of East Asiatic Design* (Vol. 1 and 2). Stone Bridge Classics. (Original work published 1912)

Finrando no kurashi to dezain. (2013). http://www.finland-design.com

Gadamer, H.-G. (1985). Truth and Method. Crossroad.

Heng. (2010). Mirror, mirror on the wall, who is the softest of them all? Evaluating Japanese and Chinese strategies in the 'soft' power competition era. *International Relations of the Asia-Pacific, 10*(2), 275-304.

Higuchi, Y. (2019). Higuchi Yûko gashû. Sâkasu. Gurafikkusha.

Hogg, C. (2006). *Top Japanese artist 'plagiarised'*. BBC News. http://news.bbc.co.uk/2/hi/asia-pacific/5049840.stm

Isao, S. (2013). Kinsei kindai manga ryakushi. In Nihon no zushô manga. Pai intânashonaru.

Kant, I. (1954). Kritik der Urteilskraft. Academic Press. (Original publication 1799)

Kôkyô, H. (1986). Tôyôga no fuhenteki shisô o motomete. In Nihonga. Zairyô to hyôgen. Bijutsu shuppansha.

Kyôko, W. (2010). Nihon bijutsushi no rinkakusen. In Furu/ima. Kurabete wakaru nippon bijutsu nyûmon. Heibonsha.

Lee, S. E. (1983). *Reflections of Reality in Japanese Art*. Cleveland Museum of Art and Indiana University Press.

Liddell, C. B. (2013). Francis Bacon: The restlessness of human existence. *Japan Times*. http://www.japantimes.co.jp/culture/2013/03/28/arts/francis-bacon-the-restlessness-of-human-existence/#.UYjG-PXb5NVY

Liu, N. (2021). *Japan's New Prime Minister Is a Demon Slayer Fan, Plans to Support Manga and Anime*. https://www.cbr.com/japan-prime-minister-demon-slayer-fan-support-manga-anime/

Mami, K. (2012). Japan, the Chaotic, and Aida Makoto. In Aida Makoto. Tensai de gomen nasai. Monument for nothing. Mori Art Museum.

Mayu, T. (2007). The Ascent of Yôga in Modern Japan and in the Pacific War. In Inexorable Modernity. Japan's Grappling with Modernity in the Arts. Lexington Books.

Miiamaaria, K., Heini, T., Sanni, S., Laura, H., & Christina, K. (2013). Reactivity of Dogs' Brain Oscillations to Visual Stimuli Measured with Non-Invasive Electroencephalography. *PLoS One, 8*(5), e61818. doi:10.1371/journal.pone.0061818 PMID:23650504

Miyashita, Y. (2006). La présence culturelle de la France au Japon et la collection Matsukata. *Relations Internationales, 2*(134), 37-53. https://www.cairn.info/revue-relations-internationales-2008-2-page-37.htm doi:10.3917/ri.134.0037

Mizuma Art Gallery. (2021). *I can't stop the patriotism.* Aikoku ga tomararenai. https://mizuma-art.co.jp/en/exhibitions/2107_aidamakoto/

Museum, A. A. (2019). The Ateneum Exhibition the Modern Woman to Travel to Japan. *Ateneum News.* https://ateneum.fi/en/news/the-modern-woman-to-japan/

Museum, M. A. (2013). Aida Makoto. Monument for Nothing. Aida Makoto. Tensai de gomen nasai. Solo exhibition catalogue. Kyôto Seigensha.

Tsuji Nobuo. (2005). *Nihon bijutsu no rekishi. Jômon kara manga-anime made.* Tôkyô daigaku shuppankai.

Nye, J. S. (2004). *Soft Power: The Means to Success in World Politics.* Public Affairs.

Osamu, H. (2007). *Nihon bijutsushi 7.* Shinchôsha.

Pes, J., & Sharpe, E. (2013). Attendance survey 2012: Tour de force show puts Tokyo on top. *The Art Newspaper,* 245.

Shimbun, M. (2013). *Kûrujapan: Nihon ryôri de shôbu.* http://mainichi.jp/select/news/20130529k0000m040065000c.html

Shinzô. (2006). *Utsukushii kuni e.* Bungei shunjû.

Somppi, S., Törnqvist, H., Hänninen, L., Vainio, O., & Krause, C. (2010). *Dogs do look at images. Eye tracking in canine cognition research.* Research team of University of Helsinki, Research Center of Animal Welfare. Paper presented in The 2nd Canine Science Forum in Vienna, Austria.

Souzou: Outsider Art from Japan. (2013). *Wellcome Collection.* http://www.wellcomecollection.org/whats-on/exhibitions/japanese-outsider-art.aspx

Sughi, A. (2006a). *Alberto Sughi, and plagiarism.* Alberto Sughi's homepage. http://www.albertosughi.com/f_prima_pagina/2006_05_30.asp

Sughi, A. (2006b). *Somewhere behind.* Alberto Sughi's blog. http://blog.absolutearts.com/blogs/archives/00000272.html

The Art Newspaper. (n.d.). *Visitor Figures 2020: top 100 art museums revealed as attendance drops by 77% worldwide.* https://www.theartnewspaper.com/2021/03/30/visitor-figures-2020-top-100-art-museums-revealed-as-attendance-drops-by-77percent-worldwide

Treat, J. W. (1996). Introduction. Japanese Studies into Cultural Studies. In J. W. Treat (Ed.), *Contemporary Japan and Popular Culture* (pp. 1–14). University of Hawai'i Press.

Wada Y. O. H. (n.d.). http://wadayoshihiko.com/profile.html

Warner, L. (1952). *The Enduring Art of Japan.* Grove Press. doi:10.4159/harvard.9780674865693

Youngs, I. (2013). *Could China save UK art galleries?* BBC News. https://www.bbc.com/news/entertainment-arts-22387987

Compilation of References

Abass, K., Ganle, J. K., & Adaborna, E. (2015). Coliform contamination of peri-urban grown vegetables and potential public health risks: Evidence from Kumasi, Ghana. *Journal of Community Health*, *41*(2), 392–397. doi:10.100710900-015-0109-y PMID:26512013

Abass, K., Ganle, J. K., & Afriyie, K. (2016). The germs are not harmful: Health risk perceptions among consumers of peri-urban grown vegetables in Kumasi, Ghana. *GeoJournal*, *84*(4), 1–15. doi:10.100710708-016-9747-6

Abbam, T., Amoako, J. F., Dash, J., & Padmadas, S. S. (2018). Spatiotemporal variations in rainfall and temperature in Ghana over the twentieth century, 1900–2014. *Earth and Space Science (Hoboken, N.J.)*, *5*(4), 120–132. doi:10.1002/2017EA000327

Abdullah, H. C., Hamed, S., Kechil, R., & Hamid, A. H. (2013). Emotional management skill at the workplace: A study at the government department in Seberang Perai Tengah. *International Journal of Social Science and Humanity*, *3*(4), 365–368. doi:10.7763/IJSSH.2013.V3.263

Abitbol, P., & Botero, F. (2005). Teoría de elección racional: estructura conceptual y evolución reciente. *Colombia internacional*, (62), 132-145.

Aboagye, D., Adu-Prah, S., & Dumedah, G. (2018). Assessing social vulnerability to biophysical hazards in the Kumasi metropolis, Ghana. *GeoJournal*, *83*(6), 1285–1299. doi:10.100710708-017-9833-4

Aboagye, D., Adu-Prah, S., & Owusu-Sekyere, E. (2019). Exposures to multiple biophysical stressors and response capacities of riparian communities in Ghana. *GeoJournal*, 1–14.

Acholiya, R. (2013). Corruption in Education System in India: A Study. *Pioneer Journal*, 100-105.

Ackerson, N. O. B., & Awuah, E. (2012). Microbial risk assessment of urban agricultural farming: A case study on Kwame Nkrumah University of Science and Technology campus, Kumasi, Ghana. *IACSIT International Journal of Engineering and Technology*, *2*(3), 356–363.

Acquaah, M., Amoako-Gyampah, K., & Jayaram, J. (2011). Resilience in family and nonfamily firms: An examination of the relationships between manufacturing strategy, competitive strategy, and firm performance. *International Journal of Production Research*, *49*(18), 5527–5544. doi:10.1080/00207543.2011.563834

Adetunde, L. A., Sackey, I., Dombirl, D. D., & Mariama, Z. W. (2015). Potential links between irrigation water microbiological quality and fresh vegetables quality in Upper East Region of Ghana. *Annual Research & Review in Biology*, *6*(6), 347–354. doi:10.9734/ARRB/2015/8273

Adger, W. (2000). Social and ecological resilience: Are they related? *Progress in Human Geography*, *24*(3), 347–364.

Afshartous, D. (2011). *Determination of sample size for multilevel model design.* Department of Statistics, UCLA. Retrieved from https://escholarship.org/uc/item/4cg0k6g0

Aftab, W., Siddiqui, F. J., Tasic, H., Perveen, S., Siddiqi, S., & Bhutta, Z. A. (2020). Implementation of health and health-related sustainable development goals: Progress, challenges and opportunities-a systematic literature review. *BMJ Global Health, 5*(8), 1–10. doi:10.1136/bmjgh-2019-002273 PMID:32847825

Ahuja, D., & Tatsutani, M. (2009). Sustainable energy for developing countries. *S.A.P.I.EN.S, 2*(1). https://journals.openedition.org/sapiens/823

Aigbogun, O., Ghazali, Z., & Razali, R. (2014). A framework to enhancesupply chain resilience the case of Malaysian pharmaceutical industry. *Global Business and Management Research, 6*(3), 219–225.

Aivaloglou, E., & Hermans, F. (2019, February 27-March 2). Early programming education and career orientation: The effects of gender, self-efficacy, motivation and stereotypes. In *Proceedings of the 50th ACM Technical Symposium on Computer Science Education* (pp. 679-685). 10.1145/3287324.3287358

Akay, A., Bargain, O., Dolls, M., Neumann, D., Peichl, A., & Siegloch, S. (2012). Happy taxpayers? Income taxation and well-being. *Income Taxation and Well-Being*, (526), 1–34.

Akrong, M. O., Ampofo, J. A., & Danso, S. K. A. (2012). The quality and health implications of urban irrigation water used for vegetable production in the Accra Metropolis. *Journal of Environmental Protection, 3*(11), 1509–1518. doi:10.4236/jep.2012.311167

Alberti, T. L. (2014). *Health literacy and health information-seeking behaviors are associated with adherence to discharge instructions (Order No. 3580089).* Available from ProQuest Dissertations & Theses Global.

Albrito, P. (2012). Making cities resilient: Increasing resilience to disastersat the local level. *Journal of Business Continuity & Emergency Planning, 5*(4), 291–297.

Aldrich, D. P., & Meyer, M. A. (2014). Social capital and community resilience. *The American Behavioral Scientist, 59*(2), 254–269. doi:10.1177/0002764214550299

Aleksić, A., Stefanović, M., Arsovski, S., & Tadić, D. (2013). An assessment of organizational resilience potential in SMEs of the process industry, a fuzzy approach. *J Loss Prevent Proc, 26*, 1238–1245. doi:10.1016/j.jlp.2013.06.004

Alencar, M. K., Johnson, K., Mullur, R., Gray, V., Gutierrez, E., & Korosteleva, O. (2017). The efficacy of a telemedicine-based weight loss program with video conference health coaching support. *Journal of Telemedicine and Telecare, 25*(3), 151–157. doi:10.1177/1357633X17745471 PMID:29199544

Alers, A., Salen, P., Yellapu, V., Garg, M., Bendas, C., Cardiges, N., Domer, G., Oskin, T., Fisher, J., & Stawicki, S. (2019). *Fundamentals of Medical Radiation Safety: Focus on Reducing Short-Term and Long-Term Harmful Exposures.* doi:10.5772/intechopen.85689

Alesina, A., & Angeletos, G. M. (2005). Fairness and redistribution. *The American Economic Review, 95*(4), 960–980. doi:10.1257/0002828054825655

Alesina, A., Di Tella, R., & MacCulloch, R. (2004). Inequality and happiness: Are Europeans and Americans different? *Journal of Public Economics, 88*(9-10), 2009–2042. doi:10.1016/j.jpubeco.2003.07.006

Alesi, P. (2008). Building enterprise-wide resilience by integrating business continuity capability into day-to-day business culture and technology. *Journal of Business Continuity & Emergency Planning, 2*, 214–220.

Compilation of References

Alexander, B., Darby, F., Fischer, K., Jack, A. A., Le Sane, C. B., Staisloff, R., & Stout, K. A. (2002). The post pandemic college and the future of: The academic enterprise, teaching and learning, the student experience, enrollment, business models and community colleges. *The Chronicle of Higher Education*.

Algert, S. J., Baameur, A., & Renvall, M. J. (2014). Vegetable output and cost savings of community gardens in San Jose, CA. *Journal of the Academy of Nutrition and Dietetics, 114*(7), 1072–1076. doi:10.1016/j.jand.2014.02.030 PMID:24751664

Ali, D. A., Figley, C. R., Tedeschi, R. G., Galarneau, D., & Amara, S. (2021, June 17). Shared trauma, resilience, and growth: A roadmap toward transcultural conceptualization. *Psychological Trauma: Theory, Research, Practice, and Policy*. Advance online publication. doi:10.1037/tra0001044 PMID:34138612

Allenby, B., & Roitz, J. (2005). Building the resilient firm: The new challenge to EHS organizations. *Environmental Quality Management, 15*(2), 27–36.

Allworth, E., & Hesketh, B. (1999). Construct-oriented biodata: Capturing change-related and contextually relevant future performance. *International Journal of Selection and Assessment, 7*(2), 97–111. doi:10.1111/1468-2389.00110

Alm, J., Jackson, B. R., & McKee, M. (1992). Estimating the determinants of taxpayer compliance with experimental data. *National Tax Journal, 45*(1), 107–114. doi:10.1086/NTJ41788949

Alm, J., McClelland, G. H., & Schulze, W. D. (1992). Why do people pay taxes? *Journal of Public Economics, 48*(1), 21–38. doi:10.1016/0047-2727(92)90040-M

Amann, B., & Jaussaud, J. (2012). Family and non-family business resilience in an economic downturn. *Asia Pacific Business Review, 18*, 203–223.

American Public Health Association (APHA). (1992). *Standard Methods for the Examination of Water and Wastewater* (18th ed.). APHA.

Amoah, P., Drechsel, P., & Abaidoo, R. C. (2005). Irrigated urban vegetable production in Ghana: Sources of pathogen contamination and health risk elimination. *Irrigation and Drainage, 54*(S1), 49–61. doi:10.1002/ird.185

Amoah, P., Drechsel, P., Abaidoo, R. C., & Henseler, M. (2007). Irrigated urban vegetable production in Ghana: Microbiological contamination in farms and markets and associated consumer risk groups. *Journal of Water and Health, 5*(3), 455–466. doi:10.2166/wh.2007.041 PMID:17878560

Anderson, P. M., & Butcher, K. F. (2006). Childhood obesity: Trends and potential causes. *The Future of Children, 16*(1), 19–45. doi:10.1353/foc.2006.0001 PMID:16532657

Andrew, S. (1998). Self-efficacy as a predictor of academic performance in science. *Journal of Advanced Nursing, 27*(3), 596–603. doi:10.1046/j.1365-2648.1998.00550.x PMID:9543047

Andrews, M. (2014). *Health literacy competencies for health professionals: A Delphi study (Order No. 3648821)*. Available from ProQuest Dissertations & Theses Global.

Anheier, H. K., & Moulton, L. (1999). Organizational failures, breakdowns, and bankruptcies: An introduction. In H. K. Anheier (Ed.), *When things go wrong: Organizational failures and breakdowns* (pp. 3–16). Sage Publications.

Annarelli, A., & Nonino, F. (2016). Strategic and operational management of organizational resilience: Current state of research and future directions. *Omega, 62*, 1–18.

Annas, G. J. (2003). HIPAA Regulations— A New Era of Medical-Record Privacy? *The New England Journal of Medicine, 348*(15), 1486–1490. doi:10.1056/NEJMlim035027 PMID:12686707

Anon. (1994). The Microbiology of Water 1994: Part 1-Drinking Water. Reports on Public Health and Medical subjects, No. 71. Methods for the Examination of Water and Associated Materials. London: HMSO.

Antonsen, S. (2009). Safety Culture and the Issue of Power. *Safety Science*, *47*(2), 183–191. doi:10.1016/j.ssci.2008.02.004

Antunes, P. (2011). BPM and exception handling: Focus on organizational resilience. *IEEE Transactions on Systems, Man, and Cybernetics*, *41*, 383–392. doi:10.1109/TSMCC. 2010.20625 04

Antwi-Agyei, P., Cairncross, S., Peasey, A., Price, V., Bruce, J., Baker, K., Moe, C., Ampofo, J., Armah, G. and Ensink, J. (2015). A farm to fork risk assessment for the use of wastewater in agriculture in Accra, Ghana. *PLoS ONE*, *10*(11), 1-19. e0142346. doi:10.1371/journal.pone.0142346

Ariani, D. W. (2016). Why do I study? The mediating effect of motivation and self-regulation on student performance. *Business Management in Education*, *14*(2), 153–178. doi:10.3846/bme.2016.329

Aristotle. (1996). *Poetics*. Penguin Books.

Armstrong, L. E., & Johnson, E. C. (2018). Water intake, water balance, and the elusive daily water requirement. *Nutrients*, *10*. doi:10.3390/nu10121928 PMID:30563134

Arrington, E. G., & Wilson, M. N. (2000). A re-examination of risk and resilience during adolescence: Incorporating culture and diversity. *Journal of Child and Family Studies*, *9*(2), 221–230. doi:10.1023/A:1009423106045

Arya, B. S. (2012). *A Comparative Study of Public and Private Health Services in Mumbai Region-Availability and Utilization Pattern* [Thesis]. S.N.D.T. Women's University, Department of Economics.

Asfaw, K., Bumpus, M., Coen, T., Edelstein, C., Rojas, A. L., Mendieta, C., . . . Vidarte, R. (n.d.). Health Service Delivery in Punjab, India. Woodrow Wilson School of Public and International Affairs.

Asgary, A., Kong, A., & Levy, J. (2009). Fuzzy-Jess expert system for indexing business resiliency. TIC-STH'09: 2009 IEEE Toronto International Conference - Science and Technology for Humanity, 153-158. https://doi.org/10.1109/TIC-STH.2009.5444516

Asiedu, B., Adetola, J., & Kissi, I. O. (2017). Aquaculture in troubled climate: Farmers' perception of climate change and their adaptation. *Cogent Food & Agriculture*, *3*(1), 1–16. doi:10.1080/23311932.2017.1296400

Ates, A., & Bititci, U. (2011). Change process: A key enabler for building resilient SMEs. *International Journal of Production Research*, *49*(18), 5601–5618. doi:10.1080/00207543.2011.563825

Ayyash-Abdo, H., Sanchez-Ruiz, M. J., & Barbari, M. L. (2016). Resiliency predicts academic performance of Lebanese adolescents over demographic variables and hope. *Learning and Individual Differences*, *48*, 9–16. doi:10.1016/j.lindif.2016.04.005

Azevedo, J. S., de Souza-Sarkis, J. E., Oliveira, T. A., & Ulrich, T. (2012). Tissue-specific mercury concentrations in two catfish species from the Brazilian coast. *Brazilian Journal of Oceanography*, *60*, 211–219.

Badreldin, H. A., & Atallah, B. (2020). Global drug shortages due to COVID-19: Impact on patient care and mitigation strategies. *Research in Social & Administrative Pharmacy*. Advance online publication. doi:10.1016/j.sapharm.2020.05.017

Bagherpour, A., & Nouri, A. (2020, October 11). COVID Misinformation Is Killing People: This "infodemic" has to stop. *Scientific American*.

Bagozzi, R. P., & Yi, Y. (1988). On the Evaluation of Structural Equation Models. *Journal of the Academy of Marketing Science*, *16*(1), 74–94. doi:10.1007/BF02723327

Bahuguna, P., Mukhopadhyay, I., Chauhan, A. S., Rana, S. K., Selvaraj, S., & Prinja, S. (2018). Sub-national health accounts: Experience from Punjab State in India. *PLoS One*, *13*(12), e0208298. Advance online publication. doi:10.1371/journal.pone.0208298 PMID:30532271

Bain, R., Gundry, S., Wright, J., Yang, H., Pedley, S., & Bartram, J. (2012). Accounting for water quality in monitoring access to safe drinking-water as part of the Millennium Development Goals: Lessons from five countries. *Bulletin of the World Health Organization*, *90*(3), 228–235. doi:10.2471/BLT.11.094284 PMID:22461718

Baker, K., Hagedorn, R. L., Hendricks, T., Clegg, E. N., Joseph, L., McGowan, M., & Olfert, M. D. (2018). Katalyst: Development of a fifth-grade novel approach to health and science experiential learning. *Science Activities*, *55*(3-4), 127–139. doi:10.1080/00368121.2018.1561406 PMID:31723307

Bandura, A. (1988). Organizational applications of social cognitive theory. *Australian Journal of Management*, *13*, 275–302. doi:10.1177/031289628801300210

Bandura, A. (1997). *Self-efficacy*. Freeman and Company.

Bandura, A. (1997). Self-efficacy: The exercise of control. *The Freeman*.

Bandura, A., & McClelland, D. C. (1977). *Social learning theory* (Vol. 1). Prentice Hall. doi:10.1177/105960117700200317

Banerjee, E. (2013). Comparative Study on Healthcare facilities produced by Government and Privately Owned Hospitals in Kolkata Municipal Corporation. *Asian Journal of Multidisciplinary Studies*, *1*(3), 7–16.

Bansal, P. T., & Corley, K. (2011). From the editors: The coming of age for qualitative research: Embracing the diversity of qualitative methods. Academy of Management Journal, 54(2), 233–237. https://doi.org/doi:10.5465/amj.2011.60262792

Baral, N. (2013, March). What Makes Grassroots Conservation Organizations Resilient? An Empirical Analysis of Diversity, Organizational Memory, and the Number of Leaders. *Environmental Management*, *51*(3), 738–749.

Baral, S., Logie, C. H., Grosso, A., Wirtz, A. L., & Beyrer, C. (2013). Modified social ecological model: A tool to guide the assessment of the risks and risk contexts of HIV epidemics. *BMC Public Health*, *13*, S293. doi:10.1186/1471-2458-13-482

Barnard, C. P. (1994). Resiliency: A shift in our perception? *The American Journal of Family Therapy*, *22*, 135–144.

Barros, V., Abdulla, A., & Boncheva, A. I. (Eds.). (2009). *Scoping meeting for an IPCC special report on extreme events and disasters: managing the risks*. WGII Technical Support Unit.

Barthes, R. (1982). The Empire of Signs. Hill & Wang.

Baseel, C. (2014). Beautiful 400-year-old garden in Okayama about to be replaced with condominium complex. *Sora News 24*. https://soranews24.com/2014/07/22/beautiful-400-year-old-garden-in-okayama-about-to-be-replaced-with-condominium-complex/

Bautron, I., & Ravaud, P. (2014). CONSORT for nonpharmacologic treatments. In D. Moher, D. G. Altman, K. F. Schulz, I. Simera, & E. Wager (Eds.), *Guidelines for reporting health research. A user's manual* (pp. 101–112). John Wiley and Sons.

Becker, M. H., & Maiman, L. A. (1975). Socio-behavioral determinants of compliance with health and medical care recommendations. *Medical Care*, *13*(1), 10–24. doi:10.1097/00005650-197501000-00002 PMID:1089182

Beck, U., & Holzer, B. (2007). Organizations in world risk society. In C. M. Pearson, C. Roux-Dufort, & J. A. Clair (Eds.), *International Handbook of Organizational Crisis Management* (pp. 3–21). Sage Publications Inc.

Beemsterboer, P. (2010). *Ethics and Law in Dental Hygiene* (2nd ed.). Saunders Elsevier.

Behavioral Economics in Child Nutrition Programs (BEN). (2018). *Smarter Lunchroom Movement.* The Cornell Center for Behavioral Economics in Child Nutrition Programs. Cornell University. Retrieved from: http://www.ben.cornell.edu/index.html

Benard, B. (1991). *Fostering resiliency in kids: Protective factors in the family, school, and community.* Department of Education.

Benjamin, W. (1969). The Work of Art in the Age of Mechanical Reproduction. In *Illuminations.* Schocken Books. Available online: https://web.mit.edu/allanmc/www/benjamin.pdf

Benjamin, W. (1970). The Author as Producer. *New Left Review, 1*(62). Available online: https://www.marxists.org/reference/archive/benjamin/1970/author-producer.htm

Bentler, P. M., & Bonnet, D. C. (1980). Significance Tests and Goodness of Fit in the Analysis of Covariance Structures. *Psychological Bulletin, 88*(3), 588–606. doi:10.1037/0033-2909.88.3.588

Berkhout, F., Hertin, J., & Gann, D. (2006). Learning to adapt: Organizational adaptation to climate change impacts. *Climatic Change, 78,* 135–156.

Bernstein, A., Bienstock, D., Hay, D., Uzunoglu, M., Zussman, G. (2004). Power Grid Vulnerability to Geographically Correlated Failures—Analysis and Control Implications. *IEEE INFOCOM 2014 Proceedings,* 2634–2642.

Bernstein, S. (2019). Being present. *Nursing, 49*(6), 14–17. doi:10.1097/01.NURSE.0000558105.96903.af PMID:31124847

Berrang-Ford, L., Ford, J. D., & Paterson, J. (2011). Are we adapting to climate change? *Global Environmental Change, 21,* 25–33.

Beugelsdijk, S., Kostova, T., Kunst, V. E., Spadafora, E., & van Essen, M. (2017). Cultural distance and firm internationalization: A meta-analytical review and theoretical implications. *Journal of Management, 44*(1), 89–130. doi:10.1177/0149206317729027 PMID:30443095

Bhamidipaty, A., Lotlikar, R., & Banavar, G. (2007). RMI: a framework for modeling and evaluating the resiliency maturity of IT service organizations. IEEE International Conference on Services Computing (SCC 2007), 300–307. https://doi.org/10.1109/SCC.2007.94

Bhamra, R., Dani, S., & Burnard, K. (2011). Resilience: The Concept, a Literature Review and Future Directions. *International Journal of Production Research, 49*(18), 5375–5393.

Bhidé, A. V. (2000). *The Origin and Evolution of New Businesses.* Oxford University Press.

Biggs, D. (2011). Understanding resilience in a vulnerable industry: The case of reef tourism in Australia. *Ecology and Society, 16*(1), 30.

Bingham, C. B., Eisenhardt, K. M., & Davis, J. P. (2007). *Opening the black box of organizational expertise: understanding what firms learn from their process experience and how that learning unfolds over time.* University of Maryland Working Paper.

Bingham, C. B., & Eisenhardt, K. M. (2011). Rational Heuristics: The 'Simple Rules' that Strategists Learn from Process Experience. *Strategic Management Journal, 32*(13), 1437–1464.

Bingham, C. B., & Haleblian, J. (2012). How Firms Learn Heuristics: Uncovering Missing Components of Organizational Learning. *Strategic Entrepreneurship Journal, 6*(2), 152–177.

Binswanger, M. (2006). Why does income growth fail to make us happier?: Searching for the treadmills behind the paradox of happiness. *Journal of Socio-Economics, 35*(2), 366–381. doi:10.1016/j.socec.2005.11.040

Birke, M., Rauch, U., Harazim, H., Lorenz, H., & Glatte, W. (2010). Major and trace elements in German bottled water, their regional distribution, and accordance with national and international standards. *Journal of Geochemical Exploration*, *107*(3), 245–271. doi:10.1016/j.gexplo.2010.06.002

Birkie, S. E., Trucco, P., & Kaulio, M. (2017). Sustaining performance under operational turbulence: The role of Lean in engineer-to-order operations. *International Journal of Lean Six Sigma*, *8*(4), 457–481.

Birkmann, J., Cardona, O. D., Carreño, M. L., Barbat, A. H., Pelling, M., Schneiderbauer, S., Kienberger, S., Keiler, M., Alexander, D., Zeil, P., & Welle, T. (2013). Framing vulnerability, risk and societal responses: The MOVE framework. *Natural Hazards*, *67*(2), 193–211. doi:10.100711069-013-0558-5

Bjørnskov, C., Dreher, A., & Fischer, J. A. (2007). The bigger the better? Evidence of the effect of government size on life satisfaction around the world. *Public Choice*, *130*(3-4), 267–292. doi:10.100711127-006-9081-5

Bjørnskov, C., Gupta, N. D., & Pedersen, P. J. (2008). Analysing trends in subjective well-being in 15 European countries, 1973–2002. *Journal of Happiness Studies*, *9*(2), 317–330. doi:10.100710902-007-9055-4

Blettner, M., Schlehofer, B., Breckenkamp, J., Kowall, B., Schmiedel, S., Reis, U., Potthoff, P., Schuz, J., & Berg-Beckhoff, G. (2008, September 19). Mobile phone base stations and adverse health effects: Phase 1 of a population-based, cross-sectional study in Germany. *Occupational and Environmental Medicine*, *66*(2), 118–123. https://www.ncbi.nlm.nih.gov/pubmed/19017702. doi:10.1136/oem.2007.037721 PMID:19017702

Blundel, R. (2013). *Quarterly Survey of Small Business in Britain Special Topic: Resilience and Recovery*. Open University. (Original work published 2013)

Boesz, C., & Lloyd, N. (2008). Investigating international misconduct. *Nature*, *452*(7188), 686–687. doi:10.1038/452686a PMID:18401384

Boin, A., & van Eeten, M. (2013). The resilient organization. *Public Management Review*, *15*(3), 429-445.

Boin, A., Hart, P., Stern, E., & Sundelius, B. (2005). *The politics of crisis management: Public leadership under pressure*. Cambridge University Press.

Boin, A., & McConnell, A. (2007). Preparing for critical infrastructure breakdowns: The limits of crisis management and the need for resilience. *Contingencies and Crisis Management*, *15*(1), 50–59.

Boin, A., & McConnell, A. (2007). Preparing for critical infrastructure breakdowns: The limits of crisis management and the need for resilience. *Journal of Contingencies and Crisis Management*, *15*(1), 50–59.

Boin, A., & van Eeten, M. J. B. (2013). The Resilient Organization—A critical appraisal. *Public Management Review*, *15*, 429–445.

Bonanno, G. A., Brewin, C. R., Kaniasty, K., & Greca, A. M. L. (2010). Weighing the costs of disaster: Consequences, risks, and resilience in individuals, families, and communities. *Psychological Science in the Public Interest*, *11*(1), 1–49. doi:10.1177/1529100610387086 PMID:26168411

Bong, M., & Hocevar, D. (2002). Measuring self-efficacy: Multitrait-multimethod comparison of scaling procedures. *Applied Measurement in Education*, *15*(2), 143–171. doi:10.1207/S15324818AME1502_02

Bonneville-Roussy, A., Bouffard, T., Palikara, O., & Vezeau, C. (2019). The role of cultural values in teacher and student self-efficacy: Evidence from 16 nations. *Contemporary Educational Psychology*, *59*, 101798. Advance online publication. doi:10.1016/j.cedpsych.2019.101798

Bonß, W. (2015). Karriere und sozialwissenschaftliche Potenziale des Resilienzbegriffs. In M. Endreß & A. Maurer (Eds.), *Resilienz im Sozialen. Theoretische und empirische Analysen* (pp. 15–31). Springer VS.

Borenstein, M., Hedges, L. V., Higgins, J. P. T., & Rothstein, H. R. (2009). *Introduction to meta-analysis*. John Wiley & Sons. doi:10.1002/9780470743386

Borman, W. C., & Motowidlo, S. J. (1993). Expanding the criterion domain to include elements of contextual performance. In N. Schmitt & W. C. Borman (Eds.), *Personnel selection in organizations*. Jossey-Bass.

Bowers, J., & Kumar, P. (2015). Students' perceptions of teaching and social presence: A comparative analysis of face-to-face and online learning environments. *International Journal of Web-Based Learning and Teaching Technologies*, *10*(1), 27–44. doi:10.4018/ijwltt.2015010103

Brady, A. C., Kim, Y. E., & Cutshall, J. (2021). The what, why, and how of distractions from a self-regulated learning perspective. *Journal of College Reading and Learning*, *51*(2), 153–172. doi:10.1080/10790195.2020.1867671

Brähler, E., Hinz, A., & Scheer, J. W. (2006). *GBB-24. Der Gießener Beschwerdebogen*. Huber.

Brahma, S. S. (2009). Assessment of construct validity in management research. *Journal of Management Research*, *9*, 59–71.

Brand, F. S., & Jax, K. (2007). Focusing the meaning(s) of resilience: Resilience as a descriptive concept and a boundary object. *Ecology and Society*, *12*, 23–39.

Branscum, P., Kaye, G., & Warner, J. (2013). Impacting dietary behaviors of children from low-income communities: An evaluation of a theory-based Nutrition Education Program. *Californian Journal of Health Promotion*, *11*(2), 43–52. doi:10.32398/cjhp.v11i2.1530

Brewer, L. (2005). The whistleblower. *Accountants Today*, 10-12.

British Standards Institution. (2006). *BS 25999-1 Code of Practice for Business Continuity Management*. British Standards Institution.

Bronfenbrenner, U. (1977). Toward an experimental ecology of human development. *The American Psychologist*, *32*(7), 513–531. doi:10.1037/0003-066X.32.7.513

Brown, A. J. (2001). Internal witness management: An art or a science? *Ethics and Justice*, *3*(2), 45–61.

Brown, K. W., Gessesse, B., Butler, L. J., & MacIntosh, D. L. (2017). Potential effectiveness of Point-of-Use filtration to address risks to drinking water in the United States. *Environmental Health Insights*, *11*. Advance online publication. doi:10.1177/1178630217746997 PMID:29270018

Bruneau, M., Chang, S., Eguchi, R. T., Lee, G. C., O'Rourke, T. D., Reinhorn, A. M., & von Winterfeldt, D. (2002). *A framework to quantitatively assess and enhance seismic resilience of communities*. Multidisciplinary Center for Earthquake Engineering Research, State University of New York at Buffalo.

Bryson, L. (1992). *Welfare and the State: Who Benefits?: Who Benefits?* Macmillan International Higher Education.

Brzezinski, M. (2019). Top incomes and subjective well-being. *Journal of Economic Psychology*, *73*, 60–65. doi:10.1016/j.joep.2019.05.003

Burke, R., & Cooper, C. (2013). *Voice and Whistle-blowing in Organizations: Overcoming Fear, Fostering Courage, and Unleashing Candour*. Edward Elgar Publishing.

Burnard, K., & Bhamra, R. (2011). Organisational resilience: Development of a conceptual framework for organisational responses. *International Journal of Production Research*, *49*(18), 5581–5599.

Burnard, K., & Bhamra, R. (2011). Organisational resilience: Development of a conceptual framework for organisational responses. *International Journal of Production Research*, *49*, 5581–5599.

Burrell, D. N. (2020). Management consulting intervention case study in a complex and toxic hospital organizational culture. *Holistica Journal of Business and Public Administration*, *11*(2), 100–114. doi:10.2478/hjbpa-2020-0022

Burrell, D. N., Bhargava, N., Duncan, T., Lindsay, P. V., Cole, C. M., & Sangle, P. (2019). Exploring the Complex Nature of Ethical Cultures in Health Care Organizations. *International Journal of Applied Research on Public Health Management*, *4*(2), 29–46. doi:10.4018/IJARPHM.2019070103

Burrell, D., Rahim, E., Juris, K., & Sette, Z. (2010). Developing knowledge transfer-oriented ethical cultures in US government agencies regulating the commercial use of nuclear power. *International Journal of Nuclear Knowledge Management*, *4*(2), 165. doi:10.1504/IJNKM.2010.032314

Byrne, B. M., Oakland, T., Leong, F. T., van de Vijver, F. J., Hambleton, R. K., Cheung, F. M., & Bartram, D. (2009). A critical analysis of cross-cultural research and testing practices: Implications for improved education and training in psychology. *Training and Education in Professional Psychology*, *3*(2), 94–105. doi:10.1037/a0014516

Camgoz, S. M., Tektas, O. O., & Metin, I. (2008). Academic attributional style, self-efficacy and gender: A cross-cultural comparison. *Social Behavior and Personality*, *36*(1), 97–114. doi:10.2224bp.2008.36.1.97

Caralli, R. A., Curtis, P. D., Allen, J. H., White, D. W., & Young, L. R. (2010). Improving operational resilience processes: The CERT® resilience management model. Proceedings - SocialCom 2010: 2nd IEEE International Conference on Social Computing, PASSAT 2010: 2nd IEEE International Conference on Privacy, Security, Risk and Trust, 1165–1170. https://doi.org/10.1109/SocialCom.2010.173

Carlson, S., Rosenbaum, D., Keith-Jennings, B., & Nchako, C. (2016). *SNAP Works for America's Children*. Center on Budget and Policy Priorities. Retrieved from: https://www.cbpp.org/research/food-assistance/snap-works-for-americas-children

Carlton, C. E. (2016). *Evaluation of health literacy as a predictor of the need for additional medical care (Order No. 10111908)*. Available from ProQuest Dissertations & Theses Global.

Carmeli, A., Gelbard, R., & Gefen, D. (2010). The importance of innovation leadership in cultivating strategic fit and enhancing firm performance. *The Leadership Quarterly*, *21*(3), 339–349. doi:10.1016/j.leaqua.2010.03.001

Carmeli, A., & Markman, G. D. (2011). Capture, governance, and resilience: Strategy implications from the history of Rome. *Strategic Management Journal*, *32*, 322–341.

Carpenter, S. R., & Brock, W. A. (2008). Adaptive capacity and traps. *Ecology and Society*, *13*(2), 40. doi:10.5751/ES-02716-130240

Carpenter, S. R., Westley, F., & Turner, M. G. (2005). Surrogates for resilience of social-ecological systems. *Ecosystems (New York, N.Y.)*, *8*, 941–944.

Carroll, A. B., & Buchholtz, A. K. (2000). *Organization and society* (4th ed.). South-Western College.

Carter, R. (2002). The impact of Public Schools on Childhood Obesity. Published: November 6, 2002. *Journal of the American Medical Association*, *288*(17), 2180. doi:10.1001/jama.288.17.2180-JMS1106-6-1 PMID:12413386

Carvalho, H., Barroso, A., Machado, V., Azevedo, S., & Cruz-Machado, V. (2012). Supply chain redesign for resilience using simulation. *Computers & Industrial Engineering*, *62*(1), 329–341.

Carver, N., Gupta, V., & Hipskind, J. (2020). *Medical Error*. StatPearls Publishing. https://www.ncbi.nlm.nih.gov/books/NBK430763/

Castleden, M., McKee, M., Murray, V., & Leonardi, G. (2011). Resilience thinking in health protection. *Journal of Public Health*, *33*(3), 369–377. doi:10.1093/pubmed/fdr027

Castro, D.C., Samuels, M., & Harman, A.E. (2013). Growing healthy kids: A community garden-based obesity prevention program. *American Journal of Preventive Medicine, 44*(3S3), S193-199. doi:10.1016/j.amepre.2012.11.024

Catalan, C., & Robert, B. (2011). *Evaluation of organizational resilience: application in Quebec*. Centre risque & performance, École Polytechnique de Montréal.

Catherine, A. (2017). Investigating the relationship between science self-efficacy beliefs, gender, and academic achievement, among high school students in Kenya. *Journal of Education and Practice*, *8*(8), 146–153.

Cénat, J. M., Noorishad, P. G., Blais-Rochette, C., McIntee, S. E., Mukunzi, J. N., Darius, W. P., Broussard, C., Morse, C., Ukwu, G., Auguste, E., & Menelas, K. (2020). Together for hope and resilience: A humanistic experience by the vulnerability, trauma, resilience and culture lab members during the COVID-19 pandemic. *Journal of Loss and Trauma*, *25*(8), 643–648. doi:10.1080/15325024.2020.1774704

Center for Disease Control and Prevention. (2019). *Childhood obesity*. Retrieved from https://www.cdc.gov/obesity/data/childhood.html

Centers for Disease Control. (2018). *Obesity. CDC Healthy Schools*. Centers for Disease Control and Prevention. Retrieved from: https://www.cdc.gov/healthyschools/obesity/index.htm

Chamlee-Wright, E. (2010). *The Cultural and Political Economy of Recovery: Social Learning in a Post-Disaster Environment* (Vol. 12). Routledge.

Chang, W., & Wong, W. (1998), Rational traditionalism: Chinese values in Singapore. In Values and Development. Centre for Advanced Studies, Faculty of Arts and Social Sciences, National University of Singapore.

Chan, J. K. (2011). Enhancing Organisational Resilience: Application of Viable System Model and MCDA in a Small Hong Kong Company. *International Journal of Production Research*, *49*(18), 5545–5563. doi:10.1080/00207543.2011.563829

Cheng, J. L. C., & Kesner, I. F. (1997). Organizational Slack and Response to Environmental Shifts: The Impact of Resource Allocation Patterns. *Journal of Management*, *23*(1), 1–18.

Cheng, P. (2007). The cultural value of resilience: The Singapore case study. *Cross Cultural Management*, *14*(2), 136–149.

Cheung-Judge, M. Y., & Holbeche, L. (2015). *Organization development: A practitioner's guide for OD and HR*. Kogan Page Limited.

Chewning, L. V., Lai, C. H., & Doerfel, M. (2012). Organizational Resilience following Disaster: A Longitudinal View of Information and Communication Technologies Use to Rebuild Communication Structure. *Management Communication Quarterly*, *27*(2), 237–263. doi:10.1177/0893318912465815

Chewning, L. V., Lai, C.-H., & Doerfel, M. L. (2013). Organizational resilience and using information and communication technologies to rebuild communication structures. *Management Communication Quarterly*, *27*, 237–263. doi:10.1177/08933 18912 46581 5

Compilation of References

Chmutina, K., Lizarralde, G., Bosher, L., & Dainty, A. (2016). Unpacking Resilience Policy Discourse. *Cities (London, England)*, *58*, 70–79. doi:10.1016/j.cities.2016.05.017

Chokshi, M., Patil, B., Khanna, R., Neogi, S. B., Sharma, J., Paul, V. K., & Zodpey, S. (2016). Health systems in India. *Journal of Perinatology*, *36*(S3, s3), S9–S12. doi:10.1038/jp.2016.184 PMID:27924110

Chowdhury, R., Ramond, A., O'Keeffe, L. M., & Shahzad, S. (2019). Environmental toxic metal contaminants and risk of cardiovascular disease: Systematic review and meta-analysis. *BMJ (Clinical Research Ed.)*, *362*, k3310. PMID:30158148

Chu, S., & Majumdar, A. (2012). Opportunities and challenges for a sustainable energy future. *Nature*, *488*(August), 294–303. doi:10.1038/nature11475 PMID:22895334

Cicchetti, D. (2010). Resilience under conditions of extreme stress: A multilevel perspective. *World Psychiatry; Official Journal of the World Psychiatric Association (WPA)*, *9*(3), 145–154. doi:10.1002/j.2051-5545.2010.tb00297.x PMID:20975856

Cicha, K., Rizun, M., Rutecka, P., & Strzelecki, A. (2021). COVID-19 and higher education: First-year students' expectations toward distance learning. *Sustainability*, *13*(1889), doi:10.3390/su13041889

Clasen, T., Prüss-Üstun, A., Mathers, C. D., Cumming, O., Cairncross, S., & Colford, J. M. Jr. (2014). Estimating the impact of unsafe water, sanitation and hygiene on the global burden of disease: Evolving and alternative methods. *Tropical Medicine & International Health*, *19*(8), 884–893. doi:10.1111/tmi.12330 PMID:24909205

Coaffee, J. (2008). Risk, resilience and environmentally sustainable cities. *Energy Policy*, *36*(12), 4633–4638.

Coates, G., McGuinness, M., Wright, N. G., Guan, D., Harries, T., & McEwen, L. (2016). SESAME: Improving Small and Medium Enterprises' Operational Response and Preparedness to Flood Events. In Management of Natural Disasters (pp. 107 – 116). WIT Press.

Coates, G., McGuinness, M., Wright, N. G., Guan, D., Harries, T., & McEwen, L. (2016). SESAME: Improving Small and Medium Enterprises' Operational Response and Preparedness to Flood Events. In Management of Natural Disasters. WIT Press.

Cobbina, S. J., Kotochi, M. C., Korese, J. K., & Akrong, M. O. (2013). Microbial contamination in vegetables at the farm gate due to irrigation with wastewater in the Tamale Metropolis of Northern Ghana. *Journal of Environmental Protection*, *4*(07), 676–682. doi:10.4236/jep.2013.47078

Cocker, F., & Joss, N. (2016). Compassion Fatigue among Healthcare, Emergency, and Community Service Workers: A Systematic Review. *International Journal of Environmental Research and Public Health*, *13*(6), 618. doi:10.3390/ijerph13060618 PMID:27338436

Cohen, J. (2008). *Statistical power analysis for the behavioral sciences*. Laurence Erlbaum Associates.

Coleman-Jensen, A., Nord, M., Andrews, M., & Carlson, S. (2012). *Household Food Security in the United States in 2011. ERR141*. U.S. Department of Agriculture, Economic Research Service.

Congressional Budget Office. (2020). *Interim Economic Projections for 2020 and 2021*. Author.

Conlon, P., Havlisch, R., Kini, N., & Porter, C. (2008). Using an Anonymous Web-Based Incident Reporting Tool to Embed the Principles of a High-Reliability Organization. In *Advances in Patient Safety: New Directions and Alternative Approaches* (Vol. 1: Assessment). Agency for Healthcare Research and Quality. https://www.ncbi.nlm.nih.gov/books/NBK43630/

Connor, K. M., & Davidson, J. R. (2003). Development of a new resilience scale: The Connor-Davidson resilience scale (CD-RISC). *Depression and Anxiety*, *18*(2), 76–82. doi:10.1002/da.10113 PMID:12964174

Constantine Brown, J. L., Ong, J., Mathers, J. M., & Decker, J. T. (2017). Compassion fatigue and mindfulness: Comparing mental health professionals and MSW Student Interns. *Journal of Evidence-Informed Social Work*, *14*(3), 119–130. doi:10.1080/23761407.2017.1302859 PMID:28388339

Cooper, M. D. (2000). Towards a model of safety culture. *Safety Science*, *36*(2), 111–136. doi:10.1016/S0925-7535(00)00035-7

Corey, C. M., & Deitch, E. A. (2011). Factors Affecting Business Recovery Immediately after Hurricane Katrina. *Journal of Contingencies and Crisis Management*, *19*(3), 170–181. doi:10.1111/j.1468-5973.2011.00642

Cornell. (2019). *Agriculture and Food Systems*. Cornell Cooperative Extension. Retrieved from: https://cce.cornell.edu/program/agriculture

Coullahan, R.; Shepherd, C. (2008). Enhancing enterprise resilience in the commercial facilities sector. *Journal of Business Continuity & Emergency Planning*, *3*(1), 5-18.

Courtemanche, G. (1988, February). The Ethics of Whistle-Blowing. *Internal Auditor*, 36–41.

Coutu, D. L. (2002). How resilience works. *Harvard Business Review*, *80*(5), 46–55.

Cox, L. (2012). Community resilience and decision theory challenges for catastrophic events. *Risk Analysis*, *32*(11), 1919–1934.

Crichton, M., Ramsay, C., & Kelly, T. (2009). Enhancing organizational resilience through emergency planning: Learnings from cross-sectoral lessons. *Journal of Contingencies and Crisis Management*, *17*(1), 24–37.

Cumming, G. S., Barnes, G., & Perz, S. (2005). An exploratory framework for the empirical measurement of resilience. *Ecosystems (New York, N.Y.)*, *8*, 975–987.

Cunha, E. M. P., Castanheira, F., Neves, P., Story, J., Rego, A., & Clegg, S. (2013). *Resilience in organizations*. Working paper.

Cunningham, E. (2016). Cultivating enlightenment: The manifold meaning of Japanese Zen gardens. *Education about. Asia*, *21*(3), 32–36.

Currence, J. (2017). *Developing Business Acumen (Making an Impact in Small Business HR)*. Society for Human Resources Management.

Curry, N., & Pillay, P. (2012). Biogas prediction and design of a food waste to energy system for the urban environment. *Renewable Energy*, *41*(May), 200–209. doi:10.1016/j.renene.2011.10.019

Dai, W., Peterson, A., & Kenney, T. (2017). Quantitative microscopy of the *Drosophila* ovary shows multiple niche signals specify progenitor cell fate. *Nature Communications*, *8*, 1244. doi:10.103841467-017-01322-9

Dalgaard-Nielsen, A. (2017). Organizational resilience in national security bureaucracies: Realistic and practicable? *Journal of Contingencies and Crisis Management*, *25*(4), 341–349. doi:10.1111/1468-5973.12164

Dalziell, E. P. (2005). Understanding the vulnerability of organizations. *Proc., 1855 Wairarapa Earthquake Symp.*, 130–135.

Dane, E. (2011). Paying attention to mindfulness and its effects on task performance in the workplace. *Journal of Management*, *37*(4), 997–1018. doi:10.1177/0149206310367948

Danes, S. M., Lee, J., Amarapurkar, S., Stafford, K., Haynes, G., & Brewton, K. E. (2009). Determinants of family business resilience after a natural disaster by gender of business owner. *Journal of Developmental Entrepreneurship*, *14*(4), 333–354. doi:10.1142/S1084946709001351

Danopoulos, E., Twiddy, M., & Rotchell, J. M. (2020). Microplastic contamination of drinking water: A systematic review. *PLoS One*, *15*(7), e0236838. doi:10.1371/journal.pone.0236838 PMID:32735575

Daughton, C. G. (2018). Monitoring wastewater for assessing community health: Sewage Chemical-Information Mining (SCIM). *The Science of the Total Environment*, *619-620*, 748–764. doi:10.1016/j.scitotenv.2017.11.102 PMID:29161600

Davidson, A. K. (2006). *A Zen life in nature: Musō Soseki in his gardens*. Center for Japanese Studies, University of Michigan.

Davidson, R. M., Lauritzen, A., & Seneff, S. (2013). Biological water dynamics and entropy: A biophysical origin of cancer and other diseases. *Entropy (Basel, Switzerland)*, *15*(12), 3822–3876. doi:10.3390/e15093822

Davis, A., Sampilo, M., Gallagher, K., Dean, K., Saroja, M., Ma, Q., He, J., Sporn, N., & Befort, C. (2016). Treating rural pediatric obesity through telemedicine vs. telephone: Outcomes from a cluster randomized controlled trial. *Journal of Telemedicine and Telecare*, *22*(2), 86–95. doi:10.1177/1357633X15586642 PMID:26026186

Day, J. R., & Anderson, R. A. (2011). Compassion fatigue: An application of the concept to informal caregivers of family members with dementia. *Nursing Research and Practice*, *2011*, 408024. doi:10.1155/2011/408024 PMID:22229086

De Backer, L., Keer, H. V., & Valcke, M. (2015). Promoting university students' metacognitive regulation through peer learning: The potential of reciprocal peer tutoring. *Higher Education*, *70*(3), 469–486. doi:10.100710734-014-9849-3

De Florio, V. (2013). On the Constituent Attributes of Software and Organizational Resilience. *Interdisciplinary Science Reviews*, *38*(2), 122–148. doi:10.1179/0308018813Z.00000000040

de Vries, H. P., & Hamilton, R. T. (2017). Why Stay? In Business and Post-Disaster Management - Business, Organisational and Consumer Resilience and the Christchurch Earthquakes. London: Routledge.

DeHart, J. (2013). Aida Makoto: Far-Sighted Visions of Near-Sighted Japan. *The Diplomat*. https://thediplomat.com/2013/05/aida-makoto-far-sighted-visions-of-near-sighted-japan

del Campana, P. (2021). *Nichiren. Japanese Buddhist monk*. Encyclopedia Britannica. https://www.britannica.com/biography/Nichiren

Deleuze, G., & Guattari, F. (1987). A Thousand Plateaus: Capitalism and Schizophrenia. University of Minnesota Press.

Dellaportas, S., Gibson, K., Alagiah, R., Hutchinson, M., Leung, P., & Van Homrigh, D. (2005). *Ethics, governance, and accountability: A professional perspective*. John Wiley & Sons, Ltd.

Demarzo, M. M. P., Cebolla, A., & Garcia-Campayo, J. (2015). The implementation of mindfulness in healthcare systems: A theoretical analysis. *General Hospital Psychiatry*, *37*(2), 166–171. doi:10.1016/j.genhosppsych.2014.11.013 PMID:25660344

Demmer, W. A., Vickery, S. K., & Calantone, R. (2011). Engendering resilience in small-and medium-sized enterprises (SMEs): A case study of Demmer Corporation. *International Journal of Production Research*, *49*, 5395–5413.

Deng, Y., & Pan, F. (2019). Dependence analysis of Sino-US trade. *Journal of Physics: Conference Series*, *1176*(4), 042093. Advance online publication. doi:10.1088/1742-6596/1176/4/042093

Denyer, D. (2017). *Organizational Resilience: A summary of academic evidence, business insights and new thinking*. BSI and Cranfield School of Management.

Deshpande, S. P. (1996). Ethical climate and the link between success and ethical behaviour: An empirical investigation of a non-profit organization. *Journal of Business Ethics*, *15*(3), 315–320. doi:10.1007/BF00382957

Desmet, B. (2018). *Supply chain strategy and financial metrics* (1st ed.). Kogan Page.

Dew, N., Goldfarb, B., & Sarasvathy, S. D. (2006). Optimal Inertia: When Organizations Should Fail. *Advances in Strategic Management*, *23*, 73-99.

Dewald, J., & Bowen, F. (2010). Storm clouds and silver linings: Responding to disruptive innovations through cognitive resilience. *Entrepreneurship Theory and Practice*, *34*(1), 197–218. doi:10.1111/j.1540-6520.2009.00312.x

Dewey, J. (1934). *Art as Experience*. Minton, Balch & Company.

Di Tella, R., & MacCulloch, R. (2008). Gross national happiness as an answer to the Easterlin Paradox? *Journal of Development Economics*, *86*(1), 22–42. doi:10.1016/j.jdeveco.2007.06.008

Diener, E. (2006). Guidelines for national indicators of subjective well-being and ill-being. *Applied Research in Quality of Life*, *1*(2), 151–157. doi:10.100711482-006-9007-x

Dluhosch, B., & Horgos, D. (2013). Trading up the happiness ladder. *Social Indicators Research*, *113*(3), 973–990. doi:10.100711205-012-0122-9

Doe, E. O., Awua, A. K., & Larbi, D. K. (2016). Microbial quality monitoring of water from a lake associated with varying human activity. *International Journal of Health Sciences*, *4*(1), 160–165.

Doern, R. (2016). Entrepreneurship and Crisis Management: The Experiences of Small Business during the London 2011 Riots. *International Small Business Journal*, *34*(3), 276–302. doi:10.1177/0266242614553863

Donaldson, L. (2001). *The contingency theory of organizations*. Sage. doi:10.4135/9781452229249

Dongre, A. S., Inamdar, I. F., & Gattani, P. L. (2017). Nomophobia: A study to evaluate mobile phone dependence and impact of cell phone on health. *National Journal of Community Medicine*, *8*(11), 688–693.

Doyle Corner, P., Singh, S., & Pavlovich, K. (2017). Entrepreneurial Resilience and Venture Failure. *International Small Business Journal*. Advance online publication. doi:10.1177/0266242616685604

Drake, G. (2015). *Health literacy: The knowledge, experience, and education of advanced practice registered nurses in Arizona (Order No. 3710735)*. Available from ProQuest Dissertations & Theses Global.

Dreyer, P., Langeland, K. S., Manheim, D., McLeod, G., & Nacouzi, G. (2016). RAPAPORT (Resilience Assessment Process and Portfolio Option Reporting Tool): Background and Method. RR-1169-AF. RAND Corporation, RR-1169-AF.

Droege, P. (Ed.). (2008). *Urban Energy Transition: From Fossil Fuels to Renewable Power*. Elsevier Ltd. doi:10.1016/B978-0-08-045341-5.00029-3

Duchek, S. (2014). Growth in the face of crisis: The role of organizational resilience capabilities. *Academy of Management Proceedings*, *2014*, 13487.

Duchek, S. (2020). Organizational resilience: A capability-based conceptualization. *Bus Res*, *13*, 215–246. doi:10.100740685-019-0085-7

Duit, A. (2016). Resilience thinking: Lessons for Public Administration. *Public Administration*, *94*, 364–380.

Duncan, C., Jones, K., & Moon, G. (1998). Context, composition and heterogeneity: Using multilevel models in health research. *Social Science & Medicine*, *46*(1), 97–117. doi:10.1016/S0277-9536(97)00148-2 PMID:9464672

Duncum, P. (1999). Case for an art education of everyday experiences. *Studies in Art Education, 40*(4), 295–311. doi:10.2307/1320551

Dyer, J. G., & McGuiness, T. M. (1996). Resilience: Analysis of the concept. *Archives of Psychiatric Nursing, 10*, 2760–282. doi:10.1016/S0883-9417(96)80036-7

Earley, P. C. (1994). Self or group? Cultural effects of training on self-efficacy and performance. *Administrative Science Quarterly, 39*(1), 89–117. doi:10.2307/2393495

Easterling, T., Kerley, K., & Wright, J. (2018). *Overweight and obesity in children and adolescents in schools – The role of school nurse.* Retrieved from: https://www.nasn.org/advocacy/professional-practice-documents/position-statements/ps-overweight

Easterlin, R. A. (2001). Income and happiness: Towards a unified theory. *Economic Journal (London), 111*(473), 465–484. doi:10.1111/1468-0297.00646

Eaton, M. J., & Dembo, M. H. (1997). Differences in the motivational beliefs of Asian American and non-Asian students. *Journal of Educational Psychology, 89*(3), 433–440. doi:10.1037/0022-0663.89.3.433

Eck, J. E., Wagner, K. L., Chapagain, B., & Joshi, O. (2019). A survey of perceptions and attitudes about water issues in Oklahoma: A comparative study. *Journal of Contemporary Water Research & Education, 168*(1), 66–77. doi:10.1111/j.1936-704X.2019.03321.x

Edgeman, R., & Williams, J. A. (2014). Enterprise self-assessment analytics for sustainability, resilience, and robustness. *The TQM Journal, 26*(4), 368–381. https://doi.org/10.1108/TQM-01-2014-0012

Eigenbrod, C., & Gruda, N. (2015). Urban vegetable for food security in cities. A review. *Agronomy for Sustainable Development, 35*(2), 483–498. doi:10.100713593-014-0273-y

Eisenhardt, K. M., & Graebner, M. E. (2007). Theory building from cases: Opportunities and challenges. *Academy of Management Journal, 50*(1), 25–32. doi:10.5465/amj.2007.24160888

Elias, R. (2008). Auditing students' professional commitment and anticipatory socialization and their relationship to whistleblowing. *Managerial Auditing Journal, 23*(3), 283–294. doi:10.1108/02686900810857721

Elliott, D. (2010). Bye Bye Kitty. In *Bye Bye Kitty. Between Heaven and Hell in Contemporary Japanese Art* (pp. 1–45). Japan Society and the Yale University Press.

Elwood, A. (2009). Using the disaster crunch/release model in building organisational resilience. *Journal of Business Continuity & Emergency Planning, 3*, 241–247.

Emilee, R., & Wilhelm-Leen, M. D. (2014). Phase angle, frailty and mortality in older adults. *Journal of General Internal Medicine, 29*(1), 147–154. doi:10.100711606-013-2585-z PMID:24002625

Encyclopedia Britannica. (n.d.). *Bakuhan system.* https://www.britannica.com/place/Japan/The-bakuhan-system

Enshûryû sadô. (n.d.). http://www.enshuryu.com

Erard, B., & Feinstein, J. (1994). The role of moral sentiments and audit perceptions in tax compliance (No. 94-03). Carleton University, Department of Economics.

Erol, O., Mansouri, M., & Sauser, B. (2009). A framework for enterprise resilience using service-oriented architecture approach. 2009 IEEE International Systems Conference Proceedings, 127–132. https://doi.org/10.1109/SYSTEMS.2009.4815785

Erol, O., Sauser, B. J., & Mansouri, M. (2010). A framework for investigation into extended enterprise resilience. *Enterprise Information Systems*, *4*(2), 111–136. doi:10.1080/17517570903474304

European Agency for Health and Safety at Work. (2014). *Calculating the costs of work-related stress and psychosocial risks: A literature review*. Publications Office of the European Union.

European Union (EU). (2015). *Final report summary - MOVE (methods for the improvement of vulnerability assessment in Europe)*. Retrieved on May, 19, 2017 from https://cordis.europa.eu/result/rcn/55194_en.html

Faimunissa Ahmed Khan, A. F. (2014, December). Comparative Study on Private and Government Hospitals working in Hyderabad. *New Man International Journal of Multidisciplinary Studies*, *1*(12).

Fakhouri, T., Hughes, J., Burt, V., Song, M., Fulton, J., & Ogden, C. (2014). *Physical Activity in U.S. Youth Aged 12-15 Years, 2012*. NCHS Data Brief. Retrieved from: https://permanent.access.gpo.gov/gpo77970/db141.pdf

Fan, X., & Sivo, S. A. (2009). Using goodness-of-fit indexes in assessing mean structure invariance. *Structural Equation Modeling*, *16*(1), 54–69. doi:10.1080/10705510802561311

FAO. (1997). Quality control of wastewater for irrigated crop production. FAO.

FAO. (2011). *Database collection of the Food and Agriculture Organization of the United Nations*. Retrieved on June 11 2017 from http://faostat.fao.org/site/354/default.aspx

Farjoun, M. (2010). Beyond dualism: Stability and change as a duality. *Academy of Management Review*, *35*(2), 202–225.

Faul, F., Erdfelder, E., Buchner, A., & Lang, A.-G. (2009). Statistical power analyses using G*Power 3.1: Tests for correlation and regression analyses. *Behavior Research Methods*, *41*(4), 1149–1160. doi:10.3758/BRM.41.4.1149 PMID:19897823

Favell, A. (2018). Aida Makoto: Notes from an Apathetic Continent. In *Introducing Japanese Popular Culture*. Routledge. Available online: https://eprints.whiterose.ac.uk/116906/1/Aida-Routledge-Final-AAM.pdf

Favell, A. (2011). *Before and After Superflat. A Short History of Japanese Contemporary Art 1990-2011*. Blue Kingfisher Limited.

Favell, A. (2018). Aida Makoto: Notes from an Apathetic Continent. In A. Freedman & T. Slade (Eds.), *Introducing Japanese Popular Culture*. Routledge. Available online https://eprints.whiterose.ac.uk/116906/1/Aida-Routledge-Final-AAM.pdf doi:10.4324/9781315723761-39

Feld, L. P., & Frey, B. S. (2002). Trust breeds trust: How taxpayers are treated. *Economics of Governance*, *3*(2), 87–99. doi:10.1007101010100032

Felin, T., Foss, N. J., Heimeriks, K. H., & Madsen, T. L. (2012). Microfoundations of Routines and Capabilities: Individuals, Processes and Structure. *Journal of Management Studies*, *49*(8), 1351–1374.

Fenellosa, E. F. (2007). *Epochs of Chinese and Japanese Art. An Outline History of East Asiatic Design* (Vol. 1 and 2). Stone Bridge Classics. (Original work published 1912)

Ferrer, R., & Klein, W. M. (2015). Risk perceptions and health behavior. *Current Opinion in Psychology*, *5*, 85–89. doi:10.1016/j.copsyc.2015.03.012 PMID:26258160

Figley, C. (1995). *Compassion Fatigue: Coping with Secondary Stress Disorder in Those Who Treat the Traumatized*. Brunner/Mazel.

Fiksel, J. (2003). Designing Resilient, Sustainable Systems. *Environmental Science & Technology*, *37*(23), 5330–5339. doi:10.1021/es0344819

Compilation of References

Finrando no kurashi to dezain. (2013). http://www.finland-design.com

Fiol, C. M., & Lyles, M. A. (1985). Organizational learning. *Academy of Management Review, 10*, 803–813.

Flach, F. F. (1997). *Resilience: How to Bounce Back When the Going Gets Tough!* Hatherleigh Press.

Flavell, J. H. (1985). *Cognitive development* (2nd ed.). Prentice Hall.

Fleming, N., Vaughan, J., & Feeback, M. (2017). Ingestion of oxygenated water enhances lactate clearance kinetics in trained runners. *Journal of the International Society of Sports Nutrition, 14*(1), 9. doi:10.118612970-017-0166-y PMID:28360825

Fleming, R. S. (2012). Ensuring organizational resilience in times of crisis. *J Glob Bus Issues, 6*, 31–34.

Folke C, Carpenter S, Walker B, Scheffer M, Elmqvist T, Gunderson L, Holling CS (2004) Regime shifts, resilience, and biodiversity in ecosystem management. Annu Rev Ecol Evol Syst, 35, 557–581. https://doi.org/ ys.35.02110 3.105711 doi:10.1146/annurev.ecols

Folke, C. (2006). Resilience: The emergence of a perspective for social–ecological systems analyses. *Global Environmental Change, 16*(3), 253–267. doi:10.1016/j.gloenvcha.2006.04.002

Formosa, C. (2015). Understanding power and communication relationships in health settings. British Journal of Healthcare Management, 21(9), 420-424.

Fornell, C., & Larcker, D. F. (1981). Evaluating structural model with unobserved variables and measurement errors. *JMR, Journal of Marketing Research, 18*(1), 39–50. doi:10.1177/002224378101800104

Franzen-Castle, L., Colby, S. E., Kattelmann, K. K., Olfert, M. D., Mathews, D. R., Yerxa, K., Baker, B., Krehibiel, M., Lehrke, T., Wilson, K., Flanagan, S. M., Ford, A., Aguirre, T., & White, A. A. (2019). Development of the *iCook* 4-H Curriculum for youth and adults: Cooking, eating, and playing together for childhood obesity prevention. *Journal of Nutrition Education and Behavior, 51*(3, 3S), S60–S68. doi:10.1016/j.jneb.2018.11.006 PMID:30851862

Freedman, D. A. (1999). Ecological inference and the ecological fallacy. *International Encyclopedia of the social &. Behavioral Science, 6*(4027-4030), 1–7.

Freeman, S. F., Hirschhorn, L., & Maltz, M. (2004). *Organizational resilience and moral purpose: Sandler O'Neill & Partners in the aftermath of 9/11/01.* Paper presented at the Annual Meeting of the Academy of Management, New Orleans, LA.

Freeman, D., Holderby-Fox, L. R., & Housepian, G. (2015). Best practices and cost controls: Improving healthcare access through innovation and communication. *Tennessee Journal Of Law & Policy, 10*(3), 108–144.

Frey, B. S., Luechinger, S., & Stutzer, A. (2009). The life satisfaction approach to valuing public goods: The case of terrorism. *Public Choice, 138*(3-4), 317–345. doi:10.100711127-008-9361-3

Frey, B. S., & Stutzer, A. (2000). Happiness, economy and institutions. *Economic Journal (London), 110*(466), 918–938. doi:10.1111/1468-0297.00570

Frey, B. S., & Stutzer, A. (2002). What can economists learn from happiness research? *Journal of Economic Literature, 40*(2), 402–435. doi:10.1257/jel.40.2.402

Frieden, J. (2020, June 10). *Lack of Health Literacy a Barrier to Grasping COVID-19*. MedPage. Retrieved from: https://www.medpagetoday.com/infectiousdisease/covid19/87002

Fu, W. (2014). The impact of emotional intelligence, organizational commitment, and job satisfaction on ethical behavior of Chinese employees. *Journal of Business Ethics*, *122*(1), 137–144. doi:10.100710551-013-1763-6

Gadamer, H.-G. (1985). Truth and Method. Crossroad.

Gaillard, J. (2007). Resilience of traditional societies in facing natural hazards. *Disaster Prevention and Management*, *16*(4), 522–544.

Galla, B. M., Shulman, E. P., Plummer, B. D., Gardner, M., Hutt, S. J., Goyer, J. P., D'Mello, S. K., Finn, A. S., & Duckworth, A. L. (2019). Why high school grades are better predictors of on-time college graduation than are admissions test scores: The roles of self-regulation and cognitive ability. *American Educational Research Journal*, *56*(6), 2077–2115. doi:10.3102/0002831219843292

Gao, C., Zuzul, T., Jones, G., & Khanna, T. (2017). Over-coming institutional voids: A reputation-based view of long-run survival. *Strategic Management Journal*, *38*, 2147–2167.

Gao, C., Zuzul, T., Jones, G., & Khanna, T. (2017). Overcoming institutional voids: A reputation-based view of long-run survival. *Strategic Management Journal*, *38*, 2147–2167. doi:10.1002mj.2649

Gao, Ch., Zuzul, T., Jones, G., & Khanna, T. (2017). Overcoming Institutional Voids: A Reputation-Based View of Long-Run Survival. *Strategic Management Journal*, *38*(11), 2147–2167.

Gao, L., & Wang, X. (2019). Healthcare Supply Chain Network Coordination Through Medical Insurance Strategies with Reference Price Effect. *International Journal of Environmental Research and Public Health*, *16*(18), 3479. doi:10.3390/ijerph16183479 PMID:31540517

Gaouette, N., Starr, B., & Salama, V. (2020). *Pentagon warns China is exploiting the coronavirus pandemic to wage 'economic warfare' on the US*. Retrieved 31 August 2020, from https://edition.cnn.com/2020/06/16/politics/pentagon-china-economic-warfare/index.html

Garmezy, N. (1991). Resiliency and vulnerability to adverse developmental outcomes associated with poverty. *The American Behavioral Scientist*, *34*, 416–430. doi:10.1177/0002764291034004003

Gasper, D. (2005). Subjective and objective well-being in relation to economic inputs: Puzzles and responses. *Review of Social Economy*, *63*(2), 177–206. doi:10.1080/00346760500130309

Gatto, N., Martinez, L., Spruijt-Metz, D., & Davis, J. (2015). L.A. Sprouts randomized controlled nutrition, cooking, and gardening programme reduces obesity and metabolic risk in Hispanic/Latino youth. *Pediatric Obesity*. Retrieved from: https://onlinelibrary-wiley-com.portal.lib.fit.edu/doi/epdf/10.1111/ijpo.12102

Geller, E. S. (1994). Ten principles for achieving a total safety culture. *Professional Safety*, *39*(9), 18–24.

Gephart, R. P. (2004). Qualitative research and the Academy of Management Journal. *Academy of Management Journal*, *47*(4), 454–462. doi:10.5465/amj.2004.14438580

Gephart, R. P., Van Maanen, J., & Oberlechner, T. (2009). Organizations and risk in late modernity. *Organization Studies*, *30*(2–3), 141–155. doi:10.1177/0170840608101474

Gereffi, G. (2020). What does the COVID-19 pandemic teach us about global value chains? The case of medical supplies. *Journal Of International Business Policy*, *3*(3), 287–301. doi:10.105742214-020-00062-w

Ghana Statistical Service (GSS), Noguchi Memorial Institute for Medical Research (NMIMR), and ORC Macro. (2004). *Ghana Demographic and Health Survey 2003*. GSS, NMIMR, and ORC Macro.

Ghana Statistical Service. (2014). *2010 Population and Housing Census, District Analytical Report: Sunyani Municipality*. Available at: http://www.statsghana.gov.gh/docfiles/2010phc/2010_POPULATION_AND_HOUSING_CENSUS_FINAL_RESULSTS.pdf

Ghoneim, F. M., & Arafat, E. A. (2016). Histological and histochemical study of the protective role of rosemary extract against harmful effect of cell phone electromagnetic radiation on the parotid glands. *Acta Histochemica, 118*(5), 478–485. doi:10.1016/j.acthis.2016.04.010 PMID:27155802

Gielnik, M. M., Spitzmuller, M., Schmitt, A., Klemann, D. K., & Frese, M. (2015). I Put in Effort, Therefore I am Passionate: Investigating the Path from Effort to Passion in Entrepreneurship. *Academy of Management Journal, 58*(4), 1012–1031.

Gillin, L. (2015). *Business acumen: In the workplace*. CreateSpace Independent Publishing.

Gilly, J. P., Kechidi, M., & Talbot, D. (2014). Resilience of organisations and territories: The role of pivot firms. *European Management Journal, 32*(4), 596–602. doi:10.1016/j.emj.2013.09.004

Gimenez, R., Hernantes, J., Labaka, L., Hiltz, S. R., & Turoff, M. (2017). Improving the resilience of disaster management organizations through virtual communities of practice: A Delphi study. *Journal of Contingencies and Crisis Management, 25*, 160–170. doi:10.1111/1468-5973.12181

Gittell, J. H., Cameron, K., Lim, S., & Rivas, V. (2006). Relationships, layoffs, and organizational resilience: Airline industry responses to September 11. *The Journal of Applied Behavioral Science, 42*, 300–329.

Glanz, K. (2018). *Social and Behavioral Theories* (pp. 1-40, Rep. No. 1). Bethesda, MD: Office of Behavioral and Social Science.

Glymph, D. C., Olenick, M., Barbera, S., Brown, E. L., Prestianni, L., & Miller, C. (2015). Healthcare Utilizing Deliberate Discussion Linking Events (HUDDLE): A Systematic Review. *AANA Journal, 83*(3), 183-188.

Goel, V. (2020). *As Coronavirus Disrupts Factories, India Curbs Exports of Key Drugs*. Retrieved 31 August 2020, from https://www.nytimes.com/2020/03/03/business/coronavirus-india-drugs.html

Goleman, D. (2005). *Emotional Intelligence*. Bantam Publishing.

Goleman, D. (2007). *Social Intelligence. Social Intelligence: The New Science of Human Relationships*. Bantam Publishing.

Good, D. J., Lyddy, C. J., Glomb, T. M., Bono, J. E., Brown, K. W., Duffy, M. K., & Lazar, S. W. (2016). Contemplating mindfulness at work: An integrative review. *Journal of Management, 42*(1), 114-142.

Gotts, N. M. (2007). Resilience, panarchy, and world-systems analysis. *Ecology and Society, 12*, 24–38.

Govinda Rao, M. M. C. (2012). Health Care Financing Reforms in India. National Institute of Public Finance and Policy.

Grace, S. O. (2016). *Nursing assessment of health literacy (Order No. 10012950)*. Available from ProQuest Dissertations & Theses Global.

Graham, C., & Felton, A. (2006). Inequality and happiness: Insights from Latin America. *The Journal of Economic Inequality, 4*(1), 107–122. doi:10.100710888-005-9009-1

Graham, C., & Pettinato, S. (2001). Happiness, markets, and democracy: Latin America in comparative perspective. *Journal of Happiness Studies, 2*(3), 237–268. doi:10.1023/A:1011860027447

Grande, O., & Trucco, P. (2008). Resilience analysis of civil defence organization: A fuzzy cognitive Map based approach. *9th International Conference on Probabilistic Safety Assessment and Management 2008, 2*, 1542–1549.

Grant, A. M., Curtayne, L., & Burton, G. (2009). Executive coaching enhances goal attainment, resilience, and workplace wellbeing: A randomized controlled study. *The Journal of Positive Psychology, 4*, 396–407. doi:10.1080/17439760902992456

Graugaard, J. (2012). A tool for building community resilience? A case study of the lewes pound. *Local Environment, 17*(2), 243–260.

Greene, K., Gabrielyan, G., Just, D., & Wansink, B. (2017). Fruit-Promoting Smarter Lunchrooms Interventions: Results From a Cluster RCT. *American Journal of Preventive Medicine, 52*(4), 451–458. doi:10.1016/j.amepre.2016.12.015 PMID:28214248

Greenfield, B., & Jensen, G. M. (2010). Beyond a code of ethics: Phenomenological ethics for everyday practice. *Physiotherapy Research International, 15*, 88–95. doi:10.1002/pri.481 PMID:20564757

Greenland, S., Senn, S. J., Rothmann, K. J., Carlin, J. B., Poole, C., Goodman, S. N., & Altman, D. G. (2016). Statistical tests, P values, confidence intervals, and power: A guide to misinterpretations. *European Journal of Epidemiology, 31*(4), 337–350. doi:10.100710654-016-0149-3 PMID:27209009

Grotberg, E. H. (Ed.). (2003). *Resilience for today: Gaining strength from adversity*. Greenwood Publishing Group., doi:10.5860/CHOICE.41-5592

Grubera, R., Axmann, S., & Schoenberg, M. H. (2005). The influence of oxygenated water in the immune status, liver enzymes, and the generation of oxygen radicals: A prospective, randomized, blinded clinical study. *Clinical Nutrition (Edinburgh, Lothian), 24*(3), 407–414. doi:10.1016/j.clnu.2004.12.007

Gunasekaran, A., Rai, B. K., & Griffin, M. (2011). Resilience and Competitiveness of Small and Medium Size Enterprises: An Empirical Research. *International Journal of Production Research, 49*(18), 5489–5509. doi:10.1080/00207543.2011.563831

Gunderson, L. H. (2000). Ecological resilience: In theory and application. *Annual Review of Ecology and Systematics, 31*, 425–439.

Gunderson, L. H., & Holling, C. S. (2002). *Panarchy: Understanding transformations in human and natural systems*. Island Press.

Gunnestad, A. (2006). Resilience in a cross-cultural perspective: How resilience is generated in different cultures. *Journal of Intercultural Communication, 11*.

Gupta, R. K., & Kumari, R. (2017). National health policy 2017: An overview. *JK Science, 19*(3), 135–136.

Gurvich, V. J., & Hussain, A. S. (2020). In and Beyond COVID-19: US Academic Pharmaceutical Science and Engineering Community Must Engage to Meet Critical National Needs. *AAPS PharmSciTech, 21*(5), 153. doi:10.120812249-020-01718-9 PMID:32449007

Hadley, J., Mowbray, T., & Jacobs, N. (2017). Examining the mediating effect of self-efficacy on approval of aggression and proactive aggression. *Journal of School Violence, 16*(1), 86–103. doi:10.1080/15388220.2015.1116993

Hagedorn, R. L., Baker, K., DeJarnett, S. E., Hendricks, T., McGowan, M., Joseph, L., & Olfert, M. D. (2018). Katalyst Pilot Study: Using Interactive Activities in Anatomy and Physiology to Teach Children the Scientific Foundation of Healthy Lifestyles. *Children (Basel, Switzerland), 5*(12), 162. doi:10.3390/children5120162 PMID:30487474

Hair, J. F., Black, W. C., Babin, B. J., & Anderson, R. E. (2010). *Multivariate data analysis* (7th ed.). Prentice-Hall.

Hall, E., Chai, W., & Albrecht, J. (2016). Relationships between nutrition-related knowledge, self-efficacy, and behavior for fifth-grade students attending Title I and non-Title I schools. *Science Direct*, *96*, 245-253. Retrieved from: https://www-sciencedirect-com.portal.lib.fit.edu/science/article/pii/S0195666315300441

Hambleton, R. K., & Patsula, L. (1998). Adapting tests for use in multiple languages and cultures. *Social Indicators Research*, *45*(1), 153–171. doi:10.1023/A:1006941729637

Hamel, G. & Välikangas, L. (2003). The quest for resilience. *Harvard Business Review*, *81*(9), 52–63.

Hamel, G., & Välikangas, L. (2003). The quest for resilience. *Harvard Business Review*, *81*(9), 52–63.

Handmer, J. W., & Dovers, S. R. (1996). A typology of resilience: Rethinking institutions for sustainable development. *Organization & Environment*, *9*, 482–511. doi:10.1177/10860 26696 00900

Hannah, S. T., Avolio, B. J., Luthans, F., & Harms, P. D. (2008). Leadership efficacy: Review and future directions. *The Leadership Quarterly*, *19*, 669–692. doi:10.1016/j.leaquea.2008.09.007

Harbaugh, W. T., Mayr, U., & Burghart, D. R. (2007). Neural responses to taxation and voluntary giving reveal motives for charitable donations. *Science*, *316*(5831), 1622–1625. doi:10.1126cience.1140738 PMID:17569866

Harvey, P., & Martinko, M. J. (2009). Attribution theory and motivation. In N. Borkowski (Ed.), *Organizational behavior, theory, and design in health care* (pp. 143–158). Jones, and Bartlett Publishers.

Hastie, R., & Dawes, R. (2009). *Rational choice in an uncertain world: the psychology of judgment and decision making*. SAGE Publications.

Haustein, E. (2014). *Management control systems in innovation companies: A contingency theory study* (Order No. 28197618). Available from ProQuest Dissertations & Theses Global. (2440376463).

Hayo, B., & Seifert, W. (2003). Subjective economic well-being in Eastern Europe. *Journal of Economic Psychology*, *24*(3), 329–348. doi:10.1016/S0167-4870(02)00173-3

Hayward, M. L. A., Forster, W. R., Sarasvarthy, S. D., & Fredrickson, B. L. (2010). Beyond Hubris: How Highly Confident Entrepreneurs Rebound to Venture Again. *Journal of Business Venturing*, *25*(6), 569–578.

Helliwell, J. F. (2003). How's life? Combining individual and national variables to explain subjective well-being. *Economic Modelling*, *20*(2), 331–360. doi:10.1016/S0264-9993(02)00057-3

Helliwell, J. F., Huang, H., Grover, S., & Wang, S. (2018). Empirical linkages between good governance and national well-being. *Journal of Comparative Economics*, *46*(4), 1332–1346. doi:10.1016/j.jce.2018.01.004

Hellriegel, D., & Slocum, J. W. Jr. (1973). Organizational design: A contingency approach. *Business Horizons*, *16*(2), 59–68. doi:10.1016/S0007-6813(73)80011-4

Hemphill, R. (2015). Medications and the Culture of Safety. *Journal of Medical Toxicology*, *11*(2), 253-6.

Heng. (2010). Mirror, mirror on the wall, who is the softest of them all? Evaluating Japanese and Chinese strategies in the 'soft' power competition era. *International Relations of the Asia-Pacific*, *10*(2), 275-304.

Herbane, B. (2015). Threat Orientation in Small and Medium-Sized Enterprises: Understanding Differences toward Acute Interruptions. *Disaster Prevention and Management*, *24*(5), 570–582. doi:10.1108/DPM-12-2014-0272

Hernández, A. L., Escobar, S. G., Fuentes, N. I. G. A. L., & Eguiarte, B. E. B. (2019). Stress, self-efficacy, academic achievement and resilience in emerging adults. *Electronic Journal of Research in Educational Psychology*, *17*(47), 129–148. https://core.ac.uk/download/pdf/286590307.pdf

Herrigel, E. (1978). *Zen in the art of archery*. Random House Inc.

Herrman, H., Stewart, D. E., Diaz-Granados, N., Berger, E. L., Jackson, B., & Yuen, T. (2011). What is resilience? *Canadian Journal of Psychiatry*, *56*(5), 258–265. doi:10.1177/070674371105600504 PMID:21586191

Hertin, J., Berkhout, F., Gann, D., & Barlow, J. (2003). Climate change and the UK house building sector: Perceptions, impacts and adaptive capacity. *Building Research and Information*, *31*, 278.

Hessami, Z. (2010). The size and composition of government spending in Europe and its impact on well-being. *Kyklos*, *63*(3), 346–382. doi:10.1111/j.1467-6435.2010.00478.x

Higuchi, Y. (2019). Higuchi Yûko gashû. Sâkasu. Gurafikkusha.

Hilpert, J. C., Stempien, J., van der Hoeven Kraft, K. J., & Husman, J. (2013). Evidence for the latent factor structure of the MSLQ: A new conceptualization of an established questionnaire. *SAGE Open*, *3*(4). Advance online publication. doi:10.1177/2158244013510305

Hilton, J., Wright, C., & Kiparoglou, V. (2012). Building resilience into systems. In SysCon 2012 - 2012 IEEE International Systems Conference, Proceedings, 638–645. https://doi.org/10.1109/SysCon.2012.6189449

Hirsch, P. M., & Levin, D. Z. (1999). Umbrella advocates versus validity police: A life-cycle model. *Organization Science*, *10*, 199–212.

Hjemdal, O., Friborg, O., Stiles, T. C., Rosenvinge, J. H., & Martinussen, M. (2006). Resilience predicting psychiatric symptoms: A prospective study of protective factors and their role in adjustment to stressful life events. *Clinical Psychology & Psychotherapy: An International Journal of Theory & Practice*, *13*(3), 194–201. doi:10.1002/cpp.488

Hobby Search. (n.d.). *Japanese commercial site for toys*. https://www.1999.co.jp

Hoffmann, V. H., Sprengel, D. C., Ziegler, A., Kolb, M., & Abegg, B. (2009). Determinants of corporate adaptation to climate change in winter tourism: An econometric analysis. *Global Environmental Change*, *19*, 256–264.

Hoffman, W., & McNulty, R. E. (2010). A business ethics theory of whistleblowing: Responding to the $1 trillion question. In M. Arszulowicz & W. Gasparski (Eds.), *Defense of proper action: The whistleblowing* (pp. 45–60). Transaction Publishers.

Hofstede, G. (1984). *Culture's consequences: International differences in work-related values* (Vol. 5). Sage.

Hogg, C. (2006). *Top Japanese artist 'plagiarised'*. BBC News. http://news.bbc.co.uk/2/hi/asia-pacific/5049840.stm

Holling, C. S. (2001). Understanding the complexity of economic, ecological, and social systems. *Ecosystems (New York, N.Y.)*, *4*, 390–405.

Hollnagel, E. (2010). How Resilient Is Your Organisation? An Introduction to the Resilience Analysis Grid (RAG). Sustainable Transformation: Building a Resilient Organization.

Hollnagel, E. (2011). Epilogue: RAG – the resilience analysis grid. In Resil. Eng. Pract. Ashgate Publishing, Ltd.

Hollnagel, E., Woods, D. D., & Leveson, N. (Eds.). (2006). *Resilience engineering: Concepts and precepts*. Ashgate Publishing Company.

Hormann, S., & Vivian, P. (2005). Toward an understanding of traumatized organizations and how to intervene in them. *Traumatology*, *11*(3), 159–169. doi:10.1177/153476560501100302

Horne, J., & Orr, J. (1998). Assessing behaviors that create resilient organizations. *Employment Relations Today*, *24*, 29–39.

Howard, S. N. (2016). *Health literacy program proposal for health care workers (Order No. 10145339)*. Available from ProQuest Dissertations & Theses Global.

Hox, J. J., Moerbeek, M., & Van de Schoot, R. (2017). *Multilevel analysis: Techniques and applications*. Routledge. doi:10.4324/9781315650982

Hromalik, C. D., & Koszalka, T. A. (2018). Self-regulation of the use of digital resources in an online language learning course improves learning outcomes. *Distance Education*, *39*(4), 528–547. doi:10.1080/01587919.2018.1520044

Huang, L., Lin, Y., Ieromonachou, P., Zhou, L., & Luo, J. (2015). Drivers and Patterns of Supply Chain Collaboration in the Pharmaceutical Industry: A Case Study on SMEs in China. *Open Journal Of Social Sciences*, *03*(3), 23–29. doi:10.4236/jss.2015.37004

Huang, N., Huang, N., & Wang, Y. (2020). US economic policy uncertainty on Chinese economy: Industry level analysis. *Applied Economics Letters*, *27*(10), 789–802. doi:10.1080/13504851.2019.1645942

Hu, L. T., & Bentler, P. M. (1999). Cutoff criteria for fit indexes in covariance structure analysis: Conventional criteria versus new alternatives. *Structural Equation Modeling*, *6*(1), 1–55. doi:10.1080/10705519909540118

Hunter, J. E., & Schmidt, F. (2004). *Methods of meta-analysis: Correcting error and bias in research findings*. Sage Publishers. doi:10.4135/9781412985031

Hussaini, I. D., Aliyu, B., Bassi, A. A., Abubakar, S. I., & Aminu, M. (2013). Assessment of health risks associated with wastewater irrigation in Yola Adamawa State, Nigeria. *International Journal of Water Resources and Environmental Engineering*, *5*(1), 54–66.

Ignatiadis, I. & Nandhakumar, J. (2007). The Impact of Enterprise Systems on Organizational Control and Drift: A Human-Machine Agency Perspective. *International Journal of Enterprise Information Systems*, *3*(3), 36-51. Doi:10.1057/palgrave.jit.2000087

ILO. (2014). Thematic Labour Overview 1: Transition to Formality in Latin America and the Caribbean (2014 ed., Thematic labour overview, pp. 1-79, Rep. No. I). Lima: International Labor Organization.

International Dunhuang Project. (n.d.). http://idp.bl.uk

Isao, S. (2013). Kinsei kindai manga ryakushi. In Nihon no zushô manga. Pai intânashonaru.

Ishak, A. W., & Williams, E. A. (2018). A dynamic model of organizational resilience: Adaptive and anchored approaches. *Corporate Communications*, *23*, 180–196.

Ismail, H. S., Poolton, J., & Sharifi, H. (2011). The role of agile strategic capabilities in achieving resilience in manufacturing-based small companies. *International Journal of Production Research*, *49*(18), 5469–5487. doi:10.1080/00207543.2011.563833

Ivannikov, M. V., Sugimori, M., & Llinás, R. R. (2017). Neuromuscular transmission and muscle fatigue changes by nanostructured oxygen. *Muscle & Nerve*, *55*(4), 555–563. doi:10.1002/mus.25248 PMID:27422738

Jaaron, A. A. M., & Backhouse, C. J. (2014). Service organisations resilience through the application of the vanguard method of systems thinking: A case study approach. *International Journal of Production Research*, *52*, 2026–2041.

Jackson, D., Firtko, A., & Edenborough, M. (2007). Personal resilience as a strategy for surviving and thriving in the face of workplace adversity: A literature review. *Journal of Advanced Nursing*, *60*(1), 1–9. doi:10.1111/j.1365-2648.2007.04412.x

Jaggar, A. M. (1989). Love and knowledge: Emotion in feminist epistemology. *An Interdisciplinary Journal of Philosophy*, *32*(2), 151–176. doi:10.1080/00201748908602185

James, E. H., & Wooten, L. P. (2005). Leadership as (un)usual: How to display competence in times of crisis. *Organizational Dynamics*, *34*, 141–152.

Jamieson, D. W. (2017). *Strategic organization design – Overview*. Lecture Presentation, Cabrini University Organizational Development Program.

Jean, A. L. (2017). *Evaluation of nurses patient engagement strategies and perceived effectiveness: Implications for health literacy (Order No. 10260578)*. Available from ProQuest Dissertations & Theses Global.

Jenson, J. D. (2011). Promoting self-regulation and critical reflection through writing students' use of electronic portfolio. *International Journal of ePortfolio*, *1*(1), 49-60.

Jentsch, V., Kantz, H., & Albeverio, S. (2006). Extreme events: magic, mysteries, and challenges. In S. Albeverio, V. Jentsch, & H. Kantz (Eds.), *Extreme events in nature and society*. Springer.

Jiang, S., Chen, Z., Wu, T., & Wang, H. (2020). Collective pharmaceutical procurement in China may have unintended consequences in supply and pricing. *Journal of Global Health*, *10*(1), 010314. doi:10.7189/jogh.10.010314 PMID:32566150

Johnson, N., & Elliott, D. (2011). Using Social Capital to Organise for Success? A Case Study of Public–Private Interface in the UK Highways Agency. *Policy and Society*, *30*, 101–113. doi:10.1016/j.polsoc.2011.03.005

Johnson, N., Elliott, D., & Drake, P. (2013). Exploring the Role of Social Capital in Facilitating Supply Chain Resilience. *Supply Chain Management*, *18*(3), 324–336. doi:10.1108/SCM-06-2012-0203

Jomova, K., & Valko, M. (2011, May). Advances in metal-induced oxidative stress and human disease. *Toxicology*, *283*(2-3), 65–87. doi:10.1016/j.tox.2011.03.001 PMID:21414382

Jose, P. E., & Bellamy, M. A. (2012). Relationships of parents' theories of intelligence with children's persistence/learned helplessness: A cross-cultural comparison. *Journal of Cross-Cultural Psychology*, *43*(6), 999–1018. doi:10.1177/0022022111421633

Joseph, S., & Linley, P. A. (Eds.). (2008). *Trauma, recovery, and growth: Positive psychological perspectives on posttraumatic stress*. John Wiley & Sons. doi:10.1002/9781118269718

Juettner, U., & Maklan, S. (2011). Supply chain resilience in the global financial crisis: An empirical study. *Supply Chain Management*, *16*, 246–259.

Jüttner, U., & Maklan, S. (2011). Supply Chain Resilience in the Global Financial Crisis: An Empirical Study. *Supply Chain Management*, *16*(4), 246–259. doi:10.1108/13598541111139062

Kacapyr, E. (2008). Cross-country determinants of satisfaction with life. *International Journal of Social Economics*, *35*(6), 400–416. doi:10.1108/03068290810873384

Kahn, W. A., Barton, M. A., & Fellows, S. (2013). Organizational crises and the disturbance of relational systems. *Academy of Management Review*, *38*, 377–396. doi:10.5465/amr.2011.0363

Kancharla, S., & Hegde, V. (2016). Inferences about supply chain practices using financial ratios. *Journal of Supply Chain and Operations Management*, *14*(1).

Kant, I. (1954). Kritik der Urteilskraft. Academic Press. (Original publication 1799)

Kantur, D., & İşeri-Say, A. (2012). Organizational resilience: A conceptual integrative framework. *Journal of Management & Organization*, *18*(6), 762–773.

Kapoor, B. (2011). *Analysis of Health & Healthcare sevices in Punjab* [Thesis]. Punjabi University, Patiala, Department of Economics.

Kates, A., & Galbraith, J. R. (2007). *Designing your organization: Using the Star Model to solve five critical design challenges*. Jossey-Bass.

Katzmarzyk, P. T., Denstel, K. D., Beals, K., Bolling, C., Wright, C., Crouter, S. E., McKenzie, T. L., Pate, R. R., Saelens, B. E., Staiano, A. E., Stanish, H. I., & Sisson, S. B. (2016). Results From the United States of America's 2016 Report Card on Physical Activity for Children and Youth. *Journal of Physical Activity & Health*, *13*(11, Suppl 2), S307–S313. doi:10.1123/jpah.2016-0321 PMID:27848726

Kaufmann, R., & Vallade, J. I. (2020). Exploring connections in the online learning environment: Student perceptions of rapport, climate, and loneliness. *Interactive Learning Environments*, 1–15. Advance online publication. doi:10.1080/10494820.2020.1749670

Kavitha, R., D. (2012). A Comparative Study on Patients' Satisfaction in Health care Services. *European Journal of Business and Management*, *4*(13).

Kawabata, T. (2003). Nichiren. When the art of the Lotus blossomed. *Japan Times*. https://www.japantimes.co.jp/culture/2003/01/22/arts/when-the-art-of-the-lotus-blossomed/

Kaygisiz, N., Shivdasani, Y., Conti, R., & Berndt, E. (2019). *The geography of prescription pharmaceuticals supplied to the U.S.: levels, trends and implications*. NBER Working Paper Series, (26524).

Kendra, J. M. (2001). *Resilience*. Internal working paper. Disaster Research Center, University of Delaware.

Kendra, J. M., & Wachtendorf, T. (2003). Elements of Resilience after the World Trade Center Disaster: Reconstituting New York City's Emergency Operations Center. *Disasters*, *27*(1), 37–53.

Kendra, J., & Wachtendorf, T. (2003). Elements of resilience after the World Trade Center disaster: Reconstituting New York City's Emergency Operations Centre. *Disasters*, *27*(1), 37–53.

Keraita & Cofie. (2014). Irrigation and Soil Fertility Management Practices. In Irrigated urban vegetable production in Ghana: Characteristics, benefits and risk mitigation (2nd ed.). International Water Management Institute (IWMI). doi:10.5337/2014.219

Khan, M. A. (2009). Auditors and the whistleblowing law. *Accountants Today*, 12-14.

Kic-Drgas, J. (2015). Communication Conflicts in an International Environment. *Global Management Journal*, *7*(1/2), 73–80.

King, R. B., & McInerney, D. M. (2016). Culture and motivation: The road travelled and the way ahead. In Handbook of motivation at school (pp. 275-279). Routledge.

King, D. D., Newman, A., & Luthans, F. (2016). Not if, but when we need resilience in the workplace. *Journal of Organizational Behavior*, *37*(5), 782–786. doi:10.1002/job.2063

Kiuchi, T., & Shireman, B. (1999). Metrics for business in the new economy: An economic change of seasons creates demands for new business metrics. *Environmental Quality Management*, *9*, 79–90.

Kizkapan, O., Bektas, O., & Saylan-Kimizigul, A. (2018). Examining self-regulation skills of elementary school students. *Cypriot Journal of Educational Science*, *13*(4), 613–624. doi:10.18844/cjes.v13i4.3569

Klassen, R. M. (2004, December). A cross-cultural investigation of the efficacy beliefs of South Asian immigrant and Anglo Canadian nonimmigrant early adolescents. *Journal of Educational Psychology*, *96*(4), 731–742. doi:10.1037/0022-0663.96.4.731

Klassen, R. M., & Kuzucu, E. (2009). Academic procrastination and motivation of adolescents in Turkey. *Educational Psychology*, *29*(1), 69–81. doi:10.1080/01443410802478622

Klein, R. J. T., Nicholls, R. J., & Thomalla, F. (2003). Resilience to natural hazards: How useful is this concept. *Environmental Hazards*, *5*, 35–45.

Knol, L., Myers, H., Black, S., Robinson, D., Awololo, Y., Clark, D., & Higginbotham, J. C. (2016). Development and Feasibility of a Childhood Obesity Prevention Program for Rural Families: Application of the Social Cognitive Theory. *American Journal of Health Education*, *47*(4), 204–214. doi:10.1080/19325037.2016.1179607 PMID:28392882

Kobori Enshû kenshûkai [Kobori Enshû Honoring Association]. (n.d.). https://www.koborienshu.org

Koewnigsbauer, K. (2018). The workplace evolution. Harvard Business Review Analytic Services.

Kôkyô, H. (1986). Tôyôga no fuhenteki shisô o motomete. In Nihonga. Zairyô to hyôgen. Bijutsu shuppansha.

Komarraju, M., Karau, S. J., & Schmeck, R. R. (2009). Role of the Big Five personality traits in predicting college students' academic motivation and achievement. *Learning and Individual Differences*, *19*(1), 47–52. doi:10.1016/j.lindif.2008.07.001

Koopaei, N. N., & Abdollah, M. (2017). Health risks associated with the pharmaceuticals in wastewater. *DARU Journal of Pharmacological Sciences*, *25*(1), 9. doi:10.118640199-017-0176-y PMID:28403898

Koren, L. (2000). *Gardens of gravel and sand*. Stone Bridge Press.

Koslowski, T. G., Geoghegan, W., & Longstaff, P. H. (2013). *Organizational Resilience: A Review and Reconceptualization*. In 33rd annual international conference of the strategic management society, Atlanta, GA.

Kota, S., & Mahoney, T. (2020). *Invent Here, Manufacture There*. Manufacturing Policy Initiative At O'neill, (20).

Kotakorpi, K., & Laamanen, J. P. (2010). Welfare state and life satisfaction: Evidence from public health care. *Economica*, *77*(307), 565–583.

KPMG. (2015). *Health care and cybersecurity: increasing threats require increased capabilities*. KPMG. https://assets.kpmg.com/content/dam/kpmg/pdf/2015/09/cyber-health-care-surveykpmg-2015.pdf

Kreft, I. G. (1996). *Are multilevel techniques necessary? An overview, including simulation studies*. Unpublished manuscript, California State University, Los Angeles.

Krippendorff, K. (2004). *Content Analysis: An Introduction to Its Methodology* (2nd ed.). Sage.

Kroeber, A. L., & Kluckhohn, C. (1952). *Culture: A critical review of concepts and definitions*. Vintage Books.

Kyôko, W. (2010). Nihon bijutsushi no rinkakusen. In Furu/ima. Kurabete wakaru nippon bijutsu nyûmon. Heibonsha.

La Porte, T. R. (1996). High reliability organizations: Unlikely, demanding and at risk. *Journal of Contingencies and Crisis Management*, *4*(2), 60–71. doi:10.1111/j.1468-5973.1996.tb00078.x

La Porte, T. R., & Consolini, P. M. (1991). Working in practice but not in theory: Theoretical challenges of "high-reliability organizations". *Journal of Public Administration Research and Theory. J-PART*, *1*(1), 19–48.

Ladizinsky, D., & Roe, D. (2010). New insights into oxygen therapy for wound healing. *Wounds: a Compendium of Clinical Research and Practice, 12*, 294300. PMID:25901579

Lake, A. A. (2011). Obesity. *Perspectives in Public Health, 131*(4), 154. doi:10.1177/1757913911413188 PMID:21888112

Lambertini, L., & Marattin, L. (2016). To adjust or not to adjust after a cost-push shock? A simple duopoly model with (and without) resilience. *Economics of Innovation and New Technology, 25*(2), 172–181. doi:10.1080/10438599.2015.1031344

Lampel, J., Bhalla, A., & Jha, P. P. (2014). Does governance confer organisational resilience? Evidence from UK employee-owned businesses. *European Management Journal, 32*, 66–72.

Langley, A. (1999). Strategies for Theorizing from Process Data. *Academy of Management Review, 24*(4), 691–710.

Lawrence, P. R., & Lorsch, J. W. (1967a). Differentiation and integration in complex organizations. *Administrative Science Quarterly, 12*(1), 1–47. doi:10.2307/2391211

Lawrence, P. R., & Lorsch, J. W. (1967b). *Organization and environment: Managing differentiation and integration.* Division of Research, Graduate School of Business Administration, Harvard University.

Layne, C. (2018, January). The US–Chinese power shift and the end of the Pax Americana. *International Affairs, 94*(1), 89–111. doi:10.1093/ia/iix249

Le Coze, J. C. (2015). *Vive la diversite! High reliability organization and resilience engineering.* doi:10.1016/j.ssci.2016.04.006

Lea, S. E., Webley, P., & Levine, R. M. (1993). The economic psychology of consumer debt. *Journal of Economic Psychology, 14*(1), 85–119. doi:10.1016/0167-4870(93)90041-I

LeBreton, M. (2015). *Implementation of a validated health literacy tool with teach-back education in a super utilizer patient population (Order No. 3700719).* Available from ProQuest Dissertations & Theses Global.

Lechner, A. (2020). "Down by the River": (Micro-)Plastic pollution of running freshwaters with special emphasis on the Austrian Danube. In M. Streit-Bianchi, M. Cimadevila, & W. Trettnak (Eds.), *Mare plasticum - The plastic sea* (pp. 141–185). Springer. doi:10.1007/978-3-030-38945-1_8

Lee, E. (2005). Whistleblowers: Heroes or villains? *Accountants Today*, 14-18.

Lee, I. M., Shiroma, E. J., Lobelo, F., Puska, P., Blair, S. N., Katzmarzyk, P. T., & the Lancet Physical Activity Series Working Group. (2012). Effect of physical inactivity on major non-communicable diseases worldwide: an analysis of burden of disease and life expectancy. *Lancet (London, England), 380*(9838), 219–229. Retrieved from: https://www.ncbi.nlm.nih.gov/pmc/articles/PMC3645500/ doi:10.1016/S0140-6736(12)61031-9

Lee, A. V., Vargo, J., & Seville, E. (2013). Developing a tool to measure and compare organizations'' resilience. *Natural Hazards Review, 14*, 29–41. doi:10.1061/(ASCH)NH.1527-6996.0000075

Lee, A., Vargo, J., & Seville, E. (2013). Developing a tool to measure and compare organizations' resilience. *Natural Hazards Review, 14*(1), 29–41.

Lee, S. E. (1983). *Reflections of Reality in Japanese Art.* Cleveland Museum of Art and Indiana University Press.

Lengnick-Hall, Beck, & Lengnick-Hall. (2011). Developing a capacity for organizational resilience through strategic human resource management. *Human Resource Management Review, 21*, 243–255.

Lengnick-Hall, C. A., & Beck, T. E. (2009). Resilience capacity and strategic agility: Prerequisites for thriving in a dynamic environment. In Resilience engineering perspectives, Volume 2. Preparation and restoration. Ashgate Publishing.

Lengnick-Hall, C. A., & Beck, T. E. (2005). Adaptive fit versus robust transformation: How organizations respond to environmental change. *Journal of Management, 31*, 738–757.

Lengnick-Hall, C. A., Beck, T. E., & Lengnick-Hall, M. L. (2011). Developing a Capacity for Organizational Resilience through Strategic Human Resource Management. *Human Resource Management Review, 21*(3), 243–255.

Leone, L. A., Fleischhacker, S., Anderson-Steeves, B., Harper, K., Winkler, M., Racine, E., Baquero, B., & Gittelsohn, J. (2020). Healthy Food Retail during the COVID-19 Pandemic: Challenges and Future Directions. *International Journal of Environmental Research and Public Health, 17*(20), 7397. doi:10.3390/ijerph17207397 PMID:33050600

Leung, R. S., Floras, J. S., & Bradley, T. D. (2006). Respiratory modulation of the autonomic nervous system during CheyneStokes respiration. *Canadian Journal of Physiology and Pharmacology, 84*(1), 61–66. doi:10.1139/Y05-145 PMID:16845891

Leveson, N., Dulac, N., Marais, K., & Carroll, J. (2009). Moving Beyond Normal Accidents and High Reliability Organizations: A Systems Approach to Safety in Complex Systems. *Organization Studies, 30*(2–3), 227–249.

Levin, I. P., Schneider, S. L., & Gaeth, G. J. (1998). All frames are not created equal: A typology and critical analysis of framing effects. *Organizational Behavior and Human Decision Processes, 76*(2), 149–188. doi:10.1006/obhd.1998.2804 PMID:9831520

Levinson, A. (2012). Valuing public goods using happiness data: The case of air quality. *Journal of Public Economics, 96*(9-10), 869–880. doi:10.1016/j.jpubeco.2012.06.007

Lewis, M. W., & Smith, W. K. (2014). Paradox as a Metatheoretical Perspective: Sharpening the Focus and Widening the Scope. *The Journal of Applied Behavioral Science, 50*(2), 127–149.

Li, C., He, C., & Lin, C. (2018). Economic Impacts of the Possible China–US Trade War. *Emerging Markets Finance & Trade, 54*(7), 1557–1577. doi:10.1080/1540496X.2018.1446131

Liddell, C. B. (2013). Francis Bacon: The restlessness of human existence. *Japan Times*. http://www.japantimes.co.jp/culture/2013/03/28/arts/francis-bacon-the-restlessness-of-human-existence/#.UYjGPXb5NVY

Liken, M. (2018). *How Teachers and Schools Can Address Childhood Obesity*. Concordia University-Portland. Retrieved from: https://education.cu-portland.edu/blog/classroom-resources/teachers-schools-childhood-obesity/

Limnios, A. M., Mazzarol, T., Ghadouani, A., & Schilizzi, S. G. M. (2014). The Resilience Architecture Framework: Four Organizational Archetypes. *European Management Journal, 32*(1), 104–116.

Limnios, E. A. M., Mazzarol, T., Ghadouani, A., & Schilizzi, S. G. M. (2014). The resilience architecture framework: Four organizational archetypes. *European Management Journal, 32*, 104–116.

Linnenluecke, M. K. (2017). Resilience in business and management research: A review of influential publications and a research agenda. *International Journal of Management Reviews, 19*(1), 4–30.

Linnenluecke, M. K., & Griffiths, A. (2010). Beyond adaptation: Resilience for business considering climate change and weather extremes. *Business & Society, 49*(3), 477–511.

Linnenluecke, M. K., & Griffiths, A. (2012). Assessing organizational resilience to climate and weather extremes: Complexities and methodological pathways. *Climatic Change, 113*, 933–947.

Compilation of References

Linnenluecke, M. K., Griffiths, A., & Winn, M. I. (2013). Firm and industry adaptation to climate change: A review of climate adaptation studies in the business and management field. *Wiley Interdisciplinary Reviews: Climate Change, 4*, 397–416.

Lissack, M. R., & Letiche, H. (2002). Complexity, Emergence, Resilience and Coherence: Gaining Perspective on Organizations and their Study. *Emergence, 4*(3), 72–94.

Liu, N. (2021). *Japan's New Prime Minister Is a Demon Slayer Fan, Plans to Support Manga and Anime.* https://www.cbr.com/japan-prime-minister-demon-slayer-fan-support-manga-anime/

Liu, Q., Luo, D., Haase, J. E., Guo, Q., Wang, X. Q., Liu, S., Xia, L., Liu, Z., Yang, J., & Yang, B. X. (2020). The experiences of healthcare providers during the COVID-19 crisis in China: A qualitative study. *The Lancet. Global Health, 8*(6), 790–798. doi:10.1016/S2214-109X(20)30204-7 PMID:32573443

Lloyd, R. (2018). *Successful integrated planning for supply chain* (1st ed.). Kogan Page.

Locher, M. (2012). *Zen gardens: The complete works of Shunmyo Masuno, Japan's leading garden designer.* Tuttle publishing.

Lomas, T., Medina, J. C., Ivtzan, I., Rupprecht, S., & Eiroa-Orosa, F. J. (2019). A Systematic Review and Meta-analysis of the Impact of Mindfulness-Based Interventions on the Well-Being of Healthcare Professionals. *Mindfulness, 10*(7), 1193–1216. doi:10.100712671-018-1062-5

Loree, D. (2020). Building corporate resilience. *Ivey Business Journal*, 2–7.

Lovell, R., Husk, K., Bethel, A., & Garside, R. (2014). What are the health and well-being impacts of community gardening for adults and children: A mixed-method systematic review protocol. *Environmental Evidence, 3*(1), 20. doi:10.1186/2047-2382-3-20

Lubian, D., & Zarri, L. (2011). Happiness and tax morale: An empirical analysis. *Journal of Economic Behavior & Organization, 80*(1), 223–243. doi:10.1016/j.jebo.2011.03.009

Luke, D. A. (2004). *Multilevel modeling.* Sage. doi:10.4135/9781412985147

Lund, P. (2012). Large-scale urban renewable electricity schemes—Integration and interfacing aspects. *Energy Conversion and Management, 63*(November), 162–172. doi:10.1016/j.enconman.2012.01.037

Luong, G., & Charles, S. T. (2014). Age differences in affective and cardiovascular responses to a negative social interaction: The role of goals, appraisals, and emotion regulation. *Developmental Psychology, 50*(7), 1919–1930. doi:10.1037/a0036621 PMID:24773101

Luthans, F., Avey, J. B., Avolio, B. J., Norman, S. M., & Combs, G. M. (2006). Psychological capital development: Toward a micro-intervention. *Journal of Organizational Behavior, 27*(3), 387–393.

Luthar, S. S. (2006). Resilience in Development: A Synthesis of Research across Five Decades. Developmental Psychopathology: Vol. 3. *Risk, Disorder and Adaptation, 739-795.*

Luthar, S. S., & Cicchetti, D. (2000). The construct of resilience: Implications for interventions and social policies. *Development and Psychopathology, 12*(4), 857–885. doi:10.1017/S0954579400004156 PMID:11202047

Luthar, S. S., & Ziegler, E. (1991). Vulnerability and competence: A review of research on resilience in childhood. *The American Journal of Orthopsychiatry, 61*(1), 6–22. doi:10.1037/h0079218 PMID:2006679

Macchia, L., & Plagnol, A. C. (2019). Life satisfaction and confidence in national institutions: Evidence from South America. *Applied Research in Quality of Life, 14*(3), 721–736. doi:10.100711482-018-9606-3

Mackey, J., Gilmore, F., Dabner, N., Breeze, D., & Buckley, P. (2012). Blended learning for academic resilience in times of disaster or crisis. *Journal of Online Learning and Teaching*, *8*(2), 122–135.

MacMillian. (2017). *Word of the Day – Resilient*. http://www.macmillandictionaryblog.com/resilient

Macpherson, A., Herbane, B., & Jones, B. (2015). Developing Dynamic Capabilities through Resource Accretion: Expanding the Entrepreneurial Solution Space. *Entrepreneurship and Regional Development*, *27*(5–6), 259–291. doi:10.1080/08985626.2015.1038598

Madni, A. & Jackson, S. (2009), Towards a conceptual framework for resilience engineering. *IEEE*, *3*(2), 181-191.

Mafabi, S., Munene, J., & Ntayi, J. (2012). Knowledge management and organisational resilience: Organizational innovation as a mediator in Uganda parastatals. *J Strategy Manag*, *5*, 57–80. doi:10.1108/17554 25121 12004 55

Magretta, J. (2012). Understanding Michael Porter: The Essential Guide to Competition and Strategy. *Harvard Business Review*.

Mahat, G., Scoloveno, M., & Ayres, C. (2014). Comparison of HIV/AIDS peer education program across two cultures. *Journal of Cultural Diversity: An Interdisciplinary Journal*, *21*(4), 152–200.

Maiden, J., Georges, J. M., & Connelly, C. D. (2011). Moral distress, compassion fatigue, and perceptions about medication errors in certified critical care nurses. *Dimensions of Critical Care Nursing*, *30*(6), 339–345. doi:10.1097/DCC.0b013e31822fab2a PMID:21983510

Maiwada, Y., & Phd, B. (2016). An Assessment of the Impact of Government Expenditure on Infrastructures: Evidence from Nigerian Health Sector Performance. *European Journal of Business and Management*, *8*(14), 2222–2839. https://iiste.org/Journals/index.php/EJBM/article/viewFile/30542/31385

Mallak, L. (1998). Putting organizational resilience to work. *Industrial Management (Des Plaines)*, *40*(6), 8–13.

Mallak, L. A. (1998). Measuring resilience in health care provider organizations. *Manpower Management*, *24*(4), 148–152. doi:10.1108/09552069810215755

Malm, H., May, T., Francis, L., Omer, S., Salmon, D., & Hood, R. (2008). Ethics, Pandemics, and the Duty to Treat. *The American Journal of Bioethics*, *8*(8), 4–19. doi:10.1080/15265160802317974 PMID:18802849

Mami, K. (2012). Japan, the Chaotic, and Aida Makoto. In Aida Makoto. Tensai de gomen nasai. Monument for nothing. Mori Art Museum.

Mamouni Limnios, E. (2011). Resilient organizations: Offense versus Defense. *25th Annual ANZAM Conference*, 7–9.

Mansfield, S. (2009). *Japanese stone gardens: Origins, meaning, form*. Tuttle Publishing.

Manyena, S. B. (2006). The Concept of Resilience Revisited. *Disasters*, *30*(4), 433–450. doi:10.1111/j.0361-3666.2006.00331.x

Manyena, S. B., O'Brien, G., O'Keefe, P., & Rose, J. (2011). Disaster resilience: A bounce back or bounce forward ability? *Local Environment*, *16*(5), 417–424.

Mara, D., & Cairncross, S. (1989). *Guidelines for the Safe Use of Water and Excreta in Agriculture and Aquaculture Measures for Public Health Protection*. World Health Organization.

Marchese, K., & O'Dwyer, J. (2014). From Risk to Resilience: Using Analytics and Visualization to Reduce Supply Chain Vulnerability. *Deloitte Review*. http://dupress.com/articles/dr14-risk-to-resilience

March, J. G., & Olsen, J. P. (1975). The Uncertainty of the Past: Organizational Learning Under Ambiguity. *European Journal of Political Research*, *3*(2), 147–171.

Marcus, A. A., & Nichols, M. L. (1999). On the edge: Heeding the warnings of unusual events. *Organization Science*, *10*, 482–499.

Mark, G., Al-Ani, B., & Semaan, B. (2009). Resilience through technology adoption: Merging the old and the new in Iraq. In *Proceedings of the 27th international conference on Human factors in computing systems*, (pp. 689-698). ACM Press.

Mark, G., & Semaan, B. (2008). Resilience in collaboration: Technology as a resource for new patterns of action. In *Proceedings of the CSCW Conference* (pp. 137-146). ACM Press.

Martin, G., Martin, P., Hankin, C., Darzi, A., & Kinross, J. (2017). Cybersecurity and healthcare: how safe are we? *British Medical Journal*, *358*.

Martin-Breen, P., & Anderies, J. M. (2011). *Resilience: A literature review*. https://opendocs.ids.ac.uk/opend ocs/handl e/20.500.12413 /3692

Martín, M. Á. G. (2002). El bienestar subjetivo. *Escritos de Psicologia*, (6), 18–39. doi:10.24310/espsiescpsi.vi6.13409

Martin, R., & Sunley, P. (2015). On the notion of regional economic resilience: Conceptualization and explanation. *Journal of Economic Geography*, *15*, 1–42.

Maruyama, G. (1998). *Basics of Structural Equation Modeling*. Sage Publishing. doi:10.4135/9781483345109

Marwa, S. M., & Milner, C. D. (2013). Underwriting corporate resilience via creativity: The pliability model. *Total Qual Manag Bus*, *24*, 835–846. doi:10.1080/14783 363.2013.79111 0

Marwa, S., & Zairi, M. (2008). An exploratory study of the reasons for the collapse of contemporary companies and their link with the concept of quality. *Management Decision*, *46*, 1342–1370. doi:10.1108/00251 74081 09119 84

Marx, M. (2014). Examining the structural challenges to communication as experienced by nurse managers in two U.S. hospital settings. Journal of Nursing Management, 22(8), 964-973. doi:10.1111/jonm.12091

Mason, S. A., Welch, V. G., & Neratko, J. (2018). Synthetic polymer contamination in bottled water. *Frontiers in Chemistry*, *6*, 4017. doi:10.3389/fchem.2018.00407 PMID:30255015

Masson, G., Vaidya, A., & Bean, M. (2020). *The coronavirus playbook: How 12 health systems are responding to the pandemic*. https://www.beckershospitalreview.com/infection-control/the-coronavirus-playbook-how-12-health-systems-are-responding-to-the-pandemic.html

Masten, A. S. (2011). Resilience in children threatened by extreme adversity: Frameworks for research, practice, and translational synergy. *Development and Psychopathology*, *23*, 493–506. doi:10.1017/S0954579411000198

Masten, A. S., Best, K. M., & Garmezy, N. (1990). Resilience and development: Contributions from the study of children who overcome adversity. *Development and Psychopathology*, *2*(4), 425–444. doi:10.1017/S0954579400005812

Masten, A. S., & Coatsworth, J. D. (1998). The development of competence in favorable and unfavorable environments: Lessons from research on successful children. *The American Psychologist*, *53*, 205–220. http://psycnet.apa.org/journals/amp/53/2/

Masten, A. S., & Obradović, J. (2007). Competence and resilience in development. *Annals of the New York Academy of Sciences*, *1094*(1), 13–27.

Masten, A. S., & Obradović, J. (2007). Competence and resilience indevelopment. *Annals of the New York Academy of Sciences*, *1094*(1), 13–27.

Mathieu, F. (2007). Running on Empty: Compassion Fatigue in Health Professionals. *Rehab Community Care Med*, *4*, 1–7.

Mathiharan, K. (2003). The fundamental right to health care. *Issues in Medical Ethics*, *11*(4), 123. PMID:16335519

Matsumoto. (1980). *Karesansui no hanashi: Mizu nakushite mizu wo tanoshimu niwa* [About *karesansui*: Enjoying gardens without water]. Heibonsha.

Matsuoka, S. (2020). Flowers, Birds, Wind, and Moon. The Phenomenology of Nature in Japanese Culture. Japan Publishing Industry Foundation for Culture.

Mayu, T. (2007). The Ascent of Yôga in Modern Japan and in the Pacific War. In Inexorable Modernity. Japan's Grappling with Modernity in the Arts. Lexington Books.

McCann, J. E., & Selsky, J. W. (2012). *Mastering turbulence: the essential capabilities of agile and resilient individuals, teams, and organizations* (1st ed.). Jossey-Bass.

McCann, J., Selsky, J., & Lee, J. (2009). Building agility, resilience, and performance in turbulent environments. *People & Strategy*, *32*, 44–51.

McCaskey, M. B. (1974). An introduction to organizational design. *California Management Review*, *17*(1), 13–20. doi:10.2307/41164556

McClelland, M. M., John Geldhof, G., Cameron, C. E., & Wanless, S. B. (2015). *Handbook of child psychology and developmental science, socioemotional processes* (Vol. 1). John Wiley & Sons. doi:10.1002/9781118963418.childpsy114

McCoy, J., & Elwood, A. (2009). Human factors in organisational resilience: Implications of breaking the psychological contract. *Journal of Business Continuity & Emergency Planning*, *3*, 368–375.

McCullough, T. (2008, May 12). The industry's strength is its resilience. Money Management Executive, p. 7.

McDaniels, T., Chang, S., Cole, D., Mikawoz, J., & Longstaff, H. (2008). Fostering resilience to extreme events within infrastructure systems: Characterizing decision contexts for mitigation and adaptation. *Global Environmental Change*, *18*(2), 310–318.

McHolm, F. (2006). Rx for compassion fatigue. *Journal of Christian Nursing*, *23*(4), 12–19. doi:10.1097/00005217-200611000-00003 PMID:17078229

McKenzie, J. F., Pinger, R. R., & Seabert, D. (2018). An introduction to community & public health. Jones & Bartlett Learning.

McLeod, G., & Nacouzi, G. (2016). Enhancing Space Resilience Through Non-Materiel Means. RAND Corporation, RR-1067-AF.

McInerney, D. M., & King, R. B. (2018). Culture and self-regulation in educational contexts. In D. H. Schunk & J. A. Greene (Eds.), Educational psychology handbook series. Handbook of self-regulation of learning and performance (pp. 485–502). Routledge/Taylor & Francis Group.

McManus, S., Seville, E., Vargo, J., & Brunsdon, D. (2008). A facilitated process for improving organizational resilience. *Natural Hazards Review*, *9*, 81–90.

McManus, S., Seville, E., Vargo, J., & Brunsdon, D. (2008). Facilitated process for improving organizational resilience. *Natural Hazards Review*, *9*, 81–90. doi:10.1061/(ASCE)1527-6988(2008)9:2(81)

Mehta, A. K. (n.d.). *Gender Responsive Budgeting: Issues related to the Health Sector in Punjab*. Retrieved December 28, 2018, from pbplanning.gov.in:http://pbplanning.gov.in/HDR/Gender%20Responsive%20Budgeting%20in%20Health%20in%20Punjab%20sent_pending.pdf

Mercado, L. (2021). *The Role of Community Gardens During the COVID-19 Pandemic*. Columbia University School of Public Health. Retrieved from: https://www.publichealth.columbia.edu/public-health-now/news/role-community-gardens-during-covid-19-pandemic

Merriam, S. B., & Mohamad, M. (2000). How cultural values shape learning in older adulthood: The case of Malaysia. *Adult Education Quarterly*, *51*(1), 45–63. doi:10.1177/074171360005100104

Meyer, A. D. (1982). Adapting to environmental jolts. *Administrative Science Quarterly*, *27*(4), 515–537.

Miceli, M. P., Near, J. P., & Dworkin, T. M. (2008). *Whistleblowing in organizations*. Routledge.

Miceli, M., & Near, J. P. (1992). *Blowing the whistle*. Lexington Books.

Miiamaaria, K., Heini, T., Sanni, S., Laura, H., & Christina, K. (2013). Reactivity of Dogs' Brain Oscillations to Visual Stimuli Measured with Non-Invasive Electroencephalography. *PLoS One*, *8*(5), e61818. doi:10.1371/journal.pone.0061818 PMID:23650504

Mikic, M., Puutio, T. A., & Gallagher, J. G. (2020). *Healthcare products trade and external shocks: The US-China trade war and COVID-19 pandemics*. ARTNeT Working Paper Series, No. 190, Asia-Pacific Research and Training Network on Trade (ARTNeT), Bangkok.

Mikušová, M. (2013). Do Small Organizations Have an Effort to Survive? Survey from Small Czech Organizations. *Economic Research-Ekonomska Istraživanja*, *264*, 59–76. doi:10.1080/1331677X.2013.11517630

Miller, D., Eisenstat, R., & Foote, N. (2002). Strategy from the Inside Out: Building Capability-Creating Organizations. *California Management Review*, *44*(3), 37–54.

Miller, D., & Friesen, P. H. (1980). Momentum and revolution in organizational adaptation. *Academy of Management Journal*, *23*, 591–614.

Miller, H. I., & Cohrssen, J. J. (2020). China's Coronavirus-Induced Paralysis Threatens U.S. Drug Supply Chain. *Missouri Medicine*, *117*(2), 86–88. PMID:32308220

Minkov, M., Dutt, P., Schachner, M., Morales, O., Sanchez, G., Jandosova, J., Khassenbekov, Y., & Mudd, B. (2017). A revision of Hofstede's individualism-collectivism dimension: A new national index from a 56-country study. *Cross Cultural & Strategic Management*, *24*(3), 386–404. doi:10.1108/CCSM-11-2016-0197

Mistry, V., Sharma, U., & Low, M. (2014). Management accountants 'perceptions of their role in accounting for sustainable development: An exploratory study. *Pacific Accounting Review*, *26*(1/2), 112–133.

Miyamoto, K. (1998). *Zusetsu: Nihon teien no mikata* [Illustrated guide to Japanese gardens]. Gakugei Shuppansha.

Miyashita, Y. (2006). La présence culturelle de la France au Japon et la collection Matsukata. *Relations Internationales*, *2*(134), 37-53. https://www.cairn.info/revue-relations-internationales-2008-2-page-37.htm doi:10.3917/ri.134.0037

Mizuma Art Gallery. (2021). *I can't stop the patriotism*. Aikoku ga tomararenai. https://mizuma-art.co.jp/en/exhibitions/2107_aidamakoto/

Mohr, J., Batalden, P., & Barach, P. (2004). Integrating patient safety into the clinical microsystem. *Quality & Safety in Health Care*, *13*(suppl 2), ii34–ii38. doi:10.1136/qshc.2003.009571 PMID:15576690

Moke, K., Chang, C. K. W., Prihadi, K., & Goh, C. L. (2018). Mediation effect of resilience on the relationship between self-efficacy and competitiveness among university students. *International Journal of Evaluation and Research in Education, 7*(4), 279–284. doi:10.11591/ijere.v7i4.15725

Momtazmanesh, S., Ochs, H. D., Uddin, L. Q., Perc, M., Routes, J. M., Vieira, D. N., Al-Herz, W., Baris, S., Prando, C., Rosivall, L., Abdul Latiff, A. H., Ulrichs, T., Roudenok, V., Aldave Becerra, J. C., Salunke, D. B., Goudouris, E., Condino-Neto, A., Stashchak, A., Kryvenko, O., ... Rezaei, N. (2020). All together to Fight COVID-19. *The American Journal of Tropical Medicine and Hygiene, 102*(6), 1181–1183. doi:10.4269/ajtmh.20-0281 PMID:32323644

Moore, T., & Lakha, R. (2004). *Tolley's Handbook of Disaster and Emergency Management: Principles and Practice*. Lexis Nexis.

Moosivand, A., Rajabzadeh Ghatari, A., & Rasekh, H. R. (2019). Supply Chain Challenges in Pharmaceutical Manufacturing Companies: Using Qualitative System Dynamics Methodology. Iranian journal of pharmaceutical research. *IJPR, 18*(2), 1103–1116. doi:10.22037/ijpr.2019.2389 PMID:31531092

Moran, K. A., & Mallak, L. A. (2016). Organizational resilience: Sustained institutional effectiveness among smaller, private, non-profit US higher education institutions experiencing organizational decline. *WOR, 54*, 267–281. doi:10.3233/WOR-16229 9

Morgan, D. (2018). Basic and Advanced Focus Groups. *Sage (Atlanta, Ga.)*.

Mori Art Museum. (2013). Aida Makoto. Monument for Nothing. Aida Makoto. Tensai de gomen nasai. Solo exhibition catalogue. Kyôto Seigensha.

Morris, D., & Matthews, J. (2014). Communication, Respect, and Leadership: Interprofessional Collaboration in Hospitals of Rural Ontario. *Canadian Journal of Dietetic Practice & Research, 75*(4), 173-179. doi:10.3148/cjdpr-2014-020

Morris, H. M. (2014). *Annals of entrepreneurship education and pedagogy*. Edward Elgar Publishing.

Morris, J., Briggs, M., & Zidenberg-Cherr, S. (2000). School-based gardens can teach kids healthier eating habits. *California Agriculture, 54*(5), 40–46. doi:10.3733/ca.v054n05p40

Morris-Suzuki, T. (1998). *Re-inventing Japan. Nation, Culture, Identity*. Routledge.

Moss, G. A. (2010). Water and health: A forgotten connection? *Perspectives in Public Health, 130*(5), 227–232. doi:10.1177/1757913910379192 PMID:21086819

Mousavi, S., & Gigerenzer, G. (2014). Risk, Uncertainty and Heuristics. *Journal of Business Research, 67*(8), 1671–1678.

Museum, A. A. (2019). The Ateneum Exhibition the Modern Woman to Travel to Japan. *Ateneum News*. https://ateneum.fi/en/news/the-modern-woman-to-japan/

Museum, M. A. (2013). Aida Makoto. Monument for Nothing. Aida Makoto. Tensai de gomen nasai. Solo exhibition catalogue. Kyôto Seigensha.

Musgrave & Woodman. (2013). *Weathering the Storm – The 2013 Business Continuity Management Survey*. London: Chartered Management Institute.

Musgrave, R. A. (1959). *Theory of public finance; a study in public economy*. Academic Press.

Musgrove, P., Zeramdini, R., & Carrin, G. (2002). Basic patterns in national health expenditure. *Bulletin of the World Health Organization, 80*(2), 134–142. doi:10.1590/S0042-96862002000200009 PMID:11953792

Nadler, D. A., & Tushman, M. (1988). *Strategic organization design: Concepts, tools & processes*. Scott, Foresman.

Nadler, D. A., & Tushman, M. L. (1990). Beyond the charismatic leader: Leadership and organizational change. *California Management Review*, *32*(2), 77–97. doi:10.2307/41166606

Najjar, N., Davis, L. W., Beck-Coon, K., & Carney Doebbeling, C. (2009). Compassion fatigue: A Review of the Research to Date and Relevance to Cancer-care Providers. *Journal of Health Psychology*, *14*(2), 267–277. doi:10.1177/1359105308100211 PMID:19237494

Nakagawara, C. (2004). The Japanese garden for the mind: The 'Bliss' of paradise transcended. *Stanford Journal of East Asian Affairs.*, *4*(2), 83–102.

National Bureau of Statistics of China. (2020). *Decline of Major Economic Indicators Significantly Narrowed Down in March*. Author.

Ndiaye, M. L., Niang, S., Pfeifer, H. R., Peduzzi, R., Tonolla, M., & Dieng, Y. (2011). Effect of irrigation water and processing on the microbial quality of lettuces produced and sold on markets in Dakar (Senegal). *Irrigation and Drainage*, *60*(4), 509–517. doi:10.1002/ird.590

Ndunda, E. N., & Mungatana, E. D. (2013). Determinants of farmers' choice of innovative risk reduction interventions to wastewater-irrigated agriculture. *African Journal of Agricultural Research*, *8*(1), 119–128.

Near, J. P., & Miceli, M. P. (1995). Effective whistleblowing. *Academy of Management Review*, *20*(3), 679–708.

Nelson, R. R., & Winter, S. G. (1982). *An evolutionary theory of economic change*. Harvard University Press.

Ngamaba, K. H., Panagioti, M., & Armitage, C. J. (2018). Income inequality and subjective well-being: A systematic review and meta-analysis. *Quality of Life Research: An International Journal of Quality of Life Aspects of Treatment, Care and Rehabilitation*, *27*(3), 577–596. doi:10.100711136-017-1719-x PMID:29067589

NHK (Nippon Hôsô Kyôkai). (2008). *Sono toki. Rekishi ga ugoita. Part 315* [Television documentary program]. https://web.archive.org/web/20081007132147/http://www.nhk.or.jp/sonotoki/2008_02.html

Nishiyama, M. (1997). *Edo Culture. Daily Life and Diversions in Urban Japan, 1600-1868* (G. Groemer, Ed. & Trans.). University of Hawai'i Press. doi:10.1515/9780824862299

Nolte, A. G., Downing, C., Temane, A., & Hastings-Tolsma, M. (2017). Compassion fatigue in nurses: A meta-synthesis. *Journal of Clinical Nursing*, *26*(23-24), 4364–4378. doi:10.1111/jocn.13766 PMID:28231623

Norris, F. H., Stevens, S. P., Pfefferbaum, B., Wyche, K. F., & Pfeffer-baum, R. L. (2008). Community resilience as a metaphor, theory, set of capacities, and strategy for disaster readiness. *American Journal of Community Psychology*, *41*(1–2), 127–150. doi:10.100710464-007-9156-6

Nutrition Education Strategies & Initiatives. (n.d.). Retrieved 2020, from https://hungerandhealth.feedingamerica.org/explore-our-work/nutrition-education-initiatives/

Nye, J. S. (2004). *Soft Power: The Means to Success in World Politics*. Public Affairs.

O'Connor, F. J., & Baratz, J. M. (2004). Some assembly required: The application of state open meeting laws to email correspondence. *George Mason Law Review*, *12*, 719.

O'Toole, M. (2002). The relationship between employees' perceptions of safety and organizational culture. *Journal of Safety Research*, *33*(2), 231–243. doi:10.1016/S0022-4375(02)00014-2 PMID:12216448

Oettingen, G. (1995). Cross-cultural perspectives on self-efficacy. In A. Bandura (Ed.), *Self-efficacy in changing societies* (pp. 149–176). Cambridge University Press. doi:10.1017/CBO9780511527692.007

Oettingen, G., & Zosuls, K. (2006). Culture and self-efficacy in adolescents. In F. Pajares & T. Urdan (Eds.), *Self-efficacy beliefs of adolescents* (Vol. 5, pp. 245–265). Information Age Publishing.

Øien, K. (2013). Remote operation in environmentally sensitive areas: Development of early warning indicators. *Journal of Risk Research*, *16*, 323–336.

Ooms, H. (1984). Early Tokugawa Ideology. In P. Nosco (Ed.), *Confucianism and Tokugawa Culture* (pp. 27–61). University of Hawai'i Press.

Ortiz-de-Mandojana, N., & Bansal, P. (2016). The long-term benefits of organizational resilience through sustainable business practices. *Strategic Management Journal*, *37*(8), 1615–1631. https://EconPapers.repec.org/RePEc:bla:stratm:v:37:y:2016:i:8:p:1615-1631

Ortiz-de-Mandojana, N., & Bansal, P. (2016). The long-term benefits of organizational resilience through sustainable business practices. *Strategic Management Journal*, *37*, 1615–1631.

Osamu, H. (2007). *Nihon bijutsushi 7*. Shinchôsha.

Oxford University Press. (2017). *Oxford Dictionaries*. Retrieved November 17, 2017, from https://en.oxforddictionaries.com/definition/organization

Ozawa, A., & Mizunuma, Y. (2006). *Nihon jûkyoshi*. Yoshikawa.

Paakkari, L., & Okan, O. (2020). COVID-19: Health literacy is an underestimated problem. *The Lancet. Public Health*, *5*(5), e249–e250. https://doi.org/10.1016/S2468-2667(20)30086-4

Pal, Torstensson, & Mattila. (2014). Antecedents of Organizational Resilience in Economic Crises – an Empirical Study of Swedish Textile and Clothing SMEs. *International Journal of Production Economics*, *147*(Part B), 410–428. doi: . doi:10.1016/j.ijpe.2013.02.031

Panter-Brick, C. (2014). Health, risk, and resilience: Interdisciplinary concepts and applications. *Annual Review of Anthropology*, *43*(1), 431–448. doi:10.1146/annurev-anthro-102313-025944

Papanek, V. (1995). *The green imperative: Natural design for the real world*. Thames and Hudson.

Pareto, V. (1906). *Manuale di economia politica*. Societa Editrice.

Parker, H., & Ameen, K. (2018). The role of resilience capabilities in shaping how firms respond to disruptions. J Bus Res, 88, 535–541. https ://doi.org/ es.2017.12.022 doi:10.1016/j.jbusr

Parker, D., Lawries, M., & Hudson, P. A. (2006). framework for understanding the development of organizational safety culture. *Safety Science*, *44*(6), 551–562. doi:10.1016/j.ssci.2005.10.004

Parsons, D. (2010). Organizational resilience. *Australian Journal of Emergency Management*, *25*(2), 18–20.

Pasteur, K. (2011). *From Vulnerability to Resilience: A Framework for Analysis and Action to Build Community Resilience*. Practical Action Publishing.

Pasupathi, M. (1999). *Socio-emotional influences on decision making: The challenge of choice-When I'm 64*. National Academies Press.

Patel, R., & Patel, H. R. (2017). A study on waiting time and out-patient satisfaction at Gujarat medical education research society hospital, Valsad, Gujarat, India. *International Journal of Community Medicine and Public Health*, *4*(3), 857. doi:10.18203/2394-6040.ijcmph20170772

Paton, D., Millar, M., & Johnston, D. (2001). Community resilience to volcanic hazard consequences. *Natural Hazards*, *24*(2), 157–169.

Paul, H., Bamel, U. K., & Garg, P. (2016). Employee resilience and OCB: Mediating effects of organizational commitment. *Vikalpa*, *41*(4), 308–324.

Pavan Srinath, P. K. (2018). *A Qualitative and Quantitative Analysis of Public Health Expenditure in India: 2005-06 to 2014-15*. The Takshila Institution.

Pawan Kumar Sharma, S. I. (2008, September). Health Care Services in Punjab: Findings of a Patient Satisfaction Survey. *Social Change*, *38*(3), 458–477. doi:10.1177/004908570803800304

Pearson, Ch. M., & Clair, J. A. (1998). Reframing crisis management. *Academy of Management Review*, *23*, 59–76.

Pelling, M. (2003). *The Vulnerabilities of Cities: Natural Disasters and Social Resilience*. Earthscan.

Pellissier, R. (2012). Innovation in a complex environment. SA Journal of Information Management, 14(1).

Pellissier, R. (2011). The Implementation of Resilience Engineering to Enhance Organizational Innovation in a Complex Environment. *International Journal of Business and Management*, *6*(1), 145–164.

Perovic, L. M., & Golem, S. (2010). Investigating macroeconomic determinants of happiness in transition countries: How important is government expenditure? *Eastern European Economics*, *48*(4), 59–75. doi:10.2753/EEE0012-8775480403

Perrier, E. (2019). Hydration for Health: So what? Ten advances in recent hydration history. *Annals of Nutrition & Metabolism*, *74*(Suppl. 3), 4–10. doi:10.1159/000500343 PMID:31203297

Pes, J., & Sharpe, E. (2013). Attendance survey 2012: Tour de force show puts Tokyo on top. *The Art Newspaper*, 245.

Peteraf, M., Di Stefano, G., & Verona, G. (2013). The Elephant in the Room of Dynamic Capabilities: Bringing Two Diverging Conversations Together. *Strategic Management Journal*, *34*(12), 1389–1410.

Petrie, B., Barden, R., & Kasprzyk-Hordern, B. (2015). A review on emerging contaminants in wastewaters and the environment: Current knowledge, understudied areas and recommendations for future monitoring. *Water Research*, *72*, 3–27. doi:10.1016/j.watres.2014.08.053 PMID:25267363

Pettit, T. J., Croxton, K. L., & Fiksel, J. (2013). Ensuring supply chain resilience: Development and implementation of an assessment tool. *Journal of Business Logistics*, *34*(1), 46–76.

Pettit, T. J., Croxton, K. L., & Fiksel, J. (2013). Ensuring Supply Chain Resilience: Development and Implementation of an Assessment Tool. *Journal of Business Logistics*, *34*(1), 46–76.

Pettit, T., Fiksel, J., & Croxton, K. (2010). Ensuring Supply Chain Resilience: Development of a Conceptual Framework. *Journal of Business Logistics*, *31*(1), 1–21.

Pfifferling, J., & Gilley, K. (2000). Overcoming compassion fatigue. *Family Practice Management*, *7*(4), 1–6.

Pfleger, P. (2015). *Healthy eaters, strong minds: What school gardens teach kids*. Retrieved from https://www.npr.org/sections/thesalt/2015/08/10/426741473/healthy-eaters-strong-minds-what-school-gardens-teach-kids

Philip Musgrove, R. Z. (2002). Basic Patterns in National Health Expenditure. *Bulletin of the World Health Organization*, *80*(2). PMID:11953792

Pieloch, K. A., McCullough, M. B., & Marks, A. K. (2016). Resilience of children with refugee statuses: A research review. *Canadian Psychology*, *57*(4), 330–339. doi:10.1037/cap0000073

Pigou, A. C. (1947). *A study in public finance*. Read Books Ltd.

Pille, R. O. (2016). *Assessing the relationship between health promotion-related health literacy and health psychology's sense of coherence in young adults (Order No. 10130915)*. Available from ProQuest Dissertations & Theses Global.

Pintrich, P. R., Smith, D. A. F., Garcia, T., & McKeachie, W. J. (1991). *A manual for the use of the Motivated Strategies for Learning Questionnaire (MSLQ)*. Technical Report (No. 91-8-004). The Regents of The University of Michigan.

Pintrich, P. R. (1989). The dynamic interplay of student motivation and cognition in the college classroom. *Advances in Motivation and Achievement: a Research Annual*, *6*, 117–160.

Plumwood, V. (2002). *Environmental Culture. The ecological crisis of reason*. Routledge.

Podsakoff, P. M., MacKenzie, S. B., Lee, J. Y., & Podsakoff, N. P. (2003). Common method biases in behavioral research: A critical review of the literature and recommended remedies. *The Journal of Applied Psychology*, *88*(5), 879–903.

Podsakoff, P. M., MacKenzie, S. B., & Podsakoff, N. P. (2016). Recommendations for creating better concept definitions in the organizational, behavioral, and social sciences. *Organizational Research Methods*, *19*, 159–203. doi:10.1177/10944 28115 62496 5

Pollack, G. (2001). *Cells, gels and the engines of life*. Ebner and Sons.

Pollio, E. W. (2018). *Health education materials: Where are the patients? (Order No. 10743845)*. Available from ProQuest Dissertations & Theses Global.

Pommerehne, W. W. (1984). Was wissen wir eigentlich über Steuerhinterziehung? *International Review of Economics and Business*, *32*, 1155–1186.

Ponomarov, S. Y., & Holcomb, M. C. (2009). Understanding the concept of supply chain resilience. *International Journal of Logistics Management*, *20*, 124–143. doi:10.1108/09574090910954873

Powdthavee, N., Burkhauser, R. V., & De Neve, J. E. (2017). Top incomes and human well-being: Evidence from the Gallup World Poll. *Journal of Economic Psychology*, *62*, 246–257. doi:10.1016/j.joep.2017.07.006

Powley, E. H. (2013). The process and mechanisms of organizational healing. *The Journal of Applied Behavioral Science*, *49*, 42–68. doi:10.1177/00218 86312 47119 2

Pross, N., Demazières, A., Girard, N., Barnouin, R., Metzger, D., Klein, A., Perrier, E., & Guelinckx, I. (2014). Effects of changes in water intake on mood of high and low drinkers. *PLoS One*, *9*(4), e94754. doi:10.1371/journal.pone.0094754 PMID:24728141

Purohit, I., Purohit, P., & Shekhar, S. (2013). Evaluating the potential of concentrating solar power generation in Northwestern India. *Energy Policy*, *62*, 157–175. doi:10.1016/j.enpol.2013.06.069

Quigley, F., & Ends, T. M. H. I. (2019). The Path to Nationalizing the U.S. Pharmaceutical Industry. *University of Michigan Journal of Law Reform*. https://ssrn.com/abstract=3496795 doi:10.2139/ssrn.3496795

Quintanilla, I., Martín, T. B., & Pardo, I. Q. (2005). *Psicología y economía*. Universitat de València.

Rabe-Hesketh, S., & Skrondal, A. (2008). *Multilevel and longitudinal modeling using Stata*. STATA press.

Rachmajanti, S., & Musthofiyah, U. (2017). The relationship between reading self-efficacy, reading attitude and EFL reading comprehension based on gender difference. *Journal of English Language, Literature, and Teaching*, *1*(1), 20–26. doi:10.17977/um046v1i1p20-26

Ram, R. (2009). Government spending and happiness of the population: Additional evidence from large cross-country samples. *Public Choice*, *138*(3-4), 483–490. doi:10.100711127-008-9372-0

Rana, A. (2013). *Job Satisfaction among Healthcare Employees in Public & Private Sector Hospitals in Punjab*. Academic Press.

Randall, M. D., & Gibson, M. A. (1990). Methodology in business ethics research: A review and critical assessment. *Journal of Business Ethics*, *9*(6), 457–471. doi:10.1007/BF00382838

Rao, M. G., & Choudhury, M. (2012). Health Care Financing Reforms in India. *Nipfp*, *100*, 34.

Rashid, S., & Yadav, S. S. (2020). Impact of the COVID-19 pandemic on higher education and research. *Indian Journal of Human Development*, *14*(2), 340–343. doi:10.1177/0973703020946700

Rastogi, R. (2020f). Intelligent Mental Health Analyzer by Biofeedback: App and Analysis. *Handbook of Research on Optimizing Healthcare Management Techniques*. doi:10.4018/978-1-7998-1371-2.ch009

Rastogi, R. (2020i). Exhibiting App and Analysis for Biofeedback Based Mental Health Analyzer. *Handbook of Research on Advancements of Artificial Intelligence in Healthcare Engineering*. Doi:10.4018/978-1-7998-2120-5

Rastogi, R. (2020m). Yajna and Mantra Science Bringing Health and Comfort to Indo-Asian Public: A Healthcare 4.0 Approach and Computational Study. *Learning and Analytics in Intelligent Systems, 13*. https://link.springer.com/chapter/10.1007%2F978-3-030-40850-3_15 doi:10.1007/978-3-030-40850-3_15

Rastogi, R., & Chaturvedi, D. K. (2020d). Intelligent Personality Analysis on Indicators in IoT-MMBD Enabled Environment. In Multimedia Big Data Computing for IoT Applications: Concepts, Paradigms, and Solutions. Springer Nature Singapore. doi:10.1007/978-981-13-8759-3_7

Rastogi, R., & Chaturvedi, D. K. (2020g). Surveillance of Type –I & II Diabetic Subjects on Physical Characteristics: IoT and Big Data Perspective in Healthcare @NCR, India. Internet of Things (IoT). doi:10.1007/978-3-030-37468-6_23

Rastogi, R., & Chaturvedi, D. K. (2020l). Tension Type Headache: IOT Applications to Cure TTH Using Different Biofeedback: A statistical Approach in Healthcare. In Biopsychosocial Perspectives and Practices for Addressing Communicable and Non-Communicable Diseases. IGI Global. doi:10.4018/978-1-7998-2139-7

Rastogi, R., Chaturvedi, D. K., & Satya, S. (2019e). Comparative Study of Trends Observed During Different Medications by Subjects under EMG & GSR Biofeedback. *IJITEE*, *8*(6S), 748-756. https://www.ijitee.org/download/volume-8-issue-6S/

Rastogi, R., Chaturvedi, D. K., Arora, N., Trivedi, P., Singh, P., & Vyas, P. (2018e). Study on Efficacy of Electromyography and Electroencephalography Biofeedback with Mindful Meditation on Mental health of Youths. *Proceedings of the 12th INDIACom*, 84-89.

Rastogi, R., Chaturvedi, D. K., Gupta, M., Sirohi, H., Gulati, M., & Pratyusha. (2020h). Analytical Observations Between Subjects' Medications Movement and Medication Scores Correlation Based on Their Gender and Age Using GSR Biofeedback. In *Pattern Recognition Applications in Engineering* (pp. 229-257). IGI Global. . doi:10.4018/978-1-7998-1839-7.ch010

Rastogi, R., Chaturvedi, D. K., Satya, S., & Arora, N. (2020n). Intelligent Heart Disease Prediction on Physical and Mental Parameters: A ML Based IoT and Big Data Application and Analysis. Learning and Analytics in Intelligent Systems, 13, 199-236. doi:10.1007/978-3-030-40850-3_10

Rastogi, R., Chaturvedi, D. K., Satya, S., Arora, N., Gupta, M., Verma, H., & Saini, H. (2020c). An Optimized Biofeedback EMG and GSR Biofeedback Therapy for Chronic TTH on SF-36 Scores of Different MMBD Modes on Various Medical Symptoms. Studies Comp. Intelligence, 841. doi:10.1007/978-981-13-8930-6_8

Rastogi, R., Chaturvedi, D. K., Satya, S., Arora, N., Gupta, M., Yadav, V., Chauhan, S., & Sharma, P. (2019i). Chronic TTH Analysis by EMG & GSR Biofeedback on Various Modes and Various Medical Symptoms Using IoT. In Big Data Analytics for Intelligent Healthcare Management. Academic Press. doi:10.1016/B978-0-12-818146-1.00005-2

Rastogi, R., Chaturvedi, D. K., Satya, S., Arora, N., Saini, H., Verma, H., & Mehlyan, K. (2018c). Comparative Efficacy Analysis of Electromyography and Galvanic Skin Resistance Biofeedback on Audio Mode for Chronic TTH on Various Indicators. *Proceedings of International Conference on Computational Intelligence &IoT (ICCIIoT)*.

Rastogi, R., Chaturvedi, D. K., Satya, S., Arora, N., Saini, H., Verma, H., Mehlyan, K., & Varshney, Y. (2018f). Statistical Analysis of EMG and GSR Therapy on Visual Mode and SF-36 Scores for Chronic TTH. *Proceedings of international Conference on 5th IEEE Uttar Pradesh Section International Conference*. 10.1109/UPCON.2018.8596851

Rastogi, R., Chaturvedi, D. K., Satya, S., Arora, N., Singh, P., & Vyas, P. (2018d). Statistical Analysis for Effect of Positive Thinking on Stress Management and Creative Problem Solving for Adolescents. *Proceedings of the 12thINDIACom*, 245-251.

Rastogi, R., Chaturvedi, D. K., Satya, S., Arora, N., Sirohi, H., Singh, M., Verma, P., & Singh, V. (2018b). Which One is Best: Electromyography Biofeedback Efficacy Analysis on Audio, Visual and Audio-Visual Modes for Chronic TTH on Different Characteristics. *Proceedings of International Conference on Computational Intelligence &IoT (ICCIIoT)*.

Rastogi, R., Chaturvedi, D. K., Satya, S., Arora, N., Trivedi, P. M., Gupta, M., Singhal, P., & Gulati, M. (2020e). MM Big Data Applications: Statistical Resultant Analysis of Psychosomatic Survey on Various Human Personality Indicators. *Proceedings of Second International Conference on Computational Intelligence 2018*. 10.1007/978-981-13-8222-2_25

Rastogi, R., Chaturvedi, D. K., Sharma, P., Yadav, V., Chauhan, S., Gulati, M., Gupta, M., & Singhal, P. (2019j). Statistical Resultant Analysis of Psychosomatic Survey on Various Human Personality Indicators: Statistical Survey to Map Stress and Mental Health. In Handbook of Research on Learning in the Age of Transhumanism (pp. 363-383). IGI Global. doi:10.4018/978-1-5225-8431-5.ch022

Rastogi, R., Chaturvedi, D. K., Sharma, S., Bansal, A., & Agrawal, A. (2018a). Audio Visual EMG & GSR Biofeedback Analysis for Effect of Spiritual Techniques on Human Behaviour and Psychic Challenges. *Proceedings of the 12th INDIACom*, 252-258.

Rastogi, R., Chaturvedi, D. K., Singhal, P., & Gupta, M. (2020o). Investigating Diabetic Subjects on Their Correlation with TTH and CAD: A Statistical Approach on Experimental Results. In *Opportunities and Challenges in Digital Healthcare Innovation*. . doi:10.4018/978-1-7998-3274-4

Rastogi, R., Chaturvedi, D. K., Verma, H., Mishra, Y., & Gupta, M. (2020a). Identifying Better? Analytical Trends to Check Subjects' Medications Using Biofeedback Therapies. *International Journal of Applied Research on Public Health Management, 5*(1), Article 2. https://www.igi-global.com/article/identifying-better/240753 doi:10.4018/IJARPHM.2020010102

Rastogi, R., Chaturvedi, D.K., Satya, S., Arora, N., Yadav, V., Yadav, V., Sharma, P., & Chauhan, S. (2019d). Statistical Analysis of EMG & GSR Biofeedback Efficacy on Different Modes for Chronic TTH on Various Indicators. *Int. J. Advanced Intelligence Paradigms*. . doi:10.1504/IJAIP.2019.10021825

Rastogi, R., Gupta, M., & Chaturvedi, D.K. (2020b). Efficacy of Study for Correlation of TTH vs Age and Gender Factors using EMG Biofeedback Technique. *International Journal of Applied Research on Public Health Management, 5*(1), Article 4. . doi:10.4018/IJARPHM.2020010104

Rastogi, R., Saxena, M., Gupta, U. S., Sharma, S., Chaturvedi, D. K., Singhal, P., Gupta, M., Garg, P., Gupta, M., & Maheshwari, M. (2019b). Yajna and Mantra Therapy Applications on Diabetic Subjects: Computational Intelligence Based Experimental Approach. *Proceedings of the 2ndedition of International Conference on Industry Interactive Innovations in Science, Engineering and Technology (I3SET2K19)*. https://papers.ssrn.com/sol3/papers.cfm?abstract_id=3515800

Rastogi, R., Saxena, M., Sharma, S. K., Muralidharan, S., Beriwal, V. K., Singhal, P., Rastogi, M., & Shrivastava, R. (2019a). Evaluation of efficacy of yagya therapy ont2- diabetes mellitus patients. *Proceedings of the 2nd edition of International Conference on Industry Interactive Innovations in Science, Engineering and Technology (I3SET2K19)*. https://papers.ssrn.com/sol3/papers.cfm?abstract_id=3514326

Rastogi, R., Saxena, M., Sharma, S. K., Murlidharan, S., Berival, V. K., Jaiswal, D., Sharma, A., & Mishra, A. (2019c). Statistical Analysis on Efficacy of Yagya Therapy for Type-2 Diabetic Mellitus Patients through Various Parameters. Advs in Intelligent Syst., Computing, 1120. doi:10.1007/978-981-15-2449-3_15

Rastogi, R., Chaturvedi, D. K., Arora, N., Trivedi, P., & Singh, P. (2017). Role and efficacy of Positive Thinking on Stress Management and Creative Problem Solving for Adolescents, *International Journal of Computational Intelligence. Biotechnology and Biochemical Engineering By Mantech Publications, 2*(2), 1–27.

Rastogi, R., Chaturvedi, D. K., Satya, S., Arora, N., Gupta, M., Saini, H., Mahelyan, K. S., & Verma, H. (2019g). Comparative Efficacy Analysis of Electromyography and Galvanic Skin Resistance Biofeedback on Audio Mode for Chronic TTH on Various Indicators. *International Journal of Computational Intelligence & IoT, 1*(1), 18–24. https://ssrn.com/abstract=3354371

Rastogi, R., Chaturvedi, D. K., Satya, S., Arora, N., Gupta, M., Singhal, P., & Gulati, M. (2019f). Statistical Analysis of Exponential and Polynomial Models of EMG & GSR Biofeedback for Correlation between Subjects' Medications Movement & Medication Scores. *IJITEE, 8*(6S), 625–635.

RastogiR.ChaturvediD. K.SatyaS.AroraN.GuptaM.SirohiH.SinghM.VermaP.SinghV. (2019h). Which one is Best: Electromyography Biofeedback, Efficacy Analysis on Audio, Visual and Audio-Visual Modes for Chronic TTH on Different Characteristics. *International Journal of Computational Intelligence & IoT, 1*(1), 25-31. Available at SSRN: https://ssrn.com/abstract=3354375

Rastogi, R., Chaturvedi, D. K., Singhal, P., & Gupta, M. (2020p). Investigating Correlation of Tension Type Headache and Diabetes: IoT Perspective in Health care. In C. Chakerborty (Ed.), *IoTHT: Internet of Things for Healthcare Technologies*. doi:10.1007/978-981-15-4112-4_4

Rathbone, E. (2012). Can we be smarter about our feelings? *University of Virginia Magazine*, 21-22.

Ray, J. L., Baker, L. T., & Plowman, D. A. (2011). Organizational mindfulness in business schools. *Academy of Management Learning & Education, 10*, 188–203. doi:10.5465/AMLE.2011.62798 929

Reb, J., Narayanan, J., & Chaturvedi, S. (2014). Leading mindfully: Two studies on the influence of supervisor trait mindfulness on employee well-being and performance. *Mindfulness, 5*(1), 36–45. doi:10.100712671-012-0144-z

Redden, G. M. (2017). *Ambulatory registered nurses' perspectives on health literacy roles and patient communication (Order No. 10257434)*. Available from ProQuest Dissertations & Theses Global.

Reeves, M., & Deimler, M. S. (2009). Strategies for winning in the current and post-recession environment. *Strat Leader, 37*, 10–17. doi:10.1108/10878 57091 10014 44

Reich, J. (2006). Three psychological principles of resilience in natural disasters. *Disaster Prevention and Management, 15*(5), 793–798.

Reinmoeller, P., & Baardwijk, N. v. (2005). The link between diversity and resilience. *MIT Sloan Management Review*, *46*, 61–65.

Repoza, K. (2020). *Why Is The U.S. So Ridiculously Dependent On China?* Retrieved 31 August 2020, from https://www.forbes.com/sites/kenrapoza/2020/04/30/why-is-the-us-is-so-ridiculously-dependent-on-china/#1b8e436b56b5

Rerup, C. (2001). Houston, we have a problem: Anticipation and improvisation as sources of organizational resilience. *Comportamento Organizacional e Gestão*, *7*, 27–44.

Rest, J. (1979). *Development in judging moral issues*. University of Minnesota Press.

Reyna, J., Hanham, J., Vlachopoulos, P., & Meier, P. (2019). A systematic approach to designing, implementing, and evaluating learner-generated digital media (LGDM) assignments and its effect on self-regulation in tertiary science education. *Research in Science Education*, 1–27. doi:10.100711165-019-09885-x

Ribeiro, L. L., & Marinho, E. L. L. (2017). Gross National Happiness in Brazil: An analysis of its determinants. *Economía*, *18*(2), 156–167. doi:10.1016/j.econ.2016.07.002

Richardson, G. E. (2002). The Metatheory of Resilience and Resiliency. *Journal of Clinical Psychology*, *58*(3), 307–321.

Richardson, G. E. (2002). The metatheory of resilience and resiliency. *Journal of Clinical Psychology*, *58*, 307–321. doi:10.1002/jclp.10020

Richardson, G. E. (2016). The applied metatheory of resilience and resiliency. In U. Kumar (Ed.), *The Routledge International Handbook of Psychological Resilience* (pp. 124–135). Routledge.

Richtnér, A., & Löfsten, H. (2014). Managing in turbulence: How the capacity for resilience influences creativity. *R & D Management*, *44*, 137–151.

Rigaud, E., Neveu, C., Duvenci-Langa, S., Obrist, M.-N., & Rigaud, S. (2013). Proposition of an organisational resilience assessment framework dedicated to railway traffic management. In *Rail Human Factors* (pp. 727–732). Supporting Reliability, Safety and Cost Reduction. doi:10.1201/b13827-97

Rijpma, J. A. (2003). From deadlock to dead end: The normal accidents-high reliability debate revisited. *Journal of Contingencies and Crisis Management*, *11*(1), 37–45. doi:10.1111/1468-5973.1101007

Riolli, L., & Savicki, V. (2003). Optimism and Coping as Moderators of the Relation Between Work Resources and Burnout in Information Service Workers. *International Journal of Stress Management*, *10*(3), 235–252. doi:10.1037/1072-5245.10.3.235

Robb, D. (2000). Building resilient organizations. *OD Practitioner*, *32*(3), 27–32.

Roberts, K. H. (1990). Some Characteristics of One Type of High Reliability Organization. *Organization Science*, *1*(2), 160.

Roberts, K. H., & Bea, R. (2001). When systems fail. *Organizational Dynamics*, *29*, 179–191.

Robertson, I. T., Cooper, C. L., Sarkar, M., & Curran, T. (2015). Resilience training in the workplace from 2003 to 2014: A systematic review. *Journal of Occupational and Organizational Psychology*, *88*(3), 533–562. doi:10.1111/joop.12120

Rose, A. (2004). Defining and measuring economic resilience to disasters. *Disaster Prevention and Management*, *13*, 307–314.

Rose, A., & Liao, S. Y. (2005). Modeling regional economic resilience to disasters: A computable general equilibrium analysis of water service disruptions. *Journal of Regional Science*, *45*, 75–112.

Rose, A., & Lim, D. (2002). Business interruption losses from natural hazards: Conceptual and methodological issues in the case of the Northridge earthquake. *Global Environmental Change, 4*, 1–14.

Rose, A., Oladosu, G., & Liao, S. Y. (2007). Business interruption impacts of a terrorist attack on the electric power system of Los Angeles: Customer resilience to a total blackout. *Risk Analysis, 27*, 513–531.

Rosenthal, U., & Kouzmin, A. (1996). Crisis management and institutional resilience: An editorial statement. *Journal of Contingencies and Crisis Management, 4*(3), 119–124.

Ross, E. (2013). *Emotion and decision making explained*. Oxford University Press.

Rudolph, J. W., & Repenning, N. P. (2002). Disaster dynamics: Understanding the role of quantity in organizational collapse. *Administrative Science Quarterly, 47*, 1–30.

Rummel, R. J. (1970). *Applied factor analysis*. Northwestern University Press.

Ruth Chandler Williamson Gallery, Scripps College. (1886). *Description of Woodblock print artwork by Chikanobu in the collection of Ruth Chandler Williamson Gallery*. https://ccdl.claremont.edu/digital/collection/cyw/id/21

Rutter, M. (1993). Resilience: Some conceptual considerations. *The Journal of Adolescent Health, 14*, 626–631. https://www.jahonline.org/issue/S1054-139X(00)X0125-5

Ryan, P. (2009). Integrated theory of health behavior change: Background and intervention development. *Clinical Nurse Specialist CNS, 23*(3), 161–172. doi:10.1097/NUR.0b013e3181a42373 PMID:19395894

Sáenz, M. J., & Revilla, E. (2014). Creating More Resilient Supply Chains. *MIT Sloan Management Review*. https://sloanreview.mit.edu/article/creating-more-resilient-supply-chains

Sahebjamniaa, N., Torabia, S. A., & Mansourib, S. A. (2015). Integrated Business Continuity and Disaster Recovery Planning: Towards Organizational Resilience. *European Journal of Operational Research, 242*(1), 261–273. doi:10.1016/j.ejor.2014.09.055

Sahoo, K., Sahoo, B., Choudhury, A. K., Sofi, N. Y., Kumar, R., & Bhadoria, A. S. (2015). Childhood obesity: causes and consequences. *Journal of Family Medicine and Primary Care, 4*(2), 187–192. Retrieved from: https://www.ncbi.nlm.nih.gov/pmc/articles/PMC4408699/ doi:10.4103/2249-4863.154628

Saito, Y. (2007). *Everyday aesthetics*. Oxford University Press. doi:10.1093/acprof:oso/9780199278350.001.0001

Salanova, M., Llorens, S., Cifre, E., & Martínez, I. M. (2012). We need a hero! Toward a validation of the healthy and resilient organization (HERO) model. *Group & Organization Management, 37*, 785–822.

Salisbury-Glennon, J. D., Wang, C.-h., Dai, Y., Jang, H. S., Collins, T. M., & Durham, K. (2021, April 8-11). *The effects of parental relationships on college students' motivation, learning strategies and metacognition during the COVID-19 global pandemic*. Poster presented at the annual meeting of the American Educational Research Association, Virtual Conference.

Salwan, P., & Gada, V. P. (2018). Antecedents of resilience: An investigation into bharat forge. *Indian Journal of Industrial Relations, 53*, 449–461.

Samurai Games Wiki. (n.d.). https://samuraigames.fandom.com/wiki/Kiyomasa_Kato

Sanfey, P., & Teksoz, U. (2007). Does transition make you happy? 1. *Economics of Transition, 15*(4), 707–731. doi:10.1111/j.1468-0351.2007.00309.x

Sanjay Basu, J. A. (2012). Comparative Performance of Private and Public Healthcar Systems in Low and Middle-Income Countries: A Systematic review. *PLoS Medicine, 9*(6). PMID:22723748

Sapountzaki, K. (2007). Social resilience to environmental risks: A mechanism of vulnerability transfer? *Management of Environmental Quality, 18*(3), 274–297.

Sarfo, R. (2018). *Relationships among health literacy, self-care, and hospital readmission status in African American adults with heart failure (Order No. 10821653)*. Available from ProQuest Dissertations & Theses Global.

Sawalha, I. H. S. (2015). Managing adversity: Understanding some dimensions of organizational resilience. *Management Research Review, 38*(4), 346–366.

Saxena, M., Kumar, B., &Matharu, S. (2018). Impact of Yagya on Particulate Matters. *Interdisciplinary Journal of Yagya Research, 1*, 1-8. doi:10.36018/ijyr.v1i1.5

Saxena, S., & Awasthi, P. (2010). *Leadership*. PHI Learning Private Limited.

Scheepers, R. A., Emke, H., Epstein, R. M., & Lombarts, K. M. (2020). The impact of mindfulness-based interventions on doctors' well-being and performance: A systematic review. *Medical Education, 54*(2), 138–149. doi:10.1111/medu.14020 PMID:31868262

Schein, E. H. (1985). Defining organizational culture. *Classics of Organization Theory, 3*, 490-502.

Schein, E. H. (1996). Organizational culture: The missing concept in organization studies. *Administrative Science Quarterly, 41*(2), 229–240. doi:10.2307/2393715

Schein, E. H. (2006). *Organizational culture and leadership* (Vol. 356). John Wiley & Sons.

Schein, E. H. (2007). The role of the founder in the creation of organizational culture. *Organization Science*, 439.

Schneider, R. (2021, October). Self-reported physical complaints are reduced upon regular use of an in-home water filter system (AcalaQuell®): A prospective, controlled, documentation study. *The Natural Products Journal, 11*(5), 673–681. doi:10.2174/2210315510999200727204959

Scholz, J. T., & Lubell, M. (1998). Adaptive political attitudes: Duty, trust, and fear as monitors of tax policy. *American Journal of Political Science, 42*(3), 903. doi:10.2307/2991734

Scholz, J. T., & Pinney, N. (1995). Duty, fear, and tax compliance: The heuristic basis of citizenship behavior. *American Journal of Political Science, 39*(2), 490–512. doi:10.2307/2111622

Scholz, U., Doña, B. G., Sud, S., & Schwarzer, R. (2002). Is general self-efficacy a universal construct? Psychometric findings from 25 countries. *European Journal of Psychological Assessment, 18*(3), 242–251. doi:10.1027//1015-5759.18.3.242

Schulman, P. R. (2004). General attributes of safe organizations. *Quality & Safety in Health Care, 13*, ii39–ii44.

Schultz, R., Hebert, R. S., Dew, M. A., Brown, S. L., Scheier, M. F., Beach, S. R., ... Nichols, L. (2007). Patient suffering and caregiver compassion: New opportunities for research, practice, and policy. *The Gerontologist, 47*(1), 4–13. doi:10.1093/geront/47.1.4 PMID:17327535

Schyns, P. (2002). Wealth Of Nations, Individual Income andLife Satisfaction in 42 Countries: A Multilevel Approach. *Social Indicators Research, 60*(1-3), 5–40. doi:10.1023/A:1021244511064

Seashore, C. N., Shawver, M. N., Thompson, G., & Mattare, M. (2004). Doing good by knowing who you are: The instrumental self as an agent of change. *OD Practitioner, 36*(3), 42–46.

Sekinishi, T. (2006). *Karesansui no haikan kôsei ni miru sansuiga no eikyô ni kansuru kōsatsu* [Investigation of the influence of *sansuiga* on *karesansui*]. Academic Press.

Senge, P. M. (2014). *The fifth discipline fieldbook: Strategies and tools for building a learning organization*. Crown Business.

Serhan, Y., & Gilsinan, K. (2020). *Can the West Actually Ditch China?* Retrieved 31 August 2020, from https://www.theatlantic.com/politics/archive/2020/04/us-britain-dependence-china-trade/610615/

Seville, E., Brunsdon, D., Dantas, A., Le Masurier, J., Wilkinson, S., & Vargo, J. (2007). Organisational resilience: Researching the reality of New Zealand organisations. *Journal of Business Continuity & Emergency Planning*, 2, 258.

Shafer, R., Dyer, L., Kilty, J., & Amos, J. (2000). *Crafting a human resource strategy to foster organizational agility: a case study* (CAHRS Working Paper #00-08). Cornell University, School of Industrial and Labor Relations, Center for Advanced Human Resource Studies.

Shahbaz, M., & Aamir, N. (2008). Macroeconomic Determinants of the Happiness of the Poor: A Case Study of Pakistan. *Journal of Economic and Social Policy*, 5, 9–27.

Sharma, A., Gupta, P., & Jha, R. (2020). COVID-19: Impact on Health Supply Chain and Lessons to Be Learnt. *Journal of Health Management*, 22(2), 248–261. doi:10.1177/0972063420935653

Sharma, S., & Prasad, F. M. (2009). Accumulation of lead and cadmium in soil and vegetable crops along major highways in Agra (India). *Journal of Chemistry*, 74, 1174–1183.

Sheffi, Y. (2005). Building a Resilient Supply Chain. *Harvard Business Review Supply Chain Strategy Newsletter*, 1(8). https://sheffi.mit.edu/sites/default/files/genmedia.buildingresilientsupplychain.pdf

Sheffi, Y. (2005). Preparing for the big one. *Supply Chain Management*, 84(5), 12 – 15. Doi:10.1049/me:20050503

Sheffi, Y. (2006). Manage risk through resilience. *Chief Executive*, 214, 28–29.

Sheffi, Y. (2007). *The resilient enterprise: Overcoming vulnerability for competitive advantage*. MIT Press.

Sheffi, Y., & Rice, J. B. (2005). A supply chain view of the resilient enterprise. *MIT Sloan Management Review*, 47, 41–48.

Shen, J. J., Cheah, C. S. L., & Yu, J. (2018). Asian American and European American emerging adults' perceived parenting styles and self-regulation ability. *Asian American Journal of Psychology*, 9(2), 140–148. doi:10.1037/aap0000099

Sheton, G. W. (2013). *Resiliency and Disaggregated Space Architectures*. White paper, Peterson AFB.

Shimbun, M. (2013). *Kûrujapan: Nihon ryôri de shôbu*. http://mainichi.jp/select/news/20130529k0000m040065000c.html

Shinzô. (2006). *Utsukushii kuni e*. Bungei shunjû.

Shufutinsky, A. (2019). Tribalism and Clone Theory in New Leaders and the Resulting Degradation of Organizational Culture. *Psychology and Behavioral Science International Journal*, 10(2).

Shufutinsky, A. (2019b). *From Salutes to Staff Meetings: A Triangulated Qualitative Inquiry Study of the Experiences of Wounded Warriors in Post-Military Corporate Positions*. ProQuest Dissertations.

Shufutinsky, A. (2020). Blackbird on a Bough: An Autoethnographic Conversation Regarding Personal Struggle, the Use-of-Self Journey, and Lessons that Inform Professional Practice. Accepted for publication in Practising Social Change (UK).

Shufutinsky, A. (2018). Organizational Assessment of a Biotechnology Firm's Safety, Health, and Environmental Department through an Organizational Development Lens. *International Journal of Interdisciplinary & Multidisciplinary Studies, 4*(3).

Shufutinsky, A., DePorres, D., Long, B., & Sibel, J. (2020). Shock Leadership Development for the Modern Era of Pandemic Management and Preparedness. *International Journal of Organizational Innovation, 13*(1), 1–23.

Shufutinsky, A., & Long, B. (2017). The Distributed Use of Self-as-Instrument for Improvement of Organizational Safety Culture. *OD Practitioner, 49*(4), 36–44.

Shufutinsky, A., Shanahan, P., Schaal, N., Madad, S., & Johnson, W. D. (2015). Applying conflict analysis and resolution strategies to assess organizational safety culture in accident investigations. *International Journal of Interdisciplinary and Multidisciplinary Studies, 2*(3), 71–90.

Shunk, D. H. (2008). Metacognition, self-regulation, and self-regulated learning: Research recommendations. *Educational Psychology Review, 20*(4), 463–467. doi:10.100710648-008-9086-3

Shuval, H. I. (1993). Investigation of typhoid fever and cholera transmission by raw wastewater irrigation in Santiago, Chile. *Water Science and Technology, 27*(3/4), 167–174. doi:10.2166/wst.1993.0341

Silverman, A. I., Akrong, M. O., Amoah, P., Drechsel, P., & Nelson, K. L. (2013). Quantification of human norovirus GII, human adenovirus, and faecal indicator organisms in wastewater used for irrigation in Accra, Ghana. *Journal of Water and Health, 11*(3), 473–488. doi:10.2166/wh.2013.025 PMID:23981876

Singh, G., Singh, R., & Thomas, E. J. (2008) Measuring Safety Climate in Primary Care Offices. In *Advances in Patient Safety: New Directions and Alternative Approaches* (Vol. 2: Culture and Redesign). Agency for Healthcare Research and Quality (US). https://www.ncbi.nlm.nih.gov/books/NBK43706/

Sitkin, S. B., See, K. E., & Miller, C. C. (2011). The paradox of stretch goals: Organizations in pursuit of the seemingly impossible. *Academy of Management Review, 36*(3), 544–566.

Slatten, L. A., David Carson, K., & Carson, P. P. (2011). Compassion fatigue and burnout: What managers should know. *The Health Care Manager, 30*(4), 326–333. doi:10.1097/HCM.0b013e31823511f7 PMID:22042140

Slavin, J. L., & Lloyd, B. (2012). Health benefits of fruits and vegetables. *Advances in Nutrition, 3*(4), 506–516. doi:10.3945/an.112.002154 PMID:22797986

Slawson, D. A. (2013). *Secret techniques in the art of Japanese gardens*. Kodansha US Publishing.

Smit, B., Burton, I., Klein, R. J. T., & Wandel, J. (2000). An anatomy of adaptation to climate change and variability. *Climatic Change, 45*, 223–251.

Smith, H. M. (2020). *Educating medical-surgical nurses to improve nursing knowledge and understanding of health literacy (Order No. 13810361)*. Available from ProQuest Dissertations & Theses Global.

Smith, K. W., & Stalans, L. J. (1991). Encouraging tax compliance with positive incentives: A conceptual framework and research directions. *Law & Policy, 13*(1), 35–53. doi:10.1111/j.1467-9930.1991.tb00056.x

Sofi, M. H., Gudi, R., Karumuthil-Melethil, S., Perez, N., Johnson, B. M., & Vasu, C. (2014). pH of drinking water influences the composition of gut microbiome and Type 1 Diabetes incidence. *Diabetes, 63*(2), 632–644. doi:10.2337/db13-0981 PMID:24194504

Somers, S. (2009). Measuring Resilience Potential: An Adaptive Strategy for Organizational Crisis Planning. *Journal of Contingencies and Crisis Management, 17*(1), 12–23.

Somers, S. (2009). Measuring resilience potential: An adaptive strategy for organizational crisis planning. *Journal of Contingencies and Crisis Management*, *17*(1), 12–23. doi:10.1111/j.1468-5973.2009.00558.x

Somppi, S., Törnqvist, H., Hänninen, L., Vainio, O., & Krause, C. (2010). *Dogs do look at images. Eye tracking in canine cognition research.* Research team of University of Helsinki, Research Center of Animal Welfare. Paper presented in The 2nd Canine Science Forum in Vienna, Austria.

Song, Y. D., & Yarbrough, T. E. (1978). Tax ethics and taxpayer attitudes: A survey. *Public Administration Review*, *38*(5), 442–452. doi:10.2307/975503

Souzou: Outsider Art from Japan. (2013). *Wellcome Collection*. http://www.wellcomecollection.org/whats-on/exhibitions/japanese-outsider-art.aspx

Spicer, M. W. (1974). *A behavioral model of income tax evasion* (Doctoral dissertation). The Ohio State University.

Spicker, P. (1995). *Social policy: Themes and approaches.* Prentice Hall.

Spillan, J., & Hough, M. (2003). Crisis Planning in Small Businesses: Importance, Impetus, and Indifference. *European Management Journal*, *21*(3), 398–407. doi:10.1016/S0263-2373(03)00046-X

Spring, H. (2020, July). Health literacy and COVID-19. *Health Information and Libraries Journal*, *37*(3), 171–172. Advance online publication. doi:10.1111/hir.12322 PMID:32672399

Sreenu, N. (2012). *A study on management of rural healthcare in Andhra Pradesh* [Thesis]. University of Hyderabad, School of Management Studies.

Sridhar, N. (2020). Effect of Chanting, Recitation of Mantras, Slokas, Duas, Music on Human Beings using EMF Radiation A Study. *Test Engineering and Management*, 83. https://testmagzine.biz/index.php/testmagzine/article/view/9212.11476-11480

Steel, Z., Marnane, C., Iranpour, C., Chey, T., Jackson, J. W., Patel, V., & Silove, D. (2014). The global prevalence of common mental disorders: A systematic review and meta-analysis 1980–2013. *International Journal of Epidemiology*, *43*(2), 476–493. doi:10.1093/ije/dyu038 PMID:24648481

Stephenson, A. (2010). *Benchmarking the Resilience of Organizations* [Unpublished PhD Thesis]. Civil and Natural Resources Engineering Department, University of Canterbury.

Stewart, D. (1996). *Organization ethics.* McGraw-Hill Companies, Inc.

Stewart, J., & O'Donnell, M. (2007). Implementing change in a public agency. *International Journal of Public Sector Management*, *20*(3), 239–251. doi:10.1108/09513550710740634

Story, M., Nanney, M. S., & Schwartz, M. B. (2009). Schools and obesity prevention: Creating school environments and policies to promote healthy eating and physical activity. *The Milbank Quarterly*, *87*(1), 71–100. doi:10.1111/j.1468-0009.2009.00548.x PMID:19298416

Strunk, K. K., & Mwavita, M. (2020). *Design and analysis in educational research: ANOVA designs in SPSS.* Routledge. doi:10.4324/9780429432798

Stutman, S., Baruch, R., Grotberg, E., & Rathore, Z. (2002). *Resilience in Latino youth.* Working Paper, Institute for Mental Health Initiatives. The George Washington University.

Suddaby, R. (2010). Editor's comments: Construct clarity in theories of management and organization. *Academy of Management Review*, *35*(3), 346–357. doi:10.5465/AMR.2010.51141319

Sughi, A. (2006a). *Alberto Sughi, and plagiarism*. Alberto Sughi's homepage. http://www.albertosughi.com/f_prima_pagina/2006_05_30.asp

Sughi, A. (2006b). *Somewhere behind*. Alberto Sughi's blog. http://blog.absolutearts.com/blogs/archives/00000272.html

Sullivan-Taylor, B., & Branicki, L. (2011). Creating resilient SMEs: Why one size might not fit all. *International Journal of Production Research*, *49*(18), 5565–5579.

Sundaravadivelu, S., & Suresh, R. (2015). Study of Physical, Mental, Intellectual andSpiritual Health of a Human Being Living in ADwelling Place Constructed According toThe Vastu Principle. *International Journal of Innovative Research in Computerand Communication Engineering*, *3*(7).

Supply Chain Risk Leadership Council. (2013). *SCRLC Emerging Risks in the Supply Chain 2013*. White paper.

Sutcliffe, K. M., & Vogus, T. J. (2003). Organizing for resilience. *Positive Organizational Scholarship*, 94-110.

Sutcliffe, K. M., & Vogus, T. J. (2003). Organizing for resilience. In K. S. Cameron, J. E. Dutton, & R. E. Quinn (Eds.), *Positive organizational scholarship: Foundations of a new discipline* (pp. 94–110). Berrett-Koehler.

Sutcliffe, K. M., & Vogus, T. J. (2003). Organizing for resilience. In K. Cameron, J. E. Dutton, & R. E. Quinn (Eds.), *Positive organizational scholarship* (pp. 94–110). Berrett-Koehler.

Suthanthiraveeran, S. (2018). The five year plans in India: Overview of Public Health Policies. *The Five Year Plans in India: Overview*.

Svalastog, A. L., Donev, D., Kristoffersen, N. J., & Gajović, S. (2017). Concepts and definitions of health and health-related values in the knowledge landscapes of the digital society. *Croatian Medical Journal*, *58*(6), 431–435. doi:10.3325/cmj.2017.58.431 PMID:29308835

Swanson, A. (2020). *Coronavirus Spurs U.S. Efforts to End China's Chokehold on Drugs*. Retrieved 31 August 2020, from https://www.nytimes.com/2020/03/11/business/economy/coronavirus-china-trump-drugs.html

Swisher, L. L., & Davis, C. M. (2005). The realm-individual-process-situation (RIPS) model of ethical decision-making. *HPA Resource*, *5*(3), 1–8.

Takano, Y., & Osaka, E. (2018). Comparing Japan and the United States on individualism/collectivism: A follow-up review. *Asian Journal of Social Psychology*, *21*(4), 301–316. doi:10.1111/ajsp.12322

Takei, J., & Keane, M. P. (2008). *Sakuteiki, visions of the Japanese garden: A modern translation of Japan's gardening classic*. Tuttle Publishing.

Taleb, N. N. (2012). *Antifragile: Things that Gain from Disorder* (Vol. 3). Random House.

Taras, V., Steel, P., & Kirkman, B. L. (2016). Does country equate with culture? Beyond geography in the search for cultural boundaries. *Management International Review*, *56*(4), 455–487. doi:10.100711575-016-0283-x

Tarundeep Singh, N. B. (2018, December 8). Health-care Utilization and Expenditure Patterns in the Rural Areas of Punjab, India. *Journal of Family Medicine and Primary Care*, *7*(1), 39–44. doi:10.4103/jfmpc.jfmpc_291_17 PMID:29915731

Taylor, D. (2020). *A Timeline of the Coronavirus Pandemic*. Retrieved 31 August 2020, from https://www.nytimes.com/article/coronavirus-timeline.html

Taylor, G. (2020). *'Wake-up call': Chinese control of U.S. pharmaceutical supplies sparks growing concern*. Retrieved 31 August 2020, from https://www.washingtontimes.com/news/2020/mar/17/china-threatens-restrict-critical-drug-exports-us/

Compilation of References

Teixeira, E. de O., & Werther, W. B. (2013). Resilience: Continuous renewal of competitive advantages. *Business Horizons*, *56*, 333–342.

Teo, W. L., Lee, M., & Lim, W.-S. (2017). The relational activation of resilience model: How leadership activates resilience in an organizational crisis. *Journal of Contingencies and Crisis Management*, *25*, 136–147. doi:10.1111/1468-5973.12179

Thakkar, M., & Davis, D. C. (2006). Risks, barriers, and benefits of EHR systems: A comparative study based on the size of the hospital. *Perspectives in Health Information Management*, *3*, 5. PMID:18066363

The Art Newspaper. (n.d.). *Visitor Figures 2020: top 100 art museums revealed as attendance drops by 77% worldwide*. https://www.theartnewspaper.com/2021/03/30/visitor-figures-2020-top-100-art-museums-revealed-as-attendance-drops-by-77percent-worldwide

The Joint Commission. (2020). *The Universal Protocol*. Retrieved from https://www.jointcommission.org/-/media/deprecated-unorganized/imported-assets/tjc/system-folders/topics-library/up_posterpdf.pdf?db=web&hash=57DC6A91EF83C142943961031B3626F9" https://www.jointcommission.org/-/media/deprecated-unorganized/imported-assets/tjc/system-folders/topics-library/up_posterpdf.pdf?db=web&hash=57DC6A91EF83C142943961031B3626F9

Thesaurus Linguae Graecae Online. (n.d.). http://www.tlg.uci.edu/lbg

Thompson, K. (2015). *A systematic guide to business acumen and leadership using dilemmas: Includes organizational health, agility, resilience, and crisis management*. CreateSpace Independent Publishing.

Thomson, S., Osborn, R., Squires, D., & Jun, M. (2013). *International Profiles of Health Care Systems*. Commonwealth Fund Pub. No. 1717. http://www.commonwealthfund.org/~/media/files/publications/fund-report/2013/nov/1717_thomson_intl_profiles_hlt_care_sys_2013_v2.pdf

Tierney, K. (2014). *The social roots of risk: Producing disasters, promoting resilience*. Stanford University Press.

Tiimub, B. M., Kuffour, R. A., & Kwarteng, A. S. (2012). Bacterial contamination levels of lettuce irrigated with waste water in the Kumasi Metropolis. *Journal of Biology, Agriculture and Healthcare*, *2*(10), 116–127.

Timmerman, P. (1981). *Vulnerability, Resilience, and the Collapse of Society: A Review of Models and Possible Climatic Application, Institute for Environmental Studies*. University of Toronto.

Tope-Banjoko, T., Davis, V., Morrison, K., Fife, J., Hill, O., & Talley, C. (2020). Academic resilience in college students: Relationship between coping and GPA. *Anatolian Journal of Education*, *5*(2), 109–120. doi:10.29333/aje.2020.529a

Torgler, B. (2003). *Tax morale: Theory and empirical analysis of tax compliance* (Doctoral dissertation). University of Basel.

Torgler, B. (2005). Tax morale in latin america. *Public Choice*, *122*(1-2), 133–157. doi:10.100711127-005-5790-4

Torun, E. D. (2020). Online distance learning in higher education: E-learning readiness as a predictor of academic achievement. *Open Praxis*, *12*(2), 191–208. doi:10.5944/openpraxis.12.2.1092

Travis, J., & Bunde, J. (2020). Self-regulation in college: The influence of self-efficacy, need satisfaction, and stress on GPA, persistence, and satisfaction. *Current Psychology (New Brunswick, N.J.)*. Advance online publication. doi:10.100712144-020-01091-7

Treat, J. W. (1996). Introduction. Japanese Studies into Cultural Studies. In J. W. Treat (Ed.), *Contemporary Japan and Popular Culture* (pp. 1–14). University of Hawai'i Press.

Trommsdorff, G. (2009). Teaching and learning guide for: Culture and development of self-regulation. *Social and Personality Psychology Compass*, *3*(5), 687–701. doi:10.1111/j.1751-9004.2009.00209.x

Trumbull, E., & Rothstein-Fisch, C. (2011). The intersection of culture and achievement motivation. *School Community Journal*, *21*(2), 25–53.

Tschumi, C. (2020). *Mirei Shigemori—rebel in the garden*. Birkhäuser. doi:10.1515/9783035621761

Tsuji Nobuo. (2005). *Nihon bijutsu no rekishi. Jômon kara manga-anime made*. Tôkyô daigaku shuppankai.

Tsukayama, H. (2015). Teens spend nearly nine hours every day consuming media. *The Washington Post*. Retrieved from: https://www.washingtonpost.com/news/the-switch/wp/2015/11/03/teens-spend-nearly-nine-hours-every-day-consuming-media/

Turnbull, S. (2002). *Samurai Invasion: Japan's Korean War, 1592-98*. Cassell & Company.

U.S. Food & Drug Administration. (2019). *Safeguarding Pharmaceutical Supply Chains in a Global Economy*. https://www.fda.gov/news-events/congressional-testimony/safeguarding-pharmaceutical-supply-chains-global-economy-10302019

Ueda, A., Nitschke, G., & Suloway, S. (1998). *The inner harmony of the Japanese House*. Kodansha International.

Ugur, E., Kara, S., Yildirim, S., & Akbal, E. (2016). Medical errors and patient safety in the operating room. *JPMA. The Journal of the Pakistan Medical Association*, *66*(5), 593–597. https://jpma.org.pk/article-details/7750?article_id=7750 PMID:27183943

Uhl-Bien, M., Marion, R., & McKelvey, B. (2007). Complexity leadership theory: Shifting leadership from the industrial age to the knowledge era. *The Leadership Quarterly*, *18*(4), 298–318.

Ungar, M. (2006). Nurturing hidden resilience in at-risk youth in different cultures. *Journal of the Canadian Academy of Child and Adolescent Psychiatry*, *15*(2), 53–58. PMID:18392194

Ungar, M. (2008). Resilience across cultures. *British Journal of Social Work*, *38*(2), 218–235. doi:10.1093/bjsw/bcl343

Ungar, M. (2013). Resilience, trauma, context, and culture. *Trauma, Violence & Abuse*, *14*(3), 255–266. doi:10.1177/1524838013487805 PMID:23645297

Ungar, M. (Ed.). (2005). *Handbook for working with children and youth: Pathways to resilience across cultures and contexts*. Sage Publications.

UN-HABITAT, Local Governments for Sustainability, and the United Nations Environment Programme. (2009). *Sustainable Urban Energy Planning: A handbook for cities and towns in developing countries*. UNEP.

UNISDR. (2015). *Making development sustainable: the future of disaster risk management. global assessment report on disaster risk reduction 2015—making development sustainable: the future of disaster risk management*. United Nations Office for Disaster Risk Reduction. Retrieved fromhttps://www.preventionweb.net/english/hyogo/gar/2015/en/gar-pdf/GAR2015_EN.pdf

United Nations Educational, Scientific and Cultural Organization. (2015). *Rethinking education: Towards a global common good?* https://unevoc.unesco.org/e-forum/RethinkingEducation.pdf

US Securities and Exchange Commission. (2018). *SEC Adopts Statement and Interpretive Guidance on Public Company Cybersecurity Disclosures*. https://www.sec.gov/news/press-release/2018-22

USAID. (2012). *Building resilience to recurrent crisis*. Available at: www.usaid.gov/sites/default/files/documents/1870/USAIDResiliencePolicyGuidanceDocument.pdf

Vaelikangas, L., & Romme, A. G. L. (2013). How to design for strategic resilience: A case study in retailing. *Journal of Organization Design*, *2*, 44–53.

Välikangas, L. (2007). Rigidity, exploratory patience, and the ecological resilience of organizations. *Scandinavian Journal of Management, 23*(2), 206–213.

Valin, H., Sands, R. D., van der Mensbrugghe, D., Nelson, G. C., Ahammad, H., Blanc, E., Bodirsky, B., Fujimori, S., Hasegawa, T., Havlik, P., Heyhoe, E., Kyle, P., Mason-D'Croz, D., Paltsev, S., Rolinski, S., Tabeau, A., van Meijl, H., von Lampe, M., & Willenbockel, D. (2014). The future of food demand: Understanding differences in global economic models. *Journal of Agricultural Economics, 45*(1), 51–67. doi:10.1111/agec.12089

van Breda, A. D. (2016). Building Resilient Human Service Organizations. *Human Service Organizations, Management, Leadership & Governance, 40*(1), 62–73. doi:10.1080/23303131.2015.1093571

van der Meer, C. A., Te Brake, H., van der Aa, N., Dashtgard, P., Bakker, A., & Olff, M. (2018). Assessing psychological resilience: Development and psychometric properties of the English and Dutch version of the resilience evaluation scale (RES). *Frontiers in Psychiatry, 9*, 169. doi:10.3389/fpsyt.2018.00169 PMID:29867601

van der Vegt, G. S., Essens, P., Wahlstrom, M., & George, G. (2015). From the editors: Managing risk and resilience. Academy of Management Journal, 58, 3. https://doi.org/ doi:10.1163/18770703-00503003

Van Der Vegt, G. S., Essens, P., Wahlström, M., & George, G. (2015). Managing risk and resilience. *Academy of Management Journal, 58*(4), 971-980.

van der Vegt, G. S., Essens, P., Wahlstrom, M., & George, G. (2015). Managing risk and resilience. *Academy of Management Journal, 58*, 971–980.

Vargo, J., & Seville, E. (2011). Crisis strategic planning for SMEs: Finding the silver lining. *International Journal of Production Research, 49*, 5619–5635.

Veenhoven, R. (2000). Well-being in the welfare state: Level not higher, distribution not more equitable. *Journal of Comparative Policy Analysis, 2*(1), 91–125. doi:10.1080/13876980008412637

Vogus, T. J., & Sutcliffe, K. M. (2007). *Organizational resilience: Towardsa theory and research agenda.* Paper presented at the Systems, Manand Cybernetics, 2007. ISIC. IEEE International Conference.

von Zerssen, D., & Petermann, F. (2011). *B-LR. Beschwerden-Liste*. Hogrefe.

Vörösmarty, C. J., McIntyre, P. B., Gessner, M. O., Dudgeon, D., Prusevich, A., Green, P., Glidden, S., Bunn, S. E., Sullivan, C. A., Liermann, C. R., & Davies, P. M. (2010). Global threats to human water security and river biodiversity. *Nature, 2010*(7315), 555–561. Advance online publication. doi:10.1038/nature09440 PMID:20882010

WadaY. O. H. (n.d.). http://wadayoshihiko.com/profile.html

Wagnild, G. M., & Young, H. M. (1993). Development and psychometric evaluation of the Resilience Scale. *Journal of Nursing Measurement*. Advance online publication. doi:10.1037/t07521-000 PMID:7850498

Wagnild, G., & Young, H. (1990). Resilience among older women. *Journal of Nursing Scholarship, 22*(4), 252–255.

Walker, B. H., Abel, N., & Anderies, J. M. (2009). Resilience, adaptability, and transformability in the Goulburn-Broken catchment. Australia. *Ecology and Society, 14*(1), 12.

Walker, B. H., & Salt, D. A. (2012). *Resilience Practice: Building Capacity to Absorb Disturbance and Maintain Function*. Island Press.

Wang, Y.-L., Liang, J., & Tsai, C.-C. (2018). Cross-cultural comparisons of university students' science learning self-efficacy: Structural relationships among factors within science learning self-efficacy. *International Journal of Science Education, 40*(6), 579–594. doi:10.1080/09500693.2017.1315780

WanjohiA. M. (2014). Social Research Methods Series: Proposal Writing Guide. https://ssrn.com/abstract=2378204

Warner, L. (1952). *The Enduring Art of Japan*. Grove Press. doi:10.4159/harvard.9780674865693

Wartick, S. (2002). Measuring corporate reputation: Definition and data. *Business & Society, 41*(4), 371–392.

Watanabe, T. (2012). The Modern Japanese Garden. In *Since Meiji: Perspectives on the Japanese Visual Arts, 1868-2000* (pp. 340-360). University of Hawai'i Press. Retrieved April 28, 2021, from https://www.jstor.org/stable/j.ctt6wqh84.19

Watts, G., & Paciga, J. J. (2011). Conscious Adaptation: Building Resilient Organizations. In T. Carmichael (Ed.), *Complex Adaptive Systems: Energy, Information, and Intelligence*. Arlington VA: AAAI Fall Symposium Series.

Wedawattaa, G., Ingirige, B., & Amaratunga, D. (2010). Building up resilience of construction sector SMEs and their supply chains to extreme weather events. *International Journal of Strategic Property Management, 14*, 362–375. doi:10.3846/ijspm. 2010.27

Weick, K. E., & Sutcliffe, K. M. (2007). Managing the unexpected: Resilient performance in an age of uncertainty (2nd ed.). San Francisco, CA: Jossey-Bass.

Weick, K. (1993). The collapse of sensemaking in organizations: The Mann Gulch disaster. *Administrative Science Quarterly, 38*, 628–652.

Weick, K. (1996). Prepare your organization for fight fires. *Harvard Business Review, 74*, 143–148.

Weick, K. E., & Sutcliffe, K. M. (2001). *Managing the unexpected: Assuring high performance in an age of complexity*. Jossey-Bass.

Weick, K. E., & Sutcliffe, K. M. (2001). *Managing the unexpected: resilient performance in an age of uncertainty*. Jossey-Bass Inc.

Weick, K. E., Sutcliffe, K. M., & Obstfeld, D. (1999). Organizing for High Reliability: Processes of Collective Mindfulness. In R. S. Sutton & B. M. Staw (Eds.), *Research in Organizational Behavior* (Vol. 1, pp. 81–123). Jai Press.

Weick, K. E., Sutcliffe, K. M., & Obstfeld, D. (2005). Organizing and the process of sensemaking. *Organization Science, 16*(4), 409–421.

Weiss, J. W. (2006). Organization ethics (4th ed.). Thompson/South West.

Weldezgina, D., & Muleta, D. (2016). Bacteriological contaminants of some fresh vegetables irrigated with Awetu River in Jimma town, Southwestern Ethiopia. *Advances in Biology, 20*(16), 1–11. doi:10.1155/2016/1526764

Welter-Enderlin, R., & Hildenbrand, B. (2006). *Resilienz. Gedeihen trotz widriger Umstände*. Carl Auer Verlag GmbH.

Welzel, C. (2013). *Freedom rising: Human empowerment and the quest for emancipation*. Cambridge University Press. doi:10.1017/CBO9781139540919

Werner, E. E. (1997). Vulnerable but invincible: High-risk children from birth to adulthood. *Acta Paedictric Supplement, 422*, 103-105. doi:.1997.tb.18356.x doi:10.1111/j.1651-2227

Westhead, P., & Batstone, S. (1998). Independent Technology-Based Firms: The Perceived Benefits of a Science Park Location. *Urban Studies (Edinburgh, Scotland), 35*(12), 2197–2219. doi:10.1080/0042098983845

Wilbanks, T. J., & Romero Lankao, P. (2007) Industry, settlement, and society. In Climate change 2007: impacts, adaptation, and vulnerability: contribution of Working Group II to the Fourth Assessment Report of the Intergovernmental Panel on Climate Change. Cambridge University Press.

Wildavsky, A. B. (1991). *Searching for Safety*. Transaction.

Wilde, J. H. (2013). *Citizen watch in the accounting department? Tax and financial reporting responses to employee whistleblowing allegations* (Order No. 3608021). Available from ProQuest Dissertations & Theses Global. (1497226692). Retrieved from https://search-proquestcom.contentproxy.phoenix.edu/docview/1497226692?accountid=35812

Williams, T. A., Gruber, D. A., Sutcliffe, K. M., Shepherd, D. A., & Zhao, E. Y. (2017). Organizational response to adversity: Fusing crisis management and resilience research streams. *The Academy of Management Annals, 11*, 733–769.

Williams, T., & Shepherd, D. (2016). Building resilience or providing sustenance: Different paths of emergent ventures in the aftermath of the Haiti earthquake. *Academy of Management Journal*. Advance online publication. doi:10.5465/amj.2015.0682

Windle, G. (2011). What is resilience? A review and concept analysis. *Reviews in Clinical Gerontology, 21*, 152–169. doi:10.1017/S0959259810000420

Winn, M. I., & Pogutz, S. (2013). Business, ecosystems, and biodiversity: New horizons for management research. *Organization & Environment, 26*, 203–229.

Winpenny, J., Heinz, I., Koo-Oshima, S., Salgot, M., Collado, J., Hernandez, F., & Torricelli, R. (2010). The Wealth of Waste: The Economics of Wastewater Use in Agriculture. Rome, Italy: Food and Agriculture Organization of the United Nations. *Water Reports, 35*. Retrieved October 10, 2018, from https://www.fao.org/docrep/012/i1629e/i1629e.pdf

Winter, S. G. (2013). Habit, Deliberation and Action: Strengthening the Micro foundations of Routines and Capabilities. *The Academy of Management Perspectives, 27*(2), 120–137.

Witmer, H., & Mellinger, M. S. (2016). Organizational resilience: Nonprofit organizations' response to change. *Work (Reading, Mass.), 54*, 255–265.

Wofford, L., Troilo, M., & Dorchester, A. (2011). Point of View: Cognitive Risk and Real Estate Portfolio Management. *Journal of Real Estate Portfolio Management, 17*(1), 69–73. doi:10.1080/10835547.2011.12089891

Wolf, J., Prüss-Ustün, A., Cumming, O., Bartram, J., Bonjour, S., Cairncross, S., & ... . (2014). Assessing the impact of drinking water and sanitation on diarrheal disease in low- and middle-income settings: Systematic review and meta-regression. *Tropical Medicine & International Health, 19*, 928–942. doi:10.1111/tmi.12331 PMID:24811732

Wong, C.-S., Law, K. S., & Huang, G.-H. (2008). On the importance of conducting construct-level analysis for multidimensional constructs in theory development and testing. *Journal of Management, 34*, 744–764.

Wood, E. M. (1972). *Mind and politics*. University of California Press. doi:10.1525/9780520332485

Woods, T., & Nies, M. (2018). Conceptual Application of the Adapted Health Belief Model to Parental Understanding of Child Weight. *Journal of Health Science & Education, 2*(4), 1-6. Retrieved from: https://www.researchgate.net/publication/327230594_Conceptual_Application_of_the_Adapted_Health_Belief_Model_to_Parental_Understanding_of_Child_Weight

Woods, D. D. (2006). Essential Characteristics of Resilience. In E. Hollnagel, D. D. Woods, & N. Leveson (Eds.), *Resilience Engineering: Concepts and Precepts* (pp. 21–34). Ashgate.

World Health Organization. (2010). *Global recommendations on Physical Activity for Health*. Retrieved from: https://www.who.int/dietphysicalactivity/global-PA-recs-2010.pdf

World Health Organization. (2019). *Childhood overweight and obesity*. World Health Organization. Retrieved from: https://www.who.int/dietphysicalactivity/childhood/en/

World Health Organization. (2019). *Patient Safety*. https://www.who.int/news-room/fact-sheets/detail/patient-safety

Wreathall, J. (2009). Measuring resilience. Resil. Eng. Perspect., 2, 95-114.

Wright, Suh, & Leggett. (2009). If at first you don't succeed: Globalized production and organizational learning at the Hyundai Motor Company. *Asia Pacific Business Review*, *15*, 163–180. doi:10.1080/13602 38070 16984 18

Wright, C., Kiparoglou, V., & Williams, M. J. (2012). A framework for resilience thinking. *Procedia Computer Science*, *8*, 45–52. doi:10.1016/j.procs.2012.01.012

Wu, Y. J., Carstensen, C. H., & Lee, J. (2020). A new perspective on memorization practices among East Asian students based on PISA 2012. *Educational Psychology*, *40*(5), 643–662. doi:10.1080/01443410.2019.1648766

Xu, H., Intrator, O., & Bowblis, J. R. (2020). Shortages of Staff in Nursing Homes During the COVID-19 Pandemic: What are the Driving Factors? *Journal of the American Medical Directors Association*, *21*(10), 1371–1377. doi:10.1016/j.jamda.2020.08.002 PMID:32981663

Yamada, S., & Hartman, E. (2020). *Shots in the dark: Japan, Zen, and the west*. The University of Chicago Press.

Yang, W., Bansal, P., & DesJardine, M. R. (2014). What doesn't kill you makes you stronger: A multi-level process theory of organizational resilience. *Academy of Management Proceedings*, *2014*(1), 13934.

Yip, S. Y., Mak, W. W., Chio, F. H., & Law, R. W. (2017). The mediating role of self-compassion between mindfulness and compassion fatigue among therapists in Hong Kong. *Mindfulness*, *8*(2), 460–470. doi:10.100712671-016-0618-5

Yohe, G., & Tol, R. S. (2002). Indicators for social and economic coping capacity: Moving toward a working definition of adaptive capacity. *Global Environmental Change*, *12*, 25–40.

Youngs, I. (2013). *Could China save UK art galleries?* BBC News. https://www.bbc.com/news/entertainment-arts-22387987

Youssef, C. M., Luthans, F., & Youssef, C. M. (2007). Emerging Positive Organizational Behavior. *Journal of Management*, *33*(3), 321–349.

Zahra, S. A., & George, G. (2002a). Absorptive Capacity: A Review, Reconceptualization, and Extension. *Academy of Management Review*, *27*(2), 185–203.

Zainuddin, M., Yasin, I. M., Arif, I., & Hamid, A. B. A. (2018, December 30-31). Alternative cross-cultural theories: Why still Hofstede? *Proceedings of International Conference on Economics, Management and Social Study*.

Zajac, E. J., Kraatz, M. S., & Bresser, R. K. (2000). Modeling the dynamics of strategic fit: A normative approach to strategic change. *Strategic Management Journal*, *21*(4), 429–453.

Zarocostas, J. (2020). How to fight an infodemic. *Lancet*, *395*(10225), 676.

Zhang, J., Norvilitis, J. M., & Ingersoll, T. S. (2007). Idiocentrism, allocentrism, psychological well being and suicidal ideation: A cross cultural study. *Omega*, *55*(2), 131–144. doi:10.2190/OM.55.2.c PMID:17944311

Zheng, P., Gray, M. J., Duan, W. J., Ho, S. M., Xia, M., & Clapp, J. D. (2020). Cultural variations in resilience capacity and post-traumatic stress: A tri-cultural comparison. *Cross-Cultural Research*, *54*(2-3), 273–295. doi:10.1177/1069397119887669

Zimmerman, B. J. (2002). Becoming a self-regulated learner: An overview. *Theory into Practice*, *41*(2), 64–70. doi:10.120715430421tip4102_2

About the Contributors

Mika Markus Merviö is Professor of International Relations at the Kibi International University, Okayama, Japan. Previously he has been working at the University of Tampere, Finland, from 1983-1995, and from which he also received his Ph.D. (International Relations). Then he moved to the International Christian University, Tôkyô, Japan as a JSPS researcher and from there to the Miyazaki International University and the University of Shimane, where he worked as a professor. From 2000 he has been working at the Kibi International University. His research interests include political and social issues, history, art and environment.

* * *

Dacosta Aboagye is an Associate Professor in environmental geography at the Department of Geography and Rural Development, Kwame Nkrumah University of Science and Technology, Kumasi, Ghana. He obtained his PhD in Geography from the University of Oklahoma, Norman, U.S.A.; Masters in Development and International Relations from Aalborg University, Aalborg, Denmark; and BA (Hons) in Geography and Resource Development from the University of Ghana, Legon, Ghana. He teaches Geomorphology, Hydrology, Hazards and Disaster Management, and Research Methods. His research interest is in exploring the various dimensions of environmental hazards and vulnerabilities, their impacts and the range of initiatives for building householder and community resilience. He is a broadly trained geographer with research and professional experience in Ghana and USA in livelihood and environmental risk assessment and disaster management.

Felix Asante is a Senior Lecturer at the Department Geography and Rural Development, Faculty of Social Sciences, KNUST. His research is in Agriculture and rural livelihoods, Climate variability/change impacts and Tourism.

Paolo Bongarzoni is an international professional with several years of corporate and teaching experience all over Europe and Australia. Before starting his academic career in Australia, he worked for Deloitte Consulting (as Strategy Senior Consultant), Daikin Europe (as Corporate Finance & Strategic Planning Executive) and he was the M&A Manager of Bombardier Transportation. He holds Doctor of Philosophy Degree in Management from SSM, a Master Degree in Finance and Management, a Post Graduate Specialization in Education and a Bachelor Degree of Business (with First Class Honors). Paolo further is an Associate CPA in Australia. He holds dual Australian/Italian Citizenship and speaks fluently English, Italian, French and Spanish. Since fall 2016, Paolo is teaching Accounting, Finance,

Strategic Management, Economics and Managerial Statistics at Swiss School of Management. Since 2018, Paolo Bongarzoni holds the position of Vice Dean at Swiss School of Management Rome Campus.

Seleste Bowers is a Licensed Clinical Social Worker in California and has her Doctorate in Health Administration. Her passions include research, education and teaching as a organizational trainer. She obtained her bachelors from San Diego Statue University, masters from University of Tennessee and her doctorate from University of Phoenix. She enjoys outdoor activities including hiking and beach adventures.

Darrell Norman Burrell is post graduate student and a 2017 graduate of the National Coalition Building Institute's (NCBI) Leadership Diversity Institute. He is a Certified Diversity Professional. He is an alumnus of the prestigious Presidential Management Fellows Program www.pmf.gov. Dr Burrell has a doctorate degree with majors in Education and Executive Leadership Coaching from A.T. Still University. Dr. Burrell has an Education Specialist (EdS) graduate degree in Higher Education Administration from The George Washington University. He has two graduate degrees one in Human Resources Management/Development and another Organizational Management from National Louis University. He also has a Master of Arts degree in Sales and Marketing Management from Prescott College. He has extensive years of university teaching experience at several universities.

Yan Dai, M.Ed. M.A., is a doctoral student in the Educational Psychology program at the Department of Educational Foundations, Leadership & Technology (EFLT), Auburn University, USA. Her research interests focus on motivation (particularly on self-efficacy and self-regulation), academic entitlement, resilience, online learning, and cross-cultural compassion study. She also works under the critical theoretical frame using ethnographic and auto-ethnographic methods.

Jessica Dávalos-Aceves is a Doctor in Economic Studies from the University of Guadalajara in Mexico. She has as well two master degrees, one in International Business from Tecnológico de Monterrey in Mexico, and other in Management from Grenoble École de Management in France. She also has a bachelor's degree in Marketing. She worked as International Business Developer from Mexican Ministry of Economy in Los Angeles, California. She performed a research stay at the École Normale Supérieure Paris and she has presented research works in workshops, including one at the Technische Universität Kaiserslautern in Germany. She has collaborated in projects from GIAGEM, a joint German-Mexican research cooperation. She won the 2021 Best Dissertation, Honorable Mention Award by the International Society for Quality-of-Life Studies for her doctoral thesis.

Adriano Ferri is a professor of Business Administration at the Swiss School of Management, Rome, Italy; from which he also received his MBA (2018-2019).

María Jesús García García is a professor at the University of Valencia. After finishing her degree in Law, she was awarded a doctoral research scholarship by the Spanish Department of Education and she went on to receive her PhD in Law from the University of Valencia. Her area of expertise is Public Law and European Union Law. María Jesús García was a fellow with the Ash Center's Government Innovation Program (Harvard University) in 2017. She has been awarded three positive research assessments by the Commission for the Assessment of Research Activity and has also been a Visiting Fellow at the Open University School of Law (United Kingdom) since 2014.

About the Contributors

Hyun Sung Jang is a Ph.D. candidate in Educational Psychology at Auburn University, USA. His research interests include the relationships between personality, motivation, and achievement goals. He also looks for cultural studies and equitable education for all students. He aims to create pedagogies for students that reflect their different backgrounds and individual needs.

Mandeep Kaur is a Senior Research Fellow pursuing Ph.D. in the Healthcare Service Quality at the Department of Commerce, Punjabi University Patiala, Punjab (INDIA). Her research interests are focused on healthcare economics, health economic modelling, service quality and customer perception. She also has masters in Commerce and awarded with first rank holder (Gold-Medalist) in merit in her master programme by the University. She worked as Assistant Professor in Sri Guru Teg Bahadur Khalsa College, Sri Anandpur Sahib, Punjab. She has volunteered as a student in NSS, RedCross and participated in various extra-curricular activities. She has attended many seminars, conferences and research methodology workshops and presented research articles with her Ph.D. supervisor.

Emmanuel Kyeremeh is a tutor at the Department of Social Studies, Berekum College of Education, Berekum, Ghana. He holds a Master of Philosophy and a Bachelor of Arts Degrees in Geography and Rural Development from the Kwame Nkrumah University of Science and Technology, Kumasi, Ghana. He also holds a Diploma in Education from the University of Education, Winneba, Ghana. His specialisations are Climatology, Environmental Management and Urban Geography. He has taught a number of courses including Natural Environment, Physical and Social Relations in Social Studies and Social Environment at the Department of Social Studies, Berekum College of Education, Berekum, Ghana, where he currently teaches. His research interests are social and biophysical vulnerabilities, health risk perceptions, climate change, and environmental resource management.

Eugene J. M. Lewis is the former Assistant Professor of Marketing at Oakwood University from 2005 to 2010. Furthermore, he still serves as Adjunct Professor teaching courses in the area Logistics/Supply Chain Management, Marketing, and Information Systems. He has worked in Academia for more than 13 years as a part-time and full-time professor. Currently, he is the International Program Manager in the Aviation Industry for the United States Army Department of Defense working in the Foreign Military Sales (FMS) arena. He has served DOD for more than 10 years and has had the opportunity to work with many government officials and dignitaries in several foreign countries.

D'Alizza Mercedes holds a BA in Political Science from the University of Colorado at Boulder, an MA in Political Science from Northwestern University, an MS in Human Resources Management from the University of Maryland, and is a licensed educator for grades 6 – 12 in the subjects of Social Studies and Spanish. Currently, Ms. Mercedes is a third-year Ph.D. Candidate in Organizational Psychology and the Chicago School of Professional Psychology. Her research investigates the Impostor Phenomenon in women of color. Currently, Ms. Mercedes serves as Adjunct Faculty at the University of Maryland Global Campus and teaches human resources and change management courses. Additionally, Ms. Mercedes serves as the Doctoral Assistant for Research Methodology and International Change Management.

Simon Regin Paxton is a lecturer at Komazawa University in Tokyo, Japan. He has an MA from Saitama University in Japanese and Asian Studies, and a PhD from Macquarie University in Interna-

About the Contributors

tional Studies. His main research interests include, kanji acquisition for non-kanji background learners of Japanese, traditional Japanese conjuring, and Japanese stone gardens.

T. Rajeshwari is a psychotherapist specializing in Nutrition and mental health. Practises freelance and has been working with children of all ages for around 35 years including as a therapist in Montessori schools. Lives in Kolkata and runs a center called Sneh Sri, which is centered on empowering women from low income backgrounds by training them to make utility products and handicrafts. Also a motivational speaker conducts workshops on effective parenting and healing meditation around the country. Also conducted nutrition and lifestyle management workshop and mind training workshop to engineers, different professionals, students and home makers. Now in a research program of " the sounds of vedic mantras and it's impact on human behaviour" with a project on yagyopathy. Treatment through ancient yagya(smokelessyagya in 10 minutes) . I'm also a karmakandi attached to AWGP. Akhilawishwa Gayatri pariwar. Also with GPYG Kolkata (Gayatripariwar youth group). She is MS in psychotherapy and dip. in Nutrition.

Rohit Rastogi received his B.E. C. S. S. Univ. Meerut, 2003. Master's degree in CS of NITTTR-Chandigarh from Punjab University. Currently he is getting a doctoral degree from the Dayalbagh Educational Institute in Agra, India. He is an associate professor in the CSE department of ABES Engineering college, Ghaziabad, India. He has won awards in a variety of areas, including improved education, significant contributions, human value promotion, and long-term service. He keeps himself engaged in various competition events, activities, webinars, seminars, workshops, projects and various other educational learning forums.

Sheelu Sagar is a research scholar pursuing her PhD in Management from Amity University (AUUP). She graduated with a Bachelor Degree of Science from Delhi University. She received her Post Graduate Degree in Master of Business Administration with distinction from Amity University Uttar Pradesh India in 2019. She is working at a post of Asst. Controller of Examinations, Amity University, Uttar Pradesh. She is associated with various NGOs - in India. She is an Active Member of Gayatri Teerth, ShantiKunj, Haridwar, Trustee - ChaturdhamVed Bhawan Nyas (having various centers all over India), Member Executive Body -Shree JeeGauSadan, Noida. She is a social worker and has been performing Yagya since last 35 years and working for revival of Indian Cultural Heritage through yagna (Hawan), meditation through Gayatri Mantra and pranayama. She is doing her research on Gayatri Mantra.

Jill Salisbury-Glennon is an Associate Professor in Educational Psychology at Auburn University, USA. Her research focuses on college students' self-regulated learning, study strategies, motivation, and the teaching and learning process.

Rainer Schneider received his PhD in psychology and sports sciences from the University of Freiburg, Germany. Following many years in the position as a senior researcher and research manager in the fields of experimental psychology, alternative medical treatments, research evaluation, and placebo effects, inter alia at the University Hospital of Freiburg and the University of Osnabrück, he founded his own research institute RECON – Research and Consulting in 2007. He publishes widely on specific and non-specific treatment effects in the field of information medicine, biomedicine, and novel therapeutic

About the Contributors

approaches. He is engaged as a scientific advisor for numerous organizations and companies both in the private and public sector.

Anton Shufutinsky, PhD, DHSc, MSPH, is a scholar-practitioner in organization development, leadership, management, occupational health and safety, environmental health, and public health. He is currently faculty of organization development & change and leadership at Cabrini University's School of Business and Professional Studies. His research foci are in organizational design, leadership development, sociotechnical systems, research methods, crisis leadership, emergency management, safety culture, and public health leadership.

Bhavna Singh is Ayurvedic Practitioner and currently acting as Principal in Ayurvedic College, Hapur, U.P., India. She has keen interest to stud the herbal and their effects on human body. She has done scientific experiments of different herbals and their vaporized state through Yajna on patient diseases. She is also fond of scientific writings and establishing Indian Vedic wisdom through logical explanations. She has been actively working in Thought Transformation movement and strongly feels that science and spirituality can move together to enrich each other. Her many papers are imprinted on various scientific journals.

Kamden Strunk is an Associate Professor of Research Methodology at Auburn University, USA. His research focuses on queer studies and LGBTQ+ people in higher education with emphasis on intersections of white supremacist cisheteropatriarchy. He also works in critical quantitative methodology and queer methodologies.

Neeti Tandon is research Scholar in Fundamental Physics at Vikram University Ujjain. She is keen researcher in Yagyopathy. She is scientist by thought and working on the study of effect of Yajna, Mantra and Yoga on mental patients, patients suffering with various diseases like diabetes, stress, arthritis, lever infection and hypertension. She is also Active Volunteer of Gayatri Parivaar and Thought Transformation Movement. She keeps herself engaged in many philanthropic activities like plantation, slum area kid education and anti addiction movement. She is gold medalist and honors through out in her education and obtained graduation and post graduation in Physics Science.

José Vargas-Hernández is research professor at Technological Institute José Mario Molina Pasquel y Henríquez, Academic Unit Zapopan. Member of the National System of Researchers of Mexico. Professor Vargas-Hernández has a Ph. D. in Public Administration and a Ph.D. in Organizational Economics. He has been visiting research at Carleton University Canada and visiting scholar at University of California Berkely. He has undertaken studies in Organisational Behaviour and has a Master of Business Administration, published four books and more than 200 papers in international journals and reviews (some translated to English, French, German, Portuguese, Farsi, Chinese, etc.) and more than 300 essays in national journals and reviews. He has obtained several international Awards and recognitions. He has also experience in consultancy. His main research is in organizational economics and strategic management. He teaches for several doctoral programs in various universities.

Chih-hsuan Wang is a faculty member at the Department of Educational Foundations, Leadership, and Technology at Auburn University, USA. She teaches research methods and data analysis courses.

Wang's current work focuses on enhancing the learning in statistics and mathematics by using technology as well as motivation assessment, and learning outcomes within an online learning environment and the impacts on the teaching and learning process. Her other research interests include STEM education, factors that influence international students' motivation and learning, and topics related to health psychology and nursing education.

Jorja Wright is a logistics manager within DoD. She focuses on efficient organizational processes and dynamic employee interactions. She received her doctoral degree in executive leadership from University of Charleston-West Virginia; her MBA from Florida Institute of Technology, concentrating in healthcare management; & her bachelor's degree in biology and a minor in chemistry from the University of Alabama-Huntsville. Dr. Wright has over 20 peer-reviewed publications and presentations on leadership, cybersecurity, logistics, and healthcare management. Dr. Wright is an innovative and talented professional with a diverse educational background focused on leadership innovation and organizational dynamics.

Index

A

anxiety 26, 34, 43, 54, 64, 68
art 14, 250, 252, 254-255, 257-258, 261, 263-268, 270-302
art history 264, 270, 279, 281, 290
art market 275, 286-287, 291-293, 298
Ayurveda 69, 73, 94

B

behaviour 15, 72, 178, 267

C

capability building 124-126, 129, 131-133, 135
capacity building 124, 150
college students 21, 23-24, 27, 30-31, 36-38
community gardening 41-43, 49, 52
community resilience 111, 114, 120, 140, 143, 149-150, 155-156, 159-160
contamination 220, 230, 232-237, 239-243, 245-249
COVID-19 1, 4, 11, 13, 16, 20-21, 23-24, 27, 31, 34, 37, 40-44, 48, 52, 75, 81-86, 204-205, 207-210, 212, 214, 216-218, 289, 293
cross-cultural comparison 21, 24, 27, 33, 35, 40
culture 1-3, 7-9, 12-19, 22-27, 29-40, 74, 79, 84-85, 115, 134-135, 253, 257-258, 261, 264, 266-268, 271-280, 284-287, 289-290, 293-297, 299-301

D

Depression 26, 34, 43, 54, 57, 215
diseases 43, 46, 49, 52, 54, 57, 69-70, 76, 88, 96, 98, 214, 231, 245
drinking water contamina 219

E

Energy Measurements 73
Enhancement of organizational resilience 104, 112
environment 2-5, 22, 24, 26, 31, 35, 41-46, 69-70, 74, 79, 84-85, 91, 100, 121, 124-131, 133, 135, 139-140, 154, 156, 158-159, 163-169, 171-174, 176-177, 183, 229-230, 232, 236, 244, 254, 256-257, 263-264, 266, 274, 276-277, 279, 281, 284, 286, 299
Everyday aesthetics 250, 257, 261

F

failures of resilience 104
food insecurity 41-42, 48, 234

G

General Welfare 178
government spending 178, 180-181, 185, 189-190, 193, 201, 203

H

happiness 178, 181-182, 186-191, 193, 200-203
hazards 2, 7, 49, 55, 80, 107, 118-120, 138, 140, 156-158, 160-161, 211, 233, 235-237, 241, 243-244, 247-248
health 1-5, 8, 11-14, 16-20, 37-38, 41-55, 58-63, 67-103, 113, 115-118, 121, 139, 141, 170-171, 175, 193, 200, 202, 208-209, 212, 214-221, 228-236, 240-241, 243, 245, 247-249, 256-257, 268, 270
health benefit 219
health complaints 219, 221, 228-229
health disparities 75, 83
health education 51, 75, 80, 85, 91
health literacy 75-86
healthcare 1-2, 4-5, 7-8, 11-17, 19, 44, 70-72, 77-81,

83-84, 87-102, 208-209, 212, 215-217, 249
Healthcare medical errors 1
healthy eating 41-43, 47, 49, 52, 234
history 74, 108, 116, 216, 219, 232, 251, 254, 263-264, 266, 269-271, 274-277, 279-282, 290, 293, 296, 300
housing 164-166, 168, 174, 248, 272, 275

I

ideology 263-265, 270, 272-274, 278, 288, 296
individual resilience 110-111, 113, 130, 132, 134, 143, 145, 151
in-home water filter 219-220, 232
interpretation 109, 148, 172, 229, 237, 263-264, 266, 271, 280, 297, 299

J

Japan 26, 38, 250-258, 261-264, 266-302

K

karesansui 250-261

L

life satisfaction 178, 184-185, 190, 200-202

M

Machine learning 74
Mantra 54, 56-58, 70, 73-74
medical group management 75
Mental Fitness 54
microbial 233-235, 237, 239, 241-244, 246-249
mimêsis 279-280, 282, 299
Mirei Shigemori 250-251, 254, 262
multi-level resilience 133, 143
museums 257, 265, 270, 275, 279, 282-283, 286-293, 301

N

nationalization 204, 214-215
Nishinaka Yukito 250, 257-259

O

OOP expenditure 87, 89, 98
organizational culture 1, 7, 9, 12-13, 17-18, 84-85, 134-135

organizational resilience 104-122, 124-140, 142-159, 163
organizational resilience analysis 104, 148
organizational systems 1, 12, 75-76, 79, 83, 108-109, 114

P

patient engagement 2, 75, 84
patient safety 1-2, 4-9, 11-14, 19-20, 80, 85
Perfectioning of Reality 279
Pharma 4.0 204, 213
Pharma shortage 204
placebo effect 219, 228
planning 25, 76, 88, 90, 98, 110, 113-115, 117, 121-122, 125, 134, 141, 151, 155, 159, 161-162, 164-167, 169-171, 173, 175, 177, 207, 217, 252, 289
politics 39, 115, 216-217, 263-266, 270, 272, 274, 276, 279-281, 284, 287, 293, 301
pollution 74, 231
public debt 178, 185, 190-191, 193
public health 1, 4, 13-14, 41-42, 48, 52, 72, 75-76, 85, 88-93, 95-96, 98-102, 115-116, 202, 209, 216, 219-220, 228-229, 232, 234, 247-249
Punjab 87-90, 92-103

R

radiation 54-56, 58, 65, 69-70, 73
representation 3, 59, 264, 266, 279-280, 282, 293, 295
resilience 19, 21-24, 26-40, 104-163, 213, 235-237, 247
Ryôanji 250

S

Sanskrit 74
self-efficacy 21-35, 37-40, 44-46, 51, 109, 111-113, 115
self-regulation 21-38, 40, 46
Sensor and IoT 74
service quality 87, 100, 153
Shunmyô Masuno 250
standard of living 88, 96, 180
stress 11-12, 15, 26, 34-35, 38-39, 49, 54, 59, 64, 68, 70, 72, 79, 105-106, 108, 117, 121, 144, 146, 152, 160, 228, 231, 235
structure 2-3, 5, 15-16, 35, 74, 87-88, 90-93, 96, 100, 125-126, 137, 154, 169, 174, 179, 186, 220-221, 228, 235, 264
Supply Chain dependance 204
Supply Chain disruption 204
sustainability 34, 117, 152, 164-167, 171, 173, 175-

Index

177, 235, 250-251, 256-257, 260, 276

T

tax burden 178, 180, 182, 191
THEORETICAL AND EMPIRICAL APPROACHES 104, 107
traditions 22, 58, 73, 263-267, 270, 272-276, 279-281, 283, 286-287, 293-299
typologies 104-105, 114

U

urban environment 164-169, 171, 173-174, 176
urban renovation 164, 166-170, 174, 176
Utilisation 87

V

values 7, 9, 22, 29, 33, 35-36, 102, 135, 145-146, 148, 152-154, 172, 175, 182, 184, 190-191, 220, 225, 231, 263-267, 271-272, 274-276, 284-285, 296
Vedic 54, 74
vegetables 44, 47-48, 233-235, 237-249, 251
visual arts 262-263, 266, 269-270, 279-282, 285-286, 290, 293-297, 299
vulnerability 34, 36, 107, 111, 116-117, 122, 131, 136, 139, 144, 148, 150-151, 159, 161-162, 212, 233-236, 246-248

Y

Yajna 54, 57, 63-65, 67-70, 73-74

Z

Zen 250-251, 253, 255, 261-262, 269-270, 273, 297

Recommended Reference Books

IGI Global's reference books are available in three unique pricing formats:
Print Only, E-Book Only, or Print + E-Book.

Shipping fees may apply.

www.igi-global.com

ISBN: 978-1-5225-8160-4
EISBN: 978-1-5225-8161-1
© 2019; 497 pp.
List Price: US$ 295

ISBN: 978-1-5225-7256-5
EISBN: 978-1-5225-7257-2
© 2019; 339 pp.
List Price: US$ 215

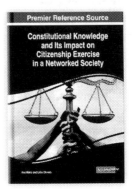

ISBN: 978-1-5225-8350-9
EISBN: 978-1-5225-8351-6
© 2019; 332 pp.
List Price: US$ 195

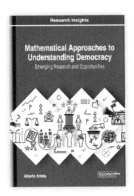

ISBN: 978-1-5225-7558-0
EISBN: 978-1-5225-7559-7
© 2019; 148 pp.
List Price: US$ 165

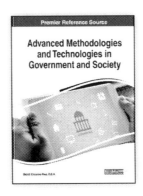

ISBN: 978-1-5225-7661-7
EISBN: 978-1-5225-7662-4
© 2019; 726 pp.
List Price: US$ 275

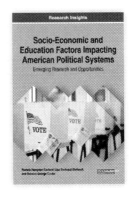

ISBN: 978-1-5225-3843-1
EISBN: 978-1-5225-3844-8
© 2018; 191 pp.
List Price: US$ 145

Do you want to stay current on the latest research trends, product announcements, news, and special offers?
Join IGI Global's mailing list to receive customized recommendations, exclusive discounts, and more.
Sign up at: **www.igi-global.com/newsletters**.

Publisher of Peer-Reviewed, Timely, and Innovative Academic Research

www.igi-global.com   Sign up at www.igi-global.com/newsletters   facebook.com/igiglobal   twitter.com/igiglobal   linkedin.com/igiglobal

Ensure Quality Research is Introduced to the Academic Community

Become an Evaluator for IGI Global Authored Book Projects

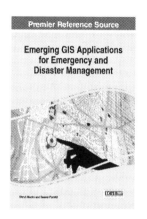 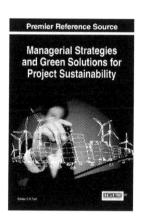  

The overall success of an authored book project is dependent on quality and timely manuscript evaluations.

Applications and Inquiries may be sent to:
development@igi-global.com

Applicants must have a doctorate (or equivalent degree) as well as publishing, research, and reviewing experience. Authored Book Evaluators are appointed for one-year terms and are expected to complete at least three evaluations per term. Upon successful completion of this term, evaluators can be considered for an additional term.

If you have a colleague that may be interested in this opportunity, we encourage you to share this information with them.

IGI Global Author Services

Providing a high-quality, affordable, and expeditious service, IGI Global's Author Services enable authors to streamline their publishing process, increase chance of acceptance, and adhere to IGI Global's publication standards.

Benefits of Author Services:

- **Professional Service:** All our editors, designers, and translators are experts in their field with years of experience and professional certifications.
- **Quality Guarantee & Certificate:** Each order is returned with a quality guarantee and certificate of professional completion.
- **Timeliness:** All editorial orders have a guaranteed return timeframe of 3-5 business days and translation orders are guaranteed in 7-10 business days.
- **Affordable Pricing:** IGI Global Author Services are competitively priced compared to other industry service providers.
- **APC Reimbursement:** IGI Global authors publishing Open Access (OA) will be able to deduct the cost of editing and other IGI Global author services from their OA APC publishing fee.

Author Services Offered:

English Language Copy Editing
Professional, native English language copy editors improve your manuscript's grammar, spelling, punctuation, terminology, semantics, consistency, flow, formatting, and more.

Scientific & Scholarly Editing
A Ph.D. level review for qualities such as originality and significance, interest to researchers, level of methodology and analysis, coverage of literature, organization, quality of writing, and strengths and weaknesses.

Figure, Table, Chart & Equation Conversions
Work with IGI Global's graphic designers before submission to enhance and design all figures and charts to IGI Global's specific standards for clarity.

Translation
Providing 70 language options, including Simplified and Traditional Chinese, Spanish, Arabic, German, French, and more.

Hear What the Experts Are Saying About IGI Global's Author Services

"Publishing with IGI Global has been *an amazing experience* for me for sharing my research. The *strong academic production* support ensures quality and timely completion." – Prof. Margaret Niess, Oregon State University, USA

"The service was *very fast, very thorough, and very helpful* in ensuring our chapter meets the criteria and requirements of the book's editors. I was *quite impressed and happy* with your service." – Prof. Tom Brinthaupt, Middle Tennessee State University, USA

Learn More or Get Started Here:

For Questions, Contact IGI Global's Customer Service Team at cust@igi-global.com or 717-533-8845

www.igi-global.com

 www.igi-global.com

Celebrating Over 30 Years of Scholarly Knowledge Creation & Dissemination

InfoSci®-Books

A Database of Nearly 6,000 Reference Books Containing Over 105,000+ Chapters Focusing on Emerging Research

GAIN ACCESS TO **THOUSANDS** OF REFERENCE BOOKS AT **A FRACTION** OF THEIR INDIVIDUAL LIST **PRICE**.

InfoSci®-Books Database

The **InfoSci®-Books** is a database of nearly 6,000 IGI Global single and multi-volume reference books, handbooks of research, and encyclopedias, encompassing groundbreaking research from prominent experts worldwide that spans over 350+ topics in 11 core subject areas including business, computer science, education, science and engineering, social sciences, and more.

Open Access Fee Waiver (Read & Publish) Initiative

For any library that invests in IGI Global's InfoSci-Books and/or InfoSci-Journals (175+ scholarly journals) databases, IGI Global will match the library's investment with a fund of equal value to go toward **subsidizing the OA article processing charges (APCs) for their students, faculty, and staff** at that institution when their work is submitted and accepted under OA into an IGI Global journal.*

INFOSCI® PLATFORM FEATURES

- Unlimited Simultaneous Access
- No DRM
- No Set-Up or Maintenance Fees
- A Guarantee of No More Than a 5% Annual Increase for Subscriptions
- Full-Text HTML and PDF Viewing Options
- Downloadable MARC Records
- COUNTER 5 Compliant Reports
- Formatted Citations With Ability to Export to RefWorks and EasyBib
- No Embargo of Content (Research is Available Months in Advance of the Print Release)

*The fund will be offered on an annual basis and expire at the end of the subscription period. The fund would renew as the subscription is renewed for each year thereafter. The open access fees will be waived after the student, faculty, or staff's paper has been vetted and accepted into an IGI Global journal and the fund can only be used toward publishing OA in an IGI Global journal. Libraries in developing countries will have the match on their investment doubled.

To Recommend or Request a Free Trial:
www.igi-global.com/infosci-books

eresources@igi-global.com • Toll Free: 1-866-342-6657 ext. 100 • Phone: 717-533-8845 x100

 www.igi-global.com

Printed in the United States
by Baker & Taylor Publisher Services